Kimberly Miller

March 2000

THE VISIBLE SELF

Global Perspectives on Dress, Culture, and Society

THE VISIBLE SELF
Global Perspectives on Dress, Culture, and Society

Joanne B. Eicher
University of Minnesota

Sandra Lee Evenson
University of Idaho

Hazel A. Lutz
University of Minnesota

Fairchild Publications

New York

Executive Editor: Olga Kontzias
Production Editor: Sylvia L. Weber
Editorial Assistant: Beth Applebome
Copy Editor: Donna Frassetto
Photo Researcher: Elsa Peterson, Ltd.
Art Director: Mary Siener
Production Manager: Priscilla Taguer

Cover Design: Lisa Klausing

Second Edition, Copyright © 2000
Fairchild Publications, Inc.

First Edition, Copyright © 1973
by Prentice-Hall, Inc.

Library of Congress Catalog Card Number: 99-75668

ISBN: 1-56367-068-2

GST R 133004424

Printed in the United States of America

BRIEF CONTENTS

Extended Contents   vii

Preface   xi

Credits for Figures   xv

I.5   *Dress as a Reflection and Sustainer of Social Reality: A Cross-Cultural Perspective* by Jean A. Hamilton and James W. Hamilton   118

Part One

THE SYSTEMATIC STUDY OF DRESS   1

1   The Classification System of Dress   2

2   Dress, Culture, and Society   32

3   Records of the Types of Dress   54

4   Written Interpretations of Dress   74

Readings for Part One   97

I.1   *The Baths* by Alev Lytle Croutier   97

I.2   *Body Ritual Among the Nacirema* by Horace Miner   100

I.3   *Eurocentrism in the Study of Ethnic Dress* by Suzanne Baizerman, Joanne B. Eicher, and Catherine Cerny   103

I.4   *Many Disciplines, Many Rewards: Inuit Clothing Research* by Betty Kobayashi Issenman   110

Part Two

PHYSICAL APPEARANCE, ENVIRONMENT, AND DRESS   125

5   Physical Appearance and Dress   126

6   Body, Dress, and Environment   148

Readings for Part Two   176

II.1   *Pressure of Menswear on the Neck in Relation to Visual Performance* by Leonora M. Langan and Susan M. Watkins   176

II.2   *Innerskins/Outerskins: Gut and Fishskin* by Pat Hickman   179

Part Three

SCALES OF CULTURE AND DRESS   185

7   Small-scale Culture and Dress   186

8   Large-scale Culture and Dress   208

9   Global-scale Culture and Dress   236

Readings for Part Three   261

III.1   *Ga'anda Scarification: A Model for Art and Identity* by Marla C. Berns   261

III.2   *They Don't Wear Wigs Here* by Barbara A. Schreier   269

III.3   *Court, Formal and Everyday Dress During the Late Ch'ing Dynasty* by A. C. Scott   273

III.4   *Transnational Biographies and Local Meanings: Used Clothing Practices in Lusaka* by Karen Tranberg Hansen   277

Part Four

ART, AESTHETICS, AND DRESS   285

10   The Art of Creating Dress   286

11   Ideals for Individual Appearance and the Art of Dress   308

12   The Art of Dress: Conformity, and Individuality   328

13   Dress and the Arts   346

Readings for Part Four   374

IV.1   *The Aesthetics of Men's Dress of the Kalabari of Nigeria* by Tonye V. Erekosima and Joanne B. Eicher   374

IV.2   *The Sweetness of Fat: Health, Procreation, and Sociability in Rural Jamaica* by Elisa J. Sobo   384

IV.3   *Scruffy is Badge of Pride, but Some Physicists Long for Cool* by Malcolm W. Browne   388

IV.4   *Signature Style: Falling Off the Fashion Train with Frida, Georgia and Louise* by Jo Ann C. Stabb   390

Part Five

DRESS AND THE FUTURE   395

14   Your Future and Dress   396

Reading for Part Five   410

V.1   *Cosmic Couture* by Elizabeth Snead   410

Bibliography   413

Index   433

EXTENDED CONTENTS

Preface   xi

Credits for Figures   xv

Part One

THE SYSTEMATIC STUDY OF DRESS   1

1   **The Classification System of Dress**   2

Dress   4

Types of Dress   7

Body Modifications   7
Body Supplements   15
*Relating Body Modifications and
  Supplements*   24

Application of the Classification System   24

Advantages of the Classification System   25

Summary   28

Study Tools   29

2   **Dress, Culture, and Society**   32

Culture   34

Society   36

The Scale of World Cultures   37

Relating Dress to Culture and Society   40

Ethnocentrism   42

Ethnic Dress   44

Contemporary Culture, Society, and Dress   45

Dress and Cultural Meanings   50

Summary   50

Study Tools   51

3   **Records of the Types of Dress**   54

Actual Artifacts   56

Visual Representations   59

Written Description and Commentary   67

Accounts of Travelers and Explorers   68
Dress History   69
Electronic Sources of Dress Information   70

Summary   70

Study Tools   71

4   **Written Interpretations of Dress**   74

Moralistic Essays, Satire, and Reform
  Literature   76

Prescriptive and Proscriptive Literature   77

Analytical Writings   84

Emergence of Anthropology   85
Increased Pace of Fashion   87
Study of Human Sexuality   87

Summary   94

Study Tools   94

Readings for Part One   97

I.1   *The Baths* by Alev Lytle Croutier   97

I.2   *Body Ritual Among the Nacirema* by Horace
       Miner   100

I.3 *Eurocentrism in the Study of Ethnic Dress* by Suzanne Baizerman, Joanne B. Eicher, and Catherine Cerny 103

I.4 *Many Disciplines, Many Rewards: Inuit Clothing Research* by Betty Kobayashi Issenman 110

I.5 *Dress as a Reflection and Sustainer of Social Reality: A Cross-Cultural Perspective* by Jean A. Hamilton and James W. Hamilton 118

Part Two

PHYSICAL APPEARANCE, ENVIRONMENT, AND DRESS 125

5 **Physical Appearance and Dress** 126

Physical Similarity 128

Physical Diversity 130

Long-term Adaptations 130
Short-term Variations 138

Summary 144

Study Tools 144

6 **Body, Dress, and Environment** 148

Physiological Adaptation to Environment 150

Habituations or Immediate Body Adjustments 152
Acclimatization 153
Physical Adaptation and Dress 154

Cultural Adaptation of the Body to Environment 155

Dress as Extensions and Modifications of the Body 160

Supplements That Extend Motor Skills and Spatial Force 161

Dress that Intervenes Between Body and Climate 166

Dress as Total Environment 170

Summary 173

Study Tools 173

Readings for Part Two 176

II.1 *Pressure of Menswear on the Neck in Relation to Visual Performance* by Leonora M. Langan and Susan M. Watkins 176

II.2 *Innerskins/Outerskins: Gut and Fishskin* by Pat Hickman 179

Part Three

SCALES OF CULTURE AND DRESS 185

7 **Small-scale Culture and Dress** 186

Small-scale Culture and Dress 188

Population, Residence, and Dress 190

Technology, Economy, and Dress 191

Social Structure, Division of Labor, and Dress 197

Polity and Dress 199

Religion and Dress 200

Summary 204

Study Tools 205

8 **Large-scale Culture and Dress** 208

Characteristics of Large-scale Cultures 210

Population, Residence, and Dress 212

Technology, Economy, and Dress 213

Social Structure, Division of Labor, and Dress 218

Polity and Dress 222

Religion and Dress 229

Summary 232

Study Tools 233

9 **Global-scale Culture and Dress** 236

Characteristics of Global-scale Cultures 239

Population, Residence, and Dress 239

Technology, Economy, and Dress   243

Social Structure, Division of Labor, and
Dress   246

Polity and Dress   249

Religion, Ideology, and Dress   256

Summary   257

Study Tools   258

Readings for Part Three   261

III.1 *Ga'anda Scarification: A Model for Art and
Identity* by Marla C. Berns   261

III.2 *They Don't Wear Wigs Here* by Barbara A.
Schreier   269

III.3 *Court, Formal and Everyday Dress During the
Late Ch'ing Dynasty* by A. C. Scott   273

III.4 *Transnational Biographies and Local
Meanings: Used Clothing Practices in Lusaka*
by Karen Tranberg Hansen   277

Part Four

ART, AESTHETICS, AND DRESS   285

10 **The Art of Creating Dress**   286

The Art of Dress   288

The Aesthetics of Dress   288

The Universality of the Art of Dress   290

Creating Forms of Dress   293

Analyzing the Meaning and Form of
Dress   297

Types of Body Supplements Used in Creating
Dress   299

Cultural Typologies of Dress   302

Summary   305

Study Tools   306

11 **Ideals for Individual Appearance and the
Art of Dress**   308

Ideals within Different Societies   310

Ghana   311
United States   313

Achieving Ideals   314

Cultural Standards for the Art of Dress   316

Change in Cultural Standards   320

Cultural Ideals in Body Form   322

Body and Dress   323

Summary   326

Study Tools   326

12 **The Art of Dress, Conformity, and
Individuality**   328

Individual Choice, Societal Influence, and the Art
of Dress   330

*Social Status and Role, Conformity, and
Dress*   332

Individuality and the Art of Dress   339

Conformity, Individuality, and Fashion in
Dress   341

Fashion Leaders   342

Summary   342

Study Tools   344

13 **Dress and the Arts**   346

Dress as an Art Form   348

Dress as an Integral Part of the Arts   350

Similarities between Stage Costume and Everyday
Dress   351

Special Requirements of Costume   354

*Accommodation to Body Action and Demands of
Performance*   354
*Adjustment to Performance Space and
Lighting*   358
Performer in Relation to the Costume   360
*Relation of Costume to the Type of
Performance*   361

Visual and Literary Arts   366

Visual Arts   366
Literary Arts   367

Artists in the Field of Design   370

Influence of Artists on Fashion   370

Summary   371

Study Tools   372

Readings for Part Four   374

IV.1   *The Aesthetics of Men's Dress of the Kalabari of Nigeria* by Tonye V. Erekosima and Joanne B. Eicher   374

IV.2   *The Sweetness of Fat: Health, Procreation, and Sociability in Rural Jamaica* by Elisa J. Sobo   384

IV.3   *Scruffy is Badge of Pride, but Some Physicists Long for Cool* by Malcolm W. Browne   388

IV.4   *Signature Style: Falling Off the Fashion Train with Frida, Georgia and Louise* by Jo Ann C. Stabb   390

Part Five

DRESS AND THE FUTURE   395

14   **Your Future and Dress**   396

Population, Residence, and Dress   398

Technology, Economy, and Dress   400

Social Structure, Division of Labor, and Dress   402

Polity, Ideology, and Dress   405

Your Future and Dress   405

Summary   407

Study Tools   408

Reading for Part Five   410

V.1   *Cosmic Couture* by Elizabeth Snead   410

Bibliography   413

Index   433

PREFACE

"What shall I wear?" "How shall I dress?" Everywhere in the world, people make daily decisions about what to wear or how to dress. Some people have more choices than others do; some people like making the decision more than others do. Our book is about the daily act of dress in cultures around the world. We use the word *dress* to emphasize a wide variety of behaviors connected to getting dressed. These behaviors include not just putting on clothing and accessories, but also grooming the body. And some examples include being dressed without wearing any clothing at all. Chapter 1 presents the definition and classification system of dress, and Chapter 2 presents a discussion of culture and society. Chapters 3 and 4 present a basis for understanding that the study of dress involves analyzing actual artifacts as well as visual representations of them and written documents about them. Even cartoons, etiquette books, and satiric writings provide us with evidence about the meaning of dress in our lives.

We present a three-pronged approach to understanding dress: its relationship to human beings as biological, aesthetic, and social animals. Chapter 5 focuses on physical appearance and dress, and Chapter 6 on the body, dress, and environment. Chapters 7, 8, and 9 present in detail concepts of the scales of world cultures as related to dress.

We tackle the idea of how people in different types of societies have different cultural practices associated with dress. In reaching the third millenium, we see an enormous variety of ways that humans dress themselves to communicate with others. We perceive differences and also similarities in the ways we as human beings organize our lives with many interrelated and complex facets. These facets include the social structures of kinship, religion, polity, and economy, along with our cultural practices related to technology, aesthetic systems, and values. In addition, our individual psychological makeup and individual emotional lives become intertwined with others.

In Chapters 10 through 13, topics related to dress as an art form are developed, ranging from personal considerations in using dress as art to analyzing the part dress plays in various recognized art forms. The book concludes with a discussion of the future of dress in Chapter 14.

In North America, as we move into the twenty-first century, the theme of cultural diversity permeates many parts of our lives. Although the particulars of dress in specific places demand sophisticated analysis and understanding of the people under study, the basic fact remains that human beings dress their bodies to communicate who they are and to receive personal satisfaction. To enable students to appreciate the complexity of dress, we draw on and integrate several disciplinary perspectives. Although the basic approach comes from the social sciences with an appreciation for physical anthropology, social anthropology, economics, and sociology, we also access information from related disciplines ranging from chemistry to art.

We have added readings to the text from a variety of sources to give students and teachers a chance for discussion and controversy. Although we use examples from all over the world, we have frequently cited specific examples from two areas of the world, the countries of India and Nigeria, where we have done fieldwork and have extensive knowledge. Examples of dress from these places provide a contrast to the all-too-familiar pictures of the dressed body in North America that we carry in our minds as participating members of this cultural perspective. Our expectation is that such largely unfamiliar sketches of dress elsewhere will provoke some new ideas about choices and variety in the lives of human beings. At the end of each part, several articles will give the student of dress a chance to explore some of the issues in the chapters in a little more depth, show how concepts introduced in the part can be applied to the dress of a particular society, or provide ethnographic information to which the reader can apply concepts from the part in order to understand the dress of a particular culture better. We indicated key concepts in italics and important terms in boldface. Important terms, discussion questions, and activities are included at the end of each chapter.

Our volume is a revision of *The Visible Self*, by Mary Ellen Roach and Joanne B. Eicher (1973). New in this revision is elaboration on the concept of dress, introduction of a discussion of ethnocentrism, ethnic dress, and the idea of cultural authentication as related to dress, as well as a new approach to understanding society and culture through an organizing scheme of small-scale, large-scale, and global-scale cultures.

ACKNOWLEDGEMENTS

Many people helped us turn the manuscript into a published book, providing support in every way, from encouragement and morale-boosting to word-processing and supplying images, library searches, editorial suggestions, and recommendations for readings.

Our foremost thanks go to Mary Ellen Roach-Higgins, whose contributions as co-author of the first edition continued to influence our work. We gratefully thank Mija Valdez, Barbara Sumberg, and Masami Suga, who worked on and critiqued early drafts of the text and bibliography. Michaele Haynes deserves special thanks for her work in revising Chapters 5 and 6. Any errors are ours, not hers. Nancy Ann Rudd made excellent and thoughtful suggestions for elaboration of the text and editing. We greatly appreciate that Betty Issenman and Jo Ann Stabb revised papers for us to use as readings, and we thank Mark Schultz for suggesting other candidates for readings.

Jennifer Yurchisin came through with superb library sleuthing skills. Many students in our courses at University of Minnesota and University of Idaho provided enthusiasm, insightful experiences, and thoughtful, sometimes challenging, questions for class discussion in analyzing dress. In addition, they suffered through early drafts of both text and reading selections. We appreciate Jennifer Stahlberg and Nancy Fulton, who were especially painstaking in giving feedback on the text.

Readers selected by the publisher were also very helpful. They include Laurie Apple, Southwest Texas State University; Linda A. Arthur, University of Hawaii at Manoa; Suzanne Loker, Cornell University; Elizabeth Lowe, Queens College; Judy K. Miler, South Carolina State University; Nancy Nelson, UNC-Greensboro; Elaine L. Pederson, Oregon State University; Nancy Ann Rudd, The Ohio State University; Sarah Schmidt, UNC-Greensboro; and Ann Stemm, Illinois State University.

Susan Torntore and Theresa Winge have been allies and colleagues in many ways. They assisted with the revision process by attending the course, suggesting edits, and spending countless hours in meticulous proofreading. Their attention to detail is exemplified in the bibliography. Fueled by chocolate, they gallantly waded through what seemed to be an unending process. Pamela Foss valiantly transposed the master bibliography into APA style. A big job!

Colleagues cheerfully supplying images included Suzanne Baizerman, Marla Berns, Margaret Issenman, and Robert Hillestad. Their contributions enhanced the illustration program that was so professionally researched by Elsa Peterson, Stephanie Clopton, and Judy K. Brody of Elsa Peterson, Ltd.

The Fairchild staff rose to many challenges in seeing the publication completed. We appreciate the efforts of Pam Kirshen Fishman and Olga Kontzias, who initially prodded us and waited patiently for the first revision. As the manuscript developed, others helped us immeasurably: Sylvia Weber, Beth Applebome, Mary Siener, and Priscilla Taguer.

Family members who were flexible when deadlines got tight and commitments needed changing include David and Emma Trayte, Tom Anderson and Elsa Lutz, and Cynthia, Carolyn, and Diana Eicher and their families. Colleagues in the School of Family and Consumer Sciences at the University of Idaho provided a particularly salutary environment for a junior faculty member to flourish. Colleagues in the Department of Design, Housing, and Apparel at the University of Minnesota continue to be critical players in each of our lives. Funds from the Regents' Professorship at the University of Minnesota strategically supported the final details for publication.

We want to acknowledge the catalytic effect of collaboration. Working together can be a hair-raising experience, but the process stretched our minds along with being valuable and energizing. We end with an observation from Paul Bohannon:

Textbooks are a difficult literary form. The author of a textbook is writing for two audiences: students and professors. It's something like children's books. Children don't buy books—adults buy books to give to children; the challenge therefore is to write a book that adults will buy and that children will like. College students do indeed buy textbooks, but they don't select them—professors do. The task is to cover what the professor thinks students should know, in a way congenial to the professor, at the same time that students find it interesting and worthwhile. (1992, p. ix)

We hope that both professors and students find this book engaging and worthwhile, but we also want critical examination that may even provoke controversy and heated discussion in- and outside the classroom.

Joanne B. Eicher
Sandra Lee Evenson
Hazel A. Lutz

CREDIT FOR FIGURES

CHAPTER 1

1.1: Photo courtesy of Professor Donald Doll, Creighton University Jesuit Community. **1.2:** Courtesy of Information Canada Photothèque. **1.5:** Photograph © Efrain J. Gonzalez, Sacred Body Art Emporium, New York. **1.7:** Corbis ©. **1.8:** Courtesy of the Haffenreffer Museum of Anthropology, Brown University. **1.9:** Michael K. Nichols/National Geographic Society Image Collection. **1.10:** Courtesy of the Federal Ministry of Information, Lagos, Nigeria. **1.11:** © UCLA Fowler Museum of Cultural History. Photo by Richard Todd. **1.12:** Paramount chief Nana Akyanfuo Akowuah Dateh II, akwanuhene and asafonhene. Photograph by Eliot Elisofon, 1970. C 2 ASH 25 Eliot Elisofon Photographic Archives, National Museum of African Art. **1.13:** Bruce Dale/National Geographic Society Image Collection. **1.14:** UCLA Fowler Museum of Cultural History. **1.15a:** © Gerry Ellis/ENP Images. **1.15b:** Isabella Tree/Hutchison Picture Library.

CHAPTER 2

2.1: AP Photo/New Evening Post, Fu Chun Wai. **2.2:** Photo by Annette Lynch, Ph.D., The University of Northern Iowa. **2.3:** AP Wide World Photo. **2.4a:** Courtesy Levi Strauss & Co. **2.4b:** Breese/Liaison Agency. **2.4c:** Based on a drawing in *Labour Pains and Labour Power* by Patricia Jeffery, Roger Jeffery, and Andrew Lyon, London: Zed Books, 1989. **2.5b:** © Wolfgang Kaehler Photography.

CHAPTER 3

3.1: Based on "Siberian Mummy Unearthed" by Natalya Polosmak, photographs by Charles O'Rear, *National Geographic*, October 1994. **3.2a and b:** Courtesy of the Art Institute of Chicago; **3.2c:** Used with the permission of the Field Museum of Natural History. **3.3:** Leksands Kulturhus Bibliotek Museum Lokalhistoriskt Arkiv, Leksand, Sweden. **3.4a:** The Granger Collection. **3.4b:** Corbis ©. **3.6:** Courtesy of Morton Salt Company, A Division of Morton-Norwich Products, Inc. **3.7a:** *Victorian Fashions and Costumes from Harper's Bazaar: 1867–1898* edited by S. Blum, Dover, 1974. **3.7b:** *Sportstyle*, February, 1996, Courtesy, Fairchild Publications.

CHAPTER 4

4.1: Reprinted with special permission of King Feature Syndicate. **4.2:** Based on drawings in *Be Beautiful: The Complete Guide to the Art of Make-Up* by Di Biggs and Maxi Meah, London: Chartwell Books, Inc., 1980 and *Style and the Man* by Alan Flusser, New York: HarperCollins, 1996. **4.4a:** Rickerby/Sipa Press. **4.4b:** © Hulton Getty/Liaison Agency. **4.4c:** © B. & C. Alexander.

CHAPTER 5

5.1: © Jeffry W. Myers/Stock Boston. **5.2:** Information Canada Photothèque. **5.3a:** Naomi Duguid/Asia Access. **5.3b:** © Mike Langford/AUSCAPE. **5.4:** © David Austen/Stock Boston. **5.5:** © 1980 Rene Burri Magnum Photos, Inc. **5.6:** *Atlas of Men* by William H. Sheldon, New York: Harper and Row, 1954. **5.7a and 5.7b:** Corbis/Lynn Goldsmith ©. **5.7c:** © Maria Valentino/Corbis Sygma.

CHAPTER 6

6.1: *Races: A Study of the Problems of Race Formation in Man*, by C. Coon, S. Garn, and J. Birdsell, Charles C. Thomas, 1950. **6.2 and 6.3:** Based on drawings in *Clothing: The Portable Environment* by Susan Watkins, Ames, IA: Iowa State University Press, 1995. **6.4:** Based on a drawing in a brochure from the University of Idaho College of Agriculture. **6.5a:** © 1998 J.Jill catalog and © 1998 Mike Donnelly. **6.5b:** Courtesy of Lenore Landry. **6.6a:** © Wolfgang Kaehler Photography. **6.6b:** © Vince Streano/The Image Works. **6.7:** Courtesy of the Museum of Contemporary Crafts of the American Craftsman's Council from *Body Covering* exhibition, April 6–June 9, 1968, National Aeronautics Space Administration, Manned Spacecraft Center, Houston, TX. **6.8 a–d:** Courtesy of Charles Miles. **6.10 a and b:** Based on drawings in *Clothing: The Portable Environment* by Susan Watkins, Ames, IA: Iowa State University Press, 1995. **6.12:** Adapted from "The Arctic Soldier: Possible Research Solutions for His Protection," by Ralph F. Guttman in *Review of Research on Military Problems in Cold Regions*, Charles R. Kalb, ed., A AL-TDR-64-28. **6.13a:** © NASA/Paul S. Howell/Liaison Agency. **6.13b:** © NASA/EPIX/Liaison Agency.

CHAPTER 7

7.1: Courtesy of Claudia Andujar, *Natural History Magazine*. **7.2:** © Michael Yamashita. **7.3:** Based on a drawing in *The Greenland Mummies* by Jens Peder Hart Hansen, Jorgen Meldgaard, and Joren Nordquist, Smithsonian Institution Press, 1991. **7.4:** The Granger Collection. **7.5:** Isabella Tree/Hutchison Picture Library. **7.6:** Jean Morris Collection, McGregor Museum, Kimberley, South Africa.

Used by permission of Mrs. M. E. Poolton and Mrs. Christine O'Brien. **7.7:** William Bond/National Geographic Society Image Collection. **7.8:** Hutchison Picture Library. **7.9:** © David Keith Jones/Images of Africa Photobank.

CHAPTER 8

8.1: Based on a drawing in *Cultural Anthropology: Tribes, States, and the Global System* by John H. Bodley, Mountain View, CA: Mayfield, 1994. **8.3a:** Based on a drawing from *Cut My Cote* by Dorothy K. Burnham, Royal Ontario Museum, 1973. **8.3b:** © Royal Ontario Museum. **8.4:** J. G. Fuller/Hutchison Picture Library. **8.5:** Victoria & Albert Picture Library. **8.6:** The Royal Collection © 1999, Her Majesty Queen Elizabeth II. **8.7:** Reproduced courtesy Dover Publications, Inc. **8.8** and **8.9:** *Strategic Atlas: A Comparative Geopolitics of the World's Powers,* by G. Chalian and J-P Rageau, maps by Catherine Petit, New York: Harper & Row Perennial Library, 1990. **8.10:** © 1996 Lise Sarfati, Magnum Photos, Inc. **8.11:** Photo Sipa Press; graphics courtesy of Time Life Syndication. **8.12a:** Based on a drawing in *Indian Clothing Before Cortes* by P. R, Anwalt, University of Oklahoma Press, 1981. **8.12b:** © Photograph by Erich Lessing. Erich Lessing/Art Resource, NY.

CHAPTER 9

9.1: © The New Yorker Collection 1997 Jack Ziegler from cartoonbank.com. All Rights Reserved. **9.5:** Dave Nagel/Liaison Agency. **9.7:** Courtesy of *Women's Wear Daily.* **9.8:** © 1995 Dennis Cox/D. E. Cox Photo Library. **9.9:** Courtesy of Hazel A. Lutz. **9.10:** © Kees/Sygma.

CHAPTER 10

10.1: AP Wide World Photo. **10.3:** Based on a drawing in "The Anthropology of Posture," by Gordon W. Hewes, *Scientific American,* Feb. 1957. **10.4a:** Corbis/Baldwin Ward ©. **10.4b** and **10.4c:** Corbis ©. **10.4d:** Corbis/Lynn Goldsmith ©. **10.5a:** Photograph courtesy, Huntington Historical Society, Huntington, NY. **10.5b:** Courtesy of *Women's Wear Daily.* **10.6:** Cartoon by Mike Luckovich, reprinted with the permission of Creators Syndicate. **10.7:** Based on a drawing in *Dress Like a Million (on Considerably Less): A Trend-Proof Guide to Real Fashion* by Leah Feldon, illustrations by Tamin Bressan, New York: Villard Books, 1994. **10.8:** Photograph by Joanne Eicher. **10.9:** Courtesy of *Women's Wear Daily.* **10.10:** Based on drawings in *Kama Kalpa or The Hindu Ritual of Love,* by P. Thomas, Bombay: D.B. Taraporevala Sons & Co. Private Ltd. Treasure House of Books.

CHAPTER 11

11.1a: Alinari/Art Resource, NY. **11.1b:** Erich Lessing/Art Resource, NY. **11.1c:** Erich Lessing/Art Resource, NY. **11.2:** Based on drawings in *Ghana's Heritage of Culture* by Kofi Atubam, Koehler and Amelang, 1963. **11.3a:** The Granger Collection. **11.3b:** Everett Collection. **11.4:** Cartoon by Mike Smith, reprinted by permission of United Feature Syndicate. **11.5a and b:** Based on drawings in *Style and the Man* by Alan Flusser, New York: HarperCollins, 1996. **11.6:** DOONESBURY © 1982 G. B. Trudeau. Reprinted with permission of UNIVERSAL PRESS SYNDICATE. All rights reserved. **11.7:** Courtesy of the British Museum. **11.8:** © 1999 Annie Leibovitz/Contact Press Images. **11.9:** Courtesy of *Women's Wear Daily.* **11.10:** Courtesy of *Women's Wear Daily.*

CHAPTER 12

12.2: B. W. Stitzer/PhotoEdit. **12.3:** Reprinted with special permission by King Feature Syndicate. **12.5 left:** Everett Collection. **12.5 right:** Photo by Lorenzo Agius for Rockport Footwear. Courtesy of World of Wonder, Hollywood, CA; The Lemonade Factory, London; and Rockport, Marlboro, MA. **12.6a:** Forrest Anderson/Liaison Agency. **12.6b:** © 1995 Dennis Cox/ChinaStock. **12.7:** AP Wide World Photo.

CHAPTER 13

13.1a and 13.1b: Courtesy of the Federal Ministry of Information, Lagos, Nigeria. **13.2:** Courtesy of Judith Lieber, Inc. Photograph by Tim Dalal Studio. **13.3a:** Courtesy of Robert Hillestad. **13.3b:** Courtesy of the Witte Museum, San Antonio, Texas. **13.4:** The Metropolitan Museum of Art, Fletcher Fund, 1944. (44.133.2). **13.5:** Carolyn J. Ngozi Eicher, 1991. **13.6a, 13.6b, and 13.6c:** Everett Collection. **13.6d:** Courtesy of the actor's agent, Peter Schub, New York. **13.7:** © Copyright The British Museum. **13.8a:** AP Photo/Rogelio Solis. **13.8b:** Copyright © 1996 Jack Vartoogian. **13.9:** Photo courtesy of Professor Donald Doll, Creighton University Jesuit Community. **13.10a and 13.10b:** Corbis ©. **13.10c:** Everett Collection. **13.11:** The Granger Collection. **13.12:** AP Photo/Anat Givon. **13.13a:** David Redfern/Retna Ltd. **13.13b:** © Index Stock and Wayne Hoy. **13.14:** Lisa Terry/Liaison Agency. **13.15:** Courtesy of the Smithsonian Institution. **13.16a:** © Amy Simms. **13.16b:** © Stine Heilman. **13.17:** Courtesy of British Film Institute Films: Stills, Posters and Designs; and Carlton International.

CHAPTER 14

14.3: © 1998. Photographed by R.A. Flynn, Inc. **14.4:** AP Photo/Lennox McLendon. **14.5:** Courtesy of *Women's Wear Daily.* **14.6:** Corbis/Robert Mountfort ©.

THE VISIBLE SELF

Global Perspectives on Dress, Culture, and Society

Part One The Systematic Study of Dress

What makes dressing the body a particularly human activity? To answer this question, we first need to have a shared definition of what it means to "be dressed." In Chapter 1 we provide a definition of dress that includes more than putting clothing on our bodies. We also include the acts that we human beings engage in when we talk about getting dressed in the morning. Ordinarily, we mean that we go through a series of processes that may involve washing all or parts of our bodies, brushing our teeth, combing our hair, applying a scented liquid of some type like lotion, aftershave, cologne or perfume, and then covering all or part of our bodies with garments and accessories. We then discuss in Chapter 2 how being dressed relates to the concepts of culture and society in order to provide an appreciation of different ways of interpreting what being dressed means.

How do we know what we know about dress? We draw from a wide array of sources. Some sources are everyday anecdotes and accounts that tell how particular individuals felt about their own way of dress. Others are scholarly writings from disciplines such as anthropology, sociology, psychology, economics, art history, and history. Some are soundly reasoned and others are impressionistic. Nevertheless, each of these approaches to the study of dress gives us some evidence about the meaning of such human acts as wearing clothes, fixing our hair, displaying jewelry, or being tattooed. One of our challenges in studying dress systematically is deciding on the accuracy of the information or its bias. In Chapters 3 and 4, we delve into various subject areas that have provided us with material for study and analysis of the dressed person, and we raise questions about assessment of different types of evidence.

1

The Classification System of Dress

OBJECTIVES

To understand the classification system of dress.

To distinguish between body modifications and body supplements.

To apply the classification system to cross-cultural examples.

HOW WE DRESS OUR bodies has significance that has intrigued people for centuries. Human beings, in every society on the globe, dress themselves for many and varied reasons, including protection of the body, extension of the body's abilities, beautification, and nonverbal communication about the wearer. However, great variation exists from one society to another in the forms of dress and their meanings. For example, the sight of adolescents in jeans and T-shirts instead of school uniforms in the United States or sarongs in another country means something different both to the wearers and to those who view them. To understand differences in dress across different societies and cultures as well as within a particular society and culture, we need a clear understanding of the concepts of dress, culture, and society. In this chapter, we present a classification system for the study of dress in different societies and cultures. We expand on the ideas of society and culture as important to the study of dress in Chapter 2.

DRESS

We view *dress* as a product and as a process that distinguishes human beings from other animals. As a product, many items are involved in dress that are a result of human creativity and technology. As a process, dressing the body involves actions undertaken to modify and supplement the body in order to address physical needs and to meet social and cultural expectations about how individuals should look. This process includes all five senses of seeing, touching, hearing, smelling, and tasting—regardless of the society and culture into which an individual is born.

Because clothing is easily seen and felt, sight and touch most quickly come to mind, as in the case of making decisions about color and texture in the clothes we wear or in the cosmetics we apply to our skins. However, our definition of dress as body modifications and body supplements includes more than clothing, or even clothing and accessories. Our definition encompasses many ways of dressing ourselves. In addition to covering our bodies, we apply color to our skins by use of cosmetics, whether paints or powders, and also apply color and pattern through tattoos. We dress our bodies by adding scent, as when we use spices, herbs, perfumes, or aftershave lotions. We also dress our bodies by eliminating actual or possible body odor when we bathe, shower, or use mouthwash. In addition, we modify taste by the application of pomades and lipsticks that can provide a pleasant sensory experience, both to ourselves and to others. Some items of dress contribute sound to our dress, as in the examples of many types of jewelry such as charms on a bracelet or pods or bells on dance anklets. Such sounds may be found to be either attractive or annoying when the wearer moves, depending on the situation. For example, cleats or stiletto-heeled shoes may seem intimidating when coming from an unidentified and unseen source (such as someone approaching on a dark street). In contrast, the same sounds may seem reassuring when associated with the familiar footsteps of a particular person. Some textiles, when worn, make sounds as our bodies move, as in the cases of taffeta or corduroy or in the example in Figure 1.1 of the girls in Dakota Indian jingle dresses.

Languages around the world have their own words and terms for items of dress and the process of dressing the body which often have value-laden ideas attached to them. In order to study the products and processes of dress both within and across cultures, we present a classification system that uses culturally neutral concepts to identify specific forms of body modifications and supplements around the world. Our *classification system for dress* organizes what we call body modifications and body supplements according to their relationship to various parts of the human body. The classification system shown in Table 1.1 is based on the definition of the dress of an individual as the assemblage of **body modifications** and **body supplements** displayed by a person and worn at a particular moment in time.[1] Dressing the body through both of these means is a total sensory system of communication that simultaneously connects an individual to some people and separates him or her from others. This system of communication through dress ordinarily precedes our verbal

Figure 1.1
Metal embellishments on the body supplements of these twins produce rich tinkling sounds at their slightest movement. They are part of the aesthetic appeal of the "jingle dress." Dakota Plains Indian, c. 1990.

communication in face-to-face interaction. Because we usually make a quick assessment of age, gender, social position, and occupation based on an individual's dress before we engage in conversation, the way a person is dressed ordinarily anchors that individual socially and culturally.

Both wearers and observers perceive characteristics of any individual's total dress through all five senses: sight, touch, smell, sound, and taste. These categories are shown across the horizontal axis of Table 1.1. Body modifications are the alterations to the body itself that relate to all five senses. Body supplements are the items that are placed upon the body, most often thought of as garments by Euro-Americans, but this category also includes jewelry and accessories. The constituent parts of an individual's dress, both body modifications and body supplements, can also be classified according to their relationships to the various parts of the body. Body supplements can additionally be characterized, as seen along the vertical axis of Table 1.1, by the way they are made or applied to the body: wrapped, suspended, or preshaped; inserted, clipped, or adhered; and handheld. We categorize body modifications according to which parts of the body they affect and body supplements according to how they relate to the human body. Both items of dress and the processes of dress can alter body processes either negatively, as in the example of a garment being too tight and physically uncomfortable, or positively, as in the example of eyeglasses improving eyesight. As we continue our study of dress, we will also understand that the context of the dress of an individual in a particular society and culture affects whether a process is viewed positively or negatively.

Throughout this book, we use the classification system to understand the power of dress within any society and culture to communicate information about individuals and groups. We turn now to presenting details and examples

6 THE VISIBLE SELF

TABLE 1.1

Classification System for Types of Dress and Their Properties

Types of Dress[a]	Color	Volume and Proportion	Shape and Structure	Surface Design	Texture	Odors and Scents	Sound	Taste
Body modifications								
Transformations of								
Hair								
Skin								
Nails								
Muscular/skeletal system								
Teeth								
Breath								
Body supplements								
Enclosures								
Wrapped								
Suspended								
Preshaped								
Combination-type								
Attachments to body								
Inserted								
Clipped or Pressure fastened								
Adhered								
Attachments to body enclosures								
Inserted								
Clipped or Pressure fastened								
Adhered								
Handheld objects								
By self								
By other								

[a]Both body modifications and body supplements can be further classified according to (a) general body locus (e.g., head, neck, trunk, arms, legs) or (b) more specific locus (e.g., lips, nose, eyelids or lashes, ears, hands, ankles, feet, breasts, genitals).
Source: Adapted from Roach-Higgins and Eicher (1992). This system is based on previous works: Roach-Higgins and Eicher (1973); Roach and Musa (1980).

of the classification system, beginning with body modifications and a discussion of the properties listed across the horizontal axis of Table 1.1. We illustrate these properties with various examples of transformations of the body. We follow the discussion of body modifications with an explanation of the various categories of body supplements.

TYPES OF DRESS

Body Modifications

The body can be temporarily or permanently physically modified in ways that change perception of the body by oneself or by others. The modifications include aspects of the body that are perceived visually such as color, volume and proportion, shape and structure, or surface design. The modifications can also change the feel, the sounds, the odors, or the tastes of the body, whether we consider how the individual experiences himself or herself or how others perceive the individual.

Color

The color of hair and skin can be changed by use of many different processes. Hair can be dyed or lightened. For example, Muslim men in India who have made the pilgrimage to Mecca dye their beards red with henna as a sign of their completion of this religious act. Skin color can be changed, too, by tattooing, powdering, painting, staining, sun-tanning, or bleaching. Elite women of the nineteenth century in Europe and North America treasured white skin and avoided sun-darkened skin by carrying parasols to shade themselves. In the United States in the 1990s, information about the dangers of too much exposure to the sun led some people to relinquish the twentieth-century idea that sun-tanning adds to beauty. In response, drug and cosmetic companies have developed an alternative to the parasol by making lotions containing elements that screen and block the tanning rays of the sun to reduce the rate of tanning. Still other developments are creams that chemically change the color of the skin so that it appears to be "tanned."

Volume and Proportion

The apparent volume and proportion of the body can be changed through various means. Wearing foundation garments such as body slimmers and minimizer bras or adding bustles or shoulder pads alters how the body looks when dressed. More permanent modifications to body volume and proportion can be created through contemporary plastic surgery to change such things as nose formation, breast size, or waist size. Bodybuilding and diet increase body volume and size, as in the case of weight lifters, football players, and other athletes. In contrast, extreme dieting and compulsive behaviors about food intake, leading to bulimia and anorexia, can reduce body size, as may be found in athletes such as gymnasts as well as cheerleaders and dancers. Hair, too, can change in volume and proportion either temporarily or permanently. Teasing and spraying with lacquers increases volume, whereas cutting with thinning scissors reduces the volume of thick hair. Application of hair thickeners, such as mud, or the attachment of hair pieces also changes the volume of hair temporarily. Hair volume may increase permanently through medical treatments to implant hair on a balding head or through treatments with medications such as Minoxidil, which cause hair to grow.

Shape and Structure

Shape and structure of portions of the body can be altered in many ways, too. For example, dressed hair and trimmed beards take on many different temporary shapes through various treatments. Cutting hair is the most common method of changing the shape of beards and hairdos in Europe and North America in the late twentieth century. However, beards in other cultures have sometimes received the range of treatments that late-twentieth-century Westerners usually associate with women's hair dressing. In many cultures around the world, both beards and hair have been brushed, rolled, bound in nets, or treated with solutions by both genders to help the body hair hold particular shapes. In the United States, for example, women's beehive hairdos of the mid-1960s and men's pointed waxed mustaches in the nineteenth century exemplify various means to achieve the desired shape and structure.

Shape and structure of other parts of the body may be changed as well as hair. Infant heads can be easily molded to achieve different shapes, such as a flat head, as seen in Figure 1.2, or a rounded one. Different shapes of corsets and girdles during the past 200 years of Western fashion history temporarily "moved" women's waists, hips, and breasts up and down and in and out. Tightly bound corsets affected a young woman's body so that a permanent

Figure 1.2
The long, tapered shape of the head of this Kwakiutl woman of Vancouver Island was achieved by binding between two padded boards during infancy. This head shape is a mark of beauty among the Northwest Coast Indians.

change to her body shape occurred during the process of growth. In contrast, modern girdles and bras change the shape of the body only when worn, but when removed, allow the body to return to its undressed shape. Figure 1.3 illustrates examples of changes in Western women's silhouette over time. Shoes with thick or high heels also make only temporary changes in the apparent height and leg length of the wearer. However, for many centuries in China, the feet of middle- and upper-class women were permanently shortened through a process of breaking and folding back the four smaller toes, irritating the skin and muscles, and binding the feet tightly with bands of cloth and snug-fitting arched shoes. This restructuring created feet 3 to 5 inches long, each said to be

Woman's corset, 1907

Women's corsets, 1917

Woman's corset, 1923

Brassiere and girdle, 1930s

Brassiere and garter belt of the 1940s

Girdles of the late 1940s and the 1950s

Bikini pants and bra, 1969

Uplift Wonderbra, 1994

Figure 1.3
Staying in fashion involves changes to body modifications as well as to body supplements. Changing fashion in undergarments has altered the relative proportion, shape, size, and emphasis upon women's hips, waists, and breasts.

shaped like a lotus bud. These permanent body modifications changed the feet of Chinese women during the early years of physical growth. Cloth bindings and the wearing of specially designed shoes maintained this ideal shape through adult life. However, these women often became unable to walk easily without the aid of a cane.

Another example of body modification arises from the occupation of Japan by U.S. forces after World War II. Japanese women who wanted to look more Western underwent eye surgery to remove the epicanthic folds in their upper eyelids. Parallel circumstances in Southeast Asia and Korea triggered this permanent body modification to eyes in later years. Men and women in the United States today restructure the shape of thighs, buttocks, chest, and hips through general exercise, bodybuilding, dieting, and plastic surgery. As long as the individual follows a diet and exercise regimen the new shape created will last. On the other hand, plastic surgery to change the shape of the breasts, laser surgery to remove unwanted hair or rejuvenate the skin, and related medical treatments give permanent results, as advertised in Figure 1.4.

Orthodontic treatments also permanently change the shape of the jaw as well as straighten the teeth, and good dental care by a dentist may aid in maintaining a youthful jawline. Moreover, false teeth maintain the illusion of a longer youthful face in aging men and women who through loss of natural teeth and depletion of bone tissue in their jaws would otherwise have foreshortened faces and more protruding lips in old age. As an example of dental treatment in another culture, women in Borneo are noted for filing down the corners of their teeth into points for beauty's sake and as part of a prewedding ritual.

Surface Design

Surface design is often applied to the body in the process of dressing and can be temporary or permanent. Temporary applications of designs include pictures painted on finger- and toenails in North American beauty salons. Another example is the dark red designs called *mehendi* (ma-HEN-dee) that are made by artfully applying a preparation of henna to stain temporary tattoo-like patterns onto the hands and feet of brides and adult women in some parts of North Africa and India.

In some cultures, painted designs stand out from the background of the portion of the body to which they are applied, such as the temporary smudges of black paint that football players wear under their eyes or the variety of face painting designs worn on various social occasions by some American Indians. In other cases, the color and design applied to skin are intended as an enhancement of the natural body, such as women's makeup in the United States at the end of the twentieth century. However, cultural practice trains our eyes to perceive specific lip and eye makeup as the natural coloration of women.

Surface design can also be made by a process of subtraction. Some young men in the 1990s created temporary designs on their scalps by cutting the hair away completely in some areas and allowing it to remain longer in other areas. Daily shaving of facial hair is also a form of design by subtraction, practiced al-

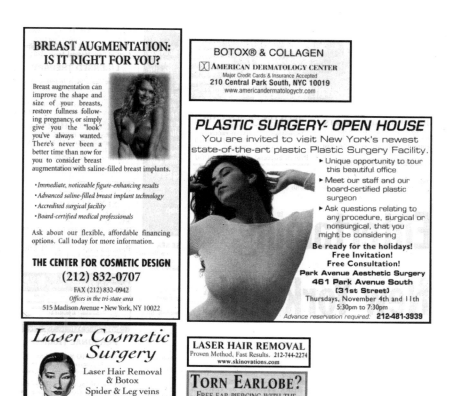
Figure 1.4
The most extensive practice of body modification for dress occurs in the United States. Plastic surgery for almost any part of the body and laser surgery are available to help individuals bring their appearance into closer alignment with cultural ideals of beauty, as these ads show. United States, 1999.

most universally by Western men in the late twentieth century along with the custom of women shaving their legs and underarm areas.

Surface design applications can be permanent, such as tattooed designs on skin, as seen in Figure 1.5. Another fashionable example among North American young people in the late twentieth century is that of inlays of gold and precious gems on teeth. Some tattoos are applied to areas of the body usually covered from view, where they may be viewed by only intimate associates, or perhaps only by the wearer. Others are meant to be viewed publicly. In some societies in the South Pacific Islands, men once received tattoos that covered their bodies from the waist to the knees. These tattoos were so complete that

Figure 1.5
With the permanent modification of his skin color and texture, through application of a tattoo design, this man can never again become completely undressed. His body modification dresses him, albeit in a minimalist manner. c. late twentieth century United States.

Stair described them as "giving the impression that the wearer had donned a suit of small clothes" (Stair as quoted in Gell, 1993, p. 52). Many tattoos are intended to enhance personal or group identity. For example, members of certain gangs in various parts of the world use tattoos to identify themselves to other members and intimate associates. By contrast, the tattoos of identification numbers on the arms of prisoners in Nazi concentration camps were used to effectively remove their personal identity by force.

Texture

Several parts of the body can undergo textural change. Hair may be curled or straightened to provide a common change in texture. Applications of lotions or oils smooth the skin in many cultures. Polish and buffing provide a smooth and shiny look to fingernails. These are all examples of temporary measures that contrast with permanent removal of wrinkles or scars through plastic surgery or face peeling. A dentist can provide a fairly smooth appearance to ridged teeth by enamel filling or capping. The scarification practiced by the Tiv people in Nigeria raises the texture of the skin into a pattern of scars that pleases both the person who is scarified and those who touch the scars (Bohannon, 1956). In addition, the design created is also more shiny and for a while lighter in color than the unscarified skin, creating visual texture for the eye as well as the tactile texture to the hand.

Odors and Scents

Body odors receive attention in the study of dress, because we engage in both the processes of addition and subtraction in regard to bodies and various odors or scents. Each of these processes usually is discussed in terms of grooming practices. When people smell something they define as unpleasant, the smell is generally called an odor, indicating a negative value. Pleasing smells that are applied to the body as part of dressing are usually called scent or fragrance, as distinct from an odor. Deodorants applied to underarms and those placed in shoes function to subtract natural body odors. Bathing with water and soap also removes the smell of body oils rising from perspiration. Simultaneously, scented body and facial soaps along with many deodorant products contribute a fragrance to the body. Hair washing products also remove odor and contribute scent in the same manner. Popular forms of scent used around the world are perfumes and colognes. In some places, such as the Middle East, smoke baths add pleasing scent to the body, as Croutier (1989) discusses in the reading for this chapter. In other places, flowers are worn, often in the hair, to add fragrance.

The mouth also receives special treatment in many cultures. For example, toothpaste and a brush are used to clean the teeth, a process which also sweetens the taste and odor of the mouth. Mint and other popular tastes in the toothpaste change how the mouth smells to any person in close physical proximity. Mouthwashes also change the breath, as do breath fresheners such as sprays or special chewing gum. In some parts of the world people chew spices to sweeten the breath. Many people in the United States often decide what to eat or avoid at mealtime based on a concern for having a pleasant-smelling breath. Though usually remote from the common definition of dressing the body, such meal decisions are about dress in the scientific sense of the word.

In rural India, for a cross-cultural comparison, people clean their mouth with a fresh-cut twig from several species of tree and bush whose sap is considered to have medicinal and cleansing qualities. The end of the twig is chewed to release the sap and turn it into a rough brush which is then used to clean the teeth. Finally, the twig is bent into a U shape to scrape the tongue from back to front. A rinsing with water usually finishes the cleansing, but in some parts of India the nasal passages are also rinsed by inhaling water through the nose and spitting it out the mouth. All these procedures affect the smell of the individual's breath, with cultural practices influencing which parts of the mouth and adjacent areas need to be cleaned.

Sound

The sounds of the body can be temporarily or permanently modified. Cultural ideals of physical movement—posture, gestures, and gait—vary widely. This modification of the body through the training of movement behavior occurs in learning the standards of one's own culture. While such behavior can be changed through conscious countertraining, it is otherwise experienced as a permanent part of the individual. The cultural training of gait and permanent body modifications, such as Chinese foot binding, become evident through sound. Each can affect the sound of a person's footsteps when stiff or hard footwear is worn. For example, Japanese women in living up to a cultural ideal of femininity often barely lift their feet as they take short steps and their shoe-covered feet make a scraping sound against the ground. North American men, in stark contrast, often stride forcefully, which becomes evident by the sharp metallic noise that is made by cleats, popularly attached to the bottom of some men's shoes in the 1950s (or by golf shoes when worn indoors). Conscious training in regard to forms of posture, gesture, and gait can take place. Poise classes for women, popular in the United States in the 1950s, taught women to sit, stand, gesture, and walk with appropriate decorum for that era. Runway models are taught the appropriate stance and gait for presentation of fashion designers' clothes. Choreographers for fashion shows often change their expectations for models' walk and posture positions from year to year, as in the fashion of crossing one foot in front of another to exaggerate hip movement. Part of an actor's training is to create posture, gestures, and gait appropriate to the character portrayed.

Other aspects of body movements that are consciously taught become evident through sound when body supplements that make sound are worn on portions of the body. Tap dancers emphasize the rhythmic sounds made by their shoes. Long fingernails, whether synthetic or natural, give a clicking noise when drummed on a tabletop for whatever reason, such as expressing impatience or boredom, or when using a computer keyboard.

The body itself may produce sound without supplements, according to culturally trained behavior, as in the example of softly padding feet, clapping hands, or snapping fingers. Performance dancers in many parts of the world dance in their bare feet in order to make percussive slapping sounds against the floor in rhythm with the music as part of the performance. In such instances, we train our bodies' movements according to specific cultural ideals and standards that relate to what is considered appropriate "dress." Sometimes, certain body sounds, such as finger snapping, may be considered appropriate in some societies and circumstances and inappropriate in others.

Training of the body also involves modeling or restricting of the sounds of natural body processes such as sneezing and coughing or releasing belches and flatulence. Some may view the cultural control of such acts as not properly falling within the study of dress. However, we can compare the importance of the dress of two North American men belching loudly, where one is wearing jeans in an informal situation and the other a tuxedo at a formal event. What is barely acceptable or humorous behavior in one case becomes totally unacceptable and unexpected behavior when the dress is formal. The imposition of controls while in public paired with the relaxation of controls while in casual or private situations, for example the suppression of a cough in the theater and the full expression of the same cough at home, indicates the range of behaviors of dressing the body for various public and private audiences.

The study of dressing the body brings us to the edge of other scientific disciplines. Thus, the study of behavior to restrain or give full vent to a belch may fall under the study of physical anthropology, just as the study of plastic surgery also falls under the heading of medicine. Yet both the control of belches and plastic surgery influence the way an individual presents the dressed self to the world.

Taste

Taste may also be involved in dressing the body. Grooming procedures for the mouth freshen the taste of the mouth as experienced by the individual. Cleaning the mouth before eating also improves the experience of the taste of the food. In India people ordinarily rinse the mouth with water before and after eating a meal. In all cultures mouth cleaning and freshening procedures alter how a person's mouth tastes when kissed, and therefore may be important in interpersonal relationships. Flavored lip glosses may also be appreciated by the one kissing as well as the one being kissed.

In regard to the mouth, we have discussed temporary procedures that recur every day, or at every meal. There are also more permanent procedures that can affect the smell and taste of the mouth. Gum disease contributes an unpleasant odor to a person's breath; successful medical treatment for the disease by a dentist can permanently improve the taste and smell of the mouth. Although some of the decisions that we make about dressing our bodies, particularly about body modifications, may be interpreted as falling in the arena of medicine rather than fashion, some individuals undertake medical treatments based on appearance, not on health.

Permanence of Modifications

Changes made to the body may be temporary or permanent. For example, lipstick can be rubbed or washed off but a tattoo cannot. Many of the temporary changes most commonly practiced are called grooming rituals and are done on a regular basis, daily, weekly, or monthly. These include such things as combing the hair, bathing, or trimming the nails.

Some modifications are semipermanent; that is, they may have a long life but are still not permanent. For example, no matter how many face-lifts a person has, wrinkles will eventually appear again. The dyeing of hair may change both color and texture and a hand lotion may smooth the texture of the skin and add a pleasant scent to the body, but both must be repeated to maintain their long-term effects. Products are often marketed based on their relative permanence. For example, an individual may see an advantage in temporary hair color, for an "undesirable" shade can be changed with the next shampooing. Similarly some women prefer to use long-wearing lipstick, which eliminates the frequent need to reapply color throughout the day. Temporary tattoos may offer the thrill of rebellion without the pain.

Body Supplements

Supplements can enclose the body, be directly attached to the body, or held for an individual by another, and they can be temporary or permanent. Body supplements can create illusions about characteristics of the body, completely obscure the body, or simply enhance it by allowing the body to be openly visible or highlighting some feature of it. People living in cold places who need to keep their bodies warm may think primarily of clothes when they think of the subject of dress. Clothes are only one form of body supplement and are primarily temporary. Many other kinds exist. For instance, women who wear costume jewelry often change their earrings from day to day, to match their clothing, whether or not their ears are pierced. These earrings supplement the body temporarily, in contrast to a supplement such as a naval ring, ordinarily not removed daily.

Enclosures

A body **enclosure** means that the supplement surrounds a portion of the body, whether or not it actually covers the body. For example, both a necklace and a neck scarf enclose the neck but only the scarf covers it. Several types of supplements enclose the body and generally fall into the common English categories of garments and jewelry. Enclosures take several forms. They include articles that are wrapped around a portion of the body, suspended from it, or preshaped to fit it.

Wrapped Primarily flat unsewn garments such as Roman togas, Indonesian sarongs, and head scarves or items such as ribbons for tying up hair, tied belts, sashes, and bandannas exemplify **wrapped enclosures**. These enclosures adjust to desired shape and fit each time they are worn. Thus they easily accommodate changes in body size and can also be easily shared and worn by individuals of different body builds. When not worn, they can be folded or laid flat for convenient storage. Sometimes a jewelry item is made in a long rope of beads or gold links, the ends unattached, and becomes a wrapped body enclosure when it is worn by wrapping or tying around the neck.

Wrapped textile garments comprise a major form of dress in many parts of the world. Typically, a wrapped body enclosure worn as a primary garment is most frequently associated with warm or hot climates, such as is characteristic of many countries in Southeast Asia and Africa. For example, many West Africans wear wrapped lower body garments, and ancient Egyptians wore garments wrapped and pleated to fit the body. Groups such as the American Plains Indians also wore wrapped buffalo robes (Fletcher & La Flesche, 1911, pp. 360–362) and later, trade blankets (Kapoun, 1992).

Wrapped enclosures are worn by many of the large population of India at the millennium. The primary garment for women is a wrapped *sari*. In addition, wrapped turbans, or head cloths, are still worn by Indian men in northern and western India. Even those adult women who wear preshaped primary garments, such as the pants called *salwar* (SAHL-war) and tunics called *kamiz* (kaa-MEEZ), also wear a suspended and wrapped cloth used as a shawl or veil, called a *dupatta* (doo-PUTT-ah), on the head. It consists of a long rectangle of cloth suspended from the head and wrapped around the upper body. Manual laboring men often wear a wrapped lower garment called a *lungi* (LOON-ghee), which consists of about 2 yards of cloth. In the first half of the twentieth century, the majority of men in India wore wrapped lower and upper body garments, before Western trousers and shirts became popular.

Suspended **Suspended body enclosures** hang from a portion of the body. These include items such as ponchos and chasubles, which are suspended from the shoulders; necklaces, which hang from the neck; and bracelets, which hang from the wrist. Earrings for pierced ears hang from the earlobes. Specific examples include amulet pouches worn suspended around the neck among some American Indian groups. Adult males in India of the "twice born" (i.e., priestly and ruling) castes wear a loop of sacred thread suspended over their shoulder and around their torso as a marker of their high social status. Young girls in some parts of India suspend a piece of jewelry from their hips with an ornament hanging in front to cover their genital area.

Preshaped **Preshaped body enclosures** are characteristic of many cultures, but they are more closely associated with European clothing, especially the tailoring tradition of both men's and women's wear in England, Europe, and North America. The Inuit (formerly called Eskimo) and other peoples dwelling in the Arctic Circle regions also have ancient traditions of preshaping garments in order to preserve the body's heat in a climate of extreme cold. Jackets, trousers, and overcoats all require a careful fitting to the body in order to achieve the European or the North American cultural ideal of appropriate dress. Many other items, outside of tailored or other cut-and-sewn textile items, are also preshaped: hats, shoes, sandals, and belts comprise a few examples. Cloth and other flat materials such as leather are not the only things to be shaped into body enclosures. Jewelry made of metals and beads may also be preshaped. Such jewelry is commonly used as body decoration in the form of rings, necklaces, and earrings. However, the same materials of metal or beads can be used to make larger preshaped enclosures that cover large portions of the body. For example, medieval European men wore chain-mail garments and metal armor for protection in battle, as Figure 1.6 shows. In South Africa, the Ndebele people wear garments made of beads rather than fabric.

    The construction of preshaped enclosures usually accommodates contours of the wearer's body; for example, a piece of metal is molded into the encircling form of a ring; pieces of cloth are seamed into tubes in the making of trousers; pieces of cloth cut with a combination of curved and straight edges are assembled as a shirt or blouse. Although some articles of jewelry such as a circle bracelet are not as accommodating of body shape as a flexible link bracelet, body size is always a factor, for the bracelet must not be so large as to fall off easily. Some garments are more preshaped than others, as in the case of a Chinese imperial dragon robe which has a loose silhouette compared to a nineteenth-century Euro-American closely fitting woman's dress, shown in Figure 1.7, or a double-breasted men's sport coat.

Combination-Type Many body enclosures simultaneously use more than one of the previously described features, and are called **combination-type body enclosures**. Very loose garments with a minimum of shaping to exact body dimensions are most accurately classified as combinations (e.g., preshaped and

Figure 1.6
This 15th century Italian suit of metal armor consists of many preshaped elements each supplementing and enclosing one or another portion of the wearer's body.

suspended), as in the Teton Dakota leather dress of Figure 1.8. Tent dresses, and tunics in many cultures, are preshaped by cutting and sewing to fit around the neck, shoulders, and arms, but are worn largely suspended from the shoulders. For outdoor wear in winter in the northern parts of North America, one form of headgear consists of a preshaped hood that is suspended from the head and its long wide ties wrapped around the neck like a scarf to enclose it. A man's necktie is preshaped but must be wrapped around the neck to be worn and tied in a particular manner. Other preshaped and wrapped body enclosures are the Colombian shawl, called *ruana* (rue-ah-nah), and the U.S. women's wraparound skirt.

Within a single dress ensemble, many different types of enclosures are worn in combination. The Indian women's sari ensemble, as seen in Figure 1.9, is a combination of a preshaped *choli* (cho-lee), or *blouz* (from blouse) as it is called in northern India, and the wrapped sari. The North American women's bathing suit ensemble is also a combination of a very preshaped swimsuit and a loosely preshaped and suspended cover-up worn when walking to and from the swimming area.

Attachments to the Body
Several items of dress may be directly affixed to different body parts. In Euro-American dress, these **attachments to the body** are most often worn as accessories or jewelry, but in other parts of the world, they sometimes are the primary type of dress.

Inserted **Inserted attachments** to the body include such things as hair pins, combs, barrettes, and flowers thrust into the hair. Hair weaving also involves insertion of real or false hair into the natural hair of an individual to increase apparent length or volume. Earrings for pierced ears, studs for pierced noses, or rings for pierced navels are examples of insertions into other parts of the body, as shown in Figure 1.10.

Figure 1.7
The preshaping of these dress and corset supplements follows the contours of the body at the waist so closely that they severely constrain it; yet the skirts of the dress and petticoat remain quite loose and voluminous around the legs.

Clipped or Pressure Fastened **Pressure fastenings** are used to clip or hold attachments onto various parts of the body. Clip earrings use a spring pressure clip or screw to attach the body supplement to the earlobe. Pince-nez, a form of eyeglasses popular in the West in the nineteenth century, were held on the bridge of the nose by the pressure of the tightly fitted frames. The monocle, popular at the turn of the century among the elite in the West, consisted of a single lens for improving eyesight that was large enough to be held in place in front of the eye by wedging it between the upper brow and the cheek bone. Hair fasteners provide ornamentation in several cultures, and especially for females in North America. For instance, a baby girl is sometimes dressed with a bow held in her hair by Velcro, or hook and loop tape, which clings to the hair.

Adhered Some body supplements are affixed to the body using a glue or mastic. These **adhered or glued attachments** include such items as false mustaches, false eyelashes, and false fingernails. In India, most adult Hindu women wear a small dot in the center of their forehead as a mark of beauty and religious affiliation. In many cases today, this mark consists of a small applied item called a *bindi* (BIN-dee), available in many fashion materials, shapes, and colors, rather than the traditional dot from red powder. Contact lenses might also be considered adhered and may also serve to modify the color of the eyes.

Figure 1.8
Leather body supplements of this type were commonly worn by women of the American Indian communities residing in the plains of central North America in the first half of the nineteenth century. They are still made and worn for special occasions today. This enclosure combines pre-shaping with suspension from the shoulders.

An attachment to the body typically covers only a very small area of the body where it is affixed. Inserted attachments may require body modification. For example, the piercing of ears is required for insertion of some kinds of earrings.

Attachments to Body Enclosures
Some items of dress in various cultures may be attached to the supplements that enclose the body. Often these are additions that play a decorative role in dress.

Inserted In North America, inserted attachments to body enclosures include, for example, cufflinks, brooches, pinned-on corsages or boutonnieres, and stud buttons for men's dress shirts. Military insignia and medals are inserted into the standard-issue uniform to communicate the wearer's rank and valor. Among the Akan of West Africa, as shown in Figure 1.11, warriors on formal occasions wear distinctive garments to which are attached diverse kinds of items, including amulets that contain important pieces of information relevant to the occupation of warrior (McNaugton, 1982).

Figure 1.9
The ensemble of body supplements commonly worn by women in much of India has two basic parts. The *choli*, a pre-shaped enclosure, covers the upper arms, shoulders, and chest. The *sari*, a wrapped enclosure, covers most of the body from head or shoulder to toe.

Figure 1.10
Dress in many cultures of the world incorporates inserted attachments to various parts of the body, as shown in this example from Nigeria.

Figure 1.11
Hunter's and warrior's
shirts in several African
societies are covered with
amulets attached to the
body enclosure by inser-
tion. Over the period of a
wearer's career, he will
collect numerous amulets
that spiritually protect
him or increase his hunt-
ing or fighting prowess.
Akan, Ghana.

Clipped or Pressure Fastened Body enclosures may have attachments affixed to them using clips or spring-loaded fasteners. **Clipped attachments** to body enclosures include men's tie clasps or clip-on bow ties. The latter are a staple of dress for little boys' formal wear in the United States and for the uniforms of food servers in restaurants. Small children in the United States often have special elastic-clip combinations that attach their mittens to the sleeve cuffs of their winter coats so the mittens are not lost when the coat is removed. In the 1950s, a woman often wore a decorative link or beaded chain with clips at each end to hold a cardigan sweater on her shoulders like a cape. Some styles of wedding dresses for North American brides include a train that can be clipped on for the ceremony and removed for dancing at the reception.

Adhered Most examples of **adhered attachments** to body enclosures in the contemporary United States are commonly applied by workers in the apparel factory rather than adhered in the home by the wearer at the time of getting dressed. For example, beads glued onto a moderately priced wedding dress are applied in the factory and the bride receives the dress already beaded. A more common everyday item is the stick-on name tag worn at large functions for easy identification.

Handheld Objects

Many important body supplements consist of **handheld objects**. Handbags and purses, for instance, are an important part of the dress of North American women when out in public. While it is considered inappropriate for a man in the United States to carry a purse, briefcases are common for both men and women. Fans have been used as a handheld body supplement by women and men in

Chinese and Japanese cultures. Among many groups, high-status individuals carry walking sticks or canes as part of their formal dress. In a more familiar example to North Americans, a bride frequently carries a bouquet of flowers in her hand.

Handheld body supplements may not always be held by the individual, but by a trusted friend, peer, or subordinate. This display of trust also lends status to the holder. During the Western wedding ceremony, for instance, the bride's bouquet is held for her much of the time by her attendant. In many African and Southeast Asian countries, an umbrella is always held by an attendant over the head of a king or chief when he appears in public. This umbrella constitutes a sign of his royal status and is a necessary part of the king's dress, as shown in Figure 1.12. The umbrella held for the president of the United States by an aide as he dashes through the rain conveys a similar meaning. Such specialized handheld objects are often indicators of status, either temporary or permanent. A bride is in a state of transition, but a king is always a ruler until death or abdication. In either case, the handheld object signifies an honored person to others present.

Figure 1.12
The royal status of Ghanian kings is indicated during their public appearances by inclusion of an elaborate umbrella in their dress. The umbrella is the king's handheld body supplement, though it is held for him by another.

Relating Body Modifications and Supplements

Many temporary and some permanent modifications to the body involve the application of body supplements. In many parts of the world, a brassiere is used to create a breast shape that changes when the garment is removed. Tight wraparound or fitted forms can simultaneously enclose the body and act as tools for reconstructing it. For example, corsets when worn over a long period of time can have the effect of permanently changing the body's shape. In the United States the wearing of narrow shoes by many women through the course of the lifetime molds the foot to a narrow shape. In contrast, in other parts of the world, people who wear sandals or remain barefoot develop a wider foot shape. Some processes of body modification require the use of body supplements, as in the use of binding cloths to aid in the reconstruction of women's feet in old China to fit a cultural ideal of small feet.

Body enclosures can create the illusion of change in body conformation. For example, shoulder pads in a suit jacket or coat make the wearer's shoulders seem broader and the hips, in contrast, proportionally smaller. Stripes placed horizontally on a body supplement may be used to draw the eye across the body to make a thin person appear wider.

APPLICATION OF THE CLASSIFICATION SYSTEM

Use of the concepts and terminology of the classification system are valuable for beginning the identification of items, processes, and ensembles of dress in a culture outside that of the researcher, writer, or intended reader of an article. Using the system prevents misunderstandings and ethnocentric judgments. For instance, the *dupatta* of northwestern India, as shown in Figure 1.13, can first be identified as a body supplement that encloses the head and the front (and sometimes back) upper torso of married women. It may be preshaped from two pieces of cloth sewn together down the middle of the *dupatta*, or it may consist of one piece of unsewn cloth. In either case, it remains a flat garment that is suspended from the top of the head and falls down the back, covering part of it. In some areas it is wrapped to cover the front of the upper torso, especially shoulders and breasts.

Use of the classification terminology in the preceding example communicates much more about the relationship to the body of the garment in question than the simple, but misleading, translation of *dupatta* into the English word "veil." A veil can refer to a garment that covers only the face, as when attached to a 1950s U.S. woman's hat (Figure 1.14), in which case it is an attachment to a body enclosure and may cover only the face or part of it. "Veil" in U.S. English also refers to the garment worn by a bride, which attaches to a headpiece and trails down her back and over the train of her gown. Ordinarily it is no longer in the front than her waist or hips. This example of a veil is suspended from a body enclosure, and is not wrapped.

Figure 1.13
The *dupatta*, or so-called "veil," is worn with the *salwar* and *kamiz* ensemble by women in South Asia; yet it covers much more than the head or face and its construction and manner of wear are culturally unique. India, second half of twentieth century.

Further development of the identification of the *dupatta* by application of the classification system would address its manner of wear and details of construction, such as color, surface design, and texture. These differentiate, for example, the *dupattas* worn by Rabari (Raw-BAR-ee) women of Gujarat (GOO-jer-aht) state or Sikh (Seekh) women living in the city of New Delhi from other ethnic wearers of similar garments in northern India.

ADVANTAGES OF THE CLASSIFICATION SYSTEM

Use of the concepts and terminology of the classification system across cultures has several advantages over culturally specific and local terms for dress found in an indigenous language. First, the classification system reduces the likelihood of using words that are inherently biased or imply cultural superiority, as is often the case in any indigenous language. We contrast two examples of dress to illustrate this point. Members of Euro-American society expect large portions of the body to be covered with clothing most of the time, and that the

Figure 1.14
We use the word "veil" to describe the piece of transparent netting covering the face of the wearer of this hat. However, it is confusing to use this culturally embedded term to describe the opaque cloth that covers a woman's face, or some other portion of her body, as in Fig. 1.13, in the cultural practices of other societies of the world.

genitals must always be covered when in public. The Nuba (NOO-ba) of northern Africa, until very recently, covered their bodies, if at all, with nothing more than color applied to the skin (Faris, 1972). The Kayapo (kai-YA-poh) (Carneiro, 1994a, 1994b) and Yanomami (yah-no-MAH-mee) (Herzog-Schröder, 1994) of Brazil similarly use color on the body and cover parts of their bodies with cloth or other supplements only on some public occasions. According to Euro-American cultural expectations, the Nuba are "undressed" or "naked," whereas according to Nuba cultural expectations, Euro-Americans might be considered "overdressed" or "compulsive about hiding the body." These examples pose the problem of how one defines "overdressed" or "naked." Use of the classification system allows us to define people as being elaborately dressed even if they are unclothed, for the classification system acknowledges that many changes can be made to the body surface through paint, tattoos, perfumes, and hair styling, which all modify the body, and thus dress it. The goal for using the classification system is to talk and write about dress without making unfair or biased judgments.

A second advantage concerns the understanding of the details of the physical form of dress items and practices and the relationship of this form to the body. Culturally specific terms subsume this information and do not make it explicit. When applied cross-culturally, they lead to misconceptions. Take the term "necklace," for example. In North America a necklace is commonly understood as an item of dress composed of small bits of metal, jewels, beads, or other material. It hangs around the neck and accessorizes the main parts of the dress, which are the garments covering the body. However, among the Samburu (Sam-BOO-roo) of central Kenya, necklaces constitute more than half of the dress of an adult female, and do not accessorize body coverings but rather constitute the body covering itself. Using the term necklace, as Figure 1.15a shows, can mislead the reader about the significant role it plays in Samburu women's dress. Similarly, describing the body covering worn by the Dugum Dani man shown in Figure 1.15b as a penis sheath does not indicate its importance in his culture. Instead, defining these items of dress as body supplements allows us to assess the coverings of the body in a more objective way than using words that ordinarily connote less significant items for Euro-

Figure 1.15
Use of conventional English dress terms to accurately name or describe any of the items worn by either of these two individuals is impossible. Use of a scientific system of dress terminology helps to open up a cross-cultural dialogue rather than foreclose discussion of cultural dress practices. (a) Samburu, Kenya. (b) Dugum Dani, New Guinea, c. 1960.

Americans. Even using the Samburu or Dugum Dani name for that item may not enhance our understanding of how much of the body is covered.

Culturally specific terms for dress items and processes also assume a social context of use for each aspect of dress. This association with the context of use enables dress to communicate information nonverbally about the social identity of the wearer. The term "skirt," for example, describes a garment worn by girls and women in North America. Anyone seeing a person wearing a skirt can, in most instances, safely assume the wearer is female except when the garment is a Scottish men's kilt. If we use the term skirt to describe Scottish men's dress, we may smile outwardly or inwardly or snicker inappropriately and wonder about slips and underwear. If we restrict ourselves to using the indigenous term kilt, we avoid making a cultural judgment, but someone unfamiliar with Scottish dress and culture will not understand what garment is involved. Thus, using the description of "preshaped and wrapped body supplement for the lower torso" from the classification system is less misleading and allows a more precise understanding.

A final advantage concerns the relationship between the complexity and detail apparent in any dress ensemble and the role of those elements of dress in nonverbal communication about the identity, activity, and particular mood of the wearer. Information about the wearer is communicated by both large and small elements of dress. A dress silhouette can help convey the wearer's gender or age, but so too can the simple placement of a ring or the use of color. Which detail is important in the communication will be determined by the context of observation. In Britain, for example, the color and design of a businessman's tie (if it is an "old school tie") may be a more critical indicator of his identity than his total ensemble of suit, shirt, tie, socks, and shoes in certain contexts. In Africa, the way a wrapper is tied or the way hair is coifed may similarly be the critical indicator of the identity of the wearer.

Body modifications or supplements alone can convey the important meaning in a particular context of observation. However, information about the identity, intents, and mood of the wearer is often conveyed by the combination of items within a dress ensemble. Relationships between the many elements create the complex meanings conveyed by dress. Scholarly terminology for analysis of dress must be culturally nonspecific, but also must convey the smallest detail of that dress so that these forms can be described and their meanings analyzed. Using a scientific definition of dress and its application through the classification system, the student of dress can achieve a level of objectivity. The seemingly strange and exotic can be studied with reduced cultural bias, as can the seemingly familiar and everyday. In this way, the analysis of people's dress can lead to a fuller understanding of their culture and everyday life.

SUMMARY

We defined dress as an assemblage of body modifications and body supplements displayed by a person. Thus, we use the term "dress" to cover the full range of things we do to the body or put on the body to get dressed. Dress includes clothing and accessories as well as grooming practices such as bathing or dyeing the hair.

These processes and items influence perception of the dressed individual through the five senses. Variations of color, texture, fragrance, materials, surface patterns, and other design variations create in dress all the variability that we enjoy through our senses and include in the idea of fashion.

Any particular change to the body or addition to the body functions in one or several ways. These include protection, beautification, extension of the body's abilities, and nonverbal communication of information about the identity and activity of the individual. The interpretation of the significance of these functional aspects of dress must occur with reference to the context within which the dress is worn. The context includes the natural and human-made physical environment, the social and political structure of human relations, and the culture in which dress is produced and worn.

According to the definition of dress of an individual as an assemblage of (1) modifications of the body and/or (2) supplements to the body, dress includes a long list of possible direct modifications of the body, such as coifed hair, colored skin, pierced ears, and scented breath, as well as an equally long list of garments, jewelry, accessories, and other types of items added to the body as supplements. Our definition of dress includes some body modifications and supplements that you may be unaccustomed to including when studying dress, such as plastic surgery to improve appearance and handheld objects such as briefcases and umbrellas. Under the classification system, a tattoo can be identified as a body modification that changes surface design and color of skin. Plaiting of hair can be seen as a modification that transforms shape and texture of hair. Trousers and a rigid bracelet are both preshaped enclosures, each with specific properties. Earrings of many shapes, textures, and colors are attachments to the body that can be either inserted in ears or clipped on with pressure. Parasols and many purses are handheld objects with innumerable variations in properties.

Using a scientific definition of dress allows us to view dress as a uniquely human product and process. We can describe types of dress using the classification system as a way to avoid cultural bias and to view objectively both the familiar and the unfamiliar. We are then better able to appreciate the wide variety of ways people all over the world dress their bodies. In Reading I.1, "The Baths" by Croutier, the dress classification system allows us to analyze items of dress and practices unfamiliar to many of us.

STUDY TOOLS

Important Terms

adhered or glued attachment (to body or body enclosure)

attachment (to body or body enclosure)

body modification

body supplement

clipped attachment (to body or body enclosure)

combination-type body enclosures

enclosures

handheld object

inserted attachment (to body or body enclosure)

preshaped body enclosure

pressure fastening (to body or body enclosure)

suspended enclosure

wrapped enclosure

Discussion Questions

1. Why is a culturally neutral language needed for identifying dress items and dress processes?
2. What types of misconceptions arise when culturally specific terminology for dress is used?
3. From your own dress practices and dress items, try to give an example of every category in the dress classification system.
4. How are body modifications and supplements interrelated? Give examples from dress in your own culture or in the cultures you see around you.

5. What aspects of dress can convey meaning? Give examples from your own dress practices and wardrobe.

6. What kinds of meanings are conveyed through dress? Give examples from your own culture of each kind of information that dress can convey non-verbally about the wearer.

7. Think about, and discuss with at least one other class member, what difference it makes if body modifications are included within the definition of dress.

8. In the same way, consider what difference it makes if an item of dress is called a diamond necklace or a preshaped, suspended, body-enclosing supplement.

9. From your own dress practices and dress items, find examples of each dress variation that is perceived through the senses. Find at least one example for each of the five senses. Refer to the horizontal axis of Table 1.1.

10. Using the dress classification system terminology, analyze which types of dress are described for urban residents in historic Turkey in Reading I.1, "The Baths."

11. What are the four basic functions that dress serves? Can you find an item in your own dress that meets all four or several of these functions? Discuss how they are interrelated in this garment.

Activities

1. Using the classification system in Table 1.1 of your text, fill in as many examples of body modifications and supplements as you can by observing the dress of your classmates. Question your classmates for examples you might not see, such as tattoos (a color modification to the skin), hair permanents (a texture modification to the hair), or bracelets (wrapped or suspended supplements that may produce sound).

2. Select one type of body supplement or modification from your own culture, such as hats, necklaces, or hair styles. Using popular and travel magazines, such as *National Geographic*, *Omni*, and foreign fashion magazines, look for that same type of dress used in cultures different from your own. Try to find as wide a range as you can in form and appearance. Look for variations in how these types of dress are used and what they mean to the people who use them. Discuss your findings in small groups. Note the similarity in general form, how difference in particular form or context of use indicate cultural differences.

3. Develop a list of body modifications and body supplements from your own culture. In small groups discuss them and separate them into lists of temporary and permanent forms of dress.

4. Develop a list of body supplements in your own culture that require body modifications or that result in modification of the body when worn over a long period of time. Discuss in small groups.

5. Develop a list of handheld items of dress from your own culture or another outside your cultural tradition. Divide them into those that are held by the wearer and those that are held by another for the wearer.

6. Develop a list of body supplements that combine types, such as suspended and wrapped, wrapped and preshaped, or preshaped and suspended. Discuss other possible combinations in small groups.

7. You may want to try out the classification system by describing a familiar item of your own dress or the process of dressing yourself today. Use the terminology to describe your cultural practices regarding hairdos and facial hair and how gender, age, and ethnic or style distinctions are indicated by the terminology of the classification systems.

8. Compare your own grooming and bathing practices with those described for Turkey in Reading I.1, "The Baths." Using the dress classification categories compare and contrast the practices. Decide whether the two sets of cultural dress practices, yours and those in Turkey, appear more similar or different when you use the classification terminology.

Note to Chapter 1

1. This definition of dress first appeared in Roach-Higgins and Eicher (1992), reprinted (excerpted) in Roach-Higgins, Eicher, and Johnson (1995). This is based on previous work in the first edition of the current text (Roach-Higgins & Eicher, 1973) and on Roach and Musa (now Campbell) (1980). Some parallel ideas are found in the work of Hillestad (1978).

2

Dress, Culture, and Society

OBJECTIVES

To define the terms culture and society.

To relate the concept of dress to culture and society.

To recognize ethnocentrism and Eurocentrism in the study of dress and how they affect our understanding of dress in other cultural groups.

To introduce globalization of dress and culture.

DRESSING THE BODY PRIMARILY changes how the individual is perceived visually. However, dress also changes or enhances the aspects of each individual that are perceived through the other four senses. Thus sound, taste, physical texture, and odor along with overall visual appearance are changed or enhanced through body modifications and body supplements. Defining dress by using the classification system of body modifications and supplements as developed in Chapter 1 is only one step in studying and understanding the importance of dress in our lives. Two additional concepts of culture and society are also needed in order to comprehend the meaning of dress in any particular place and undertake the analysis of dress as a system of nonverbal communication among human beings.

CULTURE

Culture, a concept added to the vocabulary of social science by anthropologists, relates to the way human beings are taught to behave from the time they are born. The study of culture focuses attention on those behaviors shared by a group of people who regularly interact with each other.

We define culture as the human-made material items and patterns of thought, feeling, and behavior shared by members of a group who regularly interact with each other. Culture thus includes a broad range of phenomena, both **material** and **nonmaterial** in nature. In this book, we examine the physical phenomena of dress as a prime example of material culture and relate it to nonmaterial culture, such as beliefs, values, and patterns of social interaction. *Enculturation* means learning the cultural ways that are taught to members of the group.

Beginning in the late nineteenth century, such things as tools, furniture, and items of dress—thus, material culture—were routinely collected and analyzed. However, by the mid-twentieth century, anthropological research had developed a concept of culture that defines the shared aspects of social life primarily in terms of ideas, beliefs, and values. This nonmaterial concept of culture includes learned behavior patterns, religious beliefs, ideals, standards, symbolic meanings, and expectations that are shared as the people of a society develop a heritage of common experiences. The culture shared by a people can change as current members interpret ideas, beliefs, and values in light of new experiences.

At the end of the twentieth century, many anthropologists are reintegrating the material and nonmaterial concepts of culture to examine how ideas and beliefs are embedded in material things. At the same time scholars in other disciplines have integrated the concept of culture into their own research and writing and attempt to define culture for their own purposes. Thus, many different definitions of the concept of culture now exist, each illuminating a facet of the human condition.

A material concept of culture includes something as small as a computer chip or as large as a highway system and everything human-made in between. A nonmaterial concept of culture includes things as specific as the meaning associated with a shape, such as a stop sign, or the concept of democracy. The significance of various material and nonmaterial things arises from being shared by a group of individuals.

Material and nonmaterial culture interrelate. People make material items of culture because of their ideas, beliefs, and values about how things should be made, about what looks good, and about how the finished item should function. The differences between the concepts of material and nonmaterial culture stem from a difference in focus on the item itself or on the idea that relates to making or using the item. The Scottsmen's kilts that we see in Figure 2.1 are examples of material culture. The idea that European men can wear a skirt as a body supplement without any underwear beneath it is an example of nonmaterial culture.

Figure 2.1
The difference between material and nonmaterial culture is amusingly illustrated by this photograph of a British color guard dressed in *kilts*. Kilts are examples of items of material culture. The mental idea or belief that it is appropriate to be bare beneath the kilt is an example of nonmaterial culture.

Currently the idea of one unit of people that we can call a culture, such as Japanese culture or South African culture, has come under attack. Anthropologists today point out that large societies are composed of many smaller sections or groups, sometimes called subcultures. People in each of these groups within a society do not always agree with members of other groups about values, meanings, and cultural forms. Sometimes they even hotly disagree. In the United States in the 1990s, for instance, an issue related to dress arose between animal rights activists (who oppose the use of animal furs in garments and who do not wear them or other leather products) and other individuals who wear both leather and fur products. These two groups do not share a cultural belief concerning the use of leather and fur; they share the controversy over them. The negotiation of the value attached to these products occurs in the public streets and media where animal rights protest activities occur, especially in regard to the marketplace where fur garments are sold or are worn. The negotiation is ongoing and may never come to an agreement among the competing groups.

SOCIETY

A group of individuals who interact with each other based on the sharing of many beliefs and ways of behavior is called a *society* by social scientists. The size of the group of interacting individuals who share a culture may be small or large in population and may coincide with the geographical boundaries of a nation. The word society captures the idea of people living together and sharing knowledge about their structural patterns, the system of organizing their families, and their political, economic, and religious structures. Learning about one's society is called the process of *socialization*.

In contrast to society, as we have noted, culture captures the idea of the way the people learn to behave in a particular society as they live within particular organizational structures. Historically, anthropology applied the concept of culture to the study of groups of people as members of a society as if all people lived within an area that was easily identified by geographical boundaries, having no interaction with people of other societies that had different cultures. We now know that this is not an accurate understanding. Society and culture may relate to the behavior of one interacting group of individuals or, in the world of 2000 C.E.,[1] cultural behavior and the structure of a society may be different. Thus, individuals from small and large societies may interact with individuals of other societies that are both small and large. We expand on the differences and importance for dress of people in what we call small- and large-scale cultures in Chapters 7 and 8.

The structure of societies can differ depending on population size, as we discuss in those chapters. Often, in small societies with small numbers of people, individuals will recognize almost everyone in the society and have direct contact. In contrast, in very large societies, where thousands or hundreds of thousands of individuals are organized into a shared way of life, individuals do not come into face-to-face contact with all other members of their society. Interaction is indirect and occurs through such mediators as the marketplace and the media. As individuals living in a large society, we may feel ourselves to be members of several distinct groups, each with its own culture. For example, we may speak of corporate culture, surfer culture, or student culture.

The spread of peoples around the globe in the colonial and postcolonial world has created several significant cultural **diasporas**, defined as members of a cultural group who have migrated to other places. Although they live as part of a new or different society, they exhibit allegiance to their cultural heritage and claim cultural identity connected to their heritage. Sometimes these members of the diaspora are viewed as a distinct ethnic group or subculture within the country where they reside, as in the example of the Hmong from Laos and Thailand who live in North America; see Figure 2.2. Such individuals may feel themselves to be members of both their ethnic cultural group and the larger cultural group of their country of residence, sometimes creating a conflicting sense of individual cultural identity.

The study of culture, and in particular the study of dress and culture becomes very complex in large societies. The simplistic definitions of the dress of

Figure 2.2
Donning their ethnic dress for special occasions such as a New Year's celebration connects Hmong-Americans to others in the Hmong diaspora around the world and sets them apart in a positive way from other Americans.

a culture group that were written in the nineteenth century can no longer be replicated almost anywhere in the world. Smaller groups within larger societies compete with each other in their definitions of cultural values and beliefs. Often members within these smaller groups can be described as having cultural behavior that characterizes their cultural heritage or past and sets them apart from members of other groups.

THE SCALE OF WORLD CULTURES

The concept of the *scale of world cultures* (Bodley, 1994) provides an approach to understanding the meaning of dress for people within a specific time and place—their social and cultural envirnoments. The idea of scale essentially relates to different sizes of society and the complexity of the social organization within these societies, along with the cultural beliefs and practices related to the particular society. The idea of scale describes three great divides in human history—how people differ from each other based on the complexity of organization necessary to sustain populations of differing size and different environments. We have adopted the terminology of small, large, and global to characterize the scale of world cultures. The characteristics of each cultural scale include society, economy, technology, population, polity, ideology, and dress, as listed in Table 2.1. Each of these aspects has cultural practices associated with the specific cultural system as we will elaborate upon in Chapters 7, 8 and 9.

TABLE 2.1

The Scale of World Cultures

	Small	Large	Global
Society	Egalitarian Kin-based Age grades	Ranked Class-based Castes	Class-based Literate
Economy	Subsistence Display Reciprocal exchange	Tribute tax Wealth Specialists	Markets Corporations Capitalist Consumer
Technology	Foraging Gardening Herding	Intensive Agriculture	Industrial Fossil fuel Monocrop
Population	500–1000 Low-density	10,000 or more High-density	1 million or more Urban
Polity	Acephalus Bigman Descent groups	Chiefdoms Kingdoms Empires	Nation states Supranational
Ideology	Animism Shamanism Ancestor cults	High gods Divine kings	Patriotism Monotheism Progress
Dress			

Adapted from Bodley, John H. (1994). *Cultural Anthropology: Tribes, States, and the Global System.* Mountain View, CA: Mayfield Publishing Company, p. 16.

Some analysts of society and culture, such as Bodley (1994) say that small- and large-scale societies and associated cultural behavior describe people's ways of living that existed in the past, whereas global scale describes the global cultural system to which the people of all cultures today can be linked through technology, trade, and travel. We assert that some small-scale and large-scale societies still exist with associated cultural practices that can exist simultaneously with at least some people (often youth and young adults) "hooking into" the **global-scale culture**.

Small-scale culture can be described as an egalitarian society with a subsistence economy based on maximizing resources in the local environment. **Large-scale culture** can be described as class- or caste-based, with power concentrated in a chief, king, or emperor; agriculture- and trade-created surpluses of wealth, which are taxed to support government programs. Global-scale culture can be described as literate and capitalist; technology is based on fossil fuels and computer chips that facilitate mass production and mass communication (Bodley, 1994).

Scale of both society and culture has implications for the study of dress. Because small-scale societies had small, egalitarian populations, different types of dress communicated age grade and the completion of rites of passage. By contrast, large-scale societies were hierarchical. Types of dress developed to communicate social status, wealth, and power in a large population in which individuals could not possibly know everyone else. In a global-scale culture, individuals may be members of several self-styled, small-scale, overlapping groups within a nation linked to other nations through trade and technology. The daily dress of an individual may include elements from many cultures simultaneously, such as a Mexican *huipil*, an Indian cotton gauze skirt, and Swedish clogs.

The concepts of social status and role are associated with the concepts of society and culture. **Social status** defines the individual's position or membership in any size society and in various social groups (e.g., those related to place and circumstances of birth, family, occupation, religion, political party, or leisure activities). A common distinction made in status is the division between ascribed and achieved. In **ascribed status**, position is ordinarily "a given," like gender, age, and ethnic background, and in a society such as India, caste position. In **achieved status**, position is gained through accomplishment, as in becoming an astronaut, a teacher, or a sales associate. The range of possible achieved status varies depending on the scale of society and can change throughout our life course. As we consider our own social positions, several factors arise that relate to our circumstances of birth, including the economic position, along with religious and political affiliations, of our families and our own occupational and other accomplishments.

Connected to the concept of social status is the concept of *social role*, or the behavior that accompanies social status. Thus, social status is the position an individual occupies, and social role is the behavior exhibited that relates to the social position. Social status and roles can change for some individuals in some countries over time. As children mature, they make their own places in the social structure by marrying or not, changing occupations, creating and losing fortunes, winning political office, and making decisions about religious or philosophical tenets.

No one example of a society and culture will fit exactly into one category of scale. Avoiding the cultural bias endemic to categorizing groups of people is one advantage of using scale in studying social and cultural aspects of dress. Instead of attempting to fit the example to the category, each societal example is viewed on its own terms, within the context of the global system, and traits are selected from each scale that accurately describe that group. It becomes possible to sidestep pigeonholing and stereotyping because a constellation of traits unique to that culture emerges. Dress is one lens through which this constellation can be studied and comprehended.

RELATING DRESS TO CULTURE AND SOCIETY

Culture influences the way we dress and other aspects of our behavior because human beings do not exist in isolation. We all live with other people and rely on interaction with other individuals. Members of a society encourage, and sometimes demand, that based on the cultural practices they have learned, only a specific range of resources be used to modify and supplement the body. Although most people in the United States believe in individual freedom, a belief that extends to choices in dress, certain limitations always exist that define what is appropriate dress. Appropriate dress can vary from one society and culture to another. Saudi Arabian women who are Muslim, for example, must completely cover themselves when out in public; whereas French women who are not Muslim usually leave their heads, arms, and legs bare when in public. In the first case, the religious beliefs and interpretation of the idea of "modesty" as found in the Koran affect the definition of dress. In the second example, French women who identify themselves as part of a contemporary fashion scene may decide to wear a miniskirt if that is in fashion, with a T-shirt and short haircut, leaving the head, arms, and legs uncovered. Furthermore, cultural definitions of the appropriate form of dress can also vary depending on such factors as age and situation within one specific society. For example, in North America, bibs tied around the neck for the purpose of eating a meal are considered appropriate only for babies, adults eating lobster in a restaurant, and the disabled elderly, not for adults in general who are able-bodied.

Dress constitutes one major example of material culture. Body supplements, such as trousers and shoes, are both items of material culture as well as the tools and materials involved in the processes of body modification. Similarly, chemical solutions used for curling hair and hair combs to keep hair tidy or arrange it in a particular way are items of material culture.

Dress also reflects or communicates nonmaterial culture, because how individuals are dressed and the meaning attached to their dress relates to cultural beliefs about standards of dress and symbolic values. For example, when someone decides to use a chemical solution to have a "permanent wave," the nonmaterial value associated with having curly or wavy hair becomes the impetus for using the item of material culture, in this case, the chemical solution. In another example in Euro-American cultures, an attractive body shape for an adult female usually means the woman's waist is narrower than her hips and bust; during many fashion periods, garments are designed to emphasize this type of body. This is not true in all cultures, nor always within every fashion period in Euro-American dress. In still another example that relates to funeral practices, in Japan white is considered the appropriate color for the corpse for burial whereas in North America, family members often choose a favorite garment from a wide variety of colors for burial attire of the deceased. Colors for the garments of mourners at the time of funerals vary around the world with black frequently found, sometimes in whole garments worn by mourners and sometimes only in armbands to signify grief.

To study dress we make use of both material and nonmaterial examples of culture. Some scholars are primarily interested in the physical form that dress takes and analyze the form to make deductions about the people they study. Other scholars are interested in the social context in which dress is worn and the designers' as well as the wearers' ideas and beliefs about the items of dress. When people engage in the latter approach to the study of dress, the possibility arises that items of dress may be designed that are better suited to new social and cultural situations.

The human physical body is itself a material culture construct. There are two reasons for this. First, the cultural practices of our society—sources of nutrition, types of exercise, constraints on behavior, and other means—mold our physical bodies as we mature. What we experience as natural to and good for the body are learned values we receive through the process of enculturation. For example, subsistence farmers in many parts of the world, whether they are men or women, develop strong muscles because they engage in manual farm labor from childhood. In cultures where farmwork is no longer common, many people develop strong muscles by working out in gymnasiums and by practicing weight lifting in order to achieve a body that appears trim and fit.

Second, we consciously change the form of the human physical body, temporarily or permanently, according to the accepted or expected beliefs of our society and culture regarding body ideals. For example, among many human groups, facial hair is natural to the adult male body, and some groups believe this natural proclivity should not be altered. In other groups, shaving the beard one or more times a day is expected, because a clean shaven face is considered naturally more aesthetically pleasing than a bearded one.

The particular material form that dress takes from one culture to another varies considerably. Different materials are used depending on climate, natural resources, and technology. For example, the human need to protect the head from the sun may be met by a felt cowboy hat, a cork pith helmet, and a straw boater, each fulfilling a common purpose. In this example, the silhouettes, forms, lines, and colors differ widely from place to place in relation to specific cultural and aesthetic values. In another example, the shape is seemingly the same, as in the case of a turban worn by a Sikh man in India or a high fashion model in a European fashion magazine, but the materials for each may be very different along with the meaning conveyed by the turban shape. In the matter of dress, preferences for specific textures, colors, smells, tastes, and sounds vary widely.

The beliefs and values associated with the types of dress also differ from one culture to another. The significance of a color, such as red, can differ between subgroups within a single society. For example, in the United States, a red tie may signify power, a red dress may signify sexuality, and a red bandanna may signify gang affiliation. As we study dress, we must learn to make sense of the shared fact that all human beings dress themselves in some way, but members of each group dress differently.

ETHNOCENTRISM

The definition of dress introduced in Chapter 1 allows us to begin to look at dress processes and items of dress across cultures without introducing values and biases from our own culture. When we view another culture, our attention is usually drawn to those beliefs, practices, and items that are different from our own, often viewing such differences as inferior because they are incomprehensible to us. Worse, we often misunderstand another culture when we view it through our own definitions. We call such misunderstanding and misinterpretation **ethnocentrism**; that is, the expression, in actions or judgments, of a particular cultural viewpoint as being superior to another culture. When we are **ethnocentric**, we focus on what is important in our culture or ignore important aspects of other cultures, believing our practices or values to be better than other peoples' practices or values. If we come from a European heritage and have a belief that European ways of behaving are superior, we are practicing **Eurocentrism** and can be called **Eurocentric**.

It is normal for each of us to take our own culture largely for granted; thus, we often fail to recognize our ethnocentrism. We can read the symbols in our own culture so easily that we often do not comprehend the meaning of symbols in other cultures. As a result, we can overlook or dismiss something that is important to others. Sometimes others challenge our ethnocentric judgments or acts, perhaps using anger, humor, or disgust to call attention to our inability to understand something outside of our experience, such as an item's significance, meaning, or physical form. When confronted, we can learn about the character and limits of our own culture and add to our knowledge about another culture, thus widening our understanding of variety in human behavior. Ethnocentric experiences about improper dress can provide humorous or painful stories when told later, and we may relate such incidents as examples of learning about behavior in other cultures.

Professionals in many fields make cultural blunders that relate to dress. For example, President Clinton's protocol advisers in 1994 created an ethnocentric gaffe when they misjudged the cultural significance in Indonesia of men's *batik* (ba-TEEK) shirts. President Clinton and other world leaders attending a conference in that country were each presented with an elaborate *batik* shirt by the President of Indonesia. Each received a shirt with a different *batik* motif that incorporated the national symbol of his country, especially designed by Iwan Turta, the foremost *batik* designer in Indonesia, with the American eagle design chosen for Clinton. The Indonesian host directed each of the leaders to wear this shirt for one of the conference events. President Clinton's protocol advisers interpreted the significance of the brightly colored, patterned shirt as being similar to the informal Hawaiian shirt, and instructed him to wear khaki trousers and casual shoes with the shirt, believing that the shirts signaled a casual conference event. Instead, in Indonesia, *batik* fabric is historically associated with royalty and formal events and both dark trousers and formal shoes should have been worn with this garment. Figure 2.3 shows the visual effect of this ethnocentric misinterpretation.

Another example of a well-meaning ethnocentric interpretation concerns a U.S. university teacher working in Nigeria. She invited some of her new acquaintances to lunch and set the table with a handwoven, indigenous textile she had recently purchased, which she thought attractive enough to use as a table runner. Her Nigerian luncheon guests expressed dismay, however, at the

Figure 2.3
President Clinton's dress protocol advisers ethnocentrically misinterpreted the Indonesian batik shirts presented to world leaders at the Asia-Pacific Economic Cooperation forum in 1994 as casual wear. The President's appearance at the formal event in khaki pants and casual shoes, appropriate for wearing with an American Hawaiian shirt, was taken as a political insult by the formally dressed Asian leaders.

thought of using this cloth on the table, as they used it as an underwrapper (similar to our petticoat or underpants)! This forced her to recognize the difference between her own and her guests' cultural definitions of what is appropriate for underwear and tablecloths.

One of the authors, studying anthropology in India, elicited disgust from her Indian friends once as she performed a perfectly natural American cultural act. In the absence of a washroom or water tap, she wet the corner of her handkerchief with her tongue in order to wipe off an ink-smudge on her cheek. The eight or ten people in the room with her were horrified and became silent. Then one of the more outspoken men asked rhetorically, "You can clean it with spit?" in a tone that let her know that this act was unacceptable. She learned that people in India view saliva as highly dirty. This contrasted with her U.S. culture, which has historic dress traditions such as "spit curls" for hair and "spit polish" for shining shoes. Another familiar example to North Americans is that of a mother who cleans her toddler's face with a saliva-moistened tissue or handkerchief.

Scholarly analyses of dress can also seem strange when a scholar writes about dress in another culture. For example, for anyone with a North American or European background, the cultural dress practices in the following analysis by Dar, an Indian scholar, may come as a surprise. He takes the bare feet and covered heads of his own country for granted and is surprised in contrasting those practices to customs in the West:

> In Europe, a cultural refinement of a primitive form of sex-worship requires men to keep their hats off and their shoes on, when in the presence of ladies. The removal of the hat is an act of homage to the eternal feminine, while the injunction against bare feet is a symbolic acknowledgment of women's monopoly in the field of corporeal display. (Dar, 1969, p. 138)[2]

On the one hand, ethnocentrism does not always imply that a judgment is wrong. It only implies that the judgment is made from the perspective of members of a particular culture, which may have little to do with the perspective of members of the culture that is being analyzed. On the other hand, ethnocentric judgments may be wrong. In limiting their cultural perspective, members of one society can misunderstand what they seek to understand and underestimate the complexity of other cultures. In the effort to avoid cultural bias in the study of dress, the challenge is both to suspend judgment and learn to see through the eyes of other people. Reading I.2, "Body Ritual among the Nacirema" by Miner, provides an opportunity for analysis of cultural practices related to dressing the body that may seem both familiar and unfamiliar.

ETHNIC DRESS

Our elaboration of the idea of ethnocentrism is important in understanding cultural differences and similarities in dress around the world. Many people have used words such as "tradition" and "ethnicity" to analyze cultural divisions of people, especially within societies that have large populations. These two words have become popularly used in general and have strong implications for the study of dress.

Tradition relates to cultural heritage; practices that come from the past. However, when the word "traditional" is used to refer to cultural practices or items such as dress, an assumption is often made of no change occurring or of something being fixed in the past. Thus, the word traditional is beginning to fall out of favor with scholars as a useful term, for in studying different cultures more thoroughly, we realize that what we have thought of as "unchanging" has often been modified, sometimes quickly and sometimes slowly. Ethnocentric outsiders who have observed another culture have not always been thorough in researching the past of other cultures. Anthropologists now demonstrate through their research that traditions are constantly changing and use the words "invention of tradition" to talk about the process of change or new developments occurring in the practices that people identify with their cultural past.[3]

Ethnicity relates to the idea of tradition, because the word refers to the heritage of a group of people with a common cultural background, which can include their dress. Ethnicity was initially used to understand political processes of conflict among different **ethnic groups** (people considered as having a common background) within a larger society, based on the assumption that conflict arises from differing cultural backgrounds. Sometimes ethnic groups have the potential of evolving in relationship to their history and are defined in a new way, such as Cajuns of Louisiana.[4] In another example, cultural groups once separate in their homeland sometimes merge to form a single ethnic group in the place of their migration. For example, people once designated as Blue, Striped, and White Hmong of Cambodia and Laos have begun to be simply called the Hmong in the United States (Lynch, 1995). In these two examples, the way group members dress to identify as Cajuns or Hmong can be called **ethnic dress**. Reading I.3, "Eurocentrism in the Study of Ethnic Dress" by Baizerman, Eicher, and Cerny discusses why ethnic dress is a more useful term than other alternatives in studying dress.

CONTEMPORARY CULTURE, SOCIETY, AND DRESS

As systems of travel and electronic communication increase in power and scope, members of the various cultures of the world have increasing contact with each other. The process of sharing and learning through such experiences crosses cultural boundaries. The breaching of cultural boundaries has occurred through most of human history, with a variety of destructive as well as constructive results. The extent of such cultural contact has greatly accelerated as we reach the twenty-first century.

At the beginning of the twenty-first century we face the prospect of **globalization**, the idea that similar ways of behaving are developing around the world as a result of interconnected economic, political, and technological changes, as exemplified through electronic mail, satellite television, and telephone communications, and international business. As the century progresses, the people of the world will share increasingly greater amounts of information and access to similar products and events. Though separated by the boundaries of nations and languages, many peoples of the world are becoming more closely linked. Thus we have punk or hip-hop examples of cultural behavior in many different countries, rock music that is international, and international beauty contests for Miss World and Miss Universe. The possibility of a global-scale society and the reality of global-scale culture are expanded upon in Chapter 9.

However, it is important to our introduction to the study of dress that we discuss **world dress**,[5] (Eicher & Sumberg, 1995) which we use to describe similar types of body modifications and supplements worn by many people in various parts of the world no matter where the types of dress or the people themselves originated. One example of body supplements that we classify as world dress originated as European men's shirts, cut-and-sewn shirts that have set-in sleeves, cuffs, collar, and a front placket with buttons, as shown in Figure 2.4a. This garment was introduced on many continents as a result of European colonialism from the seventeenth through nineteenth centuries when European men traveled all over the world, resulting in many variations of this basic European garment being found in different societies (see Figure 2.4b and c). It is made in different lengths, tailored loose or tight, from plain white or colored cotton or patterned wool, made with rounded tails or pleated down the front, and in many other styles. In the Philippines, the shirt is worn as part of men's formal dress ensembles, without any suit jacket; in parts of northern India as one type of a women's blouse with a sari; on the coast of Nigeria as a chief's knee-length tunic; and in other versions in many other areas. These examples are recognized as forms of Western dress in respect to origins, but they are no longer specifically European, Western, Philippine, Indian, or Japanese. If they are used with no change involved from the original men's shirt, they are examples of world dress. If changes have been introduced to transform the styling of the shirt itself or to combine it with garments not originally used in the West, we use the concept of **cultural authentication**, which we discuss more fully in Chapter 8. World dress also includes examples of garments derived from non-Western sources such as the Japanese kimono influencing Western bathrobes and dressing gowns.

Two more words especially popular in Europe and the United States to analyze culture and dress are history and fashion. **History** involves the idea of chronology or the passage of time. **Fashion** involves the idea of changes that come and go in both material and nonmaterial examples of culture, particularly in items of dress. Both history and fashion as ideas usually stress the constantly changing nature of European and American cultures, most often describing what has been thought of as a fundamental difference between Western and non-Western cultures. In the past, Eurocentric scholars have relied heavily on written history (written documentation with a chronological base), and until recently did not acknowledge the importance and relevance of oral history, thus

(a)

(c)

(b)

Figure 2.4
The basic form that we call shirt, a preshaped enclosure, has developed in many different directions as it has spread around the world. It is worn by different age and gender groups, and is viewed as appropriate for very different occasions in the various societies of the world where it is now worn.
(a) U.S. man, 1990s; (b) Philippines man;
(c) North Indian woman, c. 1980.

implying or even stating explicitly that only people from Euro-American heritages had experienced change over time. This perspective has been questioned by many scholars who have begun to recognize both the historic traditions and the dynamic nature of culture anywhere in the world. The ability of cultural practices to undergo change, whether quickly or slowly, is particularly evident in many examples of dress. As an example of material culture that is prone to change, dress items and practices are especially involved when other parts of society and culture change, especially technology. Individuals begin to reinterpret and reinvent their practices from the past to meet new challenges of life.

Sometimes the material aspects of dress change and become a long-lasting practice and sometimes they change and fade away. For instance, in the United States early in the twentieth century, use of the zipper as a garment closure replaced hooks and eyes on women's dresses and buttons and buttonholes on men's trousers in a short period of time and has continued. In contrast, in the mid-1990s, men's boxer underwear became adopted as outerwear for both male and female youth. The form of boxer shorts was combined with colorful and playfully printed cloth and then disappeared as a fashion. In an example from China in the early twentieth century, the *qi pao* (chee POW), called *cheung sam* (chay-oong SAM) in the Cantonese language, is a cut-and-sewn gown with diagonal front closing, stand-up collar, sleeves, and side slits. It developed from a loose men's garment to a slim-fitting dress for urban women which is sometimes called a "Suzie Wong" dress from a movie of that name (Garrett, 1994, pp. 102–107).

In Chapters 8 and 9 we examine more closely the relationship between world dress, ethnic dress, and fashionable dress along with whether or not there is cultural variation in the forms that world dress takes. Generally, at the end of the twentieth century, the process of deciding how to dress is becoming increasingly complex for many people around the world. We continue to use dress to define ourselves and to announce our affiliations, such as ethnicity, as we fulfill several roles in life. Thus, we move through several cultural milieus. We use dress to communicate to others which role we are emphasizing at any given time during the day or through the years. As individuals, we change from world dress, to fashionable dress, and to ethnic dress depending upon the immediate context. For example, a first-generation Laotian teenager in the United States may don traditional Hmong dress for the funeral of a family member, wear jeans to class, and wear a fashionable blue-skirted suit ensemble to a job interview. Choices of dress help this student bridge several cultural traditions within our emerging global society.

As cultures come into contact with each other through processes such as colonialism or globalization, innovative items or ensembles of dress emerge that we define as world dress and world fashion. People balance their own cultural traditions with the demands of a global society against their own desires to express individual tastes. We view the arbitrary separation of fashionable dress from ethnic dress and traditional dress from contemporary dress as an obstacle to understanding the role of culture in dress in the globalizing world. For example, Figure 2.5a and b illustrate the similarities between punk hairdos and an American Indian hairstyle. We encourage students of dress to look at all the types of dress that we see around us, whether we find examples from history or from our contemporary world, from our own culture or from the culture of others, or from a mix of all of these.

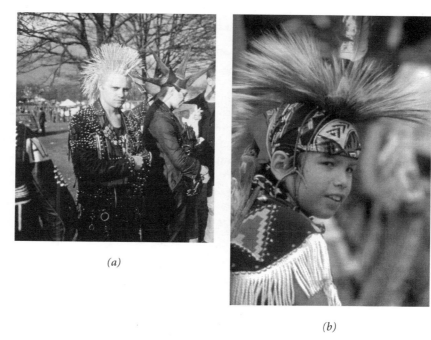

(a)

(b)

Figure 2.5
The incorporation of the "mohawk" hair style from its historical origins among
American Indians of earlier centuries into contemporary fashion by some later twentieth century youth confounds the categorization of this specific style of dress as either fashionable or ethnic dress.
(a) Youth in London, 1990s; (b) American Indian boy in dance dress.

We will discuss the similarities among human beings in Chapter 5. No
matter what our skin color, eye color, hair texture, or body build, human beings exist as one species, *Homo sapiens*, within the animal kingdom. We all
dress our bodies in some manner, and the world around us is a dynamically
changing world. However, our book emphasizes the rich differences in the use
of resources to dress the body by various groups of *Homo sapiens*, based on geographical location, history, and cultural customs. Through a cross-cultural
study of the differences in the way people dress around the world, we can appreciate the cultural significance of dress.

The study of dress in any part of the world has become a complex subject.
It is also a rich and challenging field in which to work, whether one is making
decisions about how to dress for work, play, or celebration each day; working
in the apparel or soft goods industry; or doing scholarly research on dress.

DRESS AND CULTURAL MEANINGS

Dress is a major form of material culture, and it is influenced by cultural ideas, standards, and beliefs. Both body supplements and body modifications are created in the context of culture, and the human body itself becomes a cultural construction because it is the base for these alterations and additions.

Both body modifications and body supplements are forms of dressing the body, but definitions of what constitutes appropriate dress vary widely from one culture to another. To be dressed does not require both modifications and supplements, except as defined in particular cultures. Coverage of the body with supplements can range from the minimum of a finger ring to the maximum of an encompassing robe. People in some cultures are appropriately dressed even though much of the body is exposed, as in the example of skimpy swimsuits, whether for men or women on many European and North American beaches. In contrast, some societies require certain sectors of the population to keep themselves completely hidden from the eyes of others while in public, as in the example of various types of veiled garments for women in many parts of the Middle East and Asia, and increasingly, in North America.

Meanings communicated by the types of dress may stem from the basic category of body modification or supplement or from one of its properties (such as color or shape). A composite of properties or component types, or both, comprises a total ensemble. Our terminology for dress thus must be both very specific and at the same time culturally neutral. We have presented the classification system of dress because the definition of the form and the social context of use of particular types of dress varies from one culture to another. This creates problems in using and understanding culturally specific words in any one culture to study dress.

Our culturally neutral concept of dress can be used to minimize bias and attachment of value to a dress item or practice. It also prevents the introduction of outside cultural assumptions about the form and social context of use of any dress practice or item named in a particular society. The terminology of the classification system is usable in descriptions across national and cultural boundaries, and includes all phenomena that can accurately be designated as dress. We can use the classification system as a model to study the types of dress worn by a particular individual or characteristic of a particular social group. Its use clarifies dress comparisons made between individuals or social groups to ascertain the meaning involved in the communication system of dress.

SUMMARY

The term culture includes human-made material items and patterns of thought, feeling, and behavior that members of a social group share who regularly interact with each other. The material and nonmaterial aspects of culture are interrelated as human beings make material culture items acting in response to conscious and unconscious nonmaterial culture, which they carry in their minds as beliefs, values, expectations, and emotional responses.

Ethnocentrism naturally leads observers of the dress of individuals from other cultures to misinterpret the significance and value of that dress. Ethnic dress relates to what people from a particular heritage or tradition wear at a specific time, as well as to the history of the people wearing it.

As the world grows seemingly smaller through the improvement of communications, and the integration of business on a worldwide level, the separation of cultures one from another is being challenged at the same time that awareness of other cultures is being heightened. The change in the structure of society around the world is clearly visible in dress. World dress, or general types of dress originating in one culture but now found in many cultures, is apparent in most every part of the globe. Changes in examples of dress may be analyzed historically or viewed through a contemporary lens of fashion.

STUDY TOOLS

Important Terms

achieved status	fashion
ascribed status	globalization
cultural authentication	global-scale culture
diaspora	history
ethnic dress	large-scale culture
ethnic groups	material culture
ethnicity	nonmaterial culture
ethnocentrism	small-scale culture
ethnocentric	social status
Eurocentrism	tradition
Eurocentric	world dress

Discussion Questions

1. Why do all humans engage in the act of dressing the body?
2. If all humans dress themselves for the same basic reasons, why do many of us look so different from each other?
3. Share with others in your discussion group the kinds of dress from other cultures you have seen on people you have met. Explain how you interpreted the dress they wore. Based on your example and the examples of others in your discussion group, decide how cultural differences in dress affect your interactions with others.
4. Share with others in your discussion group the range in kinds of dress from other cultures you have seen on people in photographs in magazines such as *National Geographic* or on travel shows on television. From seeing

those kinds of dress, what type of cultural life do you think the wearers of those various kinds of dress would lead? What impressions do you think those people would have of you, based on the way you are dressed? To what extent do you think these impressions are true, and to what extent do you think they are ethnocentric stereotypes?

5. According to your text, what are the limitations of words such as adornment and clothing?

6. What are the limitations of terms such as primitive, nonindustrialized, folk, and traditional?

7. Why do the authors of Reading I.3, "Eurocentrism in the Study of Ethnic Dress," favor the term ethnic dress?

8. Consider the way in which American grooming rituals, that is, American temporary and permanent body modifications, have been reported in Reading I.2, "Body Ritual Among the Nacerima." How did you react in reading about American bathing practices? How does reading this article help you understand the term ethnocentrism?

9. With reference to the Nacerima article, discuss how the use of unfamiliar language, even when it is scientific, can lead to or dispel ethnocentrism. How will reading this short ethnography about a group with whom you are familiar change the way you read other scientific articles about the dress of societies with which you are unfamiliar? Also discuss how the use of the terminology of the dress classification system alters your understanding of your own dress.

10. Following the definitions in Reading I.3, "Eurocentrism in the Study of Ethnic Dress," give examples of ethnic dress and national dress, drawing upon the dress of your family, your friends, and yourself. Would you include all of your dress within these two categories, or do you wear other kinds of dress? If so, into which other category from Reading I.3 would you put this other dress that you wear?

Activities

1. Using fashion magazines (such as *Vogue, Allure, Details*) and popular magazines (such as *National Geographic* and *Omni*), flag examples of body supplements and modifications that are similar between cultures. For example, tattoos used as a rite of passage in the Pacific and as part of a Paris fashion show; bowl haircuts characteristic of the Yanamamo of Brazil and young U.S. Amish boys. Discuss your findings in small groups. Note the similarity in form, but difference in use and meaning.

2. Select a body supplement or body modification and flag examples in catalogues and popular magazines from as many different cultural groups around the world as possible. Examples might include jeans, uniforms, bangles, skin painting, or hair dressing. Discuss your findings in small groups. Which examples might be considered ethnic dress, world dress, or world fashion?

3. Think about the various groups, large and small, that you participate in through the days, weeks, and seasons of your life. Identify which of these groups may be said to have their own culture and distinctive types of dress. Examples might be the corporate culture where you work, the ethnic community of your ancestors, and your childhood scout troop. Each of these groups may have required special dress. Document those cultural differences with family photographs or examples from your wardrobe. How distinct are these ensembles? How much overlap do you see?

4. Describe a familiar grooming ritual or dressing activity using Miner's technical writing style (as illustrated in the second reading for this chapter), avoiding ordinary words where a more abstract one will do. Think about how this broadens or changes your perception of these activities.

5. Using the definition of world dress in Chapter 2, list which cultures around the world have been the origin of body supplements or modifications that make up your own dress. If you have trouble finding items and processes whose historical origins lie outside the United States, try looking up the names of such things in a dictionary until you find some that have an association with another part of the world. It may be helpful to use the more old-fashioned names for things when looking them up; for example, look up "rouge" rather than "blush" and "trousers" rather than "pants" or "jeans."

6. Update Miner's article on Nacirema (Reading I.2) based on your understanding of contemporary Nacirema society and its cultural practices concerning the body. How have the body practices remained the same or changed since Miner wrote his analysis in 1957?

Notes to Chapter 2

1. Societies mark time using many different calendar systems. With the spread of Christianity and the rise to power of European Christian kingdoms (or empires), the terms B.C. (Before Christ) and A.D. (*Anno Domini*, "in the year of our Lord") came into common usage. In our effort to avoid Eurocentrism, we have chosen to use terms introduced recently—B.C.E. (Before the Common Era) and C.E. (Common Era)—that designate the same time frame in a nonreligious way.

2. We are indebted to Emma Tarlo (1996, p. 14) for this quote from Dar.

3. Early discussion of invention of tradition (Hobsbawm & Ranger, 1983) was applied to dress by Cohn (1983; 1989). Other responses to the demonstration of the changeable character of traditions and ethnic dress have appeared (Baizerman, 1987; Eicher, 1995; Nag, 1989; Picton, 1992, 1995; Spooner, 1986; and Tarlo, 1996).

4. This idea was brought to our attention by the research project of Jennifer Stahlberg (1998) on Cholitas of Bolivia, and we have extended it to the Cajuns of Louisiana.

5. In an initial article on this idea, Eicher and Sumberg (1995) used the term "world fashion." In Chapter 9 we comment on the distinction between world dress and world fashion.

3

Records of the Types of Dress

OBJECTIVES

To identify and evaluate the sources of information about dress, such as artifacts, visual representations, and written documentation.

To understand dress as evidence of human behavior.

AS WE CHRONICLE, SUMMARIZE, and interpret dress, we draw upon information from many different sources and disciplines, from art and art history to cultural history, social psychology, and anthropology, as well as chemistry and physics. Numerous resource materials are available: we learn about types of dress from actual items of dress, from a wide variety of visual records, including paintings and sculpture that show representations of dress, and from written descriptions by travelers and explorers, along with costume histories and electronic material from the World Wide Web (www). In each of these cases, one of the challenges confronting us as we assess evidence about dress is to consider the accuracy or bias of the evidence. We begin by discussing actual items of dress that provide direct visual inspection and evidence. *Records of dress as sources of information* serve our learning about types of dress in any society and culture and about human behavior.

ACTUAL ARTIFACTS

Real items of dress, often referred to as **artifacts** of dress, may come from archaeological digs, from personal collections, or from museum holdings. Archaeological *evidence of dress* ranges from fragments of textiles to whole garments, from beads and other items of jewelry to residues of makeup and perfume. Contemporary items of dress are readily available, along with many examples from the eighteenth and nineteenth centuries. The further back in history we delve, the more difficult the challenge of finding actual examples becomes, because much evidence from earlier eras has been destroyed or has deteriorated through time. Complete garments are rare finds by archaeologists because those made of textiles and leather usually disintegrate when buried in the earth. Thus, in general, study of actual artifacts becomes necessarily limited. Although few garments dated earlier than the seventeenth century have survived, jewelry, and other "hard" body equipment such as armor have sometimes been preserved from earlier times. Some items of body ornament, such as beads made of nonreactive minerals, have lasted for thousands of years and are identified among the possessions of prehistoric peoples. In contrast, the preservation of perishable organic materials, such as cottons, linens, silks, woolens, leathers, and furs that have been used in apparel in various parts of the world for centuries, occurs only under unusual circumstances. Extreme cold, dryness, or a fortuitous combination of environmental conditions may sometimes forestall the deteriorating effects of oxygen, light, and microorganisms and preserve clothing, or fragments, from earlier eras.

For example, undisturbed "cold storage" in the low temperatures of permanently frozen soil of northern Russia probably accounts for preservation of Old Stone Age leather and fur garments included among archeological finds reported by Russian scientists in the 1960s ("Modern Stone Age Men," 1969, p. 583; "Paleolithic Funeral," 1965, pp. 53–54). In one burial site,[1] the remains of two young boys were found clad in leather trousers and shirts and fur-lined boots. Beads of mammoth ivory decorated their apparel. In another grave, a Cro-Magnon-type man was buried in trousers and shirt of fur, also decorated with beads of mammoth ivory. Bracelets of mammoth ivory and strands of Arctic fox teeth added to his personal adornment. In the recent analysis of the body of "Otzi," the Iceman uncovered by melting ice in the Italian Alps, researchers found Otzi's leather boots were insulated with straw and that his legs bore tattoos (Spindler, 1994). Body modifications such as tattoos were also preserved on the skin of a Pazyryk woman whose 2,400-year-old tomb was inundated by water soon after her burial and remained frozen since that time in the permafrost of Siberia (Polosmak, 1994, p. 82), as seen in Figure 3.1.

The recent Chinchorro mummy finds in the desert on the coast of Chile, like many Egyptian finds, owe their preservation to arid sand (Arriaza, 1995). The cleaned and reassembled bones of the deceased were dressed and interred, some as early as 7,000 years ago. The garments, human hair "wigs," and painted masks which survived intact may represent the types of body supplements and modifications worn in life, or be special dress worn only by the deceased.

Figure 3.1
The few artifacts of dress that have survived intact from ancient times show us that beautiful and elaborate forms of dress were worn in prehistory. The discovery of a woman's grave made in the Siberian permafrost 2,400 years ago revealed both body modifications like this tattoo design and body supplements.

In ancient burial sites in Egypt and the central Andean region of South America, clothing made of several types of fibers has resisted the devastation of time because of the dryness of the desert areas in which burials were made. Flax was the fiber used almost exclusively in the textile body supplements of the ancient Egyptians, and linen tunics, shawls, loincloths, skirts, and robes were recovered from Egyptian burials in the desert. In fact, the garments found in King Tutankhamun's tomb by Howard Carter in 1922–23 were so well preserved that researchers in the 1990s were able to duplicate them and then try on the replicated garments.[2] They wanted to understand how these ancient Egyptian supplements fit the human body. By replicating the garments, they were better able to understand the functional reasons behind the garments' form of construction (Fowler, 1995, pp. B5, B7). The dress items include intricately made sandals decorated with birds and flowers made of gold and glass.

The favorable combination of burial arrangement and soil conditions in some parts of western Europe preserved body supplements and tools for body modification from an early era, whether composed of metallic or organic materials, as in the case of garments and jewelry found in remarkably good condition in Scandinavian graves of the Bronze Age (1500–1100 B.C.E.) (Broholm & Hald, 1940). In these oak coffin burial sites, some of the oldest complete garments preserved from western Europe have been discovered, along with pins, earrings, arm rings, combs, and other ornaments of bronze. Cut-and-sewn jackets and wraparound skirts, loincloths, gowns, and cloaks of woven wool were the basic garments. Men's hats were sometimes made in an intricate pile technique, women's caps by complicated braiding. Shoes, and sandals were of leather. Especially fascinating is the short, wraparound women's string skirt from Denmark dating to the fourteenth century B.C.E., because this type of string skirt is similar in form to other string skirts found elsewhere in the world (Barber, 1994, p. 57).

The people of the Central Andes had a wide variety in types of textiles according to Murra (1989). He reports that in the climate of the Central Andes area textiles do not keep well, so it was only in recent years that the extent of cultivation of wool from camelids was recognized. New archaeological and written finds together have revealed a wealth of fibers and designs in Andean textiles. Cotton and other bast fibers such as maguey, found in abundance in archaeological sites on the coastal plains of Peru, and hair fibers from animals, including the vicuna, guanaco, alpaca, and llama from the mountainous areas, were used in an array of ponchos, skirts, shirts, breechcloths, shawls, turbans, and belts (Murra, 1989, pp. 276–278). Thus it is a mistake to assume, in the absence of archaeological finds of intact body supplements, that an area of the world did not have a rich dress culture in prehistoric times. We remain ignorant only because the evidence has not yet been found.

Actual artifacts of dress give us excellent sources of information because each garment may be examined for its fiber composition and method of production. Because materials and technologies characterize certain times and places, we can learn something about the people who wore the garments. For example, before the invention of the sewing machine by Elias Howe in the mid-1800s, all garments were sewn by hand. Because hand-sewing is so time intensive, most people owned very few clothes and tended to wear them until they were well worn, even frayed. Only wealthy people owned multiple garments that did not become worn out. In many parts of the world and among many classes of people, everyday dress still does not survive use to be saved for study by later scholars. This helps explain why museums house mostly high fashion or expensive garments of the wealthy, both because of the quantity of these garments available and their condition.

Another reason that some items of dress do not survive is that the wearers do not believe that they are important enough to be saved for posterity and thus do not preserve them. We can think about listing the items of our own dress that we might save for our descendants to appreciate or contribute to a museum collection. Then we can think of listing all the things we wear that we would not bother to preserve. How much history of the dress of our own era might be lost to future generations in the second list? In the United States, curators in museums find it easy to collect designer, special occasion, and wedding dresses along with some faddish items, but difficult to collect items of dress that people wear on a daily basis and take for granted.

We can understand that artifacts have limitations as sources of evidence and information. Often we do not have information about the person owning it, how it was worn on the body, what its meaning was to the owner, or what the occasion was when worn. For example, a student in a class on historic costumes selected a party dress of her grandmother's for analysis. Based on the design and construction of the garment, she could not tell which was front and back. Even after trying the garment on, she was unsure. It was only after she found a portrait of her grandmother wearing the dress that she determined how the dress was to be worn. Consequently, visual representations such as photographs, paintings, or drawings become important sources of information about the dress of common folk and everyday dress.

VISUAL REPRESENTATIONS

For pictorial and other **visual representations** of dress we are indebted to many different kinds of artists and artisans. From the second half of the nineteenth century, the visual record has been further highly developed by photographers specializing in still photography, motion pictures, television, video, and most recently, computerized movies. For visual information previous to the development of photography, we depend mainly on the works of painters, sculptors, potters, metal workers, weavers, and engravers as seen in Figure 3.2a, b, and c. Painters include the earliest cave dwellers who created art on the walls of caves as well as their numerous descendants who record their impressions of human appearance on various surfaces. Sculptors model recognizable human forms from clay, wood, ivory, and rough chunks of stone. Potters fashion ceramics in human form or decorate clay pots with human figures. Figures such as the terra-cotta soldiers unearthed in the 1970s in Xian, China, have meticulous details that give us specific information about hairstyles and uniforms. Metal workers etch human figures on precious or base metals or cast figures in metal. The hands and tools of weavers translate threads of different color, size, and texture into pictures of humans. Engravers, lithographers, and other printers provide illustrations of people and their dressed appearance that can be made widely available.

The contributions of artisans who depend largely on the skill of their hands are considerable. At times their work constitutes the only clues we have to the nature of dress type and use in a particular era or place. With the inundation of Pompeii by the ash of Mount Vesuvius, most of their artifacts perished along with the people who created them, but the excavation of surviving interior wall paintings and mosaics are rich sources of detail into the everyday life of the citizens of Pompeii, including their dress.

Portrait art, depictions of historical events, and travelers' sketches yield some of the richest detail. A special contribution of the sixteenth century was

(a)   *(b)*   *(c)*

Figure 3.2
For evidence of dress from the era preceding the invention of photography, we must rely on the creations of artists and craft workers for visual depiction of dress.
(a) Peruvian Mochica, "Stirrup Spout head" headdress; (b) Medieval "The Last Supper Textile;" (c) Yoruba wooden statues.

the printing in Europe of costume plates depicting not only European, but also New World, Asian, and African dress. These products of the engraver's art helped to satisfy an expanded desire for recording information about these far-away lands and people. This interest in documentation developed with the enthusiasm for maritime exploration that blossomed in western Europe at this time and set a pattern for the centuries to follow. References in the Torah and Bible promoted early interest among Europeans and an awareness of remote areas in Asia and Africa, but concepts of what these places were like and how people must have looked were, for most medieval Europeans, based on legends that had been handed down from classical times. When Bible stories were illustrated, frequently the setting and the dress of the characters were European. For example, a reproduction of a nineteenth-century C.E. *Dalmalningar*, a type of Swedish folk painting, in Figure 3.3 depicts Jesus, in nineteenth-century Swedish noble dress, entering Jerusalem, which looks suspiciously like Stockholm. Thus, the folk painting tells us more about Swedish dress of that period than Biblical dress (Tonsing, 1998).

Figure 3.3
When artwork depicts historical scenes, critical skill must be exercised to interpret the evidence of dress. This depiction of Jesus entering Jerusalem shows him dressed according to the cultural expectations of the artist's era, rather than in the dress of biblical Israel. Swedish Dalmålningar, nineteenth century.

Legend was often blended with information from historians, particularly the classical Greek historian Herodotus who, for his time, had traveled rather widely in Asia Minor, Persia, the Mediterranean islands, Egypt, and Libya. Errors which he made in recording what he observed were perpetuated and compounded by later classical Roman historians, such as Solinus and Pliny who drew on him heavily for information, and sometimes added stories and legends of their own. Even as late as the end of the fifteenth century, the engravings of the Nuremberg Chronicles, which are one of the earliest products of the European printing press, reinforced classic misconceptions by representing inhabitants of remote regions of Asia or Africa as having grotesque and distorted bodies.

After the discovery of the New World, minds were unlocked as information was brought back to Europe by fifteenth- and sixteenth-century explorers and travelers. Sketches of men, women, and children brought back from many parts of the world showed that human beings in far-off lands did not have the extreme physical deviations that had so long been imagined, although they scarcely cover their bodies at all or might clothe themselves in ways very different from people in Europe. German engravings by Theodore DeBry, published in 1590 and 1591, are early examples of prints of dress from the New World, as seen in Figure 3.4a. DeBry depicted the unique dress of the American Indians of Florida and Virginia. The headdress, body painting, and tattooing, and the generally bare bodies clad only incidentally in deerskin aprons or cloaks, sometimes a strap of interwoven moss, must have seemed exotic to the Europeans. DeBry's prints of Florida were taken from paintings done by Jacques LeMoyne Demorgues and are thought to have been done from memory after Demorgues returned to France from his travels in Florida in 1564 or 1565. His prints of Virginia are adapted from watercolors done by John White, as seen in Figure 3.4b, who resided for a while with the settlers in the Roanoke colonies established by Sir Walter Raleigh between 1585 and 1587 (Lorant, 1946, p. 31). Since White's paintings were on-the-scene records, they are regarded as the earliest authentic pictorial records of aboriginal life in what is now the United States.[3]

Also important to our knowledge of dress are pictorial records that have been deliberately made in order to preserve knowledge of antiquity. For example, Francois Roger de Gaignieres' collection of sketches made between 1670 and 1688 from art work on funerary and other monuments have been a much-utilized source for redrawn illustrations in books on early French costume (Davenport, 1948, p. 485). An artist-engraver, Louis Bordeau, was commis-

(a)   (b)

Figure 3.4
The depiction of New World peoples evidenced forms of dress that seemed exotic to Europeans. A German engraving by Theodore DeBry (a), published 1590–1591 was based on works such as John White's on-the-scene painting of Indians around the Roanoke colony, 1585–1587 (b). White's works are regarded as the earliest authentic pictorial record by Europeans of aboriginal dress in what is now the United States.

sioned by Gaignieres to do the actual work which eventually passed into the hands of Louis XIV, and was finally deposited with the national archives of France, where it is still preserved.

Mercantile interest in clothing, particularly in France, began to expand as miniature representations of the newest ideas in women's fashions were sent from Paris on **fashion dolls** to centers of business throughout Europe, and even across the Atlantic to America. Use of these dolls is thought to date back to the late fourteenth century. In the seventeenth and eighteenth centuries they were a primary means for supplying the latest word in French fashion, including millinery and hair styling.

The production of **costume plates** began about 1500, and became a well-developed art in the seventeenth century. By the end of the eighteenth century, costume plates, which are after-the-fact portrayals of established modes of dress, must be distinguished from **fashion plates**, as in Figure 3.5a which, like the fashion dolls, were used to promote and publicize new fashions (Holland, 1955, pp. 21–22). Fashion plates along with costume plates differ from contemporary fashion photographs such as that of Figure 3.5b. Early dress and fashion plates included depictions of men's dress; however, these diminished in

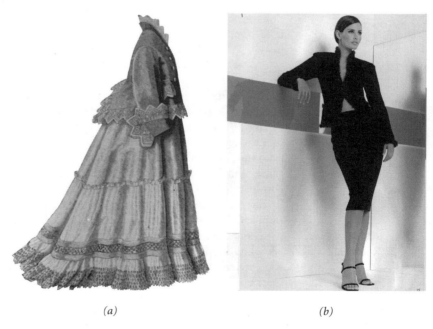

(a)   (b)

Figure 3.5
It is necessary to exercise critical skill when using fashion photographs or pictures as evidence of dress. Do they evidence dress as popularly worn or the promotion of particular forms of dress through advertising in the hope of making them popular?
(a) Fashion plate from *Godey's Lady's Book*, late 18th or early 19th century; (b) Escada catalog, 1999.

importance by the late eighteenth century, as fashion competition among Western men began to wane, and fashion display became more the province of women. Women's fashion magazines and general women's magazines, such as *The Delineator* and *Godey's Lady's Book*, that carried fashion plates, emerged at this time as forerunners of numerous publications of the nineteenth and twentieth centuries. Fashion plates were colored by hand until late in the nineteenth century, when a general change to color printing took place. An important point to remember is that artists' depictions are frequently idealized or distorted versions of the body. In photographs, photographic techniques such as airbrushing or retouching can also alter the body image.

The introduction of photography in the nineteenth century foreshadowed twentieth-century Western fashion promotion via the work of the photographer rather than the artist or copyist, although sketches reproduced through modern processes such as offset-lithography are still used in American pattern illustrations and sometimes in special artwork today. Dress history books, the evolutionary offspring of earlier collections of costume plates, have also moved to the utilization of photographs rather than drawings, although many dress history books still depend primarily on drawings and depictions of paintings and sculpture for illustration. Davenport's monumental work, *The Book of Costume*, first published in 1948, used photographs of artwork for her illustrations, and led the way for a growing number of "art books" on dress that have used improved methods of photography and printing, including color, to illustrate examples of dress.

We often believe that photographers present accuracy in their images of dress but neither their work nor that of artists or copyists can be guaranteed to mirror reality. Each may have a goal of promoting an idea rather than showing dress people actually wear. Even today, most people do not dress or pose like the models depicted in glossy high fashion magazines, which purport to predict the newest trends. Especially when conditions promote great social and economic inequalities, illustrations of dress tend to be characteristic of only those who have prestige and money. Changes in the dress of the poor have commanded relatively little interest of museums or artists earning their living by catering to the tastes of the well-to-do. A further distortion encouraged by publications on dress in the nineteenth century is the emphasis on women's dress and the downplaying of the dress of men.

Interest in publishing pictures of men's dress waned as the dress of men of the nineteenth century became increasingly drab and standardized: the growing number of middle-class businessmen devoted their time and energies to making money rather than to competing in fashion. However, the women in their families, both wives and daughters, had the time and were expected to indulge in personal display. As the prestige of royalty lessened after World War I, fashion leadership was taken by the new rich, such as bankers, industrialists, railroad barons, and their wives. A trend toward more variation and more rapid change in men's dress in the second half of the twentieth century may reflect an increase in leisure time for a greater number of men; time as well as money must be available if an individual is interested in fashion. This move toward more participation in fashionable dress has been accompanied by an increased interest in fashion illustrations showing men's dress.

Many kinds of commercial artists other than the illustrators of fashion periodicals depict dress in their paintings and drawings. For example, artists have been commissioned in many countries to paint or draw indigenous dress for postage stamps (Niubo, 1970). Commercial artists incorporate dress in their advertisements for mass media. Frequently the dress is accurate and up-to-date, providing a true historical record, as apparently indicated in Figure 3.6. At other times, aspects of dress are exaggerated or distorted in order to elicit a certain response in the reader to increase sales appeal. For example, the dress worn by actors in television advertisements for household products is often

Figure 3.6
Art in the service of commerce sometimes inadvertently depicts dress with such accuracy that it can be followed through time as a record of change in dress practice in a culture.

contextually accurate, but advertisements for fine jewelry and expensive automobiles may feature idealized dress. Similar distortion can arise in portraiture, for artists frequently idealize their subjects. Their ability to depict reality may also be limited by art conventions or the media they use.

Just as actual artifacts of dress have their advantages and disadvantages as sources of information, so do visual representations. Through photographs and paintings, we can see how garments and accessories were worn and in what combinations, but we cannot always be sure how accurately they portray actual garments. The student of dress can learn more about the dress and about the context in which it was worn when both are seen together. Figure 3.7 shows a "then and now" comparison of dress for similar purposes as depicted in fashion publications a century apart. These records help us observe changing practices in the dress of a culture over time. On the other hand, we usually cannot see from a visual record how the supplements were made.

In addition, visual representations can be posed and do not always reflect reality. In the late 1800s, young American Indian children were relocated to

Figure 3.7
Visual depiction of dress can sometimes tell us a lot about the social context in which the dress is worn and the identity of the wearer. However, such depiction cannot tell us how the body supplements were made, nor how the body modifications were achieved. (a) U.S. velveteen bicycling costume, 1894; (b) U.S. activewear for active sports and exercise, 1996.

boarding schools in an attempt to "civilize" them. Before-and-after portraits were taken of them to encourage white Americans to donate money to these schools and to a cause that seemed noble at the time. Often the "before" pictures were taken immediately after the children were taken off the train, when they looked tired and disheveled. The "after" portraits were taken in formal portrait studios, with the children dressed in Euro-American dress. In some photographs, even their skin appears whiter. In any case, both sets of portraits were carefully constructed to have maximum emotional impact on the white viewers, yet they tell us nothing about what those children really felt or believed about how they looked.

One student at the University of Minnesota tells the story of being forced by her mother to wear a traditional form of Korean dress—a *hanbok* (hawn-bock) ensemble—for a studio photograph. She found the clothing, with its tight ties around the chest and full petticoats underneath the skirt, extremely uncomfortable. When telling the story, she says she still dislikes the traditional dress of her country, and she testifies that the photograph that was taken does not represent how she normally dressed for everyday occasions while growing up in her Korean homeland. She wished she were being photographed in the dress garments that she normally wore everyday, the ones often thought of as "Western."

WRITTEN DESCRIPTION AND COMMENTARY

Since artists may deviate from exact, visual representation of dress, the accuracy of their pictures needs to be determined by cross-checking with other kinds of available data. One way to check is to consult **written descriptions** and **commentaries** on dress of the same time period, when such material is available. Diaries, accounts of travel and exploration, catalogues, biographies, novels, memoirs, essays, satires, books of history and philosophy, manuals on etiquette and personal conduct, and religious tracts are often rich sources of information on dress, even when not primarily intended for this purpose. They can provide information to help validate the authenticity of visual representations and to elucidate the meaning of dress within its contemporary setting, although they, too, may be subject to **bias**. They can also contribute original information unavailable through visual media. For example, written descriptions can tell us how an antebellum dress maintained its shape with a crinoline and why the Amish use straight pins instead of buttons as closures. Since essays, manuals on etiquette, and books on philosophy are highly interpretive, giving special points of view, their consideration will be reserved for the next chapter. The novel as a source of description about what people wear can also provide information on dress from another time period or culture. Some writers, such as Raymond Chandler in "The Little Sister," originally published in 1949, give vivid word descriptions that make the reader picture clearly what characters are wearing and how the manner of dress relates to the character, as in the description "The rimless glasses gave her that librarian's look."

Accounts of Travelers and Explorers

Travelers and explorers, sometimes intrigued and sometimes dismayed by customs that varied from their own, have provided us with many descriptions and comments on dress. These travelers' tales offer unparalleled details as a source of information about dress, but this advantage must be balanced with the singular, and often ethnocentric, viewpoint of their authors. Marco Polo's account of his thirteenth century travels in medieval Asia was initially received with skepticism in his own day, when legend seemed more believable than the remarkable tales he told. Eventually accepted as an honest account, but once again at the end of the twentieth century becoming disputed, his book is an example of a volume that, in its rich description of customs, included information on dress. References to elegant fabrics of silk and gold, however, are more numerous than references to dress itself. His ill-concealed astonishment concerning dress of women in Balashan, a province north of Afghanistan, is reported in this way:

> A peculiar fashion of dress prevails amongst the women of the superior class, who wear below their waists, in the manner of drawers, a kind of garment, in the making of which they employ, according to their means, an hundred, eighty, or sixty ells[4] of fine cotton cloth; which they also gather or plait in order to increase the apparent size of their hips; those being accounted the most handsome who are the most bulky in that part. (Polo, 1958, p. 57)

Captain Cook's journal provided Europeans with some of the first detailed information on the general appearance and dress of peoples of the South Pacific, an area little known even 250 years after Magellan's historic circumnavigation of the globe had opened the way. His account of tattooing as practiced in Tahiti, one of many stopping points on his journeys, is as follows:

> Both sexes paint their bodys, tattow, as it is called in their Language. This is done by inlaying of the Colour of Black under their skins in such a manner as to be indelible. . . . Their method of Tattowing I shall now describe. The colour they use is lampblack prepar'd from the Smoak of a kind of Oily nut, used by them instead of Candles. (Wharton, 1893, p. 93)

An example of a more opinionated traveler, one who failed to endear herself to nineteenth-century readers in the United States because of her devastatingly candid observations of their personal habits, was Mrs. Trollope. Her book on the *Domestic Manners of Americans*, published in 1832, dwells on many fine details related to grooming, dress, and appearance. Her attitude toward the accomplishments of the people she observed in this respect is well reflected in the following paragraph:

> The ladies have strange ways of adding to their charms. They powder themselves immoderately, face, neck, and arms, with pulverized starch; the effect is indescribably disagreeable by day-light, and not very favourable at any time. They are also most unhappily partial to false hair, which they wear in surprising quantities; this is the more to be lamented, as they generally have very fine hair of their own. I suspect this fashion to arise from an indolent mode of making their toilet, and from

accomplished ladies' maids not being very abundant; it is less trouble to append a bunch of waving curls here, there, and everywhere, than to keep their native tresses in perfect order. (Trollope, 1832/1949, pp. 299–300)

Dress History

In **dress history**, visual representations and written commentary meet. Dress history volumes began with the binding together of collections of costume plates whose printing followed the introduction of the printing press. They took on added dimensions as descriptive texts were added. Books by Planche (1834), Hope (1841), Fairholt (1846), and Weiss (1853, 1860–72) in the first half of the nineteenth century were forerunners of a number of books on European costume history that became popular in the last quarter of that century. Among the best known of the latter were those by Quicherat (1877), Racinet (1888), Rohrbach (1882, with lithographs by Kretschmer), and Hottenroth (1896).

The twentieth century witnessed an expanding interest in clothing customs, and many volumes on Western dress have been published. Early works increasing Westerners' knowledge of the history of non-Western dress include works on Asia, such as Fabri's (1960) and Ghurye's (1951) individual volumes on history of dress in India, Minnich's (1963) *Japanese Costume*, Scott's (1958) *Chinese Costume in Transition*, Garrett's (1994) *Chinese Clothing: An Illustrated Guide*, Fairservis's (1971) *Costumes of the East*, and Mead's (1969) *Traditional Maori Clothing*. Works on South America include Wood and Osborne's (1966) *Indian Costumes of Guatemala*, Cordry and Cordry's (1968) *Mexican Indian Costumes*, Schevill's (1992) *Maya Textiles of Guatemala*, and Hendrickson's (1995), *Weaving Identities: Construction of Dress and Self in a Highland Guatemalan Town*. These volumes provide not only text but an array of sketches, drawings, and historic and contemporary photographs of the artifacts and of the dress as worn.

More recently, increased awareness of the many cultures of the globe has produced many more publications on the history of dress of peoples outside Western culture. One notable development in many twentieth-century histories of dress, whether of Western or non-Western dress, is an increased emphasis on examination and interpretation of dress within a total social, cultural, economic, and political context. Changes in type of dress are studied in relation to other changes in a society, instead of as isolated social phenomena, and viewpoints that arbitrarily classify types as good or bad and changes as frivolous or socially undesirable are avoided. Among books on Western costume published since the mid-1940s, Davenport's (1948) *The Book of Costume* is one of the richest in explanatory detail. Boucher's (1987) *20,000 Years of Fashion: A History of Costume and Personal Adornment*, Russell's (1982) *Costume History and Style*, Roach and Musa's (1980) *New Perspectives on the History of Western Dress*, Payne, Winakor, and Farrell-Beck's (1992) *The History of Costume*, and Tortora and Eubank's (1998) *A Survey of Historic Costume* are further examples. The previously mentioned books on non-Western costume also relate clothing to various factors that provide a backdrop for understanding human behavior.

Electronic Sources of Dress Information

Visual documentation and written information on dress meet electronically on the World Wide Web. Scholars of dress create home pages as conscious and deliberate sources of information about dress. Tourist boards of countries, such as Mexico and Indonesia, incorporate visual images of ethnic and national dress into their websites to highlight their rich cultural heritages. Fashion designers and manufacturers worldwide promote their wares on the Web. Individuals create personal home pages to celebrate and communicate to friends and family major life course events, such as weddings and births, with photographs that show celebratory outfits.

The advantage of these sources is the usual combination of visual and written documentation. Often, because the images might be of family events, people are caught in the act of being themselves. If the purpose of the source is to present information on dress, images are selected for their clarity and ability to be downloaded and printed by the person who accesses the website. Also, in such cases, the critical skills necessarily brought to bear in use of published costume history books apply to the costume history websites.

The disadvantage to websites and home pages is that there is no filtering process, in the form of publishers, editors, and juries of scholars, to assess the validity and significance of the information and ideas being presented. What might appear to be a scholarly treatise may be revealed after further sleuthing to be the creation of an amateur or a clever fake. Moreover, progress in the electronic manipulation of images makes it possible to create false images easily. Sometimes important written documentation is missing. One of our students was quite frustrated upon accessing a website in which many clear photographs of a Turkish-American wedding were available, but there was no written information given. Also images on the Web are often copied from original nonelectronic sources of publication, but references to the original are not given; this constitutes a form of plagiarism and is a prosecutable offense in the United States. Direct e-mail inquiries to scholars working in the field of dress is one way to check on or ensure the accuracy of documentation found on the Web.

SUMMARY

Dress has so fascinated human beings that we have long felt the urge to record its many types; therefore, many sources of information are available to those wishing to study the types of dress throughout the ages. Actual artifacts tell us the form and manufacture of the garment, but offer little information about social context. However, examples of everyday dress rarely survive for analysis. Cave drawings, sculpture, paintings, and ceramics provide visual representations from very ancient times; and pictorial textiles and printed plates show dress from about the sixteenth century. These sources depict dress in use and convey the social context of the wearer, but often the wealthy and powerful are favored, with the dress of common folk less frequently depicted. Written accounts of travelers and explorers supplement information from visual representations and actual artifacts. Some accounts, although biased, offer perspectives characteristic of the era. Dress histories, flourishing during the last two centuries, summarize data from many of these sources. Photographs of actual objects, often in color, make modern histories of dress more exact. Contemporary works include social history and the forces behind change.

In the late twentieth century, we have many rich sources of published visual and written documentation of dress. Yet so little is written on the dress of some parts of the world, and dress is changing so rapidly in many places, that we must access as many types of records of dress as possible. We need to search for all forms of documentation of dress, whether academic scholarship or incidental visual evidence, to learn about the many ways that people dress around the world today and through history.

STUDY TOOLS

Important Terms

artifact

bias

dress history

costume plate

fashion doll

fashion plate

visual representations

written commentaries

written descriptions

Discussion Questions

1. Describe different environmental conditions under which organic dress artifacts have been preserved. Give examples.
2. Explain what can be learned from examining actual dress artifacts. What cannot be learned?
3. List the types of visual representations of dress and give examples of each.
4. What do travelers' tales contribute to our knowledge about dress? What might be a failing of travelers' accounts?
5. Why are histories of dress important sources of information?
6. In small groups examine Figures 3.4a and 3.4b carefully. How are they similar and how are they different? Paying special attention to the depiction of the fringed wrapped body supplement and the color modifications to the skin, how do you see ethnocentrism of the sixteenth-century European artist emerging in his depictions of Eastern North American natives? In what ways do you think these are an accurate depiction of sixteenth-century American Indian dress?

7. Imagine you are writing a history of dress of your family, going back six generations. What kinds of records of dress would you be able to use as evidence? First consider the evidence from your own family's heirlooms. Then, consider what other forms of evidence you could turn to when you had exhausted your own family's historical documentation.

8. In the days before photography and newspapers were in common use, what kinds of evidence of dress were produced? What are the limitations of these earlier forms of evidence of dress? What kinds of dangers or limitations are associated with modern forms of evidence of dress?

9. Many academic fields contribute to our understanding of dress. Using Reading I.4, "Many Disciplines/Many Rewards: Inuit Clothing Research," by Issenman, list the variety of disciplines that contributed to her knowledge of Inuit dress and give an example of each from the dress of your own culture.

Activities

1. Create a chart with sources of information about dress along one axis and advantages/disadvantages of each source along the other axis. Complete the chart for this chapter and for Chapter 4.

2. Examine a dress history book. List the records of the forms of dress used by the author to provide visual representations and written commentary. Compare your findings with other students. Do some dress histories appear to be more thorough than others? Explain.

3. Using your college or university catalogue, make a list of majors. Each student will select one major and call a professor from that field. Find out how that field might or does add to our knowledge about dress.

4. Select a topic related to dress, perhaps as part of your own research. Find three sources of information about the topic on the Internet. Evaluate their advantages and disadvantages as sources.

5. Select a time frame and a cultural area for studying a form of dress about which you would like to learn more, as inspiration for developing a line of dress, theater costumes, or a marketing scheme some time in your career. List the various areas of the library, such as art history or archaeology and the types of materials in which you hope to find sources of information on the dress for your selected time and culture frame. Find one example of each of at least three types of sources of information on the dress of your selected time and culture area and bring them to class to share. Try to find types of sources that you do not ordinarily use.

Notes to Chapter 3

1. Because burial sites and graves are often the only source of information about people in the ancient past, they have been a focus of archeological study. However, archaeologists have on a few occasions excavated the graves of deceased individuals

whose immediate grandchildren were still alive. The family members were naturally upset and wanted to preserve their ancestors' burial sites. Such instances occurred in the context of privileged members of society studying the history of vulnerable minority communities, such as Euro-American archaeologists studying American Indians. The culture and history of ethnic communities, made vulnerable by their second-class status, often are made the subject of archaeological studies because of this discipline's close association with anthropology, which has its origins in a science of the ethnographic other. Some members of American Indian communities feel that their history is being stolen from them by non-Indian archaeologists, and thus resist the archaeological excavation of even ancient sites in the United States. Archaeologists respond that the information stored in such ancient sites will be lost to all unless excavated, because it continues to decompose in the ground. Modern archaeologists and citizens' groups struggle to find a middle ground between the need to collect and preserve time-sensitive data and respect for the descendants of the deceased individuals being disinterred and examined. One solution has been the application of sonic and X-ray technology to the study of remains without disturbing them. In many cases, however, ancient graves are discovered in the process of ploughing the land or digging into the earth to build the foundations for new buildings or highways. In such cases the sites have already been disturbed to some degree and salvage archaeological studies are quickly made. The social group responsible for funding the construction, be it an individual developer or a transportation department of the government, does not want to bear the expense of changing the construction plans. In consideration of the number of years that human beings have existed on the earth, under most every square yard of ground there lies one of our ancestors, and it is hard to avoid bumping into them from time to time. Government bodies, archaeologists, and relevant sectors of the general public continue to try to resolve the controversy with an agreement about which types of graves are fair subjects of archaeological study.

2. The researchers replicated the garments because wearing the original garments is frowned upon by textile historians and preservationists in the late twentieth century, because irreparable harm can be done to these ancient items of dress.

3. John White's watercolors were published for the first time in Lorant's (1946) book, which also contains reprints of Theodore DeBry's engravings from both White's and Jacques Demorgues' paintings.

4. One ell equals three-quarters of a yard.

4

Written Interpretations of Dress

OBJECTIVES

To identify types of written interpretations of dress.

To recognize meanings conveyed by written interpretations.

To examine the analytical works about dress and their significance.

ALTHOUGH DRESS AND FASHION seem insignificant or superficial to some people,[1] a wide array of **analytical writing** indicates how important the topic has been across the globe and over time. Many examples of descriptive literature, philosophical treatises, moralistic essays, theoretical analyses, and research reviews and reports provide information and insights about how the way people dress relates to human needs and behavior. These *written interpretations* help us understand why some types of dress are preferred, for what purposes an individual uses dress, and what purpose dress serves within society.

MORALISTIC ESSAYS, SATIRE, AND REFORM LITERATURE

We often hear comments made about whether or not someone has dressed appropriately. Many people through the ages have recorded their approval or disapproval in writing of different types of dress on moral grounds. How these writers use dress to make a moral point reveals information for their time about meanings of dress. Reading helps us understand these people and their value systems. Sometimes **moralistic essays** from different time periods sound similar, but on close examination, the philosophical base for the arguments differs. For example, the ardent sixteenth-century Puritan, Philip Stubs, argues against the dress of his day, sounding much like Clay Geerdes, a contributor to an underground newspaper of the 1960s. Stubs said in 1595:

> For doe not the most of our . . . newfangled fashions rather deforme, then adorne us: disguise us, then become us: making us rather to resemble savage beastes and brutish Monsters, then continent, sober and chast Christians. (p. 8)

Geerdes said in 1969:

> Cosmetics do not make women beautiful, they symbolize artificiality and unnatural image, which are truly ugly masks of people unable to accept themselves as they really are. (p. 5)

As we compare the two points of view, Stubs roots his arguments in religious doctrine of his time, whereas Geerdes bases his on 1960s popular psychology about being oneself.

Sometimes, the symbolic nature of dress encourages **satire**. The satirist, as moralist, uses dress as a symbol to expose human follies and vices. For example, clothes are the medium rather than the target of nineteenth-century philosophizing in Carlyle's *Sartor Resartus* (1834), originally titled *Thoughts on Clothes*. Nevertheless, what he has to say reveals how dress is similar to other social inventions and how it can become an integral part of the social fabric of human beings:

> Clothes, from the King's mantle downwards, are emblematic, not of want only, but of a manifold cunning Victory over Want. On the other hand, all emblematic things are properly clothes, thought-woven. . . . Men are properly said to be clothed with Authority, clothed with Beauty, with curses, and the like. (pp. 72–73)

Comic strips and cartoons often ridicule or satirize the way people dress. Cartoon and caricature represent special forms of humor; they capture the basic elements of a current fashion and make them explicit through exaggeration. These two forms of satire also use dress to symbolize specific individuals or types of individuals. Scott Adams, creator of the comic strip Dilbert, dresses his characters to indicate how he views the individuals and the quirks of their behavior, as in the example of the horned hairstyle of the boss, which portrays him as a devil. Another example occurs in the comic strip Cathy, for Cathy frequently frets over decisions about dress and new fashions, picking up the theme of distress supposedly exhibited by many American women when they think about what to wear. Commonplace facts that have been overturned can also be used in cartoons as shown in Figure 4.1 about dressing like the boss.

In the second half of the nineteenth century, **reform literature** was prevalent. The Women's Dress Reform Movement, an arm of the Women's Rights Movement, made women's dress a social issue. These reformers, although ridiculed severely and frustrated in their efforts, tried to introduce Turkish-inspired trousers to replace voluminous skirts popular for women. They did not imagine the drastic changes in women's dress that finally came with the general social shifts of the 1920s in the United States and Europe.

PRESCRIPTIVE AND PROSCRIPTIVE LITERATURE

A wide range of writing involves **prescriptions** about what is proper dress for specific situations (the dos) as well as **proscriptions**, which tell readers what not to wear (the don'ts). Popular writing includes fashion magazine articles and worst-dressed lists, popular etiquette books, and books about how to dress. Examples directed to specific clientele include internal business circulars

Ironically, it was young Greg Walcraft's blind acceptance of his business school's advice to "dress like your boss" that cost him further opportunities within the corporation.

Figure 4.1
The cartoon comments on confusion in work place relationships wrought by changing gender roles. Its humor rests on a true understanding, however satirized, that the cartoonist shares with the reading public about the work dress of women in "white collar" managerial positions at the time the cartoon was published.

dictating corporate dress policy, government memos on dress protocol for political representatives when traveling abroad, and clothing selection textbooks for high schools and colleges, which were fairly common in the early and mid-twentieth century.

In countries with class distinctions, standards for appearance as indicated in etiquette books often support social differences. Frequently, upwardly mobile people use such references to learn proper dress for new social situations, such as attending a dinner party or evening event never before experienced. These prescriptions for dress usually describe some customs of the past that seemed socially useful and presumed to guarantee current social success. In America, prescriptive standards for insuring success for job interviews, for example, became especially popular after John Molloy (1975, 1977) introduced his *Dress for Success* books and newspaper columns in the 1970s, which many others copied. *Glamour* magazine features a column on "Dos and Don'ts" that began in 1939. *Glamour* (Coffey, 1979) also published a book with the subtitle "Effective dressing on the job, at home, in your community and everywhere."

Feature articles have appeared in many magazines on the topic of appropriate dress, along with a variety of instruction books on makeup and makeovers, such as *Cindy Crawford's Basic Face: A Makeup Book* (Crawford, Kashuk, & Boyes, 1996). Other publications on dress or on etiquette authored by well-known magazine cover models like Brooke Shields (1985), who later moved into TV stardom, as well as by movie stars and designers provide advice on dressing to look slender. Bob Mackie (1979) used his experience in dressing television and cinema stars like Cher, Carol Burnett, Barbra Streisand, and Bette Midler, in crafting his advice for more ordinary women about how to dress glamorously. More recently Joan Rivers (1999) wrote on aging and the popularity of plastic surgery in Hollywood to counteract the aging effect. Other popular books tell readers how to *Flatter Your Figure* (Larkey, 1992) and how to present a personal style (Klensch & Meyer, 1995; Nix-Rice, 1996).

In the nineteenth century, many pages in general manuals on etiquette described correct dress, a selling point for a book as often emphasized by a book's subtitle. Newcomers as immigrants to the United States, interested in creating a new life, consulted etiquette books for help, because cultural patterns of behavior from their past no longer seemed to fit into their new and unfamiliar cultural setting. Some people not only changed cultural traditions, but also experienced social mobility; they wanted to learn something about the social graces needed to enter a new setting or may have wanted to shed negative stereotypes of being backward or from the "old country." Clearly, people wanted to know how to behave properly in the early decades of the nineteenth century. Magazines such as *Godey's Lady's Book* included frequent suggestions on etiquette and dress, and a great demand for manuals arose that were devoted to social decorum, as the historian Arthur Schlesinger (1947) comments:

> From the late 1820s on, this literature poured forth in a never-ending stream. An incomplete enumeration shows that, aside from frequent revisions and new editions, twenty-eight different manuals appeared in the late 1850s—an average of over three new ones annually in the pre-Civil War decades. (p. 18)

Americans felt self-conscious about their manners and dress as they compared themselves with self-confident Europeans, particularly the French and English. Thus, Duffey (1876) urged her countrymen to cast off their feelings of inferiority and dependency and strike off for themselves to develop an American style of behavior. She presented her case in this way:

> We have so long borrowed our manners, like our literature, from the Old World, that we have become thoroughly imbued with the feeling that what is not European—what is not at least English—cannot be proper and right in the conduct of life. But now, in the hundredth year of our national existence, it is time we began to realize the fact that we are perfectly capable of depending upon ourselves in matters pertaining to both behavior and dress. Our civilization is American; and, all unaware of it as we are, our development of the finer and gentler traits of character is just as truly American. We should understand that the American gentleman, though he may be lacking in the exceedingly polished, almost subservient, outward forms of politeness of the Frenchman—though he may not be so self-asserting and condescending as the Englishman—is just as true a gentleman; and the type which he presents would be more acceptable to the American People. Underneath an occasional appearance of brusqueness is hidden an even greater respect for women—that touchstone of true gentility. Our national institutions themselves teach men to respect one another as those of no nation do. There is an unwritten code of manners in our best American society, and there is no better code on the face of the earth. . . . (pp. 3–4)

But deference to the English and French was hard to stifle. Americans wanted to be seen as equal to their European peers. For example, in the 1920s, Emily Post (1928) admonished men on how to dress properly:

> If you would dress like a gentleman, you must do one of two things, either study the subject of a gentleman's wardrobe until you are competent to pick out good suits from freaks, or buy only English ones. It is not Anglomania, but plain common sense to admit that, just as the Rue de la Paix in Paris is the fountainhead of fashions for women, Bond Street in London is the home of irreproachable clothes for men. (p. 597)

And the English, as well as the Americans, could bow to the French in matters of women's dress. Mrs. Merrifield (1854), an English woman in the mid-nineteenth century, complained about the influence of French fashion on the English, yet she succumbed to its power as she sprinkled her writing with French fashion terms and finally admitted a superior talent among the French by saying:

> The French, whose taste in dress is so far in advance of our own, say that ladies who are *cinquante ans sonnes* (on the wrong side of fifty), should neither wear gay colours, nor dress of slight materials, flowers, feathers, or much jewelry; that they should cover their hair, wear high dresses, and long sleeves. (p. 93)

To the extent that nineteenth-century American manuals on decorum had the goal of describing common behavior suitable for all social levels, they helped newcomers settle socially and geographically in a new place. However Schlesinger (1947) points out that the rise of a new group of moneyed people following the Civil War encouraged a lingering deference to a code of social differences. People who made fortunes overnight in such areas as mining, railroads, banking, and real estate yearned after a style of life appropriate to their newly elevated status. To provide for their needs, manuals on proper behavior were written to explain ways for developing more aristocratic behavior. These manuals helped perpetuate belief in a well-ordered society based on individuals learning to behave in a manner appropriate to their "station in life." One post–Civil War book warned:

> Never dress above your station; it is a grievous mistake, and leads to great evils, besides being the proof of an utter want of taste. (*Decorum*, 1879, p. 270)

Readjustments in society followed World War I, and the day of conspicuous consumption of the *nouveau riche*, who had dominated U.S. society in the latter part of the nineteenth century and early part of the twentieth century, was over. References to matters of adjusting appearance to indicate station in life disappeared from even the more formal and tremendously popular etiquette manuals of Lillian Eichler (1921) and Emily Post (1928). In addition, a new type of book aimed clearly at the masses instead of the leisured well-to-do appeared and was frankly aimed toward making getting along with peers as easy as possible. One of these books (Norwood, 1937), intended to produce instant etiquette, began with this forthright introduction:

> The tempo of our times demands an etiquette book designed for instantaneous reference. *The Common Sense Etiquette Dictionary* satisfies a definite and an urgent need. It contains—without padding, sermonizing or moralizing—the essentials for good-breeding. It gives a bird's eye view of the entire field of manners—all one needs to know to move gracefully, confidently, and easily among his fellows. All non-essentials have been eliminated. Etiquette is in a continual state of flux. A last year's etiquette book is more or less outmoded. Time waits for no man. Neither does etiquette. Manners move on. (p. 7)

As we move into the twenty-first century, general manuals on etiquette and popular books on the art of dress and selection of clothing move away from moralizing to suggesting how dress helps social relationships and allows an individual some personal satisfaction about "looking good." Similarly, in the 1980s a whole range of color analysis books appeared, such as Jackson's *Color Me Beautiful* (1987), that promoted choosing colors to enhance skin tone and hair color to make individuals feel more attractive because the colors chosen show them off to advantage. Such books generally apply to one society and are not necessarily usable in another; sometimes they specifically apply to only one segment of a society. They fall into the prescriptive category: they suggest dress for an individual in order to appear handsome, beautiful, or socially at ease in various places and on different occasions. For example, Karpinski (1994) gives a lot of attention to the face in his advice book for men, *Red Socks Don't Work*. He gives specific directions for selecting hairstyles and shapes of eyeglasses to complement the face and draw attention away from deficiencies. He implies an ideal facial type for men exists that all men must strive to achieve.

Boyer (1990), in *Eminently Suitable: The Elements of Style in Business Attire*, advises a short man about how to dress so that he looks taller:

> Trouser legs should taper modestly from thigh to bottom, to help give the illusion of a longer silhouette. It's a good idea for the shorter man to wear self-supporting trousers (the kind with waist tabs, rather than belt loops), or suspenders, since a belt tends to break the vertical line. (p. 97)

The viewpoint of such writers of prescriptive literature on dress are recognizable by the "shoulds" and "should nots," by the "dos" and the "don'ts," implied or real, given to the reader. Suggestions for dress are stated in a categorical way rather than as possible options. However, in a rapidly changing society such as the United States, rules for personal behavior may run the risk of being obsolete before a book ever reaches publication.

Nevertheless, some themes for proper dress persist through the decades. U.S. books published on the art or etiquette of dress reveal the stability of culture, particularly ideals for women's and men's figures and face shape, as shown in Figure 4.2. Other aspects of the ideal dressed person change over time. An idea such as the "rightness or wrongness" of human size, for example, cannot be measured by a fixed metric that applies to all societies and to all eras. Rather, height is a value in relation to the height of other members of the society in which one lives. However, in books on women's dress dated 1854 (Merrifield), 1941 (Kettunen, pp. 47–57), and 1969 (O'Sullivan, p. 14), suggestions were made about how to dress to correct for "wrong" height. What "proper" height may be is not always expressed in feet or inches; but readers, immersed in the customs of their own society, ordinarily understand the approximate measurements for "too tall" and "too short." Such books imply that the reader understands that height has something to do with personal attractiveness, perhaps even marriageability. These books offer, therefore, suggestions for socially acceptable ways of dressing that direct attention away from being an apparently undesirable height. Authors also instruct men as well as women about dressing to look tall and slim, as in the following passage by the Canadian fashion designer and master tailor, Jean-Paul LoGiacco:

> A custom-tailored coat is an elegant addition to your wardrobe. . . . The style of the coat should make you look tall and slender. The length should be to the calf, at the most no lower than five inches from the ground. The shoulders should be wider than normal for an interesting style, with a wide top, suppressed waist, and a gentle flow of fabric over the hips to complete the v-shape. (LoGiacco & Cross, 1995, p. 100)

Books on etiquette and manuals on how to dress continue to be popular in the United States with many titles in print. They are usually published for women, although not exclusively so. Men's nineteenth-century withdrawal from fashion competition is reflected in selection books as well as dress history books—books devoted to selecting men's clothes are less common than similar books for women. A 1939 volume by Stote, *Men Too Wear Clothes*, notes the difference between attention given the sexes in its title. Depending on the discretion with which they are used, prescriptive works can act as democratic,

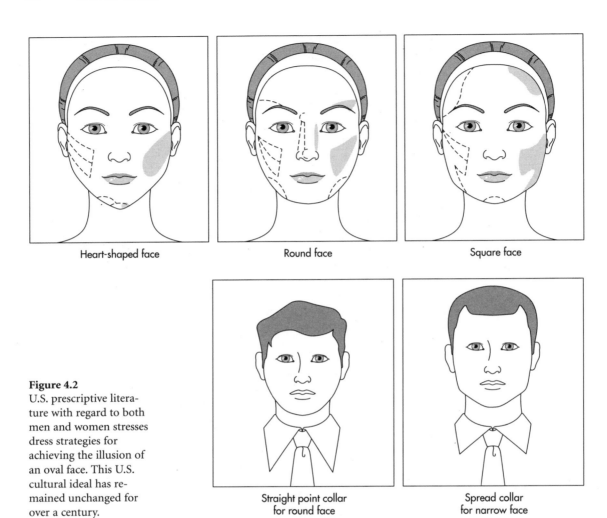

Heart-shaped face

Round face

Square face

Straight point collar
for round face

Spread collar
for narrow face

Figure 4.2
U.S. prescriptive literature with regard to both men and women stresses dress strategies for achieving the illusion of an oval face. This U.S. cultural ideal has remained unchanged for over a century.

socializing agents preparing individuals for social interaction and acceptance in social groups to which they may aspire. Two more recent books acknowledge the importance of men dressing appropriately. LoGiacco and Cross (1995) advise:

> . . . learn to plan your wardrobe so that it complements your lifestyle. Then you'll learn how to choose a custom-tailor and what to expect once you've done so. You'll learn which style and cut of clothes to choose that will best suit your proportions and taste. And you'll get to compare your own wardrobe with those of some successful top executives known for their style and dress. But most important, you'll learn how custom-tailoring can greatly improve your life and help you to achieve success—I would advise you not to settle for less. (p. 5)

Similarly, Flusser (1996) points out that dressing well can be learned when he says:

> Despite the commonly held myth that stylish men are born, not made, dressing well is an acquired skill. Becoming proficient in matters of self-attire is much like honing the talents needed to become a great golfer. While playing frequently can improve your game, until you start practicing the correct technique, your potential will always remain unfulfilled. All issues of proportion or design, as they relate to a man's individual style, should have a logical explanation. (p. xii)

Such instructions about learning what to wear, whether male or female, may give an individual an increased feeling of self-confidence if choosing the right outfit seems one way of gaining social acceptance. However, following an author's advice will not guarantee that an outfit will be appropriate for all situations or any locale. Halbreich and Wadyka (1997) indicate their point of view about this matter:

> . . . shopping and dressing is about much more than clothes. It's something you do to make yourself feel good. It should be fun. And sometimes even funny. Because if you aren't enjoying your clothes, then you really are missing the point. (p. 6)

Recognizing cultural diversity in the United States means that we are paying more attention to the possible difference in perspective of male or female, old or young, rich or poor, black or white, along with understanding regional or ethnic differences that may influence choices of dress. Particularly in matters of appropriateness for different occasions, an author's recommendations need testing and checking locally. One example that arose in the 1990s is related to the term "casual dress" and the institution of "casual Fridays" in the U.S. workplace. Originally intended to make people feel more relaxed and able to work at the end of the workweek, wearing casual dress may be interpreted as wearing anything from jeans and a T-shirt to carefully selected, color-coordinated ensembles. Therefore, explicit dress codes for casual Fridays are emerging as retailers and authors produce advice for those men and women who find themselves puzzled when deciding what is a casual outfit for work.

In addition, books on etiquette and proper dress run the risk of being quickly outdated by swiftly changing fashions. The authors often refer to an earlier time and its requirements for personal behavior and may, therefore, leave out current considerations that cause social discomfort. Sometimes, descriptions with specific detail such as widths and lengths of trousers and skirts, types of collars and cuffs, and preferred or prohibited garment colors, take on the quaint quality of being old-fashioned by the time of publication.

However, we can find these books useful because they reflect ideal patterns for behavior in a particular time for a particular group of people. Such writing serves as a rich source of social data about dress at that time. Even though the author's view may be biased or describe an ideal act that rarely occurs, the ideals demonstrate attempts to exert influence on various kinds of behavior. In addition, presenting a code of ideal behavior that represents majority inclination rather than social consensus is not likely to be acceptable to everyone within a society. More likely, someone will disagree and question the unattainable ideals. The ancient cliché that "you can't judge a book by its cover" expresses protest against prescribed rules of dress.

Books, magazines, or newspaper columns with advice about how to dress are helpful to interested readers because many people feel comfortable when understanding the rules expected for behavior. Understanding the rules or expectations about dress contributes to an orderliness in life; knowing what to wear for particular situations encourages rapport among those who understand these rules. Using visual and other sensory clues of dress to decide an individual's identity instead of a lengthy conversation, can shorten the time involved to establish a communication base. Knowing who the salespeople are in a store, based on their dress, speeds the business transaction, just as getting help from a police officer may happen more quickly if police officers are in uniform.

Books on clothing selection and dress offer opportunities to learn the aesthetic tools and standards of a specific culture and about the expectations for appropriate dress. Books that make suggestions for "how to buy" and "how to dress" in contrast to earlier books that told readers "how to sew," reflect a shift in North America to mass-produced clothes of many kinds and in vast quantity. Evaluation of how materials and manufacturing techniques affect appearance of a garment on the body receive emphasis along with suggestions for choosing among alternatives with money available. Both the earlier manuals on sewing and the more recent ones on being a good consumer emphasize arriving at the same goal of having an appearance that satisfies current ideals. The subject of ideals in dress is addressed in Chapter 11.

Some books even offer the reader the opportunity to examine one's inner mind and exorcise the demons of the "old" etiquette books with their "shoulds and should nots." For example, Goldsmith and Collins (1995) in *Simple Isn't Easy* examine how women's closets have not kept pace with their changing roles and suggest that a fresh approach to accumulating a wardrobe will simplify one's life. A philosophy of personal dress becomes a philosophy for a satisfying life.

ANALYTICAL WRITINGS

Writings that interpret dress and human behavior rather than call for dress reform or preservation of prescribed types of dress come from a variety of disciplines. The roots for this change and the expansion of behavioral studies related to dress lie within an early interest of social scientists in the phenomenon of dress. In reading this section, note how many different types of scholarly disciplines are represented in analytical writings about modifying and supplementing the body around the world. As scholars in the various basic social sciences were probing the range of human behavior, many focused part of their attention on dress and fashion. Four conditions encouraged this interest: (1) The women's dress reform movement; (2) the emergence of anthropology as a social science; (3) a discernible increase in the pace of fashion change in dress; and (4) the rise of human sexuality as a subject of scholarly research.

Emergence of Anthropology

In response to Europe's increasing contacts with non-Western peoples through European colonization of parts of Asia, Africa, and the Americas, the science of anthropology developed in Europe and North America in the late nineteenth century. Early ethnographers documented the full range of material culture items, including dress, first in drawings and written descriptions, and later through photographs, films, and videos. Social and cultural anthropologists' interest in dress largely waned by the 1930s as the discipline turned toward a more abstract concept of culture, but since the 1970s it has been rekindled along with an interest in material culture studies.

Ethnographies published before 1940 almost always included a chapter describing modes of dress. The Smithsonian Institute's *Annual Reports of the Bureau of Ethnology* (later *American Ethnology*) contain a valuable collection of research reports on American Indian societies. So, too, do early issues of *The American Anthropologist*, the journal of the American Anthropological Association, since anthropologists in the United States did fieldwork primarily on societies in North America. Early volumes of British and other European anthropological societies' journals provide rich sources of information on the nineteenth-century dress of peoples residing in their respective empires; for example, British anthropologists researched India and Africa, and the French anthropologists researched North African societies. These anthropologists, as colonial officers, recognized that effective colonial rule included understanding the dress of the various classes of people along with other aspects of their customs and behavior.

Many thorough ethnographies describe items of dress in detail sufficient to teach methods of historic reconstruction of ethnic dress. Some early reports on American Indians such as that by Fletcher and La Flesche (1911), exhibit an unusual early sophistication in the analysis of the communicative value of dress, as shown in Figure 4.3. The philosophical basis of this early work documented modes of cultural life that were expected to die out; the work was often referred to as "salvage" ethnography. Such examples must be read critically, for contemporary dress was sometimes overlooked or purposely ignored in order to document and photograph forms of cultural dress described as "unchanging" and "traditional." For example, Boas (1930) criticized the force that was apparently used to badger an informant into revealing information about historic face painting practices, thus questioning the validity of information.[2]

Occasionally ethnographers carried their research beyond the task of documentation and preservation of a record of non-Western dress, to analyze the dress in more depth. Fletcher and La Flesche's (1911) work probed the significance of different ways that Omaha men wrapped their blankets (formerly buffalo skins) on their bodies. The ethnographers recognized the existence of a

Figure 4.3
U.S. anthropologists Fletcher and La Flesche (1911) analyzed the meaning communicated by different ways of wrapping enclosures (blankets, or the historically earlier buffalo robes) within Omaha dress practice: (a) bystander observing a transaction, (b) young man waiting for his lover, (c) man addressing the tribe or council, and (d) man admonishing the tribe or council.

complex code of meaning associated with the manner in which wrapped dress is readjusted on the wearer's body according to the activity of the wearer. Unfortunately later scholars of dress ignored such analyses when anthropology abandoned the study of dress. For example, an important manuscript by Stevenson (1911) on Pueblo Indian dress remains relatively inaccessible in ethnological archives.

Monographs devoted exclusively to dress are rare but occasionally occur as in the case of Mead (1969), a New Zealand Maori looking at cultural traits within his own society. Others are Bogatyrev (1971) on Moravian Slovakia and Verity Wilson (1986) on Chinese dress. Bibliographies compiling interdisciplinary sources on African dress have also been collected (Eicher, 1969; Pokornowski, Eicher, Harris, & Thieme, 1985).

Increased Pace of Fashion

Interest in documenting or analyzing dress was aroused in response to rapid fashion changes, especially in women's clothing, as the rate of fashion change accelerated to a very discernible level. These changes occurred as nineteenth-century industrialization developed means for producing new fashions quickly and inexpensively. Invention of the sewing machine occurred at mid-century and was instrumental in both the elaboration of women's dress and the pace of changes in fashions of dress. Unraveling the mysteries of the evolving fashion system of dress that reached out both nationally and internationally became a challenge. Social psychologists, inspired by works of Tarde (1903) and Le Bon (1895), were especially interested in what generates collective changes in behavior, including influences on fashions in dress; however, economists also included fashions of dress in their realm of concern.

Study of Human Sexuality

The relation of clothing to sexual experience and interplay represented another condition that was given expression as scientific treatises on sex began to be published. Krafft-Ebing's *Psychopathia Sexualis* (1886/1965); Freud's *The Interpretation of Dreams* (1915); and Havelock Ellis's *Studies in the Psychology of Sex* (c. 1901), which was published after great controversy, opened a new era of open scientific discussion of sexuality. All of these works referred to aspects of clothing or appearance. Krafft-Ebing called attention to transvestism, the practice of gender cross-dressing, and fetishism, a sexual preoccupation related to the symbolism of specific clothing items. Freud presented ideas about clothing and analysis of the total complex of conscious and unconscious behavior involved through dreams. In *The Interpretation of Dreams* (1915) and later work he referred to the symbolism of dress. In a work heavily documented with cross-cultural and intracultural references, Ellis treated a number of topics related to dress, or undress, in a manner formerly taboo. He analyzed modesty, nudity practices, clothing fetishes, and bodily enhancements such as perfumes and bathing in their relation to human sexual behavior. Thomas's *Sex and Society* (1907, p. 201–220) also treated the subject of sexual behavior and clothes.

Although many of the writings of the social scientists are in the form of short journal articles, cumbersome to summarize on a broad scale, a fairly clear picture of social science developments in the study of dress arises when one consults published books and monographs. We turn now to a summary of the social science writing that analyzes dress in regard to the interests that stimulated development of the topic.

Ross's *Social Psychology* (1908) showed great concern with the contagion of collective behavior that results in group action. Thus, the crowd, the mob, and fashion were subjects for his attention. German sociologist Simmel (1904) also concerned himself with fashion. Both he and Ross utilized theoretical concepts that had much in common with earlier theories of collective behavior presented by Tarde and Le Bon.

Veblen, an economist and social observer, maintained in *The Theory of the Leisure Class* (1899) that dress symbolized the position of the leisured class and that women's dress served as a symbol of the status of their fathers and husbands. Wilfred Webb's *Heritage of Dress* (1912) was both within and outside the mainstream of social science of his day. He presented detailed descriptions of historical costume, but he also applied findings of psychologists to understand the effect of clothing on the individual and contributed an analysis of cultural survivals in dress, from an almost Darwinian "survival of the fittest" point of view.

Out of this incubation period early in the twentieth century, Crawley (1912), an anthropologist, published the first really comprehensive statement on dress which utilized cross-cultural examples and included analysis of such factors as gender, occupation, and religious relationships. During the rest of this decade and the next, few significant publications on dress appeared with the exception of Dearborn (1918), who wrote a monograph on the psychology of clothing. He looked at clothing in relation to the total behaving person and included detailed analysis of the effects of clothing on physiological processes as well as upon social behavior and individual attitudes and behavior. Not until the 1940s were further reports published, and these focused on the relation of clothing to physiology. In *Physiology of Heat Regulation and the Science of Clothing*, Newburgh (1949) presented many findings from studies by U.S. governmental agencies that had considered problems in design of protective clothing for survival in Arctic regions, the tropics, high altitudes, and space.

A later publication, *Clothing: Comfort and Function* by Fourt and Hollies (1970), emphasized the biophysics of clothing. More comprehensive than other publications on clothing and body physiology was Renbourn's *Materials and Clothing in Health and Disease* (1972). He touched on functions of materials and clothing, the psychology of dress, and clothing and physiology. Watkins (1984) combined her knowledge of the body and dress and produced a book that emphasized research on and design of functional clothing. Publications by anthropologists concerned with both human physical adaptation and cultural adaptation to environment, such as Cohen (1968), have complemented these works.

In the late 1920s and 1930s an upsurge of interest produced publications on the psychological, social, and cultural implications of dress. In general, changes in dress paralleled sharp breaks with social tradition at that time. For example, in the dress of women, a woman's leg fully exposed to the knee had been unknown in polite Western society since the time of the early Greek city-states. Social scientists set to work to interpret the implications of this and other drastic changes in dress.

In 1928, Nystrom presented his *Economics of Fashion*, and Hiler, an artist, wrote *From Nudity to Raiment* (1929), indicating his interest in probing existing literature for theories on origins of dress. About the same time, two books on the psychology of clothing were published: Hurlock (1929) and Flügel (1930), the latter with a decided psychoanalytic orientation. In the *Encyclopedia of the Social Sciences*, three anthropologists published classic statements related to dressing the body: Benedict (1931) on dress, Bunzel (1931) on ornament, and Sapir (1931) on fashion. Crawley's earlier essay reappeared in 1931 in a book titled *Dress, Drinks, and Drums*.

The decade of the thirties also stimulated the compilers of bibliographies such as Colas (1933), Monro and Cook (1937; see also Monro & Monro, 1957), and Hiler and Hiler (1939), whose introduction rivaled Crawley's work in its comprehensiveness. These bibliographies occurred more than 30 years after the only previous comprehensive index of costume, the catalogue of the Lipperheide library, which had classified more than 5,000 titles between 1896 and 1905.[3]

Publication decreased worldwide during the 1940s as a result of World War II. However, works from this period include those by Cunnington (1941), who drew on social science theories and referred to the necessity for considering psychological factors in the understanding of women's dress, and Bell (1947), who applied and expanded Veblen's concepts in analysis of dress. Elizabeth Hawes (1938, 1954) and Bernard Rudofsky (1947) published books in a light vein, but their tongue-in-cheek descriptions of the human pursuit of beauty reflected social sensitivity. Sheldon (1940, 1942) developed a theory about the varieties of human physical difference as related to temperament, a topic closely related to dress since body build deals with aspects of personal appearance.

In the 1950s, psychoanalytic concepts influenced the work of several students of dress. Laver (1964), frequent contributor to dress history, confessed to plunging into "the muddy waters of psychoanalysis." He adopted Flügel's (1930) concept of shifting erogenous zones as a partial explanation of fashion change. Bergler (1953) utilized the same theory in his *Fashion and the Unconscious*, as he formulated a systematic theoretical scheme for understanding dress. His scheme, grounded in psychoanalytic theory, explained that the compulsions of fashion, like other behavior, evolve from conflicting motives. In *The Importance of Wearing Clothes*, Lawrence Langner (1959) referred to Adler's refinements on psychoanalytic theory, notably his concepts of inferiority and superiority as explanatory of dress. These concepts were similar to an expanded explanation by Laver (1952, 1969) of a hierarchical principle whereby dress is used as a means of enhancing the owner's sense of importance. Laver proposed a motivational triad by adding a seduction principle that emphasized the use of dress to make an individual more desirable in the eyes of the opposite sex and a utility principle that emphasized body comfort for an individual as an important factor in dress. His principles are featured in Figure 4.4.

In the 1960s, an important shift in orientation in social science writing occurred with Stone (1962), who presented a symbolic interaction framework that proposed environmental rather than inborn influences on dress and differed from psychoanalytic writings in the 1950s. His perspective coincided with other approachs of that time such as Goffman's (1959). The latter offered a dramatic perspective in which each person is seen as playing a role that is facilitated when dressed for the part. These works, typically eclectic in orientation, applied research and theory from various social sciences in analyses of dress. Some were textbooks with a particular emphasis, such as Roach and Eicher (1965), who presented a collection of readings with a theoretical overview that emphasized understanding dress within a sociocultural context. Ryan (1966) summarized research by coordinating findings based on many different theoretical premises, classifying them according to their general social psychological significance. Anspach (1967), taking fashion as her focus, emphasized an economic viewpoint that regards clothing as a commodity. However, several writers viewed clothing not only as an economic but also as a social and psy-

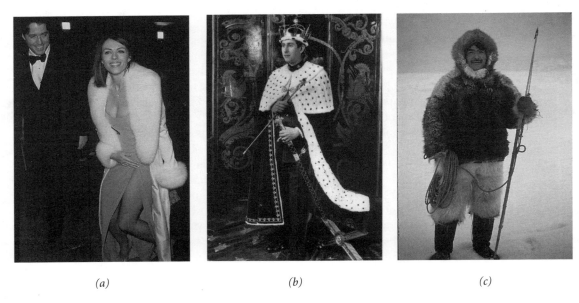

(a)   (b)   (c)

Figure 4.4
Laver's principles of dress are exemplified by three uses of the same garment form: (a) furs for luxury and seduction, United States, 1997; (b) furs as a mark of rank, Prince Charles at his investiture as Prince of Wales, 1969; and (c) furs to keep out the cold, Greenland, 20th century.

chological phenomenon. Horn (1968) and Horn and Gurel (1981) encompassed economic, social, and psychological viewpoints from the social sciences. Their work incorporates points of view from aesthetics, as well as the biological and physical sciences.

In an essay entitled *Fashion*, Blumer (1968) contributed a theory of fashion appropriate to contemporary mass society. He sees the fashion system as a complex means for facilitating orderly change within a mass society no longer able to provide identity and maintain order via social custom. Klapp (1969) directed his writing to a number of matters other than dress; however, he gave considerable attention to the problem of finding identity in mass society by proposing several means whereby a person may try to express individuality through dress. Three major concepts—awareness, symbols, and role—were used by Rosencranz (1972) for analyzing dress, whereas Polhemus and Proctor (1978) developed an argument that proposed that anti-fashion stands in opposition to the concept of fashion in understanding why people dress. The first edition of *The Visible Self* (Roach & Eicher, 1973) was published as a systematic approach to the study of dress, recognizing the many disciplines and concepts that contribute to our understanding of dress as a uniquely human activity.

European publications since 1960 have also contributed to the sociological approach to the study of dress. These include books by König (1967), Brenninkmeyer (1963), and Barthes (1983) on fashion factors. In the 1980s and 1990s, several Americans analyzed dress and human behavior, including Lurie in *The Language of Clothes* (1981), Kaiser in *The Social Psychology of Clothing* (1997), Hollander in *Seeing Through Clothes* (1978), and Cunningham and Lab in *Dress and Popular Culture* (1991) and *Dress in American Culture* (1993). Rubinstein (1995) adopted Stone's and Goffman's frameworks to develop a sociology of dress around the theme of dress codes in U.S. society.

Fashion as a word or concept began to appear in more book titles by authors from various disciplines, such as Solomon's *The Psychology of Fashion* (1985), *Women and Fashion* by Evans and Thornton (1989), *Chic Thrills: A Fashion Reader* by Ash and Wilson (1992), *On Fashion* by Benstock and Ferriss (1994), *The Face of Fashion* by Craik (1994), and Barnard's *Fashion as Communication* (1996). The ideas of identity and culture began to emerge as a focus as well in books like *Fashion, Culture, and Identity* (Davis, 1992) and *Dress and Identity* (Roach-Higgins, Eicher, & Johnson, 1995).

During the 1960s Americans increased their awareness of non-Western forms of dress by media reporting on political events in Southeast Asia and the sending of thousands of troops to fight in Vietnam and Laos. The opening of the central highlands of New Guinea for the first time in the 1950s, disclosed peoples living successfully with a basically stone age technology. Several published ethnographies resulted with pictures of men dressed in body supplements of penis sheaths, feathers, and necklaces. The discipline of anthropology rediscovered dress as a topic of serious study. A slow, but steady, stream of publications since the 1970s developed this topic, such as the Stratherns' (1971) analysis of body painting in New Guinea. Tarlo's (1996) book on the social significance of dress in India, *Clothing Matters*, indicates the tone of these recent anthropological contributions. The resurgence of interest by anthropologists provides connections with contemporary anthropological theory along with reassessment of the analysis of the types and functions of dress. Recognition of earlier work and contemporary analysis is illustrated by Hendrickson (1996) and colleagues on several examples from Africa, Perani and Wolff (1999) on art patronage as related to African textiles and dress, and Renne (1995) on the dress and cloth of the Bunu Yoruba. Other examples are Weir (1989) on dress in Palestine, Dalby (1993) on the Japanese kimono, Kawakami (1993) on Japanese immigrants in Hawaii, the reissue of Hansen's (1983) *Mongol Costumes,* and the exhaustive analysis of Boulanger (1997) on wrapping *saris* in the Indian sub-continent. Foster (1997) analyzed the references to dress in narratives collected by the formerly enslaved in the United States to present an understanding of the many different ways dress was important in the lives of African-Americans in the antebellum South. The documentation of dress as a significant cultural factor, along with new theoretical perspectives (such as the "embedding of culture" in the bodies of society's members) in volumes such as *Cloth and Human Experience* (Weiner & Schneider, 1989), provides an additional dimension to understanding human behavior as we enter the twenty-first century.

Histories of dress provide insights about reasons for dressing the body, but primarily they highlighted fashionable dress of North American and European upper-class people, especially women. Among books on Western dress published since the mid-1940s, Davenport (1948) supplies rich explanatory detail whereas Boucher (1967) supplements detail and illustrations with commentary emphasizing French fashion influence (from a somewhat antiquarian viewpoint, one that Breward [1995] calls "hemline histories"). Another trend in the late twentieth century is an increasingly global emphasis in terms of global influences on styles and fashions, placing more emphasis on the meanings and range of meanings of garments, on context and meaning, and on the uses of meanings across social and cultural groups. Dress and fashion historians are changing the underpinnings of dress history by using new historical evidence and new theories or concepts, such as modernity and postmodernism. Elizabeth Wilson (1987) and Breward (1995) are two examples of this trend in analyzing the history of fashionable European dress from the fourteenth century on. Other authors such as McCracken (1990), provide new insights with an interpretation from an industrial and economic context of global consumerism, marketing, commerce, and consumption.

Lipovetsky (1994) develops an analysis of fashion by arguing that it begins in Western society in the fourteenth century. He claims that fashion rises as a critical factor in democratic societies, for it emphasizes individuality. His book is primarily a philosophical treatise without visual representations. Polhemus (1994), however, as an anthropologist looked at the subcultures of Western fashion to present a picture of dress that moved far away from the high status viewpoint offered in earlier dress histories. Diffusion and innovation theories also contribute a different interpretation of change in fashion and dress history, in contrast to viewing such changes from an evolutionary viewpoint.

These new points of view supplement the previously mentioned books on non-Western dress in broadening our perspective on how an understanding of dress contributes to a more complete understanding of human behavior.

Clothing and textile scholars in the 1950s organized a professional association (the American College Professors of Textiles and Clothing) under the umbrella of the American Home Economics Association, which later resulted in the establishment of an independent group called the International Textile and Apparel Association (ITAA). This group publishes the *Clothing and Textile Research Journal*,[4] devoted exclusively to articles concerning textiles and dress, including the social aspects of dress. The Costume Society was organized in England in 1965, initiating an annual journal titled *Costume*. The Costume Society of America launched its organization in 1973 along with an annual publication titled *Dress*. The latter two focus on historical analyses. In 1997, a quarterly journal titled *Fashion Theory* began publication, emphasizing an interdisciplinary approach as related to the fashion process across the globe.

No doubt influenced by issues raised by the women's movement, scholars of dress in the 1980s began to examine issues of dress and gender roles; these investigators included Kidwell and Steele (1989) and Barnes and Eicher (1992). A renewed study of dress and sexuality emerged as well. Steele (1985, 1996) focused on the relationship between dress, gender, and sexuality throughout history and in contemporary Western society. Hollander further developed ideas about gender and dress in *Sex and Suits* (1994).

Other writers in a number of other fields in the late twentieth century also analyzed the relation of dress to gender role and the experience of sexuality. Feminist scholars working in the disciplines of women's studies and film criticism started to pay serious attention to dress as an outgrowth of their analysis of the social construction of gender. Naomi Wolf's (1991) discussion of "the beauty myth" exemplifies this approach. Cross-dressing has also received attention from writers interested in the definition of gender and its relationship to dress. The topic has piqued the interest of many: examples focusing on male to female "drags" include Ackroyd (1979), Kirk and Heath (1984), Woodhouse (1989), and Chermayeff, David, and Richardson (1995). Garber (1992) and Bullough and Bullough (1993) treat the topic by assessing the phenomenon of cross-dressing by both males and females. More recently, the meaning of dress in the lives of transsexuals has been treated by Griggs (1997).

From the 1980s dress historians have begun to document and analyze fashion changes in non-Western dress. For example, Garrett (1987, 1994) demonstrates that Chinese dress has a long history of fashion changes, with the "Mao suit" from 1948 through the late 1980s paralleling the social changes and development of the People's Republic of China. As we move into a new millennium and participate in an emerging global economy, dress no longer seems to be treated by academics as an insignificant or superficial phenomenon. The study of dress by scholars from many different disciplines contributes to our understanding of dress as critical to our physical well-being, as a communication of identity, and as a tool for negotiating social change.

SUMMARY

Writers throughout history have revealed to us how the form of dress has been regarded by the people of their time. Many contemporary writers describe the form of dress as right or wrong, moral or immoral, just as writers of a hundred or a thousand years ago did. A common North American phenomenon of the nineteenth and twentieth centuries has been the writing of prescriptive articles and books that have defined dress customs and prescribed appropriate dress. Many of these North American customs have been borrowed from others, particularly the English and French.

Works that have approached objective, unbiased analyses of dress and a search for understanding, rather than preservation of social custom, are mainly a product of the twentieth century. Contributors have been from many fields, including psychology, cultural anthropology, sociology, economics, women's studies, and interdisciplinary fields such as home economics and human ecology. In the second half of the twentieth century, professional organizations were formed, in part, to further the study of dress. These organizations include the Costume Society, in England, the Costume Society of America, and the International Textiles and Apparel Association. The journals published by these groups are devoted exclusively to the study of textiles and dress.

Works that have documented the types of dress of non-Western societies have come from anthropology, before 1940 and after 1970, and from dress historians who have started to document the changes in fashion of dress in non-Western societies. The relation of dress to gender role and sexuality are being explored by scholars in several fields of study.

STUDY TOOLS

Important Terms

analytical writing
moralistic essays
prescriptions (about dress)
proscriptions (about dress)
satire
reform literature

Discussion Questions

1. How has dress etiquette changed in the recent past (e.g., for weddings, work, parties, and art events)? Has society changed or have you changed?
2. Describe three reasons why written interpretations that stress understanding dress as a component of human behavior emerged in the late nineteenth century?
3. Explain how etiquette books and manuals on manners contributed to the experience of becoming a U.S. citizen in the nineteenth century.

4. Imagine you are researching a theatrical play that is set in the seventeenth century. What kinds of written records might describe what people wore in the 1600s? What other sources of information about seventeenth century dress would be helpful?

5. Imagine you are researching the dress of a specific group or nation of people. You expect variations in what anthropologists reported in 1910, 1955, and 1990. What kinds of dress information would studies from each era supply? What are their limitations? How do you account for these strengths and limitations?

6. How can Hamilton and Hamilton's study of the Karen (Reading I.5) be used as a source of information about dress. What information does it contain? What are the limitations of this reading as a source?

Activities

1. Find a cartoon that makes dress its subject and explain why it is amusing and what it conveys about the culture and society from which it comes.

2. Select and read an etiquette or "dress for success" book from any era. For whom is the book written and what is its purpose? Describe dress prescriptions. Explain how the goal of the book and its prescriptions convey social values and goals.

3. Select and read one of the analytical works described in Chapter 4. What is the author's main point about what dress means to people? Compare your findings with other students. Note any conflicting or complimentary interpretations. Can you summarize their understandings of dress into a "unifying theory?"

4. Examine a tourist or business guide to another country (e.g., *Fodor's, Let's Go, Lonely Planet*). Based on the dress etiquette and travel advice offered, create an ensemble from your existing wardrobe that would allow you to travel in that country in comfort and without offending anyone. Explain to your classmates how this ensemble is related to the values of the people of the host culture.

5. Go to the library and find two dress history books, one quite old and the other published recently. In the two books, find sections that are describing the same historical time period and place, and compare them to discover agreements and disagreements between their textual report and visual depiction of the dress of that time. Look at the sources upon which both costume histories rely in footnotes, bibliography, and actual artifacts shown. Can you explain the agreements and similarities between the two books based on the kinds of sources they used?

Notes to Chapter 4

1. See Steele (1991) for an astute analysis of this point and the introduction in Blumer (1968), which points out that fashion exists in theories of science and many other areas of thought and life in general.

2.   An editorial comment to James A. Teit's "Tattooing and Face and Body Painting of the Thompson Indians, British Columbia," in *Annual Report of the Bureau of American Ethnology 1927–1928* (vol. 45, pp. 397–439), Washington, DC: U.S. Government Printing Office.

3.   Lipperheide, Franz Joseph (1896–1905). *Katalog der Freiherrlich von Lipperheideshen Kostümbibliothek*. Berlin: F. Lipperheide.

4.   *Clothing and Textiles Research Journal*, Monument, CO: ITAA, from 1982 to present.

Readings for Part One

I.1 THE BATHS
Alev Lytle Croutier

Forty days after a baby was born, his mother and the midwife took him to the baths for the first time for a special ceremony. The midwife broke a duck's egg inside a bowl and smeared it on the baby's face. This was so done that the child would have the ability to swim as well as a duck.
—*Musahipzade Celal,* Eski Istanbul Yasayisi *(19th century)*

Women of the harem were renowned for their luminous complexions and satin skin. To wash and purify was a religious obligation. It is not surprising, therefore, that so many baths were built in the Seraglio. The sultan, the valide, and the wives all had private baths, while the other women of the harem shared a large bathhouse, which sometimes welcomed the sultan as well.

The *hamam* (Turkish bath) is an adaptation of the Byzantine bath, which itself derived from Roman *thermae*. Many of the famous baths were renovated from the Byzantine originals. While thermae were concentrated in urban areas and fashionable resorts, hamams were scattered throughout the provinces. Until recently, Roman, or Pompeiian, aqueducts were used in the baths, distributing water under the floor or through numerous foundations. A central source often heated the two adjoining hamams, with the women's bath on one side and the men's on the other.

For harem women, deprived of so many freedoms, the hamam became an all-consuming passion and a most luxurious pastime. The bathing ritual took several hours, often lasting into the evening, as Julia Pardoe describes in her *Beauties of the Bosphorus* (1830): "The heavy, dense, sulphurous vapour that filled the place and almost suffocated me—the subdued laughter and whispered conversations of . . . [the slaves'] mistresses, murmuring along in an undercurrent of sound—the sight of nearly three hundred women, only partially dressed, and that in fine linen so perfectly saturated with vapour that it revealed the whole outline of the figure—the busy slaves passing and repassing, naked from the waist upwards, and with their arms folded upon their bosoms, balancing on their heads piles of fringed or embroidered napkins—groups of lovely girls, laughing, chatting, and refreshing themselves with sweetmeats, sherbet, and lemonade—parties of playful children, apparently quite indifferent to the dense atmosphere which made me struggle for breath . . . all combined to form a picture like the illusory semblance of a phantasmagoria, almost leaving me in doubt whether that on which I looked were indeed reality, or the mere creation of a distempered brain."

When women came to call on women in other harems, they stayed for several days. Odalisques greeted and immediately escorted them to the baths to clean and refresh themselves. In her 1908 memoir, *Haremlik*, Demetra Vaka, a young Greek woman, returns to Istanbul after traveling abroad and visits her Turkish friends: "Slave women undressed us and took us to the bathing house on the shore of the sea. After the bath, we were put in loose, clean garments lent to us by the mistress."

An anonymous Italian work. *Constantinopoli e di Turchi* (1510), contains an engraving of ladies proceeding to the baths, followed by a train of slaves carrying on their heads magnificent bathing robes, towels, perfumes, and baskets full of the fruit and pastry their mistresses will consume during their long retreat at the bathhouse. For women living in harems, the bath provided a chance to go out into the world. For some, the pilgrimage afforded sufficient freedom to arrange clandestine meetings. For all, the public baths were a center for gossip and a wellspring of invented scandal. They were the women's private clubs.

At one time, the Seraglio had thirty or so baths, but today very few remain intact. Most have been torn down and converted into other rooms—the clues to their past found only in the perforated domes that signify the hamam. The two adjoining baths in the Seraglio, the sultan's and the valide sultana's, do survive—marble edifices with tall narrow columns and a skylight. Once, the floors and the walls were inlaid with the most opulent faience tiles: the water ran from brass faucets into large marble sinks, and women poured it over themselves out of bowls of silver and gold. No tubs were used because of a superstitious belief that still water contained *ifrits* (evil beings). (Indeed, the women were not permitted to recite verses from the Koran, since the baths were generally a favorite resort of ifrits and dijinns.)

Mrs. Harvey, an English woman traveling in Turkey, found the baths less than soothing: "In an instant I felt as a shrimp, if he feels at all, must feel in boiling water—I was boiled," she wrote in her *Travels* (1871). "I looked at my companion: her face was a gorgeous scarlet. In our best Turkish and in faint and imploring accents, we gasped 'Take us away!' All in vain. We had to be boiled and rubbed and boiled and rubbed we must be."

A hundred years later, the operation had not changed—at least judging from Marianne Alireza's memoir, *At the Drop of a Veil* (1971): "I sat naked on the stool while steam swirled around me, the painted cherubs watched, and I was soaped and scrubbed raw with the shredded wheat biscuit, otherwise known as a loofa, a spongelike tropical gourd. After half drowning me with her pitiless bucket rinsings. Hayat finished the deluge with cologne and powder and was as soaked as I was."

Women ladled perfumed water over one another and hennaed their hair, hands, and feet. On special occasions, like weddings, floral designs made from henna were stamped on their bodies. In his *I costumi et i modi particolari de la vita de Turchi,* Bassano da Zara details the use of henna:

> They are fond of black hair, and if any woman by nature does not possess it she acquires it by artificial means. If they are fair or grey through old age they use a red dye like that with which horses' tails are dyed. It's called Chna [henna]. The same is used on their nails, sometimes whole hand, sometimes the foot following the shape of the shoe, and again some dye the pubic region and four fingers' length above it. And for this reason they remove their hairs, considering it a sin to have any in their private parts.

"Just as in the case of henna, which is a good preventative against perspiration," N. M. Penzer reports in *The Harem* (1936), "so certain forms of eye-black [kohl, surme, kajal, tutia, etc.] give coolness to the eyes and help to prevent opthalmalia [sic], as well as being a guard against the evil eye. The meeting of the eyebrows, while considered beautiful in Mohammedan countries, is not liked among the Hindus, and in Iceland, Denmark, Germany, Greece, and Bohemia it is considered a sign of a werewolf or a vampire." The women also scrubbed their skin with pumice stone, washed their hair with egg yolks,

and used egg whites to eliminate the crow's feet around the eyes. Each woman brought to the baths an assortment of perfumes, essences, and creamy concoctions. They experimented with these and traded beauty secrets.

"It is not altogether easy to define the beauty of the Turkish women," Edmondo de Amicis declared in his 1896 travelogue *Constantinople.* "In thinking of them, I may say I always see a very white face, two black eyes, a crimson mouth, and a sweet expression. But then, they almost all of them paint, whiten their skin with almond and jasmine paste, lengthen their eyebrows with India ink, color their eyelids, powder their necks, draw circles around their eyes and put patches on their cheeks; but in all these they employ taste and discretion, unlike the belles of Fez, who use whitewash brushes to beautify themselves with."

Spices such as cloves and ginger were used not simply in cooking and making potpourries, but were rubbed on the body because the women in harems believed that certain mixtures increased powers of seduction. The English explorer Samuel Baker described how a woman would make a hole in the ground, fill it with embers of sandalwood, frankincense, and myrrh, and crouch over the hole, her clothes arranged around her as a sort of tent to capture the fumes. This ritual perfumed the body and the clothes as well as warded off the evil eye. We see an exquisite re-creation of this in the John Singer Sargent painting *Fumée d'Ambre Gris.*

Sometimes arguments arose among the women, culminating in clogs and bowls flying in the air. Sturdy bath attendants seized the culprits by the waist and threw them out into a cold courtyard to cool off. Those clogs—high-stilted wooden contraptions called *pattens*—were required footwear in the baths. Art objects, decorated with inlaid mother-of-pearl and other precious stones, pattens also preserved tender feet from the heated bath marble and reduced the danger of slipping on the wet floor. They kept the wearer well above the flowing water, protecting her skin from corrosive depilatories and other ungodly substances swirling around on the floor. They also prevented contamination by jealous djinns hiding in the secret and dark corners of the hamam.

It was considered a sin to have hair on one's private parts, and harem women, extremely observant on this point, scurried off to the hamams at the first sign of hair. They removed hair not only from their legs and underarms, but from all body crevices, even nostrils and ears. They spread themselves with a burning paste, which was later scraped off with the sharp edges of mussel shells. The paste, according to Jean Thevenot's *Travels into the*

Levant (1656), "was made of a certain mineral called *rusma*, beat into a powder, and with lime and water made into a paste, which they apply to the parts where they would have their hair fetcht off, and in less than half a quarter of an hour, all the hair falls off with the paste, by throwing hot water upon it: They know when it is time to throw water by seeing if the hair comes off with the paste; for if it be left too long sticking on the place, after it had eaten off the hair, it would corrode the flesh." Rusma contained arsenic and could tarnish the flesh unless applied meticulously. The advantage of using a depilatory rather than a razor was that the paste removed the hair at the follicle, while shaving only leveled off the surface of the epidermis, and the hair grew back faster and stronger than before.

My grandmother introduced me to *ada*, which is still a popular form of depilatory in the provinces. This simple, candylike paste of lemon and sugar is difficult to bring to the right consistency. Two parts granulated beet sugar are caramelized and added to one part lemon juice, while stirring constantly over low heat until it begins to bubble. It is removed quickly from the heat and tested by dropping a tiny ball in a glass of water. If it crystallizes, the ada is done; if it dissolves, it needs to cook longer. When ready, it is puttied in cool hands and the desired amount is spread on the hairy part of the body. Then it is vigorously pulled off, bringing the hair with it.

After hours of being steamed, scrubbed, and massaged, the bathers moved to the *tepidarium*, a resting room where the sensual pleasure of bathing culminated in sweet exhaustion and relaxation. Tepidariums had private and public rooms. After passing through a vestibule and a series of warm rooms into the center, where a fountain of tepid water splashed, women were massaged, scraped, and pumiced. In an adjoining room, they were rinsed, left to rest on mattresses, given coffee, and told the latest stories. Beautiful gilded hangings, encrusted with pearls, decorated the walls. Heavy Persian rugs and low sofas, upholstered in gold and silver embroideries and piled high with cushions, completed the decor. The women took naps, groomed each other, smoked bejew-

eled *chibuks* (very long pipes), and nibbled on slices of melon or savored delicately perfumed sherbets. "When at length they venture into the outer hall," observed Julia Pardoe in her *Beauties of the Bosphorus*, "they at once spring upon their sofas, where the attentive slaves fold them in warm cloths, and pour essence upon their hair, which they twist loosely without attempting to dislodge the wet, and then cover with handsome headkerchiefs or embroidered muslin; perfumed water is scattered over the face and hands, and the exhausted bather sinks into a luxurious slumber beneath a coverlet of satin or of cider down. The centre of the floor, meanwhile, is like a fair; sweetmeat, sherbet, and fruit merchants parade up and down, hawking their wares. Negresses pass to and fro with the dinners or *chibuks* (pipes) of their several mistresses; secrets are whispered—confidences are made; and altogether, the scene is so strange, so new, and withal so attractive, that no European can fail to be both interested and amused by a visit to a Turkish Hammam."

Bibliography

Alireza, Marianne. *At the Drop of a Veil*. Boston, 1971.

Amicis, Edmondo de. *Constantinople*, 2 vols. Philadelphia, 1896.

Bassano da Zara, Luigi. *I Costumi et i modi particolari de la vita de Turchi*. Rome, 1545.

Harvey, Mrs. *Turkish Harems and Circassian Homes*. London, 1871.

Pardoe, Julia. *Beauties of the Bosphorus*. London, 1840.

Penzer, N. M. *The Harem*. London, 1936.

Thevenot, Jean. *1655–1656 da Turkiye*. Istanbul, 1978.

Vaka, Demetra. *Haremlik*. Boston, 1909.

I.2 BODY RITUAL AMONG THE NACIREMA
Horace Miner

Most cultures exhibit a particular configuration or style. A single value or pattern of perceiving the world often leaves its stamp on several institutions in the society. Examples are "machismo" in Spanish-influenced cultures, "face" in Japanese culture, and "pollution by females" in some highland New Guinea cultures. Here Horace Miner demonstrates that "attitudes about the body" have a pervasive influence on many institutions in Nacireman society.

The anthropologist has become so familiar with the diversity of ways in which different peoples behave in similar situations that he is not apt to be surprised by even the most exotic customs. In fact, if all of the logically possible combinations of behavior have not been found somewhere in the world, he is apt to suspect that they must be present in some yet undescribed tribe. This point has, in fact, been expressed with respect to clan organization by Murdock. In this light, the magical beliefs and practices of the Nacirema present such unusual aspects that it seems desirable to describe them as an example of the extremes to which human behavior can go.

Professor Linton first brought the ritual of the Nacirema to the attention of anthropologists twenty years ago, but the culture of this people is still very poorly understood. They are a North American group living in the territory between the Canadian Cree, the Yaqui and Tarahumare of Mexico, and the Carib and Arawak of the Antilles. Little is known of their origin, although tradition states that they came from the east. . . .

Nacirema culture is characterized by a highly developed market economy which has evolved in a rich natural habitat. While much of the people's time is devoted to economic pursuits, a large part of the fruits of these labors and a considerable portion of the day are spent in ritual activity. The focus of this activity is the human body, the appearance and health of which loom as a dominant concern in the ethos of the people. While such a concern is certainly not unusual, its ceremonial aspects and associated philosophy are unique.

The fundamental belief underlying the whole system appears to be that the human body is ugly and that its natural tendency is to debility and disease. Incarcerated in such a body, man's only hope is to avert these characteristics through the use of the powerful influences of ritual and ceremony. Every household has one or more shrines devoted to this purpose. The more powerful individuals in the society have several shrines in their houses and, in fact, the opulence of a house is often referred to in terms of the number of such ritual centers it possesses. Most houses are of wattle and daub construction, but the shrine rooms of the more wealthy are walled with stone. Poorer families imitate the rich by applying pottery plaques to their shrine walls.

While each family has at least one such shrine, the rituals associated with it are not family ceremonies but are private and secret. The rites are normally only discussed with children, and then only during the period when they are being initiated into these mysteries. I was able, however, to establish sufficient rapport with the natives to examine these shrines and to have the rituals described to me.

The focal point of the shrine is a box or chest which is built into the wall. In this chest are kept the many charms and magical potions without which no native believes he could live. These preparations are secured from a variety of specialized practitioners. The most powerful of these are the medicine men, whose assistance must be rewarded with substantial gifts. However, the medicine men do not provide the curative potions for their clients, but decide what the ingredients should be and then write them down in an ancient and secret language. This writing is understood only by the medicine men and by the herbalists who, for another gift, provide the required charm.

The charm is not disposed of after it has served its purpose, but is placed in the charmbox of the household shrine. As these magical materials are specific for certain ills, and the real or imagined maladies of the people are many, the charm-box is usually full to overflowing. The magical packets are so numerous that people forget what their purposes were and fear to use them again. While the natives are very vague on this point, we can only assume that the idea in retaining all the old magical materials is that their presence in the charm-box, before which the body rituals are conducted, will in some way protect the worshipper.

Beneath the charm-box is a small font. Each day every member of the family, in succession, enters the shrine room, bows his head before the charm-box, mingles different sorts of holy water in the font, and proceeds with a brief rite of ablution. The holy waters are secured from the Water Temple of the community, where the priests conduct elaborate ceremonies to make the liquid ritually pure.

In the hierarchy of magical practitioners, and below the medicine men in prestige, are specialists whose designation is best translated "holy-mouth-men." The Nacirema have an almost pathological horror of and fascination with the mouth, the condition of which is believed to have a supernatural influence on all social relationships. Were it not for the rituals of the mouth, they believe that their teeth would fall out, their gums bleed, their jaws shrink, their friends desert them, and their lovers reject them. They also believe that a strong relationship exists between oral and moral characteristics. For example, there is a ritual ablution of the mouth for children which is supposed to improve their moral fiber.

The daily body ritual performed by everyone includes a mouth-rite. Despite the fact that these people are so punctilious about care of the mouth, this rite involves a practice which strikes the uninitiated stranger as revolting. It was reported to me that the ritual consists of inserting a small bundle of hog hairs into the mouth, along with certain magical powders, and then moving the bundle in a highly formalized series of gestures.

In addition to the private mouth-rite, the people seek out a holy-mouth-man once or twice a year. These practitioners have an impressive set of paraphernalia, consisting of a variety of augers, awls, probes, and prods. The use of these objects in the exorcism of the evils of the mouth involves almost unbelievable ritual torture of the client. The holy-mouth-man opens the clients mouth and, using the above mentioned tools, enlarges any holes which decay may have created in the teeth. Magical materials are put into these holes. If there are no naturally occurring holes in the teeth, large sections of one or more teeth are gouged out so that the supernatural substance can be applied. In the client's view, the purpose of these ministrations is to arrest decay and to draw friends. The extremely sacred and traditional character of the rite is

evident in the fact that the natives return to the holy-mouth-men year after year, despite the fact that their teeth continue to decay.

It is to be hoped that, when a thorough study of the Nacirema is made, there will be careful inquiry into the personality structure of these people. One has but to watch the gleam in the eye of a holy-mouth-man, as he jabs an awl into an exposed nerve, to suspect that a certain amount of sadism is involved. If this can be established, a very interesting pattern emerges, for most of the population shows definite masochistic tendencies. It was to these that Professor Linton referred in discussing a distinctive part of the daily body ritual which is performed only by men. This part of the rite involves scraping and lacerating the surface of the face with a sharp instrument. Special women's rites are performed only four times during each lunar month, but what they lack in frequency is made up in barbarity. As part of this ceremony, women bake their heads in small ovens for about an hour. The theoretically interesting point is that what seems to be a preponderantly masochistic people have developed sadistic specialists.

The medicine men have an imposing temple, or *latipso*, in every community of any size. The more elaborate ceremonies required to treat very sick patients can only be performed at this temple. These ceremonies involve not only the thaumaturge but a permanent group of vestal maidens who move sedately about the temple chambers in distinctive costume and headdress.

The *latipso* ceremonies are so harsh that it is phenomenal that a fair proportion of the really sick natives who enter the temple ever recover. Small children whose indoctrination is still incomplete have been known to resist attempts to take them to the temple because "that is where you go to die." Despite this fact, sick adults are not only willing but eager to undergo the protracted ritual purification, if they can afford to do so. No matter how ill the supplicant or how grave the emergency, the guardians of many temples will not admit a client if he cannot give a rich gift to the custodian. Even after one has gained admission and survived the ceremonies, the guardians will not permit the neophyte to leave until he makes still another gift.

The supplicant entering the temple is first stripped of all his or her clothes. In everyday life the Nacirema avoids exposure of his body and its natural functions. Bathing and excretory acts are performed only in the secrecy of the household shrine, where they are ritualized as part of the body-rites. Psychological shock results from the fact that body secrecy is suddenly lost upon entry into the *latipso*. A man, whose own wife has never seen him in an excretory act, suddenly finds himself naked and assisted by a vestal maiden while he performs his natural functions into a sacred vessel. This sort of ceremonial treatment is necessitated by the fact that the excreta are used by a diviner to ascertain the course and nature of the client's sickness. Female clients, on the other hand, find their naked bodies are subjected to the scrutiny, manipulation and prodding of the medicine men.

Few supplicants in the temple are well enough to do anything but lie on their hard beds. The daily ceremonies, like the rites of the holy-mouth-men, involve discomfort and torture. With ritual precision, the vestals awaken their miserable charges each dawn and roll them about on their beds of pain while performing ablutions, in the formal movements of which the maidens are highly trained. At other times they insert magic wands in the supplicant's mouth or force him to eat substances which are supposed to be healing. From time to time the medicine men come to their clients and jab magically treated needles into their flesh. The fact that these temple ceremonies may not cure, and may even kill the neophyte, in no way decreases the people's faith in the medicine men.

There remains one other kind of practitioner, known as a "listener." This witchdoctor has the power to exorcise the devils that lodge in the heads of people who have been bewitched. The Nacirema believe that parents bewitch their own children. Mothers are particularly suspected of putting a curse on children while teaching them the secret body rituals. The counter-magic of the witchdoctor is unusual in its lack of ritual. The patient simply tells the "listener" all his troubles and fears, beginning with the earliest difficulties he can remember. The memory displayed by the Nacirema in these exorcism sessions is truly remarkable. It is not uncommon for the patient to bemoan the rejection he felt upon being weaned as a babe, and a few individuals even see their troubles going back to the traumatic effects of their own birth.

In conclusion, mention must be made of certain practices which have their base in native esthetics but which depend upon the pervasive aversion to the natural body and its functions. There are ritual fasts to make fat people thin and ceremonial feasts to make thin people fat. Still other rites are used to make women's breasts larger if they are small, and smaller if they are large. General dissatisfaction with breast shape is symbolized in the fact that the ideal form is virtually outside the range of human variation. A few women afflicted with almost inhuman hyper-mammary development are so idolized that they make a handsome living by simply going from village to village and permitting the natives to stare at them for a fee.

Reference has already been made to the fact that excretory functions are ritualized, routinized, and relegated to secrecy. Natural reproductive functions are similarly distorted. Intercourse is taboo as a topic and scheduled as an act. Efforts are made to avoid pregnancy by the use of magical materials or by limiting intercourse to certain phases of the moon. Conception is actually very infrequent. When pregnant, women dress so as to hide their condition. Parturition takes place in secret, without friends or relatives to assist, and the majority of women do not nurse their infants.

Our review of the ritual life of the Nacirema has certainly shown them to be a magic-ridden people. It is hard to understand how they have managed to exist so long under the burdens which they have imposed upon themselves. But even such exotic customs as these take on real meaning when they are viewed with the insight provided by Malinowski when he wrote:

"Looking from far and above, from our high places of safety in the developed civilization, it is easy to see all the crudity and irrelevance of magic. But without its power and guidance early man could not have mastered his practical difficulties as he has done, nor could man have advanced to the higher stages of civilization."

Source: Reproduced by permission of the American Anthropological Association from *American Anthropologist 58*, June 1956. Not for further reproduction.

I.3 EUROCENTRISM IN THE STUDY OF ETHNIC DRESS
Suzanne Baizerman
Joanne B. Eicher
Catherine Cerny

In the study of costume by European and American scholars (hereafter referred to as Euroamerican[1]), fashion and Western dress have enjoyed privileged positions.[2] American and European museum costume collections, exhibitions, and university curricula largely reflect the predilections of a society that has given precedence to the status and lifestyle of the middle and upper class Euroamerican, with much less attention paid to ethnic dress.[3] With increasing emphasis on cultural pluralism, it becomes even more critical to integrate the study of ethnic dress within a broader context.[4] . . .

The Implications of Eurocentrism on the Study of Dress

Bias in the study of dress of peoples other than those of one's own culture is difficult to escape. We are taught as children that the way we dress is the way one ought to dress. For Europeans and Americans this lesson has meant that the dress of other times and other places has been studied from an ethnocentric point of view (just as a member of another culture might be biased in the study of European and American dress). The term Eurocentric, which has a pejorative connotation, refers to a provincial conception of the world based on a vantage point that "focuses overwhelmingly on European and Western cultures while giving little attention to Asia, Africa, and Latin America."[10] To counteract this, recent curriculum reform in U.S. secondary schools and university settings has focused on increasing global awareness and on addressing cultural diversity by extending the scope of study beyond Euroamerican frontiers. . . .

European experiences with the non-European world during the Age of Exploration,[12] from the fifteenth to the nineteenth century, shaped assumptions about the distinctions between Western and non-Western modes of dress. Whether based on direct observation or written accounts, portraits of the people studied and their dress often yielded inaccurate representations. European aesthetic standards and European perceptions of clothing

were applied when representing non-European modes.[13] When Westerners and non-Westerners were depicted together, their clothing suggested Western dominance and implied justification for this dominance,[14] as in Figure I.3.1.

By the nineteenth century, Darwin's theory of evolution provided one explanation of this cultural diversity.

Figure I.3.1
"Stanley and Kalulu," frontispiece, Henry M. Stanley, *How I Found Livingstone*, 1891.

Social Darwinism applied the evolution metaphor to define developmental stages to societies and their features.[15] The more politically complex and technologically advanced societies were further up the evolutionary trajectory, and hence more European, than the more simple, traditional societies.[16] Rosaldo has suggested the bias of this orientation by describing the evolutionary process as "a long, arduous journey upward, culminating in 'us.'"[17] And, we add by logical extension, "our dress."

Early twentieth century costume books linked the dress of early Europeans to the dress of non-European peoples of the world through application of this evolutionary model. Webb, writing in 1907, provided an example:

> Man has existed in a civilized condition for a comparative short time, and there remain all kinds of records and illustrations, not to mention actual clothes themselves, which can be consulted or examined. Moreover, primitive man in almost every stage of culture are, or were till quite lately, to be found somewhere in the world, and much can be gleaned from them as to the origin and uses of costume.[18]

Such notions were vital to justifying the paternal stance taken by the Western world as expansionist policies were applied to colonial societies.[19] Dress was used to secure a society's position along the evolutionary track. Webb's sketch (Figure I.3.2) of Java man and his family, selected for the frontispiece of his book, supports this type of speculation:

> Clothes proper are of a later origin, and, as we have already mentioned would only be adopted for protective purposes after man had lost the greater part of his hairy covering.[20]

At that time, Java man was the earliest known man with human physical features. The implication of this view is that dress at the more primitive stages is somehow inferior or less worthy of serious study, except to the extent that it sheds light on more advanced civilizations.

Dress was touted as a visible manifestation of the civilized state of being, of cultural superiority where advancement was defined in terms of superior economic development and global dominance. Modifying dress practices of the colonized to parallel those of the West was seen as a way of extending civilization. Social Darwinism justified the colonial attitude of the Euroamerican to other people of the world. This tone is apparent in the Carpenter's 1908 educational reader that

Figure I.3.2
"Very Early Man in Java," Plate I, Wilfred Webb, *The Heritage of Dress*, 1907, 9.

describes the dependence of the U.S. apparel industry on raw materials from other countries. Carpenter commented in the introductory chapter:

> As we journey from place to place, we shall be able to study every stage in the building up of this great industry, finding the savages of the wilds still wearing the scanty clothing of early ages, and those a little more advanced making their garments according to the rude fashions that our ancestors followed. In different countries we shall see how the materials are produced, and, in our great factories and workshops, how they are transformed into the garments sold in our stores.[21]

This account of global interdependence was framed by the assumption:

We now consider the use of clothing a sign of civilization, and look upon it as one of the chief things that mark our superiority to the rest of the animal creation, and to such of the human race as are less clad than ourselves.[22]

Thus, the notions of Social Darwinism affected the evaluations of dress and technology of other cultures. Uncut rectangular garments became precursors to more complex, cut-and-sewn forms with Western dress indicative of social and moral advancement. Backstrap looms were seen as less evolved than mechanized treadle looms.[23] As garments became more complex in design, original purposes of adornment and protection were forgotten.[24] George Darwin, son of Charles Darwin, described the way in which certain garment features, such as the notched lapels on men's jackets, were vestiges of earlier functional garments features.[25] The implication was that as one climbed the evolutionary ladder, clothing forms and technology became more complex, more like those in Western society. . . .

Paralleling the history of dress with the development of Western civilization is both misleading and detrimental to understanding the diversity of world dress. The study of Western civilization may be useful in documenting European philosophy and history, but we cannot assume that the history of Western dress follows the same trajectory. We propose a more broadly based approach that emphasizes cultural and aesthetic pluralism. . . .

Eurocentric Assumptions Inherent in Terminology

In 1980, the need for a definition of ethnic dress was addressed by Roach and Musa in "New Perspectives on the History of Western Dress." They suggested a multidisciplinary approach to the study of Western dress, specifying Western dress as "only dress that is clearly identifiable as being within the continuous sphere of influence of Western European fashionable dress."[32] They recognized that "those things called European are the end-products of hundreds of years of intermixing of elements from many cultures"[33] and that "Western" dress has been adopted by peoples outside of Europe, yet they also acknowledged the difficulty in qualifying mixtures of Western and non-Western dress" as part of Western European fashionable dress and relegated analysis of "mutations and hybrids" to the study of indigenous society. Correspondingly, they excluded clothing practices of indigenous European folk from their definition of European dress by arguing that the myriad variations were re-

sponses to provincial customs and needs, rather than to the global phenomenon of fashion. They left open, as beyond the scope of their work, specifying and discussing what did not fall into the category of Western European fashionable dress. Therefore in this paper, we focus on the residual category that, according to anthropologist Bernard Cohn, probably encompasses the dress of nine-tenths of the world's people today, not to mention those of ancient times.[34]

Efforts to describe that which lies outside fashionable Western dress have generated a profusion of terms. In addition to *ethnic*, other terms commonly used are *non-Western, peasant, folk, primitive, tribal, exotic, regional, national, non-industrial*, and *traditional*. The meanings that underlie these terms tell as much about the perceptions and attitudes of the Euroamerican who applied them as about the dress described. As we examine each term, we uncover assumptions that show the shifting relationship between Euroamericans and others outside this domain and demonstrate the scope of a Eurocentric view of the world.

Qualifying adjectives, such as *primitive, savage*, and *exotic*, often indicate dress of people less familiar or less known. They tap our own myths and fantasies, with connotations stemming from Puritan notions about pagans and heathens.[35] Labels which use these terms promote stereotypes that allow us to dehumanize the people described and distance ourselves from them. The terms *non-Western* and *non-industrial* no doubt arose in an attempt to bring a more objective, neutral approach to the study of dress, an approach that respected the cultural authenticity of a people, but at the same time acknowledged their uniqueness in a modern European world. However, as time has seen their broadening application, these terms have likewise provided a residual designation, into which the different and the unfamiliar are discarded. The prefix *non* gives them a built-in negative. Where *Western* and *industrial* are associated with the Euroamerican, and thus with the progress of civilization, the negative prefix, as in *non-Western*, implies clothing traditions that have fallen short of the standard of modernity and technological sophistication. Today, the appropriateness of this distinction is even more questionable as the reach of the modern industrial world (e.g., radio and television) extends to many remote areas.

Close attention to the term *costume* reveals it as a highly problematic one. To some, the term *costume* contains an inherent bias that differentiates the unfamiliar from the familiar. In English usage, the term *costume* often refers to exceptional dress, dress outside the context of everyday life: Halloween costume, masquerade costume, theater costume. In these contexts costume speaks to an assumed identity in opposition to everyday roles. The term *costume* is sometimes used to mean the dress of all people and identifies historic repositories (e.g., The Metropolitan Museum of Art's Costume Institute) and textbooks on the Western tradition of dress (e.g., Payne's *History of Costume*). However, clothing and adornment from other times and other places may be referred to as costume—e.g., primitive costume, ethnic costume, folk costume—to mark distance, in a Eurocentric fashion, from *our* experience.[36]

While terminology establishes boundaries between Euroamerican society and the rest of the world, it may be more difficult to see how it also validates a hierarchical relationship between a powerful Euroamerican elite and a less powerful Other. Terms such as *primitive, tribal, folk, exotic, native, indigenous*, and *peasant* may connote the patronizing perspective of the colonizer and the implied inferiority of the colonized. Furthermore, terms such as *exotic, tribal*, or *folk* seem inappropriate when applied to the courtly dress of non-European civilizations. They deny a complexity and elegance that otherwise exemplify dress, for instance, among the nobility of the Han Dynasty or of the ancient Maya, both of which developed independent of European influence. The study of dress can actually acknowledge the cultural sophistication of other societies.

At times, the dress of those ascribed this inferior status has been described as unchanging, frozen in time, unaffected by outside influences. In 1959, Bradshaw noted that many of the examples of world dress illustrated in her book "are still worn today and in some cases they have not changed for several centuries, so proving that the dress is the one most suited to its environment. . . ."[37] The term *traditional dress* connotes a static image and often provokes a romantic image. Traditional dress is often considered "authentic," implying that the dress tradition has been handed down from a past and remains free from the influence of modern civilization. Yet many current studies now acknowledge the impact of industrialization upon dress in remote parts of the world.[38]

Rather, all societies have complex histories. As Sally Price points out:

> Recent research that applies historical and anthropological sophistication to materials in Africa, Oceania, and the Americas is building a persuasive case that the nonhistorical reputation of primitive societies is a construction of

Western cultural biases and the limitations of traditional Western modes of scholarship.[39]

To counter Eurocentrism, we must recognize that contemporary styles of dress are the consequence of a history in which internal and external forces of change have selectively shaped the form. This applies equally to Euroamerican and non-Euroamerican dress. Whether or not change occurs slowly or rapidly, is internally or externally determined, dress traditions evolve to reflect social change, as new materials, technologies, and ideologies are introduced and have an impact. For example, the clothing styles of the modern Maya of Mexico and Guatemala are viewed as traditional, yet they are hybrids of indigenous Mesoamerican dress and styles introduced by Spaniards during the sixteenth through nineteenth centuries.[40] Anthony Shay aptly describes Croatian folk dress as "layered": materials, ornamentation, and garments have been added or modified in response to cross-cultural influences (including Roman, Renaissance European, and Ottoman) since initial settlement.[41] Similarly, Amish dress, with the incorporation of historic European components, has been classified as a variation of Euroamerican dress. However, like Mayan and Croatian dress, elements of dress have been borrowed, incorporated, and thus transformed into a new expression—Amish ethnic dress. All three cases exemplify a process which Tonye Erekosima and Joanne Eicher have termed *cultural authentication*.[42]

The Eurocentric view promoted the stereotype of traditional dress as a rigidly prescribed costume form with few variations to differentiate the social roles and relationships within a community. Ethnic dress was often perceived by outsiders as uniform, only linked to identification of the wearer's ethnicity. As Shelagh Weir's 1989 study of Palestinian village costume so clearly pointed out, the problem may lie with not being trained to see subtle differences.[43] Within a community, distinctions among group members can identify other categories in addition to ethnicity, such as age, marital status, religious or political affiliation.[44]

The term *national costume*, by implying geographic specificity, gives the illusion of a less value-laden term. At the same time, however, it sustains assumptions about timelessness and ethnicity. The emergence of the term can be correlated with political and social developments of nineteenth and twentieth century Europe, a time of considerable upheaval precipitated by the Industrial Revolution. The establishment of national dress signified political and/or social autonomy of a people becoming embedded in the romanticism of the period. The term reflected attempts to preserve cultural traditions and social institutions threatened by increasing modernization. Sentiment and nostalgia surrounding national dress reinforced efforts to perpetuate national identity.[45]

This connection to nation-state boundaries has made the concept of *national costume* valuable in a specific context but of limited utility as an overarching term to describe the particular variants of world dress. Today, political boundaries often blur the distinctiveness of national dress. As in the case of Yoruba dress in West Africa, geographic and cultural boundaries of a society may extend beyond the political boundaries of any one nation. The dress of certain peoples in the south of Mexico are culturally related to others in Guatemala, descendants of the ancient Maya, but political boundaries have largely separated the study of the dress of the region into "Mexican Dress" and "Guatemalan Dress." One exhibition, "Beyond Boundaries: Highland Maya Dress at the Museum of International Folk Art," successfully transcended national boundaries and examined dress across national boundaries within a culturally defined region.[46]

At first glance, the term *regional dress* has an appeal; it is neutral to Eurocentric biases, applicable to various contexts, and can trascend national boundaries. Under closer examination, the term is ambiguous, for *all* dress has regional specificity. Factors such as climate, terrain, and dress practices customize even Western dress to specific locales, communities, and subcommunities, in subtle ways. *Regional dress* as a term lacks an indication that dress is not just geographically, but also culturally defined. For example, although the form of Amish dress may vary regionally, a common ideology shared among the communities governs its overall use.[47]

We proposed earlier that the term *regional dress* was more neutral than *ethnic dress*,[48] but we now conclude that *ethnic dress* emerges as the most workable term. It is easily associated with the term *ethnic group*: "Any group of people who set themselves apart and are set apart from other groups with whom they interact or coexist in terms of some distinctive criterion or criteria which may be linguistic, racial or cultural."[49] Most often an ethnic group will have a name or ethnonym for itself.[50] Examples of ethnic dress may broadly range from the dress of the Moravians of the Czech Republic, the second generation Japanese (*nisei*) who wear *kimono* for the *Bon Odori*[51] celebration in California, or the Cakchiquel Maya of Guatemala.

Ethnic can encompass other terms, including *folk, traditional, regional,* and *non-Western.* It can be broadened to encompass defined communities such as the Amish who, because of their association with European dress elements, have not usually been characterized as ethnic. Likewise, it can encompass European dress elements found on other continents, such as the Kalabari in Nigeria or Sino-Japanese elements found in Euroamerican fashion.[52] Ethnic dress symbolizes collective identity, identifying the wearer both within and beyond the community. Further, in research settings, the term ethnic is usually associated with an emic perspective, an approach that seeks to reflect the point of view of those inside a particular culture.

However, use of the term *ethnic* has been problematic. Numerous, inconsistent, and vague definitions of the term have made it difficult to specify how narrowly or broadly the term can be applied. Because the term has generally been applied to immigrant and Third World peoples, some scholars consider that a politically charged "us versus them" hierarchy is embodied by the term.[53] Others raise the question: Are we all ethnic?[54] However, recent theoretical work in the area of ethnicity has emphasized the processual nature of the term,[55] transforming a static concept into a more dynamic one that embraces change over time.

Notes

1. We use Euroamerican to include North and South America, Australia and New Zealand as extensions of Europe.

2. Note that throughout this paper preference is given to the word "dress." We acknowledge that dress may be a troublesome term due to its association with women's garments. However, the use of dress as a gender-free reference to clothing is consistent with English usage as it appears in standard dictionaries, for example, the *Oxford English Dictionary (2nd ed.)*.

3. Similarly, we acknowledge that the study of popular dress within the Euroamerican context has been largely overlooked until recently.

4. CSA [Costume Society of America] members may recall the controversy surrounding the 1989 CSA Symposium on the topic of ethnic dress. Many members questioned the relevance or this topic.

10. Joseph Berger, "Ibn Batuta and Sitar Challenging Columbus and Piano in Schools," *New York Times,* 12 April 1989.

12. Scholars, such as George W. Stocking, *Victorian Anthropology* (New York: The Free Press, 1987) have explored the roots of historical understanding to reveal the nature and extent of assumptions that underlay European exploration and colonization.

13. See JoAnne Olian, "Sixteenth-Century Costume Books," *Dress* 3 (1977), and Eileen Ribeiro, "Introduction," in *The Historical Encyclopedia of Costume* by A. Racinet (New York: Facts on File Publication, 1988), 1–7.

14. See Margaret T. Hodgen, *Early Anthropology in the Sixteenth and Seventeenth Centuries* (Philadelphia: University of Pennsylvania Press, 1964).

15. See Cynthia R. Jasper and Mary Ellen Roach-Higgins, "History of Costume: Theory and Instruction," *Clothing and Textiles Research Journal* 5, no. 4 (Summer 1987): 1–6, for a discussion of this issue as it relates to university curriculum.

16. See Edward Burnett Tylor, *Primitive Culture: Researches into the Development of Mythology, Philosophy, Religion, Language, Art, and Custom*, 5th ed. (Boston: Estes and Lauriat, 1913). He identifies three evolutionary stages: savagery (technology consisted of stone tools and wild foods), barbarism (beginning agriculture and metallurgy), and civilization (begins with introduction of writing).

17. Renato Rosaldo, *Culture and Truth: The Remaking of Social Analysis* (Boston: Beacon Press, 1989), 31.

18. Wilfred M. Webb, *The Heritage of Dress: Being Notes on the History and Evolution of Clothes* (London: E. Grant Richards, 1907), 2.

19. Merwyn S. Garbarino, *Sociocultural Theory in Anthropology: A Short History* (New York: Holt Rinehart and Winston, 1977), 10.

20. Webb, *The Heritage of Dress*, 7.

21. Frank George Carpenter, *How the World is Clothed* (New York: American Book Co., 1908), 10.

22. Ibid., 13–14.

23. George Foster, *Culture and Conquest: America's Spanish Heritage* (New York: Viking, 1960), 107.

24. During the late nineteenth and early twentieth centuries, there was considerable scholarship questioning the functional origin(s) of dress and its relationship to contemporary circumstance. Scholars discussed the validity of theories by using non-European practices as indicative of earlier evolutionary or developmental stages. See, for example, Knight Dunlap, "The Development and Function of Clothing," *Journal of General Psychology* 1 (1928): 64–78; Edward Westermarke, *The History of Human Marriage* (New York: The Allerton Book Co., 1992); and W. I. Thomas, "The Psychology of Modesty and Clothing," *The American Journal of Sociology* 5 (1899): 246–266. That the origins of dress continues to be a concern is shown in 1980s textbooks on clothing. See Marilyn Horn and Lois M. Gurel, *The Second Skin, 3rd ed.* (Boston: Houghton Mifflin Co., 1981), 10–35.

25. George Darwin, "Development in Dress," *Macmillan's Magazine* (September 1872): 410.

32. Mary Ellen Roach and Kathleen Ehle Musa, *New Perspectives on the History of Western Dress* (New York: Nutriguides, 1980), 5.

33. Ibid.

34. Bernard Cohn, *An Anthropologist Among the Historians and Other Essays* (Oxford: Oxford University Press, 1987), 35.

35. In the late nineteenth century, the terms *primitive, barbarian,* and *savage* were used to describe those who were believed to live in early stages of social and technological development. Most were dark skinned and wore little clothing. Nudity or near nudity led to assumptions about promiscuity and immorality. The primitive, barbarian, or savage represented a contrast to Euroamericans with their own social life and was seen as ancestral to their own civilized state. The semi-clothed state of the diverse indigenous populations challenged basic assumptions about the necessity of modesty and protection in contemporary European dress. A critical discussion of these assumptions in accounting for the origins of clothing can be found in Hilaire Hiler, *From Nudity to Raiment* (London: W. and G. Foyle, 1929).

36. Using the word *costume*, especially in reference to the non-Euroamerican, also avoids dealing with the aesthetic, political, social, and economic implications of dress forms and practices within their original settings.

37. Angela Bradshaw, *World Costume* (London: Adam and Charles Black, 1959).

38. See, for example, Ronald Waterbury, "Embroidery for Tourists," *Cloth and Human Experience*, edited by Annette B. Weiner and Jane Schneider (Washington, D.C.: Smithsonian Institution Press, 1989), 243–271, and Cherri M. Pancake, "Gender Boundaries in the Production of Guatemalan Textiles," *Dress and Gender: Making and Meaning in Cultural Contexts*, ed. by Ruth Barnes and Joanne B. Eicher (Oxford: Berg Publishers, Inc., 1992), 76–91.

39. Sally Price. *Primitive Art in Civilized Places* (Chicago: University of Chicago Press, 1989), 67.

40. See Abby Sue Fisher, "Manila Galleon Trade Textiles: Cross-Cultural Influences on New World Dress," in *Textiles as Primary Sources: Proceedings of the First Symposium of the Textiles Society of America*, (Minneapolis: Textile Society of America, 1988).

41. Anthony Shay, "Traditional Costumes of Croatia: An Introductory Survey," *Ornament* 3 (1981): 14–20.

42. Tonye V. Erekosima and Joanne B. Eicher, "Kalabari Cut-Thread and Pulled-Thread Cloth: An Example of Cultural Authentication," *African Arts* 14 (February 1981): 48–51, 81.

43. Shelagh Weir, *Palestinian Dress* (London: British Museum, 1989).

44. See Petr Bogatyrev, *The Functions of Folk Costume in Moravian Slovakia* (1937; reprint, The Hague: Mouton, 1971).

45. See Hugh Trevor-Roper, "The Invention of Tradition: the Highland Tradition of Scotland," in *The Invention of Tradition*, ed. Eric Hobsbawn and Terence Ranger (Cambridge: Cambridge University Press, 1983), 15–41.

46. Nora Fisher, ed., *Beyond Boundaries: Highland Maya Dress at the Museum of International Folk Art* (Sante Fe: Museum of New Mexico Press, 1984).

47. Stephen Scott, *Why Do They Dress That Way?* (Intercourse, PA: The People's Place/Good Books, 1986).

48. See Suzanne Baizerman, Joanne B. Eicher, and Catherine Cerny, "Ethnic Dress: An Exploration of Terminology with Implications for Research and Teaching" (Paper presented at the annual meeting of the Costume Society of America, Denver, 1989).

49. Charlotte Seymour-Smith, *Macmillan Dictionary of Anthropology* (London: The Macmillan Press Ltd., 1986).

50. Colin Renfrew, *Archaeology and Language: The Puzzle of Indo-European Origins* (New York: Cambridge University Press, 1987), 216.

51. A folk dance performed in appreciation of fruitful harvest to the harvest deities. *Bon* is a particular week in August when the ancestral spirits visit the world of the living. *Odori* means dance. In *Bon Odori*, participants dressed in kimonos generally form a large circle(s) and collectively follow a choreographed dance format. The dance is commonly performed prior to, during, and after the *Bon* week.

52. See Erekosima and Eicher, "Kalabari Cut-Thread and Pulled-Thread Cloth" and Kim and DeLong, "Sino-Japanism in Western Women's Fashionable Dress."

53. See J. Sarna, "From Immigrants to Ethnics: Toward a New Theory of Ethnicization," *Ethnicity* 5 (1978): 370–78.

54. See Elizabeth Tonkin, Maryon McDonald and Malcolm Chapman, *History and Ethnicity* (New York: Routledge, 1989), 16.

55. See, for example, Malcolm Chapman, Maryon McDonald and Elizabeth Tonkin, "Introduction", *History and Ethnicity*, 1989, and Renfrew, *Archaeology and Language.*

Bibliography

Baizerman, Suzanne, Joanne B. Eicher, and Catherine Cerny. "Ethnic Dress: An Exploration of Terminology with Implications for Research and Teaching." Paper presented at the annual meeting of The Costume Society of America, Denver, 1989.

Berger, Joseph. "Ibn Batuta and Sitar Challenging Columbus and Piano in Schools." *New York Times* 12 April 1989.

Bogatyrev, Petr. *The Functions of Folk Costume in Moravian Slovakia.* 1937. Reprint. The Hague: Mouton, 1971.

Bradshaw, Angela. *World Costume.* London: Adam and Charles Black, 1959.

Carpenter, Frank George. *How the World is Clothed.* New York: American Book Company, 1908.

Chapman, Malcolm, Maryon McDonald, and Elizabeth Tonkin. "Introduction." *History and Ethnicity*, edited by Elizabeth Tonkin, Maryon McDonald, and Malcolm Chapman. New York: Routledge, 1989.

Cohn, Bernard S. *An Anthropologist Among the Historians and Other Essays.* Oxford: Oxford University Press, 1987.

Darwin, George. "Development in Dress." *Macmillan's Magazine* (September 1872): 410–416.

Erekosima, Tonye V. and Joanne B. Eicher. "Kalabari Cut-Thread and Pulled-Threat Cloth: An Example of Cultural Authentication." *African Arts* 14 (February, 1981): 48–51, 81.

Fisher, Abby Sue. "Manila Galleon Trade Textiles: Cross-Cultural Influences on New World Dress." In *Textiles as Primary Sources: Proceedings of the First Symposium of the Textile Society of America*, 131–135. Minneapolis, 1988.

Fisher, Nora, ed. *Beyond Boundaries: Highland Maya Dress at the Museum of International Folk Art.* Santa Fe: Museum of New Mexico Press, 1984.

Foster, George. *Culture and Conquest: America's Spanish Heritage.* New York: Viking, 1960.

Garbarino, Merwyn S. *Sociocultural Theory in Anthropology: A Short History.* New York: Holt Rinehart and Winston, 1977.

Hiler, Hilaire. *From Nudity to Raiment.* London: W. and G. Foyle, 1929.

Hodgen, Margaret T. *Early Anthropology in the Sixteenth and Seventeenth Centuries*. Philadelphia: University of Pennsylvania Press, 1964.

Jasper, Cynthia R. and Mary Ellen Roach-Higgins. "History of Costume: Theory and Instruction," *Clothing and Textiles Research Journal* 5, no. 4 (Summer, 1987): 1–6.

Olian, Jo Anne. "Sixteenth-Century Costume Books." *Dress* 3 (1977): 20–48.

Payne, Blanche. *History of Costume*. New York: Harper and Row, 1965.

Price, Sally. *Primitive Art in Civilized Places*. Chicago: University of Chicago Press, 1989.

Renfrew, Colin. *Archaeology and Language: The Puzzle of Indo-European Origins*. New York: Cambridge University Press, 1987.

Ribeiro, Eileen. "Introduction." In *The Historical Encyclopedia of Costume* by A. Racinet, 4–7. New York: Facts on File Publication, 1988.

Roach, Mary Ellen and Kathleen Ehle Musa (now Campbell). *New Perspectives on the History of Western Dress*. New York: Nutriguides, Inc., 1980.

Rosaldo, Renato. *Culture and Truth: The Remaking of Social Analysis*. Boston: Beacon Press, 1989.

Sarna, J. "From Immigrants to Ethnics: Toward a New Theory of Ethnicization." *Ethnicity* 5 (1978): 370–378.

Seymour-Smith, Charlotte. *Macmillan Dictionary of Anthropology*. London: The Macmillan Press Ltd., 1986.

Shay, Anthony. "Traditional Costumes of Croatia: An Introductory Survey." *Ornament* 3 (1981): 14–20, 13.

Stocking, George W., Jr. *Victorian Anthropology*. New York: The Free Press, 1987.

Tonkin, Elizabeth, Maryon McDonald, and Malcolm Chapman, eds. *History and Ethnicity*. New York: Routledge, 1989.

Trevor-Roper, Hugh. "The Invention of Tradition: the Highland Tradition of Scotland." In *The Invention of Tradition*, edited by Eric Hobsbawn and Terence Ranger, 15–41. Cambridge, Cambridge University Press, 1983.

Tylor, Edward Burnett. *Primitive Culture: Researches into the Development of Mythology, Philosophy, Religion, Language, Art, and Custom*. 5th ed. Boston: Estes and Lauriat, 1913.

Webb, Wilfred M. *The Heritage of Dress: Being Notes on the History and Evolution of Clothes*. London: E. Grant Richards, 1907.

Weiner, Annette B. and Jane Schneider. *Cloth and Human Experience*. Washington, D.C.: Smithsonian Institution Press, 1989.

Weir, Shelagh. *Palestinian Dress*. London: British Museum, 1989.

Source: Excerpted from *Dress*, vol. 20 (1993). Reprinted by permission.

I.4 MANY DISCIPLINES, MANY REWARDS: INUIT CLOTHING RESEARCH
Betty Kobayashi Issenman

Although the Inuit[1] have inhabited the North American continent, *Kalaallit Nunaat* (the ancient and modern name for Greenland), and northeastern Siberia for over 4,000 years, their apparel is little know to dwellers of non-northern lands. The garments play a key role for the Inuit: as protection, identification, and culture bearer. The Inuit passed on their technology and wisdom from generation to generation by example and through oral history and legends and have recently begun to record the ancient lore in writing and film. Both oral and written accounts are an invaluable legacy to clothing investigations.

Many physical and social sciences have contributed to the research about Inuit clothing, resulting in the enrichment of our comprehension. From the evidence at hand, we can conclude that the Inuit and their ancestors, over the millennia, created their clothing using the same basic principles of construction and containing the messages of their identity, history, artistry, and spirituality. At the same time, their empirical approach to living makes for an adaptability to allow changes in styles and materials used, according to their environment and contact with other groups.

Archaeology, Ethnology

Archaeological excavations have played a major role to help us reach these conclusions. Statuettes are one source of information as seen in a Dorset-era figurine, possibly 1,500 years old, from Devon Island, Northwest Territories (NWT), Canada. The carving depicts "a person dressed in kamiks [boots], trousers to just below the knees, double parka with the inner reaching to the hips, the outer to the waist" (Robert McGhee, written communication 1982). A distinguishing feature of some Dorset statuettes is what has been called a high, upright collar on a hoodless parka.[2]

Evidence of skin clothing manufacture from 4,000 years ago comes to us in archaeological finds of tools such as scrapers, ulus, needles and their cases, thimbles, and cut and sewn skins.

The absence of some tools, for example of bone needles, at certain archaeological sites on the Arctic coast has led social anthropologists to conclude that many ancestors of the Inuit observed the sewing restrictions whereby activities and products of land and sea were kept separate according to the prohibitions of the sea-goddess Sedna (Maxwell, 1973; 1985, p. 55). The injunctions of Sedna, the most powerful spirit who symbolized the intimate liaison between humans and sea mammals, forbade the sewing of caribou clothing at the coast.

Museology, Historians

Museologists and historians have helped disclose some of the continuities and discontinuities in Arctic clothing. The discovery at Qilakitsoq, West Kalaallit Nunaat, in 1972 by two Kalaallit (Greenlandic Inuit) hunters, of eight bodies preserved by natural mummification in a dry, cold, rock cavity ranks as one of the most valuable revelations about the forebears of the Inuit.[3] Carbon dating of the graves and artifacts point to approximately AD 1475. The sealskin jacket in the illustration, found on one of the women, is an example of the beautiful construction of skin clothing that continues to the present.

We see similar clothing 200 years later in a seventeenth-century European painting, rendered in 1654, the oldest known of Kalaallit. The painting shows four Inuit who were kidnapped that year, in a most tragic event, from the Nuuk Fiord area. The clothing appears to have the same features as that of the Qilakitsoq mummies of the fifteenth century. Evident are the woman's high, rounded, shallow hood with median stripe anchored to the main body by projections, and flaps front and back; the man's hooded coat edged with fur and the roomy, seamless, dropped shoulders; dehaired sealskin boots

with soles that come up the sides of the foot and crimped heel and toe; and the use of light and dark skins, which may symbolize the seal.

We did not know what the back of their clothing looked like until 1989, when historical research revealed that a rounded view of the prisoners' clothing had been published in 1656.[4] Tankards carved from narwhal tusk, ca. 1660, bear miniature sculptures of these Inuit with naturalistic details. The painting and the tiny carvings link the Kalaallit clothing of the fifteenth-century mummies to that of the seventeenth century. The Qilakitsoq woman's jacket manifests features found in historic Kalaallit clothing and in other parts of the Arctic.

Biochemistry

Danish biochemists who analyzed the sealskins found they had the same composition as modern Kalaallit skins. The results showed that the ringed seal has not undergone changes of the connective tissue due to environmental or genetic influences during the past 500 years (Ammitzboll et al., 1989, pp. 97–98). Moreover, the prehistoric and modern methods of dressing harp and ringed seal skins were found to be similar: scraping, washing, stretching, and drying.

Ornithology

Ornithology has disclosed a good deal about the inner parkas made of birdskins found on the Qilakitsoq mummies (Moller, 1989, pp. 33–34). Skins from five different waterfowl are placed to best advantage in these garments: cormorant, female eider, goose, red-throated loon, and mallard. Skins with short dense plumage are used at spots where warmth is most important, and more open-feathered skins are placed at wrist and neck openings to let heat out. Birdskin coats made in the second half of the twentieth century show the same careful placement of the skins.

Dentistry, Radiology

Dental anatomists and radiologists confirmed that the women of Qilakitsoq, 500 years ago, used their teeth as a third hand and as tools for skin preparation for clothing (Pedersen & Jacobsen, 1989, pp. 122–125). In the same way, many twentieth-century Inuit women prefer the better results obtained from chewing skins for boots, and from preparing sinew, the Inuit thread, by alternately rolling the split tendon on the cheek or thigh. The separated fibres are run through the teeth and tested with the tongue to find weak or broken parts.

Geology, Mineralogy

Geological and mineralogical investigations of the Qilakitsoq clothing, for example of a waterproof boot, confirmed the presence of mineral grains from places other than the site of discovery. The provenance of the grains could elucidate the travels of the group.

Conservation, Restoration

Conservators and restorers are excellent contributors to Inuit clothing research (Segal & Newton, 1990; Carlsen et al., 1995). Frozen skin clothing, found by archaeologists from the Canadian Museum of Civilization on Devon Island, NWT, is possibly 1,000 years old. Treatment to characterize, clean, and stabilize the artifacts was carried out by the Conservation Division of the Canadian Museum of Civilization and the Archaeology Section of the Canadian Conservation Institute. One of the procedures produced a child's mitten made of caribou skin. Its three-piece pattern is one found today in all the countries inhabited by the Inuit. The pattern is distinguished by the lack of seams at the base of the thumb and at the edges of the hand. A fourth piece trims the wrist with seal fur.

A crumpled piece of caribou skin came from the same site in the High Arctic. The restorative measures started in situ brought to light a hood that is most likely, from my examinations, a part of a man's parka. The treatment revealed the stitches and pattern, the appearance of which correspond to seams and designs used today. For example, the hood, made from numerous pieces of caribou skin, fur to the inside, is designed to be worn close to the head. Overcast stitches of sinew join the parts. A skin thong acts as a drawstring at the face opening. Another restored artifact, a boot, has seven vertical panels of caribou skin, fur to the outside. The sole appears to be made of dehaired sealskin, the toe is fully gathered, the heel only slightly.

Zoology, Biology

Zoology and biology have helped clothing researchers to fathom, for example, the qualities of the fur of caribou and seal, and how these skins enable northern peoples to survive. Caribou fur, like that of the polar bear, traps warmth within each hair and between the hairs, especially in the dense hairs close to the hide (McElhone, 1984, pp. 6–7; Mirsky 1988, p. 26). When a hunter wears two layers of caribou, he or she can keep warm and dry, and live comfortably even at −60°C. Inuit families continue to wear fur clothing, especially if they live on the land or go on long hunting trips in winter.

Sealskin clothing is traditionally worn in spring and summer by many Inuit groups, for sealskin weighs less than caribou skin. It is full of oil and, therefore, water repellent, and it does not shed when damp. The seal's natural insulation prevents almost all loss of heat (Mirsky, 1988, p. 26). Sealskin boots have excellent qualities: they can be made waterproof, and are lightweight and porous so that body humidity exits and the feet remain quite dry inside. They are worn in most parts of the Arctic, winter and summer.

Training and Research in the Arctic

After contact, the Inuit helped non-Inuit explorers and scientists to survive in a seemingly hostile climate. They taught the outsiders to understand their sophisticated technology and their refined cosmology. Today, Inuit and non-Inuit teachers and students continue to share their knowledge. One powerful instrument of teaching and research is Arctic College, with headquarters in Iqaluit, NWT. It has five campuses and over 30 community learning centres spread across the Canadian Arctic that train young people in the physical and social sciences.

The Government of the Northwest Territories (Canada), the majority of whose members are aboriginal people, founded the Science Institute of the Northwest Territories, now called Nunavut Research Institute. The Institute combines traditional Inuit wisdom with the knowledge of the industrial scientific community. In one project, formal training in heritage research started in 1991 with the Tungatsivvik archaeological project. As part of the Environmental Technology Program set up by Arctic College, the program cooperates with the whole community of Iqaluit, Baffin Island (Rigby & Stenton, 1992; Stenton & Rigby, 1995). Many students learn basic excavation and conservation techniques in collaboration with such organizations as Parks Canada and the Canadian Conservation Institute.

Inuit school boards and organizations, sometimes assisted by non-Inuit institutions, have established documentary and photographic archives (Aapak, 1981; Lahti, 1996). They are recording the elders' personal and group histories, legends, and wiscom about survival skills, in their own language. They are helping to train teachers, archaeologists, and museologists. Several courses seek to revitalize traditional knowledge to serve contemporary life with the elders taking a leading role (Ernerk, 1993, p. 12).

Some Puzzles

Dorset Figurines

Of course, many questions remain to be answered. For example, one puzzle concerns the Dorset figurines carved with what seems to be a high collar on a hoodless garment. Figurines excavated in widely scattered areas in the Eastern Arctic, including Kalaallit Nunaat, exhibit this style. Meterologists have established that the climate of the Dorset era was marked by cooling that continued from pre-Dorset times (Maxwell, 1985, p. 364). A hoodless parka would not give adequate protection under such conditions. Does the clothing represented on these figurines actually have a collar or has the hood been folded back to leave the wearer bare-headed? Is it possible that Dorset hunters, who are known for their elegant iconography, sought to capture a moment when, with hood thrown back, they welcome Siqiniq, the sun, or her return after the long winter night? Can these figurines—which are found, it seems, only in the Eastern Arctic—tell us something about the origin and spread of the Dorset culture?[5]

Stitches and Seams

A boot fragment made of sealskin, perhaps 1,000 years old, in the collection of the Canadian Museum of Civilization, shows traditional seams and stitches, and the seamless sole. Were these stitches and pattern the response of Siberian nomads to the climate they met in their search for new hunting grounds in less populated areas that, as it turned out, had more severe temperatures? The stitch for which Inuit seamstresses are most famous is the waterproof stitch, one version of which is called *ilujjiniq*. It is employed mainly for seams in boots and mitts. Other versions are used for gutskins—the waterproof garment made from sea mammal intestines. I would say this stitch is unequaled in the annals of needlework, and is possibly unique to the Inuit.[6]

Did the Thule culture whale-hunters of 1,000 years ago bring the boot, with its many refinements, from Alaska across the Arctic to Kalaallit Nunaat when the hunt for sea mammals became highly developed? Essentially the same stitches and seams are still in use throughout the Arctic. If we could trace the development of this stitch with its seams through time and Arctic migrations, we might find some answers to riddles about the origins of northern peoples.

The Northeast Siberian Connection

The wonderful robe of the shaman Qingailisaq, who was born in Iglulik, NWT, in the nineteenth century, presents us with another riddle. The robe was made by the shaman's wife, Ataguarjugusiq, after he had undergone a spiritual experience.[7]

The pattern is an important exception to the style worn by Canadian Inuit shamans, whose costume is that of the other members of the community except for his or her special belt and knife. The style and motifs of Qingailisaq's costume has parallels in the clothing of Siberian Koryak. It is dess-like and hoodless. The ten scallops on the lower edge of the coat have a fur mosaic border similar to the motifs on funerary hoods of the Koryak. The circular designs with blade-like projections on Qingailisaq's robe, three in front and three in back, evoke Koryak and Chukchi roundels.[8] The decorative strips that dangle from the circles have tassels of red stroud such as found in the ceremonial and shamanic clothing of the Chukchi Motifs.

The question naturally arises: How did it come to pass that an Iglulik shaman's robe echoed the ceremonial garments of the Koryak and the Chukchi? We know that some designs and motifs used on fur and skin clothing and clothing tools have ancient roots that come from the ancestors of the Inuit (Figure I.4.1).[9] Genetic, linguistic, and cultural patterns link the Inuit peoples of Northeast Asia, the North American Arctic, and Kalaallit Nunaat.[10] Some symbols found on historical clothing are used from the first century through the Thule culture—the Y, parallel lines, broken (stretched) stitch, spurred lines, dots,

Figure I.4.1

Design elements shared by Inuit and Northeast Siberians. Drawing by Margaret Issenman after Ivanov (1963), Prytkova (1976), and Levin and Potapov (1961).

circle and dot, tooth, and arrow shapes. Not yet clear is whether the spread of motifs and styles, as exemplified in Qingailisaq's costume, resulted from the collective memory as well as direct contact via trade routes and migrations, or some other reason.

Evolution of Alaskan Clothing

The evolution of Alaskan Inupiaq and Yup'ik clothing still needs elucidation. The earliest examples of Inupiaq clothing, from a group called the Kakligmiut, were brought to light in excavations from 1981 to 1983 at Utqiagvik, near Barrow, northern Alaska. A family was discovered, frozen by what is deduced to have been a catastrophic accident.[11] Analysis by radiocarbon dating for the house and its contents established a date of ca. A.D. 1510 (Dekin, 1984, p. 149). Later considerations gave pause to affirming the sixteenth-century date as positive, and until the chronology can be fully refined, the scientists wish to give a conservative estimated date as ca. A.D. 1500 to 1826 (Hall & Fullerton, 1990, pp. 270–271).

One of the thousands of artifacts uncovered at Utqiagvik is a woman's outer coat of caribou fur. It has flaps that are closer in appearance to those of Canadian *amautiit*[12] than to later Alaskan clothing, which went through at least two stylistic changes: the parka with a broad U-shaped flap front and back, and then the dresslike shape cut full (Fitzhugh & Kaplan, 1982, pp. 132–43).

North and South, Partners

Archaeologists and ethnologists, both Inuit and non-Inuit, continue to examine the material culture of northern peoples, a legacy both ancient and living. Since the late 1970s, some non-Inuit museums carried forward the earlier endeavors of individual curators and began to work with Inuit to display and interpret their patrimony. In 1987 the Assembly of First Nations (AFN) of Canada proposed to the Canadian Museum of Civilization that they jointly evaluate museum policies regarding the material and spiritual heritage of aboriginal peoples (Erasmus, 1988). The culmination of country-wide discussions resulted in 1992 with an agreement between the AFN and the Canadian Museums Association "to develop an ethical framework and strategies by which Aboriginal Peoples and cultural institutions could work together to represent Aboriginal history and culture" (Assembly of First Nations/Canadian Museums Association, 1992, p. 1).

Today, museums and other institutions cooperate with Inuit communities as equal partners both in research and interpretation of their heritage. The exhibition "Names and Lives of Nunavik," for example, which opened in 1992 in the First Nations Gallery, McCord Museum of Canadian History, Montreal, grew out of collaboration between Avataq Cultural Institute, Ludger Muller-Wille of the Department of Geography of McGill University, the renowned Taamusi Qumaq (1914–1993), the first Inuk author of an Inuktitut dictionary, and the Department of Ethnology and Archaeology of the McCord Museum.

Many disciplines have made rich contributions to Inuit clothing research. In return, this knowledge can assist physical and social scientists in the pursuit of their goals.[13]

Acknowledgments

I wish to recognize the distinguished contributions to world civilization made by the peoples of the Arctic. The hunters and seamstresses continue to fashion clothing and tools according to ancient traditions and incorporating twentieth century technology.

For the research to prepare this paper, I wish to thank the following people who shared their knowledge and archives with me, and helped with photographs, some for over a period of 15 years: Claus Andreason of the Greenland National Museum; Lydia Black of the University of Alaska, Fairbanks; John Harrington of Indian and Northern Affairs Canada; Staff of the McCord Museum of Canadian History, Montreal, in particular Jacqueline Beaudoin-Ross and Moira McCaffrey; Robert McGhee, Robert Pammett, Stacey Girling and Margery Toner of the Canadian Museum of Civilization; Gerda Moller and Poul Mork of the National Museum of Denmark; Douglas Stenton of Arctic College; Callum Thomson of the Newfoundland Museum; Beth Turcy of the State University of New York at Binghamton.

Notes

1. The peoples who were called "Eskimo" now prefer to use the word that means "people" in their own language: *Yuit* or *Yup'ik* in the coastal areas of the Chukchi Peninsula, on St. Lawrence Island, and in Central and Southwestern Alaska; *Inupiaq* in Northern Alaska; *Inuit* in the Canadian Arctic; and *Kalaallit* in *Kalaallit Nunaat* (Greenland). In order to present a unified nomenclature, the 1977 Inuit Circumpolar Conference held in Barrow, Alaska, decreed that all present-day people formerly described as Eskimos should be called Inuit.

2. For information on Dorset culture statuettes see Issenman and Rankin (1988), Meldgaard (1960), Taylor and Swinton (1967), and Thomson (1985).

3. Moller (1989) is the main source of information about the Qilakitsoq clothing. For additional insights see Ammitzboll et al. (1989), Hansen and Gullov (1989), Kalaallit Nunaata Katersugaasivia (n.d.), and Rosing (1986 [1979]).

4. A three-dimensional view of the Kalaallit prisoners' clothing was published by Olearius (1656), after he met the three kidnapped Inuit women, Kabelau, Gunneling, and Sigoko, at Gottorp (Meldgaard, 1980, p. 4). For a full account of the research about the tankards and a discussion of the clothing, see Bencard (1989).

5. The six "high-collared" figurines I know of come from Inuaarsivik, Kalaallit Nunaat; Shuldham Island, Labrador; Diana Island, Nunavik; Devon Island and Mill Island, NWT.

6. Sources of information about the waterproof stitch and seams include Pharand (1974, p. 15, Plate 10), Hadlereena et al. (1986), Issenman (1997, pp. 90–93), Manning and Manning (1944), and Oakes and Riewe (1995, p. 33).

7. Maker's name obtained by Judy McGrath, consultant to auktuutit, Inuit Women's Organization and John MacDonald, Director, Iglulik Research Institute. Descendants of the shaman in Iglulik, NWT, made three reproductions of his robe in 1982, which went to the Canadian Museum of Civilization, Hull, Quebec; the Prince of Wales Northern Heritage Centre, Yellowknife; and l'Université Laval, Ste-Foy, Québec. Documentation on the costume is found in Boas (1907), Driscoll (1983), Issenman (1985), Issenman and Rankin (1988), Rasmussen (1929), and Saladin d'Anglure (1983).

8. The American Museum of Natural History, New York City, has several examples of disk-like ornaments from the Koryak and Chukchi. These come from clothing at least one set of which is that of a shaman.

9. Sources for the study of motifs are Bronshtein (1986), Ivanov (1963), Levin and Potapov (1961), Mundkur (1984), Prytkova (1976), Rainey (1941), and Schuster (1951, 1964, 1967).

10. References for a study of parallels between native cultures of Northeast Asia and North America are found in Chaussonnet (1988), Fitzhugh and Crowell (1988), Gurvich (1979, 1988), Hatt (1934, 1969 [1914]), Ivanov (1963), Leroi-Gourhan (1946), Levin and Potapov (1961), Mundkur (1984), Schuster (1951), and Zhornitskaya (1983).

11. Turcy (1986) is the main source of information about the Utqiagvik clothing. For reports of the whole project see Lobdell and Dekin (1984), and Hall and Fullerton (1990). Kakligmiut territory consisted of a small section of the North Alaska coastal plain from Point Belcher to Point Christie, and extended approximately 50 km inland.

12. The *amauti* (pl. *amautiit*), the woman's upper garment, is distinguished from the man's parka by the *amaut* or baby pouch. The amaut, where a child spends the first 2 to 3 years, is built into the amauti at the top back, below the hood.

13. For more extensive material on any topic in the chapter see Issenman (1997b).

References

Aapak, Kailapi. (1981). About Education. *Inuktitut, 48*, 7–15.

Ammitsboll, T., Moller, R., Moller, G., Kobayashi, T., Hino, H., Asboe-Hansen, G., and Hansen, J. P. H. (1989). Collagen and glycosaminoglycans in mummified skin. In J. P. Hart Hansen & H. C. Gullov (Eds.), *The mummies from Qilakitsoq—Eskimos in the 15th century* (pp. 93–99). Man and Society Series No. 12. Copenhagen: Meddelelser om Gronland.

Assembly of First Nations/Canadian Museums Association. (1992). *Turning the page: Forging new partnerships between museums and first peoples.* Ottawa: Task Force Report on Museums and First Peoples.

Bencard, Megens (1989). Two 17th-century Eskimos at Rosenborg Palace. In J. P. H. Hansen & H. C. Gullov (Eds.), *The mummies from Qilakitsoq—Eskimos in the 15th century* (pp. 47–55). Copenhagen: Meddelelser om Gronland.

Boas, Franz (1907). Second report on the Eskimo of Baffin Land and Hudson Bay. *Bulletin of the American Museum of Natural History, 15* (2), 371–570.

Bronshtein, M. M. (1986). Typological variants of ancient Eskimo graphic ornamentation. (The problem of a cultural history of the Bering Sea Region during the first millenium BC [to the] first millenium AD). *Soviet Ethnography, 6*, 45–58, (Russian); 1–23 (Indian and Northern Affairs Canada translation, English.) Pagination given in the text refers to the original work in Russian.

Carlsen, Lars, Anders Feldthus, A., & Anne Lisbeth Schmidt (1995). The preservation of Inuit clothing collected during the Fifth Thule Expedition 1921–1924. *Arctic, 48* (4), 333–337.

Chaussonnet, Valérie. (1988). Needles and animals: Women's magic. In W. Fitzhugh & A. Crowell (Eds.)., *Crossroads of continents. Cultures of Siberia and Alaska* (pp. 209–226). Washington, DC: Smithsonian Institution Press.

Dekin, Albert A. Jr. (1984). Retrospect and prospect: Archaeology. *Arctic Anthropology, 21* (1), 149–151.

Driscoll, Bernadette (1983). *The Inuit parka: A preliminary study based on the collections of the National Museum of Man (Ottawa); the Manitoba Museum of Man and Nature; the American Museum of Natural History; and the National Museum of Natural History, Smithsonian Institution.* Master's thesis, Carleton University, Ottawa.

Erasmus, Georges. (1988). Preserving our heritage: A working conference for museums and first peoples. Opening address, Ottawa, November.

Ernerk, Peter. (1993). Inuit Silattuqsarvingat—The Inuit University of the North. In L.-J. Dorais & L. Muller-Wille (Eds.) *Social sciences in the north, Topics in Arctic social science, 1*, 11–14. Ste-Foy, Quebec. International Arctic Social Sciences Association and le Groupe d'études inuit et circumpolaires.

Fitzhugh, William, and Aron Crowell, A. (Eds.). (1988). *Crossroads of continents. Cultures of Siberia and Alaska.* Washington, DC: Smithsonian Institution Press.

Fitzhugh, William, and Susan Kaplan (1982). *Inua: Spirit world of the Bering Sea Eskimo.* Washington, DC: Smithsonian Institution Press.

Gurvich, Ilja S. (1979). An ethnographic study of cultural parallels among the aboriginal populations of Northern Asia and Northern North America. *Arctic Anthropology, 16* (1), 32–38.

———. (1986). Ethnic connections across Bering Strait. In W. Fitzhugh & A. Crowell (Eds.), *Crossroads of continents. Cultures of Siberia and Alaska* (pp. 17–23). Washington, DC: Smithsonian Institution Press.

Hadlereena, Melanie, Attima Hadlari, & Maureen Jensen. (1986). Making waterproof kamiks. Artisan: Seepola Nowdluk of Iqaluit, NWT. In Ed Hall (Ed.), *A way of life* (pp. 57–90). Yellowknife, Canada: Government of the Northwest Territories.

Hall, Edwin S., and Lynne Fullerton, (Eds.). (1990). Vol. 1. *The 1981 excavations at the Utqiaqvik archaeological site, Barrow, Alaska.* Vol. 2, *Additional reports of the 1982 investigations by the Utqiaqvik Archeology Project, Barrow, Alaska.* Vol. 3, *Excavation of a prehistoric catastrophe: A preserved household from the Utqiaqvik Village, Barrow, Alaska.* Barrow, AK: The North Slope Borough Commission on Inupiat History, Language and Culture.

Hansen, J. P. Hart, and H. C. Gullov. (Eds.). (1989). *The mummies from Qilakitsoq—Eskimos in the 15th century.* Man and Society Series No. 12. Copenhagen: Meddelelser om Gronland.

Hatt, Gudmund (1934). North American and Eurasian culture connections. *Proceedings Fifth Pacific Science Congress, 4*, 2755–2765.

———. (1969). Arctic skin clothing in Eurasia and America: An ethnographic study. Kirsten Taylor, transl. *Arctic Anthropology, 5* (2), 3–132. Originally published as *Arktiske Skinddragter i Eurasien og Amerika: En Etnografisk Studie* (Copenhagen: J. H. Schultz 1914).

Issenman, Betty Kobayashi. (1985). Inuit skin clothing: Construction and motifs. *Etudes/Inuit/Studies, (2)*, 101–119.

———. (1997a). Stitches in time: Prehistoric Inuit skin clothing and related tools. In C. Buijs & J. Oosten (Eds.), *Braving the cold: Change and continuity in Arctic clothing.* Leiden, Netherlands: Centre for Non-Western Studies, Leiden University.

———. (1997b). *Sinews of survival: The living legacy of Inuit clothing.* Vancouver: UBC Press in association with *Etudes/Inuit/Studies* of Université Laval.

Issenman, Betty, & Catherine Rankin, (1988). *Ivalu: Traditions du vêtement inuit. (Traditions of Inuit Clothing).* Montreal: McCord Museum of Canadian History.

Ivanov, Sergei Vasil'evich. (1963). *Ornament narodov Sibiri kak istoricheskiy istocknik* (Ornaments of the peoples of Siberia as an historical source) n.s.81. Moscow and St. Petersburg: Izdatel'stvo Akademii Nauka SSSR. Pagination refers to the original work in Russian (Indian and Northern Affairs translation).

Kalaallit nunaata katersugaasivia. (n.d.). *Qilakitsoq.* Nuuk: Gronlands Landsmuseum.

Lahti, Brian. (1996). The Nunavutians build a democracy. *Globe and Mail,* 4 May, p. A18.

Leroi-Gourhan, André (1946). *Archéologie du Pacifique-Nord: Matériaux pour l'étude des relations entre les peuples riverains d'Asie et d'Amérique [and Greenland].* Paris: Institut d'Ethnologie, Musée de l'Homme.

Levin, M. G., & Potapov, L. P. (Eds.). (1961). *Istoriko—etnograficheskii atlas Sibiri.* Moscow: Institut Etnografii an SSSR.

Maxwell, Moreau S. (1973). *Archaeology of the Lake Harbour District, Baffin Island.* Mercury Series, Archaeological Survey of Canada Paper No. 6. Ottawa: National Museum of Man.

———. (1985). *Prehistory of the eastern Arctic.* Orlando, FL: Academic Press.

Meldgaard, Jorgen. (1960). *Eskimo sculpture.* London: Methuen.

———. (1980). Ethnographic objects in the Royal Danish Kunstkammer. In B. Dam-Mikkelsen & T. Lundbaek, (Eds.), Gronland/Greenland pp. 1–16. Ethnographical Series No. 17. Copenhagen: Publications of the National Museum.

Mirsky, Stephen D. (1988). Solar polar bears. *Scientific American*, March, 24, 26.

Moller, G. (1989). Eskimo clothing from Qilakitsoq. In J. P. H. Hansen & H. C. Gullov (Eds.), *The mummies from Qilakitsoq—Eskimos in the 15th century* (pp. 23–46). Man and Society Series No. 12. Copenhagen: Meddelelser om Gronland.

Mundkur, Balaji (1984). The bicephalous "animal style" in Northern Eurasian religious art and its Western hemispheric analogues. *Current Anthropology, 25* (4), 451–482.

Oakes, Jill, & Rick Riewe, (1995). *Our boots: An Inuit women's art.* Vancouver: Douglas and McIntyre.

Olearius, Adam. (1656). Vermehrte Newe Beschribung der muscowitischen und persischen Reyse. In: *Von den Grunlandern* (pp. 163–179). Schleswig: n.p.

Pedersen, P. O., & Jan Jakobsen. (1989). Teeth and jaws of the qilakitsoq Mummies. In J. P. H. Hansen & H. C. Gullov (Eds.), *The mummies from Qilakitsoq—Eskimos in the 15th century* (pp. 112–130). Man and Society Series No. 12. Copenhagen: Meddelelser om Gronland.

Pharand, Sylvie. (1974). *Clothing of the Iglulik Inuit.* Research Report, Canadian Ethnology Service. Ottawa: National Museums of Canada.

Prytkova, N. F. (1976). Odezhda chukchei, koriakov i itel'menov (Chukchi, Koryak and Itelman clothing). In *Material'naia kul'tura narodov Sibiri i severa* (Material culture of the peoples of Siberia and the North), 5–88. St. Petersburg: Nauka. Pagination refers to original work in Russian (Indian and Northern Affairs Canada translation).

Rainey, Froelich G. (1941). The Ipiutak culture at Point Hope, Alaska. *American Anthropologist, 43* (3), 364–375.

Rasmussen, Knud. (1929). *Intellectual culture of the Iglulik Eskimos: Report of the Fifth Thule Expedition 1921–24.* Vol. 7, Pt. 1. Copenhagen: Gyldendalske.

Rigby, Bruce, & Douglas Stenton. (1992). Renewing the cultural spirit: Inuit study their past alongside southern archaeologists. *Arctic Circle, 2* (5), 34–36.

Rosing, Jons. (1986). *The sky hangs low.* Naomi Jackson Groves, trans. Kapuskasing, ON: Penumbra Press. Originally published as *Himlen er lav.* (Arhus, Denmark: Wormianum 1979).

Saladin d'Anglure, Bernard (1983). Ijiqqat: voyage au pays de l'invisible Inuit. *Etudes/Inuit/Studies,* (1), 67–83.

Schuster, Carl (1951). Joint marks: A possible index of cultural contact between America, Oceania, and the Far East. *Uitgave Koninklijk Instituut Voor de Tropen* (Royal Tropical Institute) 94 (39), 2–51.

———. (1964). Skin and fur mosaics in prehistoric and modern times. In *Festscrift fur Adolph E. Jensen* (pp. 559–610). Munich: K. Renner.

———. (1967). Survival of the Eurasiatic animal style in modern Alaskan Eskimo art. In S. Tax (Ed.). *Selected papers of the 29th International Congress of Americanists* (pp. 35–45). New York: Cooper Square.

Segal, Martha, & Charlotte Newton. (1990). The conservation of archaeological skin artifacts from the Canadian Arctic. *Journal of the International Institute for Conservation Canadian Group, 15,* 23–30.

Stenton, Douglas, and Bruce Rigby. (1995). Community-based heritage education, training and research: Preliminary report on the Tungasivvik Archaeological Project. *Arctic, 48* (1), 47–56.

Taylor, William E., Jr., & George Swinton. (1967). Prehistoric Dorset art. *The Beaver, 298,* 32–47.

Thomson, Callum. (1985). Dorset shamanism: Excavations in northern Labrador. *Expedition, 27* (1), 37–49.

Turcy, Beth Louise. (1986). *Traditional Kakligmiut skin clothing.* Master's thesis, State University of New York, Binghamton.

Zhornitskaya, Maria Y. (1983). *Narodnoye Choreograficheskoye Iskusstvo Korennogo Nasyelyeniya Severo-Vostoka Sibiri* (Choreographic art of the Native people of Northeast Siberia). Moscow: Nauka.

Source: Printed by permission of the author, Betty Kobayashi Issenman.

I.5 DRESS AS A REFLECTION AND SUSTAINER OF SOCIAL REALITY: A CROSS-CULTURAL PERSPECTIVE

Jean A. Hamilton
James W. Hamilton

Abstract

Traditional anthropological participant-observation and cultural interpretation can provide insight into the relationship of dress to human individual and social experience that more expedient methodologies may ignore. This interpretation of female dress of the Karen, a hill tribe in northwest Thailand, relies primarily on anthropological symbolic theory. It suggests that dress may serve as a symbolic metaphor of the relationship of the individual to the cultural system. As such, dress can be an extremely powerful symbolic way of expressing and reinforcing subtle values, relationships, and meaning in human culture. Dress can contribute to the maintenance of cultural continuity by interaction with ritual to cause individuals to want to act as they must act in order to preserve their own cultural system.

One of the most intimate manifestations of self-in-society is the presentation of the body through dress. Dress, defined by Roach and Musa (1980) as "the total arrangement of all the outwardly detectable modifications of a person's body and all material objects added to it" (p. 68), is a noun. As such, it implies an arrangement made up of material items using the body as a background canvas. Dress is also an act, a verb, and the act of dressing, of willfully behaving to achieve the state of being dressed, is a uniquely human behavior that no other higher primates exhibit. Further, a particular configuration of dress, employed in a particular cultural context, is a manifestation of the unique ability of humans to symbol.

. . . In this paper the concern is with dress as culturally directed symbolic behavior, assuming both the behaviors of dress and the physical artifacts of dress to be imbued with culturally prescribed symbolic meanings. The goal of this analysis, therefore, is to discern the cultural meaning embodied in both the behavior and the material artifacts of Karen female dress. With regard to this sort of research goal, Geertz (1973) asserted that cultural analysis is "not an experimental science in search of law but an interpretive one in search of meaning" (p. 5). This analysis concludes that Karen women's role and status as "married" or "unmarried" is critically important to the functioning of all social organization that comprises Karenness and that their dress is a nearly perfect mirror of this importance. Hence, for the Karen, dress is a critical means of presenting the body as a social entity with cultural meaning.

Methodology

. . . The research strategy is two-sided: that of data collection and that of data analysis. As is the case with other qualitative methodologies, these two processes often occur at the same time. The specific methodological tool for ethnographic analysis, like that presented in this paper, is participant-observation.

. . . The participant-observer seeks to live as intimately as possible in the cultural system under study in an attempt to understand social life "through the eyes of those who live it *in addition to* [italics added] the eyes of the scientific observer" (Edgerton & Langness, 1974, p. 3). This encourages the researcher to avoid, to the extent possible, imposing one's own values and interpretations inappropriately. At the same time, the participant-observer seeks to understand the cultural system as a whole. Here the assumption is that "cultural behaviors must not be isolated from the context in which they occur nor from any other significant aspects to which they are related" (Edgerton & Langness, 1974, p. 4).

. . . Once in the field, the researcher seeks to become accepted and trusted by both the formal and informal power structures and to master the language so that data collection can begin. The techniques of data collection likely include, but are not necessarily limited to, structured and unstructured interviews, life histories, solicited and unsolicited conversations, involvement and experience with the daily and seasonal round of activity, unobstructive observation of ongoing behavior and interaction, and observations on the production and use of material culture. From these activities, the researcher generates mounds of field notes, including a calendar of daily and seasonal activity, kinship and social relationships, analyses of decision making and political power, economic organization of production and distribution, analyses of belief systems and the supernatural, special events and celebrations, mechanisms for socialization, and attention to language structure and its use. Further, in addition to the field notes thus generated, the researcher generally keeps a more personal diary, recording his/her emotional responses and observations about the research experience.

The ethnographic data on which the analysis presented in this paper is based was collected by one of the authors during nearly two years of fieldwork on-site in a Karen tribal village in northwest Thailand. The original overriding goal was a study of culture change, specifically the analysis of "the adaptive processes whereby a tribal culture becomes incorporated within a state as the state expands into tribal areas" (Hamilton, 1976a, p. xii). The Karen village in which this study was conducted was located in a river valley slated for flooding by the Thai government in order to expand hydroelectric power in that part of the country. Hence, a number of Karen tribal and Thai peasant villages would undergo dramatic change, providing a laboratory for studying cultural disruption, assimilation, and mechanisms of cultural survival in the face of imposed change. The theoretical assumption was that culture is an interacting system and that economic change or adaptation is a most important aspect of the total process of adaptation.

The nearly two years of field work was broken into two periods, the first lasting 17 months and the second period, 10 years later, lasting 6 months. Prior to the onset of fieldwork, the researcher spent five months in Bangkok in intensive study of the Thai language, cultivation of governmental sanctions for the study, and the evaluation of potential community sites for the study. In the field, the researcher lived for 10 months in a Thai village two miles from the Karen village and commuted every day by bicycle. A Karen-Thai translator was hired until the Karen language was sufficiently mastered and the translator was no longer needed. At the end of the 10-month period, he had earned enough trust in the Karen village and propitiated the village spirits sufficiently that he was allowed to move into the Karen village and build a house there. Eventually he was ceremonially adopted as the son of the village head elder.

Using all the techniques referred to above, the researcher carefully documented (Hamilton, 1959–1961, 1969) patterns of behavior pertaining to daily life and special occasions and constructed an analysis of Karen culture as an interacting system (Hamilton, 1976a, 1976b). A later careful examination of original field notes, slides and photographs, and material artifacts provided the rich bank of data regarding dress on which the analysis that follows is based.

The following description of Karen dress and culture is synchronic; that is, the bulk of these data comes from the first period of field work, 1959–1960, and is descriptive, therefore, of the "ethnographic present," a slice of time in a place since flooded as a result of dam construction. Hence, the ethnographic description that follows is written in the present tense. The extent to which assimilation into the dominant Thai state may have altered today's reality of Karen dress and culture is not known; one suspects that change has been significant. The fact that assimilation may have occurred in no way negates the importance of these data and resultant analysis in illuminating our understanding of dress as a unique and important part of the human experience.

The Karen

The Thai are the politically dominant cultural group in the country of Thailand. Yet in the hills to the northeast and northwest are a variety of ethnic groups, culturally and linguistically distinct from the Thai. The Karen, a tribal group in Service's (1971) categories of socio-cultural complexity, are one of these ethnic groups. The three sub-groups of Karen total about 1.2 million people and traditionally occupy different ecological niches from high mountains to lower foothills between Thailand and Burma. Their primary subsistence activities revolve around rice agriculture, fishing, and some trade.

The Karen live in scattered villages throughout this area, and their villages are interspersed with villages of other ethnic groups and with those of Thai peasants. While the Karen tribal people and Thai peasants interact over issues of mutual concern to both, for example, bargaining over prices in economic exchange and sharing folk medicine practices, it should be emphasized that these are distinctly different peoples even though there has been much borrowing between them. Karen and Thai villages in the lowland areas may be near each other and have frequent contact, but a Karen village is normally composed exclusively of Karen people. It is considered quite exceptional for intermarriage or intervillage residence to occur in either Thai or Karen villages.

The 35-house Pwo (one of three Karen sub-groups) Karen village of Ban Hong, the site of this analysis, is located on the Ping River, which flows from the north into the Gulf of Siam 500 miles to the south. The village population, over the two-year period during which these data were collected, averaged 198 people, 115 of whom were female. The village is about 75 miles from the Burma border to the west and about 90 miles from Chiengmai, an old Northern Thai capital. There are several Thai villages in the general area, but the most important one to the Karen in Ban Hong is the Thai village of Wang Lung, two miles away. For most of the Karen in Ban Hong, Wang Lung village is the most immediate, primary contact with the outside world. It is also the market center for these Karen, where home-manufactured and collected goods such as baskets, eggs, fish, honey, rope, and frogs are sold and where raw materials and finished goods are purchased.

Karen economic organization is based on rice agriculture, supplemented by hunting, gathering, and fishing. Additionally, cultivated gardens provide vegetables, fruits, and tobacco, and small animals such as pigs and chickens are raised. Participation in the Thai cash economy results from the sale of woven textiles, baskets, ropes, fish, small animals, and some produce. In addition, Karen men often sell their labor to the Thai or to overland traders for cash.

Contributing to the economic organization of a Karen village are the social structural relations of family organization. The Karen of Ban Hong village, like all Karen, are matrilineal and matrilocal; that is, descent is traced exclusively through the female side of the family and residence patterns, except in rare instances, are also determined according to the wife's mother's residence. Thus, when a Karen couple marry, the new household is established near the household of the wife's mother. The new husband then becomes a member of the wife's family's work group with *her* father in charge.

Women's overt political influence, however, is at best informal. It is the village male elders (the adult male head of each household) who make decisions o[n] behalf of the welfare of the community. This group is presided over by a traditional headman whose position is normally patrilineally inherited. It is in this context that disputes are resolved and policy is established relevant to the functioning of the village.

While there has been some conversion to Christianity, especially among Karen in Burma, and while some Karen participate in Buddhist ceremonies, most Karen, and all the ones in the site village, are animists. They believe in one's individual spirits (of which there are 32 in the body), ancestral spirits, and village spirits. There are also spirits that reside in trees, the river, rice fields, and the like. Some are good and some are bad. There is much concern with controlling and propitiating spirits of all kinds in order to minimize negative happenings such as illness, crop failure, and wind damage.

Women's work varies by season. When there is harvesting to be done, that work comes first. Women also manage the daily chores of the household and perform some ritual obligations. During the rainy season most of the women's time is taken up with weaving. From their own weaving productivity they clothe themselves and their families and earn a bit of money from the sale of woven articles to Thai merchants. Weaving is *always* and *only* women's work. While some cotton is grown locally, most yarn, undyed, is purchased by the women in Wang Lung, the nearby Thai village. They purchase packaged dyes there as well, and the women, at home, dye the yarn in the colors appropriate for the item to be made.

Karen women also earn small amounts of money, primarily by consigning their woven goods to male Karen salesmen who in turn sell the products to Thai and Chinese merchants. In addition to weaving, women spend most of their time in subsistence activities, in home and family care, and in the raising and teaching of children. Some women are specialists in folk medicine techniques and midwifery. All are weaving specialists, learning to manipulate the backstrap loom when they are small children.

Karen Dress
The Production Process
Textile production for the Karen is the province of women. Young girls begin weaving at age six or seven. By the time of young adolescence a Karen girl has become

Figure I.5.1
A village gathering. Photograph by James Hamilton.

quite skilled at making all forms of clothing, bags, and blankets. By the time she must begin her own wedding dress, which is the most important woven item of her life, she is a consummate weaver and needleworker. The fabrics produced on the primitive loom are very colorful and vibrant compared to the relative drabness of Thai dress, which is produced on the two-harness horizontal loom used by Thai peasants.

The weaving process is done on a backstrap loom. The cotton yarn is dyed, sized, wrung, dried, smoothed, and wound into a ball in preparation for warping. Warping accomplished, the weaver sits on the ground under the house that has been built on stilts, the floor of which is about five to six feet above the earth. The far end of the simple loom frame consists of the warp beam that is placed horizontally on the outside of two vertical house poles. The other end of the loom frame is attached to a belt that runs behind the weaver's back.

Little is actually known about the origin or meaning of the textile motifs. When questioned, the women in Ban Hong were not able to attribute any particular meaning to the embroidered or woven designs or colors. It is the case, however, that for the Karen in the Ban Hong and surrounding areas, the design in a married woman's skirt identifies which group and village she is from (much as the Scottish tartans are said to indicate one's clan membership). In a study of a different Pwo Karen group much further isolated in the mountains, Hinton (1974) reported that "their function [i.e., skirt design] is purely decoration" (p. 34). Apparently, any conscious symbolic meaning in the textile motifs has been lost.

Karen Male Dress

Karen men have in recent years been much less constrained by tradition than have Karen women, although traditional Karen male dress is still worn by many men on ceremonial occasions and by some older men as daily attire. The traditional male dress consists of a calf-length tubular skirt woven in red stripes alternating with two black stripes that run horizontally around the body. The wearer steps into the tube, which is then folded in front and tied at the waist with a piece of rope. The skirt is most often worn with a short box-shaped white jacket with long set-in sleeves. It has a row of embroidered black and red diamonds down the center back. A second traditional blouse alternative, put on over the head, is a nearly solid red one, now worn mostly by young male children.

For everyday wear, however, most Karen men wear either the loosely tailored calf-length pants of Chinese and Thai peasants, folded, tucked, and tied at the waist, or they wear Western-style pants and shirt, all purchased as machine-made apparel. In this case the men are visually almost indistinguishable from Thai men. On any normal day, Karen men may be seen in the village dressed in traditional Karen male dress, Western Thai-style dress, or in some combination thereof.

Unlike most Thai men, however, Karen men are tattooed at puberty with geometric designs from just above the waist to just below the knees. For Karen men it is the puberty rite of tattooing that signifies adulthood. In addition, tattooing provides a magical, protective function, and it also signifies that the male is eligible for marriage. (See Van Gennep, 1960.) The tattooing is said to be sexually appealing to women; traditionally, no self-respecting Karen girl would consider marrying a man who was not tattooed. In fact, a male is not considered to be adult if he has not been tattooed. For a male, therefore, it is the body tattooing rather than any change in clothing or marital role which signifies the change in age status from child to adult. Finally, some older men, usually those who normally wear traditional Karen dress, still keep their hair long and pulled around to one side. It is then covered with a wrap-around white turban. A tuft of hair is pulled out the side of the turban and, like the tattooing, is considered to be very sensuous.

Karen Female Dress

Karen female dress is dramatic—aesthetically, symbolically, and socially. The point of this paper is that dress is an integrated phenomenon and that the levels of variation allowed and conformity demanded are culturally prescribed and provide social communication of the role and status of the individual (see Goffman, 1959; Keyes, 1979). This is most dramatically expressed in the textiles made for female dress.

Unmarried female dress. Unmarried females, regardless of chronological age, wear the same style one-piece shift dress. It consists of a plain-weave white cotton fabric and reaches from the shoulders to close to the ankles. As the basic garment is woven, a horizontal design is woven into the fabric at what will be the approximate waistline of the wearer. This "belt" consists of red bands with yellow and green geometric designs. After the basic dress construction is completed, small red and black diamonds, in a ratio of 4:1, are embroidered about two inches apart on the skirt portion of the dress from the bottom of the skirt up to hip level. These diamonds are about one-half inch long and three quarters of an inch in width. Finally, a thin red line of stitching or a red twine stitched in place outlines the slits left for the head and arms. Usually, a female has only one dress at a time. It is worn constantly, until the dress is either worn out or outgrown. By that time a new dress has been constructed in the appropriate next size.

Unmarried females, like the married women, pull their hair back into a low bun at the back of the neck. All women have pierced ears and wear necklaces and bracelets. The amount of jewelry, however, is a function of age status, unmarried "marriageable" females exhibiting the most volume and color in jewelry. Hence, marriageable females wear large colorful yarn pom-poms in their ears in addition to silver spools. As a young girl gets older, the number of bracelets she wears increases so that a marriageable female's arms may be nearly covered from wrist to shoulder with bracelets. Similarly, she wears more necklaces just prior to marriage than she will ever wear again.

Married women's dress. Of all the woven items produced by Karen weavers, it is the married woman's blouse that is the most spectacular. Every young girl must make her own married woman's skirt and blouse, and as the time approaches for her to be married she will begin the weaving process in order to have the woven skirt and woven and embroidered blouse completed on time.

Ths construction of the married woman's blouse is basically the same as the construction of the unmarried woman's sack dress except that it is shorter, designed to come to just below the waist, and that the yarn with which it is woven has been dyed black. Once the basic blouse construction is completed, an elaborate decorative embroidery process is begun which involves almost completely covering the black ground fabric with a geometric pattern of red and yellow. After the embroidery process is finished, white seeds are applied to portions of the blouse, serving as a kind of outline between geometric areas of the embroidered pattern.

The married woman's skirt is woven in two panels on the backstrap loom. The loom is warped in alternating red, orange, black, yellow, blue, and green yarns, with orange predominating. All the warp yarns have been dyed prior to weaving, but interestingly, the yarns that form the dominant orange stripe are dyed using the "ikat" technique, resulting in undyed, or white, areas within the orange stripe.

Karen female dress behavior. The dress described above for unmarried females is worn by any unmarried Karen female, *regardless* of chronological age. Since marriage is defined as the natural state of an adult person, it is expected that all girls will marry and change to married women's dress. If by chance a female never marries, she continues to wear the dress of an unmarried girl and will live her life being treated as a female child. The Karen, then, equate *adult female* with *adult married female.* Hence, the clothing and the amount of jewelry and decoration worn provide easily recognizable cues as to how a Karen female should be treated, and these symbols announce her status-position and relative age stage in Karen society.

At the appropriate time during the three-day wedding celebration, the Karen *girl* becomes a Karen *woman,* symbolized at that time by her change to the dress of an adult married woman. In reference to the role of ritual, Wolf (1966), discussing the importance of the marriage ceremony *per se* in society, observes that "we find everywhere symbols which underwrite the continuity of the household" (p. 97). For the Karen, a critical symbol is women's dress. The married couple is left alone for a few hours in order that the marriage can be consummated. Emerging with her new husband, the bride, who until that time has worn the traditional unmarried female dress, now wears married woman's dress, the only outward symbol of her newly acquired status and the dress she will wear for the rest of her life. During the next few years after her marriage, a Karen woman will gradually decrease the amount of jewelry and body decoration, which had peaked just prior to marriage, by giving these accessories to her daughters as they grow. Now married, the Karen woman is, by definition, an adult. The symbol of her new status is her beautiful and brightly colored married woman's blouse and skirt.

While there is little variation in motif, color, and final structure of each item of clothing, there are some subtle variations in the extrinsic decoration of clothing items and in body decoration according to one's relative age and social role or status. These subtle, as well as the gross, differences in dress are important markers in signaling one's role identification in the life of the community. Thus, the Karen female life cycle is characterized by specific sets of behaviors, and it is signaled and announced by dress; by the clothing's shape, pattern, and color; and by attachments to the body.

Discussion

Ritual, symbol, and material artifact all interact to provide a metaphor of Karen family life, social status, and cultural continuity. The interaction of the ritual (social event), the artifact (material item of dress), and the symbol (abstract idea) all merge during the ceremonial event of marriage. In the process, the Karen female is transformed by the material thing—her "dress" in the context of the ritual—from a girl to a woman. Thus, *things,* ma-

Figure I.5.2
The dress of the woman and two girls show the differences in dress for married and unmarried females. Photograph by James Hamilton.

terial artifacts, have a powerful influence on the socialization of individuals and in the continuance of a cultural system. There is, according to Csikszentmihalyi and Rochberg-Halton (1981), a personal, a social, and a cosmic-environmental interaction between people and symbol-laden things such that individuals are changed by the transaction. They explain that

> not surprisingly, the clothes one wears . . . are expressions of one's self, even when they act as disguises rather than reflections. But it is more difficult to admit that the things one uses are in fact part of one's self; not in any mystical or metaphorical sense but in cold, concrete actuality. . . . These signs are part of what organizes . . . [one's] consciousness, and because [one's]

self is inseparable from the sign process that constitutes consciousness . . . [the things are] as much a part of . . . self as anything can be (pp. 14–15).

Thus, *things*, material artifacts, in this case, dress, can have a powerful influence on the socialization of individuals and on the continuance of a cultural system. For Karen women, married women's dress is critical for the culturally appropriate psychological state of a woman, for the continuity of the matrilineal tradition of cultural transmission, and for our understanding of much of the cultural system.

Karen dress is, therefore, a remarkable example of the significance that dress can have in the symbolic life of self-in-society. It illuminates the importance of *things* in the dual-sided process of social differentiation and integration discussed by Csikszentmihalyi and Rochberg-Halton (1981). On the one hand, Karen dress serves as a badge, a kind of "collective representation" (Durkheim, 1976) which distinguishes groups and characterizes them in reference to other related and unrelated groups. As such, it embodies a powerful survival element, survival in the sense that the group can maintain its distinctness as a group through, among other things, its dress. This kind of group solidarity and distinctness through conformity and similarity in dress characterizes tribal groups around the world. *Things* may thus serve to unify an ethnic group by differentiating it from other groups, that is, by declaring a schism between groups, thus solidarity within groups. At the same time, however, internal integration is served as Karen dress encourages one's individual psychological adaptation to one's own cultural system by punctuating rituals that signal changes in behavior and status along with attendant responsibilities and expectations. Hence, *things*, like Karen female dress, which serve to differentiate women—married from unmarried—within the society, are important in the maintenance of internal social integration. Therefore, within a cultural system both solidarity and differentiation are maintained by the artifacts of a society. That the tradition in dress has been carried for a longer time by women is, in this case, likely a result of a culture that has matrilineal roots, one in which women are the important bearers of the culture, being defined by the group as critical in transmitting it to the next generation. . . .

The point in the Karen case is that the fact of marriage, family, child rearing, and ethnic distinctness are intimately wrapped up in being a proper Karen woman. This behavior is expressed, is reinforced, and is collectively represented by the Karen married woman's dress; its sensory impact is reinforced by the emotional content of the marriage ritual and its daily sensual—visual—reminder of role, obligation, status, and privilege provided by married woman's dress.

At the sensory pole the Karen married woman's dress is more obviously related to the perpetuation of Karen culture than is at first apparent: the wrap-around skirt is functionally advantageous to the developing size of the mother as the fetus grows; the loose blouse facilitates breast feeding much more readily than, for example, the one-piece shift dress of unmarried females. Finally, the first act of *married* coitus is intimately connected with the change to married dress. All of this further reinforces the sensory pole of symbol and ritual for Karen culture and its attributes and perpetuation.

It is naive to think that the Karen, or any other tribal group in a similar juxtaposition to a more powerful state system, can be indefinitely successful in maintaining the symbols of a separate identity and internal cultural integrity as the state expands to incorporate them. Viewed from the ethnographic present, a synchronic time slice that, while no longer necessarily extant, is useful for analytic and illustrative purposes, the Karen case provides a valuable example of the importance of dress as part of a cultural system that seeks to maximize human adaptation and the survival of that system.

Dress, as a pan-human expression of culture and, therefore, of being human, is often much more profound than is generally supposed: It can be an extremely powerful, symbolic, ritualized way of expressing and reinforcing subtle values, relationships, and meanings in human cultures. It may be that the social, ritual, and symbolic significance of human dress deserves rethinking in the context of cultural systems. Dress is often a powerful medium through which the "obligatory is converted to the desirable" (Turner, 1964, p. 32) as people are socialized, through the interaction of ritual, symbol, and artifact, to want to do—find it good to do—what they are required to do—must do—for continuation of their social reality.

References

Csikszentmihalyi, M., & Rochberg-Halton, E. (1981). *The meaning of things: Domestic symbols and the self.* Cambridge, England: Cambridge University Press.

Durkheim, E. (1976). *The elementary forms of the religious life* (2nd ed.). London: George Allen & Unwin. (First published in 1915.)

Edgerton, R.B., & Langness, L.L. (1974). *Methods and rules in the study of culture.* San Francisco: Chandler and Sharp.

Goffman, E. (1959). *The presentation of self in everyday life.* Garden City, NY: Doubleday Anchor.

Geertz, C. (1973). *The interpretation of cultures.* New York: Basic Books.

Hamilton, J.W. (1959–61). Original field notes.

Hamilton, J.W. (1969). Original field notes.

Hamilton, J.W. (1976a). *Pwo Karen: At the edge of mountain and plain.* St. Paul: West.

Hamilton, J.W. (1976b). Structure, function, and ideology of a Karen funeral in northern Thailand. In D.J. Banks (Ed.), *Changing identities in modern southeast Asia* (pp. 95–109). The Hague: Mouton.

Hinton, E.M. (1974). The dress of the Pwo Karen of north Thailand. *Journal of the Siam Society, 62*(1), 27–34.

Keyes, C. (Ed.). (1979). *Ethnic adaptation and identity.* Philadelphia: Institute for the Study of Human Issues.

Roach, M. E., & Musa, K. E. (1980). *New perspectives on the history of Western dress.* New York: Nutri-Guides.

Service, E. R. (1971). *Primitive social organization* (2nd ed.). New York: Random House.

Turner, V. (1964). Symbols in Ndembu ritual. In M. Gluckman (Ed.), *Closed systems and open minds: The limits of naivety in social anthropology* (pp. 20–51). Edinburgh: Oliver & Boyd.

Van Gennep, A. (1960). *The rites of passage* (M.B. Vizdom & S.T. Kimball, Trans.). Chicago: University of Chicago Press.

Wolf, E.R. (1966). *Peasants.* Englewood Cliffs, NJ: Prentice-Hall.

Source: Excerpted from the *Clothing and Textile Research Journal,* 1989, vol. 7, no. 2. Reprinted by permission of the International Textile & Apparel Association.

Part Two Physical Appearance, Environment, and Dress

Around the world we find many different types of bodies with some physical similarities and differences, along with social interpretations of apparent differences. In Chapter 5 we look at how dress relates to the physical body and illustrate some of the variations in physical characteristics among human beings. As a single species, human beings exhibit great similarity in body form. We each have 208 bones and more than 600 muscles. Generally, we walk upright on two legs and have two sets of opposable thumbs and a covering of skin "to keep the blood in and the rain out" (Morris, 1985, p. 11). At the same time, we demonstrate differences and variations in specific physical characteristics as a result of long-term adaptations, such as sex differentiation and race, and short-term variations such as nutrition, disease, growth, and aging. Chapter 6 assesses the relationship of dress to various types of natural environments, acknowledging that sometimes how human beings decide to dress for an environment differs from approaches of other human groups in a similar setting.

5

Physical Appearance and Dress

OBJECTIVES

To describe how all humans are similar in physical appearance.

To understand the origins of variation in physical appearance.

To recognize the physical body as the foundation upon which dress is built.

To explore how dress can be used to alter or enhance the form of the physical body to meet personal and cultural needs.

BODY SUPPLEMENTS AND MODIFICATIONS are necessarily designed in relation to the body. The body is always a part of the total appearance a person presents, yet we almost always see the human physical body dressed. Our perception of the body's physical form is obscured by the modifications and supplements that change it, cover it, or create illusions of its real form. What is the nature and range of variation of this human body?

To study dress, we begin by looking first at the human body, because dress and the body's physical characteristics interrelate. These characteristics include general body conformation (commonly called body build), facial features, amount of hair, hair texture and color, and skin texture and color. In other words, the body is the framework for dress. With this given set of physical characteristics, we modify or supplement, changing the color, texture, or form to suit us. Within the system for classification of dress, these aspects of the body are designated by reference to specific body parts—for example, head, torso, hand—and by reference to parameters along which individual bodies show variation or can be modified—for example, form, volume, texture, color, smell, and so on. In this chapter, we first consider the similarities among humans in physical appearance and then the differences. Finally, we discuss the relationship between dress and physical appearance.

PHYSICAL SIMILARITY

People tend to look more like their relatives due to the mechanics of genetics. Although the term "blood relative" is still widely used, we know that genes are the carriers of relationship, not blood. The characteristics of parents (and by extension, their parents, and so on, back through the generations) are passed along to offspring in units called genes. Genes, in conjunction with the environment and diet, regulate the growth and development of individuals. Each individual is the product of the equal genetic contributions of his or her biological father and mother. The particular combination of genetic information is unique to each individual, with the exception of identical twins. There is no correlation between genetic traits such as color of eyes and of hair, that is; blue eyes and blonde hair are not inherited as a unit.

We need to understand the concept of the gene pool before discussing human similarities and differences. A **gene pool** is the total complement of genes shared by potential reproductive members of a population. A population, the group within which one is most likely to find a mate as such, is marked by a degree of genetic relatedness (Jurmain, Nelson, Kilgore, & Trevathan, 1997, p. 104).

All humans are members of one species, **_Homo sapiens_**, and as such, display much similarity in physical characteristics. Physical diversity is apparent in the variations found in hair and skin colors, height and weight, and body proportions, as shown in Figure 5.1, but all humans share the same general body configuration. Recent genetic studies show that all humans are identical for three-quarters of the human genome, the total genetic endowment of a species (Lewontin, 1982, p. 120). The remaining one-quarter, made up of traits that have more than one variable such as skin color or height, are fairly evenly distributed (Park, 1999, p. 351).

Why didn't humans evolve into different **species** while moving across the earth and inhabiting a wide range of environments during a minimum of 200,000 years? Although we live in the subzero temperatures of the Arctic as well as the intense heat of sub-Saharan Africa, no _Homo sapiens_ population has ever been separated long enough from others to evolve into a different species. **Speciation** occurs when populations are totally separated by geographical or behavioral barriers and the separated populations adapt to the different envi-

Figure 5.1
As a single species human beings are incredibly similar in physical makeup, yet we focus on minor superficial differences when dressing ourselves or interpreting the appearance of others.

ronments through the process of natural selection. Changes occur as those organisms that are best adapted to the habitat live and reproduce the next generation, while those that are less well adapted fail to contribute their genes to the population's gene pool:

> However, while we have been spreading and moving about, no human population has been isolated long enough, or to [a] complete enough degree, to allow even moderately separate and independent genetic events to take place. During all this time, humans have in fact become increasingly mobile, and it seems fair to say that we exchange genes at most every opportunity. (Park, 1999, p. 350)

We will see in the next section that physically apparent characteristics (called **phenotypes**), such as skin color or body proportions, may be adaptations to a particular environmental condition. However, culture has been *Homo sapiens'* most important, and most flexible, adaptive mechanism to new environments (Park, 1999, p. 350). Our capacity for cultural adaptation allows our migration into varied climates of the world aided by body coverings, sheltering structures, heating, and other climate control systems that we have developed. Shanklin points out that culture's great advantage is its relative rapidity when she refers to the polar bear's need to develop genetically based adaptations to the Arctic cold such as long fur in contrast to humans use of clothing (Shanklin, 1994, p. 43).

Culture is possible because humans have evolved with a complex brain and nervous system coupled with a capacity for speech that enables us to develop and manipulate visual and verbal symbols, the heart of culture (Tanner, 1988, p. 136). Dress is a tool humans use to interface with the physical environment, pursue beauty, and communicate with each other. All human beings are capable of making artifacts to clothe and decorate our bodies and to develop a system of symbols connected with the particular aspects of dress. We discuss interrelationships among the various cultural adaptations to surroundings and to the body again in the next chapter.

PHYSICAL DIVERSITY

Long-term Adaptations

Differences and variations in physical characteristics in human beings are related to the interplay of a number of factors, including **heredity**, environmental influences, age, and development. All modern *Homo sapiens* are members of the same species and share the same general body configuration. However, even a quick glance around a typical classroom reveals that there are many physical variations in appearance from color of hair, eyes, and skin to the shape of facial features. Where does this *physical diversity* come from? Some phenotypical or physically apparent characteristics, such as skin color and body proportions, may be adaptations to environmental conditions. The adaptive value, if any, of other variations in the appearance of humans, such as color and texture of hair, is unknown.

As some of modern *Homo sapiens'* ancestors were spreading out of Africa and moving into Asia and Europe at least one million years ago, adaptations to these differing environments began to be made through natural selection. Skin color varies generally by latitude: populations closer to the equator have darker skin, while those farther away have lighter skin. There is general agreement that darker skin protects against the kind of ultraviolet (UV) ray damage exemplified by melanoma, a type of skin cancer. According to principles of natural selection, there must have been a parallel advantage to lighter skin for those populations farther away from the equator. A possible advantage is suggested by the vitamin D hypothesis. Vitamin D can lead to rickets, a skeletal deformity that in women can make childbirth difficult or impossible. Park says, "Skin color was thus seen as a balancing act—dark enough to protect from the damaging effects of UV and light enough to allow the beneficial effects" (1999, p. 322).

Darker skin as a protection against overexposure to UV is generally accepted, but the vitamin D hypothesis has recently been questioned, primarily on the basis of lack of supporting fossil evidence. Another possible explanation for an advantage to lighter skin in higher latitudes comes from military data that suggests darker skin is more subject to frostbite damage than is lighter skin (Post et al., 1975, as cited in Park, 1999, p. 322).

There are several possible correlations between environments and body proportions: generally, populations of people in extremely cold climates tend to be stockier with shorter limbs in proportion to the trunk in contrast to those in hot, arid climates, who have more linear bodies. The key is that the stockier person has less surface area per unit of mass and maintains heat better, while the linear body has more surface area and loses heat more rapidly (Park, 1999, p. 321).

Opinions differ greatly about the possible adaptive aspects of different eye forms. The **epicanthic fold**, a fold of skin that covers part or all of the edge of the upper eyelid, is common among some Asian populations (see Figure 5.2), indigenous Central American groups, and !Kung[1] of Africa. Some biologists (e.g., Cole, 1963, pp. 20–24) think it may provide protection against the cold and snow glare for Asians living in very cold regions and protection against sun glare for the !Kung living in southeastern Africa.

Whatever adaptive benefits skin color and body shape may or may not have, their evolutionary significance to specific environments took place thousands of years ago. Humans now have spread out and live in all areas of the earth except Antarctica, so why are there still populations that share similarities in physical appearances? By definition, members of a species are capable of

Figure 5.2
The epicanthic fold at the inner corner of the eye, found in several human populations in diverse areas of the globe, provides protection to the eye from harsh climate conditions. Inuit, mid-twentieth century.

interbreeding with all others of the opposite sex and producing fertile off-spring. However, human mating is not random, and for hundreds of generations people have tended to choose their partners from within their own social group or from a neighboring population:

> As a result, the physical expressions of the genes inherited from an expanding chain of parents and grandparents—most of whom lived in the same region as one another—also tend to cluster, so that there can be a great deal of variation from one geographic region to another in skin color, hair form, facial morphology, body proportions and a host of less immediately obvious traits. (Shreeve, 1994, p. 58)

This clustering of physical variations is most often in the form of a **cline**; that is, "a continuum of change from one area to another, as opposed to sudden and absolutely distinct changes" (Park, 1999, p. 349).

Examples include the people living in isolated mountain villages in the Himalayas and Australian aboriginal groups. Examine the photographs of people from two different Himalayan valleys in Figure 5.3. They are close to each other "as the crow flies," but their isolation in mountain valleys contributes to their unique appearances. Sociocultural factors such as language, religion, and

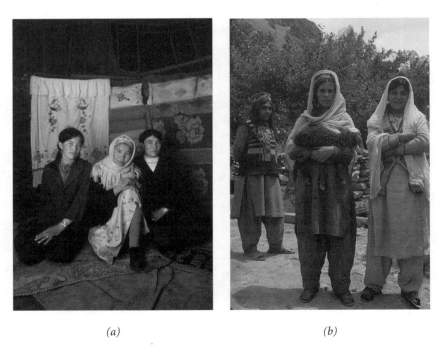

(a)   *(b)*

Figure 5.3
Geographical barriers encourage the development of distinctive gene pools in human groups otherwise living relatively close to each other on the globe, as do these people who are separated more by the height of ranges of the Himalayan Mountains than by geographical distance. (a) Kazakh women, (b) Wakhi women.

political differences may also act as barriers and slow the mingling of genes between groups. As geographical, or cultural, distance increases, physical differences between groups may increase. As physical anthropologist Alice Brues noted, "If I parachute into Nairobi, I know I'm not in Oslo" (quoted in Begley, 1995, pp. 67–69).[2] In other words, we many not notice the gradations of change in physical characteristics of humans as we travel over short geographical distances, but the changes become evident when we travel over great distances or cross major geographical divides.

Race

Racial categories such as "Caucasian" or "Negroid" are the result of human beings' attempts to identify biologically distinct groupings based upon physical appearance. A number of researchers, such as Alain Corcos, suggest that the concept of **race** did not really begin until the Age of Exploration and widespread European ship travel. Not only did Europeans come into contact with widely separated societies, but the differences in appearance were striking because travel by sea does not reveal the gradations of change in physical appearance visible to land travelers. According to Corcos, "Europeans were struck by the fact that the people they encountered appeared to be physically different from themselves and they quickly began to devise systems of classification" (1997, p. 3). The eighteenth century Swedish naturalist Linnaeus included four races of humans in his classification system of all known animals: American or red, European or white, Asiatic or yellow, and African or black. Well into the twentieth century, dozens of attempts were made to set up a specified number of racial categories based upon a selection of supposedly correlated physical traits, with skin color being most important. Some systems recognized as few as 3 races, while others enumerated as many as 200. The problem is that although some physical features are correlated in particular geographical areas, such as blonde straight hair, blue eyes, and fair skin in the Scandinavian region of Europe, where do all of the curly-haired and dark-haired Europeans fit?

There are always combinations of features or gradations of color that do not fit into the racial categories, no matter how numerous the categories. Equally dark-skinned people live in parts of Africa, Australia, India, and Melanesia, but they differ greatly in other physical traits. Many racial systems classify people in India as white or Caucasoid on the basis of hair texture and facial features, and ignore the skin color of some Indian populations that are darker than many Africans. Many Australian Aborigines have light-colored or tawny hair in combination with dark skin and broad noses, as shown in Figure 5.4—so how should they be classified? And how can one account for the differences in facial features, skin tones, and body proportions within the continent of Africa? Several studies have demonstrated that roughly 10 to 15 percent of total genetic variation is found between groups while 85 to 90 percent variation is found within a single group (Boaz & Almsvist, 1997, p. 445).

In 150 years of research on race it has not been possible to prove scientifically the existence of racial categories based upon physical appearance. Anthropologists are divided over the continued use of the racial categories,

Figure 5.4
The natural physical makeup of the dark-skinned, dark-eyed, blonde Australian Aborigine toddler differs from that of the older child only in hair color, but this aspect of the toddler's appearance challenges the validity of the racial categories. The physical makeup of many other human populations around the world similarly challenge attempts at racial categorization.

with cultural anthropologists often calling the term "race" a folk taxonomy used to classify members of a group so as to exclude some individuals systematically from full participation within their society and granting privileges to others. Some biological anthropologists believe that recognition should be made of physical variation within modern humans, but they are careful to emphasize the geographical, clinal distribution of similar traits and to point out the dangers of racist use of racial categories. In actuality, no clear-cut divisions will exist in the future, as more and more mixing of populations is taking place through the interbreeding that accompanies war, immigration, and travel. The American Anthropological Association (AAA) has summarized and taken a position on current scientific and social understanding of race.

One modern example of a well-known individual who illustrates that physical characteristics are ambiguous is the late U.S. Representative Adam Clayton Powell, Jr. He liked to tell stories from his youth about how, when his family first moved into an African-American area, even his neighbors had trouble classifying his race (Powell, 1971, p. 24); Powell concluded that it was the way that a person thinks that determines the race. Published photographs of Powell and other contemporary African-Americans testify to the fact that dress also played a role in this racial confusion (Hamilton, 1991; Haygood, 1993; Hickey & Edwin, 1965; Powell, 1971). The practice of transforming the texture of the hair in emulation of Euro-Americans, a fashion popular in the 1950s, contributed to the problem of racial classification. Only through Powell's parents' choice of residence, their active participation in the African-American church leadership and community life, and Adam's later church and political leadership in the community did the family claim and have granted membership in the black "race." Without their claim of black racial pride, they would not have been identified as black. It was more a matter of their passing for black by their behavior and self-identification in public statements rather than of passing for white (Hamilton, 1991, pp. 44–45). Relying simply on the physical appearance of the members of the Powell family, people—both black and white—wondered whether Adam was white, black, or Italian (Haygood, 1993, p. 1).

Ethnicity

Lieberman, Reynolds, and Kellum (1983, p. 72) suggest that the scientifically debatable concept of race be replaced with the term **ethnic group**, a change indicating the decreased importance of biological categories and the greater importance of culture—those values, beliefs, habits, customs, and norms that people from a common background share. Hispanic, Jewish, and Irish-American are categories based upon cultural variables such as language, religion, and shared history. Ethnic categorization is definitely not without its animosity and prejudice as is all too readily seen in the Balkans in the 1990s. However, if humans must be categorized, ethnicity is more potentially useful than race because it reflects shared culture and history rather than physical appearance, which may be widely diverse.

Ethnicity is often used as a political symbol and may be an impetus for empowerment. Dress plays an important role in this process. For example, an outgrowth of the 1960s and 1970s civil rights movement among African-Americans was the emergence of the Afro hair style as a symbol of ethnic pride. In the late twentieth century, kente cloth, a brightly colored strip-woven fabric characteristically used by powerful Ghanaian chiefs, as shown in Figure 1.12, became the flag of African-American ethnic unity. Thus the pride and power associated with a preslavery past contributed to transforming presumed racial difference into a unique ethnic identity, even though the enslaved peoples were brought to America from many West African countries. Another example is the case of the Hasidic Jews (Fig. 5.5) or differences in various American Indian groups and their types of dress.

Sex Differentiation

Just as human physical variations are obvious when one looks around a typical classroom, differences between men and women are also apparent. In addition to the appearance of external genitalia, generally, men have more facial and body hair, narrower hips, flatter buttocks, and a tendency to greater body mass. However, beyond the obvious differences in sex organs, **sex differentiation** in

Figure 5.5
The dress of Hasidic Jews communicates their specific cultural identity. Like many other human groups, they use distinctive ethnic dress to communicate a separation that extends beyond, or sometimes in spite of, the realities of their genetic closeness or distance from neighboring human populations.

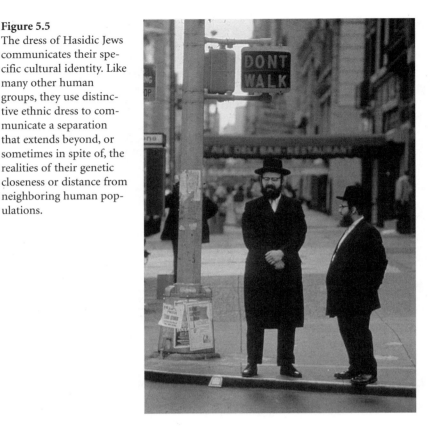

the appearance of body form is not as clear-cut as we are often led to believe. In the words of Downs and Bleibtreu (1972, p. 304), "Instead of fitting the stereotype for 'man' or 'woman,' each individual falls somewhere on a continuum running from almost 'all male' to almost 'all female' in physical characteristics." In some populations, differences between male and female body configuration appear to be greater than in others.

A secondary sex characteristic that distinguishes men from women is the amount of hair. Men are more frequently able to grow beards and they have hair on their legs, chests, stomachs, backs, and arms, as well as (around) their genitals. Women usually cannot grow beards, have almost no hair on their chests, stomachs, or back, and compared with men, have only light growths on their legs and arms (Downs & Bleibtreu, 1972, pp. 266–267). However, there is a broad range in how hirsute (hairy) men and women are. Japanese men are comparable to Europeans in the amount of hair, but many other Asian men have little body hair. Many sub-Saharan Africans, both males and females exhibit very little body hair, whereas the people of Papua New Guinea and the Ainu on the Japanese island of Hokkaidu often have much hair.

Just how much female body hair is considered acceptable differs from one culture to another. Sometimes women use body modification techniques to remove unwanted hair to achieve an image of what constitutes an ideal woman. In the United States, for example, it is a common practice for women to pluck eyebrows that are considered too bushy, to remove hair from upper lips and facial moles that starts to appear in older middle age, and to shave underarms and legs. In Muslim Turkey (Croutier, 1989) and northern Africa (e.g., Mernissi, 1994), and Muslim-influenced communities in India (Hershman, 1974), women commonly remove hair from every inch of their bodies, except for the head. This includes the fine hairs that cover the face, hair that people in the United States commonly do not notice. By contrast, among the Toda people of northern India, extensive dark facial hair is part of the aesthetic for women. These body modifications maintain the cultural definition of what is a female physical human being. In these examples, each culture identifies a different standard of female hirsutism out of the naturally occurring range of body hair exhibited by female humans.

The physical differences between the sexes can be important in the type of clothing designated as female or male. Sometimes a society may emphasize sexual characteristics, at other times it may de-emphasize them. For example, a woman's shirtwaist dress characteristic of the late 1950s with a tight waist reveals breast size and shape and makes hips appear broad even if the individual has a thick waist. In the 1970s in the United States, the fashion for disco dancing went hand-in-hand with men wearing their shirts open and displaying gold medallions glinting in a nest of chest hair. By the 1990s, grunge and hip-hop music emphasized layers of loose-fitting clothing, revealing little of the body underneath. Religious beliefs often influence how much of the body is covered for men and women. In many places, Muslim women wear garments that conceal much of their body when they go out in public.

Body Conformation

Classification of human body types is difficult since the averages of these types represented are likely to be emphasized, and people may overlook the wide range of human variations within populations. Averages and norms describe trends rather than the total picture. Downs and Bleibtreu (1972, pp. 262–263) contend that even population differences in height have been greatly exaggerated. They underscore within-group variation by pointing out that "tall" Mbuti[3] of Africa may be shorter than "short" Europeans or Japanese. Conversely, short individual Crow Indians of North America or Nilots of Africa (groups noted for their tall stature) may be taller than "tall" Europeans or Japanese.

One of the most ambitious attempts to examine human variation in body build is that of Sheldon (1940, pp. 1–5), who classified U.S. women and men of different ethnic backgrounds according to the degree to which they exhibited characteristics of three major body types: the **endomorphic** (rounded with prominent abdomen), **mesomorphic** (large boned and muscular), and **ectomorphic** (linear and slender). According to his explanation of the system as shown in Figure 5.6, all individuals are considered to have some of each of the three types of characteristics even though they may be most closely identified as one type or another. Thus, Sheldon's model can be useful in looking at people in context. For example, the subsistence economies of some small societies, such as the Agta of the Philippines, are usually high in fruits and fibers foraged from the surrounding jungle. Because their diets are low in animal fats, their bodies tend to be muscular. When comparing this body type to Sheldon's somatotypes, one might locate the Agta body somewhere between mesomorph and average.

The muscle-bound bodies of young Arnold Schwartzenegger and Lou Ferrigno shown Figure 5.7a exemplify Sheldon's mesomorph; the Japanese sumo wrestler shown in Figure 5.7b exemplifies the endomorph; and the fashion model, Kate Moss, shown in Figure 5.7c exemplifies the ectomorph. Consider other people who might exemplify Sheldon's somatotypes and the cultural and historical context within which their body forms exist.

A basic challenge in design and construction of body coverings is that the body is a three-dimensional form that bends and moves but must be fitted by flat materials such as fabrics, skins, leaves, and grasses. These materials must be suspended on, wrapped around, or fitted to the contours of the body. Cutting and sewing fabrics versus wrapping fabrics to fit the body offer different design possibilities and restrictions.

Short-term Variations

Nutrition and Disease

Both the amount and kind of food available may account for differences in body development. All people require the same nutrients in different amounts according to age, sex, activities, size, and state of health. However, everyone may not have access to all these necessary nutrients.

Climate, for example, can limit what food can be grown. In the Arctic region, where plant and animal life is limited by severe cold, the seal was long a major source of food for the Inuit who needed a diet high in calories, such as seal fat gives, to make up for heat loss. Uncooked seal is also rich in vitamins A, C, and D, among other nutrients. In areas of heavy rainfall, such as Southeast Asia, rice that can flourish in the water-soaked ground is an important food. Wheat and potatoes supply nutrients to people in other climates.

In addition to climate, technology affects the food supply. Domestication of plants and animals allows for control of the food supply that is impossible among hunters and gatherers. Inedible substances can sometime be made edible if a suitable technology is developed. Thus, poisonous, bitter cassava can be converted into an important source of food starch in tropical regions of South America, Africa, and the Malaysian archipelago through a lengthy leaching process.

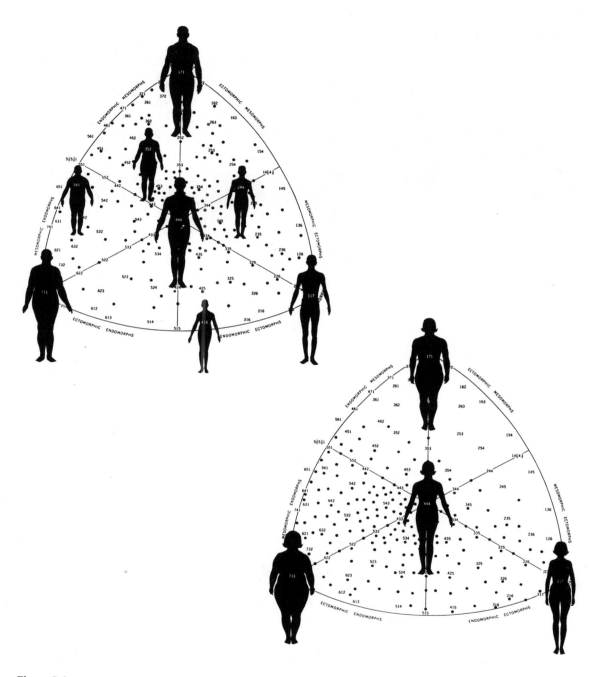

Figure 5.6

Sheldon's three somatotypes, here diagrammed separately for men and women, can be a useful tool for describing human physical appearance variation at the level of the individual.

(a)   *(b)*   *(c)*

Figure 5.7
(a) Mesomorphism is enhanced by body building. (b) Extreme endomorphism is cultivated by sumo wrestlers in Japan. (c) Late twentieth century female fashion models meet an ectomorphic ideal of beauty for North American and European women.

Once ways of preserving and transporting foods from place to place are developed, climate places fewer restrictions on the food supply; technology overcomes the restrictions. In addition, strains of staple foods like wheat and potatoes can be genetically altered to better resist pests and increase yields to feed more people. However, traditions that determine what is good or proper to eat may still limit nutrition. For instance, long-time habits and religious beliefs may prohibit the use of some nutritious foods, which can influence the shape of the body.

If improper nutrition occurs, physical appearance may deviate from that of the well-nourished body in a number of ways: height and weight may be affected, stomachs may become distended as a result of malnutrition, muscles may atrophy, skin and hair may change in color and texture, bones may be deformed, teeth may decay. In addition, skin may become very sensitive, making the feel of clothing uncomfortable. Similar changes may also occur with many kinds of body malfunctions, disease, and medical treatments from anorexia nervosa to hepatitis to chemotherapy. In North America and in Europe where being fashionably thin is promoted, young women especially are susceptible to eating disorders, such as anorexia nervosa and bulimia.

If obesity is considered beautiful, it may be encouraged and the matter of health disregarded. Obesity is related to nutrition and health, but also to ideals of beauty. Although extreme obesity places strains on the body and its organs, it may be pursued when considered aesthetically desirable.

If nutrition and disease alter appearance in ways that are considered culturally negative, individuals may make changes in their dress and ornamentation to create the illusion of the preferred body size and shape or to mask the effects of disease. Chemotherapy patients often lose their hair and make use of wigs or hats both to cover their uncharacteristic baldness and to fulfill cultural standards of appearance. Women who have undergone mastectomies also may choose to wear prostheses or to have breast reconstruction.

With improved nutrition and health care, populations become more robust. People grow taller, live longer, and stay active far beyond the norm of their ancestors. In fact, today's young adults are, on average, 2 inches taller than their parents. This change has implications for apparel manufacturers who must develop garments that fit the body. For example, the U.S. military and some clothing designers are now using body scanners to make garments that fit the human body more accurately (Gazzuolo, 1997). Nutrition and health can relate to body supplements in less promising ways. The chapter reading on tight neckwear worn by men in North America is an example of how U.S. adult male health is jeopardized by dress practices. Some doctors have reported helping patients resolve gastrointestinal discomfort by recommending that they wear pants with a larger waist measurement than they have been wearing. Physicians refer to this as the "tight pants syndrome."

Growth and Age

Each human being differs from all others in physical appearance, posture, and body movement, and the appearance of each individual also changes continuously, especially in the inevitable processes of maturation and aging. The young need new clothes as they grow and change body size and proportion, and changes in body size and conformation continue throughout life. Infant garments are often now labeled for size with age, height, weight, and length because no one of these indicators accurately captures the wide range of infant body variation. Even sizing for children's clothing presents challenges in understanding the relationship between body size and age, as shown in Figure 5.8.

During pregnancy a woman's breasts and abdomen usually enlarge significantly and breasts remain larger as long as a woman breastfeeds her child. With an emphasis on calcium intake during pregnancy and nursing, a woman's bone density may increase as well. Throughout life, the percentage of body fat changes for both men and women. The body loses fat deposits of babyhood and may add fat deposits again later. To accommodate such changes in the body, specific garments, such as maternity wear and nursing bras, have been designed, as shown in Figure 5.9.

Height may change after adulthood as skeletal changes take place. In addition, loss of subcutaneous fat deposits in the face occurs for some older people, causing facial features to develop sharper or more angular lines. Body movement gradually becomes restricted as muscle fibers change and joints no

Infant

Size	Newborn	3 month	6 month	12 month	18 month	24 month
Weight	6½-9 lbs.	10-13 lbs.	14-18 lbs.	19-22 lbs.	22½-25½ lbs.	26-29 lbs.
Height	19"-21½"	22½"-24½"	25"-27"	27½"-29"	29½"-31"	31½"-33"

Toddler

	S	M	L
	2T	3T	4T
Height	33	36	39
Chest	21	22	23
Waist	20	20½	21
Hip	22	23	24

Little Kid

	S	M	L
	4	5/6	6X/7
Height	39	45	49
Chest	23	24½	25½
Waist	21	22	22½
Hip	23	25	26

Big Kid

	S	M	L	XL
	7/8	10/12	14/16	18/20
Height	52	59	64	68
Chest	27	30	33½	36
Waist	23	25	27½	29½
Hip	28	32	34	36

Junior (Girls)

	S		M		L		XL
	3	5	7	9	11	13	15
Height	64½	65	65½	66	66½	67	67½
Chest	32½	33½	34½	35½	37	38½	40
Waist	24½	25½	26½	27½	29	30½	32
Hip	35	36	37	38	39½	41	42½

Coed (Junior/Student)

	XS	S	M	L	XL
Chest	32½-33½	34½-36½	37-39½	40½-42½	43½-45½

Student (Boys)

	S		M		L		XL	
	31	32	33	34	35	36	38	40
Height	68	68	70	70	72	72	72	72
Chest	36½	37½	38½	39½	40½	41½	43½	45½
Waist	31	32	33	34	35	36	38	40
Hip	37½	38½	39½	40½	41½	42½	44½	46½

Figure 5.8

The degree to which body shape and size change over time is evidenced by the complexity of the various sizing methods developed by clothing manufacturers. Individuals' bodies change in predictable ways as they mature and age, yet each person also constitutes a unique constellation of traits that may be difficult for mass fashion producers to fit.

longer bend or rotate as easily. Baldness and graying of hair may accompany aging, but vary according to population and sex. Women, for example, rarely become bald, whereas men frequently do. As body conformation and mobility change and as skin and hair alter, an individual may be prompted to choose different designs and colors in order to suit aesthetic tastes or to adjust to social custom in a specific society. In the United States, individuals may feel the

Figure 5.9

Special garments are sometimes made to accommodate the changes in body size and shape that accompany normal biological processes, such as pregnancy and breast feeding. Nursing bra, United States, c. 1995.

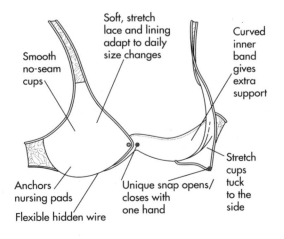

Soft, stretch lace and lining adapt to daily size changes

Curved inner band gives extra support

Smooth no-seam cups

Anchors nursing pads

Flexible hidden wire

Unique snap opens/ closes with one hand

Stretch cups tuck to the side

need to dye their gray hair or cover varicose veins by wearing slacks. In many Mediterranean countries, an older woman who is also a widow may be expected to wear black for the remainder of her days, whether or not black is pleasing with her eye, skin, and hair color. One characteristic of the aging baby boomers in the United States is a continuing interest in looking younger, as captured in Figure 5.10. Body supplements such as Nivea's "Visage Anti-Wrinkle and Firming Creme" are marketed to older baby boomers to soften the appearance of aging.

Differences in body proportions at different ages also affect design of clothing. The average young child has a head that is about one-fourth of total body length whereas an adult has a head nearer one-eighth of body length. Legs increase in proportion to body length from about one-fourth to about one-half of body length from infancy to adulthood. While male and female infants vary little in general body conformation, by adolescence the pelvis of the female has widened in proportion to the rest of the body and her breasts have developed. The male in adolescence develops broader shoulders and bulkier muscles in the upper torso. In addition, a woman's postpartum body may be more rounded and curved than before her pregnancy, requiring a change in her choices of dress. Thus, a series of body changes in height, weight, hair, skin color

Figure 5.10
In U.S. culture, dress is sometimes used to counter the physical effects of aging, as shown by this advertisement for an anti-wrinkle cream.

and texture, and general body conformation take place during each individual's life, with adjustments in clothing made in response to biological changes.

SUMMARY

Human beings are basically much alike in physical appearance because they are part of one species, *Homo sapiens*. However, differences exist in the appearance of their bodies. These differences can be attributed to the influences of environment, heredity, and the maturation and aging processes. Although heredity is fixed and the aging process inevitable, environmental influences can be modified by the application of technology. Medical care and nutrition also affect the body's development and appearance.

Differences in individual physical appearance and naturally occurring changes to the physical body arising from the human biological developmental cycle affect design and choice of dress. These choices occur within the range of the aesthetic tastes and social customs of the community within which the individual lives.

STUDY TOOLS

Important Terms

clines
ectomorphic
endomorphic
epicanthic fold
ethnic group
gene pool
heredity
Homo sapiens
mesomorphic
phenotypes
race
sex differentiation
speciation
species

Discussion Questions

1. How are all human beings physically similar? Why? How are human beings physically diverse? Why?

2. Explain and give examples of how geographical barriers and natural selection create homogeneity within human groups and among human groups.

3. Describe how nutrition and disease affect the way we look and dress.

4. What role does melanin play in human variation both among cultures and across the life span?

5. Discuss the ideas found in Sheldon's model. Explain how it could be used as a way to approach objectivity in cross-cultural research.

6. Why are skin color and hair type not the best way to categorize people?

7. Discuss the range of variation in human physical appearance across the life span and give two examples each of how the form of dress relates to these variations from aesthetic and medical perspectives.

8. What is the difference between genetic and social categories of race? What role do social categories of race play in relation to dress? Provide examples of dress—both body modifications and body supplements—that support social categories of race.

9. Compare and contrast the biological and sociological uses of the concept of race. How do these two very different concepts relate to the study of dress?

10. Discuss ways that dress is used to alter or enhance the form of the physical body for the purpose of meeting personal, cultural, and societal needs.

11. Discuss the wearing of dress shirts and neckties by men, analyzed in Reading II.1, "Pressure of Menswear on the Neck in Relation to Visual Performance" by Langan and Watkins (1987), and answer two questions: (1) how does the described menswear relate to the personal, cultural, and social needs of the wearer; (2) can you think of any womenswear that has a similar relationship to the needs of the wearer?

12. Langan and Watkins describe the detrimental effects of men's shirt collars and neckties when they constrict blood flow to the neck and head. Identify other dress practices in your culture that jeopardize health.

Activities

1. As a class, divide up into races based on similarities in, for example, hair color, then by who has a tattoo, and finally by membership in different clubs. Are the groups composed of the same people from race to race? What does this tell you about the usefulness of the term race? Is there a better way to think about similarities and differences between people?

2. Using disposable magazines and catalogues, clip pictures of men and women of varying body forms wearing dress that allows you to see their bodies (e.g., swimsuits, underwear, active wear). Sort the images into endomorphs, ectomorphs, and mesomorphs for each gender. Re-create Sheldon's chart in Figure 5.6, recognizing that few bodies are one classic morph or another. Examine the final result. Does this tell you anything about the types of bodies most apt to be photographed for popular

consumption? Assuming Sheldon's goal was a value-free method of typing human body variation, do any cultural biases inevitably appear?

3. Go back to Table 1.1 on page 6. Instead of examining how we modify and supplement our bodies, explore how environmental and hereditary influences create variation. List these sources on the vertical axis, keeping "properties" the same. Complete the chart with an example of each.

4. Using disposable magazines and catalogues, clip pictures of people with as many different skin colors as possible. Create a color spectrum with the picture of the person with the least amount of melanin at one end and the most amount of melanin at the other. Note how difficult it is to do this. What does this tell you about gene pools and heredity?

5. Select a pair of shoes—either winter boots, sandals, athletic cleats, high heels, or low-heeled shoes—and wear them throughout the entire day, no matter what your activity, in so far as it is possible without doing damage to yourself or others. As you do this, keep a journal noting how the footwear enhanced or impeded your body's physical abilities and functioning through the day. In cases when you had to exchange the footwear for something else to protect yourself or others, note the reasons for which you had to make the change. Also record how the footwear promoted or defeated your ability to meet your social and cultural requirements. Analyze your journal data as instances of meeting, or failing to meet, your physical, cultural, and social needs.

6. Imagine yourself wearing a dress shirt and necktie, if you are male, or similarly constricting women's dress, if you are female, throughout a full 24-hour day to all your activities, including sleeping and brushing your teeth. Write down all the activities in which you would find the dress uncomfortable or a hindrance to your activities. Then sort these out into three groups, according to whether they relate to your physical, cultural, or social needs. Be aware that some instances can fit into two or all three of these categories at the same time. What does this activity tell you about the relationship of dress to physical, cultural, and social needs of the individual?

7. Compare the color of skin on the underside of your forearm (where it is exposed to less sunlight) with the same area of the body on 10 other people among your close friends and family members. In each case record ahead of time, your expectation about whether or not the person compared has lighter or darker skin color than you and what hue (e.g., red to pink, yellow, blue, green, brown, etc.) you expect it to be. Then record your actual findings. When you have finished all 10, record your findings in a journal. Did you find what you expected or something unexpected? Did you learn anything new through this experiment?

8. Pair off with another person in the class who looks very different from you. Tell each other about your background and usual activities, covering the topics in Chapter 5 that relate to long-term and short-term changes or variations in physical appearance; for example, include such things as biological background, age, major illnesses, amount of exercise or physical

work, nutrition levels. Using this data, together analyze the various origins of your similarities and differences in physical appearance.

Notes to Chapter 5

1. The !Kung were formerly called bushmen by outsiders.
2. Alice Brues, noted physical anthropologist, is reported to use this image when describing our perception of the occurrence of human physical variation, according to Sharon Begley in her article "Three Is Not Enough," *Newsweek*, February 13, 1995, pp. 67–69.
3. The Mbuti and other similarly short peoples in Central Africa were formally called pygmies by outsiders.

6

Body, Dress, and Environment

OBJECTIVES

To understand the ability of the human body to adapt to small changes in the physical environment over short periods of time, through basic daily body functioning and through acclimatization.

To understand the role of dress as a tool that intervenes between the human body and natural and human-made environments.

To explore the role of dress as a cultural tool that allows human beings to survive in or explore a wide variety of environments.

THE COMFORT AND OPTIMUM functioning of our bodies depends upon the physiology of the body as we interact with the physical environment and are affected by body modifications and body supplements. The most common example of body supplement is clothing that covers the body and has the potential to be protective or have regulatory characteristics in relating to the physiological functioning of the body. Body modifications also can benefit or detract from body functioning. An example of a body modification that is beneficial to the functions of the body is laser surgery to the eyes in order to correct minor vision impairments. In contrast, a body modification that detracts from the functions of the body is filing of teeth to resemble fangs, which can puncture the lips or insides of the mouth, as in the case of some youth in North America dressing as vampires. In another example, that of piercing the tongue, the use of tongue ornaments can chip and crack teeth and create a choking hazard.

In this chapter, we discuss the flexibility of human beings in adapting to different environmental conditions that may affect comfort and functioning of the body. Some genetically based adaptations are the result of natural selection and are extremely long term. The body makes short-term adaptations itself and still others are possible because humans can produce cultural devices such as clothing, shelter, and modes of transportation. A close relationship exists between the cultural design of dress, shelter, transportation, and the environment in every society. For example, dressing for an indoor or outdoor job involves different considerations, as does making a decision about whether to walk or ride to your destination on a rainy or snowy day. Optimum human adaptation depends upon a combination of both physiological and cultural adaptation. Dress supplements that cover the body are not necessary for basic survival in moist, tropical climates, whereas they are desirable for comfort in temperate climates during cool seasons. However, some kind of clothing, shelter, or thermal control is mandatory for survival in extremely cold Arctic areas, in temperate regions in winter, and in hot desert regions of the globe. In addition, personal satisfaction and issues of modesty relate to dress in all climates, no matter how warm or cold.

PHYSIOLOGICAL ADAPTATION TO ENVIRONMENT

As we have seen in Chapter 5, extremely long-term evolutionary adaptations to different thermal environments may be the reason for variations in body build and facial features among human beings. Although the evidence is somewhat contradictory, many scientists do see a correlation between long limbs in proportion to the trunk with a hot environment and a shorter, more compact body and shorter limbs with a cold environment. For example, people such as the Australian Aborigines and the Tuareg of the Sahara, who have lived for innumerable generations in dry heat, have long-limbed lean bodies with a large amount of body surface area in proportion to their volume, to give off heat more efficiently. In contrast, the Inuit and others living around the cold Arctic Circle have shorter extremities and more compact bodies that have a relatively smaller amount of skin surface in relation to their height and volume. Therefore, their bodies give up proportionately less heat. To compare the relative skin surface of the two body types, see Figure 6.1. However, people who live in warm climates with high humidity do not exhibit the same linear look as those who inhabit dry heat. Thus, the Mbuti and other forest people of Africa and the Indians of the humid Amazon-Orinoco basin, who must cope with difficulties of evaporation in a nearly water saturated atmosphere, show no clear **physiological adaptation** in body form (Coon, Barn, & Birdsell, 1955).

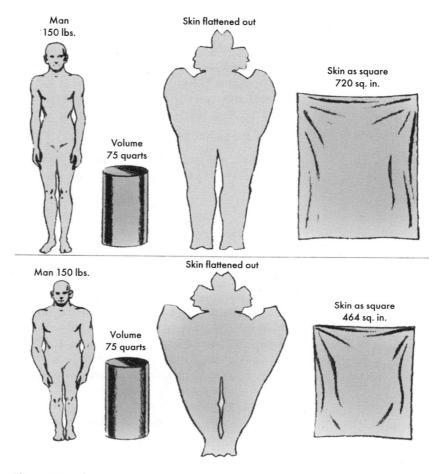

Figure 6.1
Comparison of body volume and skin surface area. If body volume is kept constant, the more linear individual will have a larger surface area. The larger area will lose heat at a faster rate, making it more difficult to survive in very cold regions.

Shorter term adaptations have been, and continue to be extremely important to humans. The body itself can make certain physiological adjustments to changes in the natural environment, particularly changes in temperature and oxygen content of the air. Many such changes take place daily as individuals move from indoors to outdoors or from rest to work, or as they are exposed to daily cyclic changes in temperature. Such short-term adjustments to a temporary environmental stimulus are referred to as **habituation**. Slightly longer-term adjustments occurring over the space of one or more days are referred to as acclimation. Examples are adjusting to a new time zone as in jet lag or tanning when exposed to more sunlight. Visitors to high altitudes acclimate within hours by increasing their respiratory and heart rates to offset the effects of hypoxia (the lowering of the level of oxygen in the blood).

Acclimatization is a long-term physiological adaptation that may take months or years and is a **genetic adaptation** (Boaz & Almquist, 1997, pp. 500–501; Jurmain, Nelson, Kilgore, & Trevathan, 1997, p. 139). Habituations and acclimatizations are the most important adaptations to environmental conditions.

Habituations or Immediate Body Adjustments

Because human beings are mammals, we are warm-blooded and possess physiological and behavioral mechanisms for maintaining internal body temperature in contrast to cold-blooded animals, which must rely on external heat to raise their body temperatures. Human beings live in a wide variety of habitats with temperatures ranging from 60°F below 0°F to in excess of 120°F. Human internal thermoregulators include sweating, shivering, and the expansion or contraction of blood vessels so that varying amounts of heat are given off with changes in temperature and humidity. However, humans still need dress and shelter for protection from extreme climate conditions.

The normal core temperature of the human body is about 98.6°F, and an individual can survive only within a very limited core body temperature range. Variations of as little as 2° to 3°F from the core temperature interfere with bodily functions and threaten life. Temperature of the body shell or skin, however, is not as critical a factor. This outer body temperature rises and falls according to environmental conditions and activities, and apparently differences as great as 20°F do not seriously disturb body functioning (*Man, Sweat*, 1969). To adapt to fluctuations in environmental temperatures, the body has means of maintaining thermal equilibrium, it can lower heat production or increase heat loss. Although humans can adapt to both excessive heat and cold, generally we cope better with heat than with cold. This is a testimony to the available evidence that suggests that earliest humans evolved in the warm-to-hot savannas of East Africa (Jurmain et al., 1997, p. 142).

Sweating is the body's major response to an increase in either the internal body temperature or surface skin temperature. Some of the approximately 1.6 million sweat glands humans possess go into action to produce a watery liquid that evaporates and cools the body surface. The salt concentration in both sweat and urine decreases so that danger of excessive salt loss, causing heat cramps, is reduced. Another heat-reducing mechanism is vasodilatation. In this response, capillaries near the skin's surface dilate to facilitate delivery of heat to the surface of the skin, where it is dissipated to prevent the body from overheating. The visible effect is flushing or an increased redness of the skin along with a feeling of warmth (Jurmain et al., 1997, p. 142).

The human body responds to cold most immediately by shivering or contracting muscles to produce more heat. "Goose bumps" are a reflexive remnant of our past when we were covered with body hair like our primate relatives. The individual hairs stand up to trap air in between and increase the insulative value. Metabolic rate is also increased and vasoconstriction of the small blood vessels near the surface of the skin occurs so that not as much heat is carried to the surface of the skin where it will be lost.

The sexes differ in certain characteristics related to thermal control (*Man, Sweat*, 1969, p. 21). Females have a thicker layer of subcutaneous fat than males and a greater number of sweat glands per unit area of the skin. Thus, females have a wider comfort range than men: 80°F to 91.4°F for women, 82.4°F to 87.9°F for men. Theoretically, women should be able to wear fewer protective body enclosures than men under similar environmental conditions without feeling discomfort. However, physical conditioning, from habitual physical work or exercise, can affect the ability of the body to make use of all these heating and cooling capacities.

Acclimatization

Today, material cultural technology has produced such completely climate controlled environments—air conditioned and heated buildings and vehicles—that many people, particularly those who can afford to do so, no longer draw upon the human body's full range of abilities to adjust physiologically to changing temperatures. Yet, there are many groups of people who still have to acclimatize to their natural surroundings in more dramatic ways.

Cold

A high metabolic rate releases more energy in the form of heat, but it requires an increase in nutrients to maintain this higher rate. People such as the Inuit who live in the chronically cold Arctic maintain a higher metabolic rate than people who live in warmer climates. The highest metabolic rates are found among the inland Inuit, whose climate is even colder than along the coast. Not coincidentally, the Inuit have the highest animal protein and fat diet of any living population anywhere in the world. Additionally, Inuit alternate between vasoconstriction, narrowing of the blood vessels to reduce heat loss at the skin surface, and vasodilatation, expansion of blood vessels to increase blood flow and warm the skin. This is a balance or compromise that prevents the frostbite that would result from continuous vasoconstriction, but does not take as much energy as vasodilatation. In contrast, Australian Aborigines maintain continuous vasoconstriction in combination with sleeping close to continuously burning fires to be comfortable at nighttime temperatures only a few degrees above freezing even though they wear extremely little clothing (Jurmain et al., 1997, p. 144). A "warming response" to extreme cold is seen in some European and Asian populations in which the hands or feet become vasodilated to increase circulation and raise the temperature (Boaz & Almquist, 1997, p. 503).

High Altitude

Today, over 25 million people live at altitudes above 10,000 feet in such places as Ethiopia, South America, and Tibet, despite the stresses placed on the body by the higher altitudes. There are permanent settlements in Tibet above 15,000 feet and in the Andes as high as 17,000 feet. Studies of these populations reveal a number of adaptations or acclimatizations that occur. Living at an altitude above approximately 10,000 feet causes a number of stresses, primarily hypoxia resulting from reduced amounts of available oxygen in the atmosphere due to lowered barometric pressure. The body must make physiological changes to use the available oxygen efficiently (Jurmain et al., 1997, p. 145). The heart, lungs, and brain bear the greatest stress brought on by the lowered oxygen.

As stated earlier in this chapter, short-term adaptations of visitors to high altitudes include an increase in breathing and heart rate. Acclimatizations, or long-term adaptations, found in people who grow up at these altitudes include the reduction, somewhere between 20 to 30 percent, in the amount of oxygen that the body absorbs. Additionally, there is greater lung capacity and larger hearts and, therefore, a tendency to larger chests.

Physical Adaptation and Dress

How do basic body adjustments, acclimatization, and genetic adaptation of the human body to the physical environment relate to dress? The answers are several and complex. Some of these are only touched upon here, but can be examined in more detail in other specialist courses of study. Others are dealt with in detail in subsequent chapters of this book.

One example concerns the basic body adaptations to changes in temperature, wind, and moisture naturally occurring in the immediate environment around an individual on any given day and through the seasons of the year. The range of behaviors they elicit from the body—perspiration and shivering—place different demands on the body supplements that we wear. The transactions of heat and moisture through the skin sometimes require forms of protective dress for survival, and more often require different forms of dress for maintenance of comfort. A primary means by which people worldwide generally adjust to changes in temperature is through change in the number of layers of clothing that is worn, in the amount of body coverage that the clothing provides, in the thickness and weave structure of the clothing, or in the fibers from which the clothing is made.

Fibers such as wool, for example, when spun into loose yarns and woven into loose, thick weave structures, can keep the body warmer than can cotton fibers, because wool fibers are scaled and somewhat curly and can be made into a cloth that holds insulative pockets of air around the body. In contrast, cotton will absorb body moisture and then release it at the touch of a breeze, so it can be woven into thin, light fabrics that cool the body by helping to take away perspiration in hot, dry climates.

Acclimatization and genetic adaptation to environment can affect dress in several ways. Since dress must accommodate the body, differences in body shape and conformation, such as accompany a growth in lung capacity in high altitude regions, or a genetic propensity to a particular body type, such as long thin legs or a compact body, will necessarily require different designs for dress to fit the body. Thus, a system of clothing sizes developed for one population will not fit all people in all populations, unless the body supplements are styled very loosely.

Such distinctive forms will also affect a regional society's ideals of beauty for the male and female human body. Body modifications and supplements are developed within a society to enhance these cultural ideals. Cultural ideals of beauty are discussed in more detail in Chapter 11.

Consistent acclimatization and genetic adaptation of a population to a specific environment can greatly alter a population's protective dress needs. For example, the Australian Aborigines previously described will not feel a need for protective clothing in cold that would have North Americans reaching for their second and third layer of garments. When we travel to a part of the world that is much colder or hotter than our home area, we often notice that we need much more or less protective clothing than members of the local society. They are better acclimatized than we to that environment and may also be genetically adapted to it because they come from a heritage of people who have lived in that environment for generations.

CULTURAL ADAPTATION OF THE BODY TO ENVIRONMENT

Although human beings can make limited adjustments, both short term and long term, to environment through physical adaptation of the body, human beings are much more remarkable for resourcefulness and versatility in **cultural adaptations**. Unlike lower animals we have little protective hair and no feathers or down; however, we can opt to be uncovered, or to cover or shelter ourselves at will. If we want to survive in an adverse climate, for example, we may devise ways for providing an artificial environment that will ensure our survival. Sometimes our survival depends upon our ability to blend into our environment, as when camouflage dress enables a hunter to get closer to the animals being hunted, or enables military personnel to fade into the landscape. Therefore the effective camouflage fabric is designed for specific settings, as seen in Figure 6.2. Our cultural adaptation through dress also allows us to help individuals weakened through ill health, age, or disability, to continue to function at higher levels of effectiveness than if they were required to rely on their physical abilities alone. For example, eyeglasses help individuals to see more clearly and a corset-like garment can provide support to a person with a bad back. Thus, we have the ability to imagine solutions to common problems and to conceive of how to go about building shelters against the elements, enter into new environments, and facilitate a fuller participation by physically weakened members of human society.

As human beings we also have the ability to create environments that are detrimental to our health, such as war or working environments that entail exposure to chemicals, radiation, or noise levels dangerous to health. In such cases we develop types of dress to help protect us in those environments. One very dramatic example of the protective role of dress and of the power of textile-

Figure 6.2
Camouflaged dress functions to visually blend its wearer into the natural environment by mimicking the color and pattern of the specific environment in which the individual intends to hide. Camouflage fabric designs for various environments: (a) woodland; (b) desert; (c) Arctic; (d) marsh.

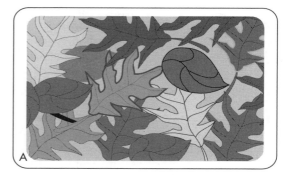

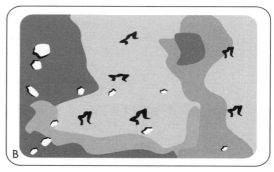

based clothing in particular is the bulletproof vest. See Figure 6.3 for an example of how the layering of special fabrics can stop a bullet. In another example of protective dress for agricultural workers, researchers have experimented with various garments and recommended specific items to protect bodies from pesticide penetration. In this case, somewhat "low-tech" dress can be worn for working with dangerous agricultural chemicals, as shown in Figure 6.4.

Another solution is to dress the body to create a compact and portable environment, which, on an elementary level, is an extension of the temperature-controlling mechanism of the body. Such cultural adaptations can be accomplished relatively swiftly and simply and are effective where physiological adaptations alone could probably never ensure survival, such as in Arctic or desert regions, under water, or in outer space. In addition, such portable environments can be developed with simple or complex technologies, although the most elaborate contrivances are seen among highly industrialized people. Thus, dress is a tool humans use to acclimatize and thrive in almost any envi-

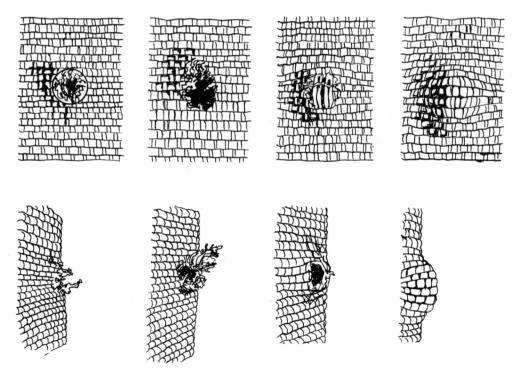

Figure 6.3
The effects of a bullet on ballistics nylon are shown for fabric layers one, four, six, and nine in two views, perpendicular (top row) and side (bottom row). The bullet was stopped at the ninth layer, giving dramatic evidence of the protective power of some forms of dress.

Figure 6.4
Due to a higher vulnerability of some parts of the body to chemical pesticides, those who work with these toxic substances should wear clothing in specific ways to ensure the dress properly protects the body.

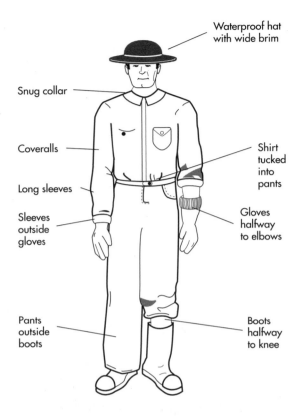

Waterproof hat with wide brim

Snug collar

Coveralls

Shirt tucked into pants

Long sleeves

Sleeves outside gloves

Gloves halfway to elbows

Pants outside boots

Boots halfway to knee

ronment. The astronaut's space suit is a familiar example, as well as suits with breathing mechanisms attached for deep-sea diving.

With our ability to create cultural devices to adapt to the environment, we can be freed from dependence on physiological or genetic adaptation and can move into and shape new environments in which we would not otherwise be able to survive. Such devices have allowed humans to enter into unusual hazardous environments, whether naturally occurring forest fires or human-made sites of radioactive or chemical accidents, for example, chlorine spillage in a wastewater plant. We can create our own shield against various stresses and threats in the physical environment. Dress can constitute one of these shields. However, dress does not isolate us completely from the physical environment, for we still operate within it.

When poorly designed, dress can create an unfavorable mini-environment within which the body is forced to function, as when the material of a body supplement does not allow sufficient range of movement or the evaporation of perspiration. In other words dress can function as an extension of the body that may simultaneously be a portable environment and a means for intervening between individual and environment. However, badly designed dress can also be a hindrance. For example, today's football and hockey players would find the old system of many separate pads—relying on stiff straps for attachment to the body—a hindrance to movement, which would badly affect their game. Today, an increased movement afforded by the development of stretchable fibers and fabrics, combined with a design that incorporates padding to protect the wearer from impact, has allowed football and hockey players to apply more force in their play while maintaining speed and agility.[1]

Another example of how dress can be a hindrance comes from the late nineteenth century, in the United States, when dress was strictly prescribed. It included the donning of long underwear in October, regardless of actual weather conditions or climate. As Fourt and Hollies (1970) emphasize:

> It is important to realize that the clothing is not just a passive cover for the skin, but that it interacts with and modifies the heat regulating function of the skin and has effects which are modified by body movement. Some of this interaction is automatic, derived from the physical properties of the clothing materials and their spacing around the body; the larger scale interactions, however, arise from conscious choice of amount and kind of clothing, and mode of wearing, especially how the clothing is closed up or left open and loose. (p. 31)

Thus they view clothing as a quasi-physiological system, which is an extension of the body and which interacts with the body, as shown in Figure 6.5a and b of hats from around the world that are used to protect the head from sun.

(a)   *(b)*

Figure 6.5
The physiological effects on the body from wearing dress are exemplified by these brimmed hats, which shield the body from the sun. They enable the wearers to see more clearly facing into the sun, slow down the rate of facial tanning, deflect the sun's heat from the shoulders, enclose perspiration on the top of the head, and produce the effect known in the United States as "hat hair." Long term effects of wearing hats include a slowing of facial wrinkling and reduction in the chance of developing cataracts or skin cancer. (a) United States, late twentieth century and (b) Hakka, near Hong Kong, mid-twentieth century.

Dress, most often clothing, serves as a mini-environment and also interacts with the body to contribute to body comfort and health. In general this comfort and health depends on maintenance of body temperature; provision of sufficient food, water, and oxygen; protection against irritation and injury from a variety of outside agents or environmental forces; and provision for freedom of movement. Clothing can prevent loss of body heat or moisture, prevent build up of excess heat, protect against bodily injury, and in very specialized cases can provide a system supplying oxygen and removing body solid wastes.

Clothing requirements for various protective and maintenance purposes, however, depend on other factors such as food intake, available shelter, and auxiliary heating or cooling systems. For protection and comfort, some balance among these factors must be maintained. If an insulated, enclosed shelter with a central heating system replaces the lean-to and open fire, obviously less clothing is required to achieve feelings of comfort. If air conditioning is introduced, warmer clothing may become necessary indoors. In cold climates, food intake can be stepped up to make more calories of heat available to the body's internal heating system. Automobiles, trains, and planes have their own controlled environments within which people can be transferred from one controlled environment to another without going outside so that clothing adjustments to changes of outside temperatures are largely unnecessary. Thus, when travelers in cold climates change airplanes in a modern airport with jetways and covered or enclosed entrances, heavy outerwear becomes virtually unnecessary until leaving the airport.

DRESS AS EXTENSIONS AND MODIFICATIONS OF THE BODY

We are born with a functioning body as our basic equipment for securing comfort, satisfaction, and survival. Our hands are good tools since we can gather food with them. Our fists and teeth can be utilized as primitive weapons for defense. Our opposable thumbs enhance our grasping ability and allow us to be tool users. Supplemented by application of our highly developed brain, our use of tools facilitates complex means of exploiting our natural environment or defending ourselves against environmental stresses or threats. As humans we conceived of how to dress ourselves, with supplements and modifications to the body that extend the effectiveness of bodily efforts or ensure comfort and survival in adverse environments. For instance we have many handheld supplements, such as purses and briefcases, that extend our ability to carry things. Body supplements worn on other parts of the body can also help us carry things. As seen in Figures 6.6a and 6.6b, the Saami hat with four peaks, called "Four Winds" hat, is used to carry small objects, similar to a carpenter's apron.[2] Each of these frees the hands to do other necessary tasks. Examples of extensions that help us survive can be as simple as a thick fabric jacket or coat of

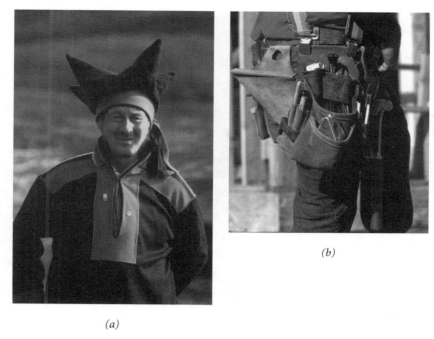

(b)

(a)

Figure 6.6
Pockets inside the pointed hat and the apron enable workers in two different societies
to extend their ability to carry small tools. (a) Saami Four Winds hat, Scandinavia and
(b) carpenter's apron, United States.

grease applied to the skin, which improve the ability of our skin to retain body
heat out in the cold air or while swimming the English Channel. Dress that extends the body's abilities can be much more complex, as the body raft shows in
Figure 6.7.

Supplements That Extend Motor Skills and Spatial Force

Two common kinds of supplements that extend a human being's motor skills
are foot and hand enclosures or attachments. Our basic means of transport are
feet and the related motor skills that make locomotion possible. Footwear is
one of the earliest cultural improvements in self-propelled transportation, and
some types of footwear are especially useful in adapting to the environment,
such as the four different kinds of soft-soled footwear used by various American Indian groups, which are depicted in Figure 6.8. The moccasin of the
American Indian provided protection against both cold and uneven terrain.
Moccasins were worn infrequently by Indians where it was warm and rained a
great deal, as in some parts of North America. Heavy rainfall, canoeing, and
fishing in the Northwest also discouraged use of the moccasin.

Figure 6.7
Dress may function simultaneously as an extension and a modification of the body.

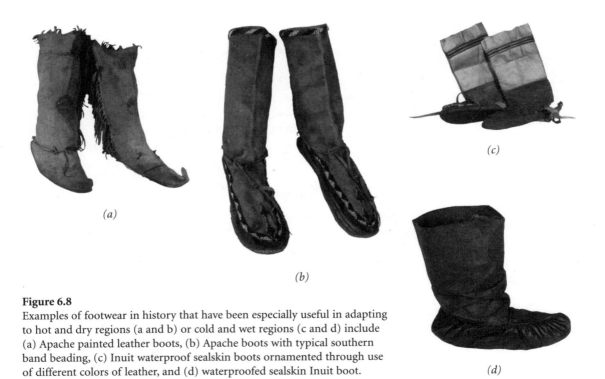

Figure 6.8
Examples of footwear in history that have been especially useful in adapting to hot and dry regions (a and b) or cold and wet regions (c and d) include (a) Apache painted leather boots, (b) Apache boots with typical southern band beading, (c) Inuit waterproof sealskin boots ornamented through use of different colors of leather, and (d) waterproofed sealskin Inuit boot.

However, the widespread use of the soft-soled moccasin in other parts of North America may relate to the use of snowshoes, for the soft sole, made of a single piece of buckskin, was easily used with snowshoes. Furthermore, although it was used beyond snowshoe areas, the moccasin's distribution corresponds closely with that of snowshoes in North America (Driver, 1969, p. 151). Bock cites the snowshoe as one of the most outstanding examples of adaptive footgear (1969, pp. 255–257), as shown in Figure 6.9. Historically it freed humans from winter isolation that severely limited communication and procuring of food: on snowshoes, a person could walk on soft snow without sinking in because the focused pressure of body weight over the foot was distributed over the broad surface of the snowshoe. Snowshoes reached their highest development in North America. In Asian and European societies, more attention was given to the development of skis, which provided greater speed with less effort (Birket-Smith, 1965, pp. 215–216).

Comparison of the culture and dress of the Saami and the Inuit, two societies inhabiting the Arctic Circle, is instructive for understanding cultural differences and dress. Environment may place demands on dress for the protection of the human body but cultural solutions can be very different. The Inuit

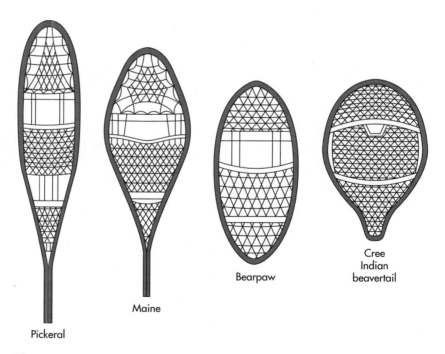

Pickeral

Maine

Bearpaw

Cree
Indian
beavertail

Figure 6.9
The snowshoe is an outstanding example of adaptive footwear. On snowshoes, a person can walk over soft snow without sinking in, facilitating faster travel on foot in winter.

historically relied on hunting for food and exclusively used animal skins for dress materials, whereas the Saami herded reindeer for a living and largely dressed themselves in fiber textiles. The protection of feet from cold and damp is very crucial in the extreme cold of their home areas, and both groups made use of animal skin for the outer layer, but used very different devices for heat insulation and keeping feet dry.

The reindeer skin shoes of the Saami packed with sedge grass provide an outstanding example of insulative footwear. Milan (1960) reports the serious attention that Saami individuals give to their foot enclosures, for he says they (the Saami)

> . . . neglect morning ablutions. . . . but devote 20 minutes to dressing the feet. First, a pair of woolen socks are put on. A roll of sedge grass is then spread out on a reindeer skin and softened by wrinkling and twisting in the hands. If the grass was used the previous day and has passed the night stuffed in the shoe, it is thoroughly dried in the warmth of the fire. A rectangular pad of grass is wrapped around the clenched fist and inserted into the shoe. It must be of the same thickness on all sides. The foot is then placed in the shoe, and by wriggling and twisting and stuffing more grass down inside the shoe, a grass sock is gradually built up. The hem of the pants is then placed outside the shoe and the plaited lace, which is perhaps three feet long is wound around the leg and secured. A Lapp (Saami) will ski hard all day and by evening the grass sock is quite damp through perspiration. His feet remain warm even while resting for long periods in cold weather. (p. 12)

The Inuit development of cut-and-sewn animal skin foot enclosures exemplifies a different approach. These alternative methods of dressing the body to adapt to extreme cold show how different societies develop unique cultural responses to solve the same problem. Oakes and Riewe (1995) describe the Inuit solution:

> Footwear consists of a combination of skin stockings, slippers, and boots made of different skins in various styles. The number and type of these layers . . . vary according to the weather, terrain, activity, and cultural group. The skins most often used to make boots are seal and caribou. Seal skin is water-resistant, making it ideal for boots worn in wet conditions. Seal skin boots vary in height from mid-calf to thigh-high and even chest-high for wading. . . . Caribou skin has thick hair which provides excellent insulation against the extreme winter cold. Footwear is made either from the caribou's body skin or leg skins. For spring and fall wear, when conditions are damp, caribou skin boots are made with seal skin soles.
>
> Feet are a difficult part of the body to keep warm and dry in the Arctic winter, due to factors such as perspiration, condensation, and wet conditions. Most hunters prefer waterproof kamiks [skin boots] rather than mass-produced rubberized or plasticized footwear, because waterproof skin boots do not build up condensation. Animal skin is porous and allows body vapors to escape, reducing the amount of moisture collected inside boots. . . . (p. 20)

Using gloves is one of the simplest ways to extend the body's mechanical capabilities. An individual's hands are excellent tools in themselves, but gloves give them protection against heat, cold, abrasion, and chemicals, thus allowing them to function under very adverse environmental conditions. Firefighters, who face high temperature from flame, can extend their mobility with fire-proof, reflective enclosures, including gloves.

The football uniform—garment, helmet, mouth guard, and shoulder pads—is an example of protective clothing that helps a player to exert and withstand force and minimize bodily injury. Similar sport examples include clothing and equipment designed for hockey, biking, and in-line skating. As women in North America have begun to participate in contact sports, such as hockey and football, protective body supplements have been developed for them that parallel items of dress for men, as seen in Figure 6.10.

Sometimes unique devices may extend body force. Navy researchers, for example, have explored the concept of a body supplement that acts as an ex-oskeleton, amplifying muscular effort and increasing ability to do heavy work by providing additional support to the grasping power of the hands and the leverage of knee, elbow, and other joints ("Man Amplifier," 1964, p. 47). The

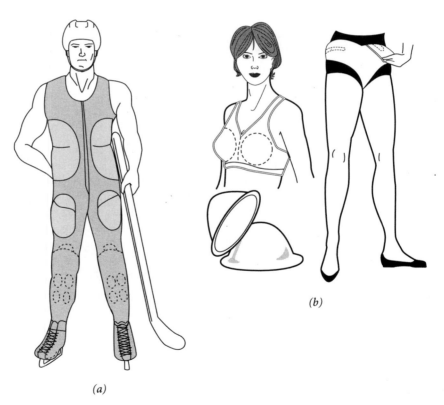

(a)

(b)

Figure 6.10
Protective clothing developed for contact sports incorporates rigid shielding devices and soft pads that are held in place against areas of the body vulnerable to injury. (a) Men's hockey protective wear; (b) Fem-Gard® breast protector and Hip-Guard® protector for women.

design principles developed for this unusual body supplement are now commonly incorporated into athletic braces to allow amateur sports players with knee joints prone to dislocation to continue to play. Artificial hands and other prosthetic devices that replace a missing body part are other unique extensions that enhance physical power and mechanical skills. Artificial teeth may be placed in the same category.

DRESS THAT INTERVENES BETWEEN BODY AND CLIMATE

Although we can survive in tropical and subtropical areas without cultural aids, we usually can be made more comfortable with inventions such as clothing and shelter. In regions with constant severe cold, or periods of cold, we must have protective aids. Often the design of body supplements, usually clothing, compromises between temperature regulation and other kinds of environmental control, since clothes must sometimes serve several protective functions at once. Thus, the enveloping robes of the nomads of the Sahara Desert not only protect against the sun's radiation but also against blowing sand. The cowboy boot protects against both rough terrain and snakebite. Other needs that may demand compromise are those of protection from dampness and from insects. Modesty requirements and desire for "attractiveness" in dress produce further compromise.

To simplify evaluations of clothing in relation to climate, Siple (1968) has proposed **clothing zones** of the world, according to layers of clothing typically required. His classification is as follows:

1. The minimum clothing zone, or the humid tropical and jungle type
2. The hot dry clothing zone, or desert type
3. The one-layer clothing zone, or subtropical or optimum comfort type
4. The two-layer clothing zone, or the temperate cool winter type
5. The three-layer clothing zone, or the temperate cold winter type
6. The four-layer maximum clothing zone, or subarctic winter type
7. The activity balance zone, or the arctic winter type (p. 389)

A layer approach to dress, compatible with Siple's delineation, has been utilized by the U.S. military services in development of a fit-together "global uniform" concept. Thus the armed services have attempted to provide "basic units for the temperate zone to which items could be added for the colder, or subtracted for the warmer, zones so that tropical gear could be close to U.S. summer equipment, and polar gear added to the U.S. winter uniform" (Fourt & Hollies, 1970, p. 23). Retailers and manufacturers such as Land's End (see Figure 6.11) have designed outdoor wear for consumers that follows a similar impetus. In the section that follows are examples of kinds of clothing adaptations in areas of the world located in different climatic zones.

In the minimum clothing zone of the tropics, dress is not designed for thermal protection. However, protection from the sun for skin and eyes, and

Figure 6.11
Some U.S. manufacturers of outdoor clothing use the concept of modifiable and layerable clothing to design garments that are adaptable to the range of climate conditions experienced through the four seasons of the temperate zone. These raincoats have button-out wool linings. How does this strategy for dress exemplify the clothing zone theory of Siple?

protection from pathogenic organisms, thorns, and insects, is likely to be related to the use of clothing. Otherwise, body enclosure is a matter of fashion and custom. Some kind of lightweight, loose garment of absorbent material, shading head gear that provides air space between hat and head, and perhaps sandals to protect the soles of the feet are probably adequate for protective purposes in the tropics.

In hot dry clothing zones, adaptations are made to strong radiation from the sun and sharp differences in day and night temperatures. Desert nomads of North Africa have worn long loose tunics of cotton or wool and added thicker wool or mohair robes that cover arms and legs. These tent-like garments allow evaporation of sweat, which is facilitated by the air currents created by walking. Solar heat can be absorbed on the surface of the garments at a distance from the body.

The !Kung of the Kalahari Desert of southern Africa have utilized a temporary body modification rather than enclosing body supplements or woven fabrics, as do the Tuareg and so many other desert peoples, in adapting to desert conditions. They appear to be partially acclimated to the daytime heat; however, scientists have not been able to determine if they have any particular physical adaptation to the nighttime cold. What is more certain is that the !Kung have developed certain unique cultural aids to help them survive and be comfortable. At night !Kung individuals curl up in skin cloaks, which they tuck in around both head and trunk, then place their feet, face, or back to the fire, and use the temporary huts they construct at each habitation site as a wind-break.

The temporary body modifications employed by the !Kung consist of temporary changes made to the surface of the skin with a set of seasonally changing treatments with various substances. The individual coats the skin "with plant juices and fats and, when obtainable, animal fat or blood, and accumulates a fine layer of Kalahari sand on the surface" (Tobias, 1968, p. 205). This "protective mail" assists adjustment to hot conditions by protection from undue absorption of solar radiation and from the desiccating effects of hot, dry winds. During the winter, an ointment made from tsama melons is smeared over the body and vigorously rubbed into the skin. "In the very dry atmosphere of the Kalahari in winter time this treatment has about the same beneficial effect as the application of cold cream to the exposed skin surfaces of the European" (Tobias, 1968, p. 205).

In the one-layer or subtropical clothing zone, climate places no great demand or restriction on dress. Thermal protection is needed for only the trunk region of the body and hands and feet require no special cover. Thus in north central Europe in the summertime, Florida in the winter, Canada in the summer, and most of the United States in the spring and fall, a single layer of clothing is sufficient to provide comfort and a wide range of materials can be used. Siple (1968, p. 403) considers this the optimum comfort zone and hypothesizes that fashion provides the details for the difference and thumbing through fashion magazines gives us the opportunity to decide if he is correct in his assessment of fashion.

The two-layer or temperate cool clothing zone frequently is humid and has occasional wet snowfalls. Southern Alaska, British Columbia, the northwest coast of the United States, and the west coast of Ireland are examples of areas that have this type of temperate, cool climate with considerable rain. Clothing must keep off rain as well as insulate against heat loss. Indians of the coastal areas of the Pacific Northwest had protective wear especially suitable for a temperate rainy climate and their activities. Their basketry hats, worn for rain and sun, were waterproof but also served to protect them from the glare of sunlit water while canoeing or fishing. Flared rain capes of shredded red-cedar bark—made to hang to just below the elbow—repelled water at the same time that they allowed arm movement for paddling canoes or engaging in other activities. Neck bands of fur prevented the harsh bark fiber from irritating the skin around the neck (Bock, 1969, pp. 438–439).

In the winter much of Europe, Asia, and Africa fall into the three- and four-layer cold-temperate and sub-Arctic clothing zones, as do Arctic and Antarctic regions in the summer. Except for some very high altitude regions, this zone is virtually absent in South America, Africa, Australia, and New Zealand.

Effective clothing for protection against cold in a sub-Arctic area must have a high insulative value when people are inactive, but a design that will allow dissipation of body heat when they are active. Otherwise the body will become heated, sweating will occur, and an accumulation of unevaporated sweat will cause chilling. Siple (1968) elaborates on problems involved in learning to use one's clothing in extreme cold as follows:

> Individuals who are exposed to low temperatures at a degree of activity insufficient to produce comfortable thermo-balance must learn a multitude of techniques which may increase the potential value of their protective clothing many times. In the first place, the body must become acclimatized so that it conserves heat to the maximum extent. Next, it is necessary that the garments are so fitted that there is the art of ventilating to avoid sweating, and in tightening closures to control too rapid loss of body heat. Each individual has to learn through experience how to perform these tasks.
>
> No amount of reading will ever make a sourdough out of a tenderfoot upon first exposure to cold. The greenhorn in regions of extreme cold is apt to suffer unmercifully, whereas the experienced person has not only learned to tolerate the cold but is efficiently making adjustments after he has started to sweat. The sourdough never reaches the point of sweating if he can avoid it. The tenderfoot who has opened his clothing or taken off a garment rarely buttons up again until he is beginning to shiver. He seems to want to impress himself or others with the appearance of being 'tough enough to take it.' The sourdough puts his clothing on and closes up before he begins to get chilled, and he stays warmer much longer. (pp. 438–439)

The general solution for what to wear in a very cold climate is, therefore, to find a lightweight material that will not load the wearer down, a way of trapping insulative dead air spaces between loose-fitting layers of clothing, and a design that can be opened up easily for releasing warm, moist air that may accumulate around the body during activity (Kennedy & Vanderlie, 1964, p. 137). Materials that breathe to allow perspiration to evaporate through the garment while protecting the body from wind and retaining heat are even better. In recent years, textile scientists have begun to create materials that can replicate the ability of animal furs, used by the Inuit, to do this.

The Inuit solution to cold has been to wear loosely fitting tailored garments of animal skins, most commonly caribou and seal, sometimes polar bear, and fox (Newburgh, 1949, pp. 9–10). Some Inuit groups also make tailored body supplements out of bird skins with the thick down and feathers intact (Oakes, 1991). A belt, worn over shirt and undershirt, which hang outside trousers, may be used to control temperature. By loosening this belt, throwing back the parka hood, and taking off mittens or a layer of garments, an Inuit can cool off. To keep warm when not moving, arms are taken out of their sleeves and put close to the body. Sweat control is very important because wet garments lose their insulative value. Therefore, garments are often taken off inside and must be carefully dried if they become wet. In North America, the development of Gore-Tex offers a similar solution through textile technology. Molecules of moisture can pass from the body through the membrane outwards, but rainwater molecules from the outside cannot pass through to the inside and saturate the body.

While the protective dress described for the Inuit was worn on a daily basis for centuries, in many parts of the world today our climate-controlled architecture provides the protection we need for most of our activities, and protective garments are reserved for sports activities and certain work activities. Technological advances in protective dress, however, often affect fashion in very large, complex societies. Dress for sports activities, for instance, have been incorporated into streetwear, as the sports garments have gained a popularity that extends beyond their limited use during sports activities. Polartech synthetic fleece garments, for example, were developed to provide thermal protection and the ability to keep a person dry from perspiration flowing during periods of high physical exertion, while remaining light in weight. The style of garments designed in this material are now worn as part of casual ensembles.

In the activity balance zone, no increase beyond four layers of garments is effective for protection; extra garments beyond this become too bulky for wear. Thus, explorers in the Arctic and Antarctic have followed the examples of what to wear in sub-Arctic weather and have utilized technological advances in materials as they have seemed appropriate. Instead of extra clothing, other types of protective measures need be taken. Activity that keeps the body's metabolic rate high enough to keep the body warm is required for survival outdoors. Figure 6.12 gives an idea of the relative size of the covering needed to protect the hands in various degrees of activity and inactivity. When covering is too thick it hampers the ability to move, thus requiring the necessity of activity balance and nutrition to keep warm.

Another possible solution is an auxiliary heating system, especially for hands and feet, which are very difficult to keep warm in extreme cold. Examples of auxiliary heating system are the hand and boot warmers and electric socks used by hunters. Otherwise, shelter and an efficient diet high in fats and carbohydrates will be required.

DRESS AS TOTAL ENVIRONMENT

Diving suits are one of the oldest types of dress that provide a total environment for the individual who is facing a hazardous environment, unsupportive of human life. More recently, some ventilated protective suits have been produced for workers needing protection against radiation, noxious gases, and dangerous chemicals.

The space suit, see Figure 6.13, is the most complicated dress that we have yet invented as a total environment. Suits for various space trips have varied; however, they all have provided ways to sustain body functions while allowing body mobility (Johnston, Carreale, & Radnofsky, 1966). They have included systems for removing metabolic heat, carbon dioxide, water vapor, urine, and fecal matter and for providing oxygen and external (gaseous) pressure. Helmets are designed to allow vision but keep out harmful radiation. The layers of the suit, including flameproof woven fabrics and aluminized plastic films, protect from meteoroids as well as the extreme heat and cold of space. The suits

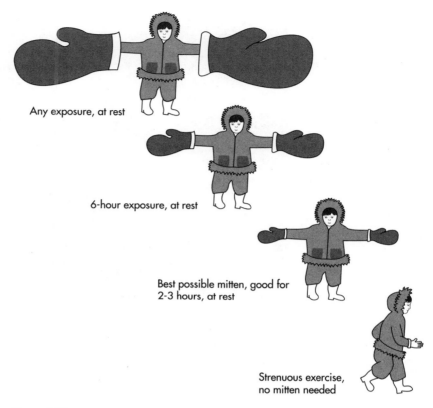

Any exposure, at rest

6-hour exposure, at rest

Best possible mitten, good for
2-3 hours, at rest

Strenuous exercise,
no mitten needed

Figure 6.12
The relative size of mittens needed for different exposure times at +20°F exemplify
the activity balance zone.

have integral bio-instrumentation systems that allow space control stations to keep constant check on blood pressure, heart action, body temperature, and respiratory rate. Microphones and headsets for interspace communication are also part of regular equipment. Because the void of space is not supportive to human life, yet offers so many opportunities for technological development, the U.S. National Aeronautics and Space Administration (NASA) continues to test garments that are lightweight and warm and allow astronauts to work with their hands. Features of dress for space were incorporated into streetwear around the time of the first major advances of the space program in the United States, and have continued to have an impact, particularly in the adoption of technology used in fabrics as well as in fasteners, such as Velcro.

Another example of dress that provides an almost total environment is the biohazard suit. Its design is based on the suit developed by NASA for work in outer space, but with the purpose of protecting the individual from harmful biological agents, such as viruses that are often airborne. The suit includes a

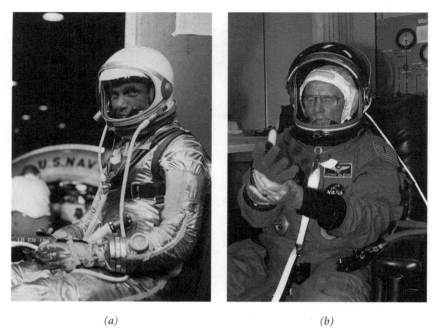

(a)   (b)

Figure 6.13
Technological improvements in space suits over time have not altered the fact that
each such body supplement functions as a controlled mini-environment. A space suit
enables its wearer to enter into the hostile environment of outer space. (a) Astronaut
John Glenn in 1964. (b) Senator John Glenn in 1998.

helmet, an oxygen supply, layers of fabric specially designed to prevent airborne pathogens from passing into the suit, and a system to create negative air
pressure. In other words, the suit has an air pressure higher than the outside
environment, which prevents airborne pathogens from entering the suit
through seams and joints in the suit. The biohazard suit is used by people
working for hospitals and for agencies such as the Centers for Disease Control,
in its laboratories and in global emergencies, such as the Ebola virus outbreak
in Zaire.

Dress for outer space creates a complete mini-environment, but this is dependent upon a supporting architectural or vehicular environment, such as the
space station or spaceship that also protects the body in outer space. Just as
dress on earth relates to the other cultural constructions, which shelter us, so
this is true in outer space. The interface between the design of shoes and the
floor allows astronauts to remain firmly attached to the floor when living or
traveling in outer space.

SUMMARY

Our adaptation to various natural environments depends to some extent on short-term adaptations to environment that our bodies can make and on genetic types of adaptation evolving through many generations. To a much larger extent, our adaptation depends on the cultural aids we can devise to supplement our basic biological equipment and to intervene between body and environment. Dress is one of the most universally used types of cultural aids or tools.

Dress can affect motor skills of individuals as well as protect them. The need for clothing as a protection against climate depends on seasonal changes as well as geographical area. In extreme cold, clothing may serve as insulative protection only if not seriously hindering body movement. For example, when clothing required for protection becomes so bulky as to prevent mobility or cause a build up of excessive heat or perspiration, other protective devices must be introduced. The space suit is an example of a type of clothing that is a portable life-support control system, providing for all needs except food and water.

STUDY TOOLS

Important Terms

acclimatization
clothing zones
cultural adaptation
genetic adaptation
habituation
physiological adaptation

Discussion Questions

1. Describe different ways the human body adjusts to changes in the physical environment. Trace this back to human biological origins.
2. Discuss dress as a cultural tool that extends human capabilities and allows humans to do more than their bodies alone could do. Give examples.
3. Which of Siple's clothing zones do you live in? How does the season or altitude affect your decision?
4. A set of snow skis and a biohazard suit are both dress that extends human capabilities. How do they accomplish this? How are they different?
5. Since dress acts as an intermediary between the human physical body and the environment in which an individual lives, the type of dress is manipulated to suit both the human's body and the environment. Select one example of both a body modification and a body supplement and analyze

for each what aspects of the dress relate to (a) the physical character or needs of the body, and (b) the demands of the physical environment.

6. How does the use of dress merely provide minimum basic requirements for comfort or survival or extend human physical abilities? Give examples for each from your own dress and from the dress of one other culture.

7. Using Reading II.2, "Innerskins/Outerskins: Gut and Fishskin," by Hickman, explain how dress can provide both physical and spiritual protection. Discuss the physical, cultural, and social needs served by Inuit fishgut rainwear.

8. Compare the Inuit fishgut coat, which is made for protection from water, as described in Reading II.2, with a garment that you wear for protection in wet weather. How does the performance of these two garments compare? How do the range of Inuits' use and your use of the respective garments compare? How do you explain the differences?

9. Consider the interplay between dress and the human-made environment in your area of the world. How does the creation of contemporary cities—with residential and work buildings, paved streets and sidewalks, sewage and storm sewers, and recreational parks and facilities—affect the social and cultural development of your dress? Think about this issue by imagining how your dress would have to change for you to thrive in an area with dirt footpaths and roads, brooks that overflow their banks in spring, and areas filled with bushes and bricks rather than lawns.

10. Imagine living in the same geographic area in which you now live but without climate control, for example, electric fans, air conditioning and heating systems, humidifiers, and dehumidifiers. Analyze and discuss how your dress would have to be altered or wardrobe expanded in order to live comfortably.

Activities

1. Bring an article of protective dress to class (e.g., a cycle helmet, surgical garb, rock climbing harness, chain saw chaps, face mask, oven mitt). Explain to the class how they are used. Speculate which materials, individually or in combination, provide the protection. Note how protective clothing is an ubiquitous part of daily life. Discuss in class whether these items are strictly functional or whether the manufacturer included aesthetic elements in their design.

2. Bring a pair of warm winter gloves or heavy work gloves to class. Don them and wear them throughout class. Take notes, zip your book bag, open a can of soda, write a note, unscrew a bolt, button a button, thread a shoelace. Consider the challenge of astronauts or biohazard technicians as they accomplish their tasks while similarly encumbered. Discuss how these gloves could be improved to facilitate body movement and function.

3. Visit a retail store specializing in sports equipment, construction, or medical supplies. List and briefly describe articles of dress designed to protect the body. What parts of the body seem to need protection more than others?

4. Find a current photograph of yourself and compare it with photographs of your predecessors—parents, grandparents, great-grandparents—at a similar age to your own. Go back as many generations as you can. From your own observations and from family oral history about the lives of these different generations, try to analyze the differences and similarities you see between your own physical appearance and body type and those of preceding generations. Use the concepts from the chapter to organize your analysis of physical appearance.

5. Wear three layers of clothing to class and keep then on through half of the class, then take off two layers half way through the class. Keep a record of the time when you feel uncomfortable (too hot or too cold) and when you find that your body has adjusted to the amount of clothing worn. At the end of the class, discuss as a group whether or not your body ever reached a state of comfort, and if so, how long it took to become comfortable after the change in clothing layers was made.

6. Make a list of 10 ability-enhancing or body-enhancing body supplements that you do not use. Look to sports and work environments and to the dress of the opposite gender for such items of dress (e.g., shin guards, bullet proof vests, skis, hard hats, hair spray, press-on nails, spike-heels). Think of and list activities in your usual weekly round of activities that might be made easier if you wore these supplements. Also imagine new, unconventional activities that these supplements would enable you to engage in.

7. Make a list of the various body movements that your think would be required of an Inuit fisherman wearing a fishgut coat. Then put on your usual rainwear and do these same movements for five minutes under a shower. Report on the success or failure of your rainwear to keep you dry. Analyze the different natural and human-made physical environment limitations that rainwear must address for the Inuit and for your own situation. How do the differences in environmental and activity requirements account for differences in the design of the two types of rainwear?

Notes to Chapter 6

1. Sometimes dress is purposely designed to hinder body movement, as in straitjackets, handcuffs, leg irons, and neck irons. In other cases dress is designed with only those movements in mind that will be required at the event to which the individual will wear the dress. Some cocktail dresses, for instance, are designed to be worn while standing without ease in the dress for the wearer to sit down without greatly stressing the fabric and destroying the design.

2. Saami is the name that the people, formerly called Lapps by outsiders, call themselves. Lapp has a derogatory connotation.

II.1 PRESSURE OF MENSWEAR ON THE NECK IN RELATION TO VISUAL PERFORMANCE
Leonora M. Langan and Susan M. Watkins

This study examined the incidence of neckwear tightness among a group of 94 white-collar working men and the effect of a tight business-shirt collar and tie on the visual performance of 22 male subjects. Of the white-collar working men measured, 67% were found to be wearing neckwear that was tighter than their neck circumference. The visual discrimination of the 22 subjects was evaluated using a critical flicker frequency (CFF) test. Results of the CFF test indicated that tight neckwear significantly decreased the visual performance of the subjects and that visual performance did not improve immediately when tight neckwear was removed.

Introduction

People have complained about the discomfort of tight clothing for centuries. From Chinese bound feet to the wasp waist of the 19th-century woman to the tight jeans and pantyhose of the present day, clothing has often been a means to force the body into a shape more closely conforming with current fashion. Although much has been said about the discomfort caused by the pressure that tight clothing places on the body, there has been little work done to link clothing pressure directly to physiological changes.

Despite complaints about discomfort, the dress shirt and tie have remained the standard uniform of men in the business world and a variety of other service and professional occupations. A number of authors have commented on indications that the pressure felt by men wearing shirts and ties is accompanied by major, immediate physiological changes. Morrow (1978, p. 80) states that "the shirt and tie are pressing against the carotid arteries of the neck, impeding blood flow to the brain." Renbourn (1972, p. 386) states that "fainting attacks are occasionally due to a sensitive carotid sinus (at the termination of the common carotid artery), pressure on which by . . . a tight collar may produce a reflex slowing

of the pulse and of fall in blood pressure." Lutz (1981, p. 326), proposing that this area needs formal investigation, suggests that tight neckwear "may produce compressive atherosclerotic angiopathy of the carotid arteries."

These statements point to blood flow restriction as a major factor in physiological changes due to neckwear pressure. If the blood flow pattern through the carotid arteries in the neck into the head is examined, one can see the potential for restriction of blood flow in the neck to affect the brain and the sensory organs. One of the first branches of the internal carotid artery, the op[h]thalmic artery, leads to the retina. The potential vision problems resulting from lack of blood supply to the eye range from a transient loss of vision due to minor retinal ischemia to the more serious problem of permanent visual damage resulting from extensive retinal ischemia and subsequent optic-nerve atrophy (Clendenin and Conrad, 1979; Hobbs, 1965). The direct relationship between blood flow in the neck and blood flow to the eye is borne out by procedures in op[h]thalmological examinations as well as in standard blood-flow diagnostic tests. For example, an ophthalmologist looks for a loss of venous pulsations that can be observed in the retina as a classic sign of carotid-artery disease. Several standard blood-flow diagnostic tests such as ocular plethysmography, supra-orbital photoplethysmography, and ophthalmodynamometry study blood pressure in the eye in order to examine blood flow through the carotid artery in the neck.

We explored the potential for tight neckwear to affect blood flow to the eye with an ophthalmologist who observed the retinal vein of a single subject using a standard, hand-held ophthalmoscope, while the tightness of a shirt collar band was increased. The subject controlled the tightening process and was asked to tighten the band only to the point that he deemed to be equal to the tightest collar he would wear. The tightness of the collar band was increased every few seconds, and the ophthalmologist observed the retinal pulsing after each tightening movement. As soon as the ophthalmologist observed cessation of the retinal pulse, the subject released the band

and retinal pulsing returned immediately. The entire procedure took less than 30 seconds. For this subject, pulsing of the retinal vein was observed to cease completely when the collar band was tightened to 1.27 cm less than the subject's unrestricted neck measurement. This indicated cessation of blood flow to the retina and the potential, over the long range, for eye damage.

Preliminary Test

In order to determine the significance of these observations, we conducted a pretest to determine whether white-collar working men wore neckwear that was tight in relation to their neck size, and, if so, how tightly it was worn.

Ninety-four white-collar working men from law offices and business firms were tested: Only company officials were notified of the test. The subjects were given no advance warning about the test, so that they would be wearing their everyday work clothing. All the subjects tested were wearing their collars buttoned and their ties secured when they were asked, at that moment, to participate in the study.

For the purposes of the pretest, neckwear was defined as "tight" if the subject's neck measured less when his shirt was buttoned and his tie knotted than it did when his neck was unrestricted. A stiffened but flexible, non-stretch measuring tape 0.64 cm wide was used to measure each man's neck. Each subject began with his dress shirt buttoned and tie knotted. The flat tape was fit between the neck and the collar just under its top edge. A coded mark was made on the stay where it overlapped to indicate the neck circumference for this measurement. The subject then loosened his tie, the tape was allowed to expand, if necessary, and a second coded mark was made on the tape. Then, the shirt was unbuttoned, the tie removed, and the tape—still lying on the original line, just below where the top edge of the collar had been—was released and marked again.

Subjects were also asked to provide additional information to help determine whether specific factors such as height/weight ratio, age range, purchaser of the shirt worn, fiber content, and length of time the shirt had been worn contributed to the incidence of tight neckwear.

The results of the pretest showed that 67% of the men tested wore tight neckwear. The average tightness was 0.48 cm, with the average portion of that due to the tie being 0.32 cm. Twelve percent of the subjects had greater than 1.27 cm of tightness. None of the factors projected to explain the reasons for tight neckwear proved to be significant influences. The fact that such a large percentage of the men tested were wearing tight neckwear convinced us that further testing on visual discrimination was merited.

Visual Discrimination Test

Subjects

Twenty-two male subjects ranging in age from 20 to the mid-60s volunteered to participate in the study. Each subject was asked to bring a tie and to wear the dress shirt that had the tightest collar he owned.

Test Method

The critical flicker frequency (known also as the critical flicker fusion or CFF test) was used to measure changes in visual discrimination (Armington, Krauskopf, and Wooten, 1978). This test measures the rapidity of a subject's visual response to the changing frequencies of a blinking light. Subjects were tested in both an ascending order (responding when the blinks were so rapid that they were perceived as a solid light) and a descending order (responding when the flicker rate slowed to a point at which the solid light appeared to be blinking again). Since the CFF test measures the timing aspects of visual performance, it is a much more sensitive test for retinal function than is a visual acuity test (E. Miller, personal communication, 1984).

Apparatus

The CFF equipment consisted of a lamp box that was secured in place on a table in front of the subject; a control box, with which the test could be started and stopped, and controlled in brightness, frequency, and slope (rate of frequency change); a subject response box; and a frequency converter with a digital read-out. The equipment was situated in a room with no windows. A floor lamp with a 40-watt bulb covered by a lamp shade was used, producing a room luminance of approximately 0.75 dekalux.

Procedure

The subjects were first given an eye examination by a licensed ophthalmologist and were checked for signs of carotid artery disease. Then, they were measured as in the preliminary test to determine the amount of collar and tie tightness for each subject.

Each subject then entered the CFF testing room and was seated in a straight-backed chair in front of the table on which the test equipment was located. The chair was situated so that in no case did a subject's eyes move farther than 84 cm from the lamp.

Each subject participated in three repetitions of three basic CFF tests, for a total of nine tests. For the first set of repetitions, the subject left his tie loosened and his shirt collar unbuttoned. For the second set of repetitions, the subject was asked to button his shirt collar and secure his tie in place. For the third set of repetitions, the subject was asked to loosen his tie and unbutton his shirt collar again.

For each test, the subject was told to look at a pencil mark on the table, which was 2.54 cm in front of the lamp light, and to press the response button the instant he saw the light become solid and non-flickering. The flicker frequency was recorded in Hz at the moment the subject pressed the response button. The equipment was then reset in a decreasing frequency mode, and the subject was asked to press the response button again when the solid light again appeared to flicker. These two increasing and decreasing frequency values were then averaged and counted as one test. Each of the remaining eight tests followed immediately after one another, with only an approximately 30-s[ec] interval needed to adjust the shirt button and tie between each of the sets of three repetitions.

A control test was also performed with 10 additional subjects. These subjects went through the regimen of nine tests, all with no collar or tie tightness. This control test was performed so that we could look at any possible effects of visual fatigue due to the test, or any visual improvement that might be due to response anticipation.

Results

Descriptive statistics for both the experimental and control groups are given in Table 1. A 2 × 3 mixed-model univariate analysis of variance was used to analyze the effect of set for each group. Each set value that was used for this analysis was the mean frequency of the three tests given to each subject under a particular test condition. The results of this ANOVA are given in Table 2. The results indicate that there was a significant decrease in CFF values between Set 1 (with no neckwear pressure) and Set 2 (with neckwear pressure) for the experimental group as compared with the control group. There was no significant difference in CFF values between Set 2 and Set 3 (after neckwear pressure was removed) for the two groups.

Conclusions

This study yielded several significant conclusions:
(1) Tight neckwear can decrease a man's visual performance as measured by the CFF test.
(2) Visual performance does not return to normal immediately after tight neckwear is removed.
(3) A large percentage of the subjects we tested (67%) wore tight neckwear.

We found it interesting that the average amount of tie tightness alone was approximately two-thirds of the total neckwear pressure. This finding points to the tie rather than the shirt as the major factor in neckwear pressure.

The implications this research holds for the relationship between visual performance and neckwear tightness could affect working men, such as computer operators, and others in a variety of fields where precise vision is important to the work. It could also provide critical information for bus drivers, pilots, and others whose vision is important for public safety.

Although this study focused on visual impairment, its findings, which link blood-flow restriction to changes in physiological function, hold implications for a variety of other sensory and cognitive functions.

TABLE 1

Means and Standard Deviations by Group and Test Conditions (in Hertz)

Test Condition	Experimental Group (N = 22)		Control Group (N = 10)	
	Mean (Hz)	S.D. (Hz)	Mean (Hz)	S.D. (Hz)
Set 1 (no neckwear pressure)	20.406	1.581	21.810	1.404
Set 2 (neckwear pressure)	19.571	1.415	21.696	1.445
Set 3 (pressure removed)	19.616	1.446	21.564	1.544

TABLE 2

ANOVA Values for All Subjects

Source	SS	df	MS	F
Group	68.72	1	68.72	11.63**
Error	177.32	30	5.91	—
Set	4.54	2	2.27	7.12**
Set 1—Set 2	3.10	1	3.10	8.64**
Error	10.73	30	0.36	—
Set 2—Set 3	0.03	1	0.03	0.09
Error	9.11	30	0.30	—
Groups × Sets	1.94	2	0.97	5.05*
Set 1—Set 2	1.79	1	1.79	4.99*
Error	10.74	30	0.36	—
Set 2—Set 3	0.11	1	0.11	0.35
Error	9.11	30	0.30	—
Within cells error	19.12	60	0.32	—

*$p < 0.05$
**$p < 0.01$

Acknowledgments

The authors would like to thank Elizabeth Miller and Richard Leavitt, ophthalmologists who contributed generously to this study. This project was supported, in part, by a grant from the special projects fund of the New York State College of Human Ecology, Cornell University, Ithaca, New York.

References

Armington, J. C., Krauskopf, J., & Wooten, B. R. (Eds.). (1978). *Visual Psychophysics and Physiology*. New York: Academic Press.

Clendenin, M. A., & Conrad, M. C. (1979). Collateral vessel development following unilateral chronic carotid occlusion in the dog. *American Journal of Veterinary Research, 40*, 87–88.

Hobbs, H. E. (1965). *Principles of ophthalmology*. New York, Elsevier.

Lutz, E. G. (1981). Tight neckwear and atherosclerotic carotid artery disease. *Journal of Clinical Psychiatry, 42*, 326.

Morrow, L. (1978, July). The odd practice of neck binding. *Time, 112*(4), 80.

Renbourn, E. T. (1972). *Materials and clothing in health and disease*. London: H. K. Lewis.

II.2 INNERSKINS/OUTERSKINS: GUT AND FISHSKIN
Pat Hickman

Looking at what cultures create, especially their textiles and clothing, is an intimate way to begin to know another people. Gut and fishskin textiles and clothing, the historic reference and inspiration for this exhibit, are not complex, structural puzzles to be analyzed. They are part of something larger, a system of belief, a unification—a hunter wearing a gut parka when hunting seal, a fisherman wearing protective clothing when catching salmon. A cycle, a wholeness and completeness exist—integrally linked to the world of the spirits. The clothing is physical and spiritual protection, made from what was available, essential to a particular way of life.

In Alaska, that vast, quiet white land, necessity served as motivation. Life was about survival. Survival clothing. Survival tools. Nothing was wasted or tossed aside as useless.

I saw my first gut parka ten years ago in a museum exhibit. I remember the stunning visual beauty, the sensation that light was coming from within. I was astounded by the idea, by the totally unexpected possibility

Figure II.2.1
Holding skins. Photograph from the San Francisco Craft and Folk Art Museum.

of someone using gut—intestines or other soft digestive organs—as a clothlike material. That overwhelming aesthetic response was the beginning of an exploration. The surprise, now, is that that initial response remains a fresh one. I still feel wonder along with a deeper understanding and appreciation.

Over the years I have studied several museum collections and the literature that mentions gut and fishskin, mostly in passing. Early ethnographers' and travelers' accounts and missionaries' and anthropologists' observations are invaluable. But in this exhibition catalogue, there are other voices I wanted to hear. I wanted the viewpoint of a native person working today in Alaska and invited Rita Pitka Blumenstein to talk directly about her own experience. John Burns answers questions from his perspective as a specialist on marine mammals. And Alice

Hoveman, a conservator, shares her understanding of the uniqueness of these materials and her concern for extending their natural life.

In most of the world, intestines and fishskins have been regarded as throwaways. There are a few, select exceptions—examples of early Ainu fishskin garments in northern Japan or fishskin clothing along the Amur River region in Russia, made and worn by the Gilyak and Goldi peoples. The *San Francisco Chronicle* reported a recent find in England: "Archeologists have discovered five condoms made of fish and animal intestines at historic Dudley Castle near Birmingham, leading them to conclude that English soldiers as far back as the 1640s took precautions against venereal disease."[1] In the words of poet Adrienne Rich, I am reminded that "History is more than the tales of our finest hours. It isn't just spoken words, verbal tradition either. Some representation of it is always being made."[2]

What attention has been paid to the clothing or textile tradition in Alaska has focused primarily on the extraordinary use of furs—striking, visually dramatic, beautiful. Economic interest in furs as a valuable commodity has assured them some historic reference. This exhibition focuses on gut and fishskin and their connectedness to a way of life in Alaska, which deserve a place in history.

Gut

Brittle archeological gut fragments from Aleut burial remains in Alaska are visible reminders of an earlier use in a previous life and time.[3] Some of the finest 18th-century Alaskan examples of gut and fishskin parkas exist in European museum collections, primarily in England, West Germany, Russia, Finland, and Denmark. In addition to two gut garments brought back from Captain James Cook's third voyage, there is artist John Webber's 1784 sketch documenting the native wearing of such a garment. . . . Cook even acquired gut parkas for his crew's use, believing the garments to be much lighter, stronger, and more waterproof than oilskins.[4]

One of the oldest and finest Aleutian gut garments in this country exists in the collection of the Peabody Museum in Salem, received there in 1835. It is a Russian-style gut cape called a "kamleika," a term applied by Russians in Alaska to a native waterproof parka made of intestines (Fig. II.2.3). It reflects early Russian contact and influence, but more than that, it's a garment with aesthetic value for its own incredibly delicate work, elegance, and refinement.

It is curious that gut, an inner membrane, has become an outer skin, tough and protective, despite its frag-

Figure II.2.2
Wearing gut parkas and carrying a catch of fish.
Photograph from the San Francisco Craft and Folk Art
Museum.

ile appearance. This transparent membrane is a thin skin
between life and death, a link between the animal and
human worlds, the worlds of giver and receiver. This
clothing represents an intimate relationship, the connection between life of the land and life of the water. There
is rawness, transformed. And there is strength and power
in the extraordinary closeness to nature.

Gut parkas were made, according to Dorothy Jean
Ray, by all Eskimos* except Central Canadian tribes.[5] The
ribbonlike gut strips, the color equality, the weightless-
ness, the thinness, and the overall garment shape are similar. All gut parkas are made with the idea of separate
strips used as a unit, joined side by side, parts becoming
a larger whole. In textile history, one is reminded of
African strip weave or patchwork quilt construction. Yet
there are also significant differences in parkas. Gudmund
Hatt suggests the gut parka evolved from the fur shirt
made out of vertical strips of fur from small animals. In
northern and eastern regions the Inupiaq gut parka is of
short, vertical lengths of intestines, seldom decorated in
the seams.[6] Elsewhere there is a horizontal placement of
the gut strips, stitched as if coiling around the body. . . .
Hatt sees this alignment as a southwestern Alaskan inno-

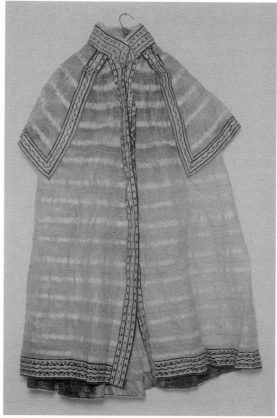

Figure II.2.3
Kamleika, a gut cape-style parka. Photograph from the
San Francisco Craft and Folk Art Museum.

vation. In either arrangement, the joining of one slit tube
to the next may be abrupt or tapered and gradual. There
is subtle but visual variation along the length of a single
gut strip, with the creamy white of the center sometimes
used as a design element.

The length and width of the gut strips vary, depending on the animal source and its size. The weight of a dry
gut parka, however long, can be as little as three ounces
or as much as seven ounces—remarkably lightweight and
"breatheable." When wet, a parka changed shape, even
got considerably longer (to contract later), but the wet-
ness did not penetrate.

Lynn Morrison, in her article, discusses the contrac-
tile quality of gut. "The gut wall is a highly ordered and
specialized tissue, like tendon. It is dense and although

---

*The belief that *Eskimo* had a pejorative meaning, "eater of raw
meat," has resulted in a shift to the self-designation of *Inuit,*
meaning "person or people," in Canada and *Inupiaq, Central
Yup'ik,* and *Siberian Yup'ik* for those native Eskimo peoples in
Alaska. . . .

pierced by capillaries *in vivo*, these close up on the death of the animal, making the material impermeable and resistant to decay. Gut is extremely tough in order to perform its biological function of contraction. It will withstand high pressure."[7]

The Siberian Yup'ik parka of St. Lawrence Island is particularly striking. Winter tanned gut, in opaque, parchmentlike strips, is preferred: this is an aesthetic choice. . . . The weather conditions elsewhere in Alaska would allow for the same freeze drying process, which causes an inflated wet gut tube to lose its transparency and become a satiny white strip. This irreversible transformation also makes the material more flexible. The membrane that results from the change from wet to dry remains nonprecious despite the appearance of satin. It is still close to its animal life.

Sinew (animal tendon) or grass were the two commonly used materials for stitching waterproof garments. Often used in combination, both could swell with moisture and keep the parka waterproof. Cotton thread, as Rita Pitka Blumenstein discusses, is now also used. G.I. Davydov writes that when a "coat is finished, the sleeves are tied together and it is filled with water. If there are no leaks, the kamleika is pronounced good."[8] The waterproof seam most frequently used is a two-thread combination, using a running stitch and parallel elements, often grasses, carried along and secured in place with the running stitch.

. . . A decorative stitch was selectively used as well— a kind of looping technique through the running stitch. And along seams frequent additions, such as short bits of colored wool yarn, were locked in place. When grass was used for stitching gut parkas, there was usually no further embellishment. According to Otto Geist, "it is by the seam that a man's raincoat and snowshirt are distinguished from a woman's. The seams of a man's raincoat are sewed on the outside, whereas a woman's coat has the seams on the underside."[9] This subtle inside and outside gender related indication is an extension of the idea of membranes as innerskins and outerskins.

Frequently a gut parka was used over other parkas, as rainshirt or snowshirt, occasionally to keep fur or feathers dry. Sometimes gut was used as a lining for waterproofing: other times gut itself was lined with trade cloth, either silk or cotton. The color of the cloth through the membrane visually contributed to the piece.

I am reminded of Scythian burial finds of felt saddle blankets lined with silk. People use the material they know best. What makes something valuable and precious is a cultural attitude toward it, dependent, traditionally, on the amount of time directly involved in production. Ingenuity abounds. The Thomas Burke Memorial Washington State Museum in Seattle has a gun jacket lined with flour sack material.

Although these gut objects were used as everyday functional articles for protection against the physical elements, they were also used extensively by the shaman. There was a widespread belief in Alaska that the garment was a spiritually protective covering.

In Eskimo art, symbolic depiction of the lifeline, the central spiritual and biological channel of an organism, is common. The soft organs, from the mouth to the anus, through the whole digestive system, are suggested.[10] The literal use of these gut membranes in protective clothing, in both functional and ceremonial ways, is directly tied to the larger belief system, a choice of materials with significant spiritual meaning.

The sound of dry gut is associated with contact with the spirit world. When a shaman was curing the sick and performing miracles "beneath the sea and in other sacred places," reference is made to the rustling sound of moving gut—the sound of a gut parka or two or three worn one on top of another.

Dorothy Jean Ray writes, "one man told me that about forty years ago, he saw a young boy who had drowned brought back to life by his father, an *angakok* (medicine man) famous throughout the North for his miraculous deeds. All were standing around, the teacher, the minister, everybody, when he shook his gutskin parka in front of his son and brought him back to this world."[11]

E. W. Hawkes said that in Labrador, when people wished to communicate with the spirits or were otherwise engaged in ceremonial performances, they always wore the gutskin raincoat because that was the dress of the spirits.[12] Ann Fienup-Riordan describes a shamanistic cure whereby "the shaman squatted in the birth position and then pulled a sick man from a prone position to a standing one by means of a tightly coiled gut raincoat. The patient then released the rope of gut and was pronounced cured."[13] A King Island boy taking his first caught bird to the men's house, dressed in a waterproof parka to keep out any harmful influence. During the important whale ceremony on Little Diomede Island, before the first whaling trip of the season, the crew put on new clothes and covered them with gutskin parkas to keep out spiritual uncleanliness."[14] On Nunivak Island and in other parts of southwestern Alaska, women wore gut parkas while cutting seal skins for use as kayak covers in order to prevent any evil from entering or afflicting the new kayaks. Men wore waterproof parkas and mittens while handling sea nets "to prevent any evil influence passing from them to the nets and keeping seal away."[15]

Chuna McIntyre tells of the "Window to the Spirit World."

"Our last breath in this life becomes our first in the next."

We Yup'ik Eskimos believe in reincarnation. Life is continuous. We are made of many lifetimes. We are essentially one with our ancestors. They live through us. They live through us without possessing or overpowering our individual selves.

From the time of *Imumi*, beyond the limits of memory, we have prepared our dead for their journey beyond, to the placed called *Pamani*, the land of "over there." There were special preparations for the spirit to travel to that world. Our dead were placed in a sitting position in a wooden box on top of the ground. They were given a piece of driftwood fashioned into a short cylinder which was placed into the clasped hand of the dead as a symbolic weapon. This was to protect them from the vicious and dangerous spirits of the sled dogs which might attack them on their way.

Over the face was placed a specially prepared seal gut Death Mask. The journey to the spirit world holds many surprises, some pleasant and some not. Seal gut is translucent, light, and resilient. You can see images and shadows through the material. It was placed over the face to protect the traveler from the surprises that may bring harm during the journey. It was essentially a transparent shield, a window to the spirit world.

In an account of his travels, 1842–44, Lt. Zagoskin mentions a memorial service for the dead, during which rain parkas made of intestine were brought as gifts for the deceased. On Nelson Island, "when guests were received from another village, for the annual mid winter dances, rolls of dried seal gut might be thrown out like streamers to the approaching kayaks."[16] Numerous significant events document the meaning and importance of gut, both in life and in death.

Fishskin

Mabel Ungudruk is a Siberian Yup'ik woman in Sitka, originally from Gambell on St. Lawrence Island. In the past, she said, when people in her village were afraid of attack, they took fish scales and smeared them on their hands and faces. The scales made them look old and shrivelled, of little interest to their enemies. This is the stuff of folk tales—that fine line between life and death, land and water, human and animal. Fishskin clothing, to someone from another culture, is only one step removed from this.

Many different kinds of fish were used for clothing and bags—dog salmon, lamprey, jack fish (pike), salmon trout, silver or king salmon, halibut, loche, grayling, and dark wolffish. Some fishskin is as thin and transparent as gut but with the literal presence or visible memory of scales. Where scales once were, there is subtle in and out play with light and shadow. The bright iridescence of wet fishskin fades in the drying process. Still, this clothing, even when dry, allows light to catch the magic of iridescence and encourages it to linger. Carefully selected alternate strips of dark and light fishskin were stitched side by side. The usual placement of tail end next to head end, with tail, head, and fins removed, holes patched, skin flattened out, and edges stitched, led to great variation, intricate fitting together, and created a shaded patchwork expanse. Natural fishskin shapes were not trimmed into equal sizes or exact shapes to fit more nearly.

Fishskin and gut do not come geographically from exactly the same places. From Fairbanks, flying north to the Arctic Circle in a small plane, the extensive snakelike river systems are visible. This is fishskin country. Just a glimpse of the much wider river ahead and one feels the unmistakable presence of the Yukon. From the mouth of the Yukon to the Kuskokwim, fishskin was used as a traditional protective material. Nelson's comment is often quoted, that "very poor people (on the lower Yukon) utilize even salmon for making their frocks."[17] It is thought that he was reflecting a bias probably from northern Eskimos who didn't use fishskin clothing. "Poor" also may mean a nonhunter: even widows and orphans could get fish.

In the summer of 1986, Louise Peter, a seventy-one-year-old Athabascan woman of Fort Yukon, Alaska, demonstrated for me her preparation and processing of fishskin for a bag as she had learned and observed from Leah Roberts, also of her village. . . . On a warm August day, outside in the yard, four king salmon, about ten pounds each, were skinned. Later the same day, Louise Peter worked with the cleaned fishskin, wet while she stitched it. Traditionally, according to Cornelius Osgood's account, fishskin was soaked in urine to promote swelling and remove fat. Louise Peter omitted this tanning, though today skins are sometimes worked with liquid detergent soap and water and wrapped in a towel to keep damp. The soft draping of the skin made it seem clothlike, except for the surprise of protruding fins— adding the visible reminder of recent life in the water.

A strip of welting, tanned caribou skin, later trimmed, was stitched with sinew in between two layers of wet fishskin, mostly to add strength and to keep the pieces from slipping and tearing. Louise Peter, in Fort Yukon, spins sinew, rolling it upward between her hands. In making the waterproof, overcast stitch, she makes an upward movement of the needle. She considers herself "up river." People living "down river," doing the same activities, she explained, would move their hands in exactly the opposite direction. While the bag is drying. Louise Peter fills it with sand or dry grass to keep its shape. When dry, such bags historically would keep out dampness and hold food or clothing.

Unity is in the idea that a fishskin bag was used for storing another form of fish—dried fish strips for food, for people or for the dogs. An old salmon skin boot was used as a bag for fish eggs. In addition to food storage, salmon skin bags were sometimes used by mourning women for keeping locks of their hair, according to Osgood.

Osgood's account of fishskin use by the Ingalik Athabascan Indians is the earliest careful documentation of process and treatment. He describes some articles made of fishskin that do not currently exist in an Alaskan collection. Reference is made to a fishskin cradle, made for a baby only after a family has lost one child by death. The salmon skin keeps away the evil spirits that caused the death of the previous child. After the first three months of a baby's life, the cradle frame is thrown away, and the salmon skin is removed, rolled up, and put away with the baby's original swaddling clothes.[18] Osgood also mentions a baby's coveralls—a one-piece suit with trousers, footwear, and a front opening. As the child grows, the fishskin suit is enlarged by cutting it in the middle and inserting a strip of fishskin. Moss is put in the seat of the garment as a diaper.

Adults wore fishskin clothing, glorious raingear and much more, as protection against rain, wind, and uncleanliness.

Tight-fitting fishskin must be wet on the fish for it to survive. Worn as clothing on a human body, it must keep out the wet. Inadequacy and vulnerability are challenged by a thin membrane. Both gut and fishskin are ingenious as a human solution for keeping the outer world, visible and invisible, from penetrating.

Notes

1. "Early British Condoms Found in Castle Dig" (*San Francisco Chronicle*. December 12, 1986), p. 36.

2. Adrienne Rich, "Resisting Amnesia" (*Ms. Magazine*, March, 1987) p. 66.

3. Ales Hrdlička. *The Aleutian and Commander Islands and Their Inhabitants* (Philadelphia: Wistar Institute of Anatomy and Biology, 1945), p. 589. Burials on Kagamil date to the late prehistoric period, around 1500 A.D.

4. J. C. Beaglehole, ed., *The Journals of Captain James Cook on His Voyages of Discovery* (Cambridge: Cambridge University Press, 1967), p. 349, n. 3.

5. Dorothy Jean Ray, "The Eskimo Raincoat" (*The Alaska Sportsman*, November, 1959), p. 13.

6. Gudmund Hatt, "Arctic Skin Clothing in Eurasia and America: An Ethnographic Study" (*Arctic Anthropology*, 1969), trans. Kirsten Taylor, p. 52.

7. Lynn Morrison, "The Conservation of Seal Gut Parkas" (*The Conservator* No. 10, 1986), p. 17.

8. G. I. Davydov, *Two Voyages to Russian America, 1802–1807* (Ontario, Canada: Limestone Press, 1977), p. 152.

9. Lola Cremens, "Eskimo Clothing on St. Lawrence Island," in *Excerpts from the Diary of Otto William Geist (Farthest North Collegian*, March, 1930), p. 8.

10. William Fitzhugh and Susan Kaplan. *Inua*, (Washington, DC): Smithsonian Institution Press, 1982, p. 201.

11. Dorothy Jean Ray, op. cit. p. 44.

12. Dorothy Jean Ray, ibid.

13. Ann Fienup-Riordan, *The Nelson Island Eskimo* (Anchorage: Alaska Pacific University Press, 1983), p. 225.

14. Dorothy Jean Ray, op. cit., p. 44.

15. Edward S. Curtis, *The North American Indian*, vol. 20 (Chicago: 1930), pp. 13, 19.

16. Ann Fienup-Riordan, op. cit., p. 225.

17. William Fitzhugh and Susan Kaplan, op. cit., p. 140.

18. Cornelius Osgood, *Ingalik Material Culture* (New Haven: Yale University Press, 1940), p. 100.

Part Three Scales of Culture and Dress

In previous chapters we have examined methods that allow us to explore the phenomenon of dress objectively. These include a scientific definition of the term dress, the classification system, and an understanding of the strengths and limitations of sources of information about dress. The concepts of social and cultural scale offer another tool for studying dress and limiting ethnocentric bias.

When we consider the topic of dress, we observe that the process of performing a body modification or donning a body supplement is more than a change or addition to the sight, smell, sound, feel, or taste of a person's experience of self and presentation of self to others. Both wearers and observers of dress make many assumptions about the meanings involved in what they perceive through the senses and do not always—or even often—think consciously about these assumptions because they are cultural. Body modifications and supplements have physical characteristics and associated cultural meanings that influence how individuals feel about themselves and interact with others. In addition, these modifications and supplements also affect how well individuals find themselves integrated into their particular scale of culture. Conversely, each scale of culture influences their dress, both as individuals and as members of a group.

When we describe the characteristics and dress practices of small- and large-scale cultures, we use the past tense to remind the reader that classic forms of these cultures originate in the historical record and represent ways of life very different from our own. At the same time, many of our examples are drawn from contemporary research on the lifeways of people in the world today, highlighting the usefulness of culture scale in appreciating the wide range of dress in the modern world.

7

Small-scale Culture and Dress

OBJECTIVES

To describe the characteristics of small-scale cultures.

To understand how these characteristics affect dress.

To explore how dress becomes a unique expression of group life.

HISTORICALLY, THE DEVELOPMENT OF *small-scale cultures* was the outcome of **sapienization**, the co-evolution of human society, language, and the human physical type that produced modern *Homo sapiens*, by at least 50,000 B.C.E. (Bodley, 1994). As humans evolved, we developed a rich social life around the immediate survival needs of the extended family, forming small-scale cultures. Some groups of people still live in cultures very similar to early small-scale settlements. This does not mean they are "living fossils" of prehistory. On the contrary, even though small-scale cultures are largely products of the past, they live on in contemporary cultures. Many groups today, such as the Masai of Kenya and Australian Aborigines accomplish the tasks of the day in time-honored ways because they are successful strategies.

SMALL-SCALE CULTURE AND DRESS

To paraphrase the column in Table 7.1, small-scale cultures were characterized by small, low-density populations. Some groups were **nomadic**, traveling in seasonal cycles within a region, foraging and hunting for food. Multifamily foraging groups of 25 to 50 people are called bands. Others lived in settlements, either gardening small plots or herding domesticated animals such as cattle,

TABLE 7.1

The Scale of World Cultures

	Small Scale
Society	Egalitarian Kin-based Age-grades
Economy	Subsistence Display Reciprocal exchange
Technology	Foraging Gardening Herding
Population	500–1000 Low-density
Polity	Acephalus Bigman Descent groups
Ideology	Animism Shamanism Ancestor cults
Dress	

Adapted from Bodley, John H. (1994). *Cultural Anthropology: Tribes, States, and the Global System.* Mountain View, CA: Mayfield Publishing Company, p. 16.

sheep, or horses. A technology of simple manual tools and an extensive knowledge of the natural environment produced enough food, clothing, and shelter for basic survival. This is known as a **subsistence economy**. People did not need or chose not to store sufficient supplies for lean times. However, some goods might have been set aside to display family prosperity or to exchange with neighbors. Often there was time for leisure activities.

Division of labor was minimal following the categories of gender, age, and ability; every individual performed a wide range of tasks to support the survival of the family and immediate community. Social structure was usually characterized by **egalitarian** relations among individuals organized into **kin-based** subgroups along the lines of marriage and family. Differences in social status were based on age, ability, and gender, as well as each individual's position in a kin group, with each individual having equal chance to experience the responsibilities and benefits of each age status. Political decisions were negotiated within and between networks of kin, there being no centralized authority to govern. This type of decentralized political system is called **acephalous**, meaning "without a head." An acephalous small-scale society is called a **tribe**. When decisions affecting the entire group needed to be made or altercations between members occurred, all adults in the community participated in the discussion and decision-making process.

Residential groups in small-scale cultures remained small in size, mobile, and flexible. Individuals lived with relatives on either the mother's or father's side and kin-based ties were maintained at great distances on both sides. This enabled the residential group to keep population density low enough for successful exploitation of natural resources without depletion. Shelter for nomadic and seminomadic communities consisted of temporary or semipermanent structures in camping sites or small settlements, respectively.

From time to time several groups or bands might have congregated at a central area to celebrate important ritual events. One such event is the *Gerewol* (GEH-ray-wall) celebration still enjoyed by the *Wodaabe* (woe-DAH-bay) who live in settlements across West Africa. Periodically, the Wodaabe gather for an event focused on matching marriageable men and women. For the Gerewol, Wodaabe men paint their faces with elaborate designs intended to enhance their unique facial features, then compete in athletic and dance competitions. Young Wodaabe women act as judges. At the conclusion of events, marriage partners are selected. Thus, the small size of the foraging band or horticultural community and the congregation of several communities for special events ensured that everyone knew everyone else within the immediate community on sight.

Religious ideology took the form of **animism**, or worship of the powers that animate aspects of the universe important to the group's survival, such as celestial bodies, geological features, and ancestors. For example, groups who lived near the water and who depended on fishing for sustenance worshipped sea creatures or water spirits. Shamans, or diviners and healers, were religious specialists, mediating between the human and the spirit worlds. Senior adults in the family performed religious and life course rituals for births, marriages, deaths, and ancestor veneration.

Even though small-scale cultures are described here as existing in the past, some contemporary cultures continue to exhibit many of these culture traits, while simultaneously taking an active part in a global system. The model of small-scale culture drawn here has many important implications for dress. As these implications emerge, we more closely examine each of the generalized characteristics listed earlier and analyze their impact on dress in detail.

POPULATION, RESIDENCE, AND DRESS

Consider population size and density. The small-scale culture in early human history had as few as 500 members, often fewer. If you count up all the people you know or have known, perhaps you will reach 500. Your personal address book may contain as many as 200 names. And each person you know is connected to other circles of acquaintance. In small-scale cultures, low population density meant that individuals probably knew or could find out through inquiry most of the people who resided in the entire geographical area in which they traveled and spent their lives. Thus, dress did not need to communicate much specific information about individual identity. People knew each other as unique individuals.

Migration in search of food, pasture, or new garden space allowed few material goods to be accumulated. This applied to dress as well; wardrobes were minimal. Groups that moved every few days owned little more than the clothes on their backs and the few permanent tools they carried on their persons. Body modifications, temporary or permanent, were an economical and efficient way to dress the body for foraging bands and herding societies. Body modifications were particularly apt in climates where the body did not require covering for protection. Moreover, temporary modifications such as body painting were an efficient method of changing dress with mood and occasion, as in Figure 7.1. Natural products of the earth, flora, and fauna were almost always at hand to be worked into a temporary paint for the body and applied with feather, twig, leaf, or finger. Sometimes, though, the band moved to a known source of products that allowed body painting. Neither the tools nor the paints for these body modifications needed to be transported when the band moved on. For example, Athabascan Indian groups frequented the "paint pots" of iron oxide, now located in the Kootenay National Park, Canada. Body supplements, too, were often made from materials immediately at hand in the natural environment.

Compared to nomads, individuals in more settled groups, who moved only seasonally to shift herds or every few years to open new gardens in the forest, had the ability to accumulate more items of dress. Several forms of supplements could be efficiently accumulated in these circumstances. Flat textiles, which were wrapped on the body, were easily folded, packed, and carried during the communities' infrequent moves. Preshaped supplements that lack contours, such as the flowing robes typical of seminomadic desert groups in sub-Saharan Africa today, were also easily packed and transported. Lastly, elaborate dress ensembles were constructed by assembling many individual elements,

Figure 7.1
Temporary body modifi-
cations, such as face and
body paint are efficient
methods of changing in-
dividual appearance with
mood and occasion. In
small-scale cultures, many
body modifications and
supplements come from
the natural environment.
The Tchi Krin, Brazil,
mid-twentieth century.

which are themselves successfully stored in a flat condition. One example is the parts of the feather and fur headdresses of Mount Hagen men and women of Highland New Guinea (Strathern & Strathern, 1971, p. 79), as seen in Figure 7.2. For people on the move, material possessions such as feathers that are lightweight, compact, and efficient in their display potential are preferred for easy storage and transport.

TECHNOLOGY, ECONOMY, AND DRESS

In a subsistence economy of small-scale cultures, each family unit provided for its own food, shelter, and clothing needs. All material needs were met by exploitation of the natural resources at hand in the near environment. The tools used were simple and required only the power of one or several cooperating individuals. However, extremely detailed knowledge of the natural environment was required, as well as knowledge of the treatment of the materials extracted for food or construction of cultural artifacts.

The Inuit ability to create boots and garments of fur that are unsurpassed for long term survival in the Arctic is recognized by the Inuit and by non-Inuit

Figure 7.2
One requirement of dress for some groups is ease of transport. In Highland New Guinea, elaborate ceremonial headpieces are created from prefabricated parts that are stored separately until assembly into their final three-dimensional form for wearing.

who choose to venture into that part of the world for exploration or sport. Indeed, Oakes and Rieve (1995) report:

> To compare the thermal properties of caribou skin and mass-produced winter clothing and footwear, we attached computerized thermometers to several parts of the bodies of fifteen volunteers, who sat in a cold chamber (-28 degrees C) for one hour without moving. Every five minutes, a computer recorded the skin temperatures of their toes, torso, cheeks, legs, and fingers. Every twenty minutes, we asked the subjects to describe how cold they felt.
>
> The test results showed that the subjects wearing caribou skin boots were comfortably warm for most of the hour, while those wearing mass-produced winter footwear became uncomfortably cold shortly after the experiment began. This experiment supports the traditional knowledge of Inuit elders, who are always telling young people to take their caribou skin kamiks [boots] with them whenever they travel on the land. (p. 19)

The required detail knowledge included the gender of the bird, the location on the animal's or bird's skin, and the season in which the animal or bird was killed because all affect the insulation value provided by the furred or feathered skin (Oakes, 1991). The design of the garment was often based on the shape of the pelt in relationship to the areas of the human body that needed protection. Reading II.2 describes how the intestines and skin of fish are used in a sophisticated manner to create garments that insulate against water, which is important for survival in the Arctic. How the type of a bird skin and its shape were used to create an Inuit anorak, a hooded jacket that pulls over the head, is pictured in Figure 7.3.

Permanent tools for manufacturing dress supplements or making body modifications were usually multipurpose, serving in other capacities as well as in dressing the body. A single tool, such as a large knife, might have been used to hunt, build shelters, cook, cut hair, scarify the skin, and manufacture cloth. In contrast, we own a wide variety of many permanent tools that are dedicated solely to dressing ourselves—either to make, repair, clean, or press clothing; or to temporarily modify our bodies.

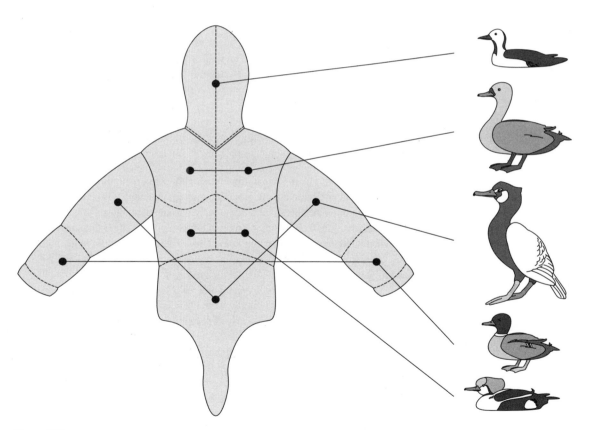

Figure 7.3
Detailed knowledge of flora and fauna makes it possible for people to use products from the environment efficiently, such as the cut of this bird skin anorak from Greenland. The skins of birds with thicker down are used to cover areas of the body more vulnerable to chill Arctic winds.

Sometime between 20,000 and 15,000 B.C.E. two new multipurpose tools—the needle and thread—were developed that had a sustained impact on dress. Archeological digs at La Gravatte, France, unearthed needles, and beads made of shell, tooth, and bone in grave sites dating to 20,000 to 26,000 B.C.E. These beads were apparently sewn onto garments, probably made of hide, because the beads appear in neat rows across the bones of the dead. As we described in Chapter 3, organic dress artifacts decompose easily and quickly, so the positioning of the beads is significant evidence of beading with needles and either sinew or twisted fiber string. String itself appears in the form of tasseled skirts etched on many of the small Upper Paleolithic (15,000 B.C.E.) figures of fecund women, called Venus figures. Physical evidence of string was found in Lascaux, the French cave famous for its Paleolithic paintings. One of the archeologists found a clod of clay that was impressed with an ancient bit of cording, with even minute fibers of the actual cording adhered to the surface. This find was carbon dated to about 15,000 B.C.E. The clay impression was so clear and detailed that it was possible to reproduce a sample of the cording (Barber, 1994).

With a needle and string, many tools can be fashioned, such as snares, fishing lines, tethers, handles, nets, carriers, and dress. One scholar, Elizabeth Wayland Barber (1994), refers to this development of twisting fiber into cord as the String Revolution and compares it to the Industrial Revolution:

> So powerful, in fact, is simple string in taming the world to human will and ingenuity that I suspect it to be the unseen weapon that allowed the human race to conquer the earth, that enabled us to move out into every econiche on the globe during the Upper Paleolithic. (p. 45)

Thus, the development of textile production, transforming naturally occurring fibers into yarns and fabrics, can be viewed as an elemental force in the success of early small-scale cultures.

In a small-scale economy, items of dress were usually made by the individual who wore them or by other members of the family or kinship group. A narrow assortment of locally available materials restricted the range of dress items and dress processes available to members of a small-scale culture. For example, when we compare dress ensembles of American Indian groups, from Baffin Island in the north to what is now Florida in the United States, differences in available materials are clearly one reason the groups are distinguished by their dress. Compare Figure 3.4a with Figure 7.4.

In some small-scale cultures, technology included gardening, herding, or the ability to capitalize on migration patterns of local wildlife. In this case, a surplus of food could be accumulated for a brief period of time. The economy in such situations was further organized around the process of displays of wealth and reciprocal exchange. Typically, wealth included food and articles of dress. The people of Mount Hagen in New Guinea (Strathern & Strathern, 1971) again provide an example. Over a period of time, families amassed and exchanged pigs, the main source of protein in their diet. Individual men collected tally markers of the history of their participation in such exchanges. The tally markers were made into necklaces, as seen in Figure 7.5, which were worn

Figure 7.4
Compare the components of dress on this sixteenth century portrait of a woman from Baffin Island to the components of dress in Figure 3.8. Differences in natural resources and climate account, in part, for differences in types of body supplements. Notice that the Baffin Island woman keeps her child tucked into the roomy hood of her parka. Painting by English artist John White, 1557.

by the men to indicate their achievements in these wealth displays. At the wealth exchanges, the men also organized displays of group dancing and dress. Such elaborate ensembles of face paint, garments, and feather headdresses as seen in Figure 7.2, might have rivaled in complexity and size anything appearing on the Las Vegas stage. Many items of dress were loaned out for the purposes of these dance-cum-dress displays, and the borrowing and returning of dress items paralleled the reciprocal exchange of pigs, but within a more narrow range of the social network. Thus, dress also functioned as the second most important form of wealth among groups that practiced display and reciprocal exchange.

The Kwakiutl people of the northwest coast of Canada practiced potlatch, a similar method of redistributing wealth in a small-scale, egalitarian society. In this example, Kwakiutl villages were not completely acephalous, but headed by chiefs, who were descended from a common powerful ancestor. Each chief attempted to validate his position and achieve status as the greatest chief among chiefs. Marvin Harris (1974) describes this rivalry:

> The prescribed manner for doing this was to hold potlaches. Each potlach was given by a host chief and his followers. The object of the potlach was to show that the host chief was truly entitled to chiefly status and that he was more exalted than the guest chief. To prove this point, the host chief gave the rival chief and his followers quantities of valuable gifts. The guests would belittle what they received and vow to hold a return potlach at which their own chief would prove that he was

Figure 7.5
The tally marker necklace worn by this Mendi man from Highland New Guinea records the number of wealth exchanges in which he has participated and signifies his degree of personal achievement.

> greater than the former host by giving back even larger quantities of more valuable gifts. (p. 114)

These valuable gifts included food, animal skins, and Hudson's Bay Company trade blankets. By 1886, Hudson's Bay blankets had replaced both food and animal skins as the primary form of valuable gift exchanged. Equivalents to potlatch exist today. After an American Indian powwow in Minneapolis, one of the authors witnessed the outgoing Powwow Princess, with the help of her supporters, pile up and give away textile and dress items including star quilts, blankets, and shirts. This act acknowledged those who had supported her through the year and was part of the thanking ceremony that precedes the announcement of the Powwow Princess for the new year.

In the technology and economy of small-scale cultures, items traded with outside groups were few in number. Trade goods were counted among the luxuries of the trading partners. The community of Dugum Dani, New Guinea highlanders studied by Heider (1970), for instance, traveled through the territory of their enemies to collect salt which they then traded with societies nearer the coast of New Guinea for other valuable items that became incorporated into dress. Such trade, or reciprocal exchange, while not very extensive in some small-scale cultures, often included a high proportion of items for use in dress and indicated the great importance of dress.

SOCIAL STRUCTURE, DIVISION OF LABOR, AND DRESS

In small-scale cultures, residential groups were organized loosely along the lines of kin relations, typically on both the male and female sides of the family. The importance of belonging to an extended kin-based group sometimes was indicated by shared forms of dress. In other words, members of the same kinship group might dress in similar ways such as a similar use and placement of color or wearing certain fabrics. For example, Reading III.1, "Ga'anda Scarification: A Model for Art and Identity," by Marla Berns describes the patterns of **scarification**, the process of creating scars through deliberate cutting of designs on the skins of young Ga'Anda women preparing for marriage. Berns states, "Hleeta (scarification) is identical on all Ga'Anda women, regardless of dialect sub-grouping, underscoring its importance as a means of ethnic consolidation and identification" (1988, p. 63). Such strategies enable members of kin groups who live at great distances to recognize the relationship that binds them when they meet.

If the group lived in a warm climate, where there was rarely any necessity to cover the body for protection, the gender and age of the individual was ordinarily apparent through physical body differences that include primary and secondary sexual characteristics. Dress became a way to highlight important aspects of the role of age and gender groups and specific individuals in relation to social occasions. In cold climates requiring much body covering for protection, dress indicates gender of the wearer and sometimes an age group, because when covered, the physical facts become inaccessible to an observer. Some indication of gender emerges in aspects of dress in all cultures whether small, large, or global in scale.

In small-scale cultures, dress was an important marker of reproductive capacity. Barber (1994) suggests that the string skirts worn by Upper Paleolithic (15,000 B.C.E.) Venus figures and probably by women themselves were not intended for warmth or modesty. Their apparent purpose was to draw the eye directly toward the center of female reproductive capacity and attract suitable mates. In addition, in many cases, mortality rates of women and their babies during childbirth were higher than experienced in the United States at the beginning of the twenty-first century. Fluctuations in food resources, disease, and differences in medical practices made it difficult to bring a healthy baby into its first year. Hence, a woman's reproductive and child rearing abilities were not taken for granted, but were considered valuable to maintaining the vitality of the group. These abilities received recognition in special types of dress. One example is the pregnancy apron used among certain South African groups as shown in Figure 7.6. Another example is the use of tattooing by the Kodi women on the island of Sumba, east of Bali. The production of cloth and the

Figure 7.6
The apron worn during pregnancy by this South African woman draws attention to her ability to bear children and her reproductive role in society. Zulu, Tugela Ferry area, 1975.

production of children are closely tied, and both are the exclusive domains of women. Hoskins relates:

> Tattooing is a female rite restricted to women who have proven their ability to reproduce. A young bride, just conceiving her first child, may have her forearms tattooed, but she cannot have her calves and thighs tattooed until she has produced several healthy children. (1989, p. 162)

The motifs tattooed on the skin are the same as the ones used on the textiles. Hoskins goes on to report that by bearing children for her husband's line, a woman acquires an enhanced rank and status. This new, achieved status qualifies her to serve as a representative of her husband's house in public events and community decisions.

Subsistence economies required individuals to perform many different kinds of tasks, but division of labor occurred only along the lines of gender, age group, and ability or inclination. Thus, each woman, generally, in the cumulative span of her life, fulfilled all the same economic functions as every other woman in the group. Women usually gathered or grew the bulk of the diet, such as nuts, berries, roots, and grains. Women also cooked and made dress items for family members. Since all women performed these functions, there was no need for dress distinctions between cooks and makers of bark cloth, for example. By contrast, consider how chefs and retail sales associates are distinguished by dress in our society. The same is true for men in foraging groups such as the Aka Pygmy in Central Africa who typically provide the bulk of the animal protein in the community's diet by hunting and fishing, but also engage in the care of very small children (Hewlett, 1991). However, there is no particular change of dress associated with hunting versus child care, since all men care for children and forage for sources of protein.

Even if dress in small-scale cultures did not need to communicate power, wealth, or status, it did serve the purpose of acknowledging the individual's transition into a new role in society. Such transitions are called **life course rituals** or **rites of passage**. Some rites of passage appear to be practiced all over the world and throughout history—blessing babies, celebrating marriage, and commemorating the dead. Rituals celebrated the adolescent boy moving from childhood into his role as warrior or initiated an adult into the role of shaman, or healer. Thus, dress marked individual accumulation of new social roles or responsibilities associated with biological growth, reproduction, and aging. Permanent body modifications, such as tattooing and scarification, that celebrate gender, biological, and social growth suit societies in which one's general social role is determined primarily by gender and age. Such groupings are called *age grades*. The Ga'Anda of Africa, as shown in Reading III.1, ritually applied permanent designs on different portions of a girl's body as she matured and the arrangements for her engagement and marriage were successfully contracted (Berns, 1988). In small-scale cultures most girls and boys matured and married no matter what else they did in life, so types of dress, such as tattoos and scarification, could be permanent. No changes of dress with the attainment of new social status need ever erase the fact that each member matured and married in the culturally prescribed manner.

Lack of elaborate and full-time divisions of labor ensured that most dress was multipurpose. The scarification designs made on the skin of Ga'Anda women served as a primary part of their dress in all their activities (Berns, 1988), as does the loincloth and breechclout used by men in many small-scale groups. A loincloth is a length of cloth wrapped around the waist and between the legs, covering the genitals, as shown on the Indian leader Gandhi pictured in Figure 10.1. A breechclout is similar and often features panels of fabric or skins suspended front and back. Indeed, such examples of dress can be described using the classification system from Chapter 1 in terms of permanent and temporary body modifications and wrapped and suspended supplements. Preshaped dress articles were primarily ceremonial, such as headdresses.

Separate dress for night wear, for different kinds of work, or for different days of the week were probably rare. As different flowers or plants came into season, daily dress might have been augmented with leaves, flowers, or body paint, but the changes were seasonal. Exceptions occurred with ceremonies and special events. Dress for these events did not represent anything as narrow as contemporary occupational uniforms in North America. Moreover, it is only in those parts of the globe where changes in the weather are so severe as to require different types of protection at different times of the year that members of such small-scale cultures could be said to have seasonal dress.

POLITY AND DRESS

As we have described in this chapter, small-scale cultures were characterized by a decentralized, or acephalous, political structure. Each member of the community contributed to the livelihood of the group. As small communities became linked by proximity or kinship relationships, social structure was organized around a **bigman**. This self-made man of influence raised his position above that of his peers, often through an aggressive round of organizing and participating in exchanges and displays of wealth, such as the potlatch described earlier. In reciprocal exchange societies the main item of wealth accumulation was also the main protein item of the diet and was eaten up, sometimes as the ending event of the display and exchange. Only the items of dress used for wealth displays survived. In such instances, dress items were inherited and used again, together with additionally amassed wealth. Dress, then, can be said to be the first form of inherited wealth, as well as the first form of private property. The bigman political position itself was not inherited, so anyone with the aptitude or influence could succeed to this role through competition. Each individual started out anew on a fairly equal footing.

Indeed, the bigman was big precisely because he could marshal so much of the community's resources into specific display events and was known for the amount of wealth items he could give or loan, including dress. Items that were loaned to one man this month were later returned. Moreover, frequent changes in political alliances ensured that individuals or groups who were on top would later find themselves displaced by others in an ongoing contest between several big men who were all relative equals, since they started out at an equal level. Thus, elaborate, rich dress was not associated with any permanent social stratification, but was a means to equalize participants.

Another way people organize themselves is by **descent groups**. A descent group is a social structure based on genealogical connections to a common ancestor. Contemporary Scottish clans are organized around a common ancestor who rose to prominence in their small-scale past. Clans are still distinguished by unique tartans carrying the clan name. In southeast Asia, the Lamaholt people living in East Flores exchange textiles as part of wedding rituals. These textiles traditionally contain patterns of ancestors linked by hands or feet and refer to a long line of descent, linking the past to the present (Barnes, 1992, p. 39).

RELIGION AND DRESS

Animism, the belief in spiritual entities found in living plants, water, mountains, and celestial bodies, characterized the religious ideology of small-scale cultures. These spiritual entities often were not depicted in anthropomorphic or human-like form. Thus, questions about the dress of spiritual beings, or gods, did not arise. The case of the family elders who have died is different. These spirits were venerated and propitiated as entities who had power to participate in the lives of the living. Because they were remembered from when they were alive on earth, these ancestors were sometimes depicted in statues dressed as the individuals were in life.

The dressing of the deceased was sometimes quite elaborate because of the belief that the deceased was entering another life and would need all the trappings of life on earth. Burial sites of ancient small-scale cultures are rich in dress articles. Examples include the Sutton Hoo ship burial in Suffolk, England (Evans, 1989), and tombs of the Pazyryk people of the Russian steppes (Polosmak, 1994), depicted in Figure 7.7. In addition, the burials, ornate head gear, textiles, and handheld objects embossed with precious metals pointed to the social stature of the deceased. We can contrast this elaborate funeral dress with that used in North America in the late twentieth century, in which cremation is becoming increasingly popular. Today, a simple set of the clothes worn by the deceased in life may be selected to dress the body before cremation, while more precious dress articles are distributed among the living family members as remembrances of the loved one.

Within the community, individual specialists served as mediators between the spirit world and the world of humans. **Shamans**, or religious specialists, took the form of healers and diviners who worked at diagnosing and healing social breeches or biological illnesses and curbing natural disasters. Typically the shaman was self-selected after a spiritual experience or when a gift for healing was revealed. An apprenticeship with an elder shaman and an initiation ritual might follow. This new role was often acknowledged and made public by some element of dress such an amulet. An amulet is an ornament or charm that carries symbolic meaning or aids in spiritual activities. Sometimes an amulet is inscribed with a symbol that acts as a shorthand reference to a prayer or incantation. Often practitioners added a supplement or modification to their dress indicating a personal relationship with the spirit who was being contacted. In some cases such dress was worn only for occasions of the shaman's divination. Other dress types, such as the application of ashes to the forehead or oils to the skin of the individual were associated with a state of grace after the shaman's intervention with the spirit world.

For most religious purposes, such as rituals associated with age grades, thanksgiving, and annual cycles, each adult male and female bore the authority and responsibility for taking religious action within the immediate family and residential group. Therefore, no special dress was required to officiate, since every adult had the same religious responsibilities. Persons likely to officiate at such a family

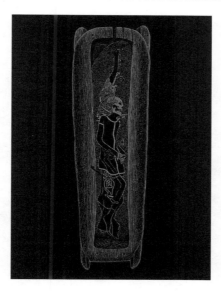

Figure 7.7
Burial sites are often rich sources of dress artifacts, such as this coffin of a Pazyryk priestess from southern Siberia, fifth century B.C.E. The coffin contained a cache of possessions a woman of influence would need in the hereafter, including wool and silk garments, a headdress, gilded ornaments, and a carved wooden hand mirror.

event were recognized by types of dress that indicated elder status, as exemplified by the Masai men pictured in Figure 7.8. At the same time, individuals who were to attend a religious event might mark their participation in the occasion by the donning of supplements created especially for the event. Mbuti women of the Ituri forest in Central Africa, for example, paint designs on new barkcloth to be worn for a religious event, but the garment merely replaced the former barkcloth garment; it was not kept in storage for special religious occasions (Meurant & Thompson, 1995).

When an individual underwent a life course transition ritual, some forms of dress became permanent markers of age-grade, as described earlier. Other types of dress were worn only for the occasion and incorporated important ritual symbolism. For instance, boys being initiated into adulthood in many of the culturally related groups around the Ituri forest in northeast Zaire had ashes rubbed on their bodies, wore grass skirts, and had a leaf pinned over their mouths for their ceremonial circumcision (Felix, 1992). Such dress ensembles were easily constructed of elements in the near environment and demonstrated a great deal of aesthetic variation. They were disposed of after the rituals were completed and the individual then donned a new item of dress, indicative of

Figure 7.8
These Masai elders have the traditional look of senior elder-hood, including a warm blanket worn as a cloak and a dignified bearing. Other dress indicators of senior status include hand-held objects such as a fly whisk made of wildbeeste tail hair and a walking staff.

new social status. In an East African example, after a Masai boy was circumcised, he had the right to wear the coiled brass ornaments and headband of blue beads of the new warrior, as in Figure 7.9.

Sometimes life course transformations were performed simultaneously on a number of individuals who together formed an age-grade. When members of an age-grade completed a life course ritual together, they shared an item of dress that distinguished them from all other age-grades, past or future, and associated them with each other. For example, among the Tiv in Nigeria, scarification styles for men changed from one generation to the next. So, an individual man's scars marked his generation to the community and created a lifelong bond with other men of his age-grade (Bohannon, 1956).

Masks were and are used in many African groups at the time of the initiation rituals. Masks depict the ideal dress of the face and head of a divinity who best embodies the role that the initiates will take on after the completion of ceremonies. The figures represent ideals or values that the initiates are expected to follow in their new roles. Masks, together with special dress, are important

Figure 7.9
Rites of passage are often associated with changes in dress. By undergoing circumcision, this young Masai man has earned the right to wear the coiled brass ornaments and head band of blue beads of a warrior.

in many other aspects of the ideological or religious life in many parts of Africa. Spiritual beings are depicted by dancers who wear masks and dress that highlight important aspects of the character of the being. The dress may not relate to dress ideals for humans, but rather may serve as an artistic depiction of ideological abstractions.

Overall, in small-scale cultures in the past and in their descendent cultures today, the social, cultural, religious, political, and economic spheres of life are closely interwoven into one rich, unified whole. The act of making and wearing dress is sometimes involved with every aspect of social and cultural life. For example, Barnes (1992) analyzed the multiple meanings involved in the weaving of cloth by women of the Angami Naga in South Asia. She found that the terminology related to important ritual headhunting activities of the Naga men also applied to Naga women's roles as weavers of cloth and bearers of children. In other words, in Naga culture, making cloth is viewed as a religious activity.

The wearing of cloth made in small-scale cultures also incorporates elements of the sacred, as when designs woven into cloth refer to spiritual entities. The religious basis for ancient Mayan designs has supported Guatemala Indians' continued production and wearing of their cultural dress. The political hierarchy in Guatemala distrusts Indian reluctance to adopt world dress, fearing underground political movements and revolution. Ironically, the state's persecution of these Indian groups has reinforced their steadfast adherence to ethnic dress and has connected them even more tightly to their ancient Mayan ancestors (Brodman, 1994). In other small-scale cultures, specific meanings of some designs are forgotten as they are encapsulated into larger neighboring cultures. Nevertheless, the designs continue to be woven for many generations.

SUMMARY

The scale of a culture and the associated cultural behaviors have broad and deep implications for the shape and character of social and cultural life. Choices of food, shelter, and dress are made within the context of scale. Describing cultural groups in terms of their unique constellations of culture traits gives the student of dress an additional method by which the lifeways of other people can be understood. At the same time, dress can be the gateway to understanding larger issues of scale.

Small-scale describes cultures that existed in the past, though some cultures today still exhibit many small-scale characteristics. Wearers of dress in such cultures made dress items themselves, using basic tools and materials at hand in the natural environment, though trade contributed a few selected materials or items. In everyday dress, distinctions were few in number, indicating primarily gender and age of wearer. Special types of dress were associated with life course rituals marking age-grade transitions and special community events. Individuals owned the dress on their bodies and little else, unless a harsh climate required more garments for specific activities. In mild climates the same dress was worn for any and all activities, day or night. Where climate was not harsh, little of the body was covered, and temporary and permanent body modifications played a more prominent role in marking social status and occasion.

STUDY TOOLS

Important Terms

acephalous
age-grade
animism
bigman
descent group
egalitarian
kin-based
life course rituals
nomadic
rites of passage
sapienization
scarification
shaman
subsistence economy
tribe

Discussion Questions

1. Define the concept of cultural scale. Explain how it can be used as a tool in the investigation of dress to avoid ethnocentrism and cultural bias.
2. What aspects of life in a small-scale culture make it unlikely that a member of that society would have a very large permanent wardrobe? Give reasons from (1) materials and methods of dress production, (2) division of labor, (3) political structure, (4) religious practice, and (5) residence patterns.
3. What aspects of small-scale cultural life parallel aspects of the life of a group, class, or job category in your contemporary society? Discuss dress strategies used by individuals that might be used by these parallel categories you named to solve dress problems in their lives.

4. Describe the steps in the scarification process explained by Berns in Reading III.1, "Ga'anda Scarification: A Model for Art and Identity." What did each step symbolize in the woman's preparation for marriage?

5. According to Berns, it was important that *hleeta* patterns were nearly identical from woman to woman among the Ga'anda and that the scars healed well. Why was this conformity important? Are there times in your culture when conformity in dress is more important than individual expression?

6. Discuss how dress becomes a unique expression of group life. Use the example of Ga'anda women's dress given in Reading III.1.

Activities

1. In small groups, make believe that you are going to take up a nomadic way of life and will have to carry with you all of the material items required for survival. Plan your wardrobe and the kind of dress processes for maximum portability and protection through all the changes of season. Discuss what your nomadic lifestyle wardrobe and dress processes would consist of and how they would change your appearance.

2. Characteristics of small-scale cultures are visible in global-scale cultures. One example is dressing alike to demonstrate kinship or age-grade. Write down occasions when people in your culture dress alike and the forms of dress they choose. In small groups, compare notes. What similarities and differences do you notice? What accounts for the differences and similarities?

3. Using the scale of world cultures in this chapter (Table 7.1), complete the row entitled "Dress." What characteristics would you identify for the dress of small-scale cultures?

4. View a documentary on a small-scale culture from materials your instructor will provide. Compare what you see and hear in the tape to the discussion of dress in small-scale cultures in the text. What are the similarities and differences?

5. Examine the *hleeta* patterns in Figure III.1.2 of Reading III.1. Using three-dimensional fabric paints, duplicate some or all of those designs onto the back of a T-shirt. After the paint dries, run your fingers over the surface of the design. Consider the similarity to touching raised patterns on a scarified skin.

6. Using the concepts regarding dress in small-scale culture given in Chapter 7 and the description of dress given in the Reading III.1, analyze the ways that Ga'anda women's dress exemplifies small-scale cultural dress.

7. Construct an imaginary dress ensemble that would identify you and your role as an adult woman. Imagine that, like scarified Ga'anda women (Reading III.1), this ensemble of modifications and supplements will be your permanent and primary dress for the rest of your life. Be true to who you really are and specific with regard to placement on the body and de-

signs selected. Finish by comparing and contrasting the elements of identity and adult role communicated by the body placement and design of the dress supplements and modifications of Ga'anda women and your imaginary ensemble. What do the differences show about Ga'anda culture and your culture?

8

Large-scale Culture and Dress

OBJECTIVES

To describe the characteristics of large-scale cultures.

To understand how these characteristics affect dress.

To explore how dress becomes a unique expression of cultural identity and group life.

To build on an understanding of culture scale as a conceptual tool for studying dress.

AS WE HAVE SEEN in Chapter 7, the concept of scale provides a method for examining the lifeways of a particular group of people. Considering scale of world cultures precludes certain forms and uses of dress and simultaneously encourages others. Conversely, by examining forms and uses of dress, we can better understand the unique constellation of societal and cultural traits that describe how a particular group of people live their lives. In this chapter, we highlight the characteristics of large-scale cultures and how dress choices were influenced by culture scale.

Once early human groups accumulated knowledge about the growth cycles of vegetation and the habits of animals in their environment, those cycles could be predicted and plants and animals could be more intensively exploited through conscious manipulation. For some groups, a nomadic life was no longer necessary for survival and agriculture developed. In such societies, people settled in villages and focused their food production efforts on farming, fishing, or trade. A few of the early agricultural cultures in the world developed into fully stratified large-scale civilizations. Such examples first arose far back in ancient history with the civilizations of ancient Mesopotamia and Egypt in the Near East and Mohenjo-Daro and Harappa in the Indus River Valley. Other centralized states and empires have developed in other areas of the globe, from Shang China (1766–1045 B.C.E.) to the Inca empire (1476–1532 B.C.E.) in present-day Peru.

Large-scale cultures represent a second great divide in human history and the sociocultural traits of these civilizations describe a very different way of life from small-scale cultures. In this case, small-scale tribal village autonomy and equality were exchanged for a second level of power in a chief or king. Adding a third level of authority to create a state and a fourth level to create an empire concentrated more power in fewer hands. The benefits of surrendering power probably originated in an attempt to reduce internal conflict or in an effort to ensure victory in war with neighboring groups (Bodley, 1994). When we discuss large-scale cultures, we include chiefdoms or kingdoms, states, and empires that existed from 10,000 B.C.E. until 1500 C.E. Thus, a tremendous range of culture traits and dress types existed within large-scale cultures, just as they did in small-scale cultures. It is important to remember that the people of many cultures today inherited cultural traits from their large-scale pasts, and we can still identify cultural traits and types of dress that sustain the vitality of these cultures in the contemporary global system.

The shift from small scale to large scale is neither inevitable nor required for cultural survival. For example, Australian Aborigines have been mobile foragers for 50,000 years. The foraging way of life is one of the most successful human adaptations to the environment. Australian Aborigines borrowed many cultural traits from New Guinea, but innovations such as farming, domesticating animals, making pottery, and using the bow and arrow were not among them. Apparently, aboriginal people did not think these technologies improved upon their existing way of life (Bodley, 1994), and they have not become a large-scale culture. Instead, they live embedded within Australia, which in itself is part of global-scale culture.

CHARACTERISTICS OF LARGE-SCALE CULTURES

The characteristics of large-scale cultures are found in Table 8.1. Many large-scale cultures were characterized by populations of 10,000 people or more; however, there was a significant range in population size from the island chiefdoms of the Pacific Ocean to the empires of Egypt. The primary population

TABLE 8.1

The Scale of World Cultures

	Large-Scale
Society	Ranked
	Class-based
	Castes
Economy	Tribute tax
	Wealth
	Specialists
Technology	Intensive
	Agriculture
Population	10,000 or more
	High-density
Polity	Chiefdoms
	Kingdoms
	States
	Empires
Ideology	High gods
	Divine kings
Dress	

Adapted from Bodley, John H. (1994). *Cultural Anthropology: Tribes, States, and the Global System.* Mountain View, CA: Mayfield, p. 16.

difference between small-scale and large-scale cultures was that in the large-scale culture, individuals could not know everyone else as an individual. People lived in some kind of permanent dwelling in rural villages clustered around at least one large city. There were many technological developments. Some originated with improving methods of acquiring food, including intensive agriculture, fishing, and trade, and employing draft animals, plows, carts, and boats. Other technological innovations expanded the creation of architectural forms, the arts, and textile products.

Large-scale economies were characterized by the generation of food supplies beyond what was needed for subsistence alone. This excess provided tribute taxes, which sustained a centralized government; trade goods used for exchange with neighboring villages; and payment for the products of specialist occupations. It was also converted into and stored as wealth by higher-status members. This wealth took the form of dress articles, works of art, and land ownership.

Division of labor followed age, gender, and ability as in small-scale cultures, but groups were also ranked by caste or class. A **caste** is a group of people who engage in a specific form of labor and who marry only within the group. Castes are ranked along a hierarchy so that some castes have greater or lesser status than others. Membership in the caste group is inherited in the same way a name is inherited. In early large-scale cultures, **class** was very similar to caste because social mobility, the ability to rise above or fall below one's social position, was limited. However, in later large-scale states, the accumulation of wealth and education made social mobility possible for some.

The political structure consisted of a centralized power, either a chiefdom, a kingdom, a state, or an empire. In a chiefdom, tribal members surrendered their equality to one person, who made decisions on behalf of the tribe. A kingdom describes the chiefs and people of several villages coalesced around one person of power. When the power of several kingdoms were unified, a state formed. An empire described a state that successfully conquered most of its neighbors. Each political structure encompassed more territory and more people as subjects.

The spiritual power of ancestors and natural forces that guided the actions of people in small-scale cultures were augmented or replaced by benevolent high gods, in human or near-human form, who were served by priests. These high gods often reigned above malevolent lesser spiritual beings or the localized spirits associated with the neighboring landscape. The belief that the power to rule was granted by high gods was called the divine right of kings and was a prominent aspect of the ideology.

POPULATION, RESIDENCE, AND DRESS

Dress in a large-scale culture differed from that of a small-scale culture. The larger size and density of communities in large-scale cultures meant that people no longer knew everyone with whom they came in contact. Consider the example of a ring of small villages or towns surrounding an urban center, which typified feudal kingdoms across Europe and China. Individuals might know everyone in their home village on sight, as well as some people directly or indirectly in nearby villages. People in villages on the other side of the urban center would be strangers; however, market days and holy days were times when everyone in the surrounding area congregated for trade in the marketplace in the urban center. Figure 8.1 diagrams the structure of an early Chinese city, including the institutions that were associated with the concentration of polity and wealth typical of urban areas in early states.

This lack of familiarity between people was an incentive to individuals to dress in a manner that provided information about family, caste, village, occupation, and wealth. Differences in caste, occupation, and wealth intersected with differences between rural and urban lifestyles, giving rise to rich diversity in dress. In addition, because most people did not travel seasonally to new hunting and gathering grounds, it was possible to accumulate more material

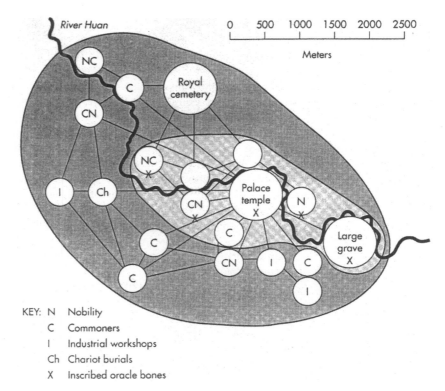

KEY:
- N   Nobility
- C   Commoners
- I   Industrial workshops
- Ch   Chariot burials
- X   Inscribed oracle bones

Figure 8.1
This diagram of a Shang Dynasty (1766–1045 B.C.E.) city in China exemplifies several differences between small-scale and large-scale cultures. Large-scale cultures feature larger populations concentrated in urban centers, a powerful leader, a religious hierarchy, and the exchange of products in a market or bazaar.

possessions, including more items of dress. It was no longer necessary to create items of dress that were light and easy to transport. Wardrobes became larger, especially among the people of upper castes and classes, who tended to be wealthier, had a wider variety of social responsibilities, and could afford to support a household staff to care for these garments. However, most common people had only one or two sets of garments, one for daily wear, and perhaps one for special occasions.

TECHNOLOGY, ECONOMY, AND DRESS

The domestication of plants and animals supported the cultivation of plant fibers, such as cotton and flax, and the use of wool for weaving into cloth. Wool and flax were two of the earliest fibers to be transformed into cloth; the ancient

Egyptians were early converters of flax into linen, the ancient Sumerians of wool. Cotton spinning and weaving developed independently in both ancient India and among the Inca. The critical component of textile production was the recognition that twisting fibers together made them stronger. This understanding by Paleolithic humans was amplified in large-scale culture into several methods of spinning fibers into yarn, including the drop spindle and foot-powered spinning wheel.

In settled, agrarian communities, dye plants were cultivated and dye colors were tested, expanded, and controlled to produce a wide variety of hues. The development of weaving techniques resulted in a wide range of textured fabrics. Examples of early loom types are shown in Figure 8.2a, b, and c. In addition, woven fabrics were further embellished with a broad scope of surface design techniques to enhance the visual interest of the piece. Portions of yarn or fabric could be bound prior to dyeing so as to resist penetration of the dye, sometimes called tie-dyeing or resist dyeing. Additional designs could be painted, printed, or embroidered onto the fabric with contrasting or complimentary colors.

Indeed the development of the textile arts from their earliest beginnings in small-scale cultures to the broad range of textiles available in large-scale cultures is one of the most significant developments in dress history. For example, India has a long and rich history of exquisite cotton textile production. Warmington claims textiles produced in kingdoms throughout India were such a significant part of Roman trade that the Roman writer Pliny lamented that India was draining away the wealth of Rome (Ramaswamy, 1985). India's reputation was based on four key elements. First, the climate and soil of central India permitted the cultivation of the highest quality long staple cotton fibers. Second, skilled spinners spun these fibers into extremely fine and strong yarns. Third,

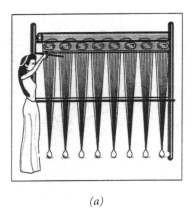
(a)

(b)

(c)

Figure 8.2
Weaving of cloth flourished in early large-scale cultures, though often the style of loom varied from place to place. Shown here are (a) upright, (b) horizontal, and (c) backstrap looms.

the yarns were dyed using vegetable dyes that were both bright and colorfast. And fourth, skilled weavers produced both basic and luxury textiles to satisfy a variety of markets. India still has a strong reputation for cotton textiles, even though the yarn is now usually mill spun and dyes are often synthetic (Evenson, 1994).

Woven fabrics were very time-consuming to create by hand, including the growing, harvesting, cleaning, spinning, dyeing, and weaving time involved. As a result, there was a tendency to be economical in the use of fabrics. Garments or portions of preshaped garments, such as sleeves, were usually created from cloth just as it came off the loom, so that there was minimal cutting, sewing, or waste of cloth. The garment might be as simple as a length of cloth wrapped around the body. The Indian *sari* and the African wrapper are examples. The *sari* is a length of cloth between 4 and 9 yards long. It drapes gracefully from pleats folded into its width and tucked into a woman's petticoat or slip. Frequently one end of the *sari* is woven or printed with an intricate pattern and this end, called the *pallau* (puh-lu), drapes over the shoulder. No cutting or sewing is required, although often a band of fabric is sewn onto the hem to add weight and grace to the fall of the skirt. The African wrapper consists of a 3-yard length of fabric wrapped around and tucked into itself at the waist. Men often wear one wrapper and women wear two—one wrapped at the low hip over a string belt and one around the waist.

The garment might include some cutting and sewing to fit the body, but still with minimal waste of fabric. The tunic exemplifies this efficiency, as pictured in Figure 8.3. It is a T-shaped garment with sleeves and an opening for the head at the top. The tunic was a common form of dress for women and men of all classes from the Greco-Roman era (c. 800 B.C.E. to 400 C.E.) to fifteenth-century Europe (Tortora & Eubank, 1998). Contemporary examples include the Indian *salwar kameez*, a tunic and trouser ensemble worn by Indian women, and the Japanese kimono, as pictured in Figure 8.4.

In a large-scale economy that produced surpluses in food and other material goods, these surpluses constituted a major form of wealth. When these surpluses were traded or converted into other products, dress itself became a communication of wealth. Many of the specialist occupations that developed in this more complex economy consisted of artisans of textiles and dress—weavers of luxurious types of cloth, furriers, lace makers, and gem cutters who created jewelry from rare and expensive materials, just to name a few. As large-scale cultures expanded and became more stratified, their members accumulated enough wealth to "waste" fabric by cutting and sewing fabric into shapes that corresponded more closely to the shape of the human body. Tailors and dressmakers emerged as a new occupational group, in the service of the wealthy.

At the same time, the development of private property occasionally included the ownership of people. Sometimes, slaves were marked by permanent body modifications, such as tattoos, to indicate ownership. Often slaves wore distinctive dress, either to communicate their status within the community or simply because their owners chose to economize on slave dress. Throughout the 3,000 years of Egyptian history, male slaves wore only loincloths as a

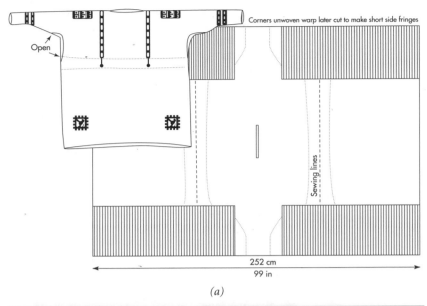

(a)

(b)

Figure 8.3

Because the hand weaving of cloth was very labor intensive, fabric was minimally shaped to fit the body with little or no waste of fabric, as exemplified by the layout of this fifth to sixth century C.E. Egyptian shirt. (a) The cloth on the loom; (b) the sewn tunic.

Figure 8.4
Economy in the use of materials and labor continue to be seen in twentieth century examples of national or traditional dress, such as these Japanese kimonos.

manifestation of their low social status (Tortora & Eubank, 1998). Slave dress in eighteenth-century America often included garments made of inexpensive fabrics such as homespun and osnaburg—fabrics woven with coarsely spun yarn in a plain weave. Homespun was made on the plantation, so it was low cost and osnaburg was often of waste fiber not suitable for other uses. Clothing discarded from the master and his family was also used by the slaves (Williams & Centrallo, 1990, p. 59). The distinctive ways in which the enslaved wore their clothing and the special manner in which they viewed clothing were important demonstrations of their refusal to accept cultural annihilation by the European community in the United States (Foster, 1997, p. 220).

Individuals of lower status were still engaged in domestic manufacture of their own daily dress. These types of dress were similar in style to those worn by the elite, but were less elaborate or were constructed of less precious materials. Also, when the family in a large-scale culture made its own dress, it was often dependent upon sources outside the family for some of the materials necessary for the completion of the finished items of dress. For example, in contemporary Afghanistan, brightly colored imported embroidery threads are purchased at the bazaar, or market, and used to embroider home-sewn dowry items. Fabric stalls in many local markets similarly demonstrate a variety of materials available globally. Itinerant traders were also a source of dress materials, peddling their wares from village to village. Even though most people in large-scale cultures were settled, the ability to carry dress articles from place to place remained an important feature of everyday life. Thus, shopping in markets or from itinerant traders for the components of dress became a practice and a source of variety for members of a large-scale culture.

As implied by these examples, one significant difference between small-scale and large-scale cultures is the concept of fashion. Fashion captures the idea of change as a process: introduction of a variation of a cultural form, its acceptance, discard, and replacement by another cultural form (Sproles, 1979). Roach-Higgins (1981) points out that an awareness of change is a necessary condition for fashion to exist. She states:

> In a society where change in cultural forms is very slow—taking several generations or even centuries—fashion is not a social reality; for members of the society, the collectivity, do not recognize and consciously share the experience of change let alone promote it. One means for determining if fashion in dress exists as a concept among a group of people is to consider fashion in relation to the life span. If people in a society are generally not aware of change in form of dress during their lifetimes, fashion does not exist in that society. (p. 128)

As the citizens of rural areas became aware of urban forms of dress, they also tended to emulate the dress of their urban cousins. At the same time, as urban dwellers accumulated more wealth, they took their dress cues from those wealthier and more powerful. Stated another way, nobility, the royal born, had the leisure time and wealth to enjoy innovation in fashionable dress. As new dress forms were created, fashion in dress would trickle down from the urban centers where nobility resided. Thus, emulation of garment styles among different groups was an element in fashion change that arose in large-scale cultures.

Where dress in small-scale cultures was egalitarian for reasons discussed in the previous chapter, dress in large-scale cultures communicates social difference. For example, as artisans specialized in the various steps of dress production, they explored the range of possibilities within one technique. A dyer might experiment with a number of different mordants, or dye fixatives, to achieve a range of subtle hues within one pigment. A weaver might combine different weights of yarn in the weft to add texture and visual interest. As people were exposed to variations and praised the work of the artisan, the artisan was encouraged to continue to innovate. Some new effects achieved great popularity until something new was offered. When the nobility decided to support these kinds of innovations, fashion in dress became a visible expression of wealth and success in the large-scale culture.

SOCIAL STRUCTURE, DIVISION OF LABOR, AND DRESS

Whereas in small-scale cultures textile and dress technologies were organized around the needs of the family and household, in large-scale cultures, they became transformed into highly specialized crafts whose products were sold in the marketplace, traded for other household goods, and used as tribute tax. **Tribute tax** was a portion of the household production given to the chief or king in exchange for protection and the maintenance of public works such as roads. Each family or extended family of textile workers became a cooperative workforce. Typically, women spun the yarns and wove the cloth, but as cloth making became a business and a livelihood, men often took up the dyeing and weaving, while children apprenticed by fulfilling preweaving tasks such as filling weaving shuttles with yarn. This division of labor continues to be true in many large-scale economies, but is by no means the rule. Among weaving families of Indian madras plaid cloth, both men and women engage in yarn preparation and weaving (Evenson, 1991).

The broad division of society into full-time occupations in castes or classes overshadowed the age, gender, and ability divisions common to small-scale cultures. Members of both caste and class status groups, whether by conscious practice or tendency, married within their own social status category. Thus, an individual's all-important social status was inherited and overrode individual abilities as a determinant of occupation. As one might imagine, this inherited social status worked in favor of group unity and prosperity, but against the individual with unique talents or with little aptitude for a particular occupation. In any case, dress emerged as the primary indicator of caste and class, facilitating or inhibiting contact between individuals of contrary castes. In other words, young men and women knew by sight who was suitable or unsuitable as a mate, according to their community standards and dress cues. In fact, communities across India are still identified by types of garments, ornaments, and tattoos. Similarly, in the United States in the antebellum, or pre-Civil War, South, a "lady" was identified by her milky-white complexion and smooth hands, characteristics which indicated that she did no manual labor and was protected from the sun and wind.

As stated earlier in this chapter, differences in the quantity and quality of materials between essentially identical styles of dress marked class differences. Garments of the noble and the commoner, which is another term for the individual not of royal birth, may be the same style, but the dress of the noble was more voluminous, made of finer fabrics, and carried more detailed embellishments than the commoner's dress. For example, the early style of the *cheung sam* was bulky and not very fitted. During the Qing Dynasty (1644–1911 C.E.), bulky clothing that used many yards of handwoven cloths displayed the wealth of middle- and upper-class women in China. In addition, the near similarity of dress styles across classes taken together with the emulation of fashion between classes may have indicated a culture in which individual mobility through the ranks of the class hierarchy had become a possibility for some people. Social mobility is also evident in the creation of **sumptuary laws** in which governments legislated dress requirements for categories of individuals. Those elements of dress that were costly, such as silk fabrics and threads of silver and gold, were restricted to the highest caste or class by law. For example, in the later years of the Roman Empire (c. 100–400 C.E.), commoners were not permitted to wear purple-dyed cloth. The cost of collecting and extracting the dye from the purpura shell was so costly that anything dyed purple was considered a luxury reserved for the high born. In another period on the other side of the globe, the fine silk kimonos "lavished with gold thread, painstaking dapple dye, and sumptuous embroidery" worn by prosperous city dwellers in early eighteenth-century Japan were outlawed by the Edo government to anyone below the *samurai*, or warrior, class. As a result, the rebellious wealthy merchant class developed a new style of understated elegance in somber-toned outer garments with opulent lining fabrics, the design of which was sometimes commissioned from famous artists (Dalby, 1993). This is another example of *trickle-down fashion*, which can occur in large-scale cultures. It is interesting to note that such challenges to distinctions of caste or class play themselves out in dress.

The existence of sumptuary laws attests to the fact that humbler folk emulated, to the extent they were able, the dress styles of the aristocracy. Sumptuary laws were enacted in response to this behavior, but sumptuary laws have never been effective for very long. As lower classes embraced the ways and means of the aristocracy, the wealthy and powerful sought new and exclusive types of dress to distinguish them from their subordinates. This constant innovation and trickle down in dress constitutes one of the bases for fashion change.

In some large-scale cultures, kings controlled the acquisition and use of fine textiles and dress by maintaining royal factories. The purpose of royal factories was to produce and supply the types of dress worn by the nobility. Because the king controlled the work of the artisans, he also controlled the distribution of their work. For example, in the world of the sixteenth- and seventeenth-century Muslim empire, robes of honor were made in royal factories and given to individuals by the emperor as a sign of their promotion into the nobility or to a higher rank within the nobility (Gordon, 1996; Hambly, 1996). Since no one else had access to the products of these factories, donning a robe of honor was a powerful and efficient way to communicate and validate an individual's new status.

Another way ranked status was evident in dress in a large-scale culture was visible in how and when the body was exposed. On the one hand, there were rules for removing some body supplements in the presence of higher ranking individuals: "In south India it was obligatory for a low-caste man to approach anyone of the upper castes or indeed for a servant his master by first stripping himself to the waist as a mark of respect" (Guha, 1983). In European countries, it was customary for a man to doff (remove) his hat to a lady and to remove his hat completely when indoors. In India during the reign of the Mughal emperors (fourteenth through nineteenth centuries C.E.) it was obligatory for individuals to cover their heads and remove their shoes in front of superiors.

On the other hand, layering of body supplements was a visible manifestation of **rank**—the greater the number of layers, the higher the rank. Examples of the importance of layering and display of multiple items of dress abound. For public occasions, noble Japanese women during the Hein period (ninth to twelfth centuries C.E.) wore many layers of kimono-like robes at one time. The colors of the robes were coordinated and the edges of the sleeves, necklines, and hems were carefully placed so that a thin strip of cloth from each robe layer was displayed (Dalby, 1993). When the Japanese crown prince was married in 1993, the vestige of this early style of Japanese noble women's dress was seen in the wedding ensemble worn by the bride; she wore a 12-layer kimono weighing about 30 pounds (Suga, 1995). In Hellenic Greece (c. 500–300 B.C.E.) sumptuary laws were passed to limit the number of garments any one person could wear at the same time in order to maintain class distinctions. The practice of layering to display social status is evident in large-scale cultures today. In India, most married women wear bangle bracelets on each wrist. The make of the bangles—plastic, glass, ivory, conch shell, silver, or gold—displays a woman's place in the social hierarchy. In Rivers State, Nigeria, the position of a Kalabari family in society is expressed in the number and quality of ancient Indian trade cloths displayed as part of a funeral celebration.

As large-scale cultures fostered a wide variety of dress forms, habits, and functions, standards for dress evolved. Rules were codified for manipulating dress, or dress gestures, to demonstrate social inequality or honor. Examples, such as doffing the hat, described previously, fall into this category of standards for the use of dress. Other examples include a Muslim woman drawing her veil over her face in modesty and humility, or a nineteenth-century European woman keeping her gloves on as a marker of both modesty and gentility. Shoes are removed before entering a Japanese or Hindu home as well as in more traditionally oriented places of business in India, and in many places when entering religious buildings, as seen in Figure 14.6. In addition, for the first time it became possible to be dressed inappropriately for a social occasion. Knowledge of the rules of dress for different events became another hurdle for the individual with high social aspirations.

As we discussed in the previous section, the expense involved in the creation of the dress differentiated upper-class wearers from lower-class wearers, as did the variety of embellishments to that dress. In medieval Europe, skilled weavers were housed at court to create ever more sumptuous cloth for the king and his family, for both everyday dress and dress worn for court occasions. Embroidery with threads of gold and silver along with precious gems decorated these exquisitely woven fabrics. Because only royalty could afford these practices, dress made a clear hierarchy of wealth and power visible to all. Kente cloth from Africa provides another example of expense in creating the dress of the highest social classes. Made by the Akan people of Ghana, it was originally woven out of imported silk cloth that was unraveled, then rewoven into strips. These narrow strips were stitched together to form one large cloth worn as a wrapper or toga-type garment by a person of high status, as in Figure 1.12. While the imported silk is an important part of kente cloth, the initial unraveling and reweaving, along with the transformation of meaning in the process, made the imported silk a symbol of royalty. Thus, the types of dress worn by the noble and powerful in a large-scale culture serve to affirm permanent, or caste, distinctions in social rank (Cole & Ross, 1977).

POLITY AND DRESS

The centralized political structure of a large-scale culture required distinctions in dress to mark the office and degree of political authority of each wearer. Insignias, or badges that identify political rank, included something as elaborate as the kente cloth described previously or a specially made medallion suspended from the neck and worn only on high holidays. Insignia of the highest ranking officials—especially chiefs, kings, and emperors—were often very ostentatious and rich. This was true not only for public appearance dress, but often also for daily dress of political leaders and their families. Of course, richness was defined in terms of what was rare or expensive to produce or obtain in the specific locale of the society in question. Yoruba kings of Nigeria have worn garments of state constructed of beads from Venice, while the Aztec rulers wore capes entirely covered in the feathers of rare colorful birds. Figure 8.5 depicts one of the squares of cloth intricately embroidered in silk with different birds worn by imperial Chinese government officials. Each bird indicated a particular government position.

When European monarchs were installed into office as absolute authority, the most sumptuous kinds of dress were a significant part of the investiture ceremony. Note that the term investiture is derived from the Latin root *investire*, which means "to clothe." Thus, the concept of royal investiture was built

Figure 8.5
Badges of office, or insignia, were used in many large-scale cultures to communicate political rank, such as this intricately embroidered square of silk sewn onto the robe of an imperial Chinese official. Different motifs represented different government positions. China, late nineteenth century.

upon the wearing of new vestments, or clothes. European monarchs wore richly detailed garments of silk brocade and velvet with gold and silver lace or embroidery. Royal robes were constructed of rare animal pelts, such as ermine and leopard, and often had such extensive trains that courtiers were required to support the weight of the trains so that the monarch could walk. Precious gems were set in crowns of gold and silver, and jewelry bedazzled the eye. Handheld insignia of state, such as scepters and orbs, left no doubt in the minds of the observers who was the power of the realm, as shown in Figure 8.6, the coronation of Peter the Great of Russia. The majesty of this regalia can also be observed when Queen Elizabeth II of England opens Parliament each year.

Centralized political authority usually required some form of military, to conquer and annex neighboring peoples, to exact tribute from agriculturists and artisans, and to maintain control of areas conquered. Thus, military uniforms developed to signify the authoritative use of power in service of the state.

Figure 8.6
The coronation regalia of Peter the Great of Russia leaves no doubt in the viewer's mind about the absolute power of the Czar. *Peter in England* by Sir Godfrey Kneller, 1698.

Such uniforms were designed to protect the soldier in combat. As seen in Figure 8.7, the Greek soldier's uniform included a helmet, leather chest and leg protectors, and a shield. Usually uniforms also carried insignia of rank to communicate degrees of authority and chain of command within the military. Uniforms and insignia continue to be visual, shorthand forms of communication, necessary in battle situations. Such insignia include the use of color, hat styles, and badges. Medals (inserted into the uniform) earned through bravery sometimes qualify a soldier for higher rank and are a clear statement to others of individual bravery and skill, within a type of dress that otherwise puts a premium on conformity.

After the initial choice to concentrate power in the authority of one individual, small-scale cultures often grew into large-scale cultures. Sometimes growing communities merged together; other times neighboring groups were assimilated through conquest. Differences in dress between the conquered and the conquerors continued, marking the variations in social position that we have called caste or class. These differences crystallized over time into what we now think of as ethnic dress (also discussed in Chapter 2), which encompasses

Figure 8.7
Military uniforms developed in large-scale cultures extended the power of the chief or king through the creation of an army. Uniforms included dress components to physically protect the soldier and to identify his position in the chain of command. Redrawn from a Greek vase, 600–400 B.C.E.

those types of dress that distinguish a group of people as culturally unique. Ethnic dress is often so identified with a specific culture that it does not enter the mainstream of dress choices for people in the larger state.

If a large-scale political entity continued to grow in size and complexity through conquest and treaty negotiations, it became an empire. Some empires developed thousands of years ago, though they controlled only small portions of the globe. For example, 3,600 years ago, the Shang Dynasty controlled much of what is now China. More recent empires were created through European colonial expansion and extended across much of the globe. In the nineteenth century it was said "the sun never set on the British Empire." Evidence of the continuing influence of imperial expansion is provided by Figure 8.8, which shows the spread of imperial languages over the globe. If we compare the size of the various empires, it is an interesting exercise to consider the extent to which various portions of the globe are still affected by the cultures of their past colonial rulers. Take for example the case of Islamic dress influence. Figure 8.9 shows the extent of the predominance of Islamic society and religion, both associated with the spread of the Islamic empire and cultural influence up to the eighteenth century C.E. In the Muslim areas highlighted, shared elements of dress might include similar definitions of which areas of the female body should be covered in public, surface design motifs that are appropriate for dress, and might extend to the way that colors are used, alone or in combination.

Colonial dress and native or indigenous dress tended to co-exist in an uneasy tension, influencing and being influenced by each other. For example, the performance dance dress of Nez Perce American Indians in twentieth century Idaho shows no clear-cut signs of influence by Euro-American dress, but the everyday dress of most Nez Perce draws very heavily, if not completely, on Euro-American dress. What was once everyday dress for many American Indian groups has become special occasion dress for events that call upon the solidarity of the ethnic community. In Figure 8.10, young Muslim women in a large Middle Eastern city combine traditional dress required by their religion with global-scale dress.

A small-scale culture continuing to survive at the margins of a large-scale culture, or incorporated into it as a salient group, may adopt dress items or dress processes from the larger group into its dress, through the mediation of its unique cultural aesthetic for dressing the body. The process of selectively borrowing a cultural object, such as an item of dress, and making it a part of the receiving culture is called *cultural authentication*. The transformation occurs at four levels. First, the object is *selected* and used. Second it is *characterized* by being given a name different from its original name to make it distinctive. Third, the object is *incorporated* into the social life of the people in a way that gives the object significance. Finally, the object is *transformed* by applied design into an object truly unique from the original object.

As an example of cultural authentication, we discuss the Kalabari people, living in the delta of the Niger river, who controlled access to the Nigerian hinterland (Eicher & Erekosima, 1995). They were consummate traders, and during the fifteenth to eighteenth centuries C.E., they had access to anything

English
French
Spanish
Portuguese
Arabic
Russian
Chinese

Figure 8.8
As large-scale cultures grew from kingdoms to empires, they exerted influence on large geographic areas. This world map, viewed from the North Pole, shows the spread of imperial languages across the globe.

European seafaring traders had to offer. As a result, the Kalabari embraced a number of exotic products—textiles, beads, canes, and hats—which they incorporated into their dress in particular ensembles for individuals of specified status. Today these same ensembles are a powerful statement of ethnic identity within the larger heterogeneous state of Nigeria. As a contrasting example, the Seminole Indians retreated into the more inaccessible areas of Florida in order to maintain a measure of independence from advancing Euro-American settlers. The Seminole continued to adopt Euro-American shirt styles, trade for cloth, and later buy sewing machines to construct a distinctive form of dress which is both new and unique to their society (Steiner, 1994). In a twist of

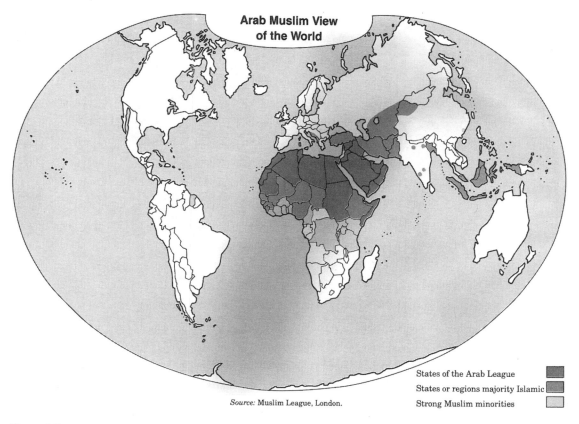

Figure 8.9
This map shows the spread of Islamic influence up to the eighteenth century C.E. In each of the areas highlighted, people share very similar ideas about dress based on the tenets and cultural practices of Islam.

irony, their detailed patchwork garments have made them famous among U.S. mainstream quilting circles in the second half of the twentieth century. Steiner (1994) details the process of cultural authentication in four cultures, including the Seminole, as they were incorporated into large-scale cultures.

Through cultural authentication, objects originating from the outside can be incorporated in a manner that retains a distinctive perspective on dress. As such, the process of cultural authentication is a powerful tool that enables the people of all groups to both grow and retain a degree of aesthetic independence in cultural contact situations, whether highly stressful or exciting to the people concerned.

Over time, as the people of small-scale cultures conquered or merged with the rule of the centralized government of a large-scale culture, they continued to retain much of their original identity, but often as an ethnic minority or underclass. This process was usually a long and protracted struggle to maintain

Figure 8.10
When the people of large-scale cultures come in contact with people of global-scale cultures, traditional dress and the dress of the global-scale culture co-exist.

dignity while adapting to a new way of life. The struggle involves much experimentation with and change in dress over a period of time. Some individuals may retain familiar styles of dress, while others incorporate new elements or adopt the dress of the new culture completely. Items of ethnic dress may eventually be incorporated in specific ways into the dress of the larger-scale culture.

Today in the hinterlands of the Amazon rainforest, the Highlands of New Guinea, the deserts of southern Africa, the jungles of South and Southeast Asia, the Arctic Circle, and other such seemingly inaccessible locales, the last remaining viable small-scale cultures have come into contact with large- and global-scale cultures which pressure them to change their ways of life. For example, the indigenous people of Central America are the descendants of the Maya who were conquered by the Spanish five centuries ago. Since that time, the adoption of world dress has been a part of the process of ongoing colonialism. Many Indians experience economic and legal discrimination, some are the victims of sustained genocidal campaigns. In Guatemala, a particularly violent conquest created a tradition of revolt among the descendents of the Maya. Wearing styles of world dress indicates affiliation with the Spanish "ladino" hierarchy; wearing ethnic dress is a blatant statement of insurrection against ladino racism. Today, the choice of whether to wear world dress or ethnic dress may determine whether the individual will live or die (Brodman, 1994). As a result of colonization and conquest, much information on the varieties of forms of dress has been, and continues today, to be lost as the habitats of the remaining small-scale cultures are taken over by resource-hungry large- and global-scale cultures that ring the globe today.

Some large-scale cultures expanded into emerging global-scale cultures, as described in the next chapter. Scott's description of ranks in the late Ch'ing dynasty in China (Reading III.3) demonstrates stratification and related dress of large-scale cultures. Other large-scale cultures waned and resumed a small-scale existence while maintaining many of the trappings of their earlier culture. After Spanish conquest of the Inca, Andean cultural traditions remained robust. Andean peasants kept their language, subsistence practices, social organization, belief structure, and material culture. The contemporary indigenous dress of the people of Choquecancha, Peru, exemplifies this in the way ancient Inca cosmology continues to be woven into the textiles used in everyday life (Seibold, 1995).

RELIGION AND DRESS

The development of a religion in which the gods are not intimately linked to everyday life or to one's family sometimes created the need for religious specialists who could communicate more effectively with these distant high gods. The priesthood as an avocation developed. In some faiths, elaborate and distinctive types of dress, called ecclesiastical dress, evolved and continue to mark priestly status, such as the dramatic orange, broad-shouldered robes of Tibetan priests. Ecclesiastical dress specific to priests or other religious practitioners indicates a special relationship with the god or gods, so it is not worn as everyday dress. Indeed, often the act of donning ecclesiastical dress is a holy act itself and facilitates the transition of the practitioner or priest from everyday action to a state of grace before god. A Roman Catholic priest still practices the ancient habit of kissing the stole, a long band of fabric, before placing it about his neck. This act is significant because the stole signifies priestly authority.

Sometimes ecclesiastical dress signals an exclusive relationship with god, such as the special daily dress of the Roman Catholic Pope, illustrated in Figure 8.11. The garb of women religious, once referred to as nuns or sisters, is also an outward manifestation of a special relationship to god and their conformity to the values of the Catholic church. The style of dress was often modest and austere, symbolizing a separation from worldly interests (Michelman, 1998). Unique styles originated from within specific communities of faith, such as the Ursuline and Benedictine orders, and reminded the wearer of the ancient tenets of the order. Many elements of Roman Catholic religious dress originated during the Byzantine Period (c. 330–1453, C.E.), when the Emperor Constantine legitimized Christianity throughout the Roman Empire.

In some large-scale cultures, the gods themselves were depicted in art and sculpture in distinctive dress. Sometimes divine dress was an elaboration of historical dress styles no longer worn by members of the community. These

Figure 8.11
This light-hearted explanation of the special daily and Sunday Mass dress of Pope John Paul II highlights the ancient origins of papal dress as an outward expression of the Pope's exclusive relationship with god.

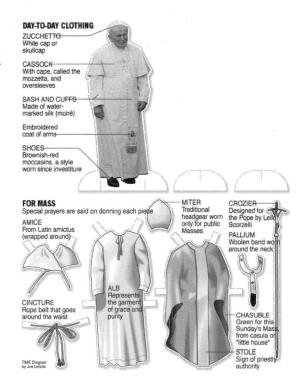

DAY-TO-DAY CLOTHING

ZUCCHETTO
White cap or skullcap

CASSOCK
With cape, called the mozzetta, and oversleeves

SASH AND CUFFS
Made of water-marked silk (moiré)

Embroidered coat of arms

SHOES
Brownish-red moccasins, a style worn since investiture

FOR MASS
Special prayers are said on donning each piece

AMICE
From Latin amictus (wrapped around)

CINCTURE
Rope belt that goes around the waist

ALB
Represents the garment of grace and purity

MITER
Traditional headgear worn only for public Masses

CROZIER
Designed for the Pope by Lello Scorzelli

PALLIUM
Woolen band worn around the neck

CHASUBLE
Green for this Sunday's Mass, from casula or "little house"

STOLE
Sign of priestly authority

TIME Diagram
by Joe Lertola

older styles associated divine figures with the earliest remembered origins of their respective cultures. As such, these artworks can be valuable sources of information about the history of dress within that culture. Consider the historical depth of the dress detailed in Figure 8.12a and b. The Mixtec goddess Tlazolteotl not only holds spindles of cotton thread, she is also wearing classical types of Mixtec dress. The illustration of Joseph, Jesus, and Mary dates from the twelfth century C.E., yet the figures wear draped garments reminiscent of Roman styles a thousand years older, roughly when the early Christian church was putting down roots. Moreover, the depiction of high gods usually embodied the highest ideals of beauty within the culture. Early images of Jesus Christ bear a striking resemblance to representations of Alexander the Great. Greek statues, such as those of Aphrodite and Achilles, were often sculpted with a proportion of ten "heads" to the body even though human bodies range from approximately six to eight heads. This means that if one were to measure the length of the head, the body would measure six to eight times that measurement.

Individuals entering sacred spaces and buildings associated with the high gods were often required to dress in a special manner for the occasion of worship and many of these prescriptions continue to demonstrate respect today. For example, in North America, many Roman Catholic women cover their heads in respect prior to entering the church sanctuary. Hindu devotees must

(a)

(b)

Figure 8.12
In some large-scale cultures, high gods are depicted in historical styles of dress, which lend honor, authority, and authenticity to the gods portrayed. A rendering of a Mixtec goddess, c. fifteenth century Mexico (a) shows her holding a spindle of cotton, which denotes cotton's cultural importance. Ceiling panels from a twelfth century church in Zillis, Switzerland (b) show the artist's understanding of the ancient dress of the infant Jesus and Virgin Mary in a scene of the flight into Egypt.

achieve ritual purity by bathing fully and wearing uncut cloth to enter the most sacred temples and gain the full benefit of their religious rituals. The placement of temples near sources of water and the digging of bathing pools at temples facilitates this requirement and allows orthodox devotees to come directly from the bath, still dripping wet in their clothes to worship at the temple. Muslims around the world must wash their faces, hands, and feet before entering a mosque to pray.

As gods become more removed from human daily life and religious specialists intervene on behalf of the faithful, dress becomes one means of intercession. The concept of ritual purity symbolizes the individual's worthiness to enter the presence of god and worship. Cleansed bodies, uncut cloth, modest dress styles, and covering parts of the body help the individual achieve a purity of thought and action as well. Thus, dress plays a crucial role in the religious life of people living in large-scale cultures.

SUMMARY

Large-scale cultures have a distinctive form of organization and associated type of culture that is markedly different from small-scale cultures. This difference is reflected in how individual members of groups dress. Large populations settled in village or urban centers meant that people no longer knew each other by sight. Dress was used to communicate information about family, caste, village, occupation, and marriage status. Permanent settlements permitted the accumulation of wardrobes and the technology to manufacture them.

Plant and animal fibers were cultivated for spinning, weaving, and dyeing into cloth. The labor-intensive nature of this process encouraged clothing styles that were economical, with little cutting, shaping, or waste of cloth. Individuals often made their own clothes, but specialists in dyeing and weaving produced dress for both commoners and nobles. Shopping for dress items at the bazaar or from itinerant traders became a source of variety in dress.

Quantity and quality of dress components emerged as indicators of wealth and social standing. When new techniques and styles were implemented by artisans, the well-to-do and high born used novelty as another manifestation of their social position and fashion in dress emerged. When people emulated dress styles of the aristocracy, fashion trickled down and new fashions were created to replace them.

When people of lower birth or rising social position adopted dress elements of their betters, sumptuary laws were enacted in an effort to keep people "in their places." Some kings controlled the production of royal factories as another means of controlling who had access to distinctive forms of dress. When the king invested an individual with a robe of honor, the robe efficiently communicated and validated this new status. Removing certain garments and the layering of garments also expressed social position relative to others.

The centralized political structure of large-scale cultures required distinctions in dress to mark the office and degree of political authority of each wearer. Insignia, uniforms, and ceremonial dress served this purpose. As small-scale cultures were incorporated into large-scale cultures, ethnic dress became one way to identify the colonized. When the people of small-scale cultures and large-scale cultures interacted, they often borrowed, changed, and incorporated articles of dress from each other. This process is called cultural authentication. Tracing the process of cultural authentication, or resistance to it, can be a useful tool in understanding the negotiation of relationships across cultural boundaries.

As religious experience shifted from individual relationships with the spirits of ancestors and natural elements to the worship of a high god or gods, religious specialists facilitated communication with the divine. Ecclesiastical dress identified religious specialists to others and helped them fulfill their role. Preparing for worship often involved purifying the body as a means to purifying the heart and donning ritually meaningful dress symbolized the individuals' worthiness to enter the presence of god.

The distinction of large-scale culture represents a second great divide in human history and describes a general way of life very different from small-scale existence. Levels of authority permitted the development of craft specialists, the accumulation of wealth, and the interaction of many different kinds of people. Dress became one means this new way of life became manifest.

STUDY TOOLS

Important Terms

caste
class
rank
sumptuary laws
tribute tax

Discussion Questions

1. Discuss the characteristics of large-scale culture and how they affect dress. Use Table 8.1 to help organize your discussion.
2. What aspects of life in a large-scale culture make it unlikely that members of that culture dress alike? Give reasons from (1) economy, (2) social structure, (3) residence patterns, (4) political conquest, and (5) religion.
3. Discuss the roles of uniforms and sumptuary laws in organizing social life in a large-scale culture.

4. Compare and contrast the way dress is affected in small- and large-scale cultures. What are the primary differences between dress in the two scales of culture?

5. Compare the dress of small-scale and large-scale cultures as a unique expression of cultural identity. How do you account for the greater variety of dress in large-scale culture, as compared to small-scale cultures? What difficulties does this variety pose when you try to summarize the unique expression of cultural identity in the dress of members of a large-scale culture?

6. Discuss how ethnic dress in a large-scale culture relates to small-scale cultures' dress.

7. Discuss characteristics of dress in large-scale culture that seem applicable to particular dress situations in your own experience. What are the underlying similarities that make this so? Use concepts from Chapter 8 to articulate your ideas.

8. What aspects of the organization of dress in large-scale cultures seem no longer applicable in your culture today? Why? Use concepts of Chapter 8 to articulate your ideas.

9. Analyze the dress changes described in Reading III.2, "They Don't Wear Wigs Here," by Barbara Schrier using the concepts of ethnic dress, cultural authentication, and fashion from Chapter 8.

10. Discuss the use of dress distinctions described in Reading III.3, "Court, Formal and Everyday Dress during the Late Ch'ing Dynasty," by A. C. Scott, analyzing their significance using concepts from Chapter 8 concerning how large-scale cultures affect dress.

11. Define the concept of cultural authentication. What are the four steps in the process?

12. Identify a detail, style, or type of dress in your culture that was culturally authenticated from another culture. Speculate on the process of cultural authentication.

Activities

1. Conduct research on the detail, style, or type of dress culturally authenticated by your culture as identified in Discussion Question 12. Were your speculations accurate?

2. In small groups, imagine you have been installed as the king or queen of a small monarchy. Design the supplements and modifications to the body used in the investiture ceremony. Describe the ceremony, focusing on when and how these vestments will be donned.

3. Characteristics of large-scale cultures are visible in global-scale culture. One example is using dress details to communicate wealth. Using pictures and advertisements from expendable fashion magazines and other sources, create a collage of the kinds of details you believe express the socioeconomic position of the wearer. In small groups, compare images. What similarities and differences do you notice? What accounts for the similarities and differences?

4. Select an item or process of dress (i.e., body supplement or modification) that is currently not worn in your own culture. If, as a designer and marketer, you were interested in introducing a new product inspired by this foreign dress into your culture, how would you use the four steps of cultural authentication model to help you organize your design and marketing ideas? Write and visually depict a plan.

5. Using Table 8.1, examine the characteristics of large-scale cultures. Complete the row entitled "Dress." What characteristics would you identify for the dress of people in large-scale cultures? Specify types and uses of dress in chiefdoms, kingdoms, states, and empires.

9

Global-scale Culture and Dress

OBJECTIVES

To describe the characteristics of global-scale culture.

To understand how these characteristics affect dress.

To explore how dress expresses group life in a global culture.

To recognize that culture scales are dynamic.

To recognize that when people of different culture scales come in contact, their affinities and conflicts are evident, in part, in dress.

THIS CHAPTER DESCRIBES *global-scale culture* and analyzes its implications for systems of dress within such a society. In Chapter 2, we compared and contrasted the concepts of *society* and *culture*. Society was described, in short, as the interactions people create to structure their lives. Culture describes the way people behave and interact with each other as they carry out their daily tasks within these structures and systems, dress being one of these behaviors.

In this chapter, we describe global-scale culture and analyze its implications for dress. What we begin to discover when we examine the characteristics listed on Table 9.1 is that, at this writing, we do not live in a single global-scale culture in which the people of all nations co-exist under one central governing

TABLE 9.1

The Scale of World Cultures

	Global
Society	Class-based
	Literate
Economy	Markets
	Corporations
	Capitalist
	Consumer
Technology	Industrial
	Fossil fuel
	Mass production
	Monocrop
Population	1 million or more
	Urban
Polity	Nation-states
	Supranational
Ideology	Patriotism
	Monotheism
	Progress
Dress	

Adapted from Bodley, John H. (1994). *Cultural Anthropology: Tribes, States, and the Global System.* Mountain View, CA: Mayfield, p. 16.

body. The closest we can come to a conceptualization of a global-scale society might be found in popular science fiction. Fans of the *Star Trek* series know that Earth, as a single entity in the future, is a member of the United Federation of Planets. However, many individual nations today can be described with a constellation of social and cultural traits that capitalize on linkages created through technology, trade, and travel. Many nations have created dynamic alliances that are mutually beneficial. Moreover, when we examine these linkages and alliances, we discover something else. If we do not live yet in a global-scale society, we do live within a global-scale culture. Through cable television, satellite communication systems, and the Internet, new and cross-cultural ideas are exchanged around the planet at the blink of an eye. Even in the smallest town in Idaho or the remotest Himalayan village, anyone with access to the Internet can download the latest in music, videos, and fashion.

One unique feature of the global system is that people of many different cultures can and do interact as part of a daily routine. The people of societies and cultures of differing scale naturally have different values and beliefs. When a small-scale culture bumps up against an emerging global-scale culture, the result can range from the mutually enriching cultural authentication of ideas and objects to the utter destruction of the small-scale culture altogether. Thus, one way to visualize scale is by examining to what extent the people of different scale cultures are interconnected to each other and by noting the quality of that interaction. The negotiation of cross-cultural relationships is often clearly and poignantly expressed in dress.

CHARACTERISTICS OF GLOBAL-SCALE CULTURES

Global-scale cultures as charted in Table 9.1, contrast sharply with small-scale cultures, for they consist of populations of one million people or more. Much of this population resides in urban centers. As people leave rural areas to find work in the city, the city grows. One urban center might expand and merge into its neighbor, forming a megalopolis. Global culture is industrialized, depending upon fossil fuels for energy. Those who continue to farm find that concentrating their efforts on the growing of one, highly specialized and hybridized monocrop that fulfills the needs of many people is more profitable than growing a variety of crops to sustain one family.

The global economy is based on the production of profit for large corporations, which focus their energies on determining and fulfilling consumer desires. Many of these consumers are literate and rank themselves according to financial income and economic well-being, rather than by bloodlines or caste. Kingdoms and empires are replaced by nation-states and nations align themselves with other nations for political or economic strength. Religious faith might remain significant to individuals, but patriotism is expected and emphasized as a right and an obligation of every citizen of each nation-state. Above all, it is the belief in progress and the application of science and reason to solve human problems that distinguishes the global-scale culture from small- and large-scale cultures.

POPULATION, RESIDENCE, AND DRESS

Each of these generalized characteristics has important implications for how individuals dress in a global-scale culture. Because the populations of global-scale cultures are so huge and people work in highly specialized jobs, dress can be used as a clear signal of social identity. The business traveler needs to identify the airline gate agent in an international airport congested with travelers from all walks of life. The judge needs to preside over the court of law and

communicate the authority of the state. The customer needs to identify the retail sales associate in a sprawling urban mall. Because many people live in vast
urban centers, obvious forms of identification like uniforms and name badges
facilitate city life with a minimum of confusion.

In addition to social identity, the citizens of a global-scale culture may feel
free to communicate individual views through dress. The ubiquitous T-shirt is
one example. All over the world, T-shirts are emblazoned with words and images that express fraternal membership, team spirit, musical taste, political
agendas, and corporate advertising. The T-shirt in Figure 9.1 expresses a humorous attitude about this popular garment. In many groups, using dress as a
primary expression of one's personal aesthetic may be valued over conformity
in dress, a subject we will address in the next section. Dress may also downplay
gender distinctions. Both men and women may wear similar kinds of dress or

Figure 9.1
The message on this T-
shirt provides a humorous
comment on message-
bearing T-shirts in gen-
eral.

they may use similar body modifications like gathering long hair into a ponytail or wearing a unisex fragrance.

Travel, for business and recreation, is a feature of global-scale culture. Many U.S. firms have offices around the world to which corporate representatives must travel from time to time. Because airline travel is competitively priced, many global-scale citizens travel to exotic ports for holidays and honeymoons. North American and European students often use their college years to backpack across Europe or Asia. Ironically, these global-scale citizens have the dress requirements of a nomadic life in common with their small-scale ancestors. Garments that are lightweight and serve multiple purposes are the mainstays of modern travelers. New fibers, fabrics, and finishes are developed to produce clothing that resists wrinkling and will launder easily and dry quickly. The globe-trotter can also select from a variety of luggage styles to suit the specific purpose of the trip, such as business, backpacking, family holiday, safari, or camping. Catalogues such as *TravelSmith* and *Orvis* offer the savvy traveler several solutions to the problem of weight and packing efficiency, from quick-dry underwear to the all-purpose black dress to the wrinkle-proof and pickpocket-proof sport coat, as pictured in Figure 9.2.

Figure 9.2

Travel for business and pleasure is a feature of global-scale culture. Designers and merchandisers in the apparel industry develop products such as this sport coat to meet the specific needs of the globetrotter.

The travel style of Japanese youth exemplifies yet another choice of tourism in a global-scale culture. Instead of a brief excursion, they move to an international city like New York where they can live an avant-garde existence quite different from their tradition-bound upbringing in Japan. "New York has beckoned as a kind of fringe Mecca, where they can buy cheap used clothing, fly their freak flag, and return home after a year or two stamped with an indelible imprimatur of hipness" (Wise, 1997, p. 34). But some Japanese youth find themselves trapped between two cultures, strange to both their American friends and their Japanese family. Nevertheless, for these young people, global-scale culture has given them the opportunity to expand their horizons.

Sometimes the collision between societies and cultures of different scale creates either forced or voluntary migrations of people from one region of the world to another. These cultural migrations are called **diasporas**. One well-documented diaspora is that of the Jews from Palestine. The area that is now a part of Israel was the point of origin for the Jewish people, among others. It was also a battleground for empires from Egypt and Rome to Islam and the Holy Roman Empire. After the fall of Jerusalem in 70 C.E., the Jews dispersed across Europe, Russia, and Asia. Christian and Islamic persecution fueled Jewish immigration to the United States and the creation of a Jewish homeland in what was then British-controlled Palestine. In spite of, or because of, the Jewish diaspora, certain types of dress have crystallized into unique dress forms and link the wearer to both history and faith. For example, the observant Jewish man will wear *tefillin* (tef-FILL-in), *tzitzit* (tseet-tseet), and *tallit* (ta-LEET) during weekday morning services. *Tefillin* are a pair of small leather cases containing scrolls of holy passages from the Torah, the Judaic book of faith. One case is tied to the forehead with the leather straps hanging down over the shoulders; the second is wrapped around the arm with the scrolls at the biceps and leather straps wrapped down toward the hand. The *tallit* is a four-cornered garment similar to a shawl worn over the shirt with *tzitzit*, or fringes, hanging down. *Tzitzit* is also the name of a garment resembling a poncho worn throughout the day under the shirt. This *tzitzit*, or *tallit katan* (ta-LEET ka-TAHN) (little *tallit*), has fringes at its four corners, which must be visible below the waistband. The wearing of these garments is commanded in the Torah, which recounts the earliest history of the Jews' relationship to god and god's commandments to them (Rich, 1999). Thus, even though people of the Jewish faith and culture are far flung, they practice the same articles of faith, with the aid of items of dress almost identical to those their ancestors used thousands of years ago.

The African slave trade is another example of a diaspora in which people from many parts of Africa were transported to labor on sugar and cotton plantations all along the East Coast of South America, the Caribbean Islands, Central America, and the United States. The presence of these immigrant cultural pockets over several generations eventually led to elements of African dress being drawn into the culture of the country in which they reside. The cultural authentication of royal Ghanaian kente cloth was described in Chapter 8. When African-Americans sought to establish their African roots in order to tap into the power a definitive ethnic origin can supply, kente cloth was culturally authenticated as a path to political ethnic solidarity. In recent years kente cloth has been drawn into world dress in the form of women's purses and hats, men's vests and bow ties, and is sold as printed yard-goods in fabric stores. The wearing of kente and African types of dress highlights African heritage and is a common badge of identity and strength. African-derived aspects of dress are found in many parts of the globe where descendants of West Africans reside.

The diaspora of ethnic groups continues today. As programs of "ethnic cleansing" are carried out in Central America, Africa, and Eastern Europe, refugees seek sanctuary across international boundaries. Some of these refugees may return to their homelands; others may remain in the countries that offered them a safe haven. The process of acculturation by many immigrant groups to North America is often visible in changes of, adaptations to, and intergenerational arguments over what is appropriate dress. Traditional styles of Laotian Hmong dress are transformed through the process of cultural authentication, outlined in Chapter 8, to reflect American and Hmong culture. In this case, older Hmong women design the garments rooted in Hmong prototypes and draw inspiration from the range of fabrics and trims available in American fabric stores. The result is a rich blend of both Hmong and American influences (Lynch, Detzner, & Eicher, 1995). Reading III.2 highlights the efforts of immigrant Jewish women to acclimate to their new world using the medium of dress. The emigration and immigration of people across international boundaries as they flee persecution or seek a better life for their children contributes to the globalization process. When people travel to new countries, by their own volition or at gunpoint, they bring with them aspects of their own culture and dress into distant areas of the world.

TECHNOLOGY, ECONOMY, AND DRESS

The predominance of a commercial market economy in which products are manufactured, bought, and sold in exchange for money produces a distinctive system for the production of apparel. Individual garments are no longer made in the home except by the hobbyist. Tailors or seamstresses continue to create custom clothing for special occasions for the well-to-do, but most clothing in the global-scale economy is mass produced. In **mass production**, textiles and apparel are manufactured in huge quantities in a factory setting. Fabric is woven and knitted from a wide range of materials drawn from agricultural, timber, and chemical sectors around the world. While every country has its own domestic textile and apparel industry, more often production processes are integrated on a global scale, with several countries contributing to the production of the final garment (Dickerson, 1995). For example, cotton grown in India might be spun into yarn and woven into cloth in the United States. The cloth might be cut in Hong Kong, the pieces assembled in Mexico, and the finished garment sold in the United Kingdom. One transnational corporation might coordinate the entire process or each of these steps might be contracted and subcontracted by a number of smaller firms. While trade is an important feature of the large-scale economy, it takes on new significance in the global-scale culture. Countries become dependent on each other to fulfill basic human needs for food, clothing, and shelter. Figure 9.3 shows the globalization of apparel manufacturing and distribution.

As a population grows and a culture embraces an industrial economy, the rhythm of daily life shifts from agrarian cycles to the time clock. When more people work outside the home there is less time to sew for the family and a greater demand for affordable ready-to-wear clothing. In order to mass-produce apparel, systems of standard sizing are necessary. Standard sizing makes it possible to cut and sew billions of garments at high speed. It also makes it possible to fit the garments to the greatest number of people. Standard sizing works well as long as a population is relatively homogeneous, with narrow ranges of variation in height, girth, and body mass. In the United States, standard sizing has been criticized because it does not serve a population rich in ethnic diversity (Lin, 1997). As a result, leading manufacturers and retailers such as Land's End and Nordstrom are carefully identifying their target markets in an effort to fit their customers well with a company-specific set of standards (Brown & Rice, 1998) as shown in Figure 9.4.

When the family farm becomes an agribusiness, the use of heavy machinery, fertilizers, and pesticides become standard practice. Dress choices must meet these new factors by protecting and safeguarding the farm worker. University extension agents recommend fitted clothing that cannot get caught

(a)   (b)

Figure 9.3
Today apparel manufacturing occurs on a global assembly line, and familiar retailers can be found in urban centers around the world. In a global-scale economy, the manufacture and distribution of mass-produced apparel products is a global enterprise.

Women

Petite 4′11″–5′3″
Regular 5′4″–5′7″
Tall 5′8″–5′11″

	X-Small	Small		Medium		Large		X-Large	
	4	6	8	10	12	14	16	18	20
Bust	33	34	35	36	37½	39	40½	42½	44½
Waist	25	26	27	28	29½	31	32½	34½	36½
Hip	35½	36½	37½	38½	40	41½	43	45	47
Rise (Pet.)	24¾	25½	26¼	27	27¾	28½	29¼	—	—
Rise (Reg.)	25¾	26½	27¼	28	28¾	29½	30¼	31	31¾
Rise (Tall)	—	—	28¼	29	29¾	30½	31¼	32	32¾
Arm (Pet.)	28½	28⅞	29¼	29⅝	30	30⅜	30¾	—	—
Arm (Reg.)	29¾	30⅛	30½	30⅞	31¼	31⅝	32	32⅜	32¾
Arm (Tall)	—	—	31½	31⅞	32¼	32⅝	33	33⅜	33¾

Women

Regular 5′4″–5′7″

	1X		2X		3X	
	16W	**18W**	**20W**	**22W**	**24W**	**26W**
Bust	42½	44½	46½	48½	50½	52½
Waist	34½	36½	38½	40½	42½	44½
Hip	45	47	49	51	53	55
Rise	29¾	30½	31¼	32	32¾	33½
Arm	31¾	32⅛	32½	32⅞	33⅛	33⅝

Men

Short 5′3″–5′7″
Regular 5′8″–6′0″
Tall 6′1″–6′3″
Big 5′8″–6′0″
Big & Tall 6′1″–6′3″

Tops	*Small*		*Medium*		*Large*		*X-Large*		*2XL*		*3XL*		
Neck	14	14½	15	15½	16	16½	17	17½	18	18½	19	19½	20
Chest	34	36	38	40	42	44	46	48	50	52	54	56	58
Arm (Reg)	32½	33	33½	34	34½	35	35½	36	35	35½	36	36½	36½
Arm (Tall)	34	34½	35	35½	36	36½	37	37½	36½	37	37½	38	38

Bottoms	*Small*		*Medium*		*Large*		*X-Large*			*2XL*		*3XL*	
Waist	28	30	32	34	36	38	40	42	44	46	48	50	52
Hip	34	36	38	40	42	44	45½	47	48½	50¼	51¾	53¼	54¾

If you're concerned about the fit of a specific garment, don't hesitate to ask our salespeople for help. They have the right answers at their fingertips.

Page 2

Questions about fit? Call for our free "Fitting Solution" sizing guide!

Figure 9.4
Standard sizing makes the mass production of billions of garments possible, but works well only with a homogenous population. Leading manufacturers and retailers in the United States use company-specific standards based on detailed knowledge of their target customers as a marketing strategy.

in moving equipment, hats that protect the head and neck from damaging effects of the sun, and coveralls designed specifically to limit skin exposure to toxic chemicals, as seen in Figure 6.4. Thus, with reference to dress as a method of protection, dress can protect the individual from innovations that make life in the global-scale culture possible. Military uniforms become an assemblage of technological defense mechanisms so that from a military point of view, dress is a tool of battle. Technicians in all fields from fire-fighting to computer manufacturing benefit from occupational dress, as discussed in Chapter 6. Indeed, one feature of global-scale culture is a reliance on occupational dress, both to communicate and fulfill one's occupation.

The massive nature of production of all goods in global culture has negative effects on the natural environment. Production of dress is no exception. Textile bleaching and dyeing processes generate harmful effluents which pollute water sources. These negative effects raise the cost of goods produced beyond what we pay for them in the marketplace, though the side effects are paid for later. Green, or environmentally safe, production is becoming more important to informed consumers of mass-produced dress. Recycled materials, such as petro-plastic pop bottles, are now restructured into fibers that are transformed into a popular sportswear fabric known as polar fleece, as pictured in Figure 9.5. One fascinating aspect of textile innovation is the development of synthetic fibers that have the comfort attributes of natural fibers, and natural fibers that have the easy-care attributes of synthetics. Examples include microfiber polyester that feels and drapes like silk, and finishing processes that reduce wrinkling in linen.

Fashion is the driving force behind the manufacturing and distribution of most dress in global-scale cultures. Cross-cultural influences, technological

Figure 9.5
Global-scale mass production of dress is detrimental to the environment, making recycled products a cost-effective choice. Polar fleece is a popular sportswear fabric made from recycled plastic soda pop bottles.

improvements, demographic shifts, and current events all contribute to the sensation that we need new wardrobes to communicate who we are in changing times. The rapid currents and cycles in fashion in a global-scale culture mean that many dress styles are obsolete before they are used up. Thus, recycling of clothing, as an environmental necessity and as a fashion force, is becoming an important consideration in dress in global-scale culture. We will address reincarnated dress in the next section.

SOCIAL STRUCTURE, DIVISION OF LABOR, AND DRESS

Because commercial enterprise drives global-scale culture, people are stratified based on their access to money and profits. One of the most visible aspects of this class stratification in the global-scale culture is extremes of poverty and wealth. Impoverished or lower income individuals own and wear fewer garments, often made of lower-quality materials. When people value material possessions, these individuals may feel the pressure to purchase quantity instead of quality garments, straining their budgets even further as affordable but poorly made garments shrink, bleed, and rapidly become unserviceable.

Wealthier and higher income individuals have the money to spend on types of dress that imply social position. They can also afford to follow fashion trends in dress and express their aesthetic tastes through garments with better cut, fit, and detail. The wealthy may hire personal servants, such as maids and valets, to aid in dressing and closet maintenance. They may also hire personal trainers to help them maintain the body form they prefer. And the very affluent may have their clothing custom made at haute couture houses in Paris by the most famous designers in the world, such as Karl Lagerfeld for Chanel, Emanuel Ungaro, and Hanae Mori.

In households headed by a single parent or in which two parents work, time is at a premium. Money is often spent to pay others to repair, launder, and press garments. Catalogues and the use of personal shoppers may be more time-efficient methods of clothing acquisition than shopping at retail stores for these families. One benefit of the mass production and importation of apparel is the availability of low-cost, high-quality clothing. As a result, sewing clothing at home is time-consuming and does not save money. It becomes a kind of artisanship solely for those who gain satisfaction from the process of creation.

When middle- and higher-income individuals tire of their garments, they may sell them in consignment stores, thus distributing better-quality apparel to people who originally would not have been able to afford such clothing. Or, used clothing is donated to charities that use the work of sorting, repairing, cleaning, and merchandising clothing to train and employ people. Used clothing is purchased by lower- and middle-income individuals for themselves and their families, by students for retro fashion statements, and by parents of rapidly growing children. The sale of secondhand clothing also transcends national boundaries, as described in Reading III.4 "Transnational Biographies and Local Meanings: Used Clothing Practices in Lusaka (Zambia)," by Karen Hansen (1995). She describes the secondhand trade in clothing from the United States and Europe to Zambia and notes that secondhand clothes are sometimes reworked to better fulfill the local aesthetic. Also, secondhand clothes from non-Western countries are reworked for sale in the West. For example, "antique" Indonesian batik wrappers are cut and sewn into jackets; Indian *saris* are cut and sewn into dresses, vests, and bed covers. These reincarnated clothes are sold through catalogues that market "ethnic" clothing and goods to a "nonethnic" market, as illustrated in Figure 9.6.

Each of these applications of used clothing has implications for the way we look to others. Because the people in many African countries wear cast-off Western dress, they may appear to Western eyes as perhaps more "poverty-stricken" than they really are. Such garments may well have been purchased for their novelty and may have cost the wearer a significant portion of income. In addition, when Euro-Americans purchase and wear reworked ethnic dress as found in mail-order catalogues, questions arise about exploiting the willingness of indigenous people to sell treasured family heirlooms for sorely needed cash.[1]

**REGAL SILK
PATCHWORK SARI ROBE**
Our luxurious silk patchwork robe
provides elegant comfort for
lounging year round. Made from
recycled authentic saris collected in
India, the rich colors and patterns
will vary and are overdyed to give
them a more muted blueish gray
hue. 100% silk, fully lined in black
rayon with matching sash. In a
generous cut for both men and
women, one size fits most.
Imported. 40"l.
F719 $69.00

Figure 9.6
When Euro-Americans purchase reworked ethnic dress, such as this jacket
made from Indian *saris*, are they contributing to the economy of a "developing" country or exploiting its people?

When garments, made of new or recycled materials, are mass-produced, the assembly-line method is often used in which each sewer completes one task in the construction process, such as sewing buttons or hems. Sewers are paid by the piece, so speed is the key to maximizing earnings. Division of labor in apparel manufacturing falls along gender lines. Women are usually sewers or sewing machine operators; supervisors and owners are usually male. However, apparel design does not appear to be gender specific.

Division of labor also occurs among countries. Many U.S. apparel manufacturers reduce labor costs by contracting their operations out, as described earlier in this chapter. The division of labor along a global assembly line benefits some workers at the expense of others. With the North American Free Trade Agreement (NAFTA), many garments intended for sale in the United States are assembled in Mexico because the Mexican worker is paid a significantly lower wage than workers of the same skill level in the United States. Although some U.S. workers feel this choice is made at the expense of their jobs, Mexican workers have access to regular work and regular paychecks. This linkage to world markets through a skilled, low-cost labor supply means that the government of Mexico brings in hard currency used to finance government development programs that in turn bring education, medical care, and reliable communication and transportation systems to its citizens. These programs are intended to stabilize economies, to make so-called developing countries less susceptible to political volatility, and to provide people with the quality of life U.S. and European workers enjoy.

Initiatives like NAFTA influence world dress. When workers in developing countries, such as Mexico, for example, earn regular incomes, they can afford to purchase for themselves the brand-name garments they may have had a hand in making. As demand for brand-name apparel and other Euro-American styles increases, *world dress*, that is, the wearing of items like blue jeans, business suits, and Birkenstock sandals, becomes more evident. And when designers search the globe for fresh ideas that will appeal to many markets, the ethnic and **national dress** of these very same countries will provide sources of inspiration for *world fashion*, which can be defined as quickly shifting styles of world dress. We can see this global sourcing of fashion design inspiration in the work of well-known designers. Yves Saint Laurent based his designs in the mid-1980s on Russian, Persian, and Mongolian fabrics and silhouettes. Norma Kamali is the latest in a long line of designers to draw ideas from India. Ralph Lauren routinely uses colors, motifs, and silhouettes originating from American Indian sources, as seen in Figure 9.7. Moreover, catalogue companies such as Peruvian Connection integrate the refined knitting skills of indigenous Peruvians with Inca-inspired motifs to create exquisite knitted garments for the Euro-American market.

POLITY AND DRESS

As nations form and reform along geographical and ethnic boundaries in the global social and cultural system, the people of almost every country, whether large or small, often feel the need to communicate national identity by means of a national costume. Because many modern nations are made up of a variety of ethnic groups, singling out one specific form of national dress can be difficult.

Figure 9.7
In a global-scale culture, fashion designers such as Ralph Lauren routinely draw inspiration from historic and contemporary small-scale and large-scale cultures, which contributes to the globalization of dress.

For example, the kingdom of Sweden is made up of a number of provinces, each with distinct provincial dress. In 1984, a national Swedish costume was designed that distilled provincial elements into a single national costume.

Subcultural groups within the nation may also develop distinctive dress, to highlight group history, religious beliefs, or ethnic identity. Up until recently, the Mao suit, seen in Figure 12.6a, was associated with the Chinese people, while Tibetan dress, pictured in Figure 9.8, and the dress of other minority peoples in China distinguished them from the larger Chinese population. There continues to be considerable pressure placed on Tibetans by the Chinese authorities to dispense with their unique dress. This is curious when at the same time the ethnic dress of the 52 Chinese minority groups is displayed at ethnic festivals. As the People's Republic of China opens itself to world trade and concurrently alters its policy on ethnic dress, it is falling back on the dress originating with the dominant cultural group, the Han Chinese. For example, the *cheung sam*, also called the *chi pao*, has often been considered the Chinese national dress for women. This choice by default of Han dress puts the cultural minorities at even greater distance from national integration than did the Mao suit.

Figure 9.8
Subculture groups within a nation may wear distinctive dress that carries religious meaning or ethnic identity, as seen in the traditional Tibetan dress pictured. Dress choices of minority groups are often points of conflict when a larger scale culture wishes to exert its authority on a small-scale culture. Tibet, 1995.

At the same time that some forms of ethnic dress are being selected for transformation into national dress, other forms of ethnic dress are being selected for transformation into high fashion. In Indonesia, dress traditions from regional cultures have been reworked into high fashion dress and marketed across Indonesia and the world. The government's promotion of its couture designers at international political summits, discussed earlier in Chapter 2, is part of Indonesia's attempt to claim political leadership in the Pacific Rim. International acceptance of Indonesian ethnic dress reworked into haute couture dress is a part of this political strategy (Boehlke, 1999).

Confirming a national identity through dress cross-cuts the promotion of tourism in some countries. There is a delicate balance between preserving and celebrating national and cultural heritage and commodifying and reifying stereotypical cultural practices in the interest of attracting tourist dollars. For example, tourists to the Melanesian island area of the South Pacific could experience local native dress by painting their faces in the same patterns as traditional masks (Douglas, 1996). In another example, the New York-based international real estate firm Julien J. Studley, Inc. rewarded its 50 most productive salespeople with a trip to the Amazon. While there, these salesmen participated in an initiation ceremony in which they were dressed in grass skirts, body paint, and feather headdresses, presumably to imitate indigenous dress (Webb, 1997). These experiences tell the tourist very little about the Melanesian and Brazilian cultures, respectively, and only encourage stereotyping of indigenous people. Yet, ethnic and national dress is often used in tourist literature to attract the traveler to lands more exotic than his or her own. On some occasions, however, international tourism leads to deeper understandings and appreciation of the dress and lifeways of other cultures. Wearing the dress of the country one is visiting, as seen in Figure 9.9, can be part of that experience. Travelers often relish and relate the pleasures of a Turkish shave, an Indian pedicure, or being measured and fitted for a custom-made silk suit in Hong Kong.

Political organization in the global-scale culture exists largely to serve economic interests. Supranational proto-governing bodies such as the United Nations (UN) and the North Atlantic Treaty Organization (NATO) work for world peace, so that the work of the General Agreement on Tariffs and Trade (GATT), the World Bank, and UNICEF can continue uninterrupted. The purpose of the GATT was to break down barriers to trade and improve access to world markets by all nations.

Developing countries have increased access to world markets and the hard currency that can make life better for their citizens. Because textile and apparel production are often the first industries in a developing country to be upgraded to global trade production levels, it is through the manufacture and trade of textiles and clothing that developing countries enter into and participate in the global economy. The disadvantage is that industrialized countries will be forced to retool their industries to compete with low-wage/high-skill countries, laying off workers in the process. Global economies are dynamic. It is important to remember that what benefits one group in one country may have a negative impact in another country, and vice versa.

Figure 9.9
When countries promote tourism, there is a delicate balance between giving tourists an authentic experience of cultural life and reinforcing stereotypes. Gag portrait of a U.S. tourist in Kashmir in local ethnic dress provided by the photographic studio, 1971.

Supranational compacts such as the UN and the GATT, along with the economic power of transnational corporations, serve two ends in the global society. They bring the people of many separate nations together into relationships that facilitate the exchange of products and ideas. At the same time, they undercut the power of the nation-state. A new global culture is created, one with looser ties to specific locales but greater access to many other areas of the world through sophisticated technologies of travel, communication, and wealth. Because associations among these people are both global and local, dress choices change. Selections are made based on the situation and with whom one expects to interact. For example, for most state occasions, the president of the United States often chooses to wear a conservative blue or gray suit, white shirt, and striped silk tie. This ensemble is worn by men around the world and is considered appropriate dress to convey respect and decorum for the event. In his home state, however, the president might choose considerably more casual attire, which honors his friends by its friendly, at-home message. For example, President Carter often appeared in jeans and work shirts, emblematic of his identification with "ordinary" Americans (Hall, 1992).

World dress emerges in the global culture. Western dress styles have been culturally borrowed or culturally authenticated by the people of countries all over the world. Business suits, jeans, uniforms, and athletic shoes are common reminders of global cultural influence on all societies and suggests a new interpretation of egalitarian dress. Global-scale culture is also evident in the prevalence and availability of designer ready-to-wear from Ralph Lauren and the late Gianni Versace. Duty-free airport shopping, mega-mall boutiques, and department store websites make "exclusive" designer products available to anyone. But, this influence works both ways. As the people of global-scale cultures go out into the world through travel and the media, they bring back dress ideas that serve as better solutions to common problems or tap into the imagination. The pajama shirt and pant outfit was once everyday wear for men from Persia to India and continues to be so in many areas. Its light color and loose flowing cut is a perfect compliment to the hot, dry climate of that area of the world. As India was being explored and dominated by European colonial powers, agents of the European East India Companies found this ensemble better suited to the climate than their own fitted, layered, wool suiting. While agents were expected to wear English-style clothing during the day to conduct business, pajamas were more comfortable dress for the evening hours. Additional examples of ethnic dress forms that are staples of world fashion and world dress today are the Mandarin collar, the sarong, and the poncho.

At this point in the globalization process, however, national dress of even the largest nations of the world are not perhaps the most commonly worn form of dress on the globe. Symptomatic of the globalization of culture, businesses are growing beyond the confines of any one nation, and the annual profits of some large international businesses are much larger than the value of the gross production of many countries. The uniforms associated with such international companies are probably the most commonly worn single form of dress around the globe, as shown in the photograph of McDonalds employees in China, in Figure 9.10. Nevertheless, in the global culture many people maintain dress forms of different cultural origins for different social occasions. Traditional, ethnic dress will be selected for life cycle rituals and local community events. National dress will be selected for state functions, and world dress is used for the world of urban employment and international events.

As world dress emerges, the citizens of small-scale cultures may feel threatened by homogenization. Some people may fear they will be swept up in a tide of globalization that will destroy their rich and ancient cultures. By contrast, and in the name of progress, political authorities may feel that certain traditions are outmoded and make them appear barbaric to the rest of the world. In many areas from Cameroon, to Indonesia, to Brazil, practices of scarification, tattooing, and body piercing have been discouraged and outlawed. Ironically, these practices have found new popularity in the United States and European countries. Some traditions are gladly abandoned in favor of ideas, methods, and dress forms that more successfully meet the needs and fulfill the tastes of a dynamic culture.

Figure 9.10
Uniforms are probably the most common type of dress worn around the world, especially those associated with international corporations. China, late twentieth century.

By contrast, the people of some large- and global-scale cultures feel so threatened by the challenges and opportunities of life in a global community, they attempt to turn back the clock to a presumably simpler existence, one seemingly more within the control of each individual. Iran has returned to a state governed by the tenets of Islam, which requires the veiling of women in public. However, in the days of the Shah, the wealthy women of Iran were well-traveled and fashionable. In 1997, the *New York Times* reported that "[t]he veil is old hat, but Muslim women give it new vogue. Now it is a fashion statement, not just a religious thing." The article goes on to report that Wafeya Sadek is a designer of custom-made veils made of velour, satin, or lace and decorated with beads and other kinds of embellishments. It would appear that once fashion becomes a part of social life, it cannot be legislated out again.

Despite the homogenous appearance of world dress, cultural differences continue to play a large role in dressing the body. Within global-scale culture, many youth attempt to rebel against the social structure their parents represent. In parts of Asia, some youth relish their global connections, yet retain their small-scale culture origins in their hearts. They don expensive, imported designer togs and frequent trendy discos. On the surface they look Western, but inside they still hold the values of their parents: respect for age and respect for the family. In one study of the cultural values of youth in Bangkok, Jakarta, Kuala Lumpur, Hong Kong, Seoul, and Singapore, it was found that world dress was associated with only marginal changes in the cultural outlook of its youthful wearers. They continued to maintain traditional filial piety values that would, for example, lead them to ask their parents to arrange their marriages (Elegant & Cohen, 1996). In Bangkok, the wearing of world dress by youth is a fashion statement that the wearer has access to expensive things, and is not a statement of cultural protest (Vatikiotis, 1996). Market researchers believe that the reason for this dissonance between outward appearance and inner ideology is nationalism. No matter what the individual in Asia looks like, each has a strong national identity that overrides other influences.

The apparent trend toward homogenous dress worldwide, especially apparent in urban youth, tends to blind us to the cultural differences that continue to exist behind the apparently shared dress. The underlying cultural differences of the wearers of world dress and world fashion constitute a veritable minefield of difficulties to individuals working in the clothing design and retailing fields. Neither stereotypes of other cultures nor assumptions of a growing cultural homogenization manifest in world dress prepare the dress professional for the challenges involved in designing or marketing dress to the world.

However, one advantage of more casual dress codes in the United States in business in the 1990s has been greater productivity and better working relationships between management and line personnel. On the other hand, arguments arise over the idea that casual dress breaks down respect for traditional bastions of knowledge and power. Some people debated that the extremely casual dress of Generation X in the classroom contributed to their expression of overall disdain for and disrespect of teachers and learning (Sacks, 1996). To combat this kind of effect, some people will emphasize patriotism and religious values. After decades of Western influence, the religious leadership of Iran has demanded a return to the traditional tenets and dress requirements of Islam, including the donning of full body garments that shroud women. Thus, as people in small-, large-, and emerging global-scale cultures interact with each other through travel, the media, trade, and the Internet, individuals are required to assess how they fit into their families and their worlds. Social role becomes fluid and dress dramatically highlights this ebb and flow. Some analysts of dress in contemporary society such as Davis (1992) and Kaiser (1997) emphasize the ambiguity of dress and fashion in regard to how difficult it becomes to assess people by their dress.

The characteristics of global-scale culture often produce the need for individuals to create versions of small-scale cultures for themselves. In the United States, sometimes the pressure of poverty fosters the development of gangs, as poor, undereducated, urban youth seek power and identity. The culture they create for themselves is described by territorial boundaries, specialized dress ensembles, a language that includes signs and posture, and rites of passage. Confusion arises when outsiders are not aware of the meanings of these cultural expressions. Are baggy pants, extra-long belts, and pagers a form of gang dress or simply junior high school fashion (Hethorn, 1995; 1999)? One department store published a fashion spread with models flashing gang signs. The store was criticized by local law enforcement for either being ignorant of the meaning of the hand gestures or for glorifying gang behavior. In any case, disenfranchised groups want to be heard, and dress is one means of expression. Other self-styled small-scale cultures might include religious groups such as the Amish or Roman Catholic religious orders for women, and other groups as diverse as the white supremacist skin-heads and New York City's Guardian Angels. In each case, dress helps the group hone its image and communicate its values to each other and the public.

RELIGION, IDEOLOGY, AND DRESS

In some emerging global-scale societies, **monotheism**, or the belief in one omniscient god is perpetuated from large-scale social structure. However, the character of this god may be substantially different from culture to culture, as we can see in modern conflicts among, and even within, believers in Christianity, Islam, and Judaism. Nevertheless, practitioners and worshippers are often distinguished by dress. In turn, dress fosters the act of worship. The ritual act of donning the *tefillin* and *tallit* by Jewish men, described earlier in this chapter, is as significant as the items themselves. Many types of ecclesiastical dress and dress practices were instituted at a time when the culture was smaller in scale, such as Roman Catholic papal and religious order habits, as discussed in Chapter 8.

In emerging global-scale culture, ecclesiastical and religious dress might be modernized to meet the needs of changing times. For example, beginning with the Second Vatican Council (Vatican II) in 1962, many Roman Catholic Church traditions were loosened with the goal of making the Church more accessible to more people. For example, orders of women religious had been easily identified by their distinctive black and white habits. After Vatican II, some women embraced less restrictive and updated styles of habit and others chose not to wear a habit at all. Many of these women religious felt the habit created a barrier between them and those they were meant to serve and were delighted to set it aside. Still other women elected to continue wearing the traditional habits of their orders, believing them to be a badge of conformity to the values of the Church and a clear statement to others of their role in the world (Michelman, 1998). Whatever their choice, belief of these women religious in their roles in the work of the Church was symbolized in dress.

In other global-scale cultures, an ideology, or an overall philosophy or way of thinking, best describes the character of cultural ideas about right and wrong. Examples include Confucianism, which is the scholarly tradition and moral order based on the teachings of Confucius (551–479 B.C.E.), and Communism, a social order characterized by the absence of class and the common ownership of the means of production based on the writings of Karl Marx. A thought-provoking instance of an ideology is the concept of the Prime Directive, which guided the quality of interspecies contact in the popular science fiction series *Star Trek*.

Ideology is evident in dress. For example, in Communist China after 1946, the Mao suit became daily dress for most Chinese. The uniform styling, fit, and narrow color range eradicated most outward status, wealth, and gender distinctions. Citizens of the United States pride themselves on their equality under democracy and the ubiquitous use of jeans seems to bear this out. Apparent equality is belied by the fact that jeans can be purchased within a huge price range, depending upon the brand name or designer label. However, when we consider the utilitarian and "rugged individualist" image associated with American jeans and note their preeminence in the pantheon of world dress, we might conclude that jeans are evidence of an ideology of global-scale culture.

The intersection of religion, ideology, gender, politics, and many of the other concepts discussed in this text appears in the complex use of the veil in Islamic culture. Some people view the veil worn by Islamic fundamentalist women as an obvious sign of oppression, a symbol of a culture that denies women the opportunity to have a political voice and economic freedom, and an obvious statement of inferiority to men. But to some Islamic women, the veil offers protection from unwanted male advances, provides a spiritual center, and is a clear rejection of Western influence (Inda, 1992). In addition to religious and social significance, the veil can also be a fashion statement. Thus, the veil has multiple meanings, some straightforward and some subtle. In her book *Veil: Modesty, Privacy and Resistance* (1999), Fadwa el Guindi describes Islamic culture as one in which veiling is intimately connected with individual ideas about a woman's identity, her body, and her community. Thus, the veil can be seen as more than a type of clothing worn exclusively by women. It is a complex statement about Islamic women's social role in a global-scale culture.

SUMMARY

Just as some small-scale cultures expand into large-scale cultures, some large-scale cultures become global, consisting of more than one million inhabitants. Many people live in urban centers and are engaged in the manufacturing of products that satisfy the diverse needs of both domestic and overseas economies. Dress becomes even more important in a global economy as a means to communicate identity and status. As countries become more dependent upon each other through trade, supranational organizations, such as NATO and UNICEF, develop to keep the peace, maintain trade linkages, and distribute the benefits of a world economy to small- and large-scale cultures.

In a global-scale economy, dress is manufactured and distributed to consumers all over the world. One hallmark of the global-scale culture is the presence of poverty. The poor in industrialized countries may own fewer garments, often of lesser quality. They may feel an economic need to sell precious family dress heirlooms to make ends meet. These heirlooms might be transformed into garments with an ethnic flavor that appeal to the wealthy, while second-hand garments from the wealthy might be sold in the marketplace for a variety of end uses.

Because of this exchange of ideas through trade, travel, and communication systems, world dress emerges. T-shirts and athletic shoes are as common as kimono-style bathrobes and clogs. The leggings and long shirt silhouette popularized by Jean-Paul Gaultier is nothing more than a Westernized version of the Indian *kameez* (ka-MEEZ) and *churidar* (CHER-ih-dar). As world dress emerges, citizens of small- and large-scale cultures may react to the threat of global encroachment by returning to traditional dress forms and standards. Ethnic dress may create solidarity among people within a society and make it more difficult for change to occur, or it may stimulate support of a cultural identity that shows resistance to former domination by colonial or neo-colonial powers. When small-, large-, and global-scale cultures collide, dress is often the stage upon which these conflicts are most visibly played out.

Cultural authentication of foreign items of dress into a small-scale culture may function as a method for a culture to resist outside pressures to change, or it may enable a culture to import desirable outside elements. Individuals in large-scale cultures also culturally authenticate elements from the small-scale cultures they incorporate or destroy. People in global-scale cultures draw fashion inspiration from both small- and large-scale cultures. In all instances, people maintain a cultural aesthetic of dress independent of the culture from which the foreign element has been selected.

The size and scope of global-scale culture prompts some people to create small-scale cultures for themselves in the form of gangs, religious orders, or political action groups.

The scale of world cultures is a continuum of culture characteristics along which individual examples blossom and decline in size and complexity as they move through time. One scale is not "better" than another, and movement from one scale to another is neither inevitable nor a sign of "progress." Global-scale culture describes the social structure of people all over the world at one point in time and space interacting with each other across many societies. Looking at dress allows us to see this interaction in sharper focus.

STUDY TOOLS

Important Terms

diaspora
mass production
monotheism
national dress

Discussion Questions

1. Using Table 2.1, the Scale of World Cultures, on page 38, explain each culture trait in your own words and give an example, either from the text or from your other reading.
2. How can the Classification System be used as a way to describe dress forms in different culture scales?

3. Are there similarities in the dress of different age groups and different ethnic dress ensembles worn in the United States that tie them together as an expression of U.S. cultural and social group life? Discuss what these various forms of dress share that expresses their group identity as members of global culture.

4. Are there similar or different ethical or experiential issues raised in the case of secondhand clothing marketed abroad or at home. Compare the information given in Reading III.4, "Transnational Biographies and Local Meanings: Used Clothing Practices in Lusaka," with your own experiences buying used clothing.

5. As a group, discuss how you acquire clothing. When you dispose of clothing, what do you do? How do you decide when to eliminate an item from your wardrobe and how do you decide what to do with it? Has your thinking about this process changed as a result of reading this chapter and the readings? Why?

6. Compare and contrast the role of ethnic and national dress in global-scale culture. If possible, give examples from your own dress.

7. Discuss the development of world dress using information from the 1500s to the present. Name as many cultures as you can that have contributed some body modification or body supplement to the development of world dress.

8. How do people in different cultures differ in the way that they discard body supplements, particularly garments? Can you see the effects of these different philosophies toward clothing in news and travel pictures in the media of people from various parts of the world? Do these different strategies for discarding garments have any global ethical implications?

Activities

1. Based on your interpretation of Chapters 7, 8, and 9, complete Table 9.1 with "Implications for Dress."

2. Collect a series of news reports that describe a conflict in the world. Include photographs, if possible. Can the conflict be described as a collision between two culture scales? Can aspects of the conflict be observed in the dress of people in the photographs?

3. Examine several issues of *National Geographic, Smithsonian,* or other similar periodical. Select reports on cultural groups and their ways of life. Describe each group by its constellation of scale traits. By examining dress, can you learn more than the report conveys? How?

4. View a documentary film assigned by your instructor. Identify the scale of the group highlighted. Can you find evidence of interaction among people from different scales? For example, if the documentary is on a small-scale culture, do you see dress forms or influences from large- or global-scale cultures? Or do you see evidence of scale changing, from one to another? Describe your understanding of what you see and hear.

5. Examine scholarly journals such as *Dress*, the *Clothing and Textiles Research Journal*, or the *Proceedings of the Textile Society of America*. Select reports that focus on dress in various culture groups. Would the application of the concept of scale clarify the thesis of the author(s)?

6. Rent a movie that is set in another time or place. Pay particular attention to the costumes. Based on dress cues and other information presented in the film, identify the scale or scales depicted. Does this understanding enhance your appreciation of the film? Why?

7. Examine the country of origin labels in your wardrobe. Make a list of all the countries in which garments were manufactured. Do some labels differentiate between fabric origin and the country of manufacture? What does this tell you about garment production in a global-scale economy?

8. Examine the sizing labels in your wardrobe. Chart how many garments use numbered sizing (10, 12, 14), measurements (length, height, or weight), and unisex sizing (S, M, L). Speculate as to why each sizing system was used. Speculate also why you may have garments in more than one size.

9. Design, describe, and depict two dress ensembles that express your national cultural and ethnic identities, respectively. Contrast them and analyze the differences between them and the significance of each ensemble, including the occasions when you would wear it.

10. Examine your own wardrobe and clothing sold in stores and mail-order catalogues for examples of garments and home furnishings that are made (or you suspect are made) from recycled clothing from foreign countries for sale in North America and Europe. Compare your response to this clothing with the clothing use described in Reading III.4.

11. Select and view a foreign film from a country outside North America or Europe with a contemporary story line. View the film for enjoyment, but also pay close attention to the dress. List evidence of global dress, as well as ways that the dress still seems foreign to you—an expression of a different ethnic or national identity.

Note to Chapter 9

1. This issue has arisen within the United States as well, when an American designer started purchasing old U.S. quilts and reconstructing them into designer coats and jackets. It generated some protest from living U.S. quilters.

Readings for Part Three

III.1 GA'ANDA SCARIFICATION: A MODEL FOR ART AND IDENTITY
Marla C. Berns

Introduction

The Ga'anda are a small group of Chadic-speaking people living in northeastern Nigeria, north of the Benue River and east of its confluence with the Gongola (Fig. III.1.1). This part of Gongola State, called the Ga'anda Hills (Aitchison et al. 1972:43, Text Map 2), is characterized by high rocky terrain punctuated with clusters of granite inselbergs, supporting a settlement pattern of dispersed hamlets. Largely due to their geographical remoteness and decentralization, little was known about the Ga'anda until recently.[1] Although their dominant artistic mode is ceramic sculpture, the scarification of women (*Hleeta*, "scarifying") is highly elaborate and contributes significantly to an understanding of Ga'anda social and art history.[2]

Ga'anda hamlets consist of numerous independent households, the heads of which are usually related through the male line.[3] Although such hamlets tend to represent patrilineal kindreds, a brother or a cousin can set up a household in another hamlet or in some other locality distant from his relatives (Meek 1931 II:380). With increases and dispersals of population over time, three rela-

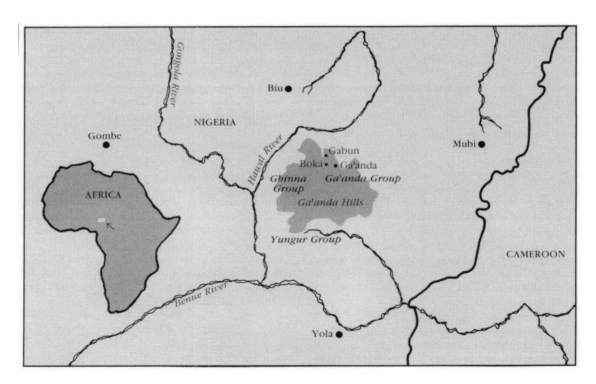

Figure III.1.1
Map: The Ga'anda Region. UCLA Fowler Museum of Cultural History.

tively independent Ga'anda subsections have emerged—Ga'anda, Gabun, and Boka—each with its own dialect. Today, much of the Ga'anda population has moved from relatively inaccessible hill sites to more centralized villages on the plains created since colonial reorganization.[4]

Each Ga'anda locality was traditionally an autonomous political unit. Authority was vested in families whose elders historically served as ritual priests and shrine custodians. Otherwise, social and economic processes were governed almost entirely by the independent decisions of household heads. The main responsibility of ritual chiefs, called Kutira, is still to preside over sacred and ceremonial activities oriented toward spirit-veneration and social integration. Today, village heads assume administrative responsibilities and judges appointed by the government of Gongola State deal with local disputes.

Each household enjoys the rewards of its own labor and enterprise. The Ga'anda are essentially subsistence agriculturalists who farm during a short rainy season (June–October) and supplement their crop yields with game killed during dry season hunts. Farmlands are inherited through the male line and are located in valleys some distance from the rugged hills where people live and where little arable land is available. Men and women grow sorghum or guinea corn, the staple of the Ga'anda diet, and women also plant smaller gardens of cow peas, cassava, and ground nuts.

Polygynous marriage is the basis of household organization and is governed by strict rules of exogamy usually involving kindreds who do not necessarily live in close proximity.[5] Therefore, marriages tend to widen spheres of geographic, as well as social and economic, interaction.

Marriages are arranged in infancy and are completed only after a demanding series of reciprocal obligations are met by the families involved. From the earliest stages on, large iron hoe blades must be given by the family of the prospective groom to that of the bride. Although no longer the case, the Ga'anda formerly regarded the blades as valuable currency and as primary markers of wealth and prestige. Large numbers of pots, gourds, and other household items are also given by the groom to his bride-to-be.

The importance of marriage is supported by the rites of personal transition both boys and girls must undergo before they are considered eligible. Girls experience a lengthy program of body and facial scarification, *Hleeta*, completed in a series of biennial stages.[6] At each stage, prescribed areas of the girl's body are cut in increasingly elaborate patterns. *Hleeta* also determines the

timing of the suitor's continuing bridewealth payments, which escalate as the scarification becomes progressively more extensive and complex. These arrangements involve long-term familial obligations, which draw on household resources for at least fifteen years.

Sometime between the ages of six and sixteen boys also go through an initiation ordeal, *Sapta*, held every seven years. No youth may marry or engage in independent economic pursuits until this three-month ordeal has been successfully completed.[7] The objective of *Sapta* is to teach boys three fundamental and interrelated skills: how to hunt and defend one's future household, how to make the tools and weapons associated with these tasks, and how to endure the hardships one might suffer in discharging these responsibilities.

Hleeta

Hleeta is accomplished in six stages, beginning when a girl is five or six years old (Fig. III.1.2). Toward the close of the dry season each year, usually in late March or April, *Hleeta* is performed by specialists in each Ga'anda locality. It is always done in a secluded area outside the hamlet, with the girl kneeling on a fixed stone, called a *dakwan fedeta* ("stone of the razor"). The elderly women (*hletenhleeta*) who do the scarification usually learn this skill from their mothers and grandmothers. They are compensated after the final marks are made with iron hoe blades, guinea corn, and tobacco. Annual permission to perform *Hleeta* must be granted by the families who historically exercise ritual control over this practice.

The patterns worked during each stage of *Hleeta* are characterized by rows of closely placed cuts that scar to form slightly raised "dots" somewhat lighter than the surrounding skin (Fig. III.1.3). To execute a row of incisions, the skin is pierced with an iron hook (*ngalkem*), its point at a right angle to the shaft, and lifted into a ridge; fine, regular lines are then deftly cut across with a triangular razor (*fedeta*). The result is a neat, delicate pattern of scars.

The first set of markings, called *hleexwira* ("scarification of the stomach"), consists of two concentric, bisected chevrons above the navel. That the first cuts made draw attention to a young girl's womb emphasizes her reproductive potential. This stage also initiates the boy's formal gifting of iron hoe blades to the girl's family.

The second stage of *Hleeta*, *hleepa?nda* ("scarification of the forehead"), entails the incision of four or five horizontal lines extending from ear to ear, the number of lines determined by the height of the girl's brow. Two years later, the third set of markings, *hlee'berixera* ("cuts

Figure III.1.2

Hleeta scarifications. Numbers correspond to stages of marking described in text and in accompanying caption. Contours of figures drawn after Chappel (1977; p. 206).

1. *hleexwira* ("scarification of the stomach").
2. *hleepa?nda* ("scarification of the forehead").
3. *hlee'berixera* ("scarification of the 'neck' of the arm [forearm]").
4. *hleefelca* ("scarification of the waist and buttocks") and *hleekersiberata* ("scarification of the back of the neck").
5. *njoxtimeta* ("cutting in places").
6. *hleefedata* ("scarification on the thighs") and *hleengup* ("scarification all-over"):
   a. *njoxta*, seven parallel lines across the upper chest, over which a row of forked branches are aligned, creating a continuous pattern (Design A); the central branch stands out from the rest, as it is a bisected arc.
   b. *?inhluuta* ("knife handle"), opposed triangles between the breasts repeating the distinctive shape of Ga'anda knife hilts.
   c. *caxi'yata*, opposed curves framing the central column of *njoxtimeta*; they take their name and shape from a round piece of calabash shell *(caxa)* used to scoop out guinea corn porridge *('yata)*.
   d. *kwardata*, the same alternation of chained lozenges and vertical lines repeated at the side of the body; informants considered *kwardata* to be the "finest" part of the design program.
   e. *shembera*, lateral lines adjoining the *hleexwira* chevrons over the navel and *kwardata* at the sides of the body; it creates another frame for a series of Design A.
   f. *kun'kanwannjinda* ("curve at the base of the navel"), a semicircle underscoring the navel and then continuing around the body as a set of three parallel lines; this curved motif balances the bisected arc worked at the top of the chest.
   g. *saxti'yera* ("ropes of rain"), closely placed vertical lines under the *kun'kanwannjinda*, which look like continuous drops of falling rain.
   h. *kwerimbete*, parallel lines following the vertical planes of the back, which intersect with the encircling band of *kun'kanwannjinda*.

© Marla Berns.

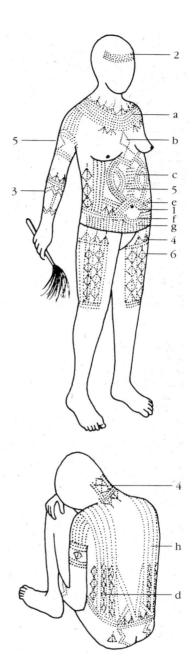

Figure III.1.3
Raised scarification markings on a Gbinna woman. Riji. 1981. © Marla Berns.

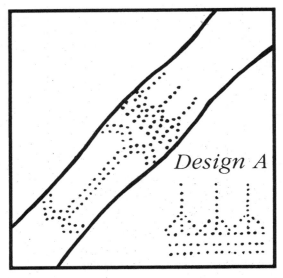

on the forearm"), is incised and involves more elaborate patterns of compact designs (Fig. III.1.4, Design A). The most distinctive element is a row of forked branches aligned over horizontal lines. This motif, which will be called Design A, is one of the few repeated elsewhere on the body, and whenever it occurs, the syntax of its two component parts is always the same. After *hlee'berixera*, the groom begins helping his in-laws on their farms, an activity he repeats each season until the girl's final marks are made. This means that a youth is effectively indentured to the bride's parents for at least eight to ten years.

The fourth stage of *Hleeta* requires repetitions of Design A to be made across the top of the thighs and buttocks (*hleefelca*) and at the base of the neck (*hleekersiberata*; Fig. III.1.4, Design B). On the nape, another distinctive, repeated motif is introduced, consisting of a lozenge or chain of lozenges framed by vertical lines, called Design B.

After these marks are made, a substantial payment in guinea corn beer (*mbaala*) is made to the bride's family. The beer is displayed in a number of ovoid gourd bowls and large, decorated pots (Fig. III.1.5). Both the number and size of these containers testify to the considerable economic investment such gifts of beer represent. Boyle (1916b: 362) explains that after the beer was delivered to the bride's father, instead of distributing it freely, he would sell it to his relatives in exchange for guinea corn. What he received, supplemented by his own surplus stocks of corn, would then be brewed into a second batch of beer. If the second brew exceeded the first in quantity, it was taken as a symbol foretelling the groom's productivity and the bride's fertility.

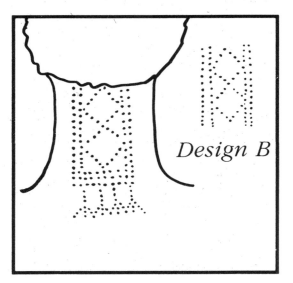

Figure III.1.4
Designs of *hleeta* scarification as described in text © Marla Berns.

The fifth stage of *Hleeta* is done when a girl is around thirteen or fourteen, called *njoxtimeta* ("cutting in places"). A column of short horizontal lines is cut down the center of the torso, branching at the top; more lines are worked at the shoulder and upper arm, framing

Figure III.1.5
Ga'anda ceremonial beer pot (*'buutiwanketa*). Ceramic.
H. 85 cm. Made by Cexawiwa Gudban, Ga'anda Town.
1981. © Marla Berns.

another unit of Design B. As the penultimate stage of *Hleeta*, the completion of *njoxtimeta* serves notice to both families that the substantial quantities of foodstuffs necessary to finalize the marriage contract must be accumulated before the last scarification can be done. The groom's family also must collect a large number of pots and calabashes to give the girl as bridewealth. In fact, the considerable economic effort such marriage payments demand often mean that the bride's family will postpone the last stage of *Hleeta* for years to extend the suitor's period of agricultural service.

Before the final phase of scarification begins, each girl must have her ears pierced and her upper and lower lips perforated. Traditionally, blades of grass were worn as daily adornment; iron or brass earrings and labrets were substituted on ceremonial occasions. (Today, no jewelry other than imported or manufactured earrings is visible on Ga'anda women.)

In March of the year when a girl's scarification is to be completed, the front of her thighs (*hleefedata*) are first marked with rows of vertically linked lozenges alternating with vertical lines (*kwardata*), a continuous multiplication of Design B. *Kwardata* shows that a contract of marriage has been officially "sealed" and prohibits any other young man from approaching the girl. Previously, other suitors may have competed for a girl's hand, and her parents might decide to favor a more promising partner.

Two months later, the girl undergoes *hleengup* ("cicatrization all over"), which involves filling in the areas of the body still left unmarked: the chest, the sides of the torso, the lower abdomen, and the back. This is a far more extensive phase of scarification than any the girl has previously experienced; it is likely that the prolongation of *Hleeta* over a number of stages prepares a girl physically and emotionally for this final ordeal.

After *hleengup* a girl observes a period of seclusion to allow the cuts to heal. She is then eligible to participate in the public festivities that conclude her marriage contract, beginning in July or August. It should be noted that one last unit of Design B can be cut into the backs of a woman's calves (*hleekante?ta*) before she completes *hleengup*. Boyle (1916b:364) indicates that these calf markings were only made if a girl procured an abortion twice while still living in her mother's compound. Although Meek (1931 II:384) does not specify that such markings were made, he does state that it was considered a "gross offence for any girl to conceive a child before this final inscription of her bodily marks." There is an apparent discrepancy between these two views, the former suggesting the marks are a further enhancement of the total *Hleeta* schema and the latter indicating they would be viewed in negative terms. Without question, for the Ga'anda, the consequences of having a child out of wedlock are severe and strong pressures are exerted to discourage premarital relations. While calf markings, done as Boyle suggests only after the second premarital pregnancy, may be permanent reminders of a girl's injudicious behavior, they are still regarded as part of a positive program of aesthetic transformation. In any case, avoiding sexual contact must have been increasingly difficult since, as indicated above, the bride's parents sometimes postponed the final stage of scarification for years.

Hleeta and Social Perpetuation

Hleeta plays a key role in the transmission and reinforcement of sociocultural values. That the markings are permanent signifies that the social transition made is irreversible. Only Ga'anda women are the carriers of this social and aesthetic message, a status suggested by the literal translation of the Ga'anda word for marriage, *kaxan nuu-nefca*, "marrying women." *Hleeta* is identical on all Ga'anda women, regardless of dialect subgrouping, underscoring its importance as a means of ethnic consolidation and identification. The consistency of this scarification program among women living in dispersed Ga'anda communities is further encouraged by the rules of exogamy and patrilocality around which social relationships are organized. And, the seriation of *Hleeta* binds the family not only to long-term domestic priorities, but to continuing social interactions that link dispersed communities. While all the economic and social implications of *Hleeta* cannot be dealt with here, it is clear that in addition to the designs visible on a woman's body, the gradual process of acquiring them is significant to their meaning.

Hleeta and *Sapta*, the boys' initiation ordeal, both acknowledge that, above all, the transition to adult status (i.e., marriageability) has been paid for in pain. During *Sapta*, for example, initiates (*wankimshaa*) are mercilessly flogged with reed switches, once to formally inaugurate the three-month ordeal and later on at least three other occasions. These whippings and a succession of other physical and psychological abuses test a boy's strength and endurance. During *Hleeta*, girls undergo a series of physical transformations that entail comparable and progressive stages of pain. The last stage of scarification, *hleengup*, causes such extensive bleeding that days of recovery are required afterward. This intense and prolonged experience tests Ga'anda girls in the same way that *Sapta* tests the boys. The ability to endure either of these experiences implies the endorsement of community spirit-guardians.

The importance of these ordeals to the socializing process is reinforced during the public festivities following the completion of *Sapta* and *Hleeta*. Every seven years community festivals, called Yoxiiwa, are held after *Sapta*; annually, independent hamlets hold an event called Yowo to honor the girls who have completed *Hleeta*. Both ceremonies include seven days of feasting and celebration. At each, special modes of self-decoration provide a dramatic visual commentary about the young peoples' commitment to Ga'anda society and their acceptance by the community and its spirit benefactors.

At the start of Yoxiiwa, each male initiate is ritually washed and then rubbed with red hematite (*mesaktariya*), the ferric oxide (Fe_2O_3) obtained locally from the "deposits left on the sides of stagnant pools as they dry up" (Boyle 1916b: 365). It is ground into a powder and made into a cosmetic paste by mixing it with sesame oil. Girls who emerge from seclusion after the completion of their final marks also smear their skin with this oily red pigment. By anointing their newly scarified skin, the subtle texture of raised scars is enhanced and accentuated. Yoxiiwa and Yowo are the only occasions when boys and girls undergo this striking ephemeral transformation. Indeed with time, the visual impact of *Hleeta* gradually diminishes as the markings fade and become almost imperceptible.

Traditionally the only clothing worn by boys and girls on these occasions is a sharply contrasting white *cache-sexe*. *Sapta* graduates wear a fiber belt, called a *talata*, which they braid themselves from strips of pith cut from particular shrubs. Girls wear a simple woven cloth apron, called a *takerker*. The combination of the colors red and white make important symbolic reference to social commitment and its link to spiritual affirmation. The application of red hematite (*mesaktariya*) draws special attention to the interface between secular and sacred realities.[8] *Mesaktariya* is a substance that identifies and activates spiritual intervention in a number of propitiatory contexts. It also is the medium that fosters direct contact between man and spirit on such occasions—smearing it over a spirit-charged vessel, which is then touched by a patient, transfers its associated healing power; dipping bows or arrows into it grants to hunters the protection of tutelary forces; and drinking it confirms the judicial authority of Ga'anda spirit "police." Rubbing the bodies of initiates with this same ritual cosmetic refers to the spiritual endorsement that has made social transitions possible as well as significant.

Hleeta Today

Scarification practices were officially outlawed in 1978 by the Gombi Local Government authority which administers the Ga'anda district. There is little doubt that this interdiction anticipates the eventual breakdown of traditional social patterns and ethnic allegiances, the covert intention of this official act of local control and national incorporation. In 1980, the new brides who danced at Xombata had not completed the final stage of *Hleeta*. Yet, they still appeared in full costume, wearing bunches of leaves tucked into the front and back of their "bikini briefs," and in spite of the fact that the other participants wore contemporary manufactured clothing. Indeed, the attention paid these young women confirms that among a significant portion of the Ga'anda population, traditional ways of life are still viable. It can be argued that Ga'anda arts will survive as long as the social and spiritual systems they support remain the ideological bases of material survival. It is significant that even the tradition of building a distinctive compound for one's new wife persists; grass panels are tied over the mud-brick walls of modern compounds to provide a suitable armature for decorative attachments.

Despite such continuities, however, it is clear that customary marriage patterns have been increasingly weakened by the antipathy of youths to prearranged marriages and to adulthood in remote Ga'anda village enclaves. Pressures to assimilate to a cosmopolitan urban culture have resulted in the concealment of ethnic markers, like scarifications, which associate the wearer with backward, "bush" societies. Girls who attend secondary schools with mixed student enrollments, in nearby or distant towns, or who hope to marry youths with a future outside the village, no longer want or need to undergo a procedure that has little relevance outside a Ga'anda context, either socially or ethnically. Often their parents offer little resistance as they, too, will benefit from this status elevation.

There has been pressure from the church since the 1950s to abandon *Hleeta*; its attitude is summarized by Margaret Nissen in her comments on the Ga'anda and the history of the Sudan United Mission in northeastern Nigeria:

> The Ga'anda girls, like their Yungur sisters, had to undergo cicatrization before marriage. But since there are a number of Christian fathers with girls ready for this ceremony, there are mature and respected people who can help the young girls in this dilemma and support them in breaking down this age-old cruel custom (1968:221).

The widespread adoption of clothing, which only became customary among the Ga'anda after the 1950s, has also contributed to the erosion of a practice that depended, in part, on visibility. Yet, the fact that *Hleeta* persisted among many Ga'anda families until its official ban in 1978 supports the contention that the process and meaning of imposing designs on a woman's body transcend aesthetics and visibility. The social history of the Ga'anda is clearly reflected in this important tradition, which may die with older generations of women, but will endure in the less ephemeral arts still preserved by the Ga'anda.

Notes

1. I conducted field research among the Ga'anda and a number of neighboring peoples living in the Gongola-Hawal Valley and adjacent areas from September 1980—June 1981 and September 1981—June 1982. This fieldwork was co-funded by the Fulbright-Hayes Doctoral Dissertation Research Abroad Program and by the International Doctoral Research Fellowship Program of the Social Science Research Council. My thanks are due to both these programs. I am also grateful to Arnold Rubin, Department of Art, UCLA, for encouraging me to continue the survey work he did in the Lower Gongola Valley in 1970–1971. During my stay among the Ga'anda (October 1980–March 1981), I was warmly received and assisted by many men and women, whom I now gratefully acknowledge. Musa Wawu na Hammandikko, my Ga'anda field assistant, should be especially thanked for his enthusiastic support and encouragement. His personal desire to preserve the Ga'anda heritage prompted him to research and write a history of the Ga'anda (1980), which Arnold Rubin and I helped to see into print with the assistance of the African Studies Center, UCLA. In addition to my lengthy treatment of the Ga'anda (1986), information on them is included in Rubin's forthcoming monograph, *Sculpture of the Benue River Valley*, and in Boyle (1915, 1961a, 1961b), Meek (1931 II), and Nissen (1968).

2. Translations of Ga'anda words have been drawn from R. Ma Newman's *Ga'anda Vocabulary*, which was produced as a part of her dissertation on the Ga'anda language (1971). Most of the vernacular terms used . . . have been checked for spelling against Newman's wordlists; words that were not included have been transcribed to the best of my ability. The following orthographic conventions for Ga'anda should be noted:

x = voiceless velar fricative	hl = voiceless lateral fricative
e = schwa	n' = voiced velar nasal
'b = glottalized "b"	'd = glottalized "d"
? = glottal stop	

3. Meek (1931 II:379–385) includes a detailed account of Ga'anda kinship and social organization.

4. The settlement pattern of the Ga'anda has made accurate census counts difficult to obtain. Meek (1931 II:369) reported 5,400 Ga'anda, while Kirk-Greene ([1958] 1969:2) later recorded 7,641. Recent popu-

lation density maps based on a 1963 census total suggest these figures should probably be adjusted to approximately 10,000–15,000 persons (at 40–60 persons per square kilometer; Aitchison et al. 1972:Text Map 12).

5. In addition to my own field notes, information on Ga'anda marriage is found in Boyle (1916b:361–366), Hammandikko (1980:13–14), and Meek (1931 II:385–386). The general pattern of marriage is the same throughout the Ga'anda region, although details vary slightly between localities.

6. The requirement that girls be scarified before marriage is noted in Hammandikko (1980:4), Meek (1931 II:384), and Nissen (1968:221). Only the article drawn from Boyle's (1916b) observations describes this procedure in any detail. Boyle also includes a number of useful drawings of the alignment of scars on the body. There are, however, a number of discrepancies between my information and that of Boyle, especially as regards which areas of the body are marked during particular stages and the specific motifs incorporated in each. It is my impression that the drawings in Boyle combine designs found on Ga'anda women with those on the Gbinna, who live west of the Ga'anda and also do full-body scarification.

7. Information on *Sapta* is drawn from oral accounts collected among Ga'anda elders in 1980–1981. Notes published by Captain Boyle (1916a) are based on his eyewitness account of an "Ordeal of Manhood" in 1913. They provide a number of useful descriptive passages, as well as some perspective on the continuity and change of this tradition in this century. Brief accounts of *Sapta* are also included in Hammandikko (1980:12–13), Meek (1931 II:378–379), and Nissen (1968:219–220).

8. Bohannan's discussion of "Beauty and Scarification amongst the Tiv" (1956 . . .) provided insights for my analysis of Ga'anda body decoration.

Bibliography

Aitchson, P. I., M. G. Bawden, D. M. Carroll, P. E. Glover, K. Klinkenberg, P. N. de Leeuw, and P. Tuley
  1972 *Land Resources of North East Nigeria*, Vol. 1. The Environment, Land Resource Study No. 9, Foreign and Commonwealth Office, Overseas Development Administration. Surrey, England.

Berns, M. C.
  1986 "Art and History in the Lower Gongola Valley, Northeastern Nigeria." Ph.D. dissertation, University of California, Los Angeles.

Bohannon, P.
  1956 "Beauty and Scarification Amongst the Tiv" *Man*, September, 56 (129): 117–121.

Boyle, C. V.
  1915 "The Lala People and other Customs." *Journal of the African Society*, October, 15(57):54–69.
  1916a "The Ordeal of Manhood." *Journal of the African Society*, April, 15(59):244–255.
  1916b "The Marking of Girls at Ga'anda." *Journal of the African Society*, July 15(60):361–366.

Chappel, T. J. H.
  1977 *Decorated Gourds in North-Eastern Nigeria*. London.

Hammandikko, M.
  1980 "History of Ga'anda/Tarihin Ga'anda." Edited and translated by M. Berns. *Occasional Paper No. 21*. African Studies Center, University of California, Los Angeles.

Kirk-Greene, A. H. M.
  1969 [1958] *Adamawa Past and Present. An historical approach to the development of a Northern Cameroons Province*. Oxford.

Meek, C. K.
  1931 *Tribal Studies in Northern Nigeria*. 2 vols. London.

Newman, R. Ma
  1971 "A Case Grammar of Ga'anda." Ph.D. dissertation, University of California, Los Angeles.

Nissen M.
  1968 *An African Church is Born: The Story of the Adamawa and Central Sardauna Provinces in Nigeria*. Denmark.

Rubin, A. et al.
  Forthcoming *Sculpture of the Benue River Valley*. Museum of Cultural History Monograph Series, Los Angeles.

III.2 THEY DON'T WEAR WIGS HERE
Barbara A. Schreier

They don't wear wigs here. These were Yekl's words of greeting to his wife, Gitl, upon her arrival in America in Abraham Cahan's story, *Yekl, A Tale of the New York Ghetto*. At the end of her long journey from Russia, Gitl puts on the sheitel not only to honor the Sabbath but to celebrate the long-awaited reunion with Yekl. The symbolism, however, is lost on her Americanized husband. During their three-year separation, he has frantically embraced the customs of his new home, changing his name to Jake and rejecting his religious heritage. The image of his bewigged wife is a painful reminder of the past he is trying to forget. From the moment that Gitl steps off the boat at Ellis Island, Jake begins his relentless criticism of her dowdy appearance. Much of his anger is directed towards Gitl's "voluminous wig of a pitch-black hue." Rejecting her protestations that she wanted to spruce "herself up for the big event," Jake flatly informs her, "They don't wear wigs here."[1] Gitl reluctantly exchanges her sheitel for a scarf; unfortunately, this also fails to meet Jake's expectations of an Americanized wife, who would naturally sport a fashionable hat. As Gitl struggles to reconcile her husband's injunctions with her religious convictions, her appearance becomes both an expression and an extension of her painful adjustment to America.

Cahan's fictional account of clothing as an outward manifestation of a character's changing social and cultural consciousness closely mirrors the experiences of many immigrant women. Recounting her arrival at Ellis Island in 1921, Ida Feldman tells the story of a fellow passenger for whom the wig played a pivotal role. Before coming to America, she received a letter from her husband cautioning her to let her hair grow because "in America you don't wear no wigs." Unfortunately, the woman contracted typhoid fever while in Poland and lost her hair; thus, she wore her sheitel on the passage over to cover her bald head. When her husband spotted her, he concluded by her appearance that she was unwilling to make the necessary sartorial adjustments, and he angrily refused to take her off of the island. Townspeople found a home for the woman and her three children; eventually she reconciled with her husband, but "she wore a wig the rest of her life."[2]

To newly arrived immigrants a change of clothes was the most visible way they could identify themselves as American Jews. This first act of initiation helped to blur the obvious differences between the "greenhorn" and the "real" Americans; it also offered tangible proof that the cultural chasm confronting the newcomers could be bridged. Learning the language would prove the ultimate test of assimilation, but mastering English often took years of study. How much easier it was to embrace the symbolic language of American clothing. It is no wonder that "great stress [was] placed upon clothes."[3] Immigrants exchanged the garments of the Old World for the fashions of the New World with the passion of individuals intent on self-transformation.

While all urban immigrants recognized clothing as the important first step of assimilation, Jewish immigrants embraced the concept with extraordinary zeal. Unlike other new émigrés who came to America with the intention of returning to the homeland, the vast majority of Jews envisioned their move as permanent. As the situation in Eastern Europe declined, Jews feared not just for their livelihoods but for their safety. Faced with the realities of political oppression, anti-Semitic Czarist restrictions, and worsening economic conditions, Jews escaped to America determined to make a new life for themselves in *di goldene medina*. Recounting his early experiences as an immigrant from the Ukraine, Dr. Morris Moel explained that coming to America "was something that you longed for and . . . even though we came under difficulties and it was somewhat difficult to adjust . . . it was the greatest land that we could imagine.[4]

The settlement pattern of Jewish immigrants also contributed to their rapid adoption of American styles. The suffering of Jews in Eastern Europe affected all socioeconomic classes, and the émigrés represented every rung in the social ladder. While much has been written about the impoverishment of the shtetl dwellers, the story must also include the Eastern European Jews who enjoyed relative prosperity. In contrast to the staggering poverty of the many Jewish peasants, other Jews earned an income much higher than the subsistence level.[5] Many lived in burgeoning industrial centers where they were exposed to new political, secular, and cultural ideas, as well as the broader world of consumption. Gill Sherrid's family enjoyed great prestige in their Russian community. His mother used to tell him about her clothing: "Everything was made to order and she was the most beautifully dressed young woman in town."[6] Gill's mother was not alone. Among the vast numbers of Jews who arrived in America between 1880 and 1920, a percentage of them came with a decidedly modern orientation.

Furthermore, nearly half of the Jewish emigrants were female, and many of them were unmarried women in their teens and twenties. Only the Irish sent a greater proportion of women to America.[7] Young Jewish women brought with them a unique set of values and concerns that was shaped as much by their Eastern European heritage as by their hopes for the future. Raised in an economy that depended upon female labor, many Jewish women came armed with experience as dressmakers or seamstresses. Willing to work, longing for an education, and aspiring to greater prosperity, this transitional generation of émigrés had the personal resources and vocational skills required to adapt to their new and strange surroundings. Certainly all newcomers had to confront the unfamiliar and deal with the pangs of separation, but youth had the advantage. Rather than struggling to transplant all of the customs of the Old Country, they willingly sought out the opportunities awaiting them. As active participants in the assimilation process, youth developed their own ethnic culture, drawing upon the past for support but eager to take on an expanded role. . . .

The urban areas where most Jews settled were lively, crowded, concrete environments that magnified sights, sounds, and smells. Although most immigrants settled in ghetto neighborhoods among other Eastern European Jews and therefore found familiar faces, language, and customs, the larger world continued to encroach upon these "centers of ethnic intensity."[11] Anna Kuthan remarked that the strangeness of her new home demanded her constant attention. "There was so many things that you can't figure out when you land here."[12] Jews who came from urban areas in Eastern Europe undoubtedly had an easier time. When asked if she found America overwhelming Rose Jaffee replied that she had little trouble adjusting because she's "seen it all before in St. Petersburg."[13] Yet while Rose remained undaunted by her first encounters with America, women from small impoverished shtetls looked at their new home with bewilderment.

Struggling with the transition, women tried to reconcile their visions of America with the stark reality of ghetto life. Home was typically a dark tenement apartment that offered only cold running water and a toilet at the end of the hall. Struggling to make ends meet, extended families crowded into two or three rooms, and women still had to take in piecework and boarders to eke out a living. For Sonia F., the garbage, noise, and crowds were painful contrasts to the "trees and cleanliness" she left behind in Kiev. Overwhelmed by homesickness, Sonia did not understand why her family had come "since it was so terrible" in the United States.[14] Back in Eastern Europe, Jews dreamed of a land of opportunity where "it would be gold in the streets, laying waiting for you."[15] Instead they found themselves in congested surroundings characterized by poverty and privation. After coming to America, Mina Friedman's mother spent her days struggling with domestic responsibilities while her husband worked sixteen hours a day in a sweatshop. The exhausting demands of "shopping from one pushcart to another, dragging up the food six flights of stairs, washing clothes in a steaming boiler," and caring for four children left little time to enjoy America's pleasures.[16]

Poverty was a particularly bitter reality to accept for those women who had left behind a life of comfort. Sara Abrams recalled that during her family's "period of reconciliation" with America, amid the conflicting emotions of peace, anger, and contentment, "a strain of sadness seemed to permeate our surroundings." The family's constant struggle for money contrasted sharply with the prosperity they had enjoyed in Poland. Sara remembered that her mother's friends would see her at the sewing machine and lament:

> The *goldene medina*. They used to tell us America was full of honey. They used to say, they shovel gold on the streets, and a woman like us, has to sit and sew, like a serving woman.[17]

Jewish women who escaped the destitution of their old home only to find themselves in another impoverished situation also felt acute frustration. Their disappointment, however, was mediated by America's promise that poverty did not have to be a life sentence. The tangible symbols of upward mobility pierced through their suffering as a talisman of the American dream. Deeply impressed by America's offering, Jews quickly developed an appetite for a new standard of living. The lyrics of "Men Shart Gold in America" pokes fun at such aspirations, but the words contain an important truth. In the song, Abie's wife agrees to follow him to America, but her acquiescence comes with strings attached. "Silks and satins I must vear ev'ry night in te-ay-ters and roast duck chickens every day no more 'herring mit potatoes' and to all dis Abie let me tell dot I must have a 'Merry Vidow' Hat." Through their acquisition of American products Jewish immigrants communicated their desire to fit into their new home; to be American, they had to look American.

Immigrants intent upon refashioning themselves did not lack for advice. Oral histories are filled with accounts of relatives who had already emigrated to this country schooling the newly arrived immigrants on the finer points of dressing. Sophie Abrams remembered going shopping with her aunt on her first day in America:

> She bought me a shirtwaist . . . and a skirt, a blue print with red buttons and a hat, such a hat I had never seen. I took my old brown dress and shawl and threw them away! I know it sounds foolish, we being so poor, but I didn't care. . . . When I looked in the mirror . . . I said, boy, Sophie, look at you now . . . just like an American.[18]

For the majority of Eastern European Jewish women, hairstyles and head coverings were the first crucial tests of looking American. The Orthodox law that required married women to cut off their hair and don a sheitel clashed with the fashionable American ideal. In the words of a fashion editor in 1905, a heavy head of hair was a woman's "crown of blessing."[19] The cult of bobbed hair belonged to the next generation of women; turn-of-the-century trend-setters took great pride in their long, luxuriant hair piled high into massive pompadours. Enormously important in the definition of female beauty, hair also carried a potent sexuality.[20] Thus, women captured their siren-like tresses into artfully arranged coiffures as a badge of maturity and respectability. The celebrated innocence of young girls enabled them to wear their hair down and often caught at the nape of the neck with an oversized stiffened bow. For Russian immigrant Fanny Gilbert, the fashion rule was absolute. "Oh my God," she recalled, "how could you go without a bow?"[21]

As a result of America's fascination with hair, the frankly artificial appearance of the coarse, stiffened wig created a clear line of demarcation between the religious old and the secular new. In his 1909 portrait of New York's Lower East Side, writer Hutchins Hapgood characterized the "Orthodox Jewess" as a drab woman, "plain in appearance, with a thick waist [and] a wig."[22] This image contrasted sharply with the "up-to-date" shopgirls whose feather-trimmed hats perched precariously on top of their fashionable hairstyles. These popular upswept styles

required long, thick hair that could be twisted and securely pinned on top of the head. For those women with less-than-voluminous tresses, artificial hairpieces known as "rats" helped create the proper illusion.

After studying Jewish immigrant girls in Chicago in 1913, Viola Paradise concluded that "almost immediately upon the girl's arrival her relatives buy for her American clothes, usually a suit, a large hat, and not infrequently, the wherewithal to fix her hair in an American fashion." Paradise went on to quote one newcomer who proudly announced: "Yes, I'm almost like an American. I have a rat for my hair."[23] . . .

Although many women discarded their wigs as a sign of American freedom, their more traditional counterparts perceived this act as a "concession to American godlessness."[25] This certainly was the case with an elderly woman who arrived at Ellis Island in 1902. Rejecting the newly purchased hat offered by her waiting relatives, she declared, "I am only an old-fashioned Jewess and I won't part with my wig. It's rather late to begin sinning."[26] Her family relented, probably because of her age. Ida Ellis's relatives were no so easily deterred. After their first week in America, Ida's parents invited family members to visit their new apartment. One of the cousins ("the Americanized one") came in, walked over to Ida's mother, and, without warning, pulled off her wig. "My mother said, 'Oh, my God! What are you doing to me?!'" to which the cousin replied, "In America you're not going to wear a wig."[27]

Discarding the wig was just the beginning of the immigrants' visual metamorphoses. Most Eastern European women arrived at Ellis Island wearing a kerchief as part of their native costume. While more elaborate head-dresses might be worn on holidays and festive occasions, the simple scarf had survived intact as part of an Orthodox Jew's costume from its beginnings in the eighteenth century.[28] Although this traditional head covering was considered an integral part of a woman's *Yiddishkeit* (Jewishness), the immigrants quickly learned that in America decorative hats were more than an accessory; they were an essential component of the feminine toilette. Turn-of-the-century hats were impressive concoctions, and a lady never appeared in public without one.

Women changed their hats to suit the occasion, the time of day, and their moods. The straw boater worn with tailored skirts and simple cotton blouses would hardly have flattered an afternoon suit or a showy evening dress. The well-stocked feminine closet contained a great variety of millinery designs, each properly stored in its own hatbox. For the new arrivals, hats became a sensitive barometer of one's fashion sense, because hat styles changed with each season. Reporting on the proliferation of millinery stores on the Lower East Side in 1900, the *New York Tribune* noted that Division Street was home to at least twenty hat shops. Sacrificing quality for quantity, these stores devised creations that met the working girl's pocketbook and her craving for a flashy accessory. Reporting that "purple and yellow is a favorite combination" because of its dramatic effect, the paper described the average East Side girl's winter hat as large and sometimes groaning "beneath the weight of nearly or quite a dozen plumes."[29]

These confections of silk, feathers, and straw evoked more than stylishness; they became a symbol of American respectability and social aspirations. When Shaya, the Russian Talmudic scholar in Abraham Cahan's story *The Imported Bridegroom*, first sees a photograph of his intended bride, he is awed by her hat. Surely this woman "in all her splendor of Grand Street millinery" must be a princess.[30] His confusion is understandable in light of prevailing customs. In some parts of Eastern Europe only women of high social status could wear hats; therefore, wearing the latest millinery fashion meant "stepping out of the serving class, and out of the ranks of the peasants."[31] For Masha, in Anzia Yezierska's autobiographical novel *Bread Givers*, it only took ten-cents worth of pink paper roses purchased from a pushcart on Hester Street to make her feel "like a lady from Fifth Avenue."[32] A fashion-conscious woman featured in a Yiddish cartoon transformed her outdated hat into an up-to-the-minute pancake style by stomping on it. Delighted with the results, she exclaimed: "Oh, my dears! How that hat suits me! My neighbor will burst with envy when she sees this special hat!"[33] . . .

When twelve-year-old Celia Adler arrived in America in 1914, she discovered that it was not enough just to wear a hat; you had to wear the right kind of hat. Traveling alone from Russia to meet her sister, she proudly wore the sailor hat given to her by a friend as a going-away present. For Celia, this hat, the first she had ever owned, "was my whole treasure." But her sister identified the old-fashioned style as the badge of a greenhorn and insisted that Celia leave the hat behind the dock at Ellis Island. "She was sure that anyone who will see me will know that I just got off the boat. And she didn't want it."[35]

Notes

1. Abraham Cahan, *Yekl: A Tale of the New York Ghetto* (New York: 1896), 34–37.

2. Ida Feldman, Ellis Island Oral History Protect, Ellis Island Immigration Museum.

3. Viola Paradise, The Jewish Immigrant Girl in Chicago. *Survey*, September 6, 1913, 703–04.

4. Dr. Morris Moel, Ellis Island Oral History Project.

5. Lucian Dobroszycki and Barbara Kirshenblatt-Gimblett, *Image Before My Eyes: A Photographic History of Jewish Life in Poland, 1864–1939* (New York: 1977), xiii.

6. Gill Sherrid, Ellis Island Oral History Project.

7. Susan A. Glenn, *Daughters of the Shtetl: Life and Labor in the Immigrant Generation* (Ithaca: 1990), 2.

. . .

11. Arthur Hertzberg, *The Jews in America: Four Centuries of an Uneasy Alliance: A History* (New York: 1989), 172.

12. Anna Kuthan, New York City Immigrant Labor History Project, Tamiment Library, New York University.

13. Interview with Rose Jaffee, 1965, courtesy of Richard Jaffee.

14. Tape I-81, New York City Immigrant Labor History Project.

15. Max and Milton Shatsky, Ellis Island Oral History Project.

16. Mina K. Friedman, "Time About No News to All," unpublished manuscript, courtesy of Alan Friedman.

17. Sara J. Abrams, "Things Trivial," American Jewish Autobiographies Collection, #92, YIVO Archives. YIVO Institute for Jewish Research.

18. Interview with Sophie Abrams, Oral History Project of the City University of New York, quoted in Elizabeth Ewen, *Immigrant Women in the Land of Dollars: Life and Culture on the Lower East Side, 1890–1925* (New York: 1985), 68.

19. "Woman's Crowning Glory," *Boston Advocate*, June 2, 1905.

20. Lois Banner, *American Beauty* (New York: 1983), 208–209.

21. Sally Goldstein, interview with Carla Reiter and Joanne Grossman.

22. Hutchins Hapgood. *The Spirit of Ghetto* (New York, 1902; reprint, Cambridge, Mass.: 1967), 72–73.

23. Paradise, "The Jewish Immigrant Girl in Chicago," 704.

. . .

25. Charlotte Baum, Paula Hyman, and Sonya Michel, *The Jewish Women in America* (New York: 1975), 205.

26. "All Right! Hurry Up," in Moses Rischin, *Grandma Never Lived in America: The New Journalism of Abraham Cahan* (Bloomington, Ind.: 1985), 143.

27. Ida Ellis, Ellis Island Oral History Project.

28. Giza Frankel, "Notes on the Costume of the Jewish Woman in Eastern Europe," *Journal of Jewish Art*, 7 (1980): 50–57.

29. *New York Tribune, Illustrated Supplement*, August 26, 1900, reprinted in Jacob Rader Marcus. *The American Jewish Woman: A Documentary History* (New York: 1981), 198–99.

30. Abraham Cahan, *The Imported Bridegroom and Other Tales of the New York Ghetto* (New York: 1898; reprint, New York: 1970), 112.

31. Doris Weatherford, *Foreign & Female: Immigrant Women in America, 1840–1930* (New York: 1986), 97.

32. Anzia Yezierska, *Bread Givers* (Garden City, New York; reprint, New York: 1975), 2.

33. From a scrapbook courtesy of Marilyn Golden.

. . .

35. Celia Adler, Ellis Island Oral History Project.

III.3 COURT, FORMAL AND EVERYDAY DRESS DURING THE LATE CH'ING DYNASTY
A. C. Scott

The various types of Chinese garments may be described under certain main headings which are given below. An understanding of these is useful when considering past and present fashions although the names used are broad in application covering as they do both male and female garments. The principal materials used for Chinese clothing in the past were silk, satin and velvet together with gauze in the summer and the ubiquitous cotton cloth which is still the universal material that it has always been, particularly in present day China. Cloth was lined, according to the style of garment and the season. For winter wear clothes were padded with raw silk and cotton wadding as of course they still are, or lined with fur. The principle behind the wearing of Chinese clothes was the use of layers of garments, in winter these layers could be increased and in the summer lightened or diminished. The point to be emphasized is that robes of similar length and cut could be worn one within the other. Naturally, there remained certain garments which were only worn as outer clothing, the final item of the layers. Broadly speaking, range in dress consisted of long gowns or robes, worn down to and often covering the feet and having sleeves; three quarter length garments also with sleeves worn over the longer dress; short jackets of waist length or just below the waist; sleeveless garments which might be waist length or longer, in the form of a kind of waistcoat worn over sleeved gowns and jackets; trousers, equally a feminine or a masculine article of dress; and skirts, invariably pleated in China. Robes and jackets were either fastened centrally down the front or else across the right breast and down the right side. The former is called *tui chin* or *tui men chin* and the latter *ta chin*. Trousers for either sex were fastened round the waist by a soft girdle and skirts which were made on the wrap over principle were also secured round the wearer's waist by tapes.

In Chinese costume terminology, which is inclined to be ambiguous in its application, the name *p'ao* is used generally and irrespective of the wearer's sex to give the idea of a long garment with sleeves and with a *ta chin* fastening, i.e. to the right. The implication behind the name *p'ao* is length, the garment reaches to the feet in a single piece and is worn as the equivalent of a European's dress or suit as the case may be, other garments may be worn over it out of doors or on ceremonial occasions. The modern Chinese woman's gown, the *ch'ang p'ao* or *ch'i p'ao* previously mentioned, immediately provides a contradiction in the rules laid down. By no stretch of the imagination could it be called long today and it is often made without sleeves in the summer. Its prototype, the Manchu ladies gown, was nevertheless a *p'ao* in the truest sense, even the modern gown when it was first introduced obeyed all the requirements for length, and so the name has stuck through all its modern deviations. Fashion's whims may carry the ladies *p'ao* to the feet again of course and for evening wear such a length is still fashionable among smart women. The ordinary long gown of Chinese men, today only seen outside the mainland, on the other hand, has never forfeited sartorial integrity as a *p'ao*, which name it still retains. When it is padded for winter wear the *p'ao* is called *mien p'ao* for both men and women. . . .

Court dress and formal dress, *ch'ao fu* and *chi fu*, together with mourning dress, *chi fu*, are all classed together under the one name *li fu*, ceremonial dress, as apart from *ch'ang fu*, everyday dress. Court dress and formal dress were not identical as we shall see, while mourning dress differed from formal dress in its uses of certain colours and dispensing with decorative insignia. . . .

As a prelude to describing the different garments worn for Court or for formal dress it is useful to enumerate the precise methods by which rank and position were indicated in costume. First there was the type of symbolism described, i.e., the use of specified motifs varying in style, placing and quantity according to the wearer's rank, secondly there was colour, different colours being prescribed for certain garments. In this connection the prerogative of the Imperial family to wear certain tones of yellow is possibly the best example of differentiation by colour. The five colours black, white, yellow, red and green represented the five elements water, metal, earth, fire and wood. Yellow was the central colour representing the earth, the centre of the universe dominated by the Emperor as the source of all power and blessing, from the earliest times yellow was therefore regarded as the Imperial colour. Thirdly there were certain types of decoration worn on the crown of the hat which were important in indicating rank.

The nine grades of official rank were each denoted by a square ornamental badge, *p'u tzu*, worn on the front and back of the surcoat. The *p'u tzu* was about twelve inches square and was adapted as insignia by the Man-

chus direct from the official styles used in the Ming dynasty. Apart from the fact that the Ming versions were slightly larger in size, the basic designs and symbolism were the same. Different designs were used by civil and military officials of equal grade, they were as follows:

	Civil	Military
1st grade	White crane	Unicorn
2nd grade	Golden pheasant	Lion
3rd grade	Peacock	Leopard
4th grade	Wild goose	Tiger
5th grade	Silver pheasant	Black bear
6th grade	Egret	Panther
7th grade	Mandarin duck	Rhinoceros
8th grade	Quail	Rhinoceros
9th grade	Paradise flycatcher	Sea horse

The unclassed grade called *wei ju liu*, literally 'not entered the stream', included those men who had hopes of promotion to the ninth grade, the first step to official advancement. They were people like junior clerks and so on. Unclassed officials of this grade were not entitled to wear a badge in Ch'ing times. On the occasions when Chinese women wore ceremonial costume they also wore the badges of their husbands' rank but with these differences, the bird emblems were common to the wives of both civil and military officials, but the female of the species was used and faced heraldically in the opposite direction to the male versions. . . .

In addition to the embroidered *p'u tzu* officials wore, in the case of formal dress, globular buttons of various colours on the crowns of their hats or, in the case of Court dress, a more elaborate ornament which contained a semi precious stone of the colour appropriate to the particular rank of the wearer. The hat decorations for the nine official grades follow:

1st grade	Plain red, coral.
2nd grade	Chased red, coral.
3rd grade	Clear blue, sapphire.
4th grade	Opaque blue, lapis lazuli.
5th grade	Clear white, rock crystal.
6th grade	Opaque white, opal.
7th grade	Plain gold.
8th grade	Figured gilt.
9th grade	Figured gilt. . . .

Court Dress, Ch'ao Fu

During the Ch'ing dynasty, Court dress, *ch'ao fu*, was the name given to the full dress worn for the highest ceremonial occasions or state events. It consisted of the following garments and accessories.

Ch'ao P'ao

This, the Court dragon robe, was a long garment reaching to the feet. It had a wide turn down collar and turn down cuffs called *ma t'i hsiu*, horse hoof cuffs, because of their shape. The *ch'ao p'ao* was firmly belted at the waist with tightly wristed sleeves and had a *ta chin* or right hand side fastening with buttons made of twisted silk cord. In a large number of cases there was a band of pleating round the centre of the garment. It was made of silk or satin with a general background colour of blue or what the Chinese call 'stone blue', *shih ch'ing*, a deep blue black. The Emperor and high Imperial family members also wore yellow versions of this robe. The garment was richly embroidered with dragon patterns and border designs which followed the rules for rank already spoken about. Although the design of the *p'ao* was strictly prescribed in its essentials there was a variety of treatment of colour, detail and texture within the limits laid down. It can be seen how rank insignia assisted that variety. The garment had slits at either side but in some of the women's robes there was also a slit at the rear, and the women's robes had also a kind of epaulette as against the straight shoulders of the men. The eighth and ninth grade officials wore a robe with a conventional all over cloud pattern in place of the dragon motifs which they were not allowed to wear. The *ch'ao p'ao* was worn over a second *p'ao* of a thinner silk material and lined according to the season.

Ch'ao Tai

Round the waist of the *ch'ao p'ao* was fastened a silk girdle, the *ch'ao tai* made of plain coloured silk, yellow for high members of the Imperial family and blue or stone blue for others. It had a jade clasp and various ornaments and pendants hung from it, made of jade, gold and silver and other materials which varied according to rank.

Wai Kua

The topmost garment worn in Court dress was a surcoat called the *wai kua*, also called the *p'u fu* or *p'u kua* in reference to the square badge, the *p'u tzu*, worn on the back and front of the garment as rank insignia by officials up to the rank of Imperial Duke, or to the single dragon roundel worn by Princes of the lower orders. This garment was three quarter length with a *tui chin* or central front opening and buttons of twisted silk cord, four in number for officials of the first grade and below, five for ranks above this. There were slits at the sides and rear the material used being silk or satin and gauze in the summer. It was edged with fur in the winter season, sable in the case of the highest ranks. The sleeves were wrist length, wide and square cut with no cuffs and the general colour of the garment was the 'stone blue' referred to, with the badge or *p'u tzu* embroidered in appropriate colours and patterns. In the *Ta Ch'ing Hui*, the Emperor's surcoat is called *kun fu* and appears to be shorter in length than the others with a slight cut away on the sleeves although in all other respects the style is the same. There were also versions of the *wai kua* which were made solely of fur for winter use; on these of course no badges were worn.

P'ei Chien

The *p'ei chien* was a shoulder cape worn over the *wai kua*. It was made of silk or satin in the same stone blue colour with a gold-woven embossed border. In winter the border was made of brown sable for civil officials down to the third grade and military officials to the second grade. Grades below this wore a velvet border. The gold border was worn in spring, summer and autumn by officials down to the seventh grade.

Ch'ao Chu

The *ch'ao chu* was a long necklace which reached to the waist and was worn over the *p'ei chien*. It was only used by officials of the fifth grade and above in the case of civil posts and by the fourth grade and upwards in military posts. Those below these ranks were not privileged to wear it. It consisted of one hundred and eight beads made of amber or similar stone with four of the beads much larger than the others, of a different material and placed at regular intervals round the necklace and a pendant which hung down the back when the necklace was worn. Two short pendants of smaller beads were attached to the left side of the necklace and a single pendant of identical length at the right side of the necklace. The position of these smaller pendants was reversed in the case of women i.e. two right and one left. The *ch'ao chu* was of Buddhist origin.

Ch'ao Kuan

The hat worn with Court dress was called *ch'ao kuan* and varied in shape according to the season. The winter version *tung ch'ao kuan* was round with a slightly conical crown and a stiff fur covered upturned brim, what in English might vulgarly be termed a 'pork pie' shape. The crown was covered with thick crimson silk floss which radiated from the apex of the hat surmounted by an ornate gold filigree support in which was fixed a precious stone of the colour appropriate to the wearer's rank. The *ling kuan*—the jade tube in which the plume was fixed was also attached to the crown of the hat. The brim of the hat was made of fur or velvet according to the rank of the wearer. The name *nuan kuan* or warm hat, was also given to this style. The summer version of the Court hat was conical in shape without a brim and made of woven rattan, the crown was covered with red silk strands and surmounted by the appropriate rank decoration as in the case of the winter hat.

Ch'ao Hsüeh

Ch'ao hsüeh, or Court boots, completed the outfit for men's court dress. They were made of black satin with high uppers and thick white soles of layered felt. They were square toed. . . . Women did not wear these of course.

Ch'ao Ch'ün

The *ch'ao ch'ün* or Court skirt was worn by women underneath the *p'ao* or dragon robe. It was made in a single piece with eighteen pleats patterned and embroidered according to rank. One for the Empress as an example, had a broad gold border round the hem patterned with *hai lung*, sea dragons. The upper part of the skirt was of crimson satin woven with a pattern of small roundels along the pleats, each roundel containing the longevity character. A similar skirt was worn by all ranks of concubines. The Chinese skirt was a wrap-over type fastened with tapes to make a girdle.

Ch'ao Kua

Over the *p'ao* women also wore a sleeveless collarless garment which was a kind of long waistcoat fastening down the front. It was called *ch'ao kua* but was also known eventually as *k'an chien erh* being a garment that was also worn informally. The Court version was heavily embroidered with the dragon and other patterns common to the *p'ao*.

Chi Fu or Formal Dress

This differed in certain points from full Court dress. It consisted of the following garments and accessories. *Mang p'ao, k'ai ch'i p'ao, ling i, tai, ch'ao chu, chi kuan* and *kuan hsüeh*. The *mang p'ao* (or *lung p'ao*) was somewhat different in style from the Court dragon robe. In the first place it had no turn down collar although it had 'horse shoe' cuffs and a right hand side opening like the Court dragon robe. Men's robes were split at the sides, front and back of the garment, the women's versions only at the sides. The pattern of the robe was different from that of the Court version. The dragon design was more in the nature of an all over pattern and the number and style of the dragons was of course according to the rules laid down. Again, blue and stone blue were the basic colours with yellow as well for the Emperor and his family.

The *wai kua*, surcoat, worn with formal dress was similar in all respects to that worn with Court dress, using the same colour and insignia. The *k'ai ch'i p'ao* was a long collarless robe with a right hand side fastening. It had horse shoe cuffs and in addition to splits at either side had a high split up the centre front and rear. It was plain coloured being yellow for the Emperor and his immediate connections, blue or cream coloured for others. The robe was made of fine silk and worn in place of the dragon robe when travelling and making visits which were not too formal or on routine business. A *tai tzu* or girdle was worn round the *k'ai ch'i p'ao*—similar to the one worn with Court dress but without the more ornate decoration and generally with two small embroidered pouches attached on either side. The *ch'ao chu* or necklace was similar to the one worn with Court dress and limited to the same ranks. Over the *k'ai ch'i p'ao* and *wai kua* was worn the *ling t'ou*. This was a stiff detachable collar rather in the style of a Western stiff collar. It was blue in colour, sometimes white, and made of fur in the winter season. The *chi kuan* or formal hat was similar in its style to the court hat except that instead of the ornate decoration which surmounted the latter a simple globular button of the appropriate rank colour was used and crimson strands of silk instead of floss on the winter version. *Kuan hsüeh*, the official boots worn with formal dress were similar to the boots worn with Court dress except that they were not square toed. The two kinds of boot were not interchangeable. . . .

Source: Excerpted from *Chinese Costume in Transition* (1958), Donald Moore. Reprinted by permission of the estate of the author.

III.4 TRANSNATIONAL BIOGRAPHIES AND LOCAL MEANINGS: USED CLOTHING PRACTICES IN LUSAKA[1]
Karen Tranberg Hansen

The extensive trade and widespread consumption in cities and towns across much of Africa of used clothing imported from the West raise questions not only about the sustainability of urban African livelihoods but also about the interplay between cultural practices and politicoeconomic forces in our late twentieth-century world. . . .

The export of used clothing from the West to developing countries such as Zambia may on first sight appear to be a textbook example of the West's continued exploitation of the rest. To be sure, the recent rapid increase of used clothing imports from the West into Zambia is a sad product of the powerless position of Zambia's textile and garment industry in a highly competitive and crowded world apparel market.[4] It is not surprising that textile and garment manufacturers' associations and unions in countries that permit commercial imports of used clothing are complaining about production decline and job losses.[5] Some observers consider used clothing as a sign of neo-colonialism that should be regulated or banned. Such viewpoints imply a direct causal connection between the decline of local textile and garment manufacturing and the growing import of used clothing. While such accounts not only simplify processes that are rather more complicated, they are also strikingly at odds with local popular sentiments.

. . . [T]hey fail to explain the popularity of used clothing and beg the question of the meanings used clothing practices assume in everyday lives among large segments of the Zambian population. Such meanings do not inhere in the commodities themselves but are constructed in interactions that involve retailers, traders and consumers in a variety of contexts. My research explores 'biographies' of used clothing from three different perspectives: regional history, political economy and social consumption. What connects these perspectives is my focus on used clothing, the ways it links different points of the world and the various meanings it is given as it flows along the path. . . .

. . . Ethnographic research that engages local actors with used clothing in a range of settings may lead to a more nuanced interpretation of the roles and meanings of used clothing for those who wear it than the condemning, denigrating or downright embarrassed commentaries by local representatives of textile and garment manufacturers and external observers.

This paper suggests some lines of inquiry into the cultural practices that surround the wearing of used clothing in Zambia. . . . For reasons of space, I discuss but a limited number of questions that go to the heart of the question of meanings. These questions concern local clothing 'theories', design and style issues and interaction with and display of clothes.

In raising these methodological concerns, I engage in a 'dialogue with evidence'.[8] That is to say that in general I draw on my extensive knowledge of Zambian urban livelihoods based on long-term research and more specifically on preliminary research I conducted into the organisation of the trade in used clothing in 1992 and 1993, principally in Lusaka, Zambia's capital. . . .

In this paper I am chiefly concerned with how things come to mean and how to interpret meaning. Since used clothing trade and consumption practices are not tied to any fixed locale but are themselves the site of this study, the field research I am proposing seeks to follow the flow of these garments into different settings and to examine the forms they assume as they become embedded in a variety of social relations. To set the background for my subsequent discussion, I first briefly sketch the contours of the international and local configuration of the used clothing trade. Then I clarify the social nature of used clothing as a constructed artefact. The remainder of the paper attempts to trace how the meanings of used clothing can be explored in a variety of contexts. . . .

Transnational Biographies: Origins and Transformations

Because every piece of used clothing has many potential future lives, the textile recycling business is extremely lucrative. An immense, profitable, but barely examined world-wide trading network ships millions of dollars worth in used clothes from Europe and North America to Third World countries and the former East Bloc.[9] While this international trade has a long history, according to news accounts it has quadrupled in scale world-wide over the last decade.[10] By some estimates, one-third or more of the people in sub-Saharan Africa now wear imported used clothing.[11]

Large quantities of worn and out-of-fashion clothes donated to charities in the West are sold to textile recyclers/bale brokers who sort and grade them for industrial uses and the second-hand clothes market, largely in the Third World. After fumigation, the clothes are compressed into bales, put in containers and shipped to wholesalers overseas. Some of these wholesalers work through agents who deal directly with the bale brokers. In the early 1990s, bales destined for Zambia were offloaded in the ports of Dar es Salaam, Beira and Durban and trucked to Lusaka where they in turn were sold, typically from warehouses, to local traders who resold them to consumers. Needless to say, there are often other steps, including cross-border smuggling, on this path.

While commercial import of used clothing has taken place for some time in Zambia, it has grown enormously in complexity and scale since the second half of the 1980s. This is in part a result of the gradual opening up of the economy during the last years of the Second Republic and of the new government's extensive liberalisation of import and foreign exchange regulations since 1991. Local textile and garment manufacturing operated in a highly protected domestic market during most of the Kaunda years.[13] Because of their outmoded plants and the growing costs of imported inputs and raw materials, most of these industries are ill-prepared both to meet the export challenge of the present liberalisation policy and to satisfy domestic needs. By and large, their products are of poor quality and too expensive for most local consumers. Because of the increasing cost of living and widespread poverty, there are few if any domestic niche markets for specialty clothing production in Zambia. What is more, fashion-conscious Zambian consumers with money to spare have always preferred foreign-produced garments to locally made clothing.[14]

Since the mid-1980s, used clothing has been spoken of as *salaula* in Zambia (selecting from a pile, in the manner of rummaging, in Bemba).[15] The *salaula* section in markets is many times larger than the food section in Lusaka and provincial towns. In the country, *salaula* is sold from small shops, hawked by itinerant traders and used widely as payment for piecework instead of cash.[16] A survey estimate from 1993 suggests that 80% of Zambia's population obtains its garments from the *salaula* market, that 95% of that market consists of commercial used clothing imports (as compared to charitable donations) and that the total import of used clothing that year came close to 32,400 tonnes.[17] 'Used clothing' includes not only garments, but also shoes, handbags, sheets, towels and draperies. In 1992 and 1993, this import involved between 10 and 12 large wholesalers, most of them Lusaka based. The majority were men of south-west Asian background, followed by Zambians, Africans from other countries and Lebanese. Several of these wholesalers came from trading firms of long standing in Zambia and some were in fact garment manufacturers who had added used clothing to their inventory.

When shipped to Zambia, used clothing already has several biographies behind it.[18] Its transformation from the West's cast-off garments into desirable clothing in Zambia involves several phases during which used clothing becomes revalorised into new objects.[19] Transactions between external suppliers and local wholesalers initiate the process through which the decommissioned use value of the West's discarded clothing is reactivated. Subsequent transformations of used garments into clothes which Zambian consumers speak of as 'new' are achieved through a variety of processes that begin at the point of resale and are made public in the ways in which clothing is put to use. Some of these transformations are plain and easy to see, for they involve alteration and recycling, while others have to be teased out of interaction. I have described some of the transformations that take place through a variety of informal practices around the selling and buying of *salaula* in some detail elsewhere.[20] . . .

Used Clothing: Things and Relationships

Few critics, in Africa and the West, have gone beyond superficially reading, condemning and deprecating the local effects of used clothing imports. Even fewer have inquired into the meanings such clothing evokes for its wearers or addressed the sometimes ambiguous roles of such clothing in everyday lives.[22]

The reasons why scholarship on markets and dress has overlooked used clothing are not hard to identify. They include, among others, a concern with centre–periphery relations and the exploitative and oppressive effects of Western institutions and forms on subaltern lives, Marx's preoccupation with commodity fetishism as a mode of 'false' representation and a hostile, if not elitist and paternalistic, stance on the global spread of mass consumption and its assumed adverse effects on local cultures. And for its part, the scholarly literature on textiles and dress has been oblivious to the social and cultural significance of Third World dealings with the West's discarded clothing.[23]

In my effort to understand the cultural issues that surround the trading and wearing of used clothing in Zambia, I seek to break with the tendency to locate the meaning of such clothing practices in the West, representing Africa only in terms of its efforts to copy and/or resist imported dress conventions. I turn instead to a body of recent scholarship for which the forms that are created in local encounters with Western commodities has been an extremely rich subject.[24] While cautious about privileging one side over the other, all these formulations imply a continuing tension, if not struggle, in the meeting between local practices and ideas and Western forms. Regardless of which formulation one chooses to apply, I suggest that this tension contributes importantly to the vitality and dynamism of the 'new' local forms whose combination of elements is always in process.

The story of used clothing consumption in Zambia is about much more than imitating Western fashion. It is also about individualised and at times idiosyncratic dress practices that are informed by local norms about social etiquette and sexual decorum. The emergent clothing system is always in process, its meanings generated in particular contexts. For clothes are not worn passively but require people's active collaboration. The presentational form,[25] the 'look' that results from this process in Zambia, does, as Hollander suggests for Western clothes,[26] have reference to pictures, to a spectrum of desirable ways of looking at any given time, which have obvious Western traces. Yet such images are also tied up with local Zambian notions of the body and sexuality, distinctions drawn by gender and generation and fuelled by the economic imperatives of everyday living and the relative power of the state. Aside from fulfilling basic clothing needs, used clothing constitutes a site where social identities are both constructed and contested. Thus dressing and dressing up, is both an end in itself and a means that may entail a certain liberatory potential.[27]

Some of the local cultural and socioeconomic issues that are at stake in used clothing consumption practices may get revealed through the angle of a recent body of anthropological work on commodities and consumption. Popular Zambian preoccupations with *salaula* richly support Appadurai's argument that commodities are socially constructed and that things have social lives.[28] Because a commodity does not always remain in the place where it was produced, it can be said to have a 'social life' whose value and meanings change as it moves through space and time. . . .

Used Clothing Practices and Meanings

My previous work has isolated some fairly widespread dress conventions that influenced how adult men and women put together clothing ensembles from the *salaula* markets during the late 1980s and early 1990s. Over and above the specifics which I describe below, there are processes involved in putting oneself together through clothing that may easily escape the gaze of the casual observer who sees *salaula* only as the West's cast-offs. The desire to be well turned-out, even if the garments are worn, makes clothes-conscious Zambians insist on immaculate ensembles whose elements are carefully laundered and ironed. Thus, detailed care for clothing is one of the processes that help to transform old clothes into new ensembles.

Aside from being spick and span and regardless of occupation and urban or rural residence, the accepted notion of how to dress makes men insist on suits, long-sleeved shirts, ties and, when of a certain age, hats for their public ensemble, even if the trousers and jacket are not matched in colour, fabric, print and styling. And leather shoes, not boots, tennis shoes or sandals, mark the man as properly put together. Irrespective of occupation and location, women insist on skirts below the knee, short sleeved loose blouses or plain dresses, on top of which a *chitenge* (printed cloth) can be worn if necessary and, when of a certain age, on headscarves and high heels [as] part of their ensemble in public. Some youth are more outgoing, flaunting the dress conventions just described, young women by wearing jeans, mini-skirts and tight fitting blouses (referred to as *sheke sheke* (the name of a beer) in 1992), and young men baggy pants, jogging suits and bermuda-length shorts referred to as '*new style*' in 1993). To be sure, dress conventions are not static but shift and are negotiated between dominant interests (the state and patriarchy) and ordinary people in ways that are influenced by the cultural politics of their time.

As a first step in considering how to tease out meanings from *salaula*, I suggest below some specific urban research sites and events in which dress and dressing up, whether in garments from the shops, the tailor or *salaula*, are getting a great deal of play. These sites and events may illuminate particularly vividly some of the disparate processes through which the meanings of clothing are constructed. . . .

Design and Style

How people put themselves together with clothes and how they create and transform styles can be explored through participant observation among tailors in different markets with different clienteles. An informal survey I conducted in 1993 shows a wide variation in the scope and volume of production in this segment of the garment industry from sweat-shop factory settings producing clothing for industrial/institutional wear to tiny one-person operations.[34] The majority of these workshops are owned and operated by men. The largest and most popular of these workshops employ both female and male seamstresses. The enterprises with which I am concerned here produce mainly for individual clients and may be distinguished into three types: workshops with several hired hands who work indoors, sewing for a largely up-scale clientele, almost exclusively women, specialising in highly stylized 'African' garments, smaller enterprises with two to three tailors who work both indoors and outdoors, sewing women's and men's garments, both 'African' and western styles and undertaking some alteration of salaula and single-person outdoor operations, often attached to markets, mainly repairing and altering salaula.

'Most people with little money', according to Hartman, 'prefer second-hand clothes to hand-made items, not because of lower cost but because of better quality and higher fashion'.[35] The widespread restyling of salaula that takes place within the bottom segment of the tailoring sector suggests that popular designs and styles are not always—or only—imported from above but are worked out with reference to local cultural and aesthetic norms of respectability and gender. Indeed mass consumption of used clothing may have a trickle-up effect that could shift the dynamics of design and style away from the apamwamba towards average consumers. To be sure, in Zambia as in the West, fashion trickles both up and down.[36]

Participant observation in tailors' workshops makes it possible to study interactions between tailors and customers about points of design and style, to discuss with tailors how style develops and to inquire with customers into what guides their decision to go to the tailor rather than the shops or the salaula market. Up-scale tailors display albums with photos of their styles, old European pattern books and European and South African magazines. Mid-level tailors rarely have their own photo albums but may produce some pages of paper with drawings of clothing styles. They also display old pattern books and magazines. Few single person tailors have any of these. Here, as with the other tailors, customers may bring a garment they want copied or they may describe what they want the tailor to sew. The extensive repair and alteration of salaula that takes place at this level is done to measure, remaking anonymous garments to fit their new owner. And some salaula of unpopular fabrics and colours are cut up, resewn and restyled into children's clothing.

Customers and tailors work hard at design and style, making garments out of local and imported fabrics and refashioning salaula to Zambian bodies, turning it into their own creation. How tailor and customer arrive at a distinct design and particular points of style may be traced through a network analysis . . . in order to reveal the channels of communication and the various influences, resources and inputs that converge into constituting particular designs and styles. Such a network might comprise a tailor's training/apprenticeship, the inspiration for his or her style, including influences from other African countries and overseas, media and TV images and customer suggestions. These networks are likely to vary considerably across the three types of workshops I identified earlier with different combinations of experiences and resources offering more or less scope for innovative designs and styles. The customer with her or his suggestions is part of the overlapping networks that form the channels of communication through which clothes, new or used, are transformed into cultural artefacts.

'Going to the tailor' thus offers close-range insights into one phase in the making of meaning of clothing. The combination of ideas that converge in the refashioning of salaula into local ensembles in turn achieves the effect of 'the latest' through ongoing interaction. This is evidenced on the street and in social gatherings, in what people wear and how and in their commentary about ensembles and the scrutiny with which they examine design and styling: Where did you buy that? Which tailor can do this pattern? Who sells Zairean prints? And where can I find 'silver' buttons?

Interaction and Display

If participant observation of the interaction between customers and tailors promises a close-up view into negotiations of designs and styles, social events of a variety of kinds offer the possibility for exploring other phases of the making of meaning. Aside from fulfilling basic clothing needs, combinations of used garments into ensembles produce important visual effects, a 'look' or presentational form that engages people's initial preoccupation with them and affects their subsequent dealings with such clothing in a variety of contexts.

Relevant settings in which to examine the verbal and observational means by which the meanings of used garments are evaluated range from domestic routines, seasonal events at which clothing features prominently such as Christmas, to life-cycle events, including 'kitchen parties'. . . . the popular bridal showers which are held in the not-so-poor parts of Zambia's urban areas. . . .

Kitchen parties are all-female events at which relatives and friends, including expatriates, come together with presents to help the bride-to-be with kitchen utensils for her new home. Invitations, often specially printed cards, are sent out to a wide range of women, including friends of friends.[39] Some of these parties are quite large, including between 100 and 200 persons; they tend to take place outdoors, in a spacious garden, on Saturday afternoons toward the end of the month, when wage-employed workers have received their paycheck. They are modelled on a loose version of initiation ceremonies and feature as party manager a senior woman marriage counsellor (*banachimbusa* in Bemba) who supposedly has instructed the bride-to-be in how to behave toward her husband, both sexually and interpersonally. One or two of these senior women manage the interpersonal relations of participants and seek to regulate their behaviour during the afternoon's activities. Helpers are active in serving food and drinks. The party gets going when the bride-to-be demonstrates her dancing skills, especially how 'to dance in bed'. Subsequent events include individual performances as each guest who cares or can be cajoled into dancing steps into the centre, commenting on the present she has brought 'for the kitchen' in terms of its importance to the marital relationship.

While some of the dances and songs performed at kitchen parties may derive from another era, these events are characterised by their ethnic heterogeneity and above all by their preoccupation with male–female relations and heterosexual norms. Ample food is served and, save in some Christian homes, such events are characterised by extensive consumption especially of beer but also of wine and alcohol-spiced punches. Given the male authoritarian atmosphere that characterises sociality across all class levels in Zambia, it comes as no surprise that men blame kitchen parties as fora where married women get drunk and indulge in social evils, such as exposing unmarried women to offensive songs about sex and gossip about extra-marital relationships.[40]

At kitchen parties, the participants' evaluation of and commentary on heterosexual behaviour extends into preoccupations with stylish appearance and dress. As a competitive presentation, a kitchen party may be viewed as a social situation set apart from everyday life in terms of place, setting and props. The focus on competitive display in sexually inflected dances, songs, gifts and clothes and the status politics that take place between women, turn kitchen parties into what Appadurai has defined as tournaments of value:

> . . . complex periodic events that are removed in some culturally well-defined way from the routine of economic life. Participation in them is . . . both a privilege . . . and an instrument of status contests . . . though such tournaments of value occur in special times and places, their forms and outcomes are always consequential for the more mundane realities of power and value in ordinary life.[41]

The 'currency' of the kitchen party's tournament of value is the female body, clothed in dress. At such parties participants evaluate and judge both behaviour and dress, collect information and trade and share insights into the sources of clothing design and style. In effect, the participants constitute a specialised knowledge group who on such occasions work out, in conflict or accommodation, the symbols and meanings which distinct clothing styles convey. . . .

Creative Tensions

The appropriation of used clothing imported from the West into dress practices in Zambia is a particularly rich research topic for exploring how contemporary urban life takes shape in the encounter with forms of economic and political power that stem from the West. Still, readers may well ask what is specifically 'Zambian' about the used clothing practices I have sketched and hinted at above. . . . Unlike reconditioned cars, television sets, computers and books, which are among the used commodities imported into Third World countries such as Zambia, used clothing has enormous crossover appeal. This is due in part to its ready availability and above all to its affordability which are making *salaula* an important, if not the chief, site of mass consumption in Zambia today. What is more, clothing reaches to the core of widespread Zambian sensibilities. Since the early days of their work in this region, Western anthropologists were struck by the active interests local people took in clothing.[44] Then, as now, clothing matters importantly in marital and sexual relationships, in same-sex and cross-sex status competitions and in economic exchange.

Today Zambians continue to pay considerable attention to clothing. Unlike in the West, where used clothing stores are a niche market that exists alongside the established garment industry, Zambia's *salaula* markets are democratising clothing access. Because of the impoverished economy, Zambians from most walks of life except the very top rely on *salaula* markets in order to satisfy both their clothing needs and their clothing desires. Save for the origin of their garments, there is nothing particularly 'Western' about how they deal with their clothes. The built-in judgemental bias of observers who condemn or deprecate this dependence on imported commodities prevent them from acknowledging what the majority of Zambians who purchase from *salaula* markets in fact are doing, namely redefining the West's used clothes as 'new' by their contexts.[45]

The ready availability of *salaula* not only fulfils the clothing needs of many poor consumers but also hints at the possibility at least temporarily of changing constraining circumstances that have to do with class, gender and generation. These circumstances constitute some of the chief local representations through which Zambians interpret clothing practices and, as such, they reduce the value of a crude post-modern reading of the used clothing story in Zambia. The cultural practices I have hinted at in suggesting how the meanings of clothes may be explored through particular events and interactions, as well as through transformations of the garments themselves, do not offer evidence of cultural fragmentation or of emptiness, of a world where anything goes. Rather, they speak vividly to and about local conundrums of everyday urban living in a rapidly transforming global world that articulate in ambiguous and contradictory ways with normative cultural ideas of gender and age. This process also grapples with a post-colonial legacy of an authoritarian one-party state that left ordinary citizens limited scope for fulfilling personal desires and at all levels of society privileged men over women. The initial optimism Zambians expressed about better opportunity and more access in their new multiparty state may well have faded,[46] yet they continue to rummage the piles of *salaula*, putting together their lives as best they can. Depending on location in class and regional terms and on gender and age, Zambians themselves read highly ambiguous meanings about freedom from wants and normative constraints into used clothing consumption and in so doing they also comment on their own localised position in a global world.

Conclusion

Anthropology today is at a particularly exciting moment due to the rapid global circulation of persons, commodities and ideas that are challenging our thinking about the specificity of culture and history and about how we do enthnography.[47] The consequences of these processes for life in cities such as Lusaka have . . . complicated effects on urban consumption patterns. . . . But that clothing, used and new, is a commodity imported from the 'West' is a different observation from contending that it means 'the same' as in its country of origin.

. . . *Salaula* wearers live in a world deeply but unevenly penetrated by the capitalist commodity form and by impressions from all over the world. Their locally informed cultural competence in dealing with used clothing transforms it into a social artefact that meets both some of their needs and expresses some of their desires. Rather than being imitations of metropolitan clothing themes, the particular characteristics of Zambian dealings with clothes are the results of highly specific historical trajectories which politically and economically have created precious little scope for a local textile and garment industry to flourish. The meanings used clothing practices assume today arise against this backdrop and in the face of deep-seated tensions within society itself—between women and men, the young and the old and ordinary people and the state.

Notes

1. This paper is based on research undertaken in Zambia, June to September 1992, funded by the University Research Grants Committee of Northwestern University and on consultancy work in Zambia and Zimbabwe, conducted in July and August 1993, for the Danish International Development Agency. . . .

4. G. Geretti and M. Korzeniewicz (eds). *Commodity Chains and Global Capitalism* (Westport, 1994).

5. In the early 1990s, labour unions in South Africa and Zimbabwe raised concerns about the growing imports of used clothing to the ILGWU, which addressed this issue, particularly the involvement of charities, at a recent international congress in Portugal. Manufacturers' associations in Zimbabwe discussed the issue of used clothing imports with the government which in turn banned commercial imports of used clothing in 1992, leaving only charitable organisations to import used clothing legally. In spite of this ban, a good deal of smuggling of used clothing into Zimbabwe takes place across the borders to Mozambique and Zambia which both allow commercial imports. Throughout 1993 and 1994 the Zambian print media have featured numerous items about the import of used clothing in which spokespersons for textile and garment manufactur-

ers associations have been much more vocal than union representatives. Letters to the editor tend overwhelmingly to describe the availability of used clothing in positive terms, emphasizing the fact that used clothing is within the purchasing power of the budgets of many poor households.

. . .

8. This is Jeremy Gould's suggestion, taken from V. Vandergeest and F. H. Buttel, 'Marx, Weber and Development Sociology: Beyond the Impasse', *World Development*, 16, 6 (1988), p. 687.

9. I have conducted extensive library searches with very minimal results. Barth van Groen and Piet Lozar, 'La Structure et l'Organisation de la Friperie a Tunis', Groupe d'Etudes Tunis, Universite Libre d'Amsterdam (1976) offer insights into the local organisation of this trade in Tunisia almost 20 years ago. S. Haggblade, 'The Flip Side of Fashion: Used Clothing Exports to the Third World', *Journal of Development Studies*, 29, 3 (1990), pp. 505–521, examined some of the economic effects of this import on the textile industry of Rwanda in the 1980s.

10. D. Todd, 'How the West's Charity Fleeces the Poor', *Toronto Star*, 13 November (1993), p. B5. I have learned more about the international configuration of this trade from the popular print media, especially newspapers, than from academic publications.

11. J. Brooke, 'International Report: Used U.S. Clothes a Best Seller in Africa', *New York Times*, Section 1, 16 February (1987).

. . .

13. M. R. Bhagavan, *Zambia: Impact of Industrial Strategy on Regional Imbalance and Social Inequality* (Uppsala, 1978); I. Karmiloff, 'Zambia', in R. Ridell (ed), *Manufacturing Africa: Performance and Prospects of Seven Countries in Sub-Saharan Africa* (London, 1990), pp. 297–336; A. Young, *Industrial Diversification in Zambia* (New York, 1973).

14. This observation applies not only to clothing and apparel but to a whole range of commodities and involves not only people of means but a broad range of the population.

15. Although the term *salaula* may have been applied to used clothing for much longer, it first drew my attention in a newspaper write-up in 1986 with the following description of a photograph: 'Ndola's Masala market, one source where *salaula* or second-hand clothes which contain polo-neck sweaters can be found'. 'Typical Scene of Zambian Market', *Sunday Times of Zambia*, 16 November (1986).

16. See G. Geisler and K. T. Hansen, 'Structural Adjustment, the Rural–Urban Interface and Gender Relations in Zambia', in N. Aslanbegui, S. Pressman and G. Summerfield (eds), *Women and Economic Transformation: Gender Impacts of Reform in Post-socialist and Developing Countries* (London, 1994), pp. 101–108.

17. Denconsult, Virkninger af Brugttoyssalg i, Udviklingslande [author's translation from Danish: Effects of Sales of Used Clothing in Developing Countries], unpublished report (1993), pp. 16, 21.

18. I. Kopytoff, 'The Cultural Biography of Things: Commodization as Process', in A. Appadurai (ed), *The Social Life of Things: Commodities in Cultural Perspective* (Cambridge, 1986), pp. 64–91.

19. Ibid., p. 73.

20. K. T. Hansen, 'Dealing with Clothing: *Salaula* and the Construction of Identity in Zambia's Third Republic', *Public Culture*, 6, 3 (1994), pp. 503–523.

. . .

22. D. Heath, 'Fashion, Anti-fashion, and Heteroglossia in Urban Senegal', *American Ethnologist*, 19, 2 (1992), pp. 19–33, is an interesting exception that casts light on the place of used clothing in Senegambian fashion.

23. Used clothing is not discussed in any of the major anthropology texts on textiles and dress, e.g. R. Barnes and J. Eicher (eds), *Dress and Gender: Making and Meaning* (London, 1992); J. Cordwell and R. A. Schwarz (eds), *The Fabric of Culture: The Anthropology of Clothing and Adornment* (Paris, 1979); A. B. Weiner and J. Schneider (eds), *Cloth and the Human Experience* (Washington, DC, 1989).

24. Notable concepts proposed to explain this process include, but are not limited to bricolage, J. Comaroff, *Body of Power, Spirit of Resistance* (Chicago, 1985), pp. 197–199); cultural brokerage, K. Barber, 'Popular Arts in Africa', *African Studies Review*, 30, 3 (1987); creolisation, U. Hannerz, 'The World in Creolisation', *Africa*, 57 (1987), pp. 546–559; heteroglossia, M. M. Bakhtin, *The Dialogic Imagination* (Austin, 1982).

25. On presentational form, see D. Miller, *Maternal Culture and Mass Consumption* (London, 1987), p. 87.

26. A. Hollander, *Seeing Through Clothes* (New York, 1978).

27. For this argument, see D. Miller, *Material Culture*, R. Wilk, 'Consumer Goods as Dialogue about Development', *Culture and History*, 7, pp. 79–100; E. Wilson,

Adorned in Dreams: Fashion and Modernity (Berkeley, 1985).

28. A. Appadurai, 'Introduction: Commodities and the Politics of Value', in A. Appadurai (ed), *The Social Life of Thines: Commodities in Cultural perspective* (Cambridge, 1986), pp. 6–11.

. . .

34. My observations show a very similar segmentation within the small-scale tailoring sector of the garment industry to that noted more than 10 years previously. See W. Hoppers, 'Towards a Differentiation of Small-scale Industry: An Example from Lusaka', *African Social Research*, 33 (1982), especially pp. 176–183.

35. M. Hartman, 'Social Relations and Access to Informal Sector Services: Some Examples from Tailors in Lusaka', unpublished seminar paper (Lusaka, n.d. [mid-to late 1980s]), p. 4.

36. J. Craik, *The Face of Fashion* (London, 1994), pp. 13, 217. . . .

39. One invitation from 1989 in my kitchen party file ends as follows: 'No Woman can be proud with a kitchen full of plastics' and one invitation from 1991 with the words: 'to brighten up this occasion, could you please contribute', inviting the guest to contribute two bottles of wine and a tray of eggs.

40. This sentence paraphrases arguments from newspapers: Letters to the Editor, 'Adolescents Should not Attend Kitchen Parties', *Zambia Daily Mail*, 27 November (1984), M. Mapulanga, 'Kitchen Parties Turned into Beer Dens', *Times of Zambia*, 5 December (1985).

41. Appadurai, 'Introduction', p. 21.

. . .

44. Although Wilson's observation that Africans in Broken Hill (Kabwe) 'are not a cattle people, nor a goat people, nor a fishing people, they are a dressed people', G. Wilson, 'An Essay on the Economics of Detribalization in Northern Rhodesia', Vol. II, *Rhodes–Livingstone papers*, no. 6 (1939), p. 18; perhaps the more striking, Richards noted in the early 1930s that rural Bemba constantly talked about clothes and took an intense interest in them. A. Richards, *Land, Labour and Diet in Northern Rhodesia* (Oxford, 1939), pp. 216–218.

45. As I have hinted at in a variety of places in the body of this paper, this is not to say that all consumers are reacting similarly to *salaula*. Segments of the population whose consumption and life-style aspirations have been particularly curtailed by the economic squeeze (for example university lecturers) may well be uneasy about admitting that in fact they purchase *salaula*.

46. During my research in Lusaka in 1992, I found this optimism expressed in the shift from the rigid safari/bush style of the 'Kaunda suit' to the double-breasted suit with tie and matching handkerchief in which the new president, F. Chiluba, dressed. That year, tailors restyling *salaula* were busy, sewing up vents and turning single-breasted jackets into double-breasted jackets which were called 'Chilubas'. See Hansen, 'Dealing', pp. 517–518.

47. On this, see A. Appadurai, 'Disjuncture and Difference in the Global Cultural Economy', *Public Culture*, 2, 2 (1990), pp. 1–24; R. Fox (ed), *Recapturing Anthropology: Writing in the Present* (Sante Fe, 1991); Sanjek, 'The Ethnographic Present'.

Source: *Journal of Southern African Studies*, vol. 21, March 1995. Reprinted by permission of Taylor & Francis Ltd., PO Box 25, Abingdon, Oxfordshire, OX14 3UE.

Part Four Art, Aesthetics, and Dress

Human beings live in various types of societies and cultures that affect what they think of as appropriate, even beautiful dress. In this section, we look at the dress as an art form in Chapter 10 by discussing various ways people dress their bodies around the world, both in modifying and in supplementing them. We also tackle the idea of ideals and standards of beauty in different places in relation to the body and to dress in Chapter 11. Similarly, in Chapter 12, we discuss the idea that all people appear to have an interest in showing by means of their dress that they conform to the expectations of others with whom they affiliate and yet display a desire to express their individuality as well. Finally, Chapter 13 focuses on how dress is used throughout a wide variety of art forms as an integral part of the many forms of art, as an art form in itself, and as a means of expression for many artists.

10

The Art of Creating Dress

OBJECTIVES

To understand dress as a distinctive art form.

To explore the human impulse to create dress.

To analyze how aesthetic relationships between dress and the body carry different meanings in different cultures and social groups.

ALONG WITH LANGUAGE, the universal human behavior of dress separates the human animal from the rest of the animal kingdom. We have the capacity to make material artifacts that we can apply to our bodies to modify them as well as to make material artifacts to supplement the body. In addition, we evaluate these body modifications and supplements as pleasing or not pleasing, which results in a system of cultural practice we call the *art of dress*. We each use artistic discretion in our everyday lives as we choose a hairstyle, consider the use of cosmetics and scent, and select styles and colors of garments and accessories to wear.

In this chapter we use the concepts art and aesthetics in discussing dress. Art is both a process and an artifact. Art as a process involves individuals carrying out activities that end in the production of artifacts whose form and composition can be assessed for the skillful arrangement of formal elements having significance to the viewer. The form has significance because it arouses a response in the viewer. Aesthetics refers to understanding how we perceive forms, their characteristics, and how we experience that response (DeLong & Hillestad, 1990, p. 33). Because human beings are aesthetic animals, the dressed body can be assessed as an art form, for aesthetic judgments are taught to members of each society. Therefore our definition of art includes the design and production of high fashion, street fashion, wearable art, and world dress along with the artistic productions found in museums, galleries, and concert halls.

THE ART OF DRESS

Our reactions to the art of dress are complex because some people do not consider the act of dressing as an art form. Such individuals may find the act of dressing of negligible or no aesthetic interest, whereas others may find the act of dressing as pleasurable and of constant interest. However, in each case, we practice the art of dress daily by design or default and our dress is evaluated, consciously or unconsciously, by others with whom we interact, and we each have the opportunity to engage daily in the act of design as well as to assess the dressed bodies of others. In addition, in some societies, professional designers and evaluators of dress exist, as do professionals who execute some of the popular body modifications, such as hairdressers and barbers, cosmetic artists, and other aestheticians. For example, the application of henna designs to the feet of a bride in Morocco, a temporary body modification, is becoming increasingly popular in the United States.

Some people are trained to create the items that modify and supplement the body, the designers and manufacturers of apparel, cosmetics, jewelry, and accessories. Other people have occupations that relate to evaluating and critiquing dress. Contemporary examples in our global culture include retail buyers who expect their choices of garments and accessories to sell, journalists for fashion magazines and newspapers, television commentators who stimulate interest in fashion and dress, and stylists who prepare models for fashion photography shoots or runway shows. Others involved are advertising agencies and other gatekeepers of fashion who promote our interest in dress.

THE AESTHETICS OF DRESS

The *aesthetics of dress* uses our five senses in the processes of dressing ourselves and perceiving others, as we pointed out in Chapter 1. We now provide more detail about the aesthetics of enhancing the appearance, scent, taste, feel, and sound of the body through dress. Our aesthetic involvement and evaluations stem from visual reactions to color, the play of light and shadow, and the relation of lines and form. Our other senses also register aesthetic responses. Our skin receives some of our earliest aesthetic experiences because our first contacts with the world are largely through the sense of touch. Infants respond to the feeling of clothes or swaddling, learn to react with pleasure to parental touch, notice feelings of being wet or dry, and learn to love the texture of a favorite toy. Combined with the other senses of sight, sound, smell, or taste, an infant's growing knowledge of the world is profoundly sensual.[1]

We find pleasure in recognizable sounds and sound patterns identifiable most commonly in art as music, poetry, and prose. The aesthetic worth of written words lies in their potential tonal qualities, rhythms, and cadence when spoken, along with any uniqueness of expression. Performing artists—musicians, poets, actors—translate the printed symbol into sound. Their dress is designed to support their presentations. Everyday dress may produce sound as well, as in the case of cleats on shoe heels, fabric rubbing against fabric, or jangling bracelets. In some places, sound-producing devices become a part of festive, ceremonial, or theatrical dress, while in other societies, such items of dress may be worn on a daily basis, or perhaps exclusively by one category of people.

Pleasant odors, such as soaps, scents (either natural as in flowers or synthetic as in perfumes), and lotions, are often an essential part of dress. In addition, some fabrics, such as raw silk, have characteristic odors that add to their aesthetic appeal. Leather gives off a distinctive odor that is developed during the processing of skins. Whether these odors are pleasing simply because of themselves, or because of the responses they elicit from their association with familiar and pleasing events and people, is debatable. Perhaps both factors are influential, as they may be in the case of those who prefer to dry clothes in the open air rather than in an automatic dryer. In all these cases, scent may stimulate pleasurable responses that in turn add to aesthetic satisfactions with the body and its dress. Early evidence of the pleasing nature of scent is suggested by the discovery of pollen and flower fragments in a Neanderthal burial site in Iraq. These finds indicate that an appropriate tribute to the dead may have been to lay them to rest in a fragrant as well as visually beautiful bed of flowers ("The Neanderthal Man," 1969, pp. 1, 47).

Therefore, the personal aesthetic of dress is associated with a pleasurable feeling or emotion that arises with stimulating sensory organs. Human beings often evaluate pleasing sensory experience as beauty. Santayana (1896/1955) stresses these qualities in all beauty:

> Beauty is a value . . . it is an emotion, an affection of our volitional and appreciative nature. An object cannot be beautiful if it can give pleasure to nobody: a beauty to which all men were forever indifferent is a contradiction in terms. This value is positive, it is the sense of the presence of something good, or (in the case of ugliness) of its absence. It is never the perception of a positive evil, it is never a negative value. (p. 49)

However, all values exist within specific cultural and historical contexts. What is beautiful to some might not be considered beautiful by all (Kupfer, 1994, p. 97). We therefore take the position that there is no universal standard of beauty.

Santayana's definition distinguishes beauty as a value different from moral value, which is also often applied to dress. Moral values may be negative as well as positive. In the case of dress, these values are often proscriptive, such as judging the wearing of torn jeans as sloppy and inappropriate, that is, judging a person on the basis of dress or physical appearance. Instead, for Santayana the pursuit of beauty strives for attaining pleasure. One way to understand beauty is to think of pleasurable, physical sensations as filtered first through our individual brains, then by our cultural sensibilities. For example, when we smell food cooking, or hear bells chiming, or notice the way someone is dressed, we first use our senses to register the experience, react personally to it, then make sense of it within a cultural context. For example, we might see the latest fashions from a famous designer such as Jean-Paul Gaultier on a television program. We might first be captivated by the movement of the models and the garments, then react by saying such garments could never be worn in real life, but finally appreciate the creativity and entertainment value of the display within the context of world fashion.

Ideas about a pleasing appearance evolve as members of a society seize upon particular forms of body and dress from which they derive pleasurable emotions. Different words and terms may exist for someone who is good looking, beautiful, pretty, or handsome. Clothing may also be assessed with these words as well as others of approval such as "neat" or "cool." Negative words are used as well, when describing a person or a garment as "ugly" or "nasty," as teenagers in the United States in the 1990s said. Different age groups and occupational groups often choose different words to talk about someone whose dress or appearance is acceptable or unacceptable. Similarly, clothing of males and females may also be described with different terminology.

As change occurs and new techniques develop to produce new forms in dress, aesthetic ideas about dress often change as well, and the words to describe acceptable or attractive dress may change. As we think of examples from the time of hippie to hip-hop subcultures, ideas about appearances and dress in North American society have subsequently changed.

THE UNIVERSALITY OF THE ART OF DRESS

Dressing the body in a pleasing way is practiced by all cultural groups, and is sometimes referred to as a cultural universal, though the form of that dress may vary greatly. Murdoch (1955) identifies the true universals of culture, not as identities in specific behavioral habits, but as similarities in classification of behavioral elements. A dogskin cloak, body paint, and tattoos represent different examples of dress in different cultures, and each can be appraised aesthetically by members of each culture.

Although a seemingly endless variety in dress exists, the common aspect appears to involve enhancement of the self. Thus, dress may consist of only a little paint, a necklace, or a waist-string, but it is an addition that, deliberately or inadvertently, draws attention to and reveals personal and social information about the individual. However, enthusiasm for dress is a personal as well as a social matter. Not all individuals are interested equally in using dress for self-enhancement. Although we are social beings and live in groups, we also have private, individual lives and we monitor group norms in deciding upon individual action. We may follow aesthetic standards of our immediate social group or of society at large or modify them to express personal, social, or philosophical ideas. We do so by using a cultural aesthetic code that others in our cultural group understand (Kupfer, 1994, p. 100). Some scholars say that culture is aesthetics. As every human being becomes enculturated, each develops an aesthetic sense, which he or she then uses to dress and respond to the dress of others. In complex cultures, a variety of aesthetic standards can co-exist that relate to different cultural and ethnic groups, different ages, and even different geographical regions within a large country, such as the United States or Russia.

People living in small-scale cultures with seemingly meager resources, meeting simple survival needs, nevertheless exercise an aesthetic sense in dressing themselves. The Fuegians, for example, who live at the frigid southern tip of South America, were picturesquely described by Charles Darwin (1958 version) in his journal that recorded observations made during the famous surveying expedition of the ship *Beagle* between 1831 and 1836. They either wore no coverings or tossed scant fur mantles of guanaco, otter, or sealskin about their shoulders in a way that seemed unlikely to keep them warm. Darwin's description of one of their leaders reveals, however, they were not without body decoration. The old man he described:

> . . . had a fillet of white feathers tied round his head, which partly confined his black, coarse, and entangled hair. His face was crossed by two broad transverse bars; one, painted bright red, reached from ear to ear and included the upper lip; the other white like chalk extended above and parallel to the first so that even his eyelids were thus colored. (p. 177)

The nomadic Aborigines of central Australia also survived under difficult environmental conditions with no coverings and only simple lean-tos of brush to protect them. Although they lived in desert conditions with night temperatures below freezing, they did not develop protective clothing. However, like the Fuegians, the Aborigines decorated their bodies with paint, scars, or emu down glued on with blood (Porteus, 1931).

The judgment that members of a small-scale culture expend all their time in meeting daily needs is ethnocentric, for often they have sizable amounts of leisure time. In some cases this time is spent in dressing for special occasions. In a classic example, Strathern and Strathern (1971) reported that men and women in Mount Hagen, New Guinea, would spend days borrowing materials and assembling their feather headdresses and preparing wigs in preparation for the special occasions of public exchanges of wealth. On the appointed day they would spend several hours painting their faces and donning the headdresses and other body supplements preparatory to the display dances associated with the wealth exchanges. People from many neighboring villages would come together for these events to participate or to observe how well the dancers' ensembles coordinated with those of others in their group.

Some coverings appear to be intended only to meet climatic demands for protection or social requirements for modesty, but they still have some element of adornment and elicit an aesthetic response from observers. Mahatma Gandhi's dress in his later life exemplified minimal cultural requirements for covering the body in Indian society; as a political statement he wore a common Indian peasant dress ensemble consisting of a plain *dhoti* (doe-TEE), or loincloth, as in Figure 10.1, sometimes with a shawl. He intended his dress to be a statement about the responsibility of the British colonial government for the poverty of India's working classes who could afford no more clothes than what enabled them to observe Indian standards of public decency (Tarlo, 1996). Yet pictures of Gandhi always show him in a sparkling white *dhoti* rather than one grayed or stained with wear, indicating, at least to non-Indians, a seeming concern with an aesthetic aspect of his dress. Moreover his white loincloth, contrasting with his brown skin, stimulated an aesthetic reaction to color in his observers. His spectacles helped him see, but as a part of his dress were also subject to an aesthetic response by others, since they became an integral part of the appearance of his face.

Both dressing the body and observing the dressed body involve physical processes as well as cultural codes that allow human beings to express and interpret visual and other sensual information about individuals. In all cultures, most people attempt to enhance their appearance in some way. In addition, people react to the aesthetic stimuli that dress provides. Although major aes-

Figure 10.1
Mahatma Gandhi's dress exemplified the minimal personal display afforded by a poor Indian peasant, yet it also evidenced aesthetic elements of concern to himself and those who observed him.

thetic reactions relate to the visual impression of the dressed body, sensitivity to sounds such as those created by jangling bracelets, the flip-flop of sandals, the swoosh of nylon wind pants, to the tastes of lip gloss, and to the odors of perfumes and lotions also are stimuli related to the appreciation of the dressed body. The art of dress may seem difficult to define, but we regard it as the relationship of body and dress recognized by members of a cultural group who use an aesthetic code to express who they are. The result gives the dressed person emotional satisfaction and has the potential to provide pleasure to both wearer and observer. However, to an outsider or someone working from a different code, the response might be fear, curiosity, or disgust. The art of dress is truly in the eye of the beholder.

CREATING FORMS OF DRESS

The classification system for dress that incorporates body modifications and body supplements as introduced in Chapter 1 illustrates that the body has certain plastic or moldable (sculptural) qualities. Hair can be straightened, curled, and forced into many different shapes, as shown in the men's haircuts in the United States in the 1990s (see Figure 10.2). Breasts, waistlines, hips, buttocks,

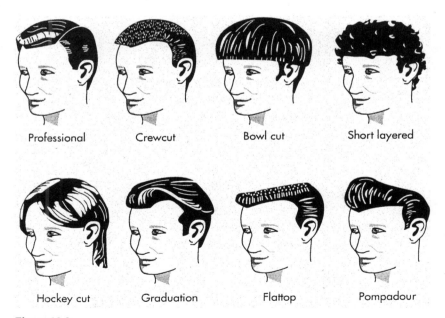

Professional   Crewcut   Bowl cut   Short layered

Hockey cut   Graduation   Flattop   Pompadour

Figure 10.2
Even with the relatively short hair worn by most men, the ease with which hair can be manipulated facilitates a great range of design possibilities. Examples of U.S. hairstyles for men in the twentieth century.

feet, and heads can be molded by massaging, surgery, or binding. Scarring and applying lotions can modify skin texture. Ears, noses, lips, and almost every conceivable body part have, in some place or at some time, been purposely re-designed by cosmetic practice or surgery, amateur or professional. Diet and ex-ercise also influence development of body form.

In addition, we can convert many materials into objects that supplement the body. Malleable metals can be made into accessories, such as jewelry, into coverings, such as helmets, or into whole garments, as in chain mail or armor. Flexible materials such as animal skins and furs along with natural and syn-thetic fibers provide us with the most widely used materials for dressing the body. Liquids are also involved in the art of dress, for often an individual's dress is started or completed with fluids: water for bathing, cosmetics or paint, as well as scents and lotions. Physically and socially, dress may be a second skin; aesthetically, however, it is a second form, if form is considered to include the total combination of aesthetic elements (color, line, value, texture, shape)[2] that a dressed body presents.

The structure of the body can be perceived independently or as a base for presentation of a total design. Thus, the impact of the aesthetic display of dress on the viewer stems from the inherent qualities (form and movement) of the human body as well as the form imposed on that body through application of external forces and materials, such as corsets, neck rings, or body building. In addition, as an independent structure, the body has observable shape, color, texture, value contrasts, and lines that define the total shape and constituent parts of shapes. In its totality, the body is made up of a number of component shapes, the legs, arms, head, neck, and trunk, arranged bilaterally on a vertical axis. Contrasting horizontal line direction is created by an alignment of shoul-ders, hips, knees, ankles, feet, eyes, mouth, and ears. Color and value contrast and texture are provided by the skin, hair, and eyes.

Changes in posture and facial gesture alter the visual impact of body and dress, as do body movements (DeLong, 1998, pp. 108–121). Both posture and movement may be greatly influenced by social customs; thus, people in differ-ent cultures may learn to stand, sit, squat, and walk in different ways, as seen in Figure 10.3. Pleasing appearance, therefore, may be recognizable more readily in those stances or movements characteristic of the culture. In Japan, women who trained to be geisha exhibit a specific cultural stance and body movement for their dress, as Dalby (1993) found out in her study of geisha. For a contrast, consider how Western fashion models in each era take particular stances and move in specific ways that demonstrate the current aesthetic ideal for presen-tation of both the ideal body and fashionable dress in the West. These move-ments and postures, and the related dress forms, are related to the roles that women play in Western society, as shown in Figure 10.4.

Aesthetic evaluation is based upon the total effect of body plus the sup-plements and modifications imposed upon it. The total effect is significant be-cause dressing the body ordinarily involves an individual making aesthetic judgments based on a desire to create an appropriate and pleasing impression. Of importance to note in today's complex world is the fact that "appropriate

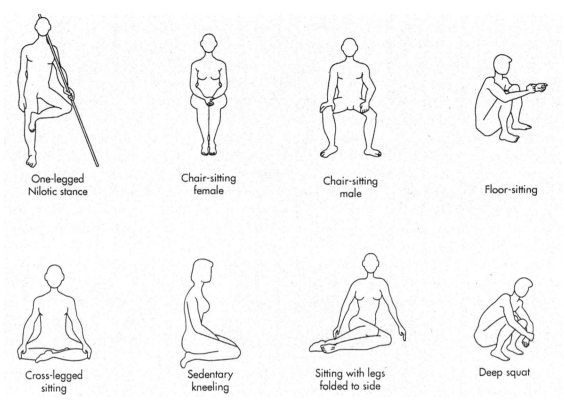

One-legged
Nilotic stance

Chair-sitting
female

Chair-sitting
male

Floor-sitting

Cross-legged
sitting

Sedentary
kneeling

Sitting with legs
folded to side

Deep squat

Figure 10.3
Beauty may be recognizable only in those postures characteristic of a culture, as seen in this selection from the many distinctive body postures found around the world.

and pleasing" dress in one group of people may be jarring and ugly to another. For example, in North America at the end of the twentieth century, the casual styles known as grunge and the wide-legged hip-hop pants worn by adolescents frequently annoyed parents and teachers and provoked public comment in newspapers and magazines controlled by adults. We find similar cases in the history of dress, such as the people called beatniks who wore black in the 1950s and the dress of punks in the 1970s. Many other instances of groups whose definitions of appropriate or pleasing dress differ from others can be found both historically and in the contemporary world.

Appreciation of the aesthetic qualities of the independent body form dates to prehistory. Among the earliest artifacts known are small carvings of unsupplemented (i.e., uncovered) figures from the Neolithic period. The totally uncovered body of male athletes, as an attractive alternate to the covered or clothed state, was notable among the early Greeks who "attached great importance to their nakedness" (Clark, 1956, pp. 23–24), especially in the Olympic games. In some cultures, the uncovered body, with only jewelry, accessories, or cosmetics

c. 1955

c. 1965

c. 1975

Figure 10.4
Changing U.S. fashion-model stances (1950s–1990s) evidence both changes in the gender expectations of women in the United States and the associated changing aesthetics of posture through which female beauty is recognized in U.S. culture.

c. 1985

c. 1997

as embellishments, is common. In this case, the body dominates and is not merely a structural base in the total visual effect that an individual presents.

In many Western cultures, strong moral sanctions against total nudity exist, and exposing the nude body in public is ordinarily considered unacceptable. Therefore, the total form of the dressed body (body plus dress) is the form most often described in aesthetic terms in such cultures. The colors, lines, shapes, and textures of the body and of dress blend to create a total form of dress that individuals often consider as unique to themselves. Figure 10.5a and b exemplify the difference between two periods of time in the contrast of the Gibson Girl's dress with the garments designed and worn by Eileen Fisher.

(a)   *(b)*

Figure 10.5
The illusion of changing body form from one fashion era to another is easily created
in cultures where standards of modesty require that much of the body be covered
with supplements. (a) U.S. studio portrait, 1890s; (b) U.S. designer Eileen Fisher in
one of her outfits, 1990s.

Indeed, individuals often become emotionally ill at ease when not dressed
in their customary dress. Figure 10.6 shows one cartoonist's portrayal of can-
didate Bob Dole in the 1996 Presidential campaign when he changed his customary suit and tie for more casual dress on the campaign trail in order to appeal to a wider audience.

ANALYZING THE MEANING AND FORM OF DRESS

In addition to aesthetic form, dress has meaning as well. Individuals often select items of dress because of the personal or public meaning that it conveys,
as in the case of the decision to wear a wedding ring. The total visual form of
the ensemble items and body modifications also conveys meanings that can be
complex or have subtle distinctions between closely related dress forms.

The total visual effect or total form of dress can be analyzed by breaking it
down into elemental aesthetic forms (colors, lines, shapes, textures), and describing how these elements are organized into particular relationships. Analyses of meaning involve the emotional, value-laden responses to the aesthetic
form of dress and understanding the reasons why certain arrangements of dress
may be thought more beautiful or appropriate than others (Kupfer, 1994). Individuals trying to explain why some arrangement is more pleasing than another

Figure 10.6
Individuals become uncomfortable when forced to abandon their customary dress for something unfamiliar, as this cartoon of the 1996 presidential campaign suggests.

may consider physiological, psychological, social, cultural, and philosophical reasons or may apply customary belief, common sense, past experience, and personal opinion.

The terms for describing aspects of color (hue, intensity, and value) along with line, shape, space, and texture, and adjectives such as horizontal, diagonal, and circular provide a language well understood by designers and artists, and generally understood by many adults in Western cultures for communication on matters of form. These terms have been developed by professionals to reach aesthetic understanding of perceived objects without the impediment of cultural bias (Fiore & Kimle, 1998). As descriptions of dress, they can be used in comparing dress cross-culturally. At the same time, many of these words are also used with specific cultural meaning and are not unbiased. Designations of specific colors, lines, shapes, spaces, and textures as "best" or ideal are culturally determined preferences, and often not applicable across cultures. Interpretations of the emotional responses of observers of these formal elements are, therefore, concerned with meaning, which is culturally taught.

TYPES OF BODY SUPPLEMENTS USED IN CREATING DRESS

Supplements to the body, as presented in the classification system, vary from culture to culture and relate to concepts of beauty and the art of dressing the body. For example, wrapped enclosures are found in many parts of the world, especially in tropical and semitropical climates. Wrapped enclosures are commonly used to cover the torso for men and women from the waist to the knees or ankles and are known by a wide variety of terms such as *saris, dhotis,* and *lungis* in India and Pakistan, as sarongs in Polynesia, as *slendangs* (SLEN-dahng) in Indonesia, as wrappers or *pagnes* (PAH-nyez) in various countries of West Africa, and by other names in many other parts of the world. Figure 10.7 provides an interpretation of a *lungi* (a man's wrapped body supplement in India) for a contemporary American woman.

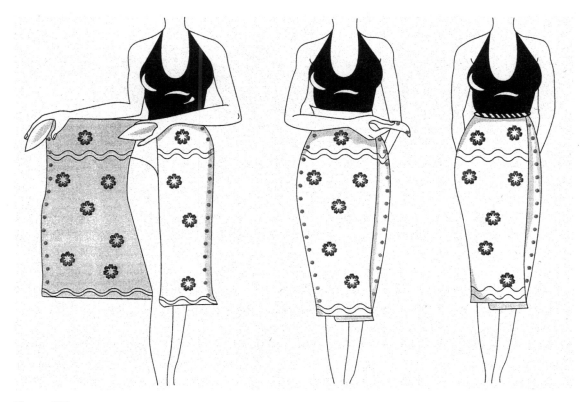

Figure 10.7
The technique for wrapping an Indian *lungi* onto the body has been adapted to a world dress fashion garment for women. "Hold the fabric behind you at waist level, leaving one side longer than the other. Fold the short side across your front. Wind the top of the long side a bit, then pull the longer, twisted side around your waist and tuck the top of the short side over the twisted part" (Feldon, 1993, p. 149).

Wrapped fabrics often enclose the head in different cultures as well and have different names for several forms, such as turbans, Indian men's *pagri* (PAH-gri), headties, and scarves. Various versions and styles exist in different places with variations for men's and women's types of headwraps. Sometimes the method of wrapping indicates marital status, as in the headties of West Indian women of Martinique, or the individual whim of the wearer or the possibility of ethnic or religious affiliation (such as the Sikh Indian men's recognizable turban or the headdress of Muslim men who have made the pilgrimage to Mecca). In some cases of wrapped garments, the fabric clings to the body, making the shape of the body predominant, as in the case of the sarong. In other examples, layers of cloth may be wrapped loosely obscuring the shape of the body, as in some examples of Indian *sari*, or the cloth is tied or tucked around the waist in such a way that the body appears plump, or perhaps even pregnant, as in the case of the Kalabari woman in Nigeria shown in Figure 10.8.

Figure 10.8
To satisfy the appearance ideals of their culture, Kalabari women pleat, fold, and wrap extra layers of cloth under their thick outer garments, which are also wrapped, to create the illusion of their cultural ideal for women—a body that is full, rounded, and fecund.

Preshaped enclosures, more than wrapped enclosures, facilitate infinite variety in the forms and artistry of dress, even down to the smallest detail as in the case of pocket styles for men's shirts or collar styles in women's blouses. Preshaped enclosures such as body stockings or a "catsuit" may also fit the body very closely. Preshaped dress can, in contrast, be constructed to surround the body loosely, as in the example of many men's and women's tailored business suits around the world. Women's dresses as well may cling to the body or stand away from it, and the various men's garments of the Middle East and Africa known as the caftan, *galibaya* (gah-lih-BAH-yah), and *djellaba* (jell-A-bah), also surround the body loosely. Such details of how a garment is wrapped or tailored, along with surface decoration, type of jewelry added, and other stylistic features frequently identify the wearer's gender, age, social status, and role in society.

The classification system emphasizes the type of dress items and processes and the placement on the body. Others systems analyze the aesthetics of dress, such as the apparel body construct system of Marilyn DeLong (1998), which assesses factors of form underlying the observer's aesthetic response to the dressed person as a whole integrated entity, viewed within the context of the environment in which it is observed.

All people across the many cultures of the world, or even all people within a single society, do not react similarly to formal elements of design even though some books about dress imply a universal understanding. For example, although Wallach (1986, pp. 114–117, 167–171) says that color combinations of "mustard/black" and "black/beige" are appropriate to or communicate the sense of, respectively, the "avant garde creator" and the "contemporary corporate" businesswoman, this is not true in every part of the world. Wallach presents only one cultural point of view and suggests only what might be true in one historical, social, and cultural setting.

Cultural bias is common in every culture. For example, in a business dress handbook entitled *Man at His Best: The Esquire Guide to Style* by Wilson (1986), the question of shirt collar styles for men is addressed:

> Narrow face (and long neck): A high collar with moderate spread will make your face look broader. Avoid long, straight collars. A collar pin can provide a forceful horizontal element, but forget about narrow ties. (p. 69)

The collar described will have the visual effect intended for the narrow face, but only in comparison to other types of collars and other facial types. The collars are themselves cultural products. More importantly, the desired effect is defined by an unstated underlying assumption about the ideal shape of the male face, an ideal no doubt specific to a particular segment of the North American population. Although the addition of a collar pin will add a horizontal line to the total visual effect, whether or not this is perceived as "forceful" depends upon the meanings attached to specific forms in the culture of the viewer. Moreover, the collar pin is a fashion accessory; its use may connote either high fashion or out-of-fashion, depending on the time period, and this message may override any other visual effect. Whether or not the illusory effect created by this dress—of a wider face—is valued as effective will depend upon the cultural context in which the person is being evaluated. The dress prescription constitutes a cultural solution for a culturally defined problem that may not exist in other parts of the world.

Emotional and cognitive reactions to the aesthetic qualities of dress are commonly recognized within all cultures. For example, the meaning of a particular item of dress can be identified within a specific culture; however, another culture may attach different meanings to the same thing. A head covering on a Muslim woman has a moral and religious meaning, which lets a man know that a woman is not available to him for social mixing; he can mix with the many women in his extended family who appear with heads uncovered in his presence within the home. In contrast, when small, transparent veils were fashionable on hats in North America and Europe, such a veil on a woman had decorative, even romantic significance that does not necessarily constitute a barrier to social interaction. Instead, a flirtatious woman might have encouraged interaction by lowering her eyes behind the veil to shape the quality of an interaction with a male.

Even in the same culture, similar types of dress may have different meanings, depending on the person and the occasion. For example, in the United States, the color black is often associated with mourning and a choice for clothing worn at funerals. Black is also the choice for the men's tuxedos worn for special evening events and for women's dresses for a festive, evening occasion. Black is currently a fashionable color for everyday dress among certain sectors of North American and European youth. The meaning of the color black is not the same in all these contexts, so each dress ensemble must be analyzed within the context of the values of its wearers and the occasions and social contexts in which they choose to wear it. Another example of difference in meaning but similarity in aesthetic results is shown in Figure 10.9. The Karl Lagerfeld dress for Chanel uses lace to decorate the skin that shows beneath it. Though visually similar to the effect of a tattoo, it does not convey a similar cultural meaning.

Furthermore, different parts of the body may have the same meaning in different cultures. For example, people in different cultures have interpreted different parts of the human body as being sexually attractive: in Japan the nape of a woman's neck is considered erotic to men; in the United States, sometimes a woman's legs, sometimes her breasts, sometimes her buttocks. Among the Mende of Sierra Leone, the sexually attractive portions of a woman's body are considered to be the buttocks and the breasts (Boone, 1986). Apparently little cross-cultural research exists on what portions of a man's body are deemed sexually attractive to women, although in the United States frequent comments, and even calendars, are produced that talk about men's "buns" (buttocks) or well-developed pectoral muscles. Apparently there is an opportunity for cross-cultural research on this topic.

CULTURAL TYPOLOGIES OF DRESS

Typologies, classifications based on type, are used in the handling of subjective data, such as cultural meanings, which are difficult to analyze with any kind of common measure. Such typologies have only a limited range of application

Figure 10.9
Visual effects very similar
to those produced by ap-
plying a tattoo onto the
skin are created by wear-
ing transparent lace over
the skin. However, the
cultural meanings of these
two forms of dress are
quite different.

and are constructed for use in a specific social group with meaning only for that group. For example, a typology describing bodies as stocky, overweight, thin, tall, and short is value laden and has serious limitations as a cross-cultural classification system. Although these words may carry a negative meaning in a particular culture, the same size body may not be perceived as overweight by people in all cultures. Some find obesity beautiful. In addition, tallness and shortness may have different connotations for men and women. This typology obviously cannot be applied to all people within a culture, let alone across cultures. Application of Sheldon's (1940) somatotypes, discussed in Chapter 5, may be a more useful tool in measuring or understanding body form. The apparel industry in the United States uses the typology of standard sizing to group women with similar proportions into like groups with terms such as juniors, queen-size, and petite that imply body size categories. Manufacturers often use various types of labels with numbers and letters to indicate sizing and as a marketing tool (Brown & Rice, 1998). Yet the individual numbers do not correspond to specific body measurements, and garments with the same number are not standardized from manufacturer to manufacturer and often fit each consumer differently.

Some authors who write advice books primarily for North American women on how to dress, such as Nix-Rice (1996), use personal style categories such as "Tailored Classic," "Sporty Natural," "High-Fashion Dramatic," and "Feminine Romantic." Nix-Rice makes strong apparel color and fabric recommendations along with hairstyle and makeup suggestions for the way women in each category should dress. In another book, Wallach (1986, pp. 133–150)

135 CHITRINI OR ART WOMAN
Second best

136 PADMINI OR LOTUS WOMAN
The most desirable type

137 HASTINI OR ELEPHANT WOMAN
The undesirable type

138 SHANKHINI OR CONCH WOMAN
The common type

Figure 10.10
Ancient Indian texts delineate a typology of four types of women on the basis of physical and psychological characteristics. These types still echo in current cultural evaluations of women's appearance in India.

defines dress ensembles for North American working women according to the type of work image a woman wants to project to indicate her personal skills, working style, and work interests. She distinguishes individuals who work in the sphere of communications as "traditional," "contemporary," and "innovative" communicators and follows these categories with specific recommendations for dress. Such **cultural typologies of dress** also exist in other cultures. For India, Thomas (1957, pp. 75–79) describes and illustrates four traditional types of women (dating to the third and fourth centuries B.C.E.): (1) *padmini* or lotus woman, (2) *chitrini* or art woman, (3) *samkhini* or conch woman, and (4) *hastini* or elephant woman as shown in Figure 10.10. Each type is characterized by certain physical and psychological attributes, with the lotus woman being the most desirable and the elephant woman the least. The meaning of any typology is ordinarily shared only by the members of a culture. Therefore, typologies involving subjective evaluation of meanings of dress may be useful but should be acknowledged as generally having a utility that is limited to a cultural setting and particular time period. Since it is difficult to create a typology that spans all physical types and cultural groups, some typologies have had limited usefulness even within a single culture because of an implicit racial or gender bias.

SUMMARY

People in all cultures pay attention to the aesthetics of dress, when dressing themselves and when viewing the dress of others. The aesthetic concern embraces primarily the visual aspects of dress, but also includes information obtainable by any of the senses. Some of the response to dress is conscious, and some is at a subconscious level. In both cases dress evokes emotional responses and communicates meanings to observers.

Types of dress are describable in aesthetic terms; they also have meanings. The total visual effect of dress can be analyzed by describing its formal aesthetic components; that is, the colors, lines, shapes, textures, and space, that body and dress present. Culturally unbiased terms for describing information gained through the other senses (e.g., smell, sight, touch, and sound) are less well developed in the analytical literature on dress. However, the physical sciences are perfectly capable of technically describing and measuring the forms of sounds, tastes, smells, and physical textures.

The degree to which the organization of the elements of dress is judged to approach the aesthetic ideal of a culture depends upon the society in which evaluations are being made. Evaluations are always made in relation to cultural ideals of the evaluator. These ideals depict the desirable rather than the achievable and may not be relevant for all segments of a particular culture. Typologies are formal classifications developed within a society and culture that help distinguish a range of ideal and less than ideal types commonly found or a range of alternative ideals from which to select. The next chapter develops the topic of ideals and standards for the art of dress.

STUDY TOOLS

Important Term

cultural typologies of dress

Discussion Questions

1. In your own words, explain Santayana's statement "Beauty is a value . . ." found on page 289 of the chapter. Discuss how the terms "beauty" and "aesthetic" differ?
2. Describe how stimulation of the senses produces an aesthetic response. How is that response filtered by our cultural orientation?
3. Compare and contrast Mende, geisha, and Euro-American ideas of beauty and the art of dress.
4. Compare the aesthetics of the dress of the Ga'Anda women described in Reading III.1 with the text comments about Mende and the Japanese geisha, first based on the cultural values and then on the values you assume exist in their cultures.
5. If beauty is in the eye of the beholder, then discuss how the universal aesthetic impulse is played out in the development of dress ensembles by yourself, one of your parents, and one of your grandparents.
6. Describe a body modification or body supplement that you and a family member of a different generation sometimes both utilize. Do you utilize these in the same or different ways? Do the similar forms of this item or modification as worn by both you and this other family member communicate the same or different meanings to yourselves and to your respective peers?
7. Using Reading IV.1, "The Aesthetics of Men's Dress of the Kalabari of Nigeria," by Tonye Erekosima and Joanne Eicher, describe the hierarchy of Kalabari men's dress. Select the *ebu, doni, woko,* or *etibo* and describe how these garments should be worn. What does adhering to Kalabari men's dress etiquette tell the viewer about the wearer?

Activities

1. Attend a public event organized by a cultural group different from your own. Examples might include an American Indian powwow, Chinese or Hmong New Year celebration, an independence day celebration such as Cinco de Mayo, or "meet the Mormons." Engage all your senses—listen to music, eat the food, observe (see, smell, hear) how people are dressed, examine dress items offered for sale. Consciously ask yourself what pleases your senses and what offends them. Talk to people and ask questions. Ask them to translate songs, describe how a food item is prepared, what different articles of ethnic dress signify. Write a paragraph describing the aes-

thetic values of the people of the culture you visited. Focus on placing what offended your senses in a cultural perspective and explaining how beauty is in the eye of the beholder.

2. Attend a museum exhibit that has dress as a component. Describe how dress is used as a canvas for artistic expression. How does the curator use dress in the exhibit? How does the curator present the body as canvas for artistic expression? Is there any advice about the power of dress you might offer the curator?

3. Construct your own typology, out of pictures and from magazines, for dress types within your society. Consider the limitation of applying this typology to people in other gender and age groups and from other societies.

4. What small aesthetic decisions do you make every day about dress? What media do you use to design yourself every day? How do your decisions vary from day to day and why? Break up into groups of three and compare your daily decisions about dress with the other two members.

Notes to Chapter 10

1. Fiore and Kimle (1998) contain many contemporary examples of this. In fact, these multisensory perceptions are thought to form the basis of language acquisition. Burns and Lennon (1993) cite Abravanel (1981): "Once a child begins to acquire conventional language . . . she names or labels information that is acquired perceptually. These stored symbols are activated whenever an object is perceived by sight or by hand, and serve to link the otherwise different and disparate forms of information" (p. 73). DeLong (1998) notes that "a sweater may be viewed as soft because we have previously experienced its softness by touch" (p. 161).

2. Variations from these terms occur. For example, form is often used instead of shape, and lightness and darkness are sometimes used instead of value. However, the meanings of all the terms are generally well agreed upon.

11

Ideals for Individual Appearance and the Art of Dress

OBJECTIVES

To identify cultural ideals of dress and body as examples of aesthetic values within each specific society.

To understand that cultural standards of dress exist within each specific society.

To examine how cultural standards and ideals differ.

To explore how dress may be manipulated to create illusions to meet standards and approach ideals of the body.

To understand widespread strategies for creating body supplements, that enhance or minimize body features (e.g., cut-and-sewn garments and wrapped garments).

IN ALL SOCIETIES, some forms of appearance are singled out as more desirable than others. As consensus develops about an ideal based on the values of members in the society, cultural ideals for pleasing appearance evolve. A **cultural ideal** is a kind of shorthand summary of aesthetic values. Because an ideal represents a set of values, it can also be seen as a goal, though often unstated. Such goals are epitomized in art, and often appear to be unobtainable. Ideals exist in every role we play and activity we engage in. "He's an ideal father," "She's the perfect boss," and "It was a perfect vacation" are common phrases that express achievement of ideals. Ideals in dress are often based on evaluations of the characteristics of both body and dress and are often achieved by only a few people. As we look at photographs of popular fashion models in North American and European magazines at the end of the twentieth century, especially female models, we see the ideals that apparently exist for their bodies include extreme thinness, in sharp contrast to the ideals for the bodies of male models, leading us to ask how such different ideals have evolved.

In some societies contests are held in which individuals compete for recognition as the most beautiful or ideal example of a man, woman, or even baby. The Miss America Pageant contest developed out of earlier nineteenth-century U.S. beauty contests, which had their precursors in Europe (Banner, 1983, pp. 249–250). However, such contests are not limited to the West. A recently popular novel by Chinese author Feng Jicai (1994), *The Three-Inch Golden Lotus*, revolves around several contests to judge the most beautiful woman's foot in the period when foot binding was still practiced in China. On another continent, that of Africa, young Wodaabe men in the country of Niger annually compete for the title of most ideal man. The Miss America Pageant contest, which began primarily as a beauty contest but has evolved into a "scholarship competition," still has contestants present themselves in evening gowns and swimsuits. Contestants also answer questions that are intended to display their intellectual capabilities. The beauty pageant format has spread throughout the world, spawning many annual beauty contests in small communities and national capitals in which distinctive cultural ideals of beauty are publicly negotiated every year (Cohen, Wilk, & Stoeltje, 1996).

We distinguish cultural ideals from **cultural standards** for beauty or attractiveness, because a standard represents something measurable and achievable by many people. When measurements can be made, reality of a standard is verified. For example, if a standard length for a woman's dress at a particular time is 10 inches from the floor, congruity with the standard can be determined, as can such U.S. standards as covering certain body parts, clean fingernails, and pressed dress shirts. On the other hand, no such exact measure can be used to determine ideal facial form. Instead, certain shapes, such as an "oval" may be singled out as more desirable in a society for a woman than a "round" face. Such ideals do imply a standard, but because they are not directly measurable, they exist as a shared goal against which individuals are evaluated and evaluate themselves.

IDEALS WITHIN DIFFERENT SOCIETIES

Ideals relate to the values that exist in a society. When applied to dress, these values connect to those physical characteristics prized by people at a particular point in time and place. Thus, sometimes a sturdy woman's figure has been considered more desirable than a slim one, for a sturdy body represents good health and the ability to undertake hard work and bear many children. In contrast, good health may easily be taken for granted where medical technology is advanced and accessible. Physical labor and child bearing are not as relevant in North America and Europe where many people work in service and white collar jobs and small family size is admired.

Antubam (1963), a Ghanaian author, contrasts historical examples of Western and Middle Eastern ideals for desirable body form. He points out that among the ancient Egyptians, the female ideal was typified by Nefertiti, c. 1370 B.C.E., who had a straight nose, long neck, oval head, and deeply set, large eyes. The Mesopotamian male ideal was that of a conqueror whose strength and power were reflected in large and often overemphasized muscles. The Greek ideals for male and female were epitomized by Apollo and Venus de Milo, both sturdy and well-formed figures. Botticelli's slender-bodied Venus exemplified the Italian Renaissance ideal, and the voluptuously ample proportions of Rubens's Venus exemplified the Northern Baroque ideal (Antubam, 1963, pp. 89–91). See Figure 11.1a, b, and c.

Ghana

As a case in point, compare and contrast the Ghanaian and North American ideals for female bodies. Ghanaians describe many parts of the body as egg-shaped ovals. The shape of the head from the top of the head to the end of the

(a)   (b)   (c)

Figure 11.1
Cultural ideals of human beauty usually differ in some respect from place to place and change over time. Notice the differences in the female bodies in these famous depictions of Venus, the goddess of beauty, from different eras and cultures in Europe. (a) Venus de Milo, Greek (130–120 B.C.E.); (b) Detail from *The Birth of Venus* by Sandro Botticelli (1444–1510); (c) *Venus before a Mirror* by Peter Paul Rubens (1577–1640).

chin is expected to look like an egg with the wider portion uppermost. Figure 11.2 illustrates this point: "Looked at from the side, the head must set on the neck at an angle of about thirty-five degrees with the top part falling back" (Antubam, 1963, p. 92). The traditional Ghanaian fertility doll (called an *Akuaba*), which is carved to ensure beauty for the unborn child, exemplifies and teaches the Ghanaian cultural ideal for the head and face:

> The Ghanaian ideal of a beautiful neck is described as follows: The neck which should have wrinkles or rings on it must fall into an elongated shape with the smaller part of it tapering towards the head. The wrinkles or rings here must be an odd number when counted to be a perfect beauty. (Antubam, 1963, p. 92)

The torso is expected to appear egg-shaped with the widest part of the oval at the neck. The egg-shaped oval is also a requirement for the thigh:

> This requirement of beauty is probably what makes Ghanaian men especially like substantial thighs and buttocks. And there is the same latent principle at work, when Ghanaians even after they have been to school and passed through the Western ideal of straight and streamlined forms, still consciously or unconsciously shoot out their buttocks, when they walk, in order that they may appear beautiful. It is fascinating to watch the so-called highly educated and refined Ghanaian ladies coming out of church, making strenuous efforts to push their buttocks out to form a concave at the back of the waist in order to appear beautiful. And, their tight Western dress stresses this point, for it shows their form more clearly. (Antubam, 1963, p. 92)

Antubam says lower legs, too, must form egg-shaped ovals with the widest part towards the knee. Mothers of female babies tie beads at the joints of the

Figure 11.2
Ghanaian ideals of feminine beauty are described by specific patterns of ovals.

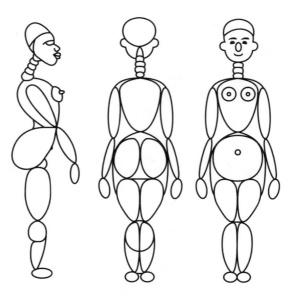

neck base, waist, elbows, wrists, knees, and ankles in an attempt to develop the muscles so that they will form an ideal shape.

United States

In contrast to Ghana, the ideal North American female form at the end of the twentieth century has been documented as tall, thin, physically fit, with large breasts, small waist and hips, and long legs. A narrow range of facial features includes a narrow nose, high cheekbones, and large eyes (Morris, Cooper, & Cooper, 1989; Rudolph, 1991). Fashion models and beauty contestants typify variations of this ideal, with models usually being thinner than beauty contestants. In recognizing cultural diversity and different ethnic groups in the United States, we can see that many cultural variations exist. Research about the bodies of African-American women reports that fuller and more rounded bodies are seen as an attractive alternative by many African-Americans to the thin, tall bodies of European-American fashion models. Even within one social group, variation in cultural ideals may exist at different points in time, as in the example of the documented changes in the relative bust, waist, and hip measurements of Miss America winners, as seen in Table 11.1. The author of *Miss America: In Pursuit of the Crown* states that in 1921, the first winner, Margaret Gorman, was 5-foot 1-inch tall with measurements of 30-25-32 (Bivans, 1991, p. 69). In contrast, she gives the measurements of the bust, waist, and hips respectively for BeBe Shopp, the winner in 1948, who measured 37-27-36. Susan Akin, the winner in 1986 (the last year the contestants' measurements were taken and publicized) measured 35-23-35 (Bivans, 1991, pp. 221–222).

Often, an ideal for a desired body may not be stated outright, but can be implied from a statement as found in a 1994 "fashion manual:"

> If your hips, buttocks, and thighs are slim you can declare this area problem free. . . . If you are heavy in these areas, read on but don't worry about it—these are the most common trouble spots for most women. Luckily, these days there are a lot of fashion remedies. The basic strategy is to draw attention *away* from trouble spots and *toward* your more alluring features. *So keep things simple in the problem area.* That means forget about flowery printed slacks and polka-dot skirts. (Feldon, 1994) (Italics in original.)

This example implies that North American readers will recognize that large female size is not a cultural preference among North Americans. The negative approach to ideals is often revealed in attention given to figure "problems." The word "overweight" connotes unattractiveness and implies physical health problems for both men and women in North America, along with the often implied negative character traits of being undisciplined and careless about diet and nutrition. A large frame may not be ideal for women, but is seen as acceptable, even preferred, for men (Rudd & Lennon, 1994, p. 167). In fact, small stature for men is viewed as a generally undesirable quality as far as ideals are concerned. Needless to say, a physical attribute becomes a problem only in reference to some cultural ideal. Although the quote from Feldon (1994) says that it

TABLE 11.1

Miss America's Statistics

Year	State	Name	Age	Height	Weight	Figure	Eyes	Hair
1921	DC	Gorman	16	5'1"	108	30-25-32	blue	blond
1925	CA	Lanphier	19	5'6"	138	34-26-37	hazel	blond
1933	CT	Bergeron	15	5'4$\frac{1}{2}$"	112	32-26-37	blue	blond
1937	NJ	Cooper	17	5'6$\frac{1}{2}$"	120	32-26-36	blue	blond
1940	PA	Burke	19	5'9"	120	34-23-35	green	brown
1944	DC	Ramey	19	5'7"	125	36-25-37	blue	red
1948	MN	Shopp	18	5'9"	140	37-27-36	hazel	brown
1952	UT	Hutchins	25	5'10"	143	36-24-36	blue	blond
1956	CO	Ritchie	18	5'6"	116	35-23-35	blue	auburn
1961	MI	Fleming	18	5'6"	116	35-22-35	green	brown
1965	AZ	Van Dyke	21	5'6"	124	36-24-36	brown	brown
1969	IL	Ford	18	5'7"	125	36-24-36	green	blond
1973	WI	Meeuwsen	23	5'8"	120	36-25-36	brown	brown
1977	MN	Benham	20	5'7"	120	35-23-35	hazel	blond
1983	CA	Maffett	25	5'7"	115	35-22-35	blue	blond
1986	MS	Akin	21	5'9"	114	35-22-35	blue	blond

Figures rounded to nearest number.
Adapted from Bivans, Ann-Marie. (1991). *America in Pursuit of the Crown*. New York: Master Media Limited, pp. 221–222.

is common for women to be "heavy" in the hips, buttocks, and thighs, the more unattainable ideal of being thinner in each of these areas is still touted as needing to be recognized by removing or dressing to conceal these "trouble spots."

Writers commenting on the art of dress often suggest that an individual modify personal body characteristics in order to resemble or approach the ideal. Names for "problem" body characteristics are usually associated with extremes of height, weight, and figure proportions, such as: tall, short, muscular, overweight, heavy, chunky, stocky, thin, out-of-proportion (large bust, round shoulders, broad shoulders, large hips). "Problems" in facial form, usually thought of as deviations from an ideal perfect oval, are also commonly described as negative types—short square, long thin, large round, long square, pointed chin, broad forehead, and high forehead. Again, we might question the logic of modifying body characteristics. As discussed in Chapter 5, physical body form is largely a result of heredity. The sturdy body cannot easily be modified to a petite and the round face cannot become oval.

ACHIEVING IDEALS

If body form does not conform to the ideal, solutions exist in some cultures that will aid in creating an illusion that conforms to the ideal. An individual may be encouraged to dress in a particular way in order to appear to have ideal form. Dress thus becomes a cultural disguise as well as an embellishment of the body (Rudd & Lennon, 1994, p. 169). Creating an illusion can be accomplished by several means:

- By enveloping the body with garments that conceal imperfect contours
- By modifying certain parts of the body that do not measure up to ideals
- By attracting attention away from the part of the body that deviates from the ideal
- By optical illusion achieved through color and line combinations in dress and cosmetics

An individual can disguise or enhance body surface with various items of apparel, hair growths, and cosmetics. In periods when beards are in fashion a man can hide less than ideal facial contours and create a new shape by the way he grows and trims his beard. Voluminous cloth wrappings will conceal body form and surface. A loose shift or tunic creates more doubt concerning body size and contours than a pair of snug-fitting trousers, and the vertical lines of these styles create the illusion of height. By contrast, a large body size is highly valued in some cultures. When a large, rounded body is desirable, as among adult Kalabari women in Nigeria, cloths are wrapped multiple times around the waist, underneath the outer garment, to make the woman's body look as large as possible, to create the illusion of the Kalabari ideal for women, as seen earlier in Figure 10.8.

To approach a cultural ideal, a body may be modified by using a body supplement like corsetry to constrict waistlines, hips, and breasts. Alternately, diet, exercise, or plastic surgery can directly change the shape of the body. The time-consuming and painful nature of these strategies is rarely questioned. As products such as body-shapers become readily available and as the cost of plastic surgery declines, more people may use these means to modify their bodies because of greater access and affordability. As cheaper technology allows more people to achieve a cultural ideal of beauty, sometimes the ideal shifts to something even more difficult to attain, and being the "most perfect" becomes the ideal.

Learning to use contrasting colors and values are processes that may be used to call attention to certain parts of the body, and thereby decrease attention to other portions of the body, because light colors advance and dark colors appear to recede. A man's white shirt and dark business suit call attention to his face and de-emphasize the rest of his body. Collars and jewelry may introduce contrasting lines and interesting details close to the face. As a result, the rest of the body and its dress become part of the background, and so-called problems such as large hips and excessive weight may not be noticed.

Similarly, cosmetics and paint may also divert attention. Black penciling around eyes draws attention away from other facial features. Lines and shadings made with powder, rouge, and paint can create the illusion of a different facial shape and bone structure, just as tweezers can shape eyebrows as in Figure 11.3a and b. Illusions of the body's structure can also be created through manipulation of the line, textures, surface design, color, shapes, and contours of covering body supplements, whether in a swimsuit, evening gown, or menswear.

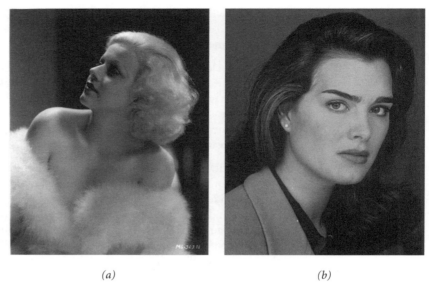

(a)   *(b)*

Figure 11.3
In the first half of the twentieth century Hollywood makeup artists popularized the technique of tweezing hair and applying color to design eyebrows that would give any woman the illusion of large, wide-set eyes, as exemplified by Jean Harlow (a) at the peak of this style. More recently, U.S. women's makeup style has stressed the "natural" look of Brooke Shields, often equally carefully crafted with tweezing, dye, or colored pencil (b).

We are trained, largely subconsciously, to understand our society's cultural aesthetics regarding the body and dress and often perceive body and dress subconsciously, since we take the aesthetics of dress for granted. The use of line combinations to create illusion in dress are most effective when the observer understands and accepts the ideal towards which the illusion strives. If cultural visual cues that create perspective are missing, the illusion may not be successful. For example, studies of the Zulus of southern Africa (Gregory, 1966, pp. 160–163) indicate that visual responses to lines are usually determined by, or greatly modified by, cultural conditioning. Westerners are highly oriented to a world of rectangles and right angles, and to parallel lines that converge by perspective, such as roads and buildings. Thus, they perceive illusion in dress that results from different straight-line relationships. In contrast, Zulus live in what has been called a circular culture, and have no such straight-line orientation or sense of converging perspective, as illustrated by the fact that they reside in round huts with round doors and plow the land in curved lines.

Line combinations also must be looked at in relation to the total visual image presented by body and dress. On one figure, the lines of a dress ensemble may create one type of effect, on another figure quite a different one, hence rules cannot be arbitrarily applied even within the same culture, let alone across cultures.

CULTURAL STANDARDS FOR THE ART OF DRESS

Anthropologists recognized rather early that cultural standards—in contrast to ideals—provide order in people's lives. Such standards enable individuals to adopt modes of behavior from a limited range of possibilities rather than from an infinite number of conceivable behaviors. As Benedict (1959) observes:

> In culture . . . we must imagine a great arc on which are ranged the possible inter-ests provided either by the human age-cycle or by the environment or by man's various activities. A culture that capitalized even a considerable proportion of these would be as unintelligible as a language that used all the clicks, all the glottal stops, all the labials, dentals, sibilants, and gutturals from voiceless to voiced and from oral to nasal. Its identity as a culture depends upon the selection of some seg-ments of this arc. (p. 24)

Cultural standards for dress limit the number of forms from which selec-tions can be made and thereby limit a person's practice of the art of dress. Specific standards, stated or unconscious, may evolve for various social or oc-cupational groups within a society, as has been spoofed in the cartoon in Figure 11.4. Underlying adherence to cultural standards for dress is the desire of individuals for social acceptance by their peers. Although individuals may not be consciously aware of this desire, they experience social discomfort when their dress is very different from that of others in their peer group.

Within specific human groups, words such as "appropriate," "proper," "in good taste," or "cool" and "neat" express approval of dress.[1] Many such words

Figure 11.4
Cultural standards of dress vary from group to group and generation to generation.

are specific to a particular time and place. For example, no matter what the decade, terms used by American teenagers or college students are not the same as those used by their grandparents. Similarly, the same word, even in the same language may not be used the same way in different countries or cultural groups. "Bad," for instance, is commonly used as a negative adjective for many things, including dress, by many people. However, youth in America began to use it in the 1990s to indicate strong approval. In addition, a word such as "appropriate" that seems the same in translation from one language to another, may not mean the same thing in different social contexts. For example, ordinarily, individuals who wear appropriate dress feel comfortable and accepted. However, social circumstances may influence whether a dress ensemble is judged inappropriate for wear and likely to cause social discomfort. When we attend an event and find ourselves inappropriately dressed, whether "over" or "under" dressed in relationship to others, we often feel embarrassed. An outsider, however, is often excused from abiding by or understanding usual social customs in dress, especially when the insiders realize the outsider does not know the rules.

Because cultural standards for appropriate dress differ markedly from place to place, and social group to social group, and because people from many cultures interact in a global society, prescriptive literature focusing on how to dress and behave in cross-cultural situations has evolved. This literature necessarily goes into small details of dress.

Figure 11.5, for example, shows some of the standard measurable relationships among the various garments that make up the white-tie-and-tails dress ensemble for men, as well as how the garments should relate to the body. Manuals of such standards are necessary in a complex social world in which

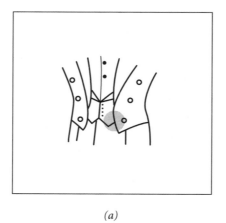
(a)

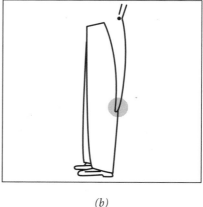
(b)

Figure 11.5
In contrast to cultural ideals, cultural standards can often be stated in measurable terms, as in these diagrams for fitting a very formal men's suit; (a) shows the correct relationship of waistcoat and jacket points, and (b) shows the correct tailcoat length.

the man who finds himself required to wear tails may not have any previous personal experience of them to guide his clothing choices. The reporter of the standard tells us that "[t]he piqué waistcoat's points should never extend below those of the tailcoat. . . . The correct back length of a tailcoat should line up with the back of a man's knee" (Flusser, 1996, p. 73).

In another example, Norine Dresser (1996), author of *Multicultural Manners: New Rules of Etiquette for a Changing Society*, relates a situation in which an individual she calls "Vladimir," who is newly arrived from Russia, waits with an interpreter in a doctor's examination room. When a casually dressed woman comes into the room and introduces herself as a nurse practitioner, Vladimir scowls and asks, "Who is this fool?" Dresser goes on to explain:

> Vladimir was put off by the nurse practitioner because of her lack of formality. She did not wear medical garb and was too friendly. This caused him to lose respect for her as a professional. Newcomers, especially from authoritarian countries, expect to see symbols of power and status from those who are treating them. Patients anticipate that any medical professional will dress in a uniform. They expect authorities to act formally and to maintain social distance." (pp. 61–62)

The lack of power and prestige symbols used by medical professionals in the United States in the late twentieth century did not fulfill the standards of appearance expected by the immigrant Russian patient.

While there is a great deal of variation in standards of dress from one culture to the next, Desmond Morris (1994) has identified three standards that appear to be valued around the world: cleanliness, health, and youth. Cleanliness, however, is defined by a group of people in regard to their own grooming practices. In many Western cultures, cleanliness is achieved through access to large amounts of water—hot and cold. This poses a particular problem for the homeless, because without a home they do not have easy access to water for bathing, oral hygiene, or washing clothes. In other cultures, cleanliness is defined and achieved in different terms. For example, among the Berber of North Africa in the first part of the twentieth century, a young girl did not bathe until just before her wedding. Nothing potentially defiling was to touch her body, so she did not expose herself by undressing to bathe until after her marriage. Premarital washing with water was restricted to washing the forearms and hands. In any culture, most people achieve some measure of cleanliness. Their success is readily measured by others in their society because the clean person looks, smells, or feels aesthetically pleasing to herself or himself as well as to others.

The second global standard of health also varies from time to time, as in the always changing charts for healthy body weight in the United States (Shapiro, 1998), and from one culture to another.[2] With adequate nutrition and health care, most people present a healthy, unblemished, vigorous body to the world. Like cleanliness, a disease-free body can be identified by the physical senses. As described in Chapter 5, we see, smell, hear, and feel the debilitating effects of many illnesses—from wounds to gum disease, coughing, diabetes, or weight loss.

The third global standard of youth may also vary from culture to culture. In small-scale cultures, a woman's youth is often related to the ability to bear many healthy children. A woman is considered old when she is no longer fertile. In global-scale cultures, youth is characterized by the young adult body, lean and fit, and able to bear children but as yet untested. Within both standards, everyone is able to fulfill the standard, but only at a certain stage during the life cycle. Youth becomes an ideal when members of a society value youth beyond its natural time frame.

CHANGE IN CULTURAL STANDARDS

Cultural standards do not mean absence of change; instead change is inevitable. Within Western fashion history the regular abandoning of one set of standards for pleasing and appropriate dress and the establishment of new standards illustrate how change occurs constantly. Some individuals act as leaders and instigate deviations and reformulate standards. Others, who are not innovators, are still sensitive to change and register their sensitivity by either encouraging or discouraging it, through their own dress decisions, thereby earning for themselves labels such as "conservative" or "liberal." However, change is valued and pursued in many areas of the world in standards for acceptable dress, and eventually both conservatives as well as liberals eventually capitulate, even if only changing to again flaunt the newer standards. Changes in standards of dress encourage both individualistic and conformist practices, for innovators want to express their apparent uniqueness by a ready willingness to change and conformists change in order to keep in step with accepted fashion norms.

To be themselves within a world of shifting standards for dress, many individuals constantly check and cross-reference, consciously or unconsciously, what is culturally valid and what can be done to maintain an attractive self-type within the current valid standards for their peer group. Fashion change exemplifies this process. Jeans, the article of dress that characterized the youth counterculture in North America in the 1960s, had become high fashion by the 1970s. By the 1980s, striped bell-bottoms, Beatle haircuts, and platform shoes had become an old-fashioned caricature. However, by 1998, some of those items of dress, among them platform shoes and bellbottoms, had become high fashion again, especially among youth in North America. The 1997 and 1999 *Austin Powers* films illustrate this change of standards when a 1970s playboy is brought back to life in the 1990s, complete with the dress and attitudes of his day. Because he has had no opportunity to follow changes in standards and adjust to them, he becomes a subject of high comedy.

An individual's likes and dislikes in regard to physical appearance and pleasing dress are not haphazard. Instead, predictable preferences depend upon the social context within which the individual learns to view the world. People learn that cultural standards are possible within specific social contexts, seldom worldwide; therefore, pleasing or appropriate appearance and dress must be understood as a social variable. Individual appearance does not exist in the absolute sense, but must be viewed in relation to a specific cultural situation. For example, Sheila Paine's memoirs (1995) of traveling from the Hindu Kush to Razgrad include her experience of learning to wear the *chador*, the all-enveloping garment Iranian women are expected to wear to divert the gaze of men. She relates:

> When I returned to London, I remarked to the man in the Foreign Office that the only advice they had given me for traveling in Iran was to take dollars in cash, but they hadn't said anything about dress.
>
> You didn't warn me that for wearing a bit of lipstick or showing a strand of hair you get forty lashes of the whip.
>
> "We thought it was seventy-two," he said. (pp. 134–135)

Faced with the particular cultural standards for dress in Iran, Paine definitely made alterations to her dress in order to survive her research trip. However, she would naturally have also exercised her personal choice in what to wear within the range of acceptability.

Standards are ordinarily assumed to be common knowledge. As the cartoon in Figure 11.6 shows, actions taken in ignorance of those standards usually lead to disaster. Occasionally, therefore, standards are stated explicitly. Often cultural dress standards are stated in published policies, such as high school or business corporation dress codes. Sometimes they are used in workshops that aim to teach individuals how to both dress attractively and meet cultural standards. National governments often provide written policies on how their international representatives should be dressed. Royal courts have issued policies on how members of the public should be dressed in order to meet the king or queen (Rundquist, 1987). Ideals also are often assumed to be common knowledge, but several ideals can exist in a society simultaneously. In addition, ideals may be presented either positively as "perfect" or negatively as problems to be addressed. They may also be expressed as ideals for pleasing body form, pleasing dress, or pleasing relationships between body and dress.

DOONESBURY   **by Garry Trudeau**

Figure 11.6
The humor of this cartoon rests on the fact that most people understand, without being told, their culture's standards for dress.

CULTURAL IDEALS IN BODY FORM

We ascertain cross-cultural variation in ideals for body types including facial forms, by looking at visual presentations of human figures, either male or female. When comparing Greek and Gothic female nudes from historical artwork, 1990s fashion figures from North America, and the women modeling swimsuits in the *Sports Illustrated* annual swimsuit issue, different body proportions are obvious. Similar variations can be noted by comparing the relative breast, waist, and hip measurements of various Venus statues with those of Barbie dolls and fashion models. Greek nude female figures fit a classical ideal that requires the same unit of distance between breasts, from breasts to navel, and from navel to division of the legs. In Gothic figures, the distance from breasts to navel is almost twice as great as that between breasts (Clark, 1956, pp. 20–21). Recently, North American fashion figures have been tall and slender, therefore rather Gothic in effect, often appearing to be $9^1/_2$ heads tall, when most people are about 8 heads tall. The *Sports Illustrated* swimsuit models are usually more rounded than the tall and angular fashion models.

The Greeks's great regard for physical perfection, which they linked with "excellence of soul or spirit," was reflected in their emphasis upon gymnastics as well as in their art (Plato, trans. 1943). The ancient Greek culture viewed the obese body negatively and idealized a slender athletic body, as shown by the evidence of the figures on a vase, as in Figure 11.7. An obese young man appears to be reproached by one of his more lithe companions. Similar variations can be noted by comparing the body proportions of the female figures in Figure 11.1a, b, and c.

Figure 11.7
Early Greek cultural idealization of the slender, athletic human figure is suggested by the rejection of the plump man depicted on this fifth century B.C.E. vase.

Ideals for body form demonstrate the power of cultural ideals within a society. Considerable consensus exists on what is the most desirable in body build, and almost everyone within a culture understands what the standards are even when they are not explicitly stated. For example, the late Diana, Princess of Wales, with her tall and leggy 5'10" figure and 36-26-36 measurements (dress size 12), was judged by both the public and popular press to be beautiful. She had evolved from dressing as a fairy-tale princess to "a more realistic image of working mother, a woman in control of her own destiny" (Graham & Blanchard, 1988, p. 10).

Body and Dress

The art of dress involves several possibilities for the relationship between dress and the body. By definition, no item of dress can be completely independent of the human form; yet a continuum exists between those that most nearly merge with body form and those that greatly diverge from body form. One option merges the body and dress, with the dress emphasizing the shape of the body. This is called **body dominant** dress. Pantyhose are an example of one such supplement. By contrast, the form of dress may diverge from the form of the body, essentially covering the body and becoming an independent form with the **body subordinate** to the dress placed on it. Some dress leaves most of the body uncovered. In such cases dress is subordinate to the body in relation to the general appearance of the resultant dressed body.[3]

However, dress that covers the body is not always body subordinate, because some forms still allow the observer to perceive the shape and form of the body clearly. A thin application of paint creates divergence in color, perhaps in texture, but not in shape, as seen in Figure 11.8 of an outfit painted on an otherwise nude body. The closer the color of the paint is to body color, the more it merges with body, the less it diverges. In such cases, dress is subordinate to the body and the body's shape remains dominant. Close-fitting flesh-colored pantyhose, for example, closely merge with body form and diverge only in texture. They do not dominate the lower torso of the body. Dress ensembles that cover most of the body can still be body dominant, through the use of body-hugging coverings or transparent fabrics, as seen in Figure 11.9.

In contrast many items of apparel seem to stand more by themselves, away from the body, as items of independent artistic merit rather than as complements to body form. In history, the human body is subordinate to the women's bustle ensemble of the 1870s and 1880s, the sixteenth-century ornate and heavily padded dress ensemble of Henry VIII, or the dragon robe of the Chinese emperor. In the contemporary period, the twentieth-century Middle Eastern men's caftan also is dress dominant, as are the robes of Roman Catholic priests and nuns in many countries, and the enclosing outer layer of dress—of conservative South Asian urban Muslin women, worn when out in public. Outerwear in cold climates is also often necessarily body subordinate. An overcoat not only covers the body but also prevents observers from gaining any sense of the shape, size, or other characteristics of the parts of the body that are covered.

Figure 11.8 (left)
Body dominant dress, such as clothing that closely follows the contours of the body revealing its shape, is easily mimicked by the application of paint onto the surface of the body. From an aesthetic standpoint, this outfit painted onto the skin of U.S. actress Demi Moore has the same appeal as the ensemble it simulates.

Figure 11.9 (right)
Body-hugging or transparent clothing, though it may cover most of the body, still reveals a lot of information about the body. Thus it is termed body dominant dress. Prada runway show, Milan, 1990s.

Dress ensembles can also combine body dominant and body subordinate elements within a single whole, drawing attention to some portions of the body while hiding, reducing, or exaggerating other portions. Figure 11.10, as example, draws attention to a woman's upper torso through the use of a closely fitting bodice, low-cut neckline, and lack of sleeves; at the same time it covers up the lower torso with a full skirt. Consider what the interplay of body subordination and dominance in different areas of the body is saying about the gender and sexuality of this figure in the context of her culture.

Shifting standards in the history of dress, for example in Europe, can be seen in the fluctuation in the form of dress that merges with, versus that which diverges from, body form. One of the sharpest shifts from dress ensembles that diverged from body form came in European dress history at the end of the eighteenth century when hoops, pompadour wigs, and stiff, heavily brocaded fabrics were abandoned for more close-fitting, less colorful body supplements. Men wore jackets and snug tubular trousers of plain colors, and some women oiled their skins so that their tubular, white, semitransparent muslin dresses would cling to their bodies (Davenport, 1948, p. 721). However change continued and by the middle of the nineteenth century, men's body contours were lost in loose-fitting suits and females concealed the lower parts of their bodies under voluminous hoop skirts.

Figure 11.10
Some forms of dress combine body dominant and body subordinate portions to draw attention to particular parts of the body. Design by Canadian-born U.S. designer Arnold Scaasi, 1990s.

Subordination of dress to body has been a persistent Western standard for men's dress for more than a hundred years. And, as commentary on women's dress makes plain, an expression of a similar standard for women's dress has occurred from time to time, though here the issue of body subordination has taken a different form. Dress that constricts the body to reduce its size is just as dominant as dress that exaggerates the body's size. Nineteenth-century dress reformers attacked both the constriction of the female torso with corsetry and the enlargement of the lower female torso with many, heavy petticoats. As long ago as 1879, Mrs. Haweis, an English woman, said that dress "shall not contradict the natural lines of the body" and "shall obey the proportions of the body" (1879, p. 32). Fluctuations over time in the accepted relationships between body and dress illustrate that whether dress is subordinate to the body or the body subordinate to dress is a matter of custom and fashion and not a timeless generalization.

SUMMARY

In all cultures, aesthetic ideals for personal appearance develop for both body form and for dress. Achievable standards also arise that enable individuals to attain some degree of the often unspoken ideals. A culture's ideals for pleasing appearance and dress change through time, so that a pleasing appearance for one era may not be the same for another, a change which is designated by the term fashion and studied in the history of dress.

If body form does not measure up to the ideal, dress may be used to remedy the situation. Several dress strategies for doing so exist. Dress can modify body form temporarily or permanently. It can hide the discrepancy by covering it up. It can draw attention away from the discrepancy. It can remove the discrepancy completely through surgical procedures. Dress can create the illusion of the ideal body.

An ideal body and ideal dress appearance in one culture may differ from the ideal in another. Around the world, there is a vast array of very different and sometimes unique ideals and sets of standards for the body and for dressing the body. Thus, what members in one culture admire is often considered bizarre, humorous, strange, or ugly by people of another culture.

STUDY TOOLS

Important Terms

body dominant
body subordinate
cultural standards
cultural ideals

Discussion Questions

1. Identify ideals and standards relating to body form, to dress, and to the dressed body that you remember from high school and compare them with those that exist in your college or university.
2. Describe and discuss the similarities and differences in body ideals between yourself and someone you know from another culture. Be specific about the physical characteristics of these body ideals. This other culture can be from another part of the world, a different generation, class, ethnic group, or subgroup within your own culture.
3. Define the difference between cultural ideals and cultural standards. Give examples of dress strategies to help a person meet cultural standard minimums and more closely approach his or her cultural ideals.
4. How does understanding the classification system of dress help you to understand ideals and standards of dress within any culture? Within your own?

5. Review the readings at the end of this part and identify the ideals and standards of dress and body form in the cultural groups discussed. What does this add to your understanding of these groups?

Activities

1. Collect ten pictures that exemplify for you the ideal of your age, gender, and social group. Examine these pictures and describe an appearance ideal based upon what features they share. Now do the same procedure for ten pictures you collect of the ideal for another age, gender, or social group. For example, collect photos of plus-size fashion models, over-50 men, or "soccer moms." Finally, compare the two ideals you have analyzed. How are they different and how are they the same?
2. Pretend that you need to dress for a special occasion such as a wedding, baptism, and friend's birthday party. With the help of your wardrobe, write down several different ensembles that you might realistically wear to that event. Remember, too, any body modifications, such as "permanents" or deodorants that you might also include. Next, analyze and list the ways that each of these dress ensembles and body modifications meet your cultural standards of dress for such an event. Finally, rate the ensembles that best achieve the cultural ideals of your social peer group.

Notes to Chapter 11

1. See also Fiore (1994): "Is 'cool' cool because it isn't beautiful? 'Cool' may refer to objects that intentionally break or disregard established criteria of formal beauty (e.g., cosmetics that create a cadaverous appearance)" (p. 10).
2. Sobo (1994) describes the Jamaican definition of a healthy body as one that is considerably heavier than the current U.S. standards for health.
3. Working simultaneously, DeLong (1998, p. 133) has also analyzed dress dominance versus body dominance.

12

The Art of Dress: Conformity and Individuality

OBJECTIVES

To recognize that individuals exercise the art of dress.

To describe how social role affects the art of dress.

To explore conformity and individuality in the art of dress.

To recognize the place of fashion in conformity and individuality in dress.

WHETHER OR NOT SELECTING and wearing dress fascinates, bores, or is of no interest to individuals, their social roles in society and associated cultural behavior also affect their choices. First, materials obtainable locally or through trade and the type of prevailing technology relate to the scale of culture and affect the limits or variety in the types of dress available. Second, an individual's social role in the society influences the daily practice of the art of dress. Third, individual characteristics and idiosyncratic preferences also play a part in choices for dress. For example, in small-scale cultures, materials may come largely from the environment and through trade with larger-scale cultures. In a global-scale culture, garments made out of synthetic fibers, woven on power looms, and assembled with automated equipment are common. A wide variety of possible examples of choices about dress exist for any individual, but potential tension always exists between individuals wanting to conform to group standards (to show affiliation) and wanting to express individuality (to show distinctiveness). In this chapter, we discuss in general the pressures for conformity, which necessarily limit choices in dress, but also acknowledge the individual characteristics that shape and influence aesthetic decisions about dress and may relate to the concept of fashion as well.

INDIVIDUAL CHOICE, SOCIETAL INFLUENCE, AND THE ART OF DRESS

Some human groups allow and encourage more leeway in aesthetic expression through dress than do others. Differences can be highlighted when comparing two groups, smaller entities, such as two occupational groups or two families. At one extreme, limited varieties of dress are prescribed within very narrow confines, as in the example of religious groups with clearly defined rules like the Mennonites, Hasidic Jews, or conservative Muslims. At another extreme, relatively little social control is exercised, and a sense of individualism may even be encouraged. For example, in day care centers for children in the United States, dress-up clothes or costumes (Figure 12.1) and opportunities to engage in imaginative role playing with items of dress are frequently part of a curriculum to nurture each child's sense of self.

In North America as elsewhere, many people think about how to dress for the day. Within the limits established in our society by our own social groups, we pick and choose outfits we believe to be appropriate for the day's specific social events and social groups. Americans prize the idea of *individuality*, and therefore many of us pride ourselves on not dressing like anyone else and strive to present ourselves as an "individual" through our dress. However, even individuals who decide not to dress like members of one group usually end up dressing like those from another group. For example, in high school, adolescents may choose to dress similarly to their friends, but different from individuals in other groups within the school. Such choices about what to wear in schools without strong dress codes often lead to discussions of youth showing clique affiliation through dress. Similarly, the physicists discussed in Reading IV.3, "Scruffy Is Badge of Pride, but Some Physicists Long for Cool," by Malcolm W. Browne, exemplifies an academic group of professionals who have informally adopted a mode of dress that no doubt distinguishes them from other peers.

Individuals who live in a large-scale culture may withdraw from one group and shift membership to another and dress is often the evidence of this shift. Such choices tend to exist only in societies with large populations, where multiple divisions of labor and differences in wealth and background provide separate and cross-cutting societal subgroups, each marked by some differentiation in dress. Thus, among people who identify themselves as religious Jews, several philosophies about adherence to Jewish law and tradition exist with implications for dress. For example, the dress of an orthodox Hasidic Jew follows

Figure 12.1
Through dress-up games, U.S. children explore fantasy lives, occupations, or hobbies that appeal to their individual selves. Such play supports the development in adulthood of that strong sense of individualism that is so culturally prized in the United States and commonly expressed by such concepts as "freedom" and "choice."

strict, specified rules for dress of both men and women as shown in an earlier image in Figure 5.6. If an individual chooses to leave this group, other groups of less conservative Jews allow the individual to fit into both a Jewish community and into the North American mainstream without the strict tenets of dress of the Hasidim.

Choice about dress in large and diverse societies such as the United States assumes that individuals understand the requirements or expectations about dress as related to an array of jobs, recreational activities, and social positions. Some people find maintaining a large wardrobe for many different situations (such as work, family activities, and leisure time) and choosing among a variety of available styles, colors, and textures of dress products pleasurable; others may find the process too time-consuming or an economic challenge. Dressing to fulfill social roles and following fashion (even when money is in short supply) provides a powerful source of self-esteem for some people. Others meet dress requirements for work and leisure with a minimal effort and minimal wardrobe, because they have different values. Etiquette and dress-for-success books discussed in earlier chapters attempt to help individuals who are unsure about dress requirements make choices. Being able to choose what we want to wear may be viewed as a freedom when compared to societies that strictly regulate individual dress.

Social Status and Role, Conformity, and Dress

The characteristics of social status serve to limit individual choices of dress, since we often dress to the standards of the group with whom we identify, as seen for example in Figure 12.2. Similar social roles encourage the act of *conformity* in dress, or dressing similarly or exactly like others, because factors of gender, family affiliation, occupation, religion, and political affiliation commonly affect individuals as they make choices about aesthetics of dress. When an individual shares participation or membership in a social group, either voluntarily or involuntarily, conformity is encouraged, particularly in relationship to standards of dress, as discussed in Chapter 11. When viewed from within the social group, the details of the dress that may set one individual apart from another are easily apparent, since all members assume the standards and focus on the range of personal choice in meeting those standards. However, when

Figure 12.2
Individual choice in dress, no matter how much encouraged within U.S. society, is always balanced with the desire to dress like others within one's group, whether that group is based on economics, age, gender, occupation, avocation, religion, politics, or any other basis of shared experience or identification.

viewed from outside, the dress of members of such a group will appear to be conforming, as for example in Figure 12.2. Also some social groups develop strictly conforming dress ensembles, or uniforms, to signify their shared social status in a particular institution or club.

Every society in the world distinguishes males from females and makes the distinction visible through gendered dress. Often individuals of one gender (most frequently men) are given more leeway or responsibility for enhancing the physical body for particular physical characteristics and emphasizing these characteristics with specific body supplements than the other gender (most frequently women). In late-twentieth-century United States, assumptions become associated with these gender distinctions. One is that most heterosexual men are thought to be less interested in dress and generally expected to display less interest in dressing to enhance their physical characteristics of color and texture in skin, eyes, or hair than most women. Instead, men are often encouraged to enhance their muscular development, physical prowess, and mental skills. Thus, a popular male body modification strategy in the United States is weight lifting, although women's interest in the activity is growing concurrently with increased participation of women in sports and professional jobs. Also, shoulder pads in men's business suits make men look physically strong and the limited range of dark colors conveys the idea of power.

In contrast, women in the workplace have been encouraged to consider choices in color, shape, and type of garments for professional business wear. They may be counseled to wear colors that will highlight eye, hair, and skin color or to wear particular styles of garments that flatter specific body shapes, thus emphasizing their physical individuality. Women's magazines offer advice about hair color or texture to enhance a woman's facial features or modify a hairstyle described as unflattering for a specific face shape. However, the late-twentieth-century trend of "corporate casual" dress in the workplace in the United States is beginning to change how both men and women dress for work, and men are finding that they have to make some of the same kinds of complicated dress choices that were previously viewed as the sole venue of women in North America. Women's increased participation in professional jobs has heightened their interest in choices of dress previously associated with menswear, and the simplicity of a jacket over a dress or with a skirt or trousers has become appealing. This type of decision brings their daily choices about what to wear closer to the decisions of men in authority in the business world and gives cartoonists good ideas for their cartoon strips, as in Figure 12.3.

Family membership also serves as a basis for social status and role behavior. Sometimes members of a family may dress alike, indicating a close relationship or shared family identity. At various times in twentieth-century North America, families have dressed their children in matching clothes, particularly if they were twins. Families traveling with small children on vacation often outfit children in the same color T-shirts for easy spotting in parks and other recreation spots. Some mothers and daughters wear matching dresses, or entire families wear coordinating outfits, to indicate their bond; some clothing catalogues offer a variety of styles to fulfill this goal, as illustrated in Figure 12.4.

Blondle: *By Dean Young and Denis LeBrun*

Figure 12.3
The recent trend for U.S. women working in upper management positions to dress in a manner previously associated only with business men is satirized in this cartoon.

In other parts of the world, families, such as co-wives, an extended kinship group or clan may wear similar dress to mark their membership. Anyone who is a member of a Scottish clan has the right to wear the clan's identifying tartan. Among the Kalabari of Nigeria, many Kalabari families own the exclusive right to particular patterns of madras plaid cottons woven in India that are associated with the trade successes of the founder of their lineage. In addition, only the Jackreese family has the right to wear a particular style of imported, European clear glass bead with a spiral design that its founding ancestor obtained through trade.

In Western society, conformity is encouraged or demanded in other ways, as when some families and institutions discourage or forbid aesthetic expression that highlights individual freedom in dress, even though others encourage, allow, or perhaps tolerate deviation. Teenagers who encounter parental objections to their attempts to define themselves through new forms of dress may feel constrained and rebel, just as teenagers and some adults protest against school or occupational uniforms. Pressure to conform may also arise in interpersonal relationships as among married couples where some spouses experience constraints from a mate who teases, ridicules, requests, or demands that his or her partner dress in a specific way. These examples of restrictions of an individual's aesthetic choices in dress may be associated with issues of control in other areas in the interpersonal relationship as well.

Especially in large- and global-scale cultures, many occupational groups distinguish themselves by dress. Such examples of occupational dress appear to encourage conformity, whether as an explicitly stated code of dress or an implicitly understood one. Both explicit and implicit codes constrain individuality, although an individual may express aesthetic judgment when the constraints or expectations for specific types of dress are minimal. Some occupational dress is rigidly defined for exclusivity, functionality, or safety. Other occupational dress is more loosely defined, depending on common experiences of people

Figure 12.4
Family membership in the United States is sometimes marked by look-alike dress.

holding the jobs. For example, military uniforms emphasize conformity, but small insignia differences reinforce the hierarchical relationships among ranks. In contrast, visual artists, musicians, and writers are often expected to show individuality and deviate from ordinary dress.

In the United States, occupations that require people to exercise their individual creativity, talents, and originality in dress on a daily basis are those in design and the performing and visual arts. Among the examples from music groups in Western society, rock artists often express a more outrageous or nonconformist individuality in dress than other musical performers. Whatever the reason for their nonconforming dress, they exert a strong appeal to youth who apparently also want to set themselves off from mainstream adults. Another example of nonconformity is that of drag queens who cross-dress to perform in public and do not meet the expectation of dressing as a male on those occasions. The pair of photographs of RuPaul in his stage costume as drag queen and in a business suit for an advertisement in Figure 12.5a and b illustrate his gender-conforming and -nonconforming roles.

Many people in the arts frequently establish a personal style that sets them off from many others in their cultures. Frank Lloyd Wright, the well-known architect, prided himself on his cape as a signature item of dress, and author Tom Wolfe prefers to wear a white suit. In Reading IV.4, "Signature Style: Falling Off the Fashion Train with Frida, Georgia, and Louise," by Jo Ann C. Stabb, we highlight three artists in North America—painters Frida Kahlo and Georgia O'Keefe along with sculptor Louise Nevelson—who established their own identities through distinctive dress.

The division of societies into stratified classes as found in North America along with several European countries, Hindu castes, or other hierarchical status groups, encourages conformity within the stratified groups, and expression of the individual's aesthetic interest through dress may be sharply curtailed. Such societal hierarchical subdivisions, found within specific political, economic, or social structures, prevents us from constructing broad generalizations that hold true for everyone within any specific society. However, each society has its own particular character within a given historical period. Members of societies under some sort of threat or societies that use force to maintain social order often restrict dress choices completely or enforce a narrow range of dress.

Figure 12.5
Two views from U.S. male model RuPaul's professional work exemplify, in a dramatic form, the concepts of both conforming and nonconforming dress.

One example of the use of dress to maintain social order comes from the government of the People's Republic of China, which was established in 1949. Chairman Mao forbid types of dress and jewelry worn during the pre-Revolutionary period because he believed they displayed and emphasized social inequalities that the new society sought to erase. In the process of fighting the old social order, a jacket and trousers that typified the Chinese peasant dress, dubbed by English speakers, the "Mao suit," was promoted for both men and women. This became a type of national dress for all individuals regardless of physique, family history, or personality type, as seen in Figure 12.6a. Thus, when President Nixon visited China in 1972 and paved the way for increased interchange with not only the United States but the rest of the world, that suit was seen in the photographs documenting the visit. As many social reform goals have been reached over time, Chinese dress restrictions have been relaxed. Individual choices in dress flourish along with a significant entry into the world of international production and trade of fashion goods. Many Chinese people in the 1990s display variety in dress and cosmopolitan fashion, as seen in Figure 12.6b.

Religious affiliation can also influence an individual's dress, for religious groups subdivide many large-scale cultures, depending on the particular situation or occasion. Many small items of dress, body supplements such as rings, pins, or necklaces, identify individuals with their religious belief. Garments as body supplements may also distinguish members of religious groups. Many communities of faith distinguish themselves from others by strong conformity in dress. The former habits of Roman Catholic nuns (Michelman, 1998), the saffron robes of Buddhist monks, and the plain dress of the Anabaptist orders are a few examples. Outward conformity in dress is an unequivocal statement of faith: "This is what I believe and I am living in harmony with those who believe and dress as I do."

In a specific example, the Amish exist as a small community of faith within the United States. For many economic, technological, social welfare, and religious purposes, they operate as an independent agricultural-based culture. Their conformity to a particular style of dress (with limited color selections, buttons and no zippers, along with specified types of hats for men and bonnets for women) serves to maintain a clear boundary between themselves and the larger society, which they perceive as a threat to their religious belief system. A man or woman in an U.S. Amish community has a limited choice of headcoverings for summer and winter wear with little or no opportunity to display an aesthetic preference. In contrast, non-Amish men and women choose to wear a hat or not, and if a baseball cap, a current choice includes wearing it forward or backward. Aesthetic considerations include a decision among many basic styles, a variety of materials, designs, colors, textures, and embellishments, such as logos. Perhaps the popularity of wearing a baseball cap backward began as an aesthetic choice.

The examples of dress within China in the Mao era and of the Amish in the United States demonstrate narrow choices that people view and experience differently. The restrictions of a central government authority imposed on

(a)

(b)

Figure 12.6

(a) At its peak of popularity in the 1970s, the "Mao suit" of the People's Republic of China, here worn by a woman and a man, helped bring an end to social inequalities by suppressing the rich array of dress practices associated with pre-communist social and economic inequalities. (b) A reduction in the totalitarian excesses of the ambitious social reconstruction schemes of several generations of communist Chinese reformers is evidenced by a loosening of dress restrictions. Since the 1980s, the Mao suit is being abandoned in favor of increasingly diverse forms of world dress.

others may seem tighter than those agreed upon from within a group, such as a community of religious believers. Although membership in various sub-groups in a society entails certain requirements and restrictions on the dress of the individual, expression of individuality may arise. However, the amount of individuality allowed may vary, as we explore next.

INDIVIDUALITY AND THE ART OF DRESS

Each individual is distinguished by a specific configuration of physical and personal characteristics along with an idiosyncratic personal history. The controversy about the influences of environment and heredity on the development of an individual has not been solved. However, the study of genetics indicates that individuals may have preferences for certain kinds of activities or behave in specific ways because of their genes. Results of the Minnesota Twin Study (Lykken et al., 1993) report that identical twins separated from birth showed a higher than normal propensity to wear a watch on the same wrist (left or right) and the same number of rings on the same fingers, even if the wrist or finger chosen is not typical in the culture in which they were separately raised. Thus, such a genetic example can relate to the art of dress for certain individuals.

Other than physical appearance, we most often conceptualize individuality in terms of personality, mood, abilities, and preferences. Personal characteristics may lead to individual choice in the details of dress, if not in the whole ensemble. When individuals create subtle dress configurations, the aesthetic details may go unnoticed by all except those who know the person well. They are, nevertheless, an expression of interest in expressing individuality. Personal desire to express individuality in dress, particularly in the United States, has been used as one argument against the use of uniforms in schools even though such use is offered by some proponents as a means to reduce gang influence and violence. Many people claim that when uniforms are strictly prescribed, individuals continue to find subtle ways to communicate identity, from how shoes are laced, to hairstyles, or the crispness of a pressed pleat.

Leisure activity in the United States is one social arena in which individual preference seems most prevalent, even though many leisure activities have expectations for appropriate garb. Baseball players must wear specialized gloves while playing the game. Guitar players develop thick calluses on the fingers of the hand with which they fret the strings; moreover, the guitarist cannot grow long fingernails on the fret hand and still play successfully. Cross-country skiing requires the wearing of garments that both insulate the body well and "breathe" out perspiration. However, there is a strong fashion aesthetic that encourages accomplished skiers to dress in garments that show off the strength and skill of their bodies. A ski enthusiast or surfer may be required to dress to a narrow code at work but enjoys flaunting the flamboyant dress and broader range of styles associated with the sport.

Leisure dress may express personal abilities and interests that are not appreciated if this apparel is worn on the job. In North American society, a T-shirt or hat with a logo can communicate a special interest, an organization of which the wearer is a member, a level of skill in a particular sport, a place to which the wearer has traveled, or what kind of pets the wearer keeps at home. In India, a young adult male interested in poetry and classical music is likely to include a bound book of plain paper as a handheld supplement to his dress. Always at hand, the book is used to write his own poems or record verses or song lyrics of others he admires, and it enables him to show his portfolio to any interested party. When on the job, the book is left at home.

Feelings about personal modesty in dress, the importance of personal display, or the value of thrift can also be indicated by an individual through choice of clothing (Kuehne & Creekmore, 1971). Some individuals find great pleasure in expressing their personal characteristics through dress; others do not. Some individuals in societies that espouse freedom in dress combine colors, textures, lines, and shapes to display their aesthetic responses, moods, and feelings. Some individuals believe that individuality should not be obvious but instead, subtle. Others may use the aesthetic art of dress to efface their individuality altogether so that they unobtrusively fit into social situations. Still others use the aesthetics of dress to draw attention to themselves. Thus, the decision to wear wrinkled clothes and mismatched colors can also be an aesthetic decision; the individual may be using the aesthetics of texture and color to project a visual image that may say: "I care about inner beauty more than outer beauty" or "I challenge the political values of this society." There are several examples of youth dress in the United States that are counter to the aesthetics of older generations, such as the burgeoning practice in the 1990s of tattooing and body piercing along with the fashion of wearing baggy clothing.

Because an observer receives only external cues concerning the inner mental and emotional state that prompted a display of dress by an individual, the observer can only guess at the intended aesthetic display. However, the observer has an internal aesthetic response, characterized by an emotional feeling toward the dress of the other. For wearer and observer alike, the subject of the emotional and aesthetic response is the human body and its dress, which has its own aesthetic qualities: different colors, textures, shapes, and dimensions. Reactions to this three-dimensional, mobile display are seldom on the basis of its aesthetic nature alone. Pure aesthetic acts of creating and contemplating dress are almost impossible because they are culturally based. Incentives to communicate various social and psychological states via aesthetics in dress invariably develop and overlap with and modify the cultural and social expression of information. Dress, therefore, usually carries several messages, those that are aesthetic and those of various kinds of social, cultural, and even psychological significance. These messages are not explicit like the written word, but subject to a range of interpretations, depending upon the perspective of the observer.

In social group situations where the range of variation in dress is very narrow, the individual who is more interested in the aesthetics of dress may pay attention to small details that are under individual control, such as fit, repair, and cleaning of garments and accessories, and personal grooming. For instance, although a nurse may be required to wear a specific color uniform at work, a very narrow range indeed, a nurse who enjoys the art of dress may pay special attention to the style and fit of garments. She may choose to contrast, for instance, a flamboyant loose top with skintight pants, or coordinate a sleek style for both top and bottom. Additional care can be taken with body grooming, makeup—if any—hairstyle, shoes, manicure, and jewelry. Another nurse may realize the value of an aesthetically pleasing appearance for job advancement and thus give attention to her dress, but not vary ensembles from day to day. A third may be fairly uninterested in personal display and merely meet the requirements of wearing a clean white uniform and refrain from such detailed care as ironing clothes, polishing shoes, or manicuring nails. Although the difference in the appearance of the three nurses may at first glance be subtle, an observer may respond quite differently to each of them. Thus, an individual can fine-tune the coordination or contrast of color, texture, line, surface design, and the like in body and dress, whether the discretionary range allowed in the particular society or situation is narrow or wide. An individual in such circumstances may be able to focus on the quality of materials of construction when other avenues of personal aesthetic expression are unavailable.

CONFORMITY, INDIVIDUALITY, AND FASHION IN DRESS

Conformity and individuality as related to the art of dress must take into consideration the concept of fashion, which relates to the idea of swiftly changing styles. Our book is not about fashion per se, but we briefly introduced various authors in Chapter 4 who have written about fashion, to point out that fashion is part of both material and nonmaterial examples of culture. We are interested in discussing fashion as a factor related to choice in dress. Blumer (1968) argues that fashion is not superficial or narrow as a topic of study, for fashion exists in thought as well as in examples of dress, food, and other habits related to everyday life. In addition, Blumer points out that when people make choices that relate to fashion, they show their awareness of and involvement in the contemporary world around them. Fashion is an important part of understanding nonverbal communication across all types of societies and cultures. When studying dress in non-Western societies, scholars concentrated on finding "traditional" garb, ornamentation, and beauty practices; thus, fashion was assumed not to exist. However, Picton (1995) states that the concept of tradition is useful, for we can acknowledge the influence of the past when discussing tradition without freezing the past into something "traditional," which implies a lack of change. Fashion becomes important in the understanding of the art of dress as related to conformity and individuality. The classic writers on fashion, including Simmel (1904) and Sapir (1931), consistently pointed out the tension between wanting to be like others in appearance and wanting to stand apart.

Those who risk expressing their individuality by pulling away from current fashion to begin another fashion successfully often become fashion leaders. One common theme in many writers about fashion has been that of fashion "trickling down" from the upper classes to the lower classes as described in Chapter 8. In response, some writers have pointed out that the opposite example is also true, that fashion items can "**trickle up**," as is the case when members of the upper classes adopt wearing the blue jeans of the working class or huaraches (woven leather sandals) worn by Mexican peasants. We prefer using Polhemus's (1994) term of "**bubble up**" to indicate such adoptions. The important point in each example, whether trickle down or bubble up, is that copying or borrowing occurs that crosses social class lines.

FASHION LEADERS

Fashion leadership is a premier example of both conforming and being individual. Existence as a **fashion leader** depends on being at the right place at the right time, but actually slightly ahead of time (Blumer, 1968). As an individual selects certain trends in design and rejects others, that individual serves as a fashion leader. Generally, only some wearers of dress exert leadership on a society-wide basis. Those who do must have highly visible ways to display their dress and must have enough wealth to afford items of dress that are noteworthy and newsworthy. Widespread visibility occurs in certain kinds of life circumstances: some people are born into well-known families, others are in high public office or are related to individuals who are in high public office. The president of the United States and family members are potential fashion leaders, although not everyone in this position has played this role. Among the presidents' wives since 1950, no doubt President Kennedy's wife, Jacqueline, was the best known for her role in fashion leadership. In an example from across the Atlantic, certainly, the late Diana, Princess of Wales, was also known for fashion leadership. Other types of people who exert fashion leadership are those who gain public attention through combinations of achievement and personal characteristics in sports, television, movies, and the theater. Fashion leaders often display personal charisma along with an interest in matters of dress. The popular singer and actress Madonna exemplifies this influence, as does rap artist Sean "Puffy" Combs, shown in Figure 12.7. Earlier examples in the entertainment field include Liberace and Elvis Presley.

SUMMARY

Every day, individual people around the world make decisions about what to wear and their aesthetic interests influence their choice of dress. Factors limiting their display of individuality or encouraging conformity in the art of dress include a society's technology, geographical locale, and trade. Together these factors limit or broaden the materials available to individuals for use in dress as well as the degree to which these materials can be manipulated and utilized.

Figure 12.7
Prominent individuals in the public eye can become fashion leaders and influence the style of dress of large numbers of people within their own nation, and sometimes around the world. U.S. rap artist Sean "Puffy" Combs has popularized the hip-hop style of dress. Here he shows solidarity with participants in New York's 1999 Puerto Rican Day parade by incorporating their flag into his shirt.

The greater the social categories within a society—groupings by gender, age group, wealth, occupation, religion, and recreational pursuit—the greater the number of choices individuals have with regard to dress. Concurrent with this increase in choice comes the challenge of defining one's own place within a complex, subdivided society. Such self-definition is accompanied by the acceptance of dress constraints or requirements for each group that one participates in. Thus, individuals around the world vary in the degree of freedom they exercise in the art of dress. They also vary in the aesthetic choices they make about dress, meeting dress norms, and maintaining dress wardrobes.

When an individual enjoys the art of dress, achieving personal distinction from other social associates may become a challenge. As individuals make conscious clothing selections and manipulate and interpret fashion details, they may see themselves as having achieved individuality. Those people outside the particular social group to which the individuals belong, however, may view members of the group as looking alike, even identical in dress, for the outsiders are not usually sensitive to the details important within the group.

Lastly, individual characteristics also play a part in deciding how to dress. Elements influencing an individual's mental and emotional state—such as physical makeup, experiences within the families of birth and marriage, and exposure to various experiences throughout life—may encourage people in the public eye to become known for their fashion leadership.

STUDY TOOLS

Important Terms

bubble up
fashion leader
trickle up

Discussion Questions

1. What is your social role? How does it differ from that of other students? How is it the same? How does dress express these similarities and differences?
2. Describe a situation in which you were required to conform to a dress code. Why was it important to conform in this situation?
3. Describe a situation in which you were expected to express your individuality through dress. How did you decide what to wear?
4. Compare and contrast the uniforms of waiters, soldiers, and Girl and Boy Scouts. How are they similar? How are they different in function and purpose?
5. Using Reading IV.1 discuss how Kalabari their dress expresses personal, family, and cultural values.
6. How does conformity in dress become nonverbal communication? How does conformity in dress ease personal interaction? How can dress be used to confuse human interaction?
7. Consider the way that you are dressed at this moment or, if you prefer, choose the way you were dressed the last time you felt you were well-dressed, including both modifications and supplements. Analyze your age, gender, class, occupation, and other aspects of your social role and then determine what aspects of your dress ensemble communicated this information about you to others.
8. Still analyzing the same dress ensemble, consider what aspects of the dress express something that is unique to you, as well as what aspects of the dress communicate your taste. If you are aware of any fashion leaders that your dress follows, such as a music or film star, give his or her name and the context in which he or she was seen wearing the particular dress item or style of dress.
9. Compare and contrast the dress of physicists, as described in Reading IV.3, and nurses in the context of individuality and conformity. How do members of each group use dress to communicate both individuality and conformity?

Activities

1. Identify a person you think is a fashion leader. What makes this person a fashion leader? How do conformity and individuality relate to being a fashion leader?

2. Identify two separate days in which you have similar schedules. On the first day, dress like "you" and record how people interact with you. On the second day, dress in a manner very different from "you" and record how people interact with you. What messages did you send with each ensemble? How were those messages interpreted? What does this tell you about the significance of dress in human interaction?

3. With reference to the comment in the text about families in the United States sometimes dressing alike, imagine a social occasion in which your entire family might unite (e.g., a grandparent celebrates a birthday). If you were expected to dress in a manner that highlighted your relationship to your family, what would you wear? Would you select items already saved by the family or would you create new dress articles?

4. Select your favorite television shows to analyze the art of dress as related to conformity and individuality. What contrasts in these examples do you find between the main character(s) and the supporting cast members?

5. Examine about a dozen issues of a fashion magazine over several years. What high fashion styles trickled down and became mainstream fashion? What fashion leaders are identified with making these styles popular?

13

Dress and the Arts

OBJECTIVES

To define the role of dress within the performing, visual, and literary arts.

To analyze the differences and similarities between costume and everyday dress.

To analyze the relationship between costume and the lighting, staging, and content of the performance.

To look at the relationship between professional artists' dress and their art.

To analyze the role of art in the design of wearable art.

To acknowledge dress as a subject of artistic expression.

THE FIRST THREE CHAPTERS of Part Four on aesthetics and dress focused on the art of dress as a personal and daily endeavor. In this chapter, we view dress as an art form, as an essential part of the literary, visual, and performing arts, and as a subject of inspiration for the arts. Many artists use dress as an expression of themselves on a daily basis as well.

DRESS AS AN ART FORM

The body, its dress, and the dressed body are legitimate forms of art in themselves. For example, in *The Body Decorated*, Victoria Ebin (1979), displays numerous examples of the decorated body on several continents, particularly from small-scale cultures. Included among the many examples of cultures where decorating the body has received anthropological analysis are the Tchikrin of Central Brazil (Turner, 1969), illustrated in Figure 7.1, and the Nuba of Africa (Faris, 1972), who decorate with body paint; the Tiv of Nigeria (Bohannon, 1956), Figure 13.1, who decorate with scars; and the Wahgi of New Guinea (O'Hanlon, 1989), who wear elaborate feathered headdresses.

The physical body, as discussed in Chapter 5, serves as an **armature**, a skeletal framework, to display various examples of apparel used as ornamental coverings, along with jewels, and many types of accessories, but is often taken for granted. However, when exhibits are mounted, such as those by the Costume Institute of the Metropolitan Art Museum, the Museum of Contemporary Crafts of the American Crafts Council, and the Victoria and Albert Museum in London, the examples of dress are usually displayed on mannequins of some type to show how dress looks when placed on a three-dimensional form.

In the United States, a burgeoning market for items of dress called **wearable art** exists. Wearable art includes garments (usually of very basic cut) that are dyed, painted, embroidered, or otherwise embellished by hand, along with items such as jewelry and accessories like women's purses (see Figure 13.2).

Figure 13.1
The artistry of dress in some societies takes the form of direct permanent application of designs onto the body, as in the scarification designs of the Tiv of northern Nigeria.

Figure 13.2
Creators of wearable art usually intend that their works, such as these intricately beaded purses, function as dress but more importantly be appreciated as art. U.S. Designer Judith Lieber, 1990s.

Wearable art is an art form set apart from other art forms because of the special relationships between the artwork, its creator, the wearer, and the viewer (Bryant & Hoffman, 1994, p. 85). Thus, garments and other items provide a medium for artists and pose exciting challenges for viewing the body and dress, as in the case of the celebration cape of Robert Hillestad in Figure 13.3a or the debutante's train in Figure 13.3b.

Body modifications can also constitute wearable art. Common contemporary examples of dress as a decorative art include people worldwide who arrange their hair in intricate designs and tattooed Americans, particularly youth, in the late twentieth century. The current popularity of tattoos has helped spawn a group of North American and European tattoo artists who may not be recognized by the fine arts establishment, but have admiring followers in North America and Europe. Their expressive work draws on the tattoo art of many parts of the world and sometimes incorporates ethnic art forms from various cultures around the world. Some tattoo artists undertake large, long-term artistic projects, such as the depiction of a father and son picking out a name on the Vietnam War Memorial, tattooed on the back of a man. Wearable art frequently distinguishes the wearers, making them more visible in any group, and can provide a means of emphasizing individuality. This is particularly the case when the wearable art is permanent, and especially when rare, as in some recent examples of diamonds or other gems being embedded in teeth (Vargo, 1998).

(a)   *(b)*

Figure 13.3
Some wearable art is created for very specific events where the wearer will be a primary focus of public attention. (a) Celebration cape by Robert Hillestad, 1997; (b) Debutante's gown with train, 1917.

Western fashion is not the only arena for dress as art. Well-known cross-cultural examples include the court dragon robes of pre-Revolutionary China (Vollmer, 1983), as in Figure 13.4, and highly decorated Japanese kimonos (Gluckman & Takeda, 1992) along with examples of tattooed and painted bodies in other cultures.

DRESS AS AN INTEGRAL PART OF THE ARTS

Dress is an important component and complement of all the arts: performing, visual, and literary. The **performing arts** include theater, dance, cinema, television, video, music, and performance art. The **visual arts** comprise painting, sculpture, photography, and printmaking. The **literary arts** include novels, drama, short stories, essays, and poetry. In analyzing dress and the arts, we include both classical and popular forms of the arts; thus, the cinema, circus, burlesque, and music groups such as rock, blues, and country music, are equally as important as opera, classical ballet, or Shakespearean drama. We also review the role of **costume** in the visual and literary arts.

When looking beyond Europe and North America to other societies in the world, we find that the arts are sometimes organized differently. Yet each soci-

Figure 13.4
Artistry in dress is well known in many cultures of the world and in many periods in history.

ety defines an area in which human artistry is recognized and encouraged and plays an important role. In other cultural forms, different body ideals will also be associated with costuming. In referring to familiar examples from within our own cultural background, we can point to the contrast between a classic ballet dancer's body, often with a short waist, small head, hyperflexible hips, long legs, and long, tapering feet as contrasted with a figure skater (an example that falls somewhere between the arts and athletics), with muscular hips and thighs that do not look bulky and can range in height. Body ideals in the performing arts tend to encourage performers whose bodies take the form that best suits the functioning of the body in performance (Barnette, 1993).

SIMILARITIES BETWEEN STAGE COSTUME AND EVERYDAY DRESS

Similarities exist between costume used in the performing arts and dress worn in everyday situations. In all life situations, dress can enhance the credibility of the individual in regard to basic social categories of age, gender, social rank, and occupation along with individual characteristics. Similarly, in the theater, dance, opera, movies, television, and the circus, credibility to the audience is necessary when the performer first appears. For example, in the circus, the ringmaster must *look* like a ringmaster, usually wearing top hat and tails.

Important in viewing dress and the arts is a discussion of the differentiation between dress and costume, for dress enhances an individual's identity, but costume conceals the true identity of the actor when portraying a character, whether or not the actor appears in full masquerade or uses costume to highlight the identity of the person being portrayed (Eicher, 1997). For example, among the Kalabari of Nigeria, male masked dancers are often sewn into their costumes in order to make sure their hands and feet are covered completely, as a means to disguise distinguishing physical characteristics that would reveal the dancer's identity to the audience, as shown in Figure 13.5. In Western theater, even though the actor's identity *as actor* is acknowledged, the costume of the actor is that of the character in the play or movie, not the dress of the individual actor, as portrayed in Figure 13.6a, b, c, and d with Dustin Hoffman in various roles as Tootsie, Little Big Man in youth and old age, and as himself.

Figure 13.5
Unlike everyday wear, dress created for use in performance arts is sometimes intentionally constructed to conceal the true identity of the person wearing it. Among the Kalabari of coastal Nigeria, dancers take on the identities of spiritual beings and their costumes must entirely cover their bodies so that their individual human identities remain a secret. Buguma, Nigeria, 1984.

Figure 13.6
Dress worn in any of the narrative performance arts must aid in the creation of the identity of the character, rather than the communication of the real identity of the performer. Actor Dustin Hoffman as (a) himself, (b) the title character in *Tootsie*, and (c) and (d) the title character in *Little Big Man*, as a young man and an old man, respectively.

An audience quickly distinguishes performers through costume, voice, and mannerism in carrying out their roles. Thus, effective costuming must communicate ideas quickly and efficiently among key characters. For example, television programs are a good example of how costumes are an efficient way to communicate with the audience, for often the actors have less than 22 minutes of a 30-minute program to tell a story. These short programs serve to create and emphasize stereotypes because the limited time does not allow each character to express and develop the full dimensions of the person portrayed and dress ordinarily serves this stereotyping.

Costumes convey a world of information such as historical time period, locale, time of day, social class, occupation, and character relationships. Costumes also point out the importance of various characters through emphasis and subordination. As an example, the male characters on the television show *Seinfeld* had body types and ways of dress that reinforced their character types and highlighted the differences in their relationships with each other. Kramer's hairstyle was a critical aspect of his wacky persona, which contrasted with the short and stocky body and manner of dress of the insecure character George.

Understanding how to create and build costumes as well as how to view costuming requires cultural knowledge of dress and aesthetic conventions. Without knowing the cultural context of a production, the viewer can miss much of the significance of performances such as Noh, as seen in Figure 13.7, and Kabuki theater in Japan, where men are the main actors and masks are used; Kathakali dance in Kerala, India, with its special type of body movements; or the Peking Opera of China, again with stylized masks that signify specific characters. In cases such as these, specialists' knowledge is mandatory for a complete understanding and appreciation of a performance.

SPECIAL REQUIREMENTS OF COSTUME

Differences between dress in the performing arts and in daily life appear more numerous than the similarities. A performer's dress must create a visual impression that will support or supplement performance; but, strangely enough, this dress may not be the same dress the audience would expect to be worn if the action were found in real life, for the demands of performance often have special requirements. Also, permanent body modifications are rarely done to performers solely for the creation of one particular role. Thus, dress illusions made by supplementing the body or temporarily modifying the body with paint are common for performances.

Accommodation to Body Action and Demands of Performance

Theatrical dress and costume must allow for body movement and comfort just as everyday dress is thought to accommodate physical movements of bodies and to be comfortable. However, the reverse may be true when for the sake of fashion or personal vanity, some individuals are willing to endure apparel that is too tight, too long, too small, or sometimes too large. In contrast, in the performing arts, two factors are involved that demand particular attention to body comfort and movement in regard to the construction of clothing. First, the

Figure 13.7
The use of character-iden-
tification markers within
a costume for a play or
film assumes the audience
shares cultural knowledge
of dress practices that will
enable them to correctly
'read' the identity markers
in the character's dress.
The character depicted by
this Noh mask can be un-
derstood only by individ-
uals encultured in the
Japanese Noh theater tra-
dition.

performers are on view to an audience and must be physically mobile and active without embarrassment. Size and fit of their garments are important as costume designers know, for too-tight trousers may rip, too-large shoes may cause
stumbling. Second, for some performing arts, such as the dance or the circus,
designers create special costumes to meet the extraordinary requirements made
of clothing as performers move, stretch, twist, and turn their bodies, often in
exaggerated ways. As an example, the design of costumes worn by ballet dancers
allows extra length at the waist for rise and fall of the chest when stretching the
arms, and armholes and sleeves are set high (Lawson & Revitt, 1958).

Total length of garments also affects mobility. Only after ballerinas began
to wear short tutus allowing great freedom in body movement were female ballet dancers able to compete with their male counterparts in dancing brilliance.
Moreover, a special development in ballet for women occurs when they dance
en pointe, using special blocked toe shoes that serve as physical extensions of
the body. The dancer can ". . . defy the laws of gravity, so to speak, by rising off
the ground on the toes and thus to create an illusion of an ethereal being differing from the rest of us earthbound humans" (Langner, 1959), as shown in
Figure 13.8a. In the case of modern dance, which has its own repertoire of classic movements, costume contrasts with that prescribed for ballet. Isadora Duncan, for example, danced in bare feet and Grecian-style flowing costumes
which, except for their length, freed the body and, in addition, emphasized
asymmetry of movement. In a contemporary example, Bill T. Jones, as shown
in Figure 13.8b, dances bare-chested, in bare feet, with loose, flowing trousers.

(a)   *(b)*

Figure 13.8
(a) Special body supplements, such as the toe shoes of female ballet dancers, extend
the dancers' physical abilities or visual presence and enhance their performance. (b)
The more exposed costuming of modern dance, as compared to ballet, is associated
with a very different repertoire of disciplined dance movements. Because a costume
can enhance or detract from a dance movement, dance costumes must be designed
with reference to the specific movements of the dance in order to be really successful.

Sometimes performance dress is designed to be so fantastic for the sake of
the performance that it becomes inconvenient and barely functions as real
dress, as in the case of the many popular "follies" stage extravaganzas of the
early twentieth century. Liberace became famous for his personal taste in ostentatious dress, and ever-more jewel-covered ensembles were created for him
as his career progressed. His garments were sometimes measured in tens of
pounds due to the weight of faux jewels embellishing them. In one performance, he blithely wore a heavy jeweled cape, as if it weighed nothing. However, he rode in a matching jewel-covered Volkswagen across the stage. This allowed him to leave the heavy cape on the automobile, which was driven
offstage as he remained to give his piano performance.

The relation of a costume to the body movements of the wearer is not
solely limited to functional requirements. Costumes for dance and athletic performances are usually designed in a form that accents the typical or most important movements of the performer's body. Tap dancers' shoes have metal
pieces attached to the soles of the shoes to emphasize the movements of the

dance with sound. Dakota dance dress, as in Figure 13.9, has many hanging fringes or suspended feathers and attached metal objects which reflect light. Together, these attachments to body enclosures exaggerate the general movements of the dancer. Many dance costumes expose the body by leaving it uncovered, as is found often in the case of performers of modern dance. The costumes of many athletic-type performances, such as figure skating, tends also to be body dominant or have elements of body dominance in it so that the physical skill of the performing body can be appreciated. Fans and judges alike can better appreciate the performance if they can see exposed portions of the body or see the body silhouette through body-conforming dress, such as the tight bodysuits or leotards and tights. Those portions of the costume that are not strictly protective or body revealing must contribute to the expression of the mood of the performance. Figure skating costumes for women are usually made of very light materials that fly around to expose the skaters legs and exaggerate the movements of leaps and spins.

Comfort and adaptation to body action are important in stage costume, but sturdiness is also required. This means strong stitching to avoid easily ripped clothes when getting in and out of a costume for a fast change between scenes. Similarly, costume for productions such as the circus need both glamour and sturdiness, as one costumer noted:

> Circus costumes take a hard beating and are exposed to more elements than the usual theatrical wardrobe. . . . They are packed and unpacked hundreds of times during the tour.
>
> Headdresses with enormous plumes and feathers must have a look of fantasy during the show, but they must pack quickly and easily. Every feather is wired to protect it from breaking. (McCormack, 1971, p. B3)

Figure 13.9
As movement is an essential element of the dance, many dance costumes are designed with features that exaggerate and draw attention to the movements of the wearer.

Performers in Broadway and London musicals, as well as in extravaganzas in Las Vegas, Reno, and Paris, also wear intricate headdresses which must be stored between performances as well as hold up from performance to performance. Some costumes have to hold up for an all-day or all-night performance. In Southern Bihar state, India, some communities hire professional sword dancers to help celebrate weddings. The sword display of the dancers echoes the general Indian cultural metaphor of bridegroom as royal prince (Indian princes always carry a sword). The dancers are expected to dance vigorously on and off for hours at a time through the day and night. Thus, their costumes must stay reliably on the body while they engage in vigorous dancing. A large portion of the costume consists of a sash securely tied and wrapped around the body, circling the body as many as ten times.

One final requirement of some stage clothing is its ability to withstand many performances without laundering. Every popular Broadway road show has elaborate and expensive costumes. Sometimes, special dry cleaners are contracted for upkeep of the costumes, but when the company is in a different town every week, spot cleaning is preferred over risking the skills of an unknown dry cleaner who may not have experience in this area. One of the authors visited the Universal Studios costume shop in Hollywood, where the costume shop director pointed out that actors' costumes are picked up each night for cleaning and returned the next morning for the next movie take. Sometimes, multiples of an actor's costume are supplied when the actor must go through scenes that demand that a piece of apparel be ripped or torn in the ensuing action.

Adjustment to Performance Space and Lighting

When the performance space involves great distance between audience and performer, theater costume design often aids effective performances. An exaggeration in some aspects of dress allows viewers from the second balcony, or highest bleachers in the circus tent, to see and understand the purpose of the costume for the performer's role. For example, a character portrayed as "small town" and not a "city sophisticate," must be immediately discerned by all members of a theater audience, seated anywhere from 10 to 70 feet away from the stage (Langner, 1959, p. 242). Fine details are unnecessary, for they may well go unnoticed by many members of the audience. Sometimes, when the distance between performer and audience is very great, costume elements are painted on using perspective techniques, such as the heavy braid one might expect as an edging on an Elizabethan gown. Exaggeration in circus and opera costume is even more mandatory, as the distance between opera and circus performers and audience members is often greater than in many other theater productions.

On the stage, cosmetics used for performers are often more intense in color than everyday makeup to allow for the distance involved between audience and actors. Movie requirements are quite different, because the audience can focus on the details of a close-up. In the early days of Hollywood, movie makers and the stars themselves were more interested in maintaining "star quality" than producing historically accurate makeup. In their efforts to perfect this star quality, makeup artists developed a "pseudo-scientific corrective makeup technique, based on the classical Greek idea of beauty" (Annas, 1987, p. 52). Thus, screen makeup can often tell us as much about the era in which the film was made as the era depicted. Note the makeup differences for three different Cleopatras in three different decades in Figure 13.10a, b, and c. In the late twentieth century, the film industry is global and many audiences are quite discerning. They expect a high level of authenticity for the price of their ticket, yet realism has its limits. Thus, even when producers aim for authenticity, they are limited in their choices by the expectations of the audience.

The amount and quality of light affects the design of costumes. The manipulation of special lighting effects make possible a much wider range of color combinations in costumes on the stage than in everyday wear. Natural light isolates color, whereas the colored illumination used for the high-tech stage tends to blend colors. Thus, on stage, colors not usually worn together and colors stronger in intensity than those worn daily may be utilized. Skilled use of lighting effects enhances the appearance of dimension in painted costume and set embellishments, making them look like they have weight and substance so they appear to be "real." In addition, lighting may in some cases actually be a part of costuming, for the color of an outfit may be created or varied by lighting. Certain iridescent effects appear only under special lighting conditions.

One cross-cultural example of a performance with limited lighting comes from rural central India where the storytelling masked dance performers called

(a)   (b)   (c)

Figure 13.10
Even when treating a historical subject like the story of Cleopatra, the U.S. film industry selects styles of dress that both enhance the particular appearance characteristics of the actor playing the role and appeal to the contemporary aesthetic sensibilities of the audience. Historical accuracy in dress becomes secondary to the task of creating a pleasing performance. This alteration of history occurs much more frequently with body modifications, such as makeup and hair styles, than with body supplements. (a) Theda Bara, 1917; (b) Claudette Colbert, 1934; (c) Elizabeth Taylor, 1963.

Chau (choe) typically perform at night in small towns and villages. Though the performances are intimate, with the audience sitting close to the dancers, the low light makes it necessary that the characters' faces be simplified down to just the essential elements. The *Chau* masks have simple, stylized faces in forms that clearly identify the mythological characters so well known to the audience from religious and folk stories.

Performer in Relation to Costume

Successful portrayal of a role depends often on an individual's costume and makeup. Charlie Chaplin is an early twentieth-century classic example of someone who successfully used costume to support his character portrayal. See Figure 13.11. As one writer comments:

> Imagine Charlie Chaplin in any outfit than his own. . . . Much thought and experiment went into its creation. Have you ever noticed how this artist wears his shabby, droll, almost pathetic costume and how he uses it to play upon your feelings? His work is an illustrious example of a great artist's use of costume. (Brauner, 1964, pp. 23–26)

Compatibility between the design of costume and how an artist perceives a role can give confidence in portrayal of that role. If an actor sees the costume as symbolic of or authentic to the role played, identification with the role is enhanced. Costumers attempt to give the actor that confidence in reproduction of costumes. However, if a costume does not coincide with an actor's visual conception of that role, the actor may suffer confusion and discomfort as the coordination of role and symbol are attempted. Lawrence Langner, founder of The Theater Guild and American Shakespeare Festival Theater at Stratford, Connecticut, claimed that "actors and actresses, and especially actresses, feel uncomfortable and unable to perform properly if they are antagonistic to the clothes they are wearing" (1959, p. 242). This antagonism may be caused by a conscious or unconscious feeling that a costume is not appropriate for the role being played. On occasion, personal vanity interferes with suggested costume designs: actors who want to enhance what they consider their most attractive features and minimize others, may react negatively to a costume that they do not feel makes them attractive.

Costume can put an actor in the mood to portray a character. Dustin Hoffman commented about the makeup used for his characterization of a 121-year-old man in the movie *Little Big Man*, "I defy anybody to put that makeup on and not feel old" ("The Old Age," 1970). Costume and makeup can also help create a mood shared between actor and audience as well as indicate change in mood. If mood is to be established convincingly, gesture, body stance, voice tones, music, and costume must complement each other, for an inharmonious detail may result in failure to establish the desired mood.

The color of a costume is a quality that is often manipulated in efforts to create mood. In American theater bright, contrasting colors and sharp differ-

Figure 13.11
Charlie Chaplin's use of specific costuming detail is central to the creation of his character in film, a fact not unrelated to the absence of sound in most of his movies. In the absence of dialogue, dress and Chaplin's interaction with his dress carried a heavier responsibility to help communicate the story.

ences in lightness and darkness are conventionally used to stress activity and gaiety. Dull and dark colors emphasize mystery or sadness. As described earlier, color can be used to focus attention onto or away from characters. Similarity in color can be used to indicate family relationships or group solidarity. For example, in productions of Shakespeare's *Romeo and Juliet*, the Capulets and the Montagues are frequently dressed in contrasting colors.

For certain theatrical or film roles, the costume or makeup has become so much a part of the character that the two become intertwined and inseparable, thus the essence of a character is the clothing for certain roles. The traditional characters of Harlequin, Pierrot and Pierrette, Peter Pan, Mary Poppins, and Mickey and Minnie Mouse have such definite costume requirements that the character is immediately recognizable because of the specific costume worn, as illustrated in Figure 13.12. The costumes for characters in the Japanese Noh drama and Kabuki theater are further examples; the costume is the character and the actor merely the "machinery" for giving the character movement. The epitome of integration of dress and role occurs in the case of these stereotyped characters; indeed, the stereotyped role may constrain the actor's freedom to be innovative and curtail personal interpretation of the role.

Relation of Costume to the Type of Performance

Costume varies greatly from one performing art to another. Each type of performance seems to demand a specific type of costume.

Figure 13.12
Some characters are immediately recognizable from the very specific dress in which they always appear.

Musical Performance

The type of music produced appears to be related to the type of dress worn by a musical performer. For example, the formal evening dress of a symphony orchestra or a chamber group has come to be associated with the formal structure of its music; the informal and spontaneous type of music produced by jazz musicians is usually typified by casual dress. However, even among these musicians, distinctions in dress can be found. For example, compare the formal attire of the Modern Jazz Quartet with the informal attire of the Brecker Brothers Band, as seen in Figure 13.13a and b.

The dress of singers often parallels the type of music they specialize in. Operatic singers such as Kathleen Battle and Placido Domingo often wear formal evening dress for concerts, while folk or country singers such as Reba McIntyre may select casual dress. Media stars like Madonna and Elton John usually choose flamboyant styles. The associations between the dress of musicians and the type of music they produce are so stereotyped that it is difficult to imagine Johnny Cash in Edwardian ruffles and lace, often worn by The Artist Formerly Known as Prince, or the Boston Symphony Orchestra in jeans and T-shirts.

Group Performance

In many areas of music and in some forms of dance the visible presence of an individual performer is subordinated to the group. A uniform costume is one means of subordinating the individual to the group effort. Visible uniformity

(a)

(b)

Figure 13.13
The dress of musicians in performance varies with the kind of music that they perform. (a) The Modern Jazz Quartet dresses formally for its performances in concert halls. (b) Many other jazz musicians, such as the Brecker Brothers Band, perform in more casual dress.

helps the audience to assess the performance as a group effort and at the same time reminds an individual performer that individual virtuosity is subsumed to group endeavor. In choirs, choruses, orchestras, dance lines, concert, and marching bands, uniformity of dress supports and enhances the appreciation of the performance by the observer. The members of a choir wear choir robes; the symphony orchestra performers, formal dress. In each case, individuality of a single performer is intentionally downplayed, except for soloists or special performers who are featured against the background of the group.

In the case of the Rockettes in Radio City Music Hall, precision dancing is the trademark, as Figure 13.14 shows. Identical costumes emphasize the precision of the dance steps and create an illusion of uniformity of execution among the dancers. Synchronized swimming teams, such as the American Women's Olympic Gold Medal winners of 1996, accentuate both athletic and artistic teamwork through identical dress—swimsuits, hair arrangements, nose plugs, and waterproof makeup.

Fantasy and the Supernatural

Some of the performing arts use a modicum of reality but strict adherence to reality is unnecessary or may even hinder achievement of a performer's artistic goal. In musicals, for example, reality is not always a desired goal; instead, fantasy and entertainment may be the major consideration. If the production

Figure 13.14
Identical costuming subordinates individual physical differences and emphasizes the uniformity of the performers' actions in the precision dancing of the Radio City Rockettes.

requires a fairy-tale effect, adherence to reality may interfere. Cowboys in the musical *Oklahoma* are usually costumed in pastel and colorful shirts rather than the drab colors that cowboys actually wore to work on the frontier. Productions known as "extravaganzas," such as Ziegfeld Follies or the Follies Bergères, also have ignored reality and emphasized fantasy in their costume. Fanciful dress may be created from feathers, beads, and sequins in an effort to create a costume that diverges as much as possible from the everyday. Burlesque and vaudeville performers sometimes also appeared in "unreal" costumes. Masquerade dancers throughout West Africa are dressed in ensembles that are unrelated to the everyday garb of the audience watching them, but instead present themselves as the fierce and fanciful or the ugly spirits of another world. Haute couture fashion designers such as Jean-Paul Gaultier and Karl Lagerfeld may supplement their runway designs with theatrical makeup, big hair, and fantastic hats and handheld objects—not because they expect their customers to dress that way, but to emphasize the theme of the line and create excitement. Each designer hopes his or her line will so thrill the press that the line will be featured in fashion magazines and trade journals such as *Women's Wear Daily*.

Another type of fantasy performance dress is required of science fiction productions, such as the television show *Star Trek*. Lennon's (1999) analysis of the gender difference that shows the dominance of men through costuming in the characters in *Star Trek* is one way of understanding the role of costuming in the series. In Reading V.1, "Cosmic Couture," Elizabeth Snead writes about details of the costuming for characters of *Star Trek*.

The reader may have limited experience with the performance fine arts analyzed in many of the examples given earlier in the chapter. However, there are many performances that are of a folk variety with which you are likely to have more exposure. A common performance example at athletic events is costuming for cheerleaders. These costumes are designed to allow cheerleaders to move easily and be highly visible. The gender differences for male and female cheerleaders are usually accommodated by their costume, with males ordinarily being covered more completely than the females, even if they are wearing shorts. This is an example of performances for which special dress is required, but does not usually fall under consideration in the arts.

Dance

Dance encompasses many types of performances around the world. Within North America, a few examples include square dancing, folk dancing, social dancing, and chorus lines. Each of these examples has specific requirements for costuming. Many examples of varied costumes exist in the specialized dance forms in other cultures, such as the Chinese lion dance, Irish step dancing, and Spanish flamenco, to name only a few. In classical ballet, symmetry of movement and symmetry in dress and hairstyle are emphasized in order to support the formal nature of the dance. In modern dance, on the other hand, free-form costumes enhance or become part of the more asymmetrical, unrestrained movements that are often used. Freedom to wear any type of costume that supports the underlying theme of the dance is stressed.

Sometimes dancing is part of another type of performance, as in the example of many kinds of parades such as Mardi Gras and Carnival costumes worn in New Orleans, Louisiana, and Mobile, Alabama, along with those in the Caribbean islands and in South America. In these examples, costumes are worn in the open street where the performers are expected to dance and move along in a parade at the same time. Frequently in these celebrations, competition exists to see who has constructed the most fantastic costume. Some of the special types of fantasy costumes place restrictions on the masked performer and, in some cases, aids for the performer's mobility are provided (such as wheels to support large wings) when constructing the costume.

VISUAL AND LITERARY ARTS

Artists who paint or draw, create sculpture, or write literature whether poetry, novels, essays, or short stories, often express the emotions, personality, and social characteristics of their subjects through dress.

Visual Arts

In the visual arts, costume may reflect current fashion or glorify the personages painted. Until the introduction of photography, sculpture and painting were major ways of recording historical events and portraying the unique appearance of individuals. On the one hand, some artists portrayed dress of common folk and aristocrats with accuracy. Such paintings can be used for documentation of the period. On the other hand, some artists who painted portraits of the wealthy and powerful enhanced their appearance with elaborate costumes in order to establish the importance and prestige of their patrons. For example, through European history, derivatives of the Greek *himation* (hy-MA-tee-on), or draped garment, were used in art works to clothe figures with honor and respect; Greek and Roman scholars were portrayed in the *himation*; the figure of Christ has been traditionally depicted in the same way. A sculpture of George Washington shows him in a classic pose clad in the *himation*, as seen in Figure 13.15. Formal portraits of Western rulers have often shown similar archaisms. Louis XIV, for example, is portrayed in costume that mixes seventeenth-century details of dress (full-bottomed wig, red-heeled shoes, and lace neckcloth) with sixteenth-century breeches.

Painters in earlier times often painted historical subjects, especially Biblical or mythological subjects, in the dress of their own period. On the other hand, the style or school of painting known as formalism of the French painter David of the eighteenth century led him to use his idea of classical Roman and Greek dress for contemporary political subjects. The Pre-Raphaelite painters of the nineteenth century favored dress that resembled that of medieval times,

Figure 13.15
Because George Washington is such an important personage in U.S. history, his dress is sometimes altered from reality in artistic depiction of him to emphasize his importance. Dress history is thus manipulated in the service of a political and social purpose.

both in their paintings and for their personal dress. Artists often decide to extend their commitment to the arts by displaying their aesthetic interest through their own manner of dress, as shown in Reading IV.4, "Signature Style: Falling Off the Fashion Train with Frida, Georgia, and Louise." There, JoAnn Stabb provides us with the examples of the dress of Frida Kahlo, Georgia O'Keeffe, and Louise Nevelson.

Visual artists sometimes use dress as the subject of the art, rather than merely representing the way their human subjects are dressed. Ami Simms, for example, has created a patchwork quilt on the subject of bikini bathing suits at the beach (Figure 13.16a). Artist Stine Heilman has created "shoes" and "purses" (handheld body supplements) out of fresh plant materials such as flowers, leaves, and vegetables or animal materials such as seashells. Obviously items of dress such as these are not meant to be worn, but instead, simply viewed (Figure 13.16b).

Literary Arts

In literature, descriptions of dress usually help depict for the reader the type of individual the author is creating, the social background, and perhaps mood. Fiction writers of both short stories and novels develop characters by describing their dress and ornamentation as well as by providing appropriate dialogue

Figure 13.16
Some visual artists make art on the subject of dress. Such artworks cannot be worn; (a) quilt on the subject of bikinis, Mary Barelli Gallagher, 1969; (b) a shoe made of vegetable matter, Stine Heilman, c. 1995.

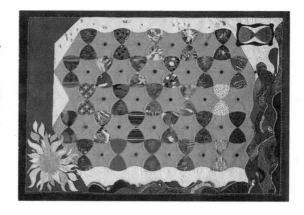

(a)

(b)

for them. In *Madame Bovary*, the appearance of gentlemen at a ball was depicted by Flaubert in such a way that the reader easily picks up clues about their social standing:

> Their clothes, better made, seemed of finer cloth, and their hair, brought forward in curls towards the temples, glossy with more delicate pomades. They had the complexion of wealth—that clear complexion that is heightened by the pallor of porcelain, the shimmer of satin, the veneer of old furniture, and that an ordered regimen of exquisite nurture maintains at its best. Their necks moved easily in their low cravats, their long whiskers fell over their turned-down collars, they wiped their lips upon handkerchiefs with embroidered initials that gave forth a subtle perfume. (1958 version, pp. 57–58)

In Chapter 3, we pointed out that providing character information through detailed descriptions of dress is a specialty of writers such as the detective fiction author Raymond Chandler. The ability of writers to convey character through dress can make or break their success. When an author can note, describe, and incorporate living detail into character and scene description, the writing comes alive to the reader. Thus, Dickens's portrayal of Miss Havisham in *Great Expectations* allowed the costumer for the movie to portray her fairly closely to Dickens's description, as shown in Figure 13.17. In their writing, poets, too, use dress as topic. Their compressed form of presentation spurs the reader to respond, often emotionally, to imagery of an individual's dress. An example is this description by the seventeenth-century poet, Herrick: "When as in silks my Julia goes, then, then, methinks how sweetly flows that liquefaction of her clothes" ("Upon Julia's Clothes" in Patrick [1963]).

Biographies and autobiographies are also part of literature. Descriptions of details of dress give historical accuracy to the portrayal of an individual. For example, Mary Barelli Gallagher (1969) documented for posterity the outfit Jacqueline Kennedy wore for the swearing-in ceremony on Inauguration Day in January 1961:

> I saw Jackie when she was finally dressed. Her outfit was captivating—a fawn-colored wool cloth coat with a little sable stand-up collar and muff to match. Her pillbox . . . matched the color of her coat. To combat the snows, Jackie wore elegant dark high-heeled, fur-trimmed boots. (p. 93)

When writing their autobiographies, individuals often provide not only accurate details about their clothing and appearance but also about their feelings related to their dress. A particularly vivid description and poignant example comes from Maya Angelou (1969):

Figure 13.17
The costuming of the character of Miss Havisham in film was easily achieved by reference to Dickens's elaborate description of her dress in his novel *Great Expectations*. Description of dress is an important part of many writers' art.

The dress I wore was lavender taffeta, and each time I breathed it rustled, and now that I was sucking in air to breathe out shame it sounded like crepe paper on the back of hearses. As I'd watched Momma put ruffles on the hem and cute little tucks around the waist, I knew that once I put it on I'd look like a movie star. (It was silk and made up for that awful color.) I was going to look like one of the sweet little white girls who were everybody's dream of what was right with the world. . . . But Easter's early morning sun had shown the dress to be a plain ugly cut-down from a white woman's once-was-purple throwaway. It was old-lady-long too, but it didn't hide my skinny legs, which had been greased with Blue Seal Vaseline and powdered with Arkansas red clay. The age-faded color made my skin look dirty like mud, and everyone in church was looking at my skinny legs. (pp. 1–2)

ARTISTS IN THE FIELD OF DESIGN

Artists are sometimes directly involved in designing dress. Mario Fortuny, a couturier of the late nineteenth and early twentieth centuries, was trained as a painter and draftsman before he became interested in clothing design and transferred his interest in color and texture to his signature pleating styles. Elsa Schiaparelli had friendships with many Surrealist painters in the 1930s. She solicited their ideas for fabric designs that she then incorporated into her clothing, and invited Salvador Dali, known for his bizarre humor, to design fabrics for her. Artwork by famous artists is also used as decorative motifs on clothing. A series of T-shirts printed with Picasso paintings were issued in the 1960s and are now collectors' items. Both Salvador Dali and Jerry Garcia, leader of the musical group The Grateful Dead, made artwork for men's neckties.

Issey Miyake is an example of an artist whose medium is dress. His work transcends fashion, often because of the technical skill behind the creation of the fabric he uses. Tiny accordion pleats, stiffening, and unusual fiber blends used in combination with cuts that are also comfortable and easy to pack and store make it difficult to define Miyake as primarily a dress designer or an artist. Similarly, Zandra Rhodes is hard to categorize as designer or artist. Her unique interpretation of cultural motifs and forms of dress recast for world fashion have an enduring appeal.

INFLUENCE OF ARTISTS ON FASHION

At various times, as when an artist develops a signature style in dress, it becomes part of the style vocabulary of the general public and can become an important fashion influence, even leading to fashion leadership. The dress of the singer Madonna provides an example, as when she wore underwear as outerwear. An earlier example comes from the movies of the 1930s, which are often cited by dress historians as having had an impact on the styles of the times (Tortora & Eubank, 1998). Another example was documented in 1945, when costume sketches and their color descriptions from that decade were intended to make the people conscious of the color mauve. Still later examples of movie influence on fashion are the slouch hat and casual menswear in the costuming of the main character, Annie Hall, in the Woody Allen film of the same name; of the white garments with Dalmatian spots on Cruella DeVille from the film *101 Dalmatians*; and the 1940s and 1950s fashions of Eva Peron in the musical *Evita*.

The dress style of poets, writers, and musicians of the hippie generation of the 1960s was also influential on later fashions, just as the black clothes of the beat generation had been earlier. The hippie clothes of the flower children inspired beads and jewelry for both males and females and flowing, flowered dresses for women. Both of these groups arose in reaction against mainstream cultural values that assumed that social mobility and success in the business world were open to all. Self-expression and wide experience within these groups were valued over conformity and material success and became codified in the dress style. Similarly, at the end of the 1990s, performers in many types of musical groups, such as heavy metal bands, also influence contemporary dress. This happens particularly in the dress of their fans when the fans attend concerts, for it is a common occurrence for concert fans to imitate the dress of the performers at that time.

SUMMARY

Dress may be viewed as a beautiful object or as an art form in itself. In addition, dress is intertwined with other art forms. In the performing arts, the dress of the performer is more accurately termed costume and serves a variety of functions necessary to the success of a particular expression of the art form. Performers' costume communicates the basic facts of age, sex, occupation, and personality to an audience as they interact with other actors on the stage. However, performers require special services from costume that are not necessary in everyday life. Thus, stage dress must accommodate body movement and be sturdily constructed; in addition, special theatrical lighting effects on costume must be considered as well as the distance between the performer and audience. The performer must find psychological support for a designated role from the costume in order to give a successful performance, or the costume by identifying the role may put special performance requirements on the performer. Some performing arts seem to require special costumes for the performers. Different types of musical and dance performances are associated with specific dress.

The visual arts and written description or commentary in the literary arts use dress to portray individual characteristics, and in the process become records of historical dress. The dress of artists across many media may also influence fashions of the times.

STUDY TOOLS

Important Terms

armature

costume

literary arts

performing arts

visual arts

wearable art

Discussion Questions

1. Describe how the body itself can be a canvas for artistic expression.
2. Describe how an article of dress can be a canvas for artistic expression.
3. Discuss the similarities and differences between performance costume and the dress of nonperformers.
4. Compare and contrast how dress is used in the art forms of painting, sculpture, and photography. How do these uses relate to use of these arts as sources of information about dress, as described in Chapter 3.
5. Why is dress important to actors in the successful portrayal of their characters?
6. Describe an occasion when you wore performance dress. How does the form of that dress relate to the form of the performance you were giving? What gave you confidence? What made you self-conscious?
7. Compare and contrast (1) dress as art, or the artistry of dress, and (2) art on the subject of dress, giving examples where possible.
8. Describe how Georgia O'Keeffe, Louise Nevelson, and Frida Kahlo used dress to create a signature style that transcended fashion (see Reading IV.4). Are there ways in which their dress also expressed or remained within the bounds of fashion of their day? How is this conscious creation of an authentic self in dress related to the discussion of conformity and individuality in dress in Chapter 12?

Activities

1. View a *Star Trek* episode or film and analyze the ways in which the costumes of the aliens are related to the kind of roles they play in the episode. How do their costumes convey information about their culture?
2. Attend an exhibition of wearable art. Analyze whether some pieces are more wearable than others. Where does "wearable" end and "art" begin? How do you think the nonwearable forms express current fashion trends or predict the dress of the future?
3. Identify a popular trend in do-it-yourself wearable art (e.g., tie-dye, embroidery, riveting, beading). Embellish a garment yourself. Write a journal entry about your inspiration, choice of garment, and technique in relation to the wearability and the artistry of the piece. Also write about how, where, and when you will find this item of dress wearable in your own life.

4.   Read a novel by your favorite author. How does the author use dress to convey character, mood, or setting? Do you think the author could use dress more effectively? Mark examples in the book and bring them to class to discuss.

5.   Select a haute couture designer from the past or present. Using color photocopies or clippings from expendable magazines, create a time line of the history of the designer's art in dress. Compare this time line with a fashion time line from a dress history book. Analyze how the designer you selected led (or predicted) fashion trends or developed along independent lines.

6.   Attend a play or dance performance and pay particular attention to the costume, or performance dress, and its relationship to the content of the performance. Also notice the use of lighting and the form (color, line texture, shape) of the staging in which the costumes are worn. Analyze how the performance dress fulfills the goals of the performance. Also consider how the dress relates to the lighting and staging. Can you think of ways the dress could have been improved to relate to the lighting, staging, or content of the performance?

IV.1 THE AESTHETICS OF MEN'S DRESS OF THE KALABARI OF NIGERIA
Tonye V. Erekosima
Joanne B. Eicher

Kalabari Dress As Ensemble

Asante uses the term African aesthetics to mean "the conscious aesthetics of people of African descent who are aware of participating in some African tradition" (1993, p. 54). Our previous analysis of Kalabari dress and the social order (Eicher and Erekosima, 1993) sets the stage for analyzing Kalabari men's dress and textiles as one example of African aesthetics. Our Kalabari data provide an in-depth analysis of the aesthetics of one group of Africans who exhibit a rich dress and textile heritage that contradicts much stereotyping of Africans. For example, Ghanaian dress and textiles are seen and used by many African Americans as representing "typical" African dress. The Kalabari data illustrate only one of many African traditions of dress that exist, for Africa is a large and complex continent.

The Kalabari case of African aesthetics in men's dress to be described here typifies a distinctive clothing tradition, that of cut-and-sewn fabrics. . . .

Within Kalabri society both male and female dress have been analyzed as indicating respectively sociopolitical and sociophysical placement of individuals in regard to their basic styles of dress (Daly, 1984; Daly, Eicher, and Erekosima, 1986; Michelman, 1987; Michelman and Erekosima, 1992; Eicher and Erekosima, 1993). In this paper, we focus on adult male dress and draw from the interviews and fieldwork of Erekosima and Eicher since 1979 (see Eicher and Erekosima, 1993 for an extensive bibliography), as well as Erekosima's (1989) focused research on Kalabari male dress which followed a preliminary analysis by Erekosima and Eicher (1981).[1] We briefly summarize the types of dress in relationship to sociopolitical meaning and elaborate on the aesthetics, etiquette and nuances understood by the Kalabari as necessary for a man's proper appearance in public.

Kalabari men, living on islands in the Niger delta of Nigeria, engaged in trade with Africans and non-Africans for centuries and treasured a variety of imported textiles that they incorporated into their daily and ceremonial lives. One of the unique aspects of their aesthetics of dress was and is their creativity in taking materials from elsewhere and subjecting them to rigorous, indigenous standards to make new ensembles that convey their own ethnic identity and concerns of societal organization.

The art of ensemble for Kalabari men characterizes most of their forms of dress with subtle distinctions and aesthetic elaborations. These distinctions and elaborations constitute efficient vises that glue together discrete and foreign-made items into a montage of Kalabari dress. We will describe and provide illustrations of the ensembles peculiar to Kalabari men, discuss their use, and analyze the expressive aspects the ensembles convey. An elaborate set of aesthetic rules about cloth and dress among the Kalabari with appropriate local nomenclature provides evidence of a sophisticated taste. Stylistic differentiation plays a key role in communicating men's roles within the social order, and a clear-cut set of aesthetic standards accompanies the practiced style differences.

The conversion of borrowed artifacts to indigenous, cultural usages, we have termed the Cultural Authentication Process (CAP). It has been postulated as a construct entailing four main steps of SCIT: Selection, Characterization, Incorporation, and Transformation (Erekosima and Eicher, 1981). The process of cultural authentication begins when a new item is introduced into a culture unfamiliar with it and becomes an item of meaningful transaction or legitimate cultural currency in the second culture.

Initially, the specific artifact is singled out from a variety of possibilities, or, in other words becomes selected. The artifact also becomes named, or characterized symbolically by members of the receiving community who acquire a shared reference in regard to it. As the object becomes associated with a definite function in the social order to solve a problem or aid in enhancing the well-being of individuals or in enriching life, it is, thereby, incorporated into the social order. Finally, when the object is transformed through creative responses to modify it so that it no longer is perceived as simply borrowed, it is then culturally authenticated. The process of cultural authentication is found throughout Kalabari life, not only in men's dress ensembles, but also in funeral display, the production of pelete bite (cut-thread cloth), and female dress. Our focus in this paper is to elaborate the examples of cultural authentication as found in the aesthetic expressions of Kalabari men's dress.

What the Kalabari of Nigeria regard as their men's traditional dress consists largely of textiles used as wrappers, garments, accessories and ornaments imported from overseas or fabricated outside their culture. The dress items include familiar Western clothing like shirts (in some modified form), trousers, accessories like hats, shoes, handkerchiefs and walking sticks as well as ornaments like gold and silver chains or studs. Some ensembles include "wrappers" and gowns of Indian textiles in combination with Western garments. Superficially, a man in such attire is not visibly wearing indigenous Nigerian dress. However, they represent to the Kalabari, objects of considerable economic value and aesthetic worth and the sociopolitical status of Kalabari males is represented by specific types of dress for age and social position.[2] Aesthetics reflect the tension between conformity and differentiation, or matter and form in cultural life. Aesthetic standards are explicitly evident within Kalabari society as specific acceptable general rules of expressive or appreciative representation. These standards include subtleties of taste that pervade the process of aesthetics and allow idiosyncratic (individual) or segmental (subgroup) emphases. Aesthetics of dress among the Kalabari also include a knowledge of the stylistic forms of dress appropriate to specific categories of people or events as well as knowledge of the transitory fashions of a specific time and place.

Kalabari aesthetics of dress exemplify African aesthetics in other realms. Practical utility merges with meaning and use. Kalabari dress is neither mere commodity or pure art.[3] This merger is the context within which we view Kalabari dress. Hence Kalabari aesthetics simultaneously encompass the pairing of sentiment and substance. African aesthetics resonates as the vantage point or basic perspective from which objects and events of reality obtain interpretation or assignments of meaningfulness in the setting of cultural lifeways.

Kalabari Men's Traditional Dress

The peculiar ensembles and the characteristic use of the imported items of dress together define Kalabari men's traditional dress. As one informant put it, Kalabari dress for men means: "to tie _injiri_ cloth, wear a garment over it, put on a hat, and pick up a walking stick" (Erekosima,

1989:337). Two major components make up the classic styles of Kalabari men's traditional dress ensembles. One is the sewn garment that covers the upper torso. The other is a length of cloth called a wrapper. When tied on the wearer, it covers the lower torso from waist to feet. The most frequently used and preferred textile for a man's wrapper is injiri, the Kalabari name for Indian madras, the plaid cotton cloth, that for centuries has been imported from India through European merchants to West Africa.

Who are the Kalabari of Nigeria whose rigid dress code for men has a strong aesthetic component? This sub-unit of the Ijo ethnic group, estimated at slightly more than one percent of the 90 million population of Nigeria, was important in the development of Nigeria: early on as fishermen, but who centuries ago turned principally into traders of salt, slaves, and palm oil. They live and have lived on a series of islands in the delta of River Niger, 4 degrees above the equator. Their overland trade with other West Africans (Alagoa, 1970) has been indicated as predating their European trading contacts with the Portuguese who came by sea in the 1400s. Later, the Dutch, French and British also arrived by sea for trade and sporadic attempts at missionary work. The 1700s and 1800s were the heyday for the Kalabari as superb traders and middlemen (for men did the trading) with the Europeans, dealing first in slaves and then in palm oil (Adams, 1823; Dike, 1956; Jones, 1963). The fortunes of the Kalabari shifted markedly after the British took political control of the geographical area that became known as Nigeria in the early 1900s. Instead of the king and chiefs being in complete control of their own political and economic affairs, they fell subject to the machinations of the British. By 1960, when independence was won for Nigeria, the Kalabari maintained pride in their ethnic heritage, but many rose to the challenge of seeing themselves as part of the larger political, economic, and geographical unit of the Nigerian polity.

Varieties of Sewn Dress and their Patterns of Use

The Kalabari word _kapa_ which stands for sewn garments, has been identified by a linguist (Jenewari, 1976) as a word in Portuguese which means dress. There is, therefore, a likely correspondence between the emergence of this sewn variant of Kalabari men's dress (in contrast to the handwoven lengths of cloth used as "wrappers") and Portuguese influence among the Kalabari starting from the early 16th century.

These Europeans clearly introduced a whole range of items of dress to the Kalabari which were both Western and non-Western (Vogt, 1975). This introduction tremendously enlarged the Kalabari wardrobe, with the Portuguese term for dress being borrowed and used in a generic way to reflect the new major development. The *injiri* cloth from India has already been cited as one such item brought in by the Portuguese (Evenson, 1991; 1993).

The records show, for instance, a documentation by Pereira in 1514 of Portuguese trade in clothing items with Benin (Ryder, 1965). A trade report by Antonio de Coyra in 1516 and then by Alvaro Frade in 1519 also attest to the same activity. Similarly, Blake (1942) describes trade with the Casa de Guinea in Lagos as reported in 1498 by Joham de Avellar and in another Casa da Guinea document of 1533. Even without the Kalabari having direct link to the Portuguese, both of these towns of Benin and Lagos were thriving market centers to which they had access at the time, as already indicated. The Kalabari trade with these ports only subsequently expanded, especially when direct trade contacts began. And the extent of the growing commerce in clothing can be inferred from the report by Davis (1954) that clothing constituted approximately 70 percent of British imports to West Africa in the 1700s.

Regarding commerce to the Niger Delta hinterland, Alagoa remarked (1970, p. 322) that:

> By the beginning of the sixteenth century . . . north-south trade was already far advanced, and carried on with huge canoes on a large scale over a long distance.

Thus was the channel kept open that led to the indirect reference about Portuguese presence in the Niger Delta hinterland by the 1600s. One European traveler (Ogilvy, 1970, p. 480) noted that there was a nobleman of Owerri, Don Antonio De Mingo, whose father had married a Portuguese woman that he had met while in Portugal and whom he brought back with him to Africa.

A more direct reference to the impact of Portuguese fashions on Kalabari society occurs in the following remarks of the British colonial administrator, Amaury Talbot, who did an ethnographic survey of the cultures of southern Nigeria in the early decades of the 20th century. In describing one of the revered deities of Kalabari society he noted (Talbot, 1932, p. 38) as follows:

> When one remembers the number of Portuguese mariners who, in old days, made their way to this part of the coast, it is not difficult to understand why the carved figure of *adumu* is here shown with the pointed mustache and

beard, the ruff and feather-trimmed hat of a don of the period when these bold seafarers first penetrated to the lower regions of the Santa Barbara [river].

The Kalabari were not merely passive recipients of borrowed forms of dress. They did not just retain or copy the Portuguese garments or treat dress as artifacts of purely material import. Their response was unlike the current unimaginative and almost passive use of Western dress by contemporary Nigerians. Among many Nigerians, over a century of adoption of modern European dress is known (Wass, 1975). Many items such as the men's suit ensemble continue to be worn with little change or modification. In addition these items are not given local names, nor modified in form or function, for they are not used in an indigenous way. In contrast, the Kalabari reacted differently to the items of dress borrowed from outside. They introduced their own words for innovations that they made, while adjusting the innovations in a practical way to fit their own perspectives of life. The result was a genuine learning situation such as Piaget and Inhelder (1969) stipulate, by which the Kalabari effected a significant adaptation of the received artifact to their deeply challenged and versatile culture. In creative response, they altered and accommodated new inputs, or adjusted their preexisting frame of reference, and brought both to an adaptive equilibrium.

This approach, earlier defined as the Cultural Authentication Process, guides our analysis of Kalabari dress. The Kalabari used a series of modified upper garments to be worn with wrapped cloth for the lower garments and added a variety of imported accessories to create a complete ensemble.

The traditional ensembles worn by Kalabari men in public are indicated by the names of the sewn garment for the upper torso that is knee-length, calf-length, or ankle-length. Kalabari traditional dress ensembles representing four ranks of the sociopolitical order are listed below in descending order of importance. The gown known as *attigra* is outside the ranking system and is described afterwards:

1. *Ebu*
2. *Doni*
3. *Woko*
4. *Etibo*

i) Describing the Ebu

The *ebu* is an ankle-length gown worn by the king (Amanyanabo) and his paramount chiefs, made of an imported plaid cotton fabric from India known as _injiri_. The style is specifically characterized by a broad, "V-shaped" front for the collar that reaches to mid-chest but is square across the back, reminiscent of the uniform of sailors. The latter were the crew of the visiting ships who rowed their smaller vessels ashore, and wore uniforms with this type of collar. Kalabari contact with European sailors and traders may have provided this key symbol of new developments in Kalabari society that resulted from stimulation from Western mercantile activity. To counter the danger to their community from the demand for slaves made by the Europeans, the Kalabari had to restructure their society radically. A monarchy coordinating expanded family trading and defense corporations emerged. The traditional extended families assimilated thousands of "strangers" from hinterland societies to evolve these new "War-Canoe Houses," and allowed the most enterprising of even these former aliens to rule over these units. Kalabari men's dress emerged to symbolize and communicate functions within such a new order.[4]

The gown is worn only with a matching piece of _injiri_ wrapper (_bite wari_). Its decor is one of simplicity, since no loud or rich accessories normally accompany it. A bowler hat or top hat is appropriate headgear, along with simple jewelry such as one solid piece of coral bead stretched across the stud-fastened mini-collar of the white shirt worn underneath. The long sleeves of the _ebu_ must be folded to slightly above the wrist, to expose the cuffs of the white shirt underneath which are usually secured with gold or silver links. A few gold rings may be worn on one or two fingers of both hands and a simple cane or walking stick held.

The _ebu_ is regarded as most fitting for the very elderly chiefs of eminent status who no longer need to assert high public visibility through ornate habiliment. They leave such projection of the image of a chief actively exercising power to those who are younger and for whom the _doni_ is a more appropriate attire than the _ebu_.

The simple style of the _ebu_ matches the status of the elder statesman who gracefully stays in the background as he offers words of wisdom and tactfully guides the strategies of the active community leaders who serve as public representatives. This perspective led to the uncontrived situation of the King (Amanyanabo) of Kalabari appearing among his Council of Chiefs at a cabinet session in 1966 as the only one amongst them wearing _ebu_.[5] Traditionally only the king and his handful of leading statesmen wore the _ebu_.

Also close discriminations are made about the quality of Indian madras, which the Kalabari call _injiri_, that

may be obtained or used. The top of the class is called "Real India" cloth, recognizable by textural qualities as well as perforation markings at the sides of the cloth. A less refined quality of _injiri_ is called "mandras or madras," and an even less durable brand of the cloth which sold rather cheaply was called Pinion. Its texture was inferior or rougher, and its colors faded readily with laundering.

ii) Describing the _Doni_

The _doni_ is an ankle-length robe worn by Kalabari notables who are chiefs (_alapu_). Made like an elongated shirt, from thick and colorful woolen material, its collar is narrow at the back with two flaps at the front. Four button-holes are centered in a front placket for display of good-sized gold or silver studs. A chain connects the studs to a brooch pinned on the left side pocket. The placket is often fashioned in a pattern called fish-gill (_sangolo_), ladder, or such other designs, with a large tab at the bottom (_doni bele_) that apparently enables the wearer to pull down the garment while walking, to straighten it out.

The sleeves of the _doni_ are slightly folded back when worn, to expose the cuffs of the white shirt that must be worn underneath it. The collar band of the shirt is fastened with a big, matching gold or silver stud, and the shirt cuffs fastened with matching links. The _doni_ is ankle-length or sometimes slightly shorter, and it must have an _injiri_ wrapper of good quality tied underneath that shows an appropriate "volume" relative to the "big" fit of the _doni_ on its wearer. The gown should not fit too closely or be too tight around the ankles.

Use of a walking stick is almost always mandatory for a man wearing the _doni_; shoes are optional. The hat need not be elaborate except during ceremonial occasions, perhaps a top hat or bowler hat. Wearing gold rings is expected. Each side of the _doni_ is slit from the hem to below the armscye, to allow for easy movement by the wearer.

Informants did not agree on the origin of the _doni_. Some insisted that it initially came from the Portuguese in its present form. These informants claimed that it was being worn by the Portuguese merchants, who gave away some in token of friendship to their leading trading partners. This item of clothing was presented as what is worn by the dons in Portugal. _Don_ was the title for a nobleman in Portuguese, as is shown by examples like the legendary Don Juan, or Don Quixote of literary fame, and of names like Don Pedro that are given to Portuguese and Spanish notables and also taken up by some Kalabari families.

Some suggested that the outstanding Kalabari traders of the period who received this gift of clothing which they called *doni* in their own dialect—were thereby being recognized as members of the league of successful entrepreneurs.

Other informants contended, however, that the word *doni* came into use only during the period of English dominance and presence in the Niger Delta, which was some time in the early eighteenth century. They insisted that the English introduced a knee-length, woolen shirt (somewhat like the later "boiled" army shirt). The Kalabari chiefs, only then emerging as a force in the internal political scene, needed to be distinguished by adopting some highly visible symbol of their status. They instructed the Sierra Leone and other repatriated black tailors on the ships at the time, to sew these for them by making them reach "down." These tailors were black men who had been repatriated from America to Africa and who had acquired artisan skills. Some became itinerant craftsmen plying the Atlantic coast and sharing their modern ways as missionaries and artisans or tradesman. Communication in any common language at the time was difficult, so the story is told that the chiefs said in a halting English: "*doni, doni*" for "down." These accounts argue that the ankle-length gown emerged as an elongated shirt that became the *doni* and the exclusive garb of Kalabari chiefs.

In examining the credibility of the first version, we found that a search through books illustrating European period dress (Evelyn, 1968) does not show anything like the *doni* being worn by the Portuguese, or any European peoples at all, from the sixteenth through to the twentieth century. The idea of an indigenous adaptive thrust using dress as a symbol of the new order, therefore, becomes more plausible or reinforced.

Whether the garment was adopted or adapted, however, the *doni* remains a Kalabari dress on account of the ensemble that forms it, and rules of etiquette associated with wearing it. Apparently such an ensemble never existed in Europe, and even differs markedly from a similar outfit worn by neighbors of the Kalabari in terms of its associated aesthetics (Erekosima, 1989).

iii) Describing the *Woko*

The garment, worn by Kalabari men in the rank of Opu Asawo, or the Gentlemen of Substance, also differs from similar garments called the *jompa* that are worn by other Niger Delta neighbors in the riverine city-states and other areas outside the Delta (as among the hinterland Igbos). This word derives from the English "jumper" but does not designate clothing that fits the same description. Among the Kalabari, however, it is called *woko*, and is made of plain-colored fabric in contrast to the figured cloths members of the other Eastern Nigerian communities use.

This form of dress probably originated from somewhere other than in Kalabari society. Bonny is a possible dispersal source for the *jompa* or *woko*, but Kalabari informants remained quite vague when discussing its origin. The Kalabari may have, again, simply devised their own unique version of the already existing outfit in order to serve some pressing internal need of status demarcation.

The Kalabari make the *woko* out of white or khaki drill and, generally today, plain terylene, wool, or serge. The colors used are yellow or beige, off-brown, or other neutral hue. This contrasts with the bright red, black, green or crimson colors criss-crossed with animal or bird motifs that characterize the *blangidi* or woolen material out of which the non-Kalabari peoples make their own equivalent of the *woko*. With the Kalabari, it is generally boorish and an anathema to wear this latter type of designed textile in the *woko* style.

The *woko* is simply-cut, hangs from the shoulders of the wearer, with front placket and no collar band. The front placket of the Kalabari *woko* or jompa is plain in contrast to the elaborate gill-pattern or ladder-design motif on the plackets of the non-Kalabari jompa, and the Kalabari *doni*. The sleeves are wide and elbow length; the garment itself is knee length. A band of the same cloth is sewn full-length at the back center of the Kalabari *woko* "to give it character," according to informants. The bottom hem is straight with side slits which are largely only stylistic. The earlier, older version of the *woko* had two front pockets and was not as long as contemporary ones. The term *woko*, which appears to have come from the Kalabari usage *wokoro-wokoro*, meaning "loose-fitting," seems an apt description for the garment.

The *woko* placket has buttonholes for three studs of gold or silver, attached to each other by a chain. A wide pocket on the left, usually sports a fluffy matching handkerchief. A walking stick is considered a necessary accessory and a straw hat or other informal head-gear like the embroidered one called "smoking cap" will be worn which is an embroidered round hat, flat on the top but decorated with tassels of metallic thread trimmings.

The *woko* is frequently worn with an *injiri* wrapper, but can also be worn with trousers, as it has been for many years. A photograph of Chief Ikiriko of Buguma said to be taken in 1917 shows him dressed with *woko* and trousers. Wearing trousers supposedly reflects a need for convenience, as when the wearer is bustling about at the beach front handling commerce and does not want to worry about the breeze lifting up his wrapper.

The Kalabari do not sew their *woko* with the cloth called *blangidi* like their neighbors use for the *jompa*. They agree in their judgment that the use of this fabric for *woko* shows poor taste. Nearer to the truth, however, may be the fact that heavily patterned and brightly colored fabrics had generally been assigned to the sewing of *doni*, to add to the full view colorfulness and commanding presence of chiefs. By sticking to only the blandly-colored fabrics for their *woko*, a clear-cut and highly distinguishable collective identity was also established for the Kalabari. A general sense of disdain for use of the supposedly garish *blangidi* to tailor a *woko* therefore sets the Kalabari apart, even though this disdain is an insular appraisal by the Kalabari about others.

A singular appreciation of this fabric is, however, in evidence for Kalabari men also have a clear ranking of *blangidi*. At the bottom of this hierarchy is a very inferior type of printed woolen cloth called *fuun* that is used only to make children's clothes. Then there are the various kinds that Kalabari women tie, like *feni*, *ologboin-gboin*, *nama-sibi*, which are largely the type used for sewing *jompa* among their neighboring peoples. Finally there are other kinds of blangidi the men consider to be heavy enough and which they will use in sewing the doni, such as *ojugbe*, *aru pike*, *okolobi torungbo*, *igbe biri* and *mene bite*.

iv) Describing the Etibo

The name *etibo* is an elision of the words "eight bob" or eight shillings which represented the cost of such a shirt brought for sale during the English period of dominance on the coast. *Etibo* is at the bottom of the hierarchy of Kalabari men's dress in the valuation of traditional dress and is associated with the bottom rank, the sociopolitical status of Asawo or the Young Men That Matter. The garment, simply a large white, long-sleeved shirt, is made of cotton. The bottom of the *etibo* has a rounded shirttail, in contrast to the straight hem of the *woko*, and the cotton material is comparatively much lighter and cheaper than the heavier woolen cloth of earlier versions. Respondents said the early examples were not usually white but colored, thick flannel material, and shorter than the current style called *etibo*. The version of the 1980s and 1990s reaches to about mid-calf, whereas the original *etibo* was knee-length.

The original, imported *etibo* appears to have simply disappeared from the market, just like several other European imported dresses that were formerly popular.

One was the "Bush Shirt," which had fur-padded parts on the shoulders and back and was made of thick wool so that it served well in keeping the cold away. Another was the Formal Dinner Shirt, with the buttonholes inserted in the wide front placket (*ekpe kuro*).

The contemporary etibo appears to have emerged from being the undershirt (*sheti*) that chiefs wore beneath their *doni* and *ebu*. Some of these Kalabari chiefs of the recent past were very big and tall people whom the European shirt ill-fitted. These men, such as Chiefs Jim George (died 1943), Inko-Tariah (died 1943), Graham Douglas (died 1949), Walter Okorosa (died 1958) as well as Okoma Tom George (died in 1950s), therefore, ordered their own shirts to be sewn to size locally. Before long, such "trendy" shirts went on to become the single, outside garb of the lower status young men and took on the name *etibo*. Its use specifically enjoyed a boost after the Nigerian Civil War of 1967–1970.

The *sheti* worn underneath other garments by chiefs had a detached collar as well as one buttonhole for a stud and for cuff links, and was not the regular shirt worn by Europeans. Some informants called it the imported English "Crown Shirt," for which the local terminology "Krama Sheti" appears to have been substituted.

The new *etibo* took closely after its forerunner in not having a collar, and in always having a cloth loop at the center of the back yoke. Its sleeves have buttons, not buttonholes for links; this change accommodates the decreased concern for prestige among younger men, although a shirt pocket was added to permit display of colorful handkerchiefs. *Etibo* is worn only with a single stud, as opposed to three worn with the *woko* and four with the *doni*. It can also be worn with any pair of trousers, although an injiri wrapper is the only correct accompaniment to the garment when one is dressing formally as Kalabari.

The *etibo* has become the focus of connoisseurship of *injiri*-tying styles because it allows more of the wrapper to be seen. Skill is required to manipulate the slim gingham piece (*injiri ikiba*), two yards long and one yard wide. Tying the cloth around the waist must be carefully done in order that the wrapper does not appear to be tied carelessly and too loosely, thus inviting a comment about careless appearance (*biri ayi sima*). Normally the bottom edge of the injiri wrapper should be at least 2 inches above the instep (*buo ikara*). However, this general rule is offset by the opportunity to display a variety of cloth tying styles that modify the rule, indicating the wearer as one thoroughly at home with cultural knowledge and etiquette of men's dress as discussed later.

v. Describing the *Attigra*

The *attigra* ensemble does not fit into the set of four which we have described that marks the Kalabari political hierarchy, but derives its great importance simply as the foremost ceremonial or dancing garb of the Kalabari as leisure-loving people. The *attigra* also attests to the primacy the Kalabari give to culture over politics, for cultural events have continued to be important and resilient in Kalabari life even as their political structure has become subordinated to that of the larger polity of Nigeria. The contrived dazzle of an *attigra* outfit is, therefore, another Kalabari original, along with its companion *ajibulu* hat that produces an effect of a balance in bulk. One informant described the wearer of this hat as holding forth like a masquerade, and amply filling the vista with his dazzle upon appearing (Erekosima, 1989:339).

Attigra is the Kalabari designation for a Northern Nigerian, handwoven cotton robe with Arab-influenced embellishments of embroidery that came into Kalabari hands before the country of Nigeria came into being. The Kalabari word "*attigra*" is formed as an elision of the usage "Atta Igarra," which derives from the words "Attah of Igalla." This king of an ancient kingdom at the northern limits of the Niger Delta (Miles, 1936) with which the Kalabari chiefs carried on their early trade was described by informants as the donor of the outfit to his contemporary Kalabari nobility, and the dress was then named after him. A more fashionable contemporary version is made from velvet material that is imported from India, usually embroidered with gold or silver threads. The *attigra* is primarily distinguished by having open sleeves that are about one third the length of the garment. The rich fabrics used are cut amply to give bulk to the wearer and to provide an image of the wearer as munificent. Matching velvet material is tied as a wrapper beneath the velvet *attigra* and shows below its hem, where it reaches to the lower calf or ankle. If the homespun variety of *attigra* from Northern Nigeria is chosen, then a matching wrapper of gingham plaid cloth called *injiri* is worn.

To wear the early form of *attigra*, for instance, a man must have either an English top-hat or the imposing indigenous creation of the ajibulu hat. A circlet of tiger's teeth (*siri aka*) or of cowry shells around the neck is a required accessory to accentuate the *ajibulu* hat. The contemporary velvet version is usually worn with an *ajibulu* and layers of coral beads bedecking the neck, imported mainly from Italy. Underneath either gown, the man must wear a European-style long-sleeved shirt and underneath that, a singlet (cotton u-neck, knit undershirt). It is normal to wear heavy gold rings on several fingers with this outfit.

Because shoes are viewed as restrictive of dance steps, being barefoot is preferred; but if shoes are worn, socks are generally not worn. To complete this outfit, a decorated fan (*ye biri efenge*) should be held in the right hand, and an elephant tusk (*oworowo*) or other material of tusk shape, made of glass or cowry shells, must be held in the left hand. Walking sticks and canes are not used when wearing *attigra*. . . .

Political Change and Its Influence on Kalabari Men's Dress

As the power of the king and the chiefs as Heads of the Canoe-Houses began to wane under the impact of British colonialism, their control over those under them became lessened. Subordinates of the actual Heads of War-Canoe Houses got to be appointed by the British administrator in certain cases to exercise power over everyone following an administrative change in the 1920's. The move spelt a death-knell to Kalabari traditional authority and initiated a marked era of individualism. The rule of the previous indigenous political regime collapsed accordingly, and along with it went strict adherence to some of the practices it had sustained, including those related to dress as a visible expression of sociopolitical rank. Not only were Kalabari men generally relieved of their previous allegiance but they had an opportunity to pursue broader identities and affinities when they were ushered into a new framework of an independent Nigerian state in 1960. Consequently changes, not only in aspects of the clothing that constitute Kalabari men's dress ensembles, but also in their patterns of use, have occurred. The old order has changed and its significant symbols have been diminished. We have identified six changes in the aesthetic standards as follows:

1. The *attigra*, for instance, has been shown to have changed from a traditional handwoven cotton material with stitched-on designs to richly embroidered, factory-produced velvets worn with heavy coral beads. This style, which was introduced from about 1914, also came with a distinctive, Indian-Sikh type of headgear having a streamer running down the back. This form of dress may not be strictly considered contemporary given the time of its introduction by people like Chief Charles Inko-Tariah, but it is not traditional. It may be labeled simply as a modern response to current industrial life in contrast to the life of the trader during the mercantile era. It particularly reflected the incidence of personal style as a result of pronounced individuation in Kalabari society.

2. The *ebu* as it is used today by chiefs shows the impact of modern trends. Partly because its cotton material

is lighter than that of the woolen *doni* and is more suited to the tropical conditions of the delta climate, and also because it is less demanding to wear in terms of required accompanying accessories, virtually any chief wears it on choice today with little adherence to established protocol.

3. The *doni*, too, is more regularly worn with shoes today as all chiefs are not expected to be expert dancers as they were in the past, and showing off the feet for dancing has not retained its importance. The several long gold chains that were frequently found worn with the *doni* in pictures of earlier chiefs seem to have, in turn, disappeared. There is a greater orientation toward economy and practical personal considerations, and less involvement with group norms and display.

A new form of dress is appearing on Kalabari users, called *kala doni* (the mini-*doni*). It is virtually like the doni or sometimes the contemporary *etibo*, except that it is often made of light woolen material instead of white cotton. It has the characteristic Kalabari decorations for a *doni* put on it. These are, in particular, the decorated chest in the form of *sangolo* (fish-gill) or *lada* (ladder) frills on both sides of the strip marking the button-holes. Then there is the flap (*bele*) sewn on underneath the strip. This outfit dispenses, however, with requirements like being worn with a shirt underneath it.

Kalabari chiefs are increasingly found wearing this dress as semi-formal out-door gear instead of the *woko*. A few chiefs, of course, condemn the use of the newfangled kala-doni that has neither place nor fit.

4. The *woko* is innovatively worn today with trousers that are made of the same material as the top garment. Previously a white or khaki *woko* or one made with some plain woolen material would be preferably worn with in-jiri, or else trousers of serge or wool that only color-matched the upper apparel.

The *woko* is also being worn now by Kalabari young men (rather than being seen as the outfit suitable only for their elders) with a lace inner shirt (similar to the Yoruba men's buba that is topped by an agbada upper garment). This innovation is apparently reflective of fairly comfortable financial standing, and may be a contemporary Nigerian fashion. The neighboring Ikwerre people appear to be the ones introducing this fashion.

Another aspect of this trend toward greater fancifulness among Kalabari young men is the increasing introduction of decorative chest designs on their *woko*. This was clearly unacceptable earlier to the Kalabari, and was more characteristic of their neighbors like the Okrika.

An even more forbidden practice that middle class Kalabari young men are beginning to adopt is the wearing of *woko* sewn with *blangidi* of *feni* or *namasibi*. This is the fashion that has been popularized by men in the Bonny, Opobo, and Nembe societies. The Kalabari men adopting this form of dress still use these only in the townships, and wear them because they are more expensive (showing them to be well-off) and are colorful, unlike the generally drab type preferred traditionally by Kalabari etiquette.

5. The contemporary *etibo*, as shown earlier, is a rather recent innovation starting around the 1950s, which got its latest boost since the 1970s. In addition to its adoption, the younger generation of Kalabari males who are about the age of new secondary-school graduates are avid consumers of this etibo as well as other fashions that are emerging as Nigerian forms.

6. Adoptions have arisen from other Nigerian traditional forms of dress, such as those of the Yoruba or Hausa. One case is the *danshiki* or short, embroidered or tie-dyed garment that is worn with trousers. Other examples are the loose-fitting *buba* or *bariga* gowns derived from Yoruba and Hausa sources respectively worn with tight trousers that hug the legs closely, usually made of the same material as the upper garment. New fashionable versions of such male dress which appear in silk or other modern fabrics, cut to contemporary taste by Nigerian fashion designers, are quite frequently seen being worn by Kalabari young men on the streets of Buguma.

Thus Kalabari young men have rapidly adopted some of the styles and current fashions from their various neighbors. Male members of Kalabari society appear committed to explore new options of identity as represented through dress, no doubt as a continuation of their willingness to combine cultural development with a political focus.

In the setting of contemporary Nigeria, however, it is not only the Kalabari who are responding to change and adopting the forms of dress of their neighbors. Kalabari men's dress is also being widely adopted by new users outside its traditional cultural circles. Many young men from the communities of Ahoada, Abua, Engenni, Ikwerre and several other places of the Rivers State have been seen wearing the *etibo* to go to work in government offices, or stroll about on the streets of Port Harcourt, the state capital in the 1980s and 1990s. Similarly, the "traditional dress" claimed by the bulk of hinterland Igbos today, of a *woko* (*jompa*) made with *blangidi*, *feni*, or *namasibi* design and worn with regular European trousers, comes from the societies of the Niger Delta city-states. Contemporary Igbo chiefs have also shown a penchant for adornment in the <u>doni</u> worn with Benin or Yoruba-derived headgear especially, and beads, when passing off as royalty.

Our research indicates not only Kalabari responsiveness but also their aesthetic creativity as a result of their interaction with members of Western society and exposure to items of dress from Western culture. The Kalabari also interacted extensively with members of other African cultures and were exposed to other African items of dress. Systematic, aesthetic rules of dress developed. These were clearly understood and practiced within Kalabari society, for the dress codes paralleled the social order. However, there has been a recent loosening of attachment to the protocols of Kalabari appearance. As our data suggest, even the chiefs or community leaders have not been conservative custodians of the "good, old ways." However, there is no suggestion that the Kalabari, as purveyors of an African aesthetic in men's dress have diminished interest. Vigorous interest and animated discussion continues among them concerning the "rights" and "wrongs" of dress and the appropriateness of new styles and fashions.

We have added another dimension to the aesthetic knowledge relating to dress as cultural heritage in the diverse continent that is Africa. We caution against oversimplified or glib references to and descriptions about "Africa" through profiles that are too limited and narrow. In addition, with the concept of the Cultural Authentication Process, we have demonstrated that the use of materials and artifacts from other cultures is a dynamic and creative process that indicates strong aesthetic commitments and choices.

Endnotes

1. Our data were collected during eight field trips by Eicher, three of which overlapped with Erekosima who is Kalabari. He collected data as participant observer over a number of years. In addition, his dissertation research included an eight week, detailed pedestrian survey, 20 formally structured interviews, 10 informal interviews as well as conversation and discussion about men's dress. Eicher's research included taped interviews, informal discussion recorded in written field notes, and slides documenting daily and ceremonial dress for all eight trips.

2. Elsewhere (Eicher and Erekosima, 1993). In the context of African cultural continuity and change with the Nigerian Kalabari as a case study, we analyzed Kalabari use of textiles and dress to communicate social order in four main dimensions: 1) The order of sociopolitical ranks as assigned to a predominately male gender, 2) The reproductive and socialization order that is predominately female, 3) The ritual order of funerals, and 4) The ceremonial order of masquerades and dance.

3. A parallel example is given by Ingold, Riches, and Woodburn (1991) who claim that for the Kalahari Bushmen of southern Africa, the two perspectives of utility and art merge in regard to the animals they hunt for food and also depict in their exquisite cave paintings.

4. For details see Erekosima, 1989.

5. This was during Eicher's first visit to the island of Buguma. She took a photograph of the King and his Council of Chiefs at that time that documents this statement.

References

Adams, Capt. J. (1823). *Remarks on the country extending from Cape Palmas to the River Congo*. London.

Alagoa, E. J. (1970). Long distance trade and states in the Niger Delta. *Journal of African History, 2*(3), 405–419.

Asante, M. K. (1993). Location theory and African aesthetics, in Welsh-Asante, K., Ed., *The African aesthetic: Keeper of the tradition*. Westport, CN: Greenwood Press.

Blake, J. H. (1942) Ed. *Europeans in West Africa, 1450–1560*. London: Hakluyt Society.

Daly, M. C. (1984). *Kalabari female appearance and the tradition of Iria*. Unpublished doctoral dissertation, University of Minnesota, Minneapolis.

Daly, M. C., Eicher, J. B., and Erekosima, T. V. [1986] Male and female artistry in Kalabari dress. *African Arts, 19*(3), 48–51, 83.

Davis, R. (1954). English foreign trade, 1600–1700. *Economic History Review, 7*, 150–166.

Dike, O. (1956). *Trade and politics in the Niger Delta 1830–1885: An introduction to the economics and political history of Nigeria* (1962 ed.). London: Oxford University Press.

Eicher, J. B. and Erekosima, T. V. (1993, April). *Taste and 19th Century patterns of textile use among the Kalabari of Nigeria*. Paper presented at Dartmouth College conference "Cloth, the World Economy, and the Artisan: Textile Manufacturing and Marketing in South Asia and Africa, 1780–1950", Hanover, New Hampshire.

Erekosima, T. V. (1989). *Analysis of a learning resource for political integration applicable to Nigerian secondary school social studies: The case of Kalabari men's traditional dress.* Unpublished doctoral dissertation, Catholic University of America, Washington, D.C.

Erekosima, T. V. and Eicher, J. B. (1981, February). Kalabari cut-thread and pulled-thread cloth: An example of cultural authentication. *African Arts, 14*(2), 8–51, 81.

Evelyn, H. (1968). *History of Costume: Tracing Spanish, Dutch, English and French costumes from peasant to court attire from the 15th century to the 20th century.* Vols. 1–3.

Evenson, S. (1991). *The manufacture of madras in South India and its export to West Africa: A case study.* Unpublished Master's thesis, University of Minnesota, Minneapolis.

Evenson, S. (1993, April). *The export of Indian madras plaids: Shifting patterns of exchange.* Paper presented at Dartmouth College Conference "Cloth, the World Economy, and the Artisan: Textile Manufacturing and Marketing in South Asia and Africa, 1780–1950," Hanover, New Hampshire.

Ingold, T., Riches, D., and Woodburn, J., (1991). *Hunters and Gatherers,* New York: Berg Publishers.

Jenewari, C. E. (1976). Identification of ethnolinguistic units in early European records: The case of Kalabari. *Journal of Niger Delta Studies, 1,* 9–18.

Jones, G. I. (1963). *The trading states of the Oil Rivers: A study of political development in eastern Nigeria.* London: Oxford University Press.

Michelman, S. O. (1987). *Kalabari female and male aesthetics: A comparative visual analysis.* Unpublished Master's thesis, University of Minnesota, Minneapolis.

Michelman, S. O. and Erekosima, T. V. (1992). Kalabari dress in Nigeria: Visual analysis and gender implications. In R. Barnes and J. B. Eicher (Eds.), *Dress and gender: Making and meaning in cultural context.* Oxford and Providence: Berg Publishers.

Miles, C, (1936). A Nigerian kingdom: Some notes on the Igalla Tribe in Nigeria and their divine king. *Journal of the Royal Anthropological Institute of Great Britain and Ireland, 66,* 393–435.

Ogilvy, J. (1970). *Africa, being an accurate description.* London: Translation of Dapper.

Pereira, D. P. (1937). *Esmeraldo de situo orbis.* London: Hakluyt Society.

Piaget, J. and Inhelder, B. (1969). *The psychology of the child.* New York: Basic Books.

Ryder, A. F. C. (1965). Dutch trade on the Nigerian coast during the 17th century. *Journal of the Historical Society of Nigeria, 3,* 195–210.

Talbot, P. A. (1932). *Tribes of the Niger Delta: Their religion and customs* (1967 ed.). New York: Barnes and Noble.

Vogt, J. (1975). Notes on the Portuguese cloth trade in West Africa, 1480–1540. *International Journal of African Historical Studies, 8*(4), 623–651.

Wass, B. M. (1975). *Yoruba dress: A systematic case study of five generations of Lagos family.* Unpublished doctoral dissertation, Michigan State University, East Lansing.

Welsh-Asante, K. (Ed.). (1993). *The African aesthetic: Keeper of the tradition.* Westport, CN: Greenwood Press.

Source: Excerpted from *ITAA Special Publication #7.* Reprinted by permission of the International Textile & Apparel Association.

IV.2 THE SWEETNESS OF FAT:
HEALTH, PROCREATION, AND SOCIABILITY IN RURAL JAMAICA
Elisa J. Sobo

In the United States there is a well-known saying that you can't be too rich or too thin, but in rural Jamaica, amassing wealth and keeping slim have antisocial connotations. Ideally, relatives provide for each other, sharing money and food. Because kin share wealth, no one gets rich; because kin feed each other, no one becomes thin. Cultural logic has it that people firmly tied into a network of kin are always plump and never wealthy.

Especially when not well liked, thin individuals who are neither sick nor poor are seen by their fellow villagers as antisocial and *mean* or stingy.[1] These individuals do not create and maintain relationships through gift-giving and exchange. They hoard rather than share their resources. Their slender bodies bespeak their socially subversive natures: thinness indicates a lack of nurturant characteristics and of moist, procreative vitality—things on which a community's reproduction depends.

Rural Jamaicans' negative ideas about thinness are linked with their ideas about health. As Sheets-Johnstone points out, "The concept of the body in any culture and at any time is shaped by medical beliefs and practices" (1992:133). Notions concerning health can profoundly influence the interactive and symbolic communications made through out bodies. These notions greatly influence the ideal standards set for bodies and affect the ways we experience, care for, and shape (or try to shape) our bodies and those of others (Browner 1985; Ehrenreich and English 1979; Nichter and Nichter 1987; Payer 1988).

Importantly, notions about health are—in a very tangible way—notions about body ideals, and they have social meaning. Health traditions do not exist in isolation from other realms of culture, such as gender relations and economy (Farmer 1988; Jordanova 1980; Martin 1987), nor are they isolated from extracultural influences, such as ecology and global political conditions (Farmer 1992; Vaughan 1991). Often, ideas about the body and its health are put forward as rationalizations or ideological supports for conditions, such as class and gender inequalities or personal maladjustments (e.g., Kleinman 1980; Laws et al. 1985; Lock 1989; Scheper-

Hughes 1992). In this chapter, I describe the traditional health beliefs that inform understandings of body shape in rural Jamaica, and I trace the connections between these ideas and Jamaican understandings about sociability (see also Sobo 1993b).

For rural Jamaicans, the ideal body is plump with vital fluids, and maintaining the flow of substances through the body is essential for good health. Taylor (1992) argues that an emphasis on maintaining a continuous, unimpeded flow through the body is common among those who value reciprocity and emphasize the obligation kin have to share with each other, which Jamaicans do. Sickness occurs when the flow is blocked or otherwise "anomic" (Taylor's term, 1988); individual pathologies are homologous with social pathologies, caused by disturbances in the flow of mutual support and aid. . . .

Methods and Setting

Research for this chapter was carried out in a coastal village of about eight hundred people in the parish of Portland, where I lived for a year in 1988 and 1989 (see Sobo 1993b for a full account of the research). Data were collected through participant-observation and interviews that took place in community settings and in private yards. I also solicited drawings of the body's inner workings from participants.

Like most Jamaicans, the majority of the villagers were impoverished descendants of enslaved West Africans.[3] Many engaged in small-scale gardening, yet few could manage on this alone. To supplement their meager incomes, people also took in wash, hired themselves out for odd jobs, engaged in part-time petty trade like selling oranges, and relied on relatives for help.

Jamaican villages typically consist of people brought together by ancestry, or by proximity to a shop or postal agency. In some cases, they are organized around an estate where village members sell their labor. Households are often matrifocal (see Sargent and Harris 1992: 523; Smith 1988: 7–8), and nonlegal conjugal unions and visiting relationships (in which partners reside separately) are common. Houses are generally made of wood planks and zinc sheeting; often they lack plumbing and electricity. People build their houses as far apart as possible, but they are usually still within yelling distance of a neighbor.

Body Basics

Jamaicans value large size, and they *build* the body by eating. Different foods turn into different bodily components as needed, either for growth or to replenish substances lost through work and other activities. Comestibles that do not so much build the body but serve to make people feel full are called *food*. In common Jamaican usage, *food* means only tubers—belly-filling starches not seen as otherwise nutritious.

Blood is the most vital and the most meaning-invested bodily component. It comes in several types. When unqualified by adjective or context, the word *blood* means the red kind, built from thick, dark liquid items such as soup, stout, and porridge and from reddish edibles such as tomatoes. Red wine, also referred to as tonic wine, can be used to build blood, and blood is sometimes called wine. Some think that the blood of *meat-kind*, such as pork or beef, is directly incorporated into human blood; others say that meat's juices build blood. Wild hog meat, redder than regular pork, is supernutritious and vitality boosting because wild hogs feed mainly on red-colored roots, said to be beneficial blood-builders. People point out that meat-kind left sitting out or from which all vital fluid has drained (as when cooked for a long time in soup) loses its nutritive value and serves only as *food* to *fill belly*.

Sinews, another type of blood, comes from okra, fish eyes, and other pale slimy foods, such as egg white or the gelatinous portions of boiled cow skin or hoof. *Sinews* refers to, among other substances, the joint lubricant that biomedical specialists call synovial fluid, which resembles egg white. Sinews is essential for smooth joint movements and steady nerves. The functioning of the eyes depends on sinews too: the eyes are filled with it and glide left and right and open and shut with its aid. Sinews, also associated with procreation, is found in sexual effluvia and breast milk. Many call sinews *white blood*, as opposed to red.

People have less elaborate ideas about what edibles other bodily components are made of. Vitamins, contained in the strengthening tablets and tonics that are popular and easily available, build and fatten. Some Jamaicans argue that meat-kind builds muscles. Most agree that corn meal builds flesh. A few suggest that milk builds bones, at least in children but not necessarily in adults whose bones have already developed.

The most important part of the inner body is the *belly*, where blood is made. This big cavity or bag extends from just below the breast to the pelvis. The belly is full of bags and tubes, such as the *baby bag* and the *urine tube*. A main conduit leads from the top of the body through the belly to the bottom, with tributary bags and tubes along its length. Sometimes, tube and bag connections are not tightly coupled. A substance improperly propelled can meander off course, slide into an unsuitable tube or bag, lodge, and cause problems.

Food Sharing and Social Relations

In reviewing the social significance and health benefits of big size cross-culturally. Cassidy (1991) found that socially dominant individuals who are enmeshed in sound relationships are usually large. Bigness tends to ensure reproductive success and survival in times of scarcity, and plumpness is generally considered attractive. According to Brink (1989), such is the case in many of the West African societies from which people were taken to Jamaica as slaves. In these societies, those who can afford to do so seclude their adolescent girls in special "fattening rooms" and, after a period of ritual education and heavy eating, the girls emerge fat, attractive, and nubile.

In Jamaica, where a respected adult is called a *big man* or a *big woman*, good relations involve food sharing, and people on good terms with others are large. Weight loss signals social neglect. A Jamaican seeing someone grow thin wonders about the sorts of life stresses that have caused the weight loss (rather than offering congratulations for it and attributing it to a "good" diet, as many middle- and upper-class people in the United States do).

In the ideal Jamaican world, mothers feed their children, kin feed kin, and lovers feed each other. Men involved with women put on pounds from the meals their women serve them. Likewise, women display the status of their relations with their measurements; the breadth of the *backside* is particularly symbolic. Villagers noticed when a woman named Meg began to *mauger down* (get thin, grow meager) and lose her once-broad bottom; they knew—and they broadcast—that her affair with a rich old man had ended as she apparently no longer received food or resources from him.

Food sharing is a part of good social relations, and it, as well as other kinds of sharing, ends when people fall out. People with *something between them* (i.e., strife) both cease to give gifts and refuse to receive them. For instance, they refuse food from each other (often because they fear being poisoned; Sobo 1992). A disruption in the flow of goods and services signals the disintegration of a relationship.[4] Sister Penny knew that her relationship with Mister Edward was in trouble on the day he refused and sent back the dinner that she regularly prepared and had her daughter carry down the road to him at his mother's house, where he lived.

Good relationships and good eating go hand in hand, but plumpness depends on more than mere food—it depends on pleasant household conditions. Living in a household where *the conditions* (that is, the group dynamics) are harmonious and agreeable ensures both physical and mental vitality. No matter what they eat, unhappy people who live where *the conditions* are unpleasant lack energy, and they *draw down* (get thin) as fat *melts off*.

When a young woman named Amy lost weight and grew lackadaisical, villagers knew that she and her live-in boyfriend were having problems. Indeed, Amy's young man had taken up with his sister's boyfriend's sister. Amy's declining physical state and lethargy indicated this change in the conditions. Even with plenty to eat, a person in her position would lack energy and pull down mauger because, as one woman commenting on the situation explained, "people with worries can't fat." . . .

Thinness

Like cleanliness and balance, plumpness is important for good health. Few rural Jamaicans want to reduce. Diet foods and beverages are only seen in bigger towns. People generally assume that they are meant for diabetics, because no one should wish to be thin. Thinness is associated with ideas antithetical to those that "good" fat connotes. Thinness and fatness are to each other as the lean, dry, white meat of a chicken is to its fatty, moist, dark parts—the parts that most eaters prefer. Ideas about infertility and unkindness are linked with the notion of thinness. People taunt others by saying they will dry up and grow thin from antisocial *meanness*. Their observations of the elite and those in power who are light-skinned and whom they see as thin reinforce this belief.

Thin people are understood to lack the vitality associated with moist and juicy "good" fat. Like an erect penis or breasts plumped with milk, like a fat juicy mango, the body seems more vital when full of fluid and large in size. While too much blood or food overburdens the body and can rot and cause sickness, as noted above, *dry* bodies have no vital nature at all (low levels of bodily fluids and fat can lead women to have trouble conceiving). A slim person, especially a slim woman, is called *mauger*—mea-

ger and powerless—as if not alive at all and, like a mummy or an empty husk, far beyond that powerfully dangerous state of decay. A thin, dry body reveals a person's non-nurturant nature and his or her lack of social commitment. . . .

Sociable Plumpness

Meanings attributed to personal appearances are context-specific, and circumstances such as personal vendettas affect which meanings get linked with whose bodies. The good as well as the bad can be highlighted. For example, a thin individual can escape ridicule if his or her svelte shape is caused by working long and hard for the benefit of others. As a general rule, however, and especially when a slender person's behavior gives others cause to disparage him or her, the thin person is cast in a bad light as lacking the willingness and the capability for giving life. The individual is branded selfish and mean, and people point to his or her body's dry, husklike nature as a confirmation of these antisocial, nonprocreative leanings. Like the person too rich, the person too thin—whether through circumstance or choice—is seen to shirk his or her social duties to share with and nurture kin. The thin individual is seen to contribute little to society, and the shape of his or her body is used to bear witness to this.

The condition of a person's relationships is inferred by others when they observe and comment on the state of his or her body. In turn, people try to mold the shapes of their bodies in order to affect the inferences other people make. Bordo (1990) explores mainstream U.S. dieting and body sculpting through exercise with this notion (and typical U.S. ideas about self-control) in mind. While mainstream Americans prefer regimes that lead to thinness, Jamaicans attempt to fatten their bodies (and those of others whom they *care* or *response* for). Both types of manipulations are efforts to construct and promote oneself as a sociable, desirable individual within a given cultural context.

A fuller understanding of the interactive dimension of body sculpting and the reading of bodily shape opens one avenue to the study of the cultural aspects of ideas about nutrition and the standards for physical beauty and health. The study of traditional health beliefs and social and moral ideals exposes much of the logic behind body shapes and the regimes people attempt to adhere to in order to affect them.

The life-affirming, prosocial associations of the plump body in Jamaica are expressed in the traditional saying that "What don't fat, kill; what don't kill, fat."

Foods or events either fatten or bring death. People try to stay fat because the plump body is healthily dilated with vital lifeblood and because it suggests to others that one is kind, sociable, and happy to fulfill obligations to kin and community. Thinness is ultimately linked with death, but the fat person's body is richly fertile, and the fat person is judged a nurturant and constructive member of a thriving network of interdependent kin.

Acknowledgments

This chapter is part of a larger study of Jamaican health traditions and their uses; ideas and information presented in this chapter are discussed more fully in my book, *One Blood* (Sobo 1993b) and in various articles (1993a, 1992, 1995). The research and much of the writing were carried out with the guidance of F. G. Bailey. Tom Csordas, Mark Nichter, Nicole Sault, William Wedenoja, and Drexel Woodson provided thoughtful comments and suggestions.

Notes

1. Many of the institutional and structural barriers to class mobility remain invisible to most of the people that they hinder, and blame for impoverishment is frequently placed on fellow villagers (Austin 1984).

3. For this reason, and because many urban dwellers were born rurally (see Brody 1981: 101) or have rural mind-sets (Brody 1981: 69), and also because many elite, modernized Jamaicans retain traditional beliefs, I often refer to the participants simply as Jamaicans.

4. Drexel Woodson notes that people who have had a falling out—people with *something between them* (strife)—do, in fact, continue to give and receive *something*—ire, enmity, or spleen. The flow of enmity between individuals marks a shift in the relationship's character (D. Woodson, personal communication).

References

Bordo, S. 1990. "Reading the Slender Body." In *Body/Politics*, ed. M. Jacobus, E. F. Keller, and S. Shuttleworth, pp. 83–112. New York: Routledge.

Brink, P. J. 1989. "The Fattening Room among the Annang of Nigeria." *Medical Anthropology* 12:131–143.

Brody, E. 1981. *Sex, Contraception, and Motherhood in Jamaica*. Cambridge: Harvard University Press.

Browner, C. H. 1985. "Traditional Techniques for Diagnosis, Treatment, and Control of Pregnancy in Cali, Colombia." In *Women's Medicine: A Cross-Cultural Study of Indigenous Fertility Regulations*, ed. L. F. Newman, pp. 99–123. New Brunswick, N.J.: Rutgers University Press.

Cassidy, C. M. 1991. "The Good Body: When Bigger is Better." *Medical Anthropology* 13:181–213.

Ehrenreich, B., and D. English. 1979. *For Her Own Good: 150 Years of the Experts' Advice to Women*. London: Pluto Press.

Farmer, P. 1988. "Bad Blood, Spoiled Milk: Bodily Fluids as Moral Barometers in Rural Haiti." *American Ethnologist* 15(1):62–83.

———. 1992. *AIDS and Accusation: Haiti and the Geography of Blame*, Berkeley: University of California Press.

Jordanova, L. J. 1980. "Natural Facts: A Historical Perspective on Science and Sexuality." In *Nature, Culture, and Gender*, ed. C. P. MacCormack and M. Strathern, pp. 42–69. New York: Cambridge University Press.

Kleinman, A. 1980. *Patients and Healers in the Context of Culture: An Exploration of the Borderland between Anthropology, Medicine, and Psychiatry*. Berkeley: University of California Press.

Laws, S., V. Hay, and A. Eagan. 1985. *Seeing Red: The Politics of Premenstrual Tension*. London: Hutchinson.

Lock, M. 1989. "Words of Fear, Words of Power: Nerves and the Awakening of Political Consciousness." *Medical Anthropology* 11:79–90.

Martin, E. 1987. *The Woman in the Body: A Cultural Analysis of Reproduction*. Boston: Beacon Press.

Nichter, M., and M. Nichter. 1987. "Cultural Notions of Fertility in South Asia and Their Impact on Sri Lankan Family Planning Practices." *Human Organization* 46(1):18–27.

Payer, L. 1988. *Medicine and Culture: Varieties of Treatment in the United States, England, West Germany, and France*. New York: Henry Holt.

Sargent, C., and M. Harris. 1992. "Gender Ideology, Child Rearing, and Child Health in Jamaica." *American Ethnologist* 19:523–537.

Scheper-Hughes, N. 1992. *Death without Weeping: The Violence of Everyday Life in Brazil*. Los Angeles: University of California Press.

Smith, R. T. 1988. *Kinship and Class in the West Indies: A Genealogical Study of Jamaica and Guyana*. New York: Cambridge University Press.

Sobo, E. J. 1992. " 'Unclean Deeds': Menstrual Taboos and Binding 'Ties' in Rural Jamaica." In *Anthropological Approaches to the Study of Ethnomedicine*, ed. M. Nichter, pp. 101–126. New York: Gordon and Breach.

———. 1993a. "Bodies, Kin, and Flow: Family Planning in Rural Jamaica." *Medical Anthropology Quarterly* 7(1):50–73.

———. 1993b. *One Blood: The Jamaican Body*. Albany: State University of New York Press.

———. 1995. "Abortion Traditions in Rural Jamaica." *Social Science and Medicine*.

Taylor, C. C. 1988. "The Concept of Flow in Rwandan Popular Medicine." *Social Science and Medicine* 27(12):1343–1348.

———. 1992. "The Harp That Plays by Itself." In *Anthropological Approaches to the Study of Ethno-medicine*, ed. M. Nichter, pp. 127–147. New York: Gordon and Breach.

Vaughan, M. 1991. *Curing Their Ills: Colonial Power and African Illness*. Stanford: Stanford University Press.

Source: Nicole Sault (Ed.). (1994) *Many Mirrors: Body Image and Social Relations*. Piscataway, N.J.: Rutgers University Press. Reprinted with the permission of the author.

IV.3 SCRUFFY IS BADGE OF PRIDE, BUT SOME PHYSICISTS LONG FOR COOL
By Malcolm W. Browne

Cops carry badges, doctors wear stethoscopes, royalty wield fly whisks and scepters, and prominent citizens of France display the rosette of the Legion d'Honneur in their buttonholes.

Even scientists sometimes like to proclaim their occupations with visible symbols, although finding unobstrusive ways to display (and celebrate) one's calling is becoming harder with the passing years.

There was a time when scientists, technicians, architects and engineers carried slide rules protruding from their jacket pockets. Slide rules were useful for making rough-and-ready calculations, of course, but they were also emblems of professional identity. Using all the scales on a good slide rule required some knowledge of logarithms, algebra and trigonometry, and the mere possession of one of these elegant instruments (especially a top-of-the-line Keuffel & Esser) was thought by some to suggest intelligence and education.

But with the advent of electronic calculators, slide rules vanished, and no substitute icon of professional status was available; plastic pocket protectors bulging with marking pens make rotten badges.

For physicists, however, there was another, albeit subtle, way to proclaim membership in a professional community that scorns conventional social images. Physicists often get into the habit of looking somewhat scruffy, and scruffiness in itself is a badge.

Many people have noticed that a hint of limited means characterizes meetings of physicists, as it did at an international conference of particle physicists in Japan last month. A handful of university department chairmen wearing jackets and ties generally turn up at such gatherings, but for most of the other participants, the dress is faded jeans, sneakers or climbing boots, sport shirts (frequently worn under backpacks stuffed with papers and books) and sometimes, baseball caps.

Caps emblazoned with the logo of the John Deere tractor maker are sometimes seen around physics meetings these days, although the most famous of physicists' headgear was Dr. J. Robert Oppenheimer's trademark porkpie hat, worn while he was director of Los Alamos National Laboratory.

The impoverished look of many physicists, particularly young ones, is not merely an affectation. Good jobs in physics—the kind that lead to university tenure—are few, and scientists living on post-doctoral fellowships often have trouble making ends meet. The cost of travel to a physics conference leaves little money for frills, and casual style is not merely an expression of Caltech physics chic; it is dictated by very tight budgets.

But the simple attire favored by many physicists has come under assault. In a letter published this month by the magazine *Physics Today*, Dr. Jeremy Levy of the University of Pittsburgh has called upon colleagues to clean up their act, not only by modernizing the conference gadgetry used at their meetings but by dressing to look like influential citizens.

"For too long," Dr. Levy wrote, "we have neglected our own shabby appearance, all the time wondering why enrollment in our discipline is dropping. We need to educate the public about the significance, the importance and the fascination of fundamental and applied physics research. And we need to look cool doing it."

Dr. Levy is not alone in this view. In his book on the art of oral scientific presentation, "Dazzle 'Em With Style," Dr. Robert R. H. Anholt of Duke University's Medical Center wrote that proper attire is as important for job applicants in the sciences and speakers at scientific meetings as white coats are for doctors making their rounds.

"Although most physicians do not need to wear a white coat unless they are in the habit of frequently spilling their coffee," he wrote, "many patients would feel uncomfortable if the attending physician did not wear one. The white coat is part of the professional image."

Dr. Levy deplored a perceived shortage at physics meetings of Internet facilities, laser pointers, liquid-crystal projection displays and other up-to-date devices, saying that these deficits have a negative effect on the public image of physicists. "We have discovered and invented so many wonderful things, yet we look and act like losers," he wrote.

But style critics like Dr. Levy overlook an important aspect of professional shabbiness of attire: It has become a part of the scientist's public persona.

Nearly a century ago Arthur Conan Doyle, a medical doctor who avidly followed developments in science, endowed one of his fictional characters, Professor Summerlee in "The Lost World," with a stereotypical image that still resonates. "Among his minor peculiarities," Doyle wrote of Professor Summerlee, "are that he is careless as to his attire" and "unclean in his person."

This was hardly true of famous physicists in the early part of the 20th century, at least when they posed for photographs. Lord Rutherford, Niels Bohr, Wolfgang Pauli and other giants of the profession appear impeccably tailored. Even Albert Einstein in early photographs is dressed in dark suits with starched wing collars and a watch chain.

But fashion changed.

In Einstein's later life the world began to see the tousle-haired creator of relativity theory wearing a sweatshirt, pedaling a bicycle or roguishly sticking out his tongue.

Dr. Levy's admonition to physicists to dress better is likely to have a mixed reception.

Physicists, having spent as many years pursuing an education and an apprenticeship as have medical doctors, often find themselves with ill-paid jobs and lacking the prestige society accords to healers.

Most people have no idea what physicists do, and their public image, physicists acknowledge, needs polishing. But physics is a kind of priesthood, in which a semblance of poverty is more a badge of pride than a dishonor.

"I don't pay much attention to clothes," a young experimenter remarked, "but I'd look silly wearing a suit at a physics meeting, even if I had room for one in my suitcase. I guess we care more about substance than image."

IV.4 SIGNATURE STYLE: FALLING OFF THE FASHION TRAIN WITH FRIDA, GEORGIA AND LOUISE
Jo Ann C. Stabb

Three famous artists of the twentieth century—Georgia O'Keeffe, Louise Nevelson and Frida Kahlo—deliberately used their clothing to extend their artistic expression and develop a 'signature style,' evidence that personality characteristics and personal presentation can be integrated and synthesized into an 'authentic self'. Highly independent and individualistic, each of these three women developed a personal image through the use of costume elements that transcended fashion. Their 'signature style' also related to their philosophy of art and paralleled their other visual creative endeavors. All three resisted fashion in clothing as they resisted merging into the "isms" of 20th century of art movements, yet their generation was the first to bring a significant female presence to the visual arts.

Georgia O'Keeffe

Georgia O'Keeffe (1888–1986) is well known for her paintings of enlarged flower forms, sculptural desert landscapes and stark natural elements interpreted with great freedom ranging from precise realism to poetic abstraction. This same "paring down" to essential shapes and forms characterized her dress as well, which was dominated by stark black and white shapes capturing the essence of form.

Born the eldest daughter in a family of strong matriarchs in a mid-western farming community, Georgia was part of the legacy of capable frontier women. She sought independence and solitude from the beginning . . . it was her nature. She also gravitated to her father and appropriated many of his tastes and habits, according to her biographer Laurie Lisle. "She preferred his love of the land, for instance, to her mother's world of learning." (Lisle, 1980, pg. 13)

As a child, the solitary hours of play nurtured her imagination and they also strengthened her natural inclination to have things her own way. She wanted to be distinct. For instance, only wearing white stockings when her little sisters were not wearing theirs. "From the time I was a little girl, if my sisters wore their hair braided, I wouldn't wear mine braided," Georgia recalled. "If they wore ribbons, I wouldn't. And I'd think they'd look better without it too." (Lisle, 1980, pg. 11).

Numerous accounts attest to her preference for plain, dark or black clothing alternating with white in the summer. This started early, perhaps as a result of being enrolled in a convent school and later an Episcopal Institute where school uniforms dominated her wardrobe. But those were rather brief episodes of imposed uniform dressing.

She was enrolled in art classes in which she did charcoal drawings—rich black on white and declared her intent to become an artist by age 13. In 1914 at age 26 she studied in New York for nine months and met Alfred Stieglitz, famed photographer and owner of Gallery 291. Through this association she became aware of the powerful abstraction in black-and-white photography. All of these elements helped to form her basic aesthetic sensibilities.

Later, as she accepted a teaching position in South Carolina, she continued to pursue her art work. Dissatisfied, she realized that there were abstract shapes in her mind, integral to her imagination, unlike anything she had been taught. "This thing that is so close to you, often you never realize it's there," she explained later. "I visualize things very clearly. I could see a whole string of things I'd like to put down but I'd never thought of doing it because I'd never seen anything like it." Thus, toward the end of her twenty-seventh year she started all over again, in the simplest way, with charcoal. "It was like learning to walk," she recalled. (Lisle, 1980, pg. 66)

During that fall of 1916, Georgia taught two classes in design to younger students and afternoon classes in 'costuming' and 'interior decoration' to Home Economics majors at West Texas State Normal College. She later explained, "When I taught art, I taught it as the thing everyone has to use." She told them that there was "art in the line of a jacket and in the shape of a collar as well as in the way one addressed a letter, combed one's hair, or placed a window in a house." (Lisle, 1980, pg. 78) As the only teacher from the East, she was immediately typecast as a Bohemian by the staid community. For one thing, she preached the importance of straight lines in women's dress rather than the customary corseted curves of 1916. She herself always wore loose garments in either black or white, sometimes with a dark green smock." (Lisle, 1980, pg. 78)

She loved to walk, and tromped around in heavy, flat walking shoes, and usually just combed her dark hair straight back, caring little for conventional styles with curls. Although her emphasis on simplicity could be quite austere, she once confided to a friend that she lined her plain woolen skirts with pure silk, reflecting her deep sensuality that was most profoundly expressed in her paintings of flowers. And once when Georgia posed for a faculty photograph, she wore her habitual black dress with a white collar—but with a large flower flamboyantly pinned to the bodice. (Lisle, 1980, pg. 78)

It was the impact of the West Texas sky and the enormous expanse of space that inspired her boldest experiments in abstraction and simplification, resulting in a series of intensely colorful watercolors, despite Stieglitz's advice to stay with black and white. She had invented a way to express her intense response to nature: simple, straightforward shapes and colors, daring compositions, spontaneous and intuitive . . . for which Stieglitz held her first one-woman show in 1917, and which *The Christian Science Monitor* reviewer Henry Tyrrell hailed as [follows:] "Now perhaps for the first time in Art's History, the style is the woman." (Lisle, 1980, pg. 85).

Georgia O'Keeffe continued this life-long pursuit of documenting nature based on this breakthrough, with an emphasis on basic, fundamental forms, timeless and honest in her eyes, that similarly led her to prefer simple shapes for her clothing and personal appearance. By the time Stieglitz got to know Georgia, her signature black dress with a little touch of white at the throat was well established.

"She believed that, in order to paint, she felt she needed simplicity around her, to help keep her head clear and uncluttered. Georgia had sewn most of her own clothes out of the finest fabrics, often sewing when she wanted time to think. She made blouses from luxurious white silk, white cotton nightgowns with white embroidery and petticoats edged with white lace. She wore a black wool coat in cold weather with a collar that buttoned up to her chin and black gloves of the best leather. At one time she also wore a pair of black bloomers under a black tentlike tunic. "Throughout the years, when asked the reason for her monotone clothing—considered odd for a painter—she gave several answers all containing some truth. Once she said that if she began to choose colors to wear, she would have no time to pick any to paint. Another time she explained that she was so sensitive to color that if she wore a red dress, she would feel obliged to live up to its flamboyance. She claimed she like being cloaked in anonymity. "There's something about black," she remarked. "You feel hidden away in it." Deadly-serious black also served to transmit the message that she was not to be treated frivolously or flirtatiously. Also, she must have realized that if all her clothes were one color, they would match and she would achieve a look of maximum elegance with a minimum of time and money." (Lisle, 1980, pg. 147) Black cloaks and kimono type dresses became her 'uniform.'

Even her penthouse apartment in New York City was extremely spare, as were her subsequent homes in New Mexico, with minimal furnishings indicating this same precision and paring down of her environment so she could focus on making art. As she stated: "Nothing is less real than realism—details are confusing. It is only by selection, by elimination, by emphasis, that we get the real meaning of things." (Lisle, 1980, pg. 278)

Louise Nevelson

Louise Nevelson (1899–1988) represents the opposite of Georgia O'Keeffe's paring down to elemental forms, in both dress and art work. She has been hailed as the "Empress of Modern Art" and "Queen of Assemblage," a term for the invented forms from found objects and materials that she incorporated into sculpture.

Born in a provincial Russian town near Kiev in 1899, she immigrated to America with her family when she was five. They settled in Rockland, Maine, where as foreigners and Jews, they were ostracized by Eastern society.

According to her biographer Laurie Lisle, her father built a business on scavenging and peddling junk. She called them "antiques." Even as a child, she gathered pebbles, sticks, marbles and other trinkets to display in little boxes. Her scavenging instinct derived directly from his example. From her mother, who indulged herself and her three daughters in elegant fabrics and fashion, she got her sense of "flair." "My mother knew fashion, she knew the line." (Nevelson, 1976, pg. 13) This ostentation presented an image directly opposite of what Rocklanders respected: modesty, understatement, and Puritan propriety. As Louise recalled, "That was her art, her pride and her job . . . my mother wanted us to dress like Queens." (Lisle, 1990, pg. 30)

Louise absorbed the lesson that extravagant display was a form of feminine self-expression. Disliking the tight-fitting, restrictive fashions of the day, and too inventive and impatient to sew from a pattern or wait for a dress-maker to stitch a garment, she often created outfits by arranging and pinning fabrics, tying white embroidered aprons around herself like blouses and wearing store-bought hats at unusual angles on her head. (Lisle, 1990, pg. 31)

At age twenty, to escape from Maine, she married a wealthy New York businessman and moved to Manhattan. There she studied art with some of the best teachers of the time, and remembers that they dressed with a distinction that appealed to her—especially a "Miss Cleveland" who had a memorable purple hat and matching coat. (Nevelson, 1976, pg. 24)

As Nevelson states in her book of recollections entitled *Dawns + Dusks* edited by Diana MacKown, "I had the foresight to understand that all of these arts were pretty much one. All of them were essential; one supported the other. I felt I was fortifying the whole structure." (Nevelson, 1976, pg. 35) She supplemented her visual art lessons with dance and movement instruction.

As her dedication to art grew, she abandoned her husband and neglected her son. She left her child with her mother and traveled to Europe to study art, and in 1931 went to Hans Hofmann in Germany, where she really began to understand Cubism. As she states: "I saw the first Picassos and it gave me a definition of structure of the world and every object in the world. Without Picasso giving us the cube, I would not have freed myself for my own work. Picasso changed our thinking and he gave us structure—of course when you recognize that, you can vary it, but that's your foundation. It gave me order in a visual sense. It gave me definition for the rest of my life around the world. Hofmann taught positive and negative space. Light and shadow. The cube transcends and translates nature into structure." (Nevelson, 1976, pg. 44)

Nevelson felt that everything she did was a creative act . . . and that she could pursue her life as an exciting, glamorous woman. "I could have played the role of the down-and-out artist, but I wanted to have fun . . . and I always dressed with a flair." (Nevelson, 1976, pg. 70) In some ways, the ultra-feminine persona that she created through the lavish presentation of herself contradicted her massive, powerful sculptures that carried a masculine assertiveness. However, upon analyzing the design elements and the creative process, there are many parallels, including intuitive combinations of disparate elements that create a holistic harmony.

During the Second World War, a period of great poverty and despair, she began using found objects. "Anywhere I found wood, I took it home and started working with it. I had all this wood lying around and I began to move it around, I began to compose. I began to respond to the 'livingness' of wood—its textures." As she states, "I feel that what people call by the word scavenger is really a resurrection. It's a translation and a transformation, both. That's the magic." (Nevelson, 1976, pg. 76) She would then paint these compositions all one color— black, white or gold—to unify the multiplicity of parts. "I gave the work order; I neutralized it by one tone . . . to see the forms more clearly." (Nevelson, 1976, pg. 123)

As Nevelson explained, "The excitement of my life is when I'm working and making decisions; when I put things together and how I put them together. I call that the livingness or essence of aliveness." (Nevelson, 1976, pg. 123) "When I clean my house, now for me, it is just not cleaning. When I have a cleaning woman or man, they do it to make the house clean. I do it for a higher order. Same thing when I put myself together or create something to wear. I love to put things together. My whole life is one big collage. Every time I put on clothes, I am creating a picture, a living picture, for myself . . . I like clothes that are upholstered. I like that you build up your clothes, and build up, and even the hat. You can do it two-dimensionally, you can do it three-dimensionally, and every time I do it, when I go back to my work, I use that again." (Nevelson, 1976, pg. 184)

"When I went to the warehouse, I didn't want to wear anything that I couldn't mess up. I had a red skirt that was an Indian squaw skirt that I got in Albuquerque some years ago. Then I put on a blue denim, washed-out jacket. And then there was a belt, it's red, it's leather, and I put it around my neck like a necklace. Then I put one of those laboring kerchiefs around my head. Blue, I think. I created a harmony. If anyone'd seen me, I was dressed according to my dimension. I feel the clothes that I have worn all my life have been freedom, a stamp of freedom—because I've never conformed to what is being worn." (Nevelson, 1976, pg. 185)

"Let's break tradition. That's exactly why I dress the way I do. I love old robes. I think I was the first person to wear a sixteenth century Mandarin Chinese robe on top of a blue denim work shirt. I project something. For me clothes and presentation of self is a projection of a total personality." (Nevelson, 1976, pg. 187)

Another feature of her signature style for which she became famous were her frankly fake eyelashes. "I don't use anything else: only my eyes. I don't feel dressed without my eyelashes. I don't wear one pair . . . I glue several pairs together and then put them on. I like it and it's dramatic, so why not?" (Nevelson, 1976, pg. 187)

As she approached the age of seventy, she spent a great deal of time and thought on her appearance. In earlier years she had been accustomed to the easy attention and power a strikingly beautiful woman commands. She continued to dramatize her appearance more than ever in the last two decades of her life. The designer Scassi offered to dress her after seeing her wearing a floor length sable coat over a pair of blue jeans and work shirt. Showing her tailored black suits, Louise remarked that she was "not the Scarsdale matron type." He remembered replying "You are absolutely right! You are the Empress of Art—and we must dress you as the Empress of Art." "Now you've got it" she agreed. (Lisle, 1990, pg. 263)

Rapport was established as he offered rich brocades, silks and velvets. He designed an evening gown from a geometric pattern of cut black velvet backed by black satin that resembled a Nevelson creation. Subsequent evening outfits made up of black tulle, black sequins, black lace and other opulent materials enabled Louise to maintain elegance and self-expression simultaneously. She collaborated with Scaasi on her wardrobe, but he set the limits. She was one of a very small number of his customers whose urge for self-expression was stronger than their concern for appropriateness. According to him, he would frequently say, "No, I think we've gone far enough." (Lisle, 1990, pg. 264)

She was described as "some ancient Gypsy who'd wandered from her wagon" . . . as she took to wearing a Moroccan chieftain's coat or a fringed and feathered African ceremonial robe. She liked to mix prints and patterns as well as styles, a mink-trimmed purple snakeskin jacket with denim work clothes, a gold lame skirt with a lumberjack shirt. She dressed in layers—a silk jersey Scaasi jumpsuit as long johns ("the most expensive underwear that anyone had ever worn," Scaasi proclaimed with exasperation) under an evening gown for warmth. She also wore an enormous black straw hat, a ten-gallon cowboy hat, or a velvet jockey cap with formal evening clothes. He realized that she was a unique creature who dressed in a kind of environment," he recalled. Louise proclaimed, "I'm what you call a real collage!" (Lisle, 1990, pg. 265)

Frida Kahlo

Frida Kahlo (1907–1954), the third example of signature style, was born in Mexico, the product of a marriage between a German immigrant father and a Mexican mother.

Throughout her life, she relentlessly sought to establish her identity through a series of 55 self portraits painted between the age of 19 and the time of her death at age 46. In these works, the combination of surrealistic imagery, her Mexican heritage and her political beliefs were synthesized and symbolized through costume elements. Her strong feminist stance also played a role. But it was her husband, Diego Rivera, who first suggested she wear the native Tehuana costumes "to enhance her magnetic beauty" and well as hide her right leg which had been deformed by polio when she was six years old. These costumes became a theme in her work that expressed her own biological, cultural, and historical heritage.

"In every facet of life, Kahlo took a stance of defiance—against conventions of behavior and dress, against circumscribed roles for women, against foreign imperialism and political oppression and finally against pain, illness and death." (Lowe, 1991, p. 20) She suffered a series of drastic physical incapacities, including the case of polio, and a near fatal accident at age eighteen, when the bus she was riding collided with a trolley car. The impact caused a metal handrail to break loose and she was pierced through the pelvis. The accident had deep psychic and physical consequences for the remainder of her life. Although she recovered sufficiently to lead a fairly active and productive life, she was continually plagued by pain and a series of frequent (a total of 32) surgeries during the next 28 years.

Her use of the Tehuana Mexican costume dating from 1929 after her marriage at age 22 was combined with other indigenous elements—especially jewelry made from fragments of Aztec and Mayan beads—to capture and express her political support for the Mexican populist movement. Over and over again in life and in her paintings she portrayed herself in the dramatic costume of her Mexican heritage, the long embroidered frilled dresses and fringed shawls (*rebozos*) characteristic of the Tehuantepec region of Mexico, a region known for its strong matriarchal culture. Her artwork was associated with the popular Mexican '*retablos*' or votive paintings in which a stage in the tragedy of the victim is illustrated. These involved graphic expressions of her introspective fears using physically specific symbols, often clothing. "While she undoubtedly did wish to make a point about her cultural heritage, she also made the costume her very own individual uniform. In certain paintings the dress is used as a personal symbol, and in the case of *My Dress Hangs There* (1933) and *Memory* (1937), it is made to stand in as a surrogate figure for Kahlo herself. Kahlo's depiction of herself in long dresses was also not confined to Tehuantepec or Mexican clothes. In a number of pictures, such as *Frida and Diego Rivera* (1931), her dress is more whimsically archaic than archetypally regional. In *The Two Fridas* (1939), she wears a Victorian lace blouse reminiscent of that worn by her own mother and grandmother, and contrasts it with a relatively simple, bold Tehuana-style dress. In both paintings her costume is idiosyncratic, combining rustic, populist, old-fashioned, folkish and historical elements" into a deliberately individual look. (Milner, 1995, pg. 14)

The individualistic nature of her costume parallels her artwork and reflects a synthesis of personal philosophy, values, and a clear understanding of the legacy she would leave. As it became synonymous with her self-image, it enabled Kahlo to achieve and control her construction of self as both subject and object. In this synergy, it became part of her self-affirming iconography.

In each case, these individual artists transcended the fashion of their time and reflected complete integration with their aesthetic and creative philosophies. Their various signature styles evoke a true synthesis of an 'authentic self' whose visual presentation parallels their other creative endeavors.

As a final test of this integrative process, when asked what they would like to be in their next life, they each responded accordingly:

> Georgia O'Keeffe: "A blonde, And I would like to have a very high soprano voice." (Kotz, 1977, pg. 40).

> Louise Nevelson: "Louise Nevelson!" (Nevelson, 1976, pg. 190)

> Frida Kahlo, in the final entry in her diary, wrote: "I hope the leaving is joyful—and I hope never to return." (Kahlo, 1995, pg. 285)

Bibliography

Berry, M. (1988). Georgia O'Keeffe. New York: Chelsea House.

Garcia, R. (1983). *Frida Kahlo: A Bibliography*. Berkeley: University of California Press.

Giboire, C. (Ed.). (1990). *Lovingly, Georgia: The Complete Correspondence of Georgia O'Keeffe and Anita Pollitzer*. New York: Simon & Schuster Inc.

Grimberg, S. (1989). *Frida Kahlo*, Dallas: Southern Methodist University.

Herrera, H. (1983). *Frida: A Biography of Frida Kahlo*, New York: Harper & Row.

Kahlo, F. (1995). *The Diary of Frida Kahlo: An Intimate Self-Portrait*, New York: Harry Abrams.

Kotz, M.L. (1977). "A day with Georgia O'Keeffe," *ARTnews, 76*(10), December, pp. 36–45.

Lisle, L. (1990). *Louise Nevelson, A Passionate Life*, New York: Summit Books.

Lisle, L. (1990). *Portrait of an Artist: A Biography of Georgia O'Keeffe*, New York: Seaview Books.

Lowe, S.M. (1991). *Frida Kahlo*, New York: Universe Publishing.

Milner, F. (1995). *Frida Kahlo*, New York: Smithmark.

Nevelson, L. (1976). *Dawns + Dusks*, D. MacKown (Ed.), New York: Charles Scribner's Sons.

Peters, S. W. (1991). *Becoming O'Keeffe: The Early Years*, New York: Abbeville Press.

Pollitzer, A. (1988). *A Woman on Paper: Georgia O'Keefe*, New York: Simon & Schuster.

Schwartz, C. (1983). *Nevelson and O'Keeffe: Independents of the Twentieth Century*, New York: Nassau County Museum of Fine Art.

Stellweg, C. (1992). *Frida Kahlo: The Camera Seduced*, San Francisco, Chronicle Books.

Source: Reprinted with the permission of the author.

Part Five Dress and the Future

Throughout this text we have proposed a systematic method of studying dress. We have introduced concepts such as the definition of dress, the classification system, and the concept of scales of society, which can be used as tools to understand our dress, the dress of others, and to avoid ethnocentric bias. Just as we used these tools to examine the aesthetics of dress in the past and present all over the world, we can also use these concepts to think about the future of dress.

In Chapter 9, we distinguished between global-scale society and global-scale culture. We argued that in many ways we already live in a highly integrated global culture, but a single global-scale society was an idea that existed only in science fiction. We can see efforts at unification, such as the implementation of the European Community with its single currency, but complete globalization may not occur in our lifetimes. Whether or not we come to live in a global-scale society, we will be able to count on the use of world dress, national dress, and ethnic dress as a distinctive human behavior to help us find our place in the world.

14

Your Future and Dress

OBJECTIVES

To consider concepts used in the study of dress to think about the future of dress.

To recognize that dress is a dynamic aspect of culture.

To consider how you will use the concepts and examples presented in this text in your life and work.

WHAT WILL DRESS BE like in the future? Will dress be necessary? Will current trends continue, move in new and different directions, or backtrack? When the authors of the first edition of this textbook considered these questions, they forecast increasing mechanization in apparel production, the development of new fibers and methods of clothing production, and what we now recognize as world dress (Roach & Eicher, 1973). In addition, they highlighted the predictions of designer John Weitz, who speculated that in the year 2068 we will live in a temperature-controlled, dirt-free environment and we will not have to consider seasonal changes in selecting our clothing. Weitz predicted that both men and women will wear two one-piece garments, one called "unders," with the features of the kinds of undergarments we wear today, and the other, "overs," which will be decorative and will be used as a status symbol ("What fashion designer," 1968, p. 199). Weitz's conception is illustrated in Figure 14.1. With the prevalence of leggings, tights, and sports bras for women and sweat pants and T-shirts for both men and women, topped with designer sweaters and jackets, we might say this prediction has already come to pass. Perhaps we will cycle away from this look, and cycle back again by 2068.

One way to think about the *future of dress* is to return to Table 2.1, the Scale of World Cultures. What traits will describe societies in the future? What are the implications for dress? We conclude with some of our speculations.

POPULATION, RESIDENCE, AND DRESS

As global-scale societies expand, they may break up into smaller units again. Their citizens may retreat, geographically or ideologically, to less settled areas to find their roots as a way of dealing with global-scale expansion, thus creating new kinds of small-scale societies. In the United States, as many sections of urban centers have become increasingly dense, dirty, and unsafe, city dwellers have moved their families to less-crowded, rural settings (Pooley, 1997). Because late-twentieth-century communication, information, and transportation systems are so well-developed, people living away from urban centers can easily stay connected to the rest of the world. If increasing numbers of workers telecommute, a daily work wardrobe of business dress, as thought of in the late 1990s, may become obsolete. However, if the line between casual and work wear blurs, perhaps the difference between casual and evening wear will sharpen. People may decide to dress up when they go out, initiating a return to stylish, joyful, formal wear for any nonwork event.

Dress could become even more international, both in its similarity and in its difference. As more people travel for business and pleasure and as more designers roam the globe for inspiration, the exchange of ideas will be even more dynamic than at present. An international business ensemble may emerge, with compo-

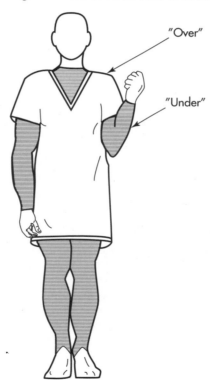

"Over"

"Under"

Figure 14.1
In 1968, the designer John Weitz predicted this style of dress for men and women in 2068. How do his speculations compare to dress today?

nents to satisfy every cultural proscription. At the same time, people may discover the benefits of national or ethnic dress, and the marketing of national
dress can become more commonplace, as exemplified by this 1997 catalogue
offering in Figure 14.2.

Tourism may even become the vehicle for the preservation of cultures,
which often is expressed by members of ethnic groups who want to emphasize
their ethnic heritage and identity. As the residents of large-scale societies with
many small-scale cultures embedded in them understand that tourists wish to
visit their countries largely for what makes them different, or even exotic, government officials may undertake programs that preserve the lifeways of all
their citizens, including textile production methods done by hand and ethnic
dress ensembles. Citizens may rediscover for themselves ways of dressing that
had lost favor in the expansion from small- to large-scale. They may choose to
wear ethnic or historical dress for their own satisfaction, not as a stereotype to
attract tourists, but as a genuine return to dress practices that enhance spiritual
and group unity. We can see an example of this in the Dakota teenager who not
only learns the Jingle Dance, but also makes her own costume and beads the

Figure 14.2
At the turn of the twenty-
first century, the marketing of national and ethnic
dress to an international
market is common. The
cut and construction of
this *salwar kameez* distributed by the J. Peterman
catalogue, and purchased
by one of the authors, is
almost identical to those
tailor-made in India for
use as daily dress.

headband, moccasins, and pouch by hand in traditional Santee Sioux motifs. In the postmodern era, when many people are disenchanted with politics and feel their voices in government are not heard, rebuilding community and ethnic foundations may seem to be a better use of time and energy. Dress is one place to start.

TECHNOLOGY, ECONOMY, AND DRESS

The manufacturing and distribution of dress products will be profoundly altered by applications of technology. If fossil fuels and mass production are characteristics of global-scale culture, perhaps microchip and custom production will characterize production in the future as people desire more individuality.

Synthetic fibers and fabrics, such as Tencel and Supplex, have been engineered to be almost as comfortable and aesthetically pleasing as natural fibers. Even polyester has been improved so that is it almost indistinguishable from silk.

Jane Schneider (1994) recounts the ins and outs of polyester within the context of global fiber competition. She remembers when synthetic fabrics were hailed as liberating modern miracles for their quick drying, no-iron qualities and brilliant hues. She notes the late-twentieth-century distaste for polyester and traces it to other cultural movements, such as the "back to nature" values of the 1960s hippie counter-culture; oversaturation of polyester in the 1970s leading to "fashion indigestion" and to intense global competition from natural fiber coalitions. By the end of the twentieth century, engineering synthetic fibers to meet specific end uses was viewed as vital to the national interest. Schneider concludes that shifting economic and technological systems work in tandem with changing consumer values.

Natural fibers have been engineered and processed to be as easy care and durable as synthetics. One kind of cotton, called Fox Fiber, grows naturally in colors. Through sophisticated plant breeding, a range of hues has been developed, all of them able to be processed with modern textile machines. Currently, the hues are very muted, but they become brighter with each washing. Perhaps in the future the range of colors will be even broader and the intensity of colors, brighter. Natural fibers might also be genetically engineered with antibacterial properties to fight the odors associated with activewear or to provide protection from ultraviolet light. In any case, it is likely that textile chemists and geneticists will combine their talents to create fibers, yarns, and fabrics with built-in properties that combine durability, ease of care, and aesthetic properties in ways we can barely imagine. Overall, many innovations, such as organically grown, naturally colored cotton and the processes used to create Tencel, have much less negative impact on the environment than traditional agricultural and dyeing methods. Earth-friendly products already have a market in the United States. As the quantity of natural resources dwindles, earth-friendly garments may be the only choice. In any case, these fiber wars will play themselves out on the runways of the twenty-first century.

In the future, we may see a return to custom-made apparel. For example, The Custom Foot in White Plains, New York, offers shoes individually made with the help of electronics. The customer selects a shoe style and a leather or fabric choice from among the many hundreds of prototypes and samples in the store. An **infrared scanner** takes a photograph of each foot and a computer converts specific data points on each photograph into measurements. Each foot is scanned separately, so feet that are different shapes or sizes can be accommodated easily. The measurements and the order are sent electronically to the factory in Tuscany, Italy, and ideally, in 3 to 4 weeks, the shoes arrive (Abend, 1996, pp. 49–54; Lehmann-Haupt, 1998, pp. 168–169). Levi Strauss offers a similar **mass-customization** service with its Personal Pair jeans. In this case, the customer tries on a prototype pair of jeans to determine individual fit and styling preferences. The jeans are cut and assembled individually for each customer and are sent to the customer's home in about 2 weeks. It is only a matter of time before the price of mass-customization is reduced, especially with the enhanced application of computer technology and laser cutting, which can cut individual garments in seconds. In the future, production processes may be so fully integrated with consumer preferences that the customer will be able to add or subtract individual style and detail preferences, adding flare to a skirt or a distinctive lapel to a jacket. The customer will be the designer.

The infrared methods of taking body measurements described here will be improved to capture many more measurements quickly. As a result, it will be possible to fit garments more closely to the body than previously possible with industrial production. One reason that garments in recent years have been so loosely fitted is to make the assembly-line production process more streamlined and therefore less costly, keeping clothing prices low. With mass-customization, this concern is eliminated and garments can been fitted to the exact preferences of the consumer, as illustrated in Figure 14.3. Historically, fashion change follows technological change. Perhaps infrared scanning and mass-customization will create a trend toward more fitted clothing. We can see the beginning of this trend in the blending of Lycra into tailored garments, permitting greater fit with improved comfort.

When we consider the application of computer technology to dress, there is no limit to the imagination. Garments might be fitted with microchips that light up a ball gown as you walk, allow you to listen to your favorite radio station on a dress with electronic field sensors sewn into its stripes, or inform you of your heart rate as you exercise (Thrasher, 1998, p. 124). In the future, could we wear a sound effect, such as the waves lapping on the shore, as part of dress the way we wear cologne?

Along with mass customization and telecommunication, **on-line shopping**, making selections and purchases on the World Wide Web will have a profound effect on the distribution of dress. Shopping centers and mega-malls may still be the place to see and be seen in one's sartorial efforts, but the nature of retailing will change. Storefronts will be used to display only samples and prototypes, eliminating crowded racks and clearance corners. Salespeople may be required to be more knowledgeable about fit and aesthetic considerations,

Figure 14.3
The application of computer technology to every phase of garment manufacturing makes mass-customization possible. The equipment shown here scans the customer's body and produces a three-dimensional image that provides information for a customized pattern.

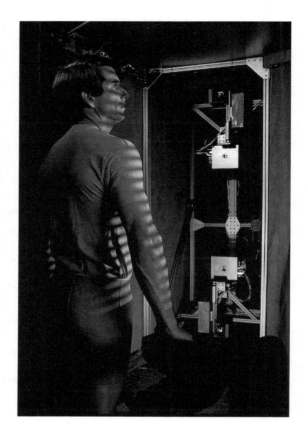

in addition to sales techniques. Shopping on-line may become so interactive that the customer can see three-dimensional images of garments on a body with similar proportions.

SOCIAL STRUCTURE, DIVISION OF LABOR, AND DRESS

As each country finds its niche in the global apparel economy, the division of labor among countries probably will expand. Each country might specialize in particular production methods with workers contributing their unique expertise to the production process, resulting in articles of dress that are an optimum balance between cost and quality for the consumer. In the global assembly line, not all articles of dress may be made by machine. Different countries may choose to return to training their workers in textile and apparel technologies from the heritage of their pasts, preferring to invigorate textile traditions and the artisans that produce them. One current example is India, with an economic policy that supports handwoven textiles, such as *saris* from the town of

Kanchipuram and block prints from Bagru for the domestic market. In the future, appreciation for these textile traditions may become the hallmark of taste. Handcrafted textiles and apparel may be imported by the affluent to serve as indicators and repositories of wealth. A global assembly line will not necessarily lead to homogenization of dress, and it may revive small-scale traditions.

If many parts of the production process occur globally, production managers will need to be multilingual and fluent in the language of dress. Global dress etiquette may emerge, along with a global travel uniform, that emphasizes respect for the people of any country one might travel through. Such etiquette would include a broad understanding of different cultural requirements concerning body modesty, along with various cultural definitions of sexual attractiveness and gender ideals. It will also include cultural variations in dress gestures of respect and subordination for purposes of correctly behaving in international venues.

The cost of cosmetic surgery may continue to decrease and may become so affordable as to become a standard and an expectation. As a result, individuals may quickly tire of the ability to live up to cultural ideals of beauty and the inevitable similarity in appearance. Perhaps they will begin sculpting their bodies, as did Michael Jackson and the woman surgically altering her face and body to look like Barbie, into their own highly individual idea of beauty. By contrast, rebellious youth might use cosmetic surgery as a form of protest that challenges established beauty ideals, much as tattooing and body piercing are now popular.

If forestalling the visible signs of aging becomes commonplace, the natural aging process may become such a novelty that it will begin to be valued as a unique expression of a life lived and of personal identity. Appreciation of the role of genetics and heredity in our lives appears to be increasing. Perhaps the U.S. obsession with the tall, slim female body and the muscular, athletic male body will subside. People may learn to appreciate their bodies as expressions of their ethnic heritage.

Exquisite materials and workmanship may replace the use of designer labels as markers of garment cost and communicators of individual social rank. In an information-based society, knowledge of quality tailoring and dressmaking may supersede the more blatant ability to purchase a designer label as an indicator of status. Understated elegance may convey affiliation more than corporate logos.

At present, there are over four billion people living on our planet. Many countries are slowing the growth of their individual populations, but the earth's population is still growing (Naisbitt & Aburdene, 1990, p. 30). This poses an interesting question for the student of dress. Will people want to enhance their similarity to or their individuality from the surrounding masses? To keep one's individuality alive in a swelling crowd may require an amplification of dress—taking the possibilities of the classification system to its limits (Morris, 1985, p. 19). We have already witnessed fashion trends in fluorescent colors, big hair, and full-body tattoos. Against this urge to stand out is the need to communicate membership in a group, to feel that you are not truly alone and isolated in the masses. Today we often choose to wear team sweatshirts, jewelry with religious symbols, or details that highlight our ethnic heritage. How will the conflicting needs of expressing individuality and group identity play themselves out in an increasingly dense population?

In the future, we may seek membership in several self-styled small-scale cultures, each with a unique style of dress. Who we are at the moment might be encapsulated in our choice of the group to which we will conform. Or, total individuality may be the standard. We might be expected to craft our own unique presentation that captures and communicates who we are as individuals, as suggested by Dennis Rodman's dress choices in Figure 14.4. Others will evaluate the success of our ensembles not by how successfully we live up to a cultural ideal, but by how accurately the ensemble represents who we really are. In any case, we may see the beginning of new ideas about what it means to express individuality and group membership.

Figure 14.4
In the future, total individuality in dress may be the norm. Celebrities like Dennis Rodman already use flamboyant dress to develop an individualistic public image.

POLITY, IDEOLOGY, AND DRESS

If patriotism and a deep regard for one's country characterizes the global-scale society, perhaps a revival of appreciation for ethnic origin will become the defining orientation for most people in the future. This may mean that in the United States, not only new immigrants but also third- and fourth-generation Americans of various heritages will incorporate more visible elements of their heritage into everyday life, including dress (Sontag & Dugger, 1998). Two forces may facilitate this flowering of ethnically-based differences in dress within all nations around the globe. First, improved communications means immigrants and their descendants will be better able to stay in touch with or reconnect with their "home" culture, particularly within diaspora groups. Second, as people jockey for position in a global culture, they may find that their ethnic origins give them higher status or a greater sense of belonging than their current nationality.

Multinational corporations with facilities and interests in many countries may increase their power and in the future play a larger role in international peacekeeping than individual governments or supranational organizations such as NATO or the United Nations. If the production of goods takes place in many different countries, political instability in one country could hold up production and trade to all the others. As countries become more dependent on each other for products, it is to be hoped that peace will flourish. During peaceful times, artisans of all types prosper, including artisans of dress.

YOUR FUTURE AND DRESS

In this text, we have attempted to identify similarities in the ways people throughout the world and over time create and use dress. We use dress as physical and spiritual protection, to establish social roles and cultural identity, and as a means of expressing individual and group aesthetic sensibilities. Thus, we can begin to see beyond our surface diversity to an understanding of what it means to be human. This appreciation of the potential of dress will be useful to you in any field of study or work you pursue.

Any aspect of apparel design, manufacturing, and merchandising requires a focused eye on the target customer. We know there is a world full of people with varying body proportions, skin tones, and aesthetic preferences. It is the job of the designer, product developer, marketer, and retailer to be sensitive to the needs and tastes of diverse markets. As Gwen O'Neal (1998) implied in her study of the African-American aesthetic, you probably will not be able to sell Laura Ashley English country garden prints to many African-American customers. In fact one designer for Nike contrasted the North American and European markets for athletic wear by describing differences in the proportional use of prints. She stated that in the United States, prints are usually used as accents to solid-color body wear. In Europe, solid colors are used as accents to overall-print body wear. Moreover, sensitivity to cultural values can help prevent gaffes, such as the use of holy verses from the Koran as motifs on sexually alluring dresses, as seen in Figure 14.5. Instead, garments that respect local customs can help pave the way for international goodwill, as exemplified by the dress of the late Diana, Princess of Wales, in Figure 14.6.

An examination of the similarities and differences in dress among cultural groups is useful in teaching and museum work. When students can identify different types of dress with similar uses or similar types of dress with different meanings, they will develop an appreciation for the range of human experience. Examining how dress has changed over time in response to changing ideals and standards of beauty, technological innovation, and world events brings history and the arts alive, especially when historical or reproduction garments can be touched, examined, or even tried on. The study of dress can also be used informally by parents and teachers to help children and young adults make sense of complex concepts such as gender, race, conformity, and individuality.

Figure 14.5
Concepts presented in this text can help anyone living and working in a global community recognize and avoid inappropriate choices related to dress, such as the designer Karl Lagerfeld's use of verses from the Koran on a sexually provocative gown.

Figure 14.6
When Diana, the Princess of Wales, visited the Al-Azhar mosque in Cairo, she demonstrated respect for Islamic cultural values by wearing a modest dress buttoned high on the neck and with full-length sleeves, covering her head, and removing her shoes.

While it is unlikely that we will ever dress completely alike or completely differently, it seems certain that we will retain the use of dress as a tool for survival, as a communicator of social status and role, and as an expression of aesthetic values as part of the human condition. Dress is a powerful force in human interaction. Although taken for granted by many people and not always appreciated as a significant aspect of human life, dress conveys a myriad of ideas about the wearers and their perspectives about their world.

SUMMARY

One way to think about dress in the future is to consider the concepts described throughout this text and speculate on their use in Table 2.1. In the future, as global societies expand and the world's population grows, people may create their own small-scale cultures or return to an appreciation of their ethnic origins. In this case, dress will emphasize a specific group identity. Dress could also become more international, both in its similarities and in its differences. Some people might choose to wear a particular national dress, even if they are not from that country. An international business ensemble may emerge, with components to satisfy every cultural proscription.

The manufacturing and distribution of dress products will be profoundly altered by the application of technology. Fibers and fabrics will be developed with properties that make them more comfortable and easy care than they are now. Garments will be custom-made, with the customer specifying fit, fabric, and styling details. Mass-customization and on-line shopping will have a profound change on apparel retailing. Storefronts will display only samples and prototypes from which the customer can make selections, prior to placing an order on-line.

Cultural ideas about ideals and standards of personal appearance may change as the cost of cosmetic surgery decreases and the appreciation of ethnic identity increases. Exquisite materials and workmanship may replace the use of designer labels as status markers. How we express individuality and group membership will change as patriotism is subsumed by ethnic identity. Multi-national corporations will take over the task of international peacekeeping in an effort to maintain global systems of production and trade, enhancing the exchange of ideas about who we are and how dress can be used to find our places in the world.

STUDY TOOLS

Important Terms

infrared scanner
mass-customization
on-line shopping

Discussion Questions

1. Using Table 2.1, the Scale of World Cultures, add a fourth column titled "Future." Fill in the table, speculating on the traits of a possible global-scale culture in the future and implications for dress.
2. Review the concepts discussed in the text and readings. How can the use of these concepts make speculations about the future of dress plausible?
3. Based on your readings and discussions in class, identify current social trends that are expressed, in part, through dress. How will these trends play out in the near future and how will dress convey the shifts?
4. How will the cultural analysis of dress help you in your career by aiding in (1) understanding the dress of your co-workers and people you come in contact with, (2) understanding how to dress yourself, and (3) solving problems in the designing, manufacturing, or retailing of dress?
5. How do you think the progress of globalization of the societies of the world will affect the designing, manufacturing, and retailing of dress? What role do you think cultural differences in dress in the future will play in your dress and your career?

6. Brainstorm some fanciful ideas of dress in the future.
7. Discuss the ways in which the costumes for *Star Trek* both reflected contemporaneous fashion and predicted dress trends of the future. In what ways did the costumes successfully predict fashion trends that later came into being? In what ways did they fail?

Activities

1. Read a book that predicts directions for the new century, such as *Megatrends 2000* by John Naisbitt and Patricia Aburdene or *Generations: The History of America's Future, 1584–2069* by William Strauss and Neil Howe. Discuss implications for dress.
2. View a movie that takes place in the future. Describe what people are wearing. How did the types of materials and forms of dress convey a futuristic setting? Is it a pessimistic or optimistic view of the future? Speculate about why the costume designer and director selected the overall look.
3. Working individually or in small groups, and using expendable magazines, cut out photographs that exemplify the concepts addressed in this text and in class. Paste them onto a piece of poster board in any order that makes sense to you. Compare your results with the rest of the class. Did some concepts seem to have more impact on some people than others? Why? How will you use the concepts mastered from this text in the future?
4. Sketch and develop the specifications for an ensemble of the future. Consider the target customer's lifestyle and how and when the ensemble will be worn and engineered.

Reading for Part Five

V.1 COSMIC COUTURE
Elizabeth Snead

When *Star Trek* premiered in 1966, the cast made its debut boldly wearing what no one had worn before. The virile male crewmembers on board the starship Enterprise explored the universe in lean, body-hugging velour shirts and slim black pants. Their female colleagues were clad in incredibly tight, shockingly short, colorful mini-skirted uniforms paired with sexy, alien-kicking boots, while those seductive extraterrestrial vamps the crew often encountered wore revealing outfits that defied all laws of gravity.

In those days, the possibility of wearing such provocative clothing in professional situations seemed a trillion light-years away. Heavens, we didn't even know from Lycra back then!

Yet now, almost 30 years later, short, shiny, stretchy, see-through styles are commonplace in fashion-forward cities. Many women go to the mall, to work, or out on the town dressed like Lt. Uhura. And many men do the same in athletic, color-blocked, casual separates strikingly similar to Capt. Kirk's uniform.

So whodathunkit?

There's a theory in fashion that futurewear is never as far out (or as far off) as society presumes. And if *Star Trek* reflects what we may wear tomorrow, then it warrants close attention. What will hang in the closets of the 23rd and 24th centuries? We've seen a preview, and it looks pretty darn sexy. Or does it?

One need only watch the original *Star Trek's* spin-offs—*The Next Generation, Deep Space Nine*, and *Voyager*—to see that our society's fears and fantasies have changed immensely since the '60s. Gone are the sporty men's threads and revealing women's outfits of the original *Trek*. In their place is the almost ubiquitous unisex unitard. Has outer space been invaded by the intergalatic PC police?

Well, sort of.

Captain's Log, Stardate 1995: Robert Blackman is the costume designer for the current *Star Trek* TV series and movies. After 20 years in theater, he came aboard $5\frac{1}{2}$ years ago for the third season of *TNG* and is responsible for the evolution of the show's look. He admits, "The

minis and go-go boots are certainly stages that I have tried to get away from."

Oh, well. It was fun while it lasted.

And what fun it was. Gene Roddenberry recruited costume designer Bill Theiss to concoct clothing for the original *Trek*. A Stanford University design graduate. Theiss had been a costumer for *The Donna Reed Show, The Dick Van Dyke Show, My Favorite Martian*, and *General Hospital*. On *Star Trek*, however, he let his imagination run wild.

Theiss's male uniforms made the men of the Enterprise appear ready for action and adventure, but his designs for the women of *Trek* were decidedly less utilitarian. Strongly influenced by the work of the high-fashion designers of his day—Pierre Cardin's A-line constructions; Paco Rabanne's metal minis and chain-link shifts; Andre Courreges's color-blocked micro-minis, plastic boots, and fishnet stockings—Theiss outfitted his females in alluring and intriguing costumes that were nothing short of out-of-this-world. Those he designed for women aliens displayed incredible feats of artistry and construction—so much so that, in the '60s, viewers tuned in for the scantly clad space babes the way they now salivate over those fashion-conscious *Melrose Place* manhunters. Think of the original *Star Trek* as *Babewatch in Space*.

Remember the slashed, barely-there tunic worn by the sexy, green-tinted Orion slave woman (Susan Oliver) in "The Menagerie"? Or the gleaming gossamer Greek gown with *no* visible means of support worn by an Enterprise anthropologist (Leslie Parrish) in "Who Mourns for Adonais?" Both illustrated Theiss's theory that it was not the amount of skin shown that mattered: it was which parts of the body were revealed. Instead of exposing breasts and derrieres, he showed off unexpected areas of the female form such as rib cages, midriffs, lower backs, and hipbones.

"Bill [Theiss] was obviously influenced by his time, as I am by mine." says Blackman. "I modify the more avant-garde designers, specifically Issey Miyake, and Rei Kawakubo for Commes des Garcons."

Though some longtime Trekkers often bemoan the increasing political correctness of the attire for female characters in *TNG, DS9*, and *Voyager* (the women's revolution, it seems, really *is* being televised). Blackman explains his feminist view, "All the technicians here are primarily women, so you become sensitive to the issue. It's become my issue. My point of view about how the world should look has definitely changed."

As a result, he consistently puts women actors in body-molding stretch jumpsuits (he hates the word "catsuit"). "It's still provocative, still 'T&A,'" he says, "But I do look forward to a time when we can get rid of the very male notion of female sexuality."

Sometimes he'll slide a dress over the jumpsuit: "It allows a woman to do anything—sit, straddle, walk the hallways of a space station—without worrying that an alien wind will blow her skirt up."

Of course, it's hard to ignore the allure of sexually suggestive fashion when you're trying to attract 18- to 24-year-old male viewers. "But if I'm handed a script that says 'she's naked and he's not.' I complain that it makes no sense," says Blackman, who nevertheless admits that his favorite designs are "anything for Majel Barrett. She's a mature, sexy, and provocative woman, and those are delights from start to finish."

Blackman acknowledges the enormous task of constantly designing and redesigning 24th-century clothing. "Obviously, a handful of things are predetermined. And there's the matter of theatrics versus reality. I mean, you can't put everyone in NASA spacesuits. That's not very romantic or very heroic."

Heroic is a word that Blackman often uses. For men, he believes, the trait is established visually with costumes that sculpt impressively broad shoulders, muscular chests, and trim waists. "Realistically, most men have a roll here or there," he says. "But I believe that, in the future, humans will have a better understanding of nutrition than we do now and people will be more concerned about their bodies. They'll be more physically fit."

To suggest that scenario, Blackman gives male and female characters an equal amount of underpinning—though in different places. While the women's suits have interior padded bras with seamless cups, the men's middles are well-constricted. "I use a fabric called 'power net'—a middleweight girdle fabric—to make T-shirts that go under the suits, I also put two or three layers of it at the waist."

He puts to final rest the rumor that William Shatner ever wore a girdle. He will not wear a girdle, I tried. "He categorically did not, does not, will not." Blackman explains how the story got started. "Shatner told me that during the filming of the original series, he once broke two ribs over a weekend and he asked the costumer for an Ace bandage to protect them. It came out in the trades as a girdle."

Another tool that Blackman uses to create the illusion of the physically fit hero is color blocking. "Jagged-edge color blocking is a fascinating technique that allows you to deal with a variety of body types," he explains. "You put the break in a confusing line so you can't really tell where the waistline is. The sides are dark, so you can't see the shape of the person, but you get the appearance of added shoulder width because of the horizontal color across the shoulder, which makes the actor look more heroic." (Are you listening, Calvin?)

One change obvious to even the most casual viewer is the transition from the two-piece dress uniforms of *TNG* to the one-piece fatigues of *DS9*. According to Blackman, the style evolved because of the differences between the two shows. In *TNG*, he says, there is more mental activity, while in *DS9* there's more physical action. "The formality, dignity, and sophistication of *The Next Generation's* suits did not work for *DS9*." says Blackman. "The *DS9* crew are up to their elbows in the grit and grime of the space station. The gray T-shirt visible underneath also breaks up the suit and makes it more casual, more vulnerable, and less armored."

There's also been a painstakingly slow evolution from the spandex uniforms that prevailed when Blackman first came aboard to the wool ones that he compares to "24th-century Eisenhower jackets" to the current jumpsuit.

When Blackman arrived, the actors were ranting—some rather loudly—about the spandex. "The stretch ran up and down the fabric, not across, so the pants would bag at the knees and put pressure on the foot as the stirrup cut into it," Blackman remembers. "Patrick Stewart told me it was throwing his back out. He had marks on his shoulders and had to go to the chiropractor every week because he was in constant pain." What's more, spandex doesn't breathe well, so it's very, very hot. And it retains odor. Not a pleasant combination. That's why Blackman began designing one-piece wool uniforms for the men—but there were still problems. The actors couldn't perform the action required in the script, for example, because wool doesn't stretch very well. "It was a technical and fashion nightmare," says Blackman. "We tried a lot of prototypes with nothing but complaints from the actors." During the third season of *TNG*, Blackman came up with two-piece wool uniforms for the men. But the women in space didn't look as good in the wool, "So we went back to spandex for them," he says. This time, though, he solved the stretch dilemma, having it run around the body rather than up and down. "We cut it differently and found a way to piece the fabric together," Blackman explains.

Fabric isn't all that has been altered over the years: Colors have been added, changed, and taken away; piping around the yoke has been removed: and necklines have risen from the trachea to the Adam's apple, where they now remain. Even the uniforms worn by the old guard in the first four *Trek* movies, which were designed by Robert Fletcher, were modified by Blackman for *Star Trek: Generations*. "I have tremendous respect for continuity and for the other costumers' work," says Blackman. "But these men [the original actors] are not built the way they were 20 years ago. So I dropped the jackets to suit length and kept a long leg to give them more dignity. After all, they *are* like career army officers."

Though there's a slight military feel to the current uniforms, Blackman insists it's not intentional. "The Bajorans, Cardassians, and Romulans are *meant* to look very military, but you have to think of the people in the Federation like American Airlines pilots. It's more a uniform for a civilian organization."

Blackman says the basic uniforms are so simple they're the equivalent of the proverbial little black dress, "which," he says, "is the hardest thing to design." And fit. Because of all the individualized underpinnings, fittings are torturously arduous, and the whole process has to

happen in practically the blink of an eye. "Usually it's a 48-hour deal," says Blackman. "I get the actor one day, do measurements, and the design is done. Sometimes we talk about the look we're shooting for, sometimes I just do it—sketch it and get the fabric. A day later the actor comes in for a fitting in the unfinished garment. He or she will stand around for half an hour and mess around in it. Then we finish it."

And as for the story beyond the ultimate *Star Trek* emblem, the Com badge? In the original series, the now-trademarked boomerang-shaped badge was just a cheesy-looking embroidered gold patch. "We came up with a metal badge for the movies. *TNG, DS9*, and *Voyager*," says Blackman, "and it eventually evolved into a communicator. These days, it's made of resin and held in place with velcro. It's rather like Barbie growing up."

Predictably, the badge is the most highly sought-after item, on and off the set. "We've had to install an elaborate and baroque check-out system," says Blackman with a chuckle. "But they're always disappearing."

Source: Star Trek: *Four Generations of Stars, Stories, and Cosmic Couture* (Spring 1995). Reprinted with permission from TV Guide. © TV Guide Magazine Group, Inc. TV Guide is a registered trademark of TV Magazine Group, Inc.

Bibliography

Abend, Jules. (1996, October). Custom-made for the masses: Is it time yet? *Bobbin, 38*(2), 49–54.

Ackroyd, Peter. (1979). *Dressing up, transvestism and drag, the history of an obsession.* New York: Simon & Schuster.

American Anthropological Association Executive Board. (1998, September). AAA statement on race. *Anthropology Newsletter, 39*(6), 3.

Angelou, Maya. (1969). *I know why the caged bird sings.* New York: Bantam Book Edition.

Annas, Alicia. (1987). The photogenic formula: Hairstyles and makeup in historical films. In Edward Maeder (Ed.), *Hollywood and history: Costume design in film.* New York: Thames & Hudson.

Anspach, Karlyne. (1967). *The why of fashion.* Ames, IA: Iowa State University Press.

Antubam, Kofi. (1963). *Ghana's heritage of culture.* Leipzig: Koehler and Amelang.

Arriaza, Bernardo. (1995). Chile's Chinchorro mummies. *National Geographic, 187*(3), 68–89.

Ash, Juliet, & Wilson, Elizabeth (Eds.). (1992). *Chic thrills: A fashion reader.* London: Pandora.

Baizerman, Suzanne. (1987). *Textiles, traditions and tourist art: Hispanic weaving in northern New Mexico.* Unpublished doctoral dissertation, University of Minnesota, St. Paul.

Baizerman, Suzanne, Eicher, Joanne B., & Cerny, Catherine. (1993). Eurocentrism in the study of ethnic dress. *Dress, 20,* 19–32.

Banner, Lois W. (1983). *American beauty.* Chicago: University of Chicago Press.

Barber, Elizabeth W. (1994). *Women's work: The first 20,000 years.* New York: Norton.

Barnard, Malcolm. (1996). *Fashion as communication.* London: Routledge.

Barnes, Ruth. (1989). *The ikat textiles of Lamalera: A study of an eastern Indonesian weaving tradition.* Leiden: E. J. Brill.

Barnes, Ruth. (1992). Women as headhunters: The making and meaning of textiles in a Southeast Asian context. In Ruth Barnes & Joanne B. Eicher (Eds.), *Dress and gender: Making and meaning in cultural contexts* (pp. 29–43). New York: Berg.

Barnes, Ruth, & Eicher, Joanne B. (Eds.). (1992). *Dress and gender: Making and meaning in cultural contexts.* New York: Berg.

Barnette, Martha. (1993, August). The perfect body. *Allure*, 106–113, 146.

Barthes, Roland. (1983). *The fashion system.* Berkeley, CA: University of California Press.

Begley, Sharon. (1995, February 13). Three is not enough. *Newsweek*, 67–69.

Bell, Quentin. (1947). *On human finery.* London: Hogarth Press.

Benedict, Ruth. (1931). Dress. In *Encyclopedia of the social sciences* (Vol. 5, pp. 235–237). New York: Macmillan.

Benedict, Ruth. (1959). *Patterns of culture.* Boston: Houghton Mifflin Co.

Benstock, Shari, & Ferriss, Suzanne. (1994). *On fashion.* New Brunswick, NJ: Rutgers University Press.

Bergler, Edmund. (1953). *Fashion and the unconscious.* New York: Robert Brunner.

Berns, Marla. (1988). Ga'Anda scarification: A model for art and identity. In Arnold Rubin (Ed.), *Marks of civilization* (pp. 57–76). Los Angeles: Museum of Cultural History, University of California Los Angeles.

Birket-Smith, Kaj. (1965). *The paths of culture.* Madison, WI: University of Wisconsin Press.

Bivans, Ann-Marie. (1991). *Miss America: In pursuit of the crown.* New York: Mastermedia Limited.

Blumer, Herbert. (1968). Fashion. In Edward Sills (Ed.), *International encyclopedia of the social sciences* (Vol. 26, pp. 341–345). New York: Macmillan & Free Press.

Boas, Franz. (1930). [Editorial comment to] James A. Teit's Tattooing and face and body painting of the Thompson Indians, British Columbia. *Annual report of the Bureau of American Ethnology 1927–1928* (Vol. 45, pp. 397–439). Washington, DC: U.S. Government Printing Office.

Boaz, Noel T., & Almquist, Alan J. (1997). *Biological anthropology: A synthetic approach to human evolution.* Upper Saddle River, NJ: Prentice Hall.

Bock, Philip K. (1969). *Modern cultural anthropology.* New York: Alfred A. Knopf.

Bodley, John H. (1994). *Cultural anthropology: Tribes, states, and the global system.* London: Mayfield.

Boehlke, Heidi. (1999). *Indigenous textiles and fashion in new order Indonesia.* Unpublished doctoral dissertation, University of Minnesota, St. Paul.

Bogatyrev, Petr. (1971). *The functions of folk costume in Moravian Slovakia.* Paris: Mouton.

Bohannon, Paul J. (1956). Beauty and scarification amongst the Tiv. *Man*, *56*(129), 117–130.

Bohannon, Paul. (1992). *We, the alien: An introduction to cultural anthropology*. Prospect Heights, IL: Waveland Press.

Boone, Sylvia Ardyn. (1986). *Radiance from the waters: Ideals of feminine beauty in Mende art*. New Haven: Yale University Press.

Borcherding, David. (1993, March/April). Nanofashion. *Utne Reader*, p. 129–130.

Boucher, Francois. (1987). *20,000 years of fashion: A history of costume and personal adornment*. New York: Harry N. Abrams.

Boulanger, Chantal. (1997). *Saris: An illustrated guide to the Indian art of draping*. New York: Shakti Press International.

Boyer, G. Bruce. (1990). *Eminently suitable: The elements of style in business attire*. New York: Norton.

Brauner, Leon. (1964, October). Character portrayal through costume. *Proceedings of the Eleventh Conference of College Teachers of Clothing, Textiles and Related Arts* (pp. 23–26). Western Region, Utah State University.

Brenninkmeyer, Ingrid. (1963). *The sociology of fashion*. Winterthur: P. G. Keller.

Breward, Christopher. (1995). *The culture of fashion: A new history of fashionable dress*. Manchester: Manchester University Press.

Brodman, Barbara. (1994). Paris or perish: The plight of the Latin American Indian in a westernized world. In Shari Benstock & Suzanne Ferriss (Eds.), *On fashion* (pp. 267–283). New Brunswick, NJ: Rutgers University Press.

Broholm, H. C., & Hald, Margrethe. (1940). *Costumes of the Bronze Age in Denmark*. Copenhagen: Nyt Nordisk Forlag.

Brown, Malcom W. (1998, July 21). Scruffy is a badge of pride, but some physicists long for cool. *The New York Times*, p. B10.

Brown, Patty, & Rice, Janet. (1998). *Ready-to-wear apparel analysis*. Upper Saddle River, NJ: Merrill.

Bryant, Nancy O. & Hoffman, Elizabeth. (1994). A critical framework for exploring the aesthetic dimensions of wearable art. In Marilyn Revell DeLong & Ann Marie Fiore (Eds.), *Aesthetics of textiles and clothing: Advancing multi-disciplinary perspectives* (pp. 84–96). ITAA Special Publication #7. Monument, CO: International Textile and Apparel Association.

Brydon, Anne, & Niessen, Sandra (Eds.). (1999). *Consuming fashion: Adorning the transnational body*. Oxford: Berg.

The buffalo budget. (1997, November 15). *Indian Express*, n. p.

Bullough, Vern L., & Bullough, Bonnie. (1993). *Cross-dressing, sex, and gender*. Philadelphia: University of Pennsylvania Press.

Bunzel, Ruth. (1931). Ornament. In *Encyclopedia of the social sciences* (Vol. 1, pp. 496–497). New York: Macmillan.

Burns, Leslie Davis, & Lennon, Sharron J. (1994). The look and the feel: Methods for measuring aesthetic perceptions of textiles and apparel. In Marilyn Revell DeLong & Ann Marie Fiore (Eds.), *Aesthetics of textiles and clothing: Advancing multi-disciplinary perspectives* (pp. 120–130). ITAA Special

Publication #7. Monument, CO: International Textile and Apparel Association.

Callaway, Helen. (1992). Dressing for dinner in the bush: Rituals of self-definition and British imperial authority. In Ruth Barnes & Joanne B. Eicher (Eds.), *Dress and gender: Making and meaning* (pp. 232–247). Oxford: Berg.

Carlyle, Thomas. (1834). *Sartor resartus.* New York: Odyssey Press.

Carneiro, Robert L., & Tobias, Stephen F. (1963). The application of scale analysis to the study of cultural evolution. *Transactions of the New York Academy of Sciences, ser. II, 26*(2), 196–207.

Carneiro, Robert L. (1994a). Manioc: The reigning crop. In Göran Burenhult (Gen. Ed.), *Traditional peoples today: Continuity and change in the modern world* (pp. 202–204). San Francisco: HarperSanFrancisco.

Carneiro, Robert L. (1994b). The blowgun: The silent, deadly tube. In Göran Burenhult (Gen. Ed.), *Traditional peoples today: Continuity and change in the modern world* (pp. 204–209). San Francisco: HarperSanFrancisco.

Chandler, Raymond. (1988 version). *The little sister.* New York: Vintage Books.

Chermayeff, Catherine, David, Jonathan, & Richardson, Nan. (1995). *Drag diaries.* New York: Umbra Editions.

Clark, Kenneth. (1956). *The nude.* New York: Pantheon Books.

Coffey, Barbara (Ed.). (1979). *Glamour's success book: Effective dressing on the job, at home, in your community, everywhere.* New York: Simon & Schuster.

Cohen, Colleen B., Wilk, Richard, & Stoeltje, Beverly. (1996). *Beauty queens on the global stage: Gender, contests, and power.* New York: Routledge.

Cohen, Yehudi A. (1968). *Man in adaptation: The biosocial background.* Chicago: Aldine.

Cohn, Bernard. (1983). Representing authority in Victorian India. In E. Hobsbawm & T. Ranger (Eds.), *The invention of tradition* (pp. 165–209). Cambridge: Cambridge University.

Cohn, Bernard S. (1989). Cloth, clothes, and colonialism: India in the nineteenth century. In Annette B. Weiner & Jane Schneider (Eds.), *Cloth and human experience* (pp. 303–353). Washington, DC: Smithsonian Institution Press.

Colas, René. (1933). *Bibliographie générale du costume et de la mode.* Paris: R. Colas. Monro.

Cole, Herbert, & Ross, Doran. (1977). *The arts of Ghana.* Los Angeles: UCLA Museum of Cultural History.

Coon, Carlton S., Barn, Stanley M., & Birdsell, Joseph B. (1955). Adaptive changes in the human body. In E. Adamson Hoebel, Jesse D. Jennings, & Elmer R. Smith (Eds.), *Readings in anthropology* (2nd ed., pp. 88–92). New York: McGraw-Hill.

Corcos, Alain F. (1997). *The myth of human races.* East Lansing, MI: Michigan State University Press.

Cordry, Donald, & Cordry, Dorothy. (1968). *Mexican Indian costumes.* Austin, TX: University of Texas Press.

Craik, Jennifer. (1994). *The face of fashion: Cultural studies in fashion.* London: Routledge.

Crawford, Cindy, Kashuk, Sonia, & Boyes, Kathleen. (1996). *Cindy Crawford's basic face: A makeup work book.* New York: Broadway Books.

Crawley, Ernest. (1912). Dress. In James Hastings (Ed.), *Encyclopedia of religion and ethics* (Vol. 5, pp. 40–72). New York: Charles Scribner's Sons.

Crawley, Ernest. (1931). *Dress, drinks, and drums.* Theodore Besterman (Ed.). London: Methuen.

Creager, Ellen. (1998, August 30). Respect for the uniform. *Detroit Free Press,* pp. G1–2.

Croutier, Alev Lytle. (1989). *Harem: The world behind the veil* (pp. 70–79, 81, 83–87, 89–91). New York: Abbeville Press.

Cunningham, Patricia, & Lab, Susan Voso. (1991). *Dress in popular culture.* Bowling Green: Bowling Green State University Popular Press.

Cunningham, Patricia, & Lab, Susan Voso. (1993). *Dress in American culture.* Bowling Green: Bowling Green State University Popular Press.

Cunnington, C. W. (1941). *Why women wear clothes.* London: Faber and Faber.

Dalby, Liza. (1993). *Kimono: Fashioning culture.* New Haven, CT: Yale University Press.

Damhorst, Mary Lynn, Miller, Kimberly A., & Michelman, Susan O. (Eds.). (1999). *The meanings of dress.* New York: Fairchild.

Dar, S. N. (1969). *Costumes of India and Pakistan: Historical and cultural study.* Bombay: D. P. Taraporevala.

Darwin, Charles. (1958 version). *The voyage of the Beagle.* New York: Bantam Books.

Davenport, Millia. (1948). *The book of costume.* New York: Crown.

Davis, Fred. (1992). *Fashion, culture, and identity.* Chicago: University of Chicago Press.

Dearborn, George Van Ness. (1918). The psychology of clothing. *The Psychological Monographs, 26*(1), 1–72.

Decorum. (1879). New York: J. A. Ruth.

DeLong, Marilyn Revell. (1987). The way we look. Ames, IA: Iowa State University Press.

DeLong, Marilyn Revell. (1998). *The way we look: Dress and aesthetics* (2nd ed.). New York: Fairchild.

DeLong, Marilyn Revell, & Hillestad, Robert. (1990). *Proceedings: Special Topics Session, Aesthetics of Apparel: Subject, Form, and Content,* Annual Conference of the Association of College Professors of Textiles and Clothing. Denver, CO.

Dickerson, Kitty G. (1997). *Textiles and apparel in the global economy.* Englewood Cliffs, NJ: Prentice Hall.

Douglas, Ngaire. (1996). *They came for savages: 100 years of tourism in Melanesia.* Alstonville, NSW, Australia: Southern Cross University Press.

Downs, James F., & Bleibtreu, Herman K. (1972). *Human variation* (Rev. ed.). Beverly Hills, CA: Glencoe Press.

Dresser, Norine. (1996). *Multicultural manners: New rules of etiquette for a changing society.* New York: Wiley.

Driver, Harold, E. (1969). *Indians of North America* (Rev. 2nd ed.) Chicago: University of Chicago Press.

Duffey, Mrs. E. G. (1876). *Our behavior, a manual of etiquette and dress of the best American society.* Philadelphia: J. M. Stoddard.

Ebin, Victoria. (1979). *The body decorated.* London: Thames & Hudson.

Eicher, Joanne B. (1969). *African dress: A select and annotated bibliography of Sub-Saharan countries.* Lansing, MI: African Studies Center, Michigan State University Press.

Eicher, Joanne B. (Ed.). (1995). *Dress and ethnicity: Change across space and time.* Oxford: Berg.

Eicher, Joanne B. (1997). Classification of dress and costume for African dance. In Esther Dagan (Ed.), *The spirit's dance in Africa* (pp. 94–97). Montreal: Galerie Amrad African Art Publication.

Eicher, Joanne B., & Erekosima, Tonye V. (1995). Why do they call it Kalabari?: Cultural authentication and the demarcation of ethnic identity. In Joanne B. Eicher (Ed.), *Dress and ethnicity* (pp. 139–164). Oxford: Berg.

Eicher, Joanne B., & Sumberg, Barbara. (1995). World fashion, ethnic, and national dress. In Joanne B. Eicher (Ed.), *Dress and ethnicity* (pp. 295–306). Oxford: Berg.

Eichler, Lillian. (1921). *Book of etiquette: Vol. 2.* Oyster Bay, NY: Nelson Doubleday.

el Guindi, Fadwa. (1999). *Veil: Modesty, privacy and resistance.* Oxford: Berg.

Elegant, Simon, & Cohen, Margot, with reports by Jayasankaran, S., Gilley, Bruce, Lee, Charles, & Hiebert, Murray. (1996, December 5). Rock solid. *Far Eastern Economic Review,* 50–52.

Ellis, Havelock. (1936). *Studies in the psychology of sex.* New York: Modern Library.

Erekosima, Tonye V. & Eicher, Joanne B. (1994). The aesthetics of men's dress of the Kalabari of Nigeria. In Marilyn Revell DeLong & Ann Marie Fiore (Eds.), *Aesthetics of textiles and clothing: Advancing multi-disciplinary perspectives* (pp. 185–199). ITAA Special Publication #7. Monument, CO: International Textile and Apparel Association.

Evans, Angela Care. (1986). *The* Sutton Hoo *ship burial.* London: British Museum Publications.

Evans, Elizabeth, & Thornton, Minna. (1989). *Women and fashion: A new look.* London: Quartet Books.

Evenson, Sandra Lee. (1991). *The manufacture of madras in South India and its export to West Africa: A case study.* Unpublished master's thesis, University of Minnesota, St. Paul.

Evenson, Sandra Lee. (1994). *A history of Indian madras manufacture and trade: Shifting patterns of exchange.* Unpublished doctoral dissertation, University of Minnesota, St. Paul.

Fabri, Charles. (1960). *A history of Indian dress.* Calcutta: Orient Longmans.

Fairholt, F. W. (1846). *Costume in England.* London: Chapman and Hall.

Fairservis, Walter A., Jr. (1971). *Costumes of the East*. Riverside, CT: Chatham Press.

Faris, James C. (1972). *Nuba personal art*. London: Duckworth.

Feldon, Leah. (1994). *Dress like a million (on considerably less): A trend-proof guide to real fashion*. New York: Villard Books.

Felix, Marc L. (1992). *Ituri: The distribution of polychrome masks in Northeast Zaire*. Munich: Verlag Fred Jahn.

Feng, Jicai. (1994). *The three-inch golden lotus* (David Wakefield, Trans.). Honolulu: University of Hawaii Press.

Fiore, Ann Marie. (1994). Aesthetics: The James Dean of textiles and clothing. In Marilyn Revell DeLong & Ann Marie Fiore (Eds.), *Aesthetics of textiles and clothing: Advancing multi-disciplinary perspectives* (pp. 7–12). ITAA Special Publication #7. Monument, CO: International Textile and Apparel Association.

Fiore, Ann Marie, & Kimle, Patricia Ann. (1998). *Understanding aesthetics for the merchandising and design professional*. New York: Fairchild.

Flaubert, Gustave. (1950 version). *Madame Bovary* (Eleanor Mary Aveling, Trans.). New York: Modern Library.

Fletcher, Alice, & La Flesche, Francis. (1911). The Omaha tribe: Language of the Robe. *Annual Report of the Bureau of American Ethnology 1905–1906* (Vol. 27, pp. 360–362). Washington, DC: U.S. Government Printing Office.

Flügel, J. C. (1930). *The psychology of clothes*. London: Hogarth Press.

Flusser, Alan. (1996). *Style and the man: How and where to buy fine men's clothes*. New York: HarperCollins.

Foster, Helen Bradley. (1997). *New raiments of self: African American clothing in the antebellum South*. Oxford: Berg.

Fourt, Lyman, & Hollies, Norman R. S. (1970). *Clothing: Comfort and function*. New York: Marcel Dekker.

Fowler, Brenda (1995, July 25). Forgotten riches of King Tut: His wardrobe. *New York Times*, pp. B5, B7.

Freud, Sigmund. (1915). *The interpretation of dreams*. New York: Macmillan. (Original work published 1900).

Freud, Sigmund. (1943). *A general introduction to psychoanalysis*. (From lectures presented 1915–1917). Garden City, NY: Garden City.

Gallagher, Mary Barelli. (1969). *My life with Jacqueline Kennedy*. New York: Paperback Library Edition.

Garber, Marjorie. (1992). *Vested interests: Cross-dressing and cultural anxiety*. New York: Routledge.

Garrett, Valery M. (1987). *Traditional Chinese clothing in Hong Kong and South China, 1840–1980*. New York: Oxford University Press.

Garrett, Valery M. (1994). *Chinese clothing: An illustrated guide*. New York: Oxford University Press.

Garrett, Valery M. (1995). The cheung sam — its rise and fall. *Costume: The Journal of the Costume Society, 29*, 88–94.

Gazzuolo, Edith B. (1997). *Garments of Light* [Video]. New York: Fairchild.

Geerdes, Clay. (1969, October 1). I'm ugly and I'm proud. *Kaleidoscope*, 5.

Gell, Alfred (1993). *Wrapping in image: Tattooing in Polynesia.* New York: Oxford University Press.

Ghurye, G. S. (1951). *Indian costume.* Bombay: Popular Prakashan.

Gluckman, Dale C., & Takeda, Sharon S. (1992). *When art became fashion: Kosode in Edo-period Japan.* Los Angeles: Los Angeles County Museum of Art.

Goffman, Erving. (1959). *The presentation of self in everyday life.* New York: Anchor Doubleday.

Goldsmith, Olivia, & Collins, Amy Fine. (1995). *Simple isn't easy: How to find your personal style and look fantastic every day.* New York: HarperPaperbacks.

Gordon, Stewart. (1996, October). *Integration of the Khilat ceremony into Hindu courts, 1600–1800.* Paper presented at the 25th Annual Conference of South Asia, Madison, Wisconsin.

Graham, Tim & Blanchard, Tamsin. (1998). *Dressing Diana.* New York: Welcome Rain.

Gregory R. L. (1966). *Eye and brain.* New York: McGraw-Hill.

Griggs, Claudine. (1997). *S/he: Changing sex and changing clothes.* Oxford: Berg.

Guha, Ranajit. (1983). *Elementary aspects of peasant insurgency in colonial India.* Delhi: Oxford University Press.

Halbreich, Betty & Wadyka, Sally. (1997). *Secrets of a fashion therapist: What you can learn behind the dressing room door.* New York: HarperCollins.

Hall, Lee. (1992). *Common threads: A parade of American clothing.* Boston: Little, Brown.

Hambly, Gavin R. G. (1996, October). *From Bukhara to Delhi: The transmission of kingly pomp and circumstance.* Paper presented at the 25th Annual Conference of South Asia, Madison, Wisconsin.

Hamilton, Charles (1991). *Adam Clayton Powell, Jr.: The political biography of an American dilemma.* New York: Atheneum.

Hamilton, Jean A., & Hamilton, James W. (1989). Dress as a reflection and sustainer of social reality: A cross-cultural perspective. *Clothing and Textiles Research Journal, 7*(2), 16–22.

Hansen, Henny Harald. (1983). *Mongol costumes.* Great Britain: Thames & Hudson.

Hansen, Karen Tranberg. (1995, March). Transnational biographies and local meanings: Used clothing practices in Lusaka. *Journal of Southern American Studies, 21*(1), 1–10.

Harris, Marvin. (1974). *Cows, pigs, wars, and witches: The riddles of culture.* New York: Random House.

Haweis, Mary Eliza. (1879). *The art of dress.* London: Chatto and Windus.

Hawes, Elizabeth. (1938). *Fashion is spinach.* New York: Random House.

Hawes, Elizabeth. (1954). *It's still spinach.* Boston: Little, Brown.

Haygood, Wil. (1993). *King of the cats: The life and times of Adam Clayton Powell, Jr.* New York: Houghton Mifflin Co.

Heider, Karl G. (1970). *The Dugum Dani: A Papuan culture in the highlands of West New Guinea.* Viking Fund Publications in Anthropology, Vol. 49. New York: Wenner-Gren Foundation for Anthropological Research, Inc.

Hendrickson, Carol. (1995). *Weaving identities: Construction of dress and self in a highland Guatemala town*. Austin, TX: University of Texas Press.

Hendrickson, Hildi. (Ed.). (1996). *Clothing and difference: Embodied identities in colonial and post-colonial Africa*. Durham, NC: Duke University Press.

Hershman, P. (1974). Hair, sex, and dirt. *Man 9*(2), 266–267, 274–298.

Herzog-Schröder, Gabriele. (1994). The Yanomami: Amazon survivors in peril. In Göran Burenhult (Ed.), *Traditional peoples today: Continuity and change in the modern world* (pp. 210–211). San Francisco: Harper San Francisco.

Hethorn, Janet. (1995). Kids and gang fashion vs. fear. *UC Davis Magazine*, 4.

Hethorn, Janet. (1999). *A street guide to gang identity* [On-line]. Available: http://gangid.ucdavis.edu.

Hewlett, Barry S. (1991). *Intimate fathers: The nature and context of Aka Pygmy paternal infant care*. Ann Arbor, MI: University of Michigan Press.

Hickey, Neil & Edwin, Ed (1965). *Adam Clayton Powell and the politics of race*. New York: Fleet Pub. Corp.

Hickman, Pat. (1987). *Innerskins/Outerskins: Gut and fishskin*. San Francisco: San Francisco Craft and Folk Art Museum.

Hiler, Hilaire. (1929). *From nudity to raiment*. New York: E. Weyhe.

Hiler , Hilaire, & Hiler, Meyer. (1939). *Bibliography of costume*. New York: H. W. Wilson.

Hillestad, Robert. (1978). The underlying structure of appearance. *Dress, 5*, 117–125.

Hobsbawm, Eric, & Ranger, Terrence (Eds.). (1983). *The invention of tradition*. Cambridge: Cambridge University.

Holland, Vyvian. (1955). *Hand coloured fashion plates 1770 to 1899*. London: B. T. Batsford.

Hollander, Anne. (1972). *Seeing through clothes*. New York: Viking Press.

Hollander, Anne. (1994). *Sex and suits*. New York: Alfred A. Knopf.

Hope, Thomas. (1841). *Costume of the ancients*. London: Henry G. Bohn. (Original work published 1809).

Horn, Marilyn J. (1968). *The second skin: An interdisciplinary study of clothing*. Boston: Houghton Mifflin.

Horn, Marilyn, & Gurel, Lois. (1981). *The second skin: An interdisciplinary study of clothing* (2nd ed.). Boston: Houghton Mifflin.

Hoskins, Janet. (1989). Why do ladies sing the blues? Indigo dyeing, cloth production, and gender symbolism in Kodi. In Annette B. Weiner & Jane Schneider (Eds.), *Cloth and human experience*, (pp. 141–173). Washington: Smithsonian Institution Press.

Hottenroth, Fr. (1896). *Le costume chez les peuples anciens et modernes: Nouvelle Serie*. Paris: Armand Guerinet.

Hurlock, Elizabeth B. (1929). *The psychology of dress*. New York: Ronald Press.

Inda, Jules. (1992, March/April). Behind the veil debate. *Utne Reader*, 23–26.

Ingrassia, Michele, with Springen, Karen & Samuels, Allison. (1995, April 24). The body of the beholder. *Newsweek*, 66–67.

Issenman, Betty Kobayashi. (1998). *Many disciplines/Many rewards: Inuit clothing research.* Edited from a paper presented at the 20th Annual Meeting and Symposium of the Costume Society of America, Montreal, June 1994.

Jackson, Carole. (1987). *Color me beautiful.* New York: Ballantine Books.

Johnson, Kim K. P., & Lennon, Sharron J. (1999). *Appearance and power.* Oxford and New York: Berg.

Johnston, Richard S., Correale, James V., & Radnofsky, Matthew I. (1966, February). *Space suit development status* (Report No. TND-3291). Washington, DC: National Aeronautics and Space Administration.

Jurmain, Robert, Nelson, Harry, Kilgore, Lynn, & Trevathan, Wenda. (1997). *Introduction to physical anthropology* (7th ed.). Belmont, CA: West/Wadsworth (International Thompson).

Kaiser, Susan. (1997). *The social psychology of clothing: Symbolic appearances in context* (Rev. 2nd ed.). New York: Fairchild.

Kapoun, Robert W. (1992). *The language of the robe: American Indian trade blankets.* Salt Lake City, UT: Gibbs-Smith Pub.

Karpinski, Kenneth J. (1994). *Red socks don't work: Messages from the real world about men's clothing.* Imanassa Park, VA: Impact.

Kawakami, Barbara F. (1993). *Japanese immigrant clothing in Hawaii, 1885–1941.* Honolulu: University of Hawaii Press.

Kennedy, S. J., & Vanderlie, Jan H. (1964, December). Enhancing the effectiveness of the individual in the arctic through clothing and equipment. *Review of research on military problems in cold regions* (Report No. TD-64-28). Arctic Aeromedical Laboratory.

Kettunen, Marietta. (1941). *Fundamentals of dress.* New York: McGraw-Hill.

Kidwell, Claudia Brush, & Steele, Valerie (Eds.). (1989). *Men and women: Dressing the part.* Washington, DC: Smithsonian Institution Press.

Kirk, Kris, & Heath, E. (1984). *Men in frocks.* London: GMP Publishers.

Klapp, Orrin E. (1969). *Collective search for identity.* New York: Holt, Rinehart & Winston.

Klensch, Elsa, with Meyer, Beryl (1995). *Style.* New York: Berkeley Publishing Group.

König, René. (1967). *Kleider und leute, zur soziologie der mode.* Frankfurt: Fischer Bücherei.

Krafft-Ebing, Richard Von. (1965). *Psychopathia sexualis.* New York: Bell. (Original work published in 1886 by Stuttgart).

Kuehne, Sue Hundley, & Creekmore, Anna M. (1971, October). Relationships among social class, school position, and clothing of adolescents. *Journal of Home Economics, 63*(7), 555–556.

Kupfer, Joseph. (1994). Clothing and aesthetic experience. In Marilyn Revell DeLong & Anne Marie Fiore (Eds.), *Aesthetics of textiles and clothing: Advancing multi-disciplinary perspectives* (pp. 97–104). ITAA Special Publication #7. Monument Colorado: International Textile and Apparel Association.

Langan, Leonora M., & Watkins, Susan M. (1987). Pressure of menswear on the neck in relation to visual performance. *Human Factors, 29*(1), 67–71.

Langner, Lawrence. (1959). *The importance of wearing clothes*. New York: Hastings House.

Larkey, Jan. (1991). *Flatter your figure*. New York: Simon & Schuster.

Laver, James. (1952). *Clothes*. London: Burke.

Laver, James. (1964). *Museum piece*. Boston: Houghton Mifflin.

Laver, James. (1969). *Modesty in dress*. Boston: Houghton Mifflin.

Lawson, Joan, & Revitt, Peter. (1958). *Dressing for the ballet*. London: Adam and Charles Black.

Le Bon, Gustave. (1895). *The crowd*. London: T. Fischer Unwin.

Lehmann-Haupt, Rachel. (1998, April). Techno tailor. *Vogue*, 168–170.

Lennon, Sharron J. (1999). Sex, dress, and power in the work place: 'Star Trek, The Next Generation.' In Kim K. P. Johnson & Sharron J. Lennon (Eds.), *Appearance and Power* (pp. 103–126). Oxford: Berg Publishers.

Lennon, Sharron J., & Burns, Leslie Davis (Eds.). (1993). *Social science aspects of dress: New directions*. Monument, CO: International Textile and Apparel Association.

Lewontin, R. (1982). *Human diversity*. New York: Scientific American Books.

Lieberman, Leonard, Reynolds, Larry, & Kellum, Robert. (1983). Institutional and socio-cultural influences on the debate over race. *Catalyst, 15*, 45–73.

Lin, Tiehong. (1997, December). *A new approach to incorporating posture into apparel sizing of pants for women 50 and older*. Unpublished master's thesis, Washington State University, Pullman.

Lipovetsky, Gilles. (1994). *The empire of fashion: Dressing modern democracy*. Princeton, NJ: Princeton University Press.

Lipperheide, Franz Joseph. (1896–1905). *Katalog der freiherrlich von lipperheideshen kostümbibliothek*. Berlin: F. Lipperheide.

LoGiacco, Jean-Paul, & Cross, Geoff. (1995). *Dress to kill*. Toronto: Jean-Paul LoGiacco.

Lorant, Stefan. (1946). *The new world*. New York: Duell, Sloan & Pearce.

Lykken, D. T., Bouchard, T. J., Jr., McGue, M., & Tellegen, A. (1993). Heritability of interests: A twin study. *Journal of Applied Psychology, 78*, 640–661.

Lynch, Annette. (1995). Hmong American New Year's dress: The display of ethnicity. In Joanne B. Eicher (Ed.), *Dress and ethnicity: Change across space and time* (pp. 255–269). Oxford: Berg.

Lurie, Alison. (1981). *The language of clothes*. New York: Random House.

MacLaury, Robert E. (1987). Color-category evolution and Shuswap yellow-with-green. *American Anthropologist, 89*, 107–124.

Mackie, Bob with Bremer, Gerry. (1979). *Dressing for glamour*. New York: A & W Publishers.

Man amplifier. (1964, June 1). *Newsweek, 53*(22), 47.

Man, sweat, and performance. (1969). Rutherford, NJ: Consumer Products Division, Becton Dickinson & Co.

Mattera, Joanne (Ed.). (1992). *Glamour dos and don'ts hall of fame: Fifty years of good fun and bad taste*. New York: Villard Books.

McCormack, Patricia. (1971, March 26). Circus attire design keyed to maintenance. *Lansing State Journal*, B3.

McCracken, Grant. (1990). *Culture and consumption: New approaches to the symbolic character of consumer goods and activities.* Bloomington, IN: Indiana University Press.

McKeon, Patricia. (1995, March). It's the accessories, stupid. *Harper's Magazine, 290*(1738), 13.

McNaughton, Patrick. (1982). The shirts that Mande hunters wear. *African Arts, 15*(3), 54–58, 91.

Mead, S. M. (1969). *Traditional Maori clothing.* Auckland: A. H. and A. W. Reed.

Mernissi, Fatima. (1994). *Dreams of trespass: Tales of a harem girlhood.* Reading, MA: Addison-Wesley.

Merrifield, Mrs. (1854). *Dress as a fine art.* London: Author Hall, Virture.

Meurant, Georges, & Thompson, Robert Farris. (1995). *Mbuti design: Paints by Pygmy women of the Ituri Forest.* New York: Thames & Hudson.

Michelman, Susan O. & Erekosima, Tonye V. (1992). Kalabari dress in Nigeria: Visual analysis and gender implications. In Ruth Barnes & Joanne B. Eicher (Eds.), *Dress and gender: Making and meaning* (pp. 164–182). Oxford: Berg.

Michelman, Susan. (1998). Breaking habits: Fashion and identity of women religious. *Fashion Theory, 2*(2), 165–192.

Milan, Frederick A. (1960, October). *Swedish Lappland: A brief description of the dwellings and winter-living techniques of the Swedish mountain Lapps* (Report No. TR 60-7). Arctic Aeromedical Laboratory.

Miner, Horace. (1956). Body ritual among the Nacirema. *American Anthropologist, 58*, 503–507.

Minnich, Helen Benton. (1963). *Japanese costume.* Rutland, VT: Charles E. Tuttle.

Modern stone-age men. (1969, December 20). *Science News, 96*, 583.

Molloy, John T. (1975). *Dress for success.* New York: Warner Books.

Molloy, John T. (1977). *The woman's dress for success book.* New York: Warner Books.

Monro, Isabelle S. & Cook, Dorothy E. (1937). *Costume index.* New York: H. W. Wilson.

Monro, Isabelle S. & Monro, K. M. (1957). *Costume index and supplement.* New York: H.W. Wilson.

Morris, A., Cooper, T., & Cooper, P. (1989). The changing shape of female fashion models. *International Journal of Eating Disorders, 8*, 593–596.

Morris, Desmond. (1985). *Bodywatching: A field guide to the human species.* New York: Crown.

Morris, Desmond. (1994). *The human animal: A personal view of the human species.* London: BBC Books.

Murdoch, George P. (1955). Universals of culture. In E. Adamson Hoebel, Jesse D. Jennings, & Elmer R. Smith (Eds.), *Readings in anthropology* (pp. 4–5). New York: McGraw-Hill.

Murra, John V. (1989). Cloth and its function in the Inka state. In Annette B. Weiner & Jane Schneider (Eds.), *Cloth and human experience,* (pp. 275–302). Washington, DC: Smithsonian Institution Press.

Nag, D. (1989). *The social construction of handwoven tangail sari in the market of Calcutta* (Vols. 1 & 2). Unpublished doctoral dissertation, Michigan State University, East Lansing.

Naisbitt, John, & Aburdene, Patricia. (1990). *Megatrends 2000: Ten new directions for the 1990s.* New York: William Morrow.

The Neanderthal man liked flowers. (1969, June 13). *New York Times*, pp. 1, 47.

Newburgh, L. H. (Ed.). (1949). *Physiology of heat regulation and the science of clothing.* Philadelphia: W. B. Saunders. (Reprint, New York: Hafner, 1968).

New York University, Film Library (Producer). (1952). *Bathing babies in three cultures* [Film]. (Available from Center for Media Services).

Niubo, F. Torrella. (1970). Postage stamps with textile motifs. *CIBA Review, 2*, 10–30.

Nix-Rice, Nancy. (1996). *Looking good: A comprehensive guide to wardrobe planning, color, and personal style development.* Portland, OR: Palmer/Pletch Publishing.

Norwood, Heywood. (1937). *Common sense etiquette dictionary.* Emmaus, PA: Rodale.

Nystrom, Paul H. (1928). *Economics of fashion.* New York: Ronald Press.

Oakes, Jill. (1991). *Coats of eider.* Hull, Québec: Canadian Museum of Civilization.

Oakes, Jill, & Riewe, Rick. (1995). *Our boots: An Inuit women's art.* New York: Thames & Hudson.

O'Hanlon, Michael. (1989). *Reading the skin: Adornment, display and society among the Wahgi.* London: Trustees of the British Museum by British Museum Publications.

The Old Age of Dustin Hoffman. (1970). *Life, 69,* 78.

O'Neal, Gwendolyn. (1998). African-American aesthetic of dress: Current manifestations. *Clothing and Textile Research Journal, 16*(4),167–175.

O'Sullivan, Joan. (1969). *How to be well dressed.* Garden City, NY: Nelson Doubleday.

Paine, Sheila. (1995). *The Afghan amulet: Travels from the Hindu Kush to Razgrad.* New York: A Wyatt Book for St. Martin's Press.

Paleolithic funeral. (1965, February). *Scientific American, 212*(2), 53–54.

Park, Michael Alan. (1999). *Biological anthropology* (2nd ed.). Mountain View, CA: Mayfield.

Patrick, J. Max (Ed.). (1963). *The complete poetry of Robert Herrick.* New York: New York University Press.

Payne, Blanche, Weinakor, Geitel, & Farrell-Beck, Jane. (1992). *The history of costume: From ancient Mesopotamia through the twentieth century.* New York: HarperCollins.

Perani, Judith, & Wolff, Norma H. (1999). *Cloth, dress and art patronage in Africa.* Oxford and New York: Berg.

Picton, J. (1992, February). Tradition, technology, and Lurex: Some comments on textile history and design in West Africa. *History, design, and craft in West African strip-woven cloth: Papers presented at a symposium organized by the National Museum of African Art, Smithsonian Institution, February*

18–19, 1988 (pp. 13–52). Washington, DC: The National Museum of African Art.

Picton, J. (1995). Technology, tradition and Lurex: The art of textiles in Africa. In J. Picton (Ed.), *The art of African textiles: Technology, tradition and Lurex* (pp. 6–31). London: Barbican Art Gallery.

Planche, James R. (1834). *History of British costume*. London: C. Cox.

Plato. (1943 version). *The republic*. (Benjamin Jowett, Trans.). New York: Books, Inc.

Pokornowski, Ila M., Eicher, Joanne B., Harris, Moira F., & Thieme, Otto. (1985). *African dress II: A select and annotated bibliography*. Lansing, MI: African Studies Center, Michigan State University.

Polhemus, Ted. (1994). *StreetStyle: From sidewalk to catwalk*. London: Thames & Hudson.

Polhemus, Ted, & Proctor, Lynn. (1978). *Fashion and anti-fashion: An anthropology of clothing and adornment*. London: Thames & Hudson.

Polo, Marco. (1958 version). *The travels of Marco Polo*. New York: Orion Press.

Polosmak, Natalya. (1994). A mummy unearthed from the pastures of heaven (photograghs by Charles O'Rear). *National Geographic, 186*(4), 80–103.

Pooley, Eric. (1997, December 8). In search of a better life. *Time 150*, 24. [On-Line]. Available: http://www.pathfinder.com/time/magazine/1994/dom/971208/cover1.html.

Porteus, Stanley. (1931). *The psychology of a primitive people*. New York: Longmans, Green.

Post, Emily. (1928). *Etiquette, the blue book of social usage*. New York: Funk and Wagnalls. (Original work published 1922).

Postman, Neil. (1992). *Technopoly: The surrender of culture to technology*. New York: Alfred A. Knopf.

Powell, Adam Clayton, Jr. (1971). *Adam by Adam: The autobiography of Adam Clayton Powell, Jr.* New York: Dial Press.

Quicherat, J. (1877). *Histoire du costume en France depuis les temps les plus reculés jusqu'a la fin du XVIII siècle*. Paris: Librairie Hachette et Cie.

Racinet, Albert Charles. (1888, August). *Le costume historique* [Historic costume]. Paris: Firmin-Didot.

Ramaswamy, Vijaya. (1985) *Textiles and weavers in medieval South India*. Delhi: Oxford University Press.

Renbourn, E. T. (1972). *Materials and clothing in health and disease*. London: H. K. Lewis.

Renne, Elisha P. (1995). *Cloth that does not die: The meaning of cloth in Bunu social life*. Seattle, WA: University of Washington Press.

Rich, Tracey. (1999). *Judaism 101* [On-line]. Available: http://www.JEWFAQ.org/signs.html.

Rivers, Joan. (1999). *Don't count the candles: Just keep the fire lit!* New York: HarperCollins.

Roach, Mary Ellen, & Eicher, Joanne B. (Eds.). (1965). *Dress, adornment and the social order*. New York: John Wiley.

Roach, Mary Ellen, & Eicher, Joanne B. (1973). *The visible self: Perspectives on dress*. Englewood Cliffs, NJ: Prentice Hall.

Roach, Mary Ellen, & Musa (now Campbell), Kathleen. (1980). *New perspectives on the history of western dress*. New York: Nutriguides.

Roach-Higgins, Mary Ellen. (1981). Fashion. In George Sproles (Ed.), *Perspectives of fashion*. Minneapolis: Burgess.

Roach-Higgins, Mary Ellen, & Eicher, Joanne B. (1992). Dress and identity. *Clothing and Textiles Research Journal, 10*(4), 1–8.

Roach-Higgins, Mary Ellen, Eicher, Joanne B., & Johnson, Kim K. P. (1995). *Dress and identity*. New York: Fairchild.

Rohrbach, Carl. (1882). *Die trachten der volker vom beginn der geschichte bis zum neunzehnten jahrhundert gezeichnet* [Costume of all nations from the earliest times to the nineteenth century] (lithographs by A. Kretschmer). London: Henry Sothern.

Rosencranz, Mary Lou. (1972). *Clothing concepts: A social-psychological approach*. New York: Macmillan.

Ross, Edward A. (1908). *Social psychology*. New York: Macmillan.

Rubinstein, Ruth P. (1995). *Dress codes: Meanings and messages in American culture*. Boulder, CO: Westview Press.

Rudd, Nancy Ann, & Lennon, Sharon J. (1994). Aesthetics of the body and social identity. In Marilyn Revell DeLong & Ann Marie Fiore (Eds.), *Aesthetics of textiles and clothing: Advancing multi-disciplinary perspectives* (pp. 163–175). ITAA Special Publication #7. Monument, CO: International Textile and Apparel Association.

Rudofsky, Bernard. (1947). *Are clothes modern?* Chicago: Paul Theobald. (An updated version is titled *The unfashionable human body* and is published by Garden City: Doubleday, 1971).

Rudolph, B. (1991, October 7). Beauty and the bucks. *Time, 138*(14), 38–40.

Rundquist, Angela. (1987). Presentation at court in Sweden 1850–1962. *Anthropology Today, 3*(6), 2–6.

Russell, Douglas A. (1982). *Costume history and style*. Upper Saddle River, NJ: Prentice Hall.

Russell, Douglas A. (1985). *Stage costume design: Theory, technique, and style* (2nd ed.). Englewood Cliffs, NJ: Prentice Hall.

Ryan, M. S. (1966). *Clothing, a study in human behavior*. New York: Holt, Rinehart & Winston.

Sacks, Peter. (1996). *Generation X goes to college: An eye-opening account of teaching in postmodern America*. Peru, IL: Carus.

Santayana, George. (1955 version). *The sense of beauty*. New York: Dover. (Original work published 1896).

Sapir, Edward. (1931). Fashion. In *The encyclopedia of the social sciences* (Vol. 6, pp. 139–144). New York: Macmillan.

Schevill, Margot Blum. (1992). *Maya textiles of Guatemala*. Austin, TX: University of Texas Press.

Schlesinger, Arthur M. (1947). *Learning how to behave*. New York: Macmillan.

Schneider, Jane. (1994). In and out of polyester: Desire, disdain and global fibre competitions. *Anthropology Today, 10*(4), 2–10.

Schreier, Barbara A. (1994). They don't wear wigs here. *Becoming American women: Clothing and the Jewish immigrant experience, 1880–1920.* Chicago: Chicago Historical Society.

Scott, A. C. (1958). *Chinese costume in transition.* Singapore: Donald Moore.

Seibold, Katharine E. (1995). Dressing the part: Indigenous costume as political and cultural discourse in Peru. In *Contact, crossover, continuity: Proceedings of the fourth biennial symposium of the Textile Society of America, 1994* (pp. 319–329). Los Angeles, CA: Textile Society of America.

Seymour-Smith, Charlotte. (1986). *Macmillan dictionary of anthropology.* London: Macmillan Reference Books.

Shanklin, Eugenia. (1994). *Anthropology and race.* Belmont, CA: Wadsworth.

Shapiro, Laura. (1998). Fat, fatter: But who's counting? *Newsweek 131*(24), 55.

Sheldon, W. H. (1940). *The varieties of human physique.* New York: Harper and Brothers.

Sheldon, W. H. (1942). *The varieties of temperament.* New York: Harper and Brothers.

Shields, Brooke. (1985). *On your own.* New York: Villard Books.

Shreeve. James. (1994, November). Terms of estrangement. *Discover 15*(11), 56–63.

Simmel, Georg. (1904, October). Fashion. *International Quarterly, 10,* 130–155.

Singh, K. S. (1993). Identification markers of communities (map). In *An anthropological atlas* (People of India, National Series Vol. XI, p. 21). Delhi, India: Oxford University Press for Anthropological Survey of India.

Siple, Paul A. (1968). Clothing and climate. In L. H. Newburgh (Ed.), *Physiology of heat regulation and the science of clothing* (pp. 389–442). New York: Hafner.

Snead, Elizabeth. (1995, Spring). Cosmic couture in *Star Trek:* Four generations of stars, stories, and, strange new worlds. *TV Guide Collector's Edition,* 70–76. Radnor, PA: News America Publications.

Sobo, Elisa J. (1994). The sweetness of fat: Health, procreation, and sociability in rural Jamaica. In Nicole Sault (Ed.), *Many mirrors: Body image and social relations* (pp. 132–144, 150–154). New Brunswick, NJ: Rutgers University Press.

Solomon, Michael, R. (1985). *The psychology of fashion.* Lexington, MA: Lexington Books.

Sontag, Deborah, & Dugger, Celia W. (1998, July 19). The new immigrant tide: A shuttle between worlds. *New York Times,* pp. 1, 12–14.

Spindler, Konrad. (1994). *The man in the ice.* New York: Harmony Books.

Spooner, B. (1986). Weavers and dealers: The authenticity of an Oriental carpet. In A. Appadurai (Ed.), *The social life of things: Commodities in cultural perspective* (pp. 195–235). Cambridge: Cambridge University Press.

Sproles, George. (1979). *Fashion: Consumer behavior toward dress.* Minneapolis: Burgess.

Stabb, Jo Ann C. (1996). *Signature style: Falling off the fashion train with Frida, Georgia and Louise.* Unpublished manuscript edited for this text.

Stahlberg, Jennifer. (1998). *Everyday dress of the Cholitas in La Paz, Bolivia, as a means to retain ethnic identity.* Unpublished undergraduate research paper for DHA 3212, Cultural Perspectives on Dress, University of Minnesota.

Steele, Valerie. (1985). *Fashion and eroticism: The ideals of feminine beauty from the Victorian era to the Jazz age.* New York: Oxford University Press.

Steele, Valerie. (1991, April) The F word. *Lingua Franca 2,*16–20.

Steele, Valerie. (1996). *Fetish: Fashion, sex, and power.* New York: Oxford University Press.

Steiner, Christopher Burghard. (1994). Technologies of resistance: Structural alteration of trade cloth in four societies. *Zeitschrift fur Ethnologie, 119,* 75–94.

Stevenson, Matilda Coxe. (1911). *Dress and adornment of the Pueblo Indians,* Ms. no. 2093. Bureau of American Ethnology Archives. Washington, DC: National Anthropological Archives.

Stone, Gregory P. (1962). Appearance and the self. In Arnold M. Rose (Ed.), *Human behavior and social processes: An interactionist approach* (pp. 86–118). New York: Houghton Mifflin.

Stote, Dorothy. (1939). *Men too wear clothes.* New York: Frederick A. Stockes.

Strathern, Andrew, & Strathern, Marilyn. (1971). *Self-decoration in Mount Hagan.* London: Gerald Duckworth.

Strauss, William, & Howe, Neil. (1992). *Generations: The history of America's future, 1584–2069.* New York: Morrow Publishers.

Stubs, Philip. (1595). *The anatomie of abuses.* London: Richard Johnes.

Suga, Masami. (1995). Exotic west to exotic Japan: Revival of Japanese tradition in modern Japan. In Joanne B. Eicher (Ed.). *Dress and ethnicity: Change across space and time* (pp. 95–115). Oxford: Berg.

Tanner, Nancy Makepeace. (1988). Becoming human, our links with our past. In T. Ingold (Ed.), *What is an animal?* (p. 136). London: Unwin Hyman.

Tarde, Gabriel. (1903). *The laws of imitation* (Elsie Clews Parsons & Elsie Clews, Trans.). New York: Henry Holt.

Tarlo, Emma. (1996). *Clothing matters: Dress and identity in India.* Chicago: University of Chicago Press.

Taylor, Penny (Ed.). (1988). After 200 years: Photographic essays of Aboriginal and Islander Australia today. Cambridge: Cambridge University Press and Canberra: Australian Institute of Aboriginal Studies.

Teit, James A. (1927–1928). Tattooing and face and body painting of the Thompson Indians, British Columbia. *Annual Report of the Bureau of American Ethnology,* Vol. 45, pp. 397–439. Washington, DC: U.S. Government Printing Office.

Thomas, P. (1957). *Kama Kalpa or the Hindu ritual of love.* Bombay: D. B. Taraporevala Sons.

Thomas, William I. (1907). *Sex and society.* Chicago: University of Chicago Press.

Thrasher, Elizabeth. (1998, February). Computer couture. *Vogue*, 124.

Tobias, Phillip V. (1968). Bushman hunter-gatherers: A study in human ecology. In Yehudi A. Cohen (Ed.), *Man in adaptation: The biosocial background* (pp. 196–208). Chicago: Aldine.

Tonsing, Ernst F. (1998). Moses Swede. *Sweden & America*, pp. 14–16.

Tortora, Phyllis G., & Eubank, Keith. (1998). *A survey of historic costume: A history of western dress* (3rd ed.). New York: Fairchild.

Trollope, Frances. (1949). *Domestic manners of Americans*. New York: Alfred A. Knopf.

Turner, Terence. (1969, October). Tchikrin: A central Brazilian tribe and symbolic language of bodily adornment. *Natural History, 78*(8), 50–59, 70.

Vatikiotis, Michael. (1996, December 5). Children of plenty: Parents spoil their kids— to show off new-found wealth. *Far Eastern Economic Review*, 54–55.

Veblen, Thorstein. (1899). *The theory of the leisure class*. New York: Macmillan.

Visser, Margaret. (1997). *The way we are: The astonishing anthropology of everyday life*. New York: Kodansha International.

Vollmer, John E. (1983). *Decoding dragons: Status garments in Ch'ing dynasty China*. Eugene, OR: University of Oregon Museum of Art.

Wallach, Janet (1986). *Looks that work*. New York: Viking.

Watkins, Susan M. (1984). *Clothing: The portable environment*. Ames, IA: Iowa State University Press.

Watkins, Susan M. (1995). *Clothing: The portable environment*, (2nd ed.). Ames, IA: Iowa State University Press.

Webb, Alex. (1997). *Amazon: From the floodplains to the clouds*. New York: Monocelli Press.

Webb, Wilfred Mark. (1912). *The heritage of dress*. London: Times Book Club. (Original work published 1907).

Weiner, Annette B., & Schneider, Jane. (Eds.). (1989). *Cloth and human experience*. Washington, DC: Smithsonian Institution Press.

Weir, Shelagh. (1989). *Palestinian costume*. London: British Museum.

Weiss, Hermann. (1853). *Geschichte des kostüms*. Berlin: F. Dümmler.

Weiss, Hermann. (1860–1872). *Kostümkunde*. Stuttgart: Ebner und Seubert.

Wharton, W. J. L., Captain (Ed.). (1893). *Captain Cook's journal during his first voyage around the world made in H. M. Bark "Endeavor" 1768–71*. London: Elliot Stock.

What fashion designer John Weitz sees ahead. (1968, April). *Textile World 118*, 4, 199.

Williams, Gloria, & Centrallo, Carol. (1990). Clothing acquisition and use by the colonial African American. In Barbara M. Stark, Lillian O. Holloman, & Barbara K. Nordquist (Eds.), *African American dress and adornment: A cultural perpsective* (pp. 51–68). Dubuque, IA: Kendall Hunt.

Wilson, Elizabeth. (1987). *Adorned in dreams: Fashion and modernity*. Berkeley, CA: University of California Press.

Wilson, Verity. (1986). *Chinese dress*. London: Victoria and Albert Museum.

Wilson, William. (1986). *Man at his best: The Esquire guide to style*. Reading, MA: Addison-Wesley.

Wise, Jeff. (1997, February 13). Escape to New York. *Far Eastern Economic Review 160*(7), 34–35.

Wolf, Naomi. (1991). *The beauty myth: How images of beauty are used against women.* New York: Anchor Books Doubleday.

Wood, Josephine, & Osborne, Lilly De Jongh. (1966). *Indian costumes of Guatemala.* Graz, Austria: Akademische Dracku, Verlagsanstalt.

Woodhouse, Annie. (1989). *Fantastic women: Sex, gender, and transvestism.* Brunswick, NJ: Rutgers University Press.

INDEX

A

Aboriginal dress, 61–62, *62*
Accessories, 5, 18
Acclimatization, 151, 152, 153–54
Acculturation, 243
Accuracy of evidence, 55
Acephalous political structure, 189, 195, 199
Achieved social status, 39
Achilles, 230
Ackroyd, Peter, 93
Actors, 14, 289, 352, *353*
Adams, Scott, 76
Adhered attachments
    to the body, 19–20
    to body enclosures, 22
Adler, Alfred, 89
Advertising, *63*
    accuracy and distortion, 65–66
Advertising agencies, 288
Aesthetics, 91, 407
    of dress, 288–90, 294
Afghanistan, 217–18
Africa, 92, 243
    dress in, 87
African-Americans, 92, 242–43, 405
African or black race, 133
Aftershave lotions, 4
Agata people, Philippines, 138
Age, 28, 141–44
Age of Exploration, 133
Age grades, 39, 199, 201, 202, 203
Aging, 78, 141–43, *143*, 403
Agrarian cycles, 244
Agribusinesses, 244
Agricultural cultures, 120
Airbrushing, 64
Airline travel, 241
Akan people, Ghana, 221
Aka Pygmy, Central Africa, 198
Akin, Susan, 313, *314*
Alexander the Great, 230
Allen, Woody, 371
Alliances, national, 238
Altitude, 151–52, 153–54

American Anthropological Association (AAA), 134
The American Anthropologist, 85
American College Professors of Textiles and Clothing, 93
American Crafts Council, Museum of Contemporary Crafts, 348
American Ethnology, 85
American Home Economics Association, 93
American Indians, 10, 73
    boarding schools, 66–67
    dress differences, 135
    engravings of, 61–62, *62*
    ethnic dress, 85, *86*
    research reports, 85
    sources for fashion design, 249, *249*
    wrapped buffalo robes, 16, 85, *86*
American or red race, 133
American Shakespeare Festival Theater, 360
Amish people, 67, 256, 337
Amulet pouches, 17
Amulets, 20, *22*, 201
Anabaptist groups, 337
Analytical writings, 75, 84–93
Ancestor worship, 189, 200, 212
Angami Naga people, South Asia, 204
Angelou, Maya, 369–70
Anglomania, 79
Animal rights activists, 35
Animals, domesticating, 210
Animism, 189, 200
Annie Hall (film), 371
Annual cycles, 201
Annual Reports of the Bureau of Ethnology, 85
Anorexia nervosa, 7, 140
Anspach, Karlyne, 90
Anthropologists, 34, 35, 92
Anthropology, 55
    emergence as a social science, 85–87
Anthropomorphic form, 200
Antibacterial properties, 400
Anti-wrinkle cream, 143, *143*

Antubam, Kofi, 311–13
Apache boots, *162*
Aphrodite, 230
Apollo, 311, *311*
Apparel manufacturing, 248, 303, 397, 405
Apparel design, 405
Archaeological digs, 56, 57, 194
Arctic region, 17, 138
Armature, 348
Armor as artifacts, 56
Art and art history, 55, 64, 211
Art of dress, 287–307
Artifacts of dress, 56–59, 287
Artificial environment, 153, 155, 170
Artisans of textile and dress, 215, 218, 220, 247, 402, 405
Artists and artisans, 59, *60*, 64, 298
Artists and fashion, 370–71
Art patronage, 92
Arts
    textile, 214
    see also Dress and the arts
Ascribed social status, 39
Ash, Juliet and Elizabeth Wilson, 91
Asia, 71, 131
Asiatic or yellow race, 133
Assembly lines, *244*, 248, 401
Athabascan Indian groups, 190
Athletic braces, 166
Athletic competitions, 189
Athletic shoes, 253
Attachments to the body, 18–20
Attachments to body enclosures, 20, 22
Austin Powers films, 320
Australian Aborigines, 132, 133, *134*, 187
    body proportions, 150
    foraging way of life, 210
    protective dress, 155, 291

B

Badges of office, 222, *222*
Baffin Island, American Indians, 194, *195*
Baggy clothing, 340

Balashan, Afghanistan, 68
Baldness, 7, 142
Balkans, 135
Ballet dancers, 351, 355, *356*, 365
Bandannas, 16
Bangkok, 254–55
Bara, Theda, *359*
Barbers, 288
Barbie dolls, 322, 403
Barnard, Malcolm, 91
Barnes, Ruth, 93
Barrettes, 18
Barthes, Roland, 91
Baseball caps, 337
Bathing, 4, 13, 88, 294, 319
Bathing pools, 232
Batik shirts, Indonesia, 42–43, *43*
Batik wrappers, Indonesia, 247
Battle, Kathleen, 362
B.C.E. (Before the Common Era), 53
Beads, 17, 22, 56
Beagle (ship) expedition, 291
Beards, 8
Beat generation, 371
Beatniks, 295
Beautification of the body, 3
Beauty, 289–90
Beauty contests, 210, 313
Beauty ideals, 155
Beauty myth, 93
Behavior, collective, 88
Belches, 14
Beliefs, 34
Bell, Quentin, 89
Belts, 17
Benedict, Ruth, 89
Benedictine order, 229
Benstock, Shari and Suzanne Feriss, 91
Berber people, North Africa, 319
Bergler, Edmund, 89
Bias
   of evidence, 55
   racial and gender, 305
   in written descriptions, 67
   see also Cultural bias
Bible, 60
Biblical subjects, 366
Bibliographies, 89
Bibs, 40
Bigman, 200
Biking, 165
Bindi, 19
Biographies, 67
Biohazard suits, 171–72
Biological parents, 128
Bird skin anoraks, 193, *193*
Bird skins, 169
Births, 189, 199
The Birth of Venus (Botticelli), 311, *311*
Bivans, Ann-Marie, 313, *314*
Black, for mourning, 302

Bleaching skin, 7
Blood vessel expansion and contraction, 152, 153
Blouz, 18
Blumer, Herbert, 91, 341
Bodley, John H., 39
Body abilities, 3
Body action and demands of performance, 354–58
Body beautification, 3
Bodybuilding, 7, 10, 41, 294, 333
Body dominant, 323–25, *324*, *325*
Body, dress, and environment, 149–75
   see also Environment
Body fat, 141
Body hair, 136
Body modifications, 4, 5, 6, 7–15, 293
   relating with body supplements, 24
   as wearable art, 349
   see also Bodybuilding; Body painting; Body piercing; Tattoos
Body movement, 141–42, 294, *295*
Body odor, 4, 13, 400
Body painting, 7, 323, *324*
   New Guinea, 91
   Nuba of Africa, 348
   in small-scale cultures, 190, *191*
Body piercing, 253, 340, 403
Body processes, natural, 14
Body protection. *See* Protective dress
Body raft, 161, *162*
Body scanners, 141
Body shape ideals, 40, 41
Body stockings, 301
Body structure, 294
Body subordinate, 323–25, *325*
Body supplements, 4, 5, 6, 15–23, *20*, 293, 299–302
   attachments to the body, 18–20
   attachments to body enclosures, 20, 22
   creating illusion, 314–16
   enclosures, 16–20
      combination type, 17–18
      preshaped, 17, 301
      suspended, 17
      wrapped, 16–17, 215, 299–300, *299*
   handheld objects, 22–23, 160
   relating with body modifications, 24
Body temperature, 152, 160
Body types, 127, 137–38, *139*, *140*, 303
Bondo people, India, 26, *27*
Bone density, 141
Books, 69
Bordeau, Louis, 62–63
Borneo women, filing teeth, 10
Boston Symphony Orchestra, 362
Botticelli, Sandro, *The Birth of Venus*, 311, *311*
Boucher, Francois, 69, 92
Boulanger, Chantal, 92
Boutonnieres, 20

Bow and arrow, 210
Boxer underwear, 48
Boyer, G. Bruce, 81
Bracelets, 17
   jangling, 289
   mammoth ivory, 56
Brand names, 248, 257
Brassieres, 9, *9*, 24
Breastfeeding, 141, *142*
Breast reconstructions, 141
Breath fresheners, 13
Brecker Brothers Band, 362, *363*
Breechclouts, 199
Brenninkmeyer, Ingrid, 91
Breward, Christopher, 92
Bridal bouquets, 23
Bridal veils, 24
Briefcases, 22, 160
Broadway road shows, 358
Bronze Age, Scandinavian graves, 58
Brooches, 20
Brues, Alice, 133, 147
Bubble-up fashion, 342
Buddhist monks, 337
Bulimia, 7, 140
Bulletproof vests, 157, *157*
Bullough, Bonnie, 93
Bullough, Vern L., 93
Bunu Yoruba, 92
Bunzel, Ruth, 89
Burial attire, 41, 200–201, *201*
   see also Burial sites and graves; Funerals
Burial sites and graves, 72, 200–201, *201*
   see also Burial attire; Funerals
Burlesque performers, 365
Burnett, Carol, 78
Bushmen, 147
Business dress
   codes for, 321
   in the future, 398
   suits, 253, 301
   women, 333, *334*
Bustle ensemble, 7, 323
Buttons, 337
Byzantine Period, 229

C
Caftans, 301, 323
Cajuns of Louisiana, 45, 53
Camouflage dress, 155, *156*
Cancer, skin, 130
Canes, 23
Caribou, 164, 169, 192
Caricature, 76
Carlyle, Thomas, 76
Carnival costumes, 366
Carpenter's apron, 160, *161*
Carter, Howard, 57
Carter, Jimmy, 252
Cartoons, 76–77, *77*

Cash, Johnny, 362
Caste, 212, 219, 239, 336
Casual dress codes, United States, 255, 333
Casual Fridays, 83
Catalogues, 67, 241, 247, 249
Cataracts, *159*
Cathy (comic strip), 76
Caucasian, 133
Cave dwellers, 59
C.E. (Common Era), 54
Celebratory outfits, 70
Centers for Disease Control, 172
Central Africa, Aka Pygmy, 198
Central America, 243
Central Andes and Peru, textiles, 58
Centralized government, 211, 212, 222
Ceremonial circumcision, 202
Ceremonies, 199
Chador, Iran, 321
Chain-mail garments, 17
Chandler, Raymond, 368
    "The Little Sister," 67
Chanel, 247, 302
Chaplin, Charlie, 360, *361*
Charities, 247
Chasubles, 17
Chau, India, 359
Cheerleaders, 365
Chemical accidents, 158
Chemicals, 155
    see also Protective dress
Chemistry, 55
Chemists, 400
Chemotherapy patients, 141
Cher, 78
Chermayeff, Catherine, 93
Cheung sam, China, 48, 219, 250
Chiefdoms, 210, 212
Childbearing, 197, 311
Child rearing abilities, 197
Children's clothing, sizing, 141, *142*
Chile, Chinchorro mummy, 56
China
    dress of government officials, 222
    222
    dress in, 87
    feudal kingdoms, 212
    national dress for women, 250
Chinchorro mummy, Chile, 56
Chinese lion dance, 365
Ch'ing Dynasty, China, 229
Chi pao, China, 250
Choirs, 364
Choli, 18, *21*
Cholitas of Bolivia, 53
Choquecancha, Peru, 229
Choruses, 364
Christianity, 242, 256
Circular culture, Zulu people, 316
Circumcision

ceremonial, 202
    Masai of Kenya, 203, *203*
Circus costumes, 355, 357, 358
Civil rights movement, 135
Clans, Scottish, 200
Clapping hands, 14
Class, 212, 219, 336
Classification system of dress, 3–31, 185, 293
    advantages of, 25–28
    applications of, 24–25
    Classification System for Types of
        Dress and Their
        Properties, 6
    culturally neutral concept, 50
    see also Body modifications; Body
        supplements
Cleanliness, 319
Cleats, 14
Cleopatras, 359, *359*
Climate, 138
    interventions between body and
        climate, 166–70
Cline, 132
Clinton, Bill, 42–43, *43*
Clip-on bow ties, 22
Clipped or pressure fastened
    attachments to the body, 19
Clipped or pressure fastened
    attachments to body enclosures, 22
Clothing selection textbooks, 78
Clothing sizes, 154
Clothing and Textile Research Journal, 93
Clothing zones, 166–70
Cocktail dresses, 175
Cohen, Yehudi A., 89
Colas, René, 89
Colbert, Claudette, *359*
Cold, 153, 160
    see also Acclimatization
Cold-blooded animals, 152
Collar styles, 301, 315
Collective behavior, 88
Colognes, 13
Colonial expansion, Europe, 225, *226*
Colonialism, 48, 85, 228–29
Color, 288, 298, 315
    body modifications, 7
    in costume, 360–61
    cultural meanings of, 41, 42, 302
    of eyes, 19
    in future dress, 400
    and lighting, 359
    printing, 64
Color analysis books, 80
Color Me Beautiful (Jackson), 80
Combination type enclosures, 17–18
Combs, 18
Combs, Sean "Puffy," 342, *343*
Comic strips, 76–77, *77*
Commercial art, 65, *65*

Commercial market economy, 243
Commoners, 219
Communication
    with dress, 85, *86*
    nonverbal, 3, 27–28, 33
    sensory system, 4–5, 33
    verbal, 4–5
Communism, 256
Concert bands, 364
Conformity and individuality, 240, 320, 329–45
    conformity, 332–39, *332*
    fashion, 341–42
    fashion leaders, 341–42
    individuality, 339–41
    societal influence, 330–39
    see also Individuality
Confucianism, 256
Consignment stores, 247
Constantine (emperor), 229
Consumers, 239
Contact lenses, 19
Contemporary culture and society, 45–46, 210
    globalization, 45–46, 48
Contemporary mass society, 91
Contemporary society, small-scale culture, 190
Cook, Captain, 68
Cook, Dorothy E., 89
Copyists, 64
Corcos, Alain, 133
Corduroy, 4
Corporate dress policy, 78
Corporations, 239, 252, *254*, 405
Corsages, 20
Corsets, 8–9, *9*, 19, 24, 315, 325
Cosmetic artists, 288
Cosmetics, 4, 287, 315
Costume, 350
Costume Institute, Metropolitan Art
    Museum, 348
Costume (journal), 93
Costume plates, 60, 63–64, 69
Costume Society of America, 93
Cotton, 58, 154, 213, 214–15, 243, 400
Coughing, 14
Country singers, 362
Cowboy boots, 166
Craft workers, 62
Craik, Jennifer, *The Face of Fashion*, 91
Crawford, Cindy, Sonia Kashuk, and
    Kathleen Boyes, 78
Crawley, Ernest, 88, 89
Creating forms of dress, 293–97
Creation of illusions, 314–16
Cro-Magnon-type man, 56
Cross-cultural influences, fashion, 245–46
Cross-cultural misconceptions, 26
Cross-cultural relationships, 239, 318

Cross-cultural studies, 49, 298, 322
Cross-dressisng, 87, 93, 336, *336*
Crowns, 223
Crow tribe, 137
Cufflinks, 20
Cultural adaptation of the body to
    environment, 155–60
Cultural anthropologists, 134
Cultural authentication, 46, 225–27, 239,
    243
Cultural bias, 25–26, 28, 40, 50, 185,
    298, 301
    see also Ethnocentrism
Cultural boundaries, 45
Cultural diversity, United States, 83
Cultural expectations in dress, 4
Cultural history, 57
Cultural ideals, 309–10
    of beauty, 403
    in body form, 322–25
    in Ghana, 311–14
    United States, 313–14
    within different societies, 310–14
    see also Ideals
Culturally neutral concepts in
    classification system of dress, 4, 50
Cultural standards, 310, 317–20
    change in, 320–21, 406
Cultural typologies of dress, 302–5,
    304
Cultural universals, art of dress,
    290–93
Culture, 34–35
    and adaptation, 129
    contemporary, 45–50
    definition, 34, 237
    development of, 130
    and dress, 40–42, 50
    embedding of, 92
    and ethnicity, 135
    and identity, 91
    subcultures, 35
    see also Global-scale culture; Large-
    scale culture; Scale of world
    cultures; Small-scale culture;
    Society
Cunningham, Patricia and Susan Voso
    Lab, 91
Cunnington, C.W., 89
Current events, 246
Customer, target, 405
Custom Foot, 401
Custom production, 400, 401
    see also Mass customization
Custom-tailoring, 82

D
Dakota dance dress, 357, *357*, 399–400
Dakota Indian jingle dresses, 4, *5*
Dalby, Liza, 92
Dali, Salvador, 370

Dalmalningar, Sweden, 60, *61*
Dance competitions, 189
Dance lines, 364, *364*
Dance performance, 365–66
Dancers, 14
Dar (Indian scholar), 44, 54
Darwin, Charles, 291
Davenport, Millia, 66, 69, 92
David (French painter), 366
David, Jonathan, 93
Day care centers, 330, *330*
Dearborn, George Van Ness, 88
Deaths, 189, 199
    dressing of the deceased, 200–201,
    201
DeBry, Theodore, 61–62, *62*, 73
Debutante's train, 349, *350*
Decentralized political systems, 189,
    199
Deep-sea diving. *See* Diving suits
Deerskin, 64
DeLong, Marilyn, 301
Democratic societies, 92
Demographic shifts, 246
Demorgues, Jacques LeMoyne, 62, 73
Denmark, string skirts, 60
Dental care, 10, 15
Deodorants, 13
Descent groups, 200
Designer labels, 257, 403
Developing countries, 248, 251
Dhoti, India, 292, 299
Diana, Princess of Wales, 323, 406,
    407
Diaries, 67
Diasporas, 36, *37*, 242–43, 405
    see also Migration
Dickens, Charles, *Great Expectations*,
    368–69, *369*
Dieting, 7, 10, 294, 315
    see also Nutrition
Dilbert (comic strip), 76
Disease, 138–41
Disenfranchised groups, 255–56
Diversity, physical, 130–44
Divine figures and dress, 229–30
Divine right of kings, 212
Diviners, 189, 201
Diving suits, 157, 158, 170
Division of labor
    future of dress, 402–4
    global-scale culture, 246–49
    large-scale culture, 212, 218–21, 330
    small-scale culture, 189, 197–99
Djellaba, 301
Dole, Bob, 297, *298*
Domestication of animals, 210, 213
Domestication of plants, 213
Domingo, Placido, 362
Dragon robe, China, 323, 350, *351*
Drag queens, 336, *336*

Dress
    as an art form, 348–50
    as an integral part of the arts, 350–51
    camouflage, 155, *156*
    complexity and detail, 27–28
    contemporary culture and society,
    45–50
    and cultural meanings, 50
    culture and society, 33–54
    definition, 4–6
    ecclesiastical, 229, *230*
    ethnic, 44–45, 48, 399, *399*
    everyday, 58–59, 72
    fashionable, 48
    functional, 88
    global-scale culture, 38–39, 46, 48,
    228, 237–60
    history books, 64
    history of, 69–70, 92
    and human behavior, 57
    large-scale culture, 38–39, 209–35
    leisure, 339–40
    national, 248, 249–51, *250*, 253, 399, *399*
    occupational, 245
    power of, 5
    protective, 3, 88, 154, *154–60*, 155,
    156–59, 245
    reasons for, 3, 4
    records of, 55–73
    reincarnated, 246
    small-scale culture, 38–39, 187–207
    and social rank, 221, *222*
    sport activities, 170
    symbolism of, 87
    terminology, 25–28
    as a tool, 130
    as total environment, 170–72
    types of, 7–24
    Western and non-Western, 69, 92
    world, 46–48
Dress (annual), 93
Dress and the arts, 347–73
    see also Arts
Dress codes
    school and business, 321, 330
    United States, 91
Dresser, Norine, 319
Dressmakers, 215, 403
Dress-up clothes, 330, *330*
Duffey, Mrs. E.G., 79
Dugum Dani people, New Guinea, 26,
    27, 196
Duncan, Isadora, 355
Dupatta, 16, 24, 25, *25*
Dyeing fabric, 214, 215
Dye plants, 214

E
Ear piercing, 20
Earrings, 16, 17, 18, 19
Eastern Europe, 243

East Flores, Lamaholt people, 200
Ebin, Victoria, 348
Ebola virus, 172
Ecclesiastical dress, 229, *230*
Economic viewpoint, 90, 92
Economy
    future of dress, 400–402
    global-scale culture, 239, 243–46, 251
    large-scale culture, 211, 213–18
    small-scale culture, 191–97
Ectomorphic body type, 137–38, *139*,
    140
Edo government, Japan, 220
Egalitarian dress, 253
Egalitrian society, 189, 195, 210, 218
Egypt, 210
    archaeological digs, 56, 57
    flax into linen, 214
    slaves' dress, 215, 217
Egyptian shirt, 215, *215*
Eicher, Joanne B., 93
Eichler, Lillian, 80
Elders, 200, 202, *202*
Electric socks, 170
Electronic sources of dress information,
    70
el Guindi, Fadwa, *Veil: Modesty, Privacy
    and Resistance*, 257
Elizabeth II, queen of England, 223
Ellis, Havelock, *Studies in the Psychology
    of Sex*, 87–88
E-mail, 70
Embedding of culture, 92
Embroidered fabric, 214
Emotional meaning of dress, 297, 298,
    302, 340
Empires, 210, 212, 225, 239
Enclosures, 16–20
Enculturation, 34
    body shape ideals, 41
Endomorphic body type, 137–38, *139*,
    140
England, 79
Engravers, 59, 60
Engravings of American Indians, 61–62,
    62
Environment
    artificial, 153, 155, 170
    cultural adaptation of the body,
        155–60
    negative effects on, 155, 245, 400
    physiological adaptation, 150–55
    portable, 157, 158
    temperature, 152–53
    see also Body, dress, and environment
Epicanthic fold, 10, 131, *131*
Equality under democracy, United
    States, 257
Ermine, 223
Erogenous zones, 89
Eskimos. *See* Inuit tribe

Essays, 67
Ethnic cleansing, 243
Ethnic dress, 44–45, 225, 399, *399*, 404
    marketing of, 247, *248*
    and national dress, 250–51, *250*
    and tourism, 399
    and world and fashionable dress, 48
Ethnic groups, 36, *37*, 45, 135, 227–28,
    405
Ethnic heritage, 403
Ethnicity, 45, 135
Ethnocentrism, 42–45, 70
    see also Cultural bias
Etiquette manuals, 67, 77, 78, 80, 83, 84
Euro-American cultures
    bare feet and covered heads, 44
    body shapes, 40
    changing nature of, 46–47
    closely fitting woman's dress, 17, *19*
    nakedness and overdressing, 25–26
Eurocentrism, 42, 54
Europe
    colonial expansion, 225, *226*
    comparisons with dress in the United
        States, 79
    costume history, 69
    dress of monarchs, 222–23, *223*
    feudal kingdoms, 212
    men's shirts, 46, *47*
    preshaped enclosures, 17
    printing press, 61
    publications, 91
    tattooing in, 253
European East India Companies, 253
European or white race, 133
Evans, Elizabeth and Mina Thornton, 91
Evening wear, 398
Everyday dress, 58–59, 70
Evita (film), 371
Evolutionary adaptations, 150
Exaggeration in costumes, 358
Exchange of goods, 194, 195, 196–97,
    211
    see also Trade
Exercise, 10, 294, 315
Extension agents, 244
Extension of the body's abilities, 3
Extensions and modifications of the
    body, 160–66
Extravaganzas, 356, 358, 365
Eyebrows, 315, *316*
Eyeglasses, 5, 19, 155
Eyes, color of, 19
Eye surgery, 10, 149

F
Fabri, Charles, 69
Face peeling, 12
Facial features, 127, 313, 333
Facial hair, 41
Facial shapes, 80, 81, *82*, 301, 310, 314

Facial wrinkling, 159
Faical gestures, 294
Fairholt, F.W., 69
Fairservis, Walther A., Jr., 69
False eyelashes, 19
False fingernails, 19
False mustaches, 19
False teeth, 10, 166
Family events, 70
Family membership, 333–34, *335*, 361
Fans, 22
Fantasy and the supernatural, 364–65
Farming, 194, 210
Fashion, 46, 288
    books on, 91
    concept of, 218
    cross-cultural influences, 245–46
    and ethnic dress, 251
    global influences, 92
    haute couture, 247, 365
    men's, 63–65, 81–83
    pace of change in, 85, 87, 341
    retro, 247
    runway models, 14
    runway shows, 288, 365
    trickle-down, 220
    and world and ethnic dress, 48
Fashion design, 70, 248–49, 288
Fashion designers, 298
Fashion dolls, 63
Fashion leaders, 320
Fashion magazines, 77, 288
Fashion models, 294, *296*, 310, 313, 322
Fashion photographs, 63, *63*, 288
Fashion plates, 63–66, *63*
Fashion shows, 14
Fashion Theory (journal), 93
Feet, 24
    henna designs, 288
    see also Foot binding in China
Feminist scholars, 93
Feng Jicai, 310
Ferrigno, Lou, 138, *140*
Fertilizers, 244
Fetishism, 87, 88
Feudal kingdoms, 212
Figure problems, 313
Figure skaters, 351, 357
Film criticism, 93
Film industry, 359, *359*
Fingernails, 12, 14
Firefighters, 164–65, 245
Fisher, Eileen, *296*, *297*
Fishing, 310
Flat textiles, 190
Flatulence, 14
Flaubert, Gustave, *Madame Bovary*, 368
Flavored lip glosses, 15
Flax, 59, 213, 214
Fletcher, Alice, 85, *86*
Florida, Seminole Indians, 226–27

Flower children, 371
Flowers, 13, 18, 23
Flügel, J.C., 89
Flushing, 152
Flusser, Alan, 83
Folk taxonomy, 134
Follies Bergères, 365
Follies stage extravaganzas. *See* Extravaganzas
Football uniforms, 158–59, 165
Foot binding in China, 9–10, 13, 24, 310
Footsteps, 14
Footwear, 161–64, *162*, *163*, 170
Foraging, 210
Formalism school of painting, 366
Fortuny, Mario, 370
Fossil fuels, 239, 400
Foster, Helen Bradley, 92
Foundation garments, 7, 8–9, *9*, 24
Fourt, Lyman and Norman R.S. Hollies, 88
Fox, 169
Fox Fiber, 400
Fox teeth, 56
Fragrances, 13
France, 79
Freud,Sigmund, 87
Frostbite, 131
Fuegian people, South America, 291
Functional dress, 88
Funerals
    colors for mourners and burial attire, 41, 302
    see also Burial attire; Burial sites and graves
Furniture, 34
Furriers, 215
Furs, 35, *90*, 223, 294
Future of dress, 397–409
    polity and ideology, 405
    population and residence, 398–400
    social structure and division of labor, 402–4
    technology and economy, 400–402

G
Gaignieres, Francois Roger de, 62–63
Gait, 13–14
Galibaya, 301
Gallagher, Mary Barelli, *368*, 369
Gandhi, Mahatma, 199, 292, *292*
Gang dress, 255
Gangs, tattoos, 12
Garber, Marjorie, 93
Garcia, Jerry, 370
Gardening, 194
Garments, 16
Garrett, Valery M., 69, 93
Gaultier, Jean-Paul, 290, 365
Geishas, Japan, 294

Gem cutters, 215
Gender, 28
    and apparel manufacturing, 248
    cross-dressisng, 87, 93, 336, *336*
    and dress, 93, 240–41, 333
    work dress, *77*
Gene pool, 128, *132*
General Agreement on Tariffs and Trade (GAFF), 251, 252
Generation X, 255
Genetic adaptation, 152
Geneticists, 400
Genitals, covering, 17, 26
Genocidal campaigns, 228
Geographical barriers, 132, *132*
Geographical boundaries, 36
Gerewol celebration, 189
Ghana
    Akuaba (fertility doll), 312
    chiefs in, 135
    female ideal, 311–13, *312*
Ghurye, G.S., 69
Gibson Girl's dress, 296, *297*
Girdles, 8–9, *9*
Glamour (magazine), 78
Glenn, John, *172*
Global influences, fashion, 92
Globalization, 45–46, 48
Global-scale culture and dress, 38–39, 46, 48, *228*, 229, 237–60
Global trade, 243–44, *244*
Global travel uniforms, 403
Gloves, 164–65, 221
Godey's Lady's Book, 63, 64, 78
Goffman, Erving, 90, 91
Goldsmith, Olivia and Amy Fine Collins, 84
"Goose bumps," 152
Gore-Tex, 169
Gorman, Margaret, 313, *314*
Gothic female figures, 322
Governments, 405
The Grateful Dead, 370
Graying of hair, 142–43
Great Expectations (Dickens), 368–69, *369*
Greco-Roman era, 215
Greece
    female ideals, 311, *311*, 322, 359
    himation, 366, *367*
    male ideals, 311, 322, *322*
    military uniforms, 224, *224*
    Olympic games, 295
Greek statues, 230
Green production, 245
    see also Environment
Griggs, Claudine, 93
Grooming practices, 13, 15, 340
Group identity, 404
Group norms, 291
Group performance, 362, 364

Growth and age, 141–43
Grunge, 295
Guanaco, 291
Guardian Angels, 256
Guatemala Indians, Mayan designs, 204, 228
Gujarat people, India, 25
Gum disease, 15
Gurel, Lois, 91
Gymnastics, 322

H
Habituations of immediate body adjustments, 151, 152–53
Hair
    amount, texture, and color, 127, 130
    attachments to the body, 18
    body, 136
    color, 7
    cultural meaning in styles of, 28
    dyeing, 15
    facial, 41
    fasteners, 19
    graying of, 142–43
    implantations, 7
    men's haircuts, 293, *293*
    permanent waves, 40
    punk, 48, 49
    removal of, 10, *10–11*
    shape and structure, 8
    styles of, 48, *49*, 135, 287
    texture, 12
    volume and proportion, 7
    washing, 13
    weaving, 18
Hairdressers, 288
Hakka people, Hong Kong, 159
Hanbok, Korea, 67
Han Chinese, 250
Handbags, 22
Handcrafted textiles, 403
Handcuffs, 175
Hand enclosures, 161, 164–65, 170, *171*
Handheld objects, 22–23, 160, *202*, 223
Hand lotion, 15
Hands, 160
Hand-sewing, 58
Hansen, Henny Harald, 92
Harappa, Indus River Valley, 210
Harlequin, 361
Harlow, Jean, *316*
Harris, Marvin, 195
Hasidic Jews, 135, *136*, 330–31
Hats, 17, 58, 141, 159, *159*
    Amish people, 337
    removal of, 220, 221
    Saami Four Winds, 160, *161*
Haute couture, 247, 365
Hawaii, Japanese immigrants in, 92
Haweis, Mary Eliza, 325

Hawes, Elizabeth, 89
Heaby metal bands, 371
Head cloths, 16
Headdresses, 199, 291, 300, 348, 357, 358
Headhunting, 204
Head scarves, 16
Headties, 300
Headwraps, 300
Healers, 189, 201
Health, 319
Heat cramps, 152
Heath, E., 93
Height, 81, 137, 141, 303
Heilman, Stine, 367, *368*
Hein period, Japan, 220–21
Hellenic Greece, 221
Hemline histories, 92
Hendrickson, Carol, 69
Hendrickson, Hildi, 92
Henna designs, feet, 288
Henry VIII, 323
Herbs, 4
Herding animals, 194
Heredity, 130, 403
Herodotus, 61
Herrick, Robert, 369
Hierarchy, 212
High altitude, 151–52, 153–54
High gods, 212, 229
Highland New Guinea, Mount Hagen
    people, 191, *192*, 194–95, *196*, 291
Hiler, Hilaire, 89
Hiler, Meyer, 89
Hillestad, Robert, 349, *350*
Himalayas, 132, *132*
Himation, Greece, 366, *367*
Hindu castes, India, 336
Hip-hop, 295, *343*
Hippie to hip-hop subcultures, 290, 371,
    400
Hispanic, 135
Historical accuracy, 359, *359*
Historical events, 59, 366
History, 46–47
History books, 67
History of dress, 69–70, 92
Hleeta (scarification), 197
Hmong-Americans, 36, *37*, 45, 48
Hockey uniforms, 158–59, 165, *165*
Hoffman, Dustin, 352, *353*, 360
Hollander, Anne, 91, 93
Holy days, 212
Homeless people, 319
Homespun fabrics, 217
Homo sapiens, 49, 128, 129, 130, 187
Hong Kong, 254–55
Hoop skirts, 324
Hope, Thomas, 69
Horn, Marilyn, 91
Hottenroth, Fr., 69
Howe, Elias, 58

Hudson's Bay blankets, 196
Huipil, Mexico, 39
Human behavior and dress, 57
Human mating, 132
Human sexuality
    attractive parts of the body in
        different cultures, 302
    and dress, 93, 403
    research in, 85, 87–88
Human size, 81
Humor, 76
Hurlock, Elizabeth B., 89
Hypoxia, 152, 154

I
Idealized photographs, 64
Ideals, 34
    of beauty, 155, 351, 403
    see also Cultural ideals; Ideals for
        individual appearance and the art
        of dress
Ideals for individual appearance and the
    art of dress, 309–27
    acheiving ideals, 314–16
    body dominant and body
        subordinate, 323–25
    change in cultural standards, 320–21
    cultural ideals, 309–10
    cultural ideals in body form, 322–25
    cultural standards, 310, 317–20
    ideals within different societies,
        310–14
        Ghana, 311–14
        United States, 313–14
Identical twins, 128
Identity and culture, 91
Ideology, 256, 256–57
    future of dress, 405
    see also Religion
Illusion creation, 314–16
Immigration, 78, 134, 242, 243, 405
Imperial languages, 225, *226*
Inca cotton, 214
Inca empire, 210, 229
India, 44, 71, 253
    adult males priestly and ruling classes,
        17
    bangle bracelets, 221
Indians. *See* American Indians; India
Individuality, 403, 404
    expression through dress, 91, 240, 291
    United States, 330
    see also Conformity and individuality
Indonesia, 70
    ethnic dress, 251
Indus River Valley
    Harappa, 210
    Mohenjo-Daro, 210
Industrial economies, 244
Industrial Revolution, 194
Infant garments, 141

Infants, 288–90
Infrared scanner, 401, *402*
Initiation rituals, 201, 203
In-line skating, 165
Innovators, 320
Inserted attachments to the body, 18, *21*
Inserted attachments to body enclosures,
    20
Insignias, 222, *222*
Interbreeding, 132
Intergenerational arguments, 243
Internal conflicts, 210
International peacekeeping, 405
International representatives dress codes,
    321
International Textile and Apparel
    Association (ITAA), 93
Internet, 238, 239, 255
    see also World Wide Web (www)
Interventions between body and climate,
    166–70
Inuit people, 17, *131*, 138
    body proportions, 150
    boots, *162*
    dress, 163–64, 169, 191–93, *193*
    metabolic rate, 152, 153
Invention of tradition, 45, 53
Investiture ceremonies, 222–23,
    223
Iran, 254, 255
    chador, 321
Iraq, Neanderthal burial site, 289
Irish-American, 135
Irish step dancing, 365
Islam, 242, 254, 255, 256, 257, *407*
Islamic empire, 225, *227*
Italian Renaissance ideal, 311, *311*
Itinerant traders, 218

J
Jackson, Carole, 80
Jackson, Michael, 403
Jakarta, 254–55
Jamaica, 327, 384–88
Japan
    marriage of crown prince (1993),
        221
    nape of the neck, 302
    women's walk, 14
    young people, 242
Jazz, 362, *363*
Jeans, 253, 257, 320, 401
Jerusalem, 242
Jesus Christ, 60, *60*, 366
Jesus, Mary, and Joseph, 230, *231*
Jet lag, 151
Jewelry, 4, 5, 16, 294
    as artifacts, 56
    attachments to the body, 18
    gem cutters, 215
    preshaped, 17

Jews, 135, 242
  women, 243
  see also Hasidic Jews; Judaism
Jingle Dance, Dakota people, 399–400
Job interviewss, 78
John, Elton, 362
John Paul II (pope), 229, *229*
Jones, Bill T., 355, *356*
Journalists, 288
Journals, society, 85
J. Peterman catalogue, *399*
Judaism, 256
  see also Jews
Julien J. Studley, Inc., 251

K
Kabuki theater, Japan, 354, 361
Kahlo, Frida, 336, 367, 393–94
Kaiser, Susan, *The Social Psychology of Clothing*, 91
Kalabari people, Nigeria, 221, 225–26, 300, *300*, 315, 352, *352*, 374
Kamali, Norma, 249
Kamiks (skin boots), 164, 192
Kamiz, 16, *25*
Karpinski, Kenneth, Jr., 80
Kashmir, *252*
Kathakali dance, India, 354
Kawakami, Barbara F., 92
Kayapo people, Brazil, 26
Kazakh tribe, *132*
Kente cloth, 135, 221, 222, 242–43
Kidwell, Claudia Brush, 93
Kilts, 27, 34, *35*
Kimono, 46, 94, 215, *217*, 350
Kin-based groups, 189, 197
Kingdoms, 210, 212, 239
King Tutankhamun's tomb, 57
Kirk, Kris, 93
Klapp, Orrin E., 91
König, René, 91
Kootenay National Park, Canada, 190
Koran, 40, 406, *406*
Korea, *hanbok*, 67
Krafft-Ebing, Richard Von, *Psychopathia Sexualis*, 87
Kretschmer, A., 69
Kuala Lampur, 254–55
!Kung of Africa, 131, 147
  temporary body modifications, 167–68
Kwakiutl tribe, Vancouver Island, 8, *8*, 195

L
Labor, low-cost, 248, 251
Lace makers, 215
Ladino racism, 228
La Flesche, Francis, 85, *86*
Lagerfeld, Karl, 247, 302, *302*, 365, 406, *406*
La Gravatte, France archaeological digs, 194

Lamaholt people, East Flores, 200
Land ownership, 211
  see also Private property
Land's End, 166, *167*, 244
Langer, Lawrence, 89, 360
Language, 130, 287
Languages, 4
  imperial, 225, *226*
Laos, 91
  Hmong people, 36, *37*, 45, 243
Lapps. *See* Saami people
Large-scale culture and dress, 38–39, 209–35
  subgroups, 330–31, 399
Larkey, Jan, 78
Laser surgery, 10, *11*
Laura Ashley prints, 405
Lauren, Ralph, 249, *249*, 253
Laurent, Yves Saint, 249
Laver, James, 89, 90
Laver's principles of dress, 90, *90*
Layering clothing
  to display social status, 220–21
  for warmth, 154, 166
Leaders in fashion, 320
Leather, 35, 56, 58, 289
Legends, 61
Leg irons, 175
Leisured class, 88
Leisure dress, 339–40
Leisure time, 189, 218, 291
Lennon, Sharron J., 365
Leopard, 223
Levi Strauss, 401
Liberace, 342, 356
Lieber, Judith, *349*
Life course rituals, 189, 199, 202, 203, 253
Lighting, 358–60
Linen, 57, 214, 245
Linnaeus, Carolus, 133
Lipovetsky, Gilles, 92
Lipperheide, Franz Joseph, 89, 96
Lipperheide library, 89
Lipsticks, 4, 15, 293
Literary arts, 350, 367–70
Lithographers, 59
Little Big Man (film), 352, *353*, 360
"The Little Sister" (Chandler), 67
LoGiacco, Jean-Paul, 81, 82
Loincloths, 199, 215, 292
Long-term adaptations, 130–38
Looms, 214, *214*
Lorant, Stefan, 73
Louisiana Cajuns, 45
Louis XIV, 63
Louis XVI, 366
Luggage styles, 241
Lungi, 16, 299, *299*
Lurie, Alison, 91
Lycra, 401

M
McCracken, Grant, 92
McDonalds, 253, *254*
McIntyre, Reba, 362
Mackie, Bob, 78
Madame Bovary (Flaubert), 368
Madonna, 342, 362, 370
Madras plaid, 219, 334
Magazines, fashion, 77, 288
Magellan, Ferdinand, 70
Maids, 247
Makeup, 10
Malnutrition, 140
Mammals, 152
Mammoth ivory
  beads, 56
  bracelets, 56
Mandarin collar, 253
Mande tribe, West Africa, 20, *22*
Mannequins, 348
Maori, New Zealand, 87
Mao suit, China, 93, 250, 256, 337, *338*
Marching bands, 364
Mardi Gras, 366
Maritime exploration, 60
Market days, 212
Marketplace, 36
Marriages, 189, 199
Martinique, 300
Marx, Karl, 256
Mary Poppins, 361
Masai of Kenya, 187, 202, *202*
  circumcision, 203, *203*
Masks, 56, 204
Masquerade dancers, 352, *352*, 365
Mass customization, 401, *402*
  see also Custom production
Mass-produced clothes, 84
Mass production, 243, 244, *244*, 247, 248, 400
Mass society, 91
Mastectomies, 141
Material culture, 34
  and art of dress, 287
  and dress, 40–42, 50
  studies in, 85
Material goods, in small-scale cultures, 190
Maternity wear, 141, *142*
Mayan designs, Guatemala Indians, 204, 228
Mbuti
  Africa, 137, 147
  barkcloth garments, 202
  physiological adaptations, 150
Mead, Margaret, 87
Mead, S.M., 69
Meaning and form of dress, 297–98
Medals, 224
Media, 36
Medieval Europe, metal armor, 17, *18*

Medieval "Last Supper Textile," *60*
Megalopolis, 239
Mega-malls, 401
Mehendi, North Africa and India, 10
Melanoma, 130
Memoirs, 67
Men, 333
    body hair, 136
    fashion for, 63–65, 81–83
    height, 81
    sexually attractive body parts, 302
    subordination of dress to body, 325
    thermal control, 153
Mende people of Sierra Leone, 302
Mennonites, 330
Merchandising, 405
Merrifield, Mrs., 79
Mesomorphic body type, 137–38, *139,
    140*
Mesopotamia, 210
Mesopotamian male ideal, 311
Metabolic rate, 152, 153
Metal armor, 17, *18*, 294
Metal workers, 59
Metropolitan Art Museum, Costume
    Institute, 348
Mexico, 70, 248
    huipil, 39
Mickey and Minnie Mouse, 361, *361*
Microchips, 400, 401
Microfiber polyester, 245
Middle East, smoke baths, 13
Midler, Bette, 78
Migration, 45, 190, 242
    see also Diasporas
Military uniforms. *See* Uniforms
Minnesota Twin Study, 339
Minnich, Helen Benton, 69
Minoxidil, 7
Miss America Pageant, 310
Miss America statistics, 313, *314*
Mixtec goddess, Tlazolteotl, 230, *231*
Miyake, Issey, 370
Moccasins, 161–64, *163*
Modern dance, 355, *356*, 357, 365
Modernism, 92
Modern Jazz Quartet, 362, *363*
Modesty, 150, 292, 340, 403
Mohenjo-Daro, Indus River Valley,
    210
Molloy, John, 78
Monocles, 19
Monotheism, 256
Monro, Isabelle S., 89
Monro, K.M., 89
Moore, Demi, *324*
Moralistic essays, 76
Moravian Slovakia, 87
Mori, Hanae, 247
Morocco, henna designs, 288
Morris, Desmond, 319

Mosaics, 59
Moss, Kate, 138, *140*
Motion pictures, 59
Motor skills, 161–66
Mount Hagen people, Highland New
    Guinea, 191, *192*, 194–95, *196*, 291
Mouth, 13, 15
Mouthwash, 4, 13
Mughal emperors, India, 220
Multinational corporations, 405
Museum of Contemporary Crafts,
    American Crafts Council, 348
Museums, 56, 58–59, 64
Museum work, 406
Music, 289, 335
Musical groups, 371
Musical performance, 362
Musicals, 358
Muslim empire, 220
Muslims, 330
    men, 7, 300
    religious rituals, 232
    women, 40, 137, 221, 225, *228*, 302,
        323
Muslim Turkey, 137
Mustaches, 8
Mythological subjects, 366

N
Nakedness, 26
Name badges, 240
Name tags, 22
National Aeronautics and Space
    Administration (NASA), 171
National alliances, 238
National costume, 249
National dress, 248, 249–51, *250*, 253,
    399, *399*
National Geographic, 57
Nationalism, 255
Nation-states, 239, 252
Native Americans. *See* American Indians
NATO. *See* North Atlantic Treaty
    Organization
Natural body processes, 14
Natural fibers, 294, 400
Natural selection, 129, 130, 150
Naval rings, 16, 18
Nazi concentration camp tattoos, 12
Ndebele people, South Africa, 17
Neanderthal burial site, Iraq, 289
Near East, 210
Neck irons, 175
Necklaces, 16, 17, 26, *27*
Neck scarves, 16
Neckties, 18
    artwork for, 370
    color and design, 28
Neckware, tight, 141
Needles for sewing, 194
Nefertiti, 311

Negroid, 133
Neolithic period, 295
Nevelson, Louise, 336, 367, 391–93
Newburgh, L.H., 88
New Guinea, 91, 196, 210, 348
New World, 61
New Zealand, Maori, 87
Nez Perce, American Indians, 225
Nigeria
    shirts, 46
    underwear and tablecloths, 43–44
Night wear, 199
Nike, 405
Nixon, Richard M., 337
Nix-Rice, Nancy, 304
Nobility, 218, 219
Noh theater, Japan, 354, *355*, 361
Noise levels, 155
Nomadic groups, 188, 210
Nonmaterial culture, 34
    and dress, 40–42
Nonverbal communication, 3, 27–28,
    33
Non-Western cultures, 46
    and emergence of anthropology, 85
Non-Western dress, 69, 91, 93
Nordstrom, 244
North America, 17, 41
North American Free Trade Agreement
    (NAFTA), 248
North Atlantic Treaty Organization
    (NATO), 251, 405
Northern Baroque ideal, 311, *311*
Northwest Coast Indians, *8*
Nose studs, 18
Nouveau riche, 80
Nuba people, Africa, 26, 348
Nudity practices, 88, 295–96
Nuns, 229, 323, 337
Nuremberg Chronicles, 61
Nursing bras, 141, *142*
Nutrition, 138–41
    in cold climates, 153, 160
    see also Dieting
Nystrom, Paul H., 89

O
Obesity, 140–41, 303
Occupational dress, 245
Occupational uniforms, 334
Occupations, 219
Odors and scents, body modifications,
    13
O'Keefe, Georgia, 336, 367, 390–91
Oklahoma (musical), 365
Old Stone Age, 56
Olympic games, Greece, 295
Omaha tribe, 85, *86*
Onassis, Jacqueline Kennedy, 342, 369
O'Neal, Gwen, 405
101 Dalmations (film), 371

On-line shopping, 401–2
Opera, 358, 362
Opposable thumbs, 160
Oral history, 46–47
Orbs, 223
Orchestras, 363, 364
Organic dress artifacts, 194
Organizational structures, 36
Orthodontic treatment, 10
Orvis (catalogue), 241
Osnaburg fabrics, 217
Otter, 291
"Otzi" the Iceman, 56
Overcoats, 323
Overdressing, 26
"Overs and unders," 397–98, *398*
Overweight, 313
Oxygen, 154

P

Pagnes, West Africa, 299
Pagri, India, 300
Paine, Sheila, 321
Paintings, 55, 64, 68, 366
Painting skin. *See* Body painting
Paint pots of iron oxide, 190
Pajama shirt, 253
Paleolithic era, 194
Palestine, 92, 242
Pallau, India, 215
Pant outfits, 253
Pantyhose, 323
Parades, 366
Parasols, 7
Parents, single and working, 247
Patchwork garments, 227
Patchwork quilts, 367, *368*
Patriotism, 239, 405
Payne, Blanche, Geitel Weinakor, and
    Jane Farrell-Beck, 69
Pazyryk people, Siberia, 56, 201, *201*
Peddlers, 218
Peking Opera, China, 354
Penis sheath, 26, *26*, 91
People's Republic of China. *See* China
Perani, Judith, 92
Performance dancers, 14
Performance space and lighting, 358–60
Performers and costume requirements,
    360–61
Performing artists, 289
Performing arts, 335, 350
Perfumes, 4, 13, 88
Perishable organic materials, 56
Permanent body modifications, 7, 15, 215
    and body supplements, 24
    surface design, 11–12
Permanent dwellings, 211
Permanent waves for hair, 40
Peron, Eva, 371
Persia, 253

Personal collections, 56
Personal grooming, 340
Personal Pair jeans, 401
Personal shoppers, 247
Personal style categories, 304
Personal trainers, 247
Perspiration. *See* Sweating
Peru
    Choquecancha, 229
    textiles, 58
Peruvian Connection (catalogue), 249
Peruvian Mochica headdress, *60*
Pesticides, 157, *157*, 244
Peter the Great, Russia, 223, *223*
Peter Pan, 361
Petro-plastic pop bottles, 245
Phenotypes, 129
Philippines, 46, *47*, 138
Photographs, 68
    idealized, 64
Photography, 58, 66, 366
Physical adaptation and dress, 154–55
Physical appearance and dress, 127–47
    physical diversity, 123, ref. 128, *129*,
        130–44
        long-term adaptations, 130–38
        body conformation, 137–38
        ethnicity, 135
        race, 133–35
        sex differentiation, 135–37
        short-term variations, 138–44
        growth and age, 141–44
        nutrition and disease, 138–41
    physical similarity, 128–30
Physical movement, 13
Physical needs for dress, 4
Physical similarity, 128–30
Physics, 57
Physiological adaptation to
    environment, 150–55
Picasso, Pablo, 370
Pickpocket-proof sport coats, 241
Pictorial records, 62
Piercing ears, 20
Pierrot and Pierrette, 361
Pince-nez, 19
Plagiarism, 70
Planche, James R., 69
Plants, domestication of, 213
Plastic surgery, 7, 10, *11*, 12, 78, 294, 315
    cost of, 403
    facelifts, 15
Pliny, 61, 214
Pocket styles, 301
Poetry, 289
Poise classes, 14
Polar bear, 169
Polar fleece, 245, *246*
Polartech synthetic fleece garments,
    170
Polhemus, Ted, 91, 92

Polity
    future of dress, 405
    global-scale culture, 239, 249–56
    large-scale culture, 210, 212, 222–29
    small-scale culture, 189, 199–200
Pollution, 245
Polo, Marco, 68
Polyester, 400
Polynesia, 299
Pomades, 4
Pompadour wigs, 324
Pompeii, 59
Ponchos, 17, 253
Population and residence, 398–400
    future of dress, 398–400
    global-scale culture, 239–43
    large-scale culture, 210–11, 212–13
    small-scale culture, 190–91
Portable environment, 157, 158
Portrait art, 59, 66
Postage stamps, 65
Post, Emily, 79, 80
Postmodernism, 92
Posture, 294, *295*
Potlatch, 195–96, 200
Potters, 59
Pottery, 210
Poverty, 246, 255
Powdering skin, 7
Powell, Adam Clayton Jr., 134–35
Power, 210
Powwow Princess, 196
Prada runway show, Milan, *324*
Pregnancy, 141, *142*
Pregnancy apron, 197, *198*
Prehistoric peoples, 56, *57*
Pre-Raphaelite painters, 366
Prescriptive literature, 77–84, 318
Preshaped enclosures, 17, 301
Presley, Elvis, 342
Priesthood, 212, 229, 323
Prince, The Artist Formerly Known as, 362
Printers, 59
Printing, color, 64
Printing press, 69
Private audiences, versus public
    audiences, 14
Private property, 215
    see also Land ownership
Proctor, Lynn, 91
Proscriptive literature, 77–84, 290
Prose, 289
Prosthetic devices, 141, 166
Protective dress, 3, 88, 154, 154–60, 155,
    156–59, 219, 245, 292–93
Prototypes, 401
Psychoanalytic theory, 89
Public audiences, versus private
    audiences, 14
Public works maintenance, 219
Pueblo people, 87

Punk dress, 295
Punk hairdos, 48, *49*
Puritans, 76
Purple-dyed cloth, 219–20
Purpura shell, 220
Purses, 22, 160, 348, *349*
    as art objects, 367, *368*
Pygmies, 147

Q
Qing Dynasty, China, 219
Qi pao, China, 48
Queen Elizabeth II, 223
Quicherat, J., 69
Quilting circles, 227, 260

R
Rabari people, India, 25
Race, 133–35
Racinet, Albert Charles, 69
Radiation, 155, 158
Radio City Rockettes, 364, *364*
Raleigh, Sir Walter, 62
Rank, 220
Ready-to-wear clothing, 244
Records of dress as sources of
    information, 55–73
Recycled clothing, 245, 246
Reform literature, 77
Refugees, 243
Reincarnated dress, 246
Reindeer, 164
Religion, 34, 40
    global-scale culture, 239, 256–57
    large-scale culture, 212, 229–32
    small-scale culture, 189, 200–204
    see also Ideology
Religious groups, 256, 330, 337–39
    see also specific religions
Religious rituals, 232
Religious tracts, 67
Renbourn, E.T., 88
Renne, Elisha P., 92
Replicating garments, 57
Reproductive capacity, 197
Residential groups, 189, 197
Resist dyeing, 214
Resource materials, 55
Retailers, *244*, 247, 288
Retro fashion, 247
Rhodes, Zandra, 370
Ribbons, 16
Richardson, Nan, 93
Rickets, 130
Rites of passage, 39, 189, 199, 201–3,
    203, 255
Ritual events, 189, 201–3
Ritual purity, 232
Rivers, Joan, 78
Roach-Higgins, Mary Ellen, Joanne B.
    Eicher, and Kim K.P. Johnson, 91

Roach, Mary Ellen and Joanne B. Eicher,
    90, 91
Roach, Mary Ellen and Kathleen Musa,
    69
Roanoke colonies, 62
Rock artists, 335
Rockettes of Radio City Music Hall, 364,
    364
Rodman, Dennis, 404, *404*
Rohrbach, Carl, 69
Roles, social, 39
Roman Catholics, 229, *229*, 230, 256,
    323, 337
Roman Empire, 219, 229
Roman togas, 16
Romeo and Juliet (Shakespeare), 361
Rosencranz, Mary Lou, 91
Ross, Edward A., 88
Royal courts, 321
Royal factories, 220
Royalty, 64
Ruana, 18
Rubens, Peter Paul, *Venus before a
    Mirror*, 311, *311*
Rubinstein, Ruth P., 91
Rudofsky, Bernard, 89
Runway models, 14
Runway shows, 288, 365
RuPaul, 336, *336*
Rural areas, 212, 218, 239, 398
Russell, Douglas A., 69
Russia
    archeological finds, 56
Ryan, M.S., 90

S
Saami people, 175
    dress, 163–64
    Four Winds hat, 160, *161*
Sacred spaces and buildings, 230, 232
Sadek, Wafeya, 254
Salespeople, 401
Salt, 196
Salwar, 16, *25*
Salwar kameez, India, 215, *399*
Samples, 401
Samurai, Japan, 220
Sandals, 57
Santee Sioux motifs, 400
Sapienization, 187
Sapir, Edward, 89
Sari, 16, 18, *21*, 92, 215, 247, 299, 300,
    402–3
Sarong, 16, 253, 299, 300
Sashes, 16
Satellite communication systems, 238
Satires, 67, 76
Scaasi, Arnold, 325
Scale of world cultures, 37–40, 185, 209
    table, *38*, 398
    see also Culture; Global-scale culture

and dress; Large-scale culture and
    dress; Small-scale culture and dress
Scandinavian graves, Bronze Age, 58
Scarification, 12, 197, 261–68, 348, *348*
    discouraging, 253
    in rites of passage, 199, 203
Scents and odors, 4, 13, 287, 293
Scepters, 223
Schevill, Margot Blum, 69
Schiaparelli, Elsa, 370
Schlesinger, Arthur, 78, 79
Schneider, Jane, 400
School dress codes, 321, 330
School uniforms, 334, 339
Schreier, Barbara A., "They Don't Wear
    Wigs Here," 268
Schwartzenegger, Arnold, 138, *140*
Science, 239
Science fiction, 365
Scottish clans, 200, 334
Scottish kilts, 27, 34, *35*
Sculptors, 59
Sculpture, 55, 64, 366
Seals, 138, 164, 169, 291
Seamstresses, 243
Seasonal dress, 199
Seasons, 154, 397
Secondhand clothing, 247
Seduction principle, 90
Seinfeld (television show), 354
Self-enhancement, 291
Self-esteem, 331
Seminole Indians, Florida, 226–27
Senses, 5, 6, 33, 288–90
Sensory system of communication, 4–5
Seoul, 254–55
Servants, 247
Sewing machines, 60, 87
Sex differentiation, 135–37
Sexuality. *See* Human sexuality
Shah of Iran, 254
Shakespeare, William, *Romeo and Juliet*,
    361
Shamans, 189, 199, 201
Shang Dynasty, China, 210, 212, *212*,
    225
Shape and structure, body
    modifications, 8–10
Shawls, 18
Sheldon, W.H., 89, 137–38, *139*, *140*,
    303
Shelter, 189
Shields, Brooke, 78, *316*
Shirts, European mens's, 46, *47*
Shivering, 152, 154
Shoes, 9, 17
    as art objects, 367, *368*
    cleats on, 289
    leather, 60
    removal of, 221
Shopp, BeBe, 313, *314*

Shoppers, personal, 247
Shopping centers, 401
Short-term variations, 138–44
Shoulder pads, 7, 24, 333
Showering, 4
Siberia, 56, *57*, 201, *201*
Signature style in dress, 370–71
Sikh people, India, 25, 41
Silk, 289
Simms, Ami, 367, *368*
Singapore, 254–55
Single parents, 247
Siple, Paul A., 166, 169
Sisters, 229
Sizes, clothing, 154, 244, *245*, 303
Skeletal changes, 141
Skin, 4, 288
    color, 7, 127, 130
    comparison of body volume and skin
        surface area, 150, *151*
    grease applied to, 161
    heat regulating function of, 159
    texture, 12, 127
    see also Body painting
Skin cancer, 130, *159*
Skin-heads, 256
Skirts, 27
Skis, 163
Slaves, 242
    Egyptian slave dress, 215, 217
    permanent body modifications, 215
    in United States, 92, 217
Slendangs, Indonesia, 299
Small-scale culture and dress, 38–39,
    187–207
Smithsonian Institute, 85
Smoke baths, Middle East, 13
Snapping fingers, 14
Sneezing, 14
Snowshoes, 163, *163*
Social customs, 91
Social expectations in dress, 4
Social identity, 239
Social interaction, 34
Socialization, 36
Social mobility, 78, 212, 219
Social psychology, 55
Social roles, 39, 329, 332–39, 405
Social science theories, 89, 90
Social status, 17, 39, 219, 332–39
Social structure and division of labor
    future of dress, 402–4
    global-scale culture, 246–49
    large-scale culture, 212, 218–21
    small-scale culture, 189, 197–99
Social tradition, 89
Societal hierarchical subdivisions, 336
Society, 36–37
    definition, 36, 237
    democratic, 92
    small and large societies, 36–37

    see also Culture; Scale of world
        cultures
Society journals, 85
Sociocultural context, 90
Solinus, 61
Solomon, Michael R., 91
Sonic technology, 73
Sound, 289
    body modifications, 4, 5, 13–15
South America
    archaeological digs, 57
    dress history, 69
Southeast Asia, 91
    umbrellas, 23
    wrapped garments, 16
South Pacific, 68
Space suits, 157, 158, 170, 172, *172*
Spanish flamenco, 365
Specialized jobs, 239
Speciation, 128
Species, 128, 130
Speech, 130
Spices, 4, 13
Spinning wheels, 214
Sport activities dress, 170
Sport coats, 241, *241*
Sports Illustrated swimsuit issue, 322
Stage costumes, 351–54
    requirements of, 354–66
Stage and screen makeup, 358–59, *359*
Staining skin, 4
    see also Body painting
Standards, 34, 332
Standards of dress, universal, 319–20
Standard sizing. *See* Sizes, clothing
Star quilts, 196
Star Trek, 238, 256, 365, 410–12
State occasions, 252, 253
States, 210, 212
Status, social, 39
Status symbols, 397
Steele, Valerie, 93
Stereotyping, 40
    immigrants, 78
    indigenous people, 251, *252*, 399
    of musicians, 362
    in television, 354
    in theater, 361
Stone age technology, 91
Stone, Gregory P., 90, 91
Storefronts, 401
Stote, Dorothy, *Men Too Wear Clothes*, 81
Straitjackets, 175
Stratherns, Andrew, 91
Stratherns, Marilyn, 91
Streisand, Barbra, 78
String Revolution, 194
String skirts, Denmark, 58
Stripes, 24
Stubs, Philip, 76
Stud buttons, 20

Students, 241
Stylists, 288
Subcultures, 35, 42, 92
    dress in, 250, *250*
    hippie to hip-hop, 290
    large-scale culture and dress, 330–31,
        399
Subsistence economies, 189, 191, 198, 211
Sumeria, wool, 214
Sumo wrestlers, 138, *140*
Sumptuary laws, 219–21
Sun-tanning, 7
Supplements, handheld, 160
Supplex, 400
Supranational organizations, 405
Surface design, body modifications,
    10–12
Surface design techniques, 214
"Susie Wong" dress, 48
Suspended enclosures, 17
Sutton Hoo ship burial, Suffolk,
    England, 201
Sweating, 13, 152, 153, 154, 169, 170
Sweden, 250
    Dalmalningar, 60, *61*
Sword dancers, India, 358
Symbolic interaction framework, 90
Symbolic meanings, 34
Symbolism of dress, 87
Synchronized swimming teams, 364
Synthetic fibers, 245, 294, 329, 397, 400

T
Tactile texture, 12
Taffeta, 4
Tailors, 215, 243, 403
Tallit, 242
Tallit katan, 242
Tally markers, 194–95, *196*
Tanning, 151
Tap dancers, 14
Tap dancers' shoes, 356
Target customer, 405
Tarlo, Emma, *Clothing Matters*, 91
Tartans, 200
Taste, 4, 293
Tattoos, 4, 7, 11–12, *12*
    cultural meanings of, 302, *303*
    designs, *57*
    discouraging, 253
    Kodi women on Sumba Island,
        197–98
    "Otzi" the Iceman, 56
    Pazyryk woman, 56
    permanence of, 15
    in rites of passage, 199
    on slaves, 215
    South Pacific Islands, 11–12, 70
    Tahiti, 70
    as wearable art, 349
    on young people, 340, 403

Taxes, tribute, 211, 219
Taylor, Elizabeth, *359*
Tchikrin people, Brazil, 191, 348
Teaching, 406
Technological changes, 45–46, 48, 406
Technology
    and dress, 245–26, 329
    and food, 138, 140
    future of dress, 400–402
    global-scale culture, 239, 243–46, 251
    large-scale culture, 211, 213–18
    small-scale culture, 191–97
Teeth, 10, 11, 12
    cleaning, 13
    false, 10, 166
    filing of, 149
    gems in, 349
Tefillin, 242
Telecommuting, 398
Television, 59, 238, 288
    stereotyping in, 354
Temperature
    body, 152, 160
    environmental, 152–53
Temporary body modifications, 7, 15
    and body supplements, 24
    surface design, 10–11
Tencel, 400
Terra-cotta soldiers, China, 59
Teton Dakota tribe leather dress, 18, *20*
Textile arts, 214
Textile production, 243–46, *244*
    development of, 194, 214
    methods of, 399
    retooling, 251
Textiles, 4
    Central Andes and Peru, 58
    disintegration of, 56
    flat, 190
Textile technology, 169, 170, 218–19
Texture, body modifications, 12
Thailand, Hmong people, 36, *37*
Thanksgivings, 201
Theater Guild, 360
Thomas, William I., 88
Thread for sewing, 194
Tibet, 250, *250*
Tibetan priests, 229
Tie clasps, 22
Tied belts, 16
Tie-dyeing, 214
Tight neckware, 141
"Tight pants syndrome," 141
Time zones, 151
Tiv people, Nigeria, 12, 203, 348, *348*
Tlazolteotl, Mixtec goddess, 230, *231*
Toda people, India, 137
Tongue piercing, 150
Tools, 34
    made with string, 194
Tool users, 160

Tootsie (film), 352, *353*
Torah, 60, 242
Tortora, Phyllis G. and Keith Eubank, 71
Tourism, 251, 399
Trade, 197, 210, 329
    global, 243–44, *244*, 251
    see also Exchange of goods
Tradition, 44–45
Transparent fabrics, 323, *324*
Transparent lace, 302, *303*
Transsexuals, 93
Transvestism, 87
Travel, 134
Travel dress, 241–42, *241*
Travelers' sketches, 61
Travel and exploration accounts, 67, 68–69
TravelSmith (catalogue), 241
Travel uniforms, 403
Tribes, 189
Tribute taxes, 211, 219
Trickle-down fashion, 220, 342
Trickle-up fashion, 342
Trollope, Frances, *Domestic Manners of Americans*, 68
Trouble spots of the body, 314
T-shirts, 240, *240*, 370
Tunics, 215, *216*
Turareg of the Sahara, 150, 167
Turbans, 16, 41, 300
Turkey, Muslim, 137
Turta, Iwan, 43
Twin study, 339
Tzitzit, 242

U
Ultraviolet (UV) light, 130, 400
Umbrellas, 23
Underclass, 227–28
"Unders and overs," 397–98, *398*
Underwear, boxer, 48
Underwear and tablecloths, Nigeria, 43–44
Ungaro, Emanuel, 247
Unhealthy environment, 155
UNICEF, 251
Uniforms, 84, 240, 253, *254*, 333
    global travel, 403
    in group performances, 362, 364, *364*
    medical symbols of power and status, 319
    military, 166, 223–24, *224*, 245, 335
    military insignia and medals, 20, 335
    nurse, 341
    occupational, 334
    school, 334, 339
United Nations (UN), 152, 251, 405
United States
    antebellum lady, 219
    cultural diversity, 83
    dress codes, 91, 255, 333

dress compared to European dress, 79
    equality under democracy, 257
    female ideal in, 313–14
    individuality, 330
    migration to, 242
    military uniforms, 166
    Miss America statistics, 313, *314*
    president, 23, 252, 342
    slaves in, 92
    tattooing in, 253
    women's legs, breasts, and buttocks, 302
Universals of culture, art of dress, 290–93
Universal standards of dress, 319–20
Universal Studios, 358
Upper Paleolithic era, 194, 197
Urban areas, 212, 218, 239, 240, 398
Ursuline order, 229
Used clothing, 247

V
Valets, 247
Values, 34, 154–55, 289–90, 297, 309
Vancouver Island, Kwakiutl tribe, 8, *8*, 195
Varicose veins, 143
Vasodilation and vasoconstriction, 152, 153
Vatican II, 256
Vaudeville performers, 365
Veblen, Thorstein, 88, 89
Vegetation growth cycles, 210
Veils, 24, *25*, *26*, 50, 154, 221, 257, 302
Velcro, 171
Venus before a Mirror (Rubens), 311, *311*
Venus de Milo, 311, *311*
Venus figures, 194, 197, 311, *311*, 322
Verbal communication, 4–5
Versace, Gianni, 253
Victoria and Albert Museum in London, 348
Video, 61
Vietnam, 91
Vision impairments, 149
Visual arts, 335, 350, 366–67
Visual representations, 55, 59–66
    advantages and disadvantages, 66–67, *68*
Visual texture, 12
Vitamin D, 130
Volume and proportion, body modifications, 7

W
Wahgi people, New Guinea, 348
Wakhi tribe, *132*
Walking sticks, 23
Wallach, Janet, 301, 304–5
War, 134, 155, 210

Wardrobes
  large-scale culture, 213
  small-scale culture, 190
Washington, George, 366, *367*
Water pollution, 245
Watkins, Susan M., 88
Wealth, 246–47, 330
  displays of, *192*, 194, 195, 200
  forms of, 211, 214
Wearable art, 348–49, *349*, *350*
Weavers, 59, 215
Weaving, 214, 214
Webb, Wilfred, 88
Wedding dress trains, 22
Wedding rings, 297
Weiner, Annette B. and Jane Schneider,
  92
Weir, Shelagh, 92
Weiss, Hermann, 71
Weitz, John, 397–98, *398*
West Africa
  Mande tribe, 20, *22*
  pagnes, 299
  wrapped garments, 16
Western cultures, 46
Western dress, 69, 92
  subcultures, 92
  and world dress, 253
White, John, 62, *62*, 73
White supremacist skin-heads, 256
White-tie-and-tails, 318–19, *318*
Wigs, 58, 141, 268
  New Guinea, 291
Wildlife migration patterns, 194, 210
Wilson, Elizabeth (1987), 92
Wilson, Verity, 87
Wilson, William, 301
Wodaabe people, Africa, 189, 310
Wolfe, Tom, 336

Wolff, Norma H., 92
Wolf, Naomi, 93
Women, 333
  body hair, 137
  business dress, 333, *334*
  cultural ideals for, 311, *311*
  cultural typologies in India, *304*, 305
  Euro-American closely fitting dress,
    17, *19*
  female ideal in Ghana, 311–13, *312*
  height, 81
  Jewish, 243
  makeup, 10
  Muslim, 40, 137, 221, 225, *228*, 302,
    323
  protective wear, 165, *165*
  roles in Western society, 294, *296*
  sexually attractive body parts, 302
  shaving legs and underarms, 11
  silhouettes, 9
  thermal control, 153
  veils, 24, *25*, *26*, 50, 154, 221, 257
  work dress, *77*
  wraparound skirt, 18
Women religious, 229, 256, 323, 337
Women's Dress Reform Movement, 77,
  84
Women's Rights Movement, 77, 93
Women's studies, 93
Women's Wear Daily, 365
Woodhouse, Annie, 93
Wood, Josephine and Lilly De Jongh
  Osborne, 71
Wool, 58, 154, 213, 214
Work dress of women, *77*
Working parents, 247
World Bank, 251
World cultures. *See* Scale of world
  cultures

World dress, 46–48, 253, 397
  and brand-name apparel, 248
  and ethnic and fashionable dress, 48
  in the future, 398
  homogenous trends, 254, 255
  studies on, 254–55
  and Western dress, 253
  and world fashion, 53, 248
World fashion, 53, 248, 290
World markets, 251
  see also Trade
World Wide Web (www), 55, 70, 253,
  401
  see also Internet
Wrapped enclosures, 16–17, 18, *21*, 215,
  299–300, *299*
Wright, Frank Lloyd, 336
Wrinkling, 241
Written descriptions and commentaries,
  67–72
Written history, 46–47
Written interpretations of dress, 75–96

X
X-ray technology, 73

Y
Yanomami people, Brazil, 26
Yoruba kings, Nigeria, 222
Yoruba wooden statues, 60
Young people, 242, 254–55, *334*, 335, 340
Youth, 319

Z
Zaire, 172
Ziegfeld Follies, 365
Zippers, 48, 337
Zones, clothing, 166–70
Zulu people, 316